Cases on Adoption, Diffusion, and Evaluation of Global E-Governance Systems:

Impact at the Grass Roots

Hakikur Rahman
ICMS, Bangladesh

Information Science REFERENCE

INFORMATION SCIENCE REFERENCE
Hershey · New York

Director of Editorial Content: Kristin Klinger
Director of Book Publications: Julia Mosemann
Acquisitions Editor: Lindsay Johnston
Development Editor: Joel Gamon
Publishing Assistant: Milan Vracarich Jr.
Typesetter: Natalie Pronio
Production Editor: Jamie Snavely
Cover Design: Lisa Tosheff

Published in the United States of America by
Information Science Reference (an imprint of IGI Global)
701 E. Chocolate Avenue
Hershey PA 17033
Tel: 717-533-8845
Fax: 717-533-8661
E-mail: cust@igi-global.com
Web site: http://www.igi-global.com

Library of Congress Cataloging-in-Publication Data

Cases on adoption, diffusion, and evaluation of global e-governance systems : impact at the grass roots / Hakikur Rahman, editor.
p. cm.
Includes bibliographical references and index.
Summary: "This book accommodates theories, issues and methodologies for designing, implementing and operating e-government systems, presenting cases covering a variety of services and applications that have been improving the governance of nations and economies"--Provided by publisher.
ISBN 978-1-61692-814-8 (hardcover) -- ISBN 978-1-61692-816-2 (ebook) 1. Internet in public administration--Case studies. 2. Public administration--Information technology--Case studies. 3. Communication in public administration--Technological innovations--Case studies. I. Rahman, Hakikur, 1957-
JF1525.A8C365 2010
352.3'802854678--dc22

2010016501

British Cataloguing in Publication Data
A Cataloguing in Publication record for this book is available from the British Library.

Table of Contents

Section 2
Operation, Management and Innovation

Section 3
Knowledge Management and Research

Detailed Table of Contents

This chapter discusses about basic issues on establishing grass roots e-government management through community practices and provides thoughts on technical, logical, managerial and policy issues. As a case it discusses about a global United Nations Development Programme (UNDP) project, Sustainable Development Networking Programme (SDNP) Bangladesh.

This chapter based on the research argues that national ICT policy should aim to provide formalized services across a nation while recognizing the importance of localized specific services. Focusing on Indian context, the chapter discusses about various mission mode projects under national e-governance plan.

This chapter is discussing various capacity development initiatives aiming at integrated environmental assessment and reporting at the sub-global level, using format of e-Learning. As a case from United Nations Environment Programme (UNEP), this research has developed a blended learning, Train-the-Multipliers program to train facilitators with the argument that this form of e-Learning implementation has clearly demonstrated potential in advancing e-governance.

This research presents a model which depicts the critical role of Chief Information Officers (CIOs) and assists in understanding the demands and effectiveness of CIOs in the public sector. The chapter explores the literature on public sector CIO addressing personal and professional characteristics focusing the State Government in Australia.

The chapter discusses on various activities the public authorities need to take when assisting vision impaired people, especially in the field of e-Government. This research has put forward a study, what steps the Finnish and German authorities have taken to support vision impaired people.

This chapter describes experiences acquired during a research work conducted as part of the European project Tell Me, supporting the pan-European creation of Living Labs. The project envisages supporting e-governance, by providing a new form of cooperation between government, enterprises, citizens and academia for a successful transfer of e-Government, e-Democracy and e-Services.

Foreword

Information communication technologies (ICTs) are recognised to be great catalysers for development and if well appropriated can accelerate the achievement of the Millennium Development Goals (MDG's) in today's technology–driven globalize world where knowledge management is rapidly becoming the centrefold of the emerging development paradigm.

A general anatomy of service industry discloses that there are many best management practices in the public and private sectors with the application of information technology. They are respectively dealing with the commercial situation and serving the various stakeholders with a sophisticated network of information technology. Ultimately, both the public and private sectors can improve their performance and add value to their services in order to meet those challenges in the industry.

The advent of ICT should be able to provide the Government administrative systems and all the stakeholders with the opportunity to better exchange information between them and to obtain within the shortest possible time, reliable data for efficient decision making in the public service system. At the same time, the system should be able to contribute to their national economies.

In conclusion, the introduction and use of ICTs in Public Administration, health, education and other utility services may help the process of transparency, but only if it is accompanied by a great simplification of language and administrative practices and if it is able to give important information with concision.

A casebook on e-Governance systems focusing adoption, diffusion and evaluation of various success cases around the globe would stand as a landmark in the arena of grass roots e-governance. This casebook will not only act as a guide for the practitioners, but also act as a white book to design and operate appropriate e-Government action plans in local, national, regional and global context.

This casebook will find its usefulness to development practitioners, researchers, policy initiators, academics and individuals as a valuable knowledge content for gaining knowledge to establish grass roots e-governance systems.

Roger Haw Boon Hong

Roger Haw Boon Hong *Professor of Corporate Social Responsibility, Ansted University (BVI) & ISBM (Netherlands). Founder cum Chairman, Ansted Social Responsibility International Award (ASRIA) Knight Grand Cross of the Order (Malta). Fellowship/Board members of IMS (UK), SSM & SNN (UK), IAL (UK), CHRRF(Switzerland), AAICL (Australia), UFI (Belgium), IDH (India), BASCSD (Bulgaria), ASWAM (Poland), AAE (Argentina), IACPS (USA)*

Preface

E-government, refers to the utilization of new information and communication technologies (ICTs) by governments being applied to the full range of government functionalities (OECD, 2001). These are the government activities that take place by digital processes over a computer network, usually the Internet, between the government and members of the public. It is the process of transforming the government, so that the use of the Internet and electronic processes become central to the way that government operates. In broader sense, e-government is the use of information technology to provide citizens and organizations with more convenient access to government information and services, and offer delivery of public services to citizen, businesses, and others who are working in the public sector (Bridges dot org, 2003; Kunstelj & Vintar, 2004; Scapin, 2009).

E-Governance is a network of organizations to incorporate government, non-government, profit, nonprofit, not-for-profit, civil societies, research entities, development actors and private sector entities. In the e-governance arena there are no distinct boundaries. The model for e-governance could be a one-stop portal, where citizens have the choice to access variety of information and services the government offers (Garson, 2006).

This casebook has tried to accommodate theories, issues and methodologies in designing, implementing and operating e-government systems. Furthermore, as the acclamation of the e-government systems in various countries, e-governance has been reported to be improved through many services. This casebook also covers a variety of services and applications across the globe that has been improving the overall governance of nations and economies. E-government and e-governance is not a new subject to the contemporary researchers, academics and to the new global leaders. Therefore, the casebook has been concise in synthesizing the theoretical analysis, but focuses more to pragmatic implementations, and emphasizes on e-government systems for targeted to the grass roots e-governance.

OBJECTIVES AND MISSION

This casebook has tried to give a thorough look into hypothetical and empirical aspects of the e-government systems with in-depth analysis of various e-government implementations, put forward several successful e-government projects across the world, and justify the enhancement of e-governance in the society, nation and globe through appropriate implementation of e-government systems. Overall objective and mission of this casebook is to assist its readers to understand the basic natures and aspects of e-government systems; able to design secured, privacy upholded and safe system that would be self empowered, independent, accountable, responsive, easily accessible and transparent; learn to utilize the e-government systems through comprehensive design, easier functionality, optimum output, less costly, time saving and simple. The mission is to guide its readers in establishing e-government projects focusing grass roots e-governance to empower the people at large for improved governance.

TARGET AUDIENCE

Being a casebook on e-government systems, it has manuscripts covering aspects of the e-society, such as e-learning, e-procurement, e-health, e-democracy, e-complaint, e-emergency, and other e-applications and e-services. Therefore, this book will be useful to the development partners, policy makers, government and non-government staffs, knowledge managers, researchers, academics and individuals. Furthermore, readers of this casebook will be enlightened with various e-government methods and systems across the world, learn about their characteristics, implementation, operation and evaluation plans including technical aspects of e-governance like, infrastructure, legislations, management, evaluation and benchmarking.

ORGANIZATION OF THE CASEBOOK

The casebook has been divided into three sections. First section focuses on foundation, benchmarking and evaluation of e-government projects or programmes discussing laws, jurisdictions, and policy matters related to e-government; benchmarking of e-government system; assessment of e-government policies and systems; comprehensive analysis of e-government implementations; performance and effectiveness measurement of e-government system; and examine their strengths and weaknesses. This section has four chapters, and all of them has tried to focus design, policy, assessment, performance and effectiveness issues on their illustrated cases.

Chapter 1 sets out with basic discussions about establishing grass roots e-government management through community practices and provides thoughts on technical, logical, managerial and policy issues. Governance systems nowadays do not only enclave simply the dissemination of government regulations and directives to their stakeholders, but also target to improve their knowledge and capacity. This research feels that to improve the governance system, inclusion of grass roots participants are necessary and nurturing of community practices targeting to raise their knowledge and skills through an adoptive e-governance framework that would enhance the process. It put forwards a global case, SDNP of UNDP in local perspectives, focusing SDNP Bangladesh.

To strengthen further, Chapter 2 argues that national ICT policy should aim to provide formalized services across a nation while recognizing the importance of localized specific services. Focusing on Indian context, this chapter discusses about various mission mode projects under national e-governance plan (NeGP), and mentions that manifestation of such approach has resulted in 100,000 common service centers (CSC) in rural areas. Furthermore, it is expected that through these CSCs, rural citizens would be benefited to raise their livelihood standards and this process may contribute for effective governance.

Among these formalized services, one essential element is to reach the people at large with faster mechanism of transaction, in terms of information delivery or concluding a financial transaction. Chapter 3 discusses about use of e-filing system that has been introduced in Malaysia. Along this context, this research has made some critical assessment of the system on security, usefulness, easy of access and users' retention. The research has also made recommendations to improve the e-filing system focusing e-governance.

The first section concluded with Chapter 4, which highlighted on various policy issues, objectives and action plans of two success cases in Asia on promoting grass roots e-governance. This chapter focuses on two cases (e-Sri Lanka and e-Korea), which penetrated the grass roots reaching out to the community level; act as catalyst to strengthen their national economy and government. The research emphasizes that cumulative human development through community approach would be the next level of knowledge dynamics across the world. It also argues that as much the country provides thrust on capacity development initiatives at the grass roots, the country has more opportunity to achieve better governance.

Next section forms the core part of this casebook and incorporates six cases focusing on operation, management and innovation aspects of e-government projects or programmes discussing designing of e-government system giving in-depth look into the e-government structure and processes; adoption of appropriate solutions and utilities providing technological and procedural form of the solution; and inclusion of decision supports tools and techniques.

Chapter 5 put forwards a case on the re-organization of the Dutch emergency response sector. It involves the diffusion and implementation of new communication and information technologies (ICTs), the introduction of safety regions and the establishment of co-located emergency response rooms (ERRs). The impact of the reorganization is illustrated by two embedded case studies: new ICTs in the safety-regions Hollands-Midden and Amsterdam-Amstelland. What the case shows is that the implementation of new ICTs in the Dutch safety-sector is not just a matter of technological skills, but of a mutual shaping of the ICTs and the organizations to enhance platform of e-governance, in this aspect the emergency response system serves as an important element.

Chapter 6 is discussing about application development for government purposes, and evaluation of projects utilizing various software technologies like, analogy, crisp and fuzzy estimation and measure models. As a case study from Czech Republic, the chapter introduces selected methods designed for complexity estimation. Each method is introduced first, then its step-by-step computation procedure is described and finally suggestion of software was made, which is supported by computation procedure. However, efforts are given about the implementation of this form of estimation approach in the area of ICT governance, especially at the grass roots e-governance.

Along this application development, easily accessible, simple, user friendly, robust, transparent, responsive and secured applications are essential in establishing multi-dimensional e-government systems. Next three chapters are illustrating the adoption of open source software in building e-government models; improving financial transparency by utilizing web interactions; and improving public service performances through e-complaints via web interfaces. These three cases are from Turkey.

On the way of creating a level playing field in terms of competition and resources, role of free and open source software (FOSS) is gaining its importance in many aspects of information technology systems. FOSS has been increasingly used both in public and private organizations in order to contain costs, increase software transparency, reliability, information security, and many other reasons. Chapter 7 has tried to identify and examine the arguments and actors, who have promoted and opposed the use of FOSS in the Turkish public sector. It also analyzes how these actors organize the processes of adoption and presents the discourses that they used to affect the open source-related policy decisions. In this context, the main aim is to link FOSS to the e-government processes, intending this manuscript as an enabler literature for grass roots e-governance improvement.

Fiscal transparency today is considered as an essential element of good governance. It has been found that e-government technologies, especially the Internet are supportive to the efforts on the part of governments offering unprecedented opportunities to public administrations enabling the dissemination of fiscal information and improving the e-governance system. Chapter 8 is discussing a case of Turkey, where reforms been made through new laws in early 2000 containing various legal and institutional regulations to improve fiscal transparency and encourage the public administrators to use websites to enhance fiscal transparency. This chapter, within the context of evaluating the endeavors in question, examines the websites of municipalities in Turkey in terms of fiscal transparency and eventually presents some suggestions for the improvement of the e-governance system.

To reach out the people at large of a community or a nation, it is imperative to have a common platform of interaction. This applies both to top-bottom interactions, or bottom-top interactions, despite nowadays, it has been argued that there should be both ways of interaction in each channel. Discussing about reaching to the national hierarchy from the bottom level, vice versa, Chapter 9 talks about how an NGO may have its place in e-governance model. This chapter is focused on a project from Turkey, 'Sikayetimiz.com', which is an e-complaint on-line model providing various support services to the people at large, discussed about its transformation stages leading to this format, and put forward some important managerial and organizational issues including operational challenges.

Last chapter of this section is on utilizing community knowledge records to improve healthcare system, as an enabler of e-governance. Chapter 10 investigates the potential of community knowledge records (CKRs) in the electronic transformation for healthcare provision in Macau. Of specific interest is the electronic governance (e-governance) context to examine the various ICTs for personalized healthcare support, such as the electronic health (or e-health) records (EHR). This chapter explores the context of citizens' e-health provision, including the EHRs considered as the digital records of personal medical history, accumulated from cradle to death.

Finally, section three focuses on knowledge management and research, featuring learning and knowledge development; economic empowerment, social empowerment, and sustainable development; and some more lessons learned from various global e-governance systems. This section comprises of four cases, one from UNEP, one from Australia, one from Greece and the last one consists of a research case based on studies conducted in Finland and Germany. The first one, discusses on environmental issues, the next one discusses about the character of Chief Information Officer in the public sector as a role model in improving e-governance, the third one is a research case on an European project, and the final one discusses about an extremely challenging issue on e-governance, which is delivering the benefits of electronic government to the vision impaired communities.

In the days of global warming, environmental issues represent some of the world's greatest crises and at the same time, most significant opportunities. The United Nations Environment Programme (UNEP) is a global leader in tackling such issues, and UNEP's Global Environmental Outlook (GEO) relies on contributions from many experts from all regions of the world. Because capacity development is critical to UNEP's ability to fulfill its mandate, UNEP collaborated with the International Institute for Sustainable Development (IISD) to commission more than 50 experts to develop training resources for integrated environmental assessment and reporting at the sub-global level. Chapter 11 is discussing these capacity development issues using format of eLearning. This research has further developed a blended learning, Train-the-Multipliers program to train facilitators. The research argues that this form of eLearning implementation has clearly demonstrated potential and is advancing e-governance at global, regional, national and sub-national levels in the area of environmental assessment and reporting.

Chapter 12 presents a model which depicts the critical role of Chief Information Officers (CIOs) and assists in understanding the demands and effectiveness of CIOs in the public sector. The chapter explores the literature on public sector CIO addressing personal and professional characteristics. It also reviews the literature pertaining to the responsibilities and career advancement and future directions in Government departments. The authors adopt a qualitative methodology by which semi-structured interviews are conducted with CIO representatives from a State Government in Australia. From collation of the interview results, utilizing a 'mind mapping' strategy, the chapter identifies a model that adequately reflects the critical factors required for a public sector CIO. The chapter concludes that there are certain unique characteristics and responsibilities that a public sector CIO must possess yet a private sector CIO does not require. The chapter also acknowledges the importance of outlining a future direction of the role; something which is neglected by the literature.

Vision impaired people are in a distinctive disadvantage when using computer screens based on visual presentation of data. Furthermore, their situation becomes increasingly critical, as most society services, such as e-Commerce, e-Business, e-Health, and e-Government are on-line. However, effective ICT can open up new communication channels and functionalities for even totally blind people, which would not have been available for them otherwise. Chapter 13 discusses on the activities public authorities need to take when assisting vision impaired people, especially in the field of e-Government. This research has put forward a study, what the Finnish and German authorities have made to support vision impaired people.

Chapter 14 describes experiences acquired during a research work conducted as part of the European project Tell Me (www.tellmeproject.eu). The project envisaged to support the pan-European creation of Living Labs as new forms of cooperation between government, enterprises, citizens and academia for a successful transfer of e-Government, e-Democracy and e-Services state-of-the art applications, solutions, know-how and best practices. This chapter explores the potential of providing an existing system (DEMOS) allowing moderated and goal-oriented discourses between the citizens and the policy makers to become parts of open-ended ventures to allow the creation of collaborative networks for electronic democracy.

CONCLUSION

As mentioned above, electronic government (e-government) is the provision of government information and services in the networked environment, intended to make government more accessible to citizens, businesses and other government agencies. However, most of the e-government systems at the earlier stages are being built to exactly mimic the age-old conventional procedures or processes, and virtually computerized the traditional methods and procedures. The notion was to minimize the design and implementation cost and at the same time to expedite the transformation process faster, without much entering into basic research. The electronic solutions were implanted into government offices without looking into the transformational aspects (mental, organizational, physical, logical, technological, economical, cultural, working style, etc.) and not providing the entire eco-system for long-term sustenance (Timonen, O'Donnell & Humphreys, 2003; Accenture, 2004; Katre, 2007; Paul, 2008).

At the same time, most of the early implementers were naïve in formulating e-government system, and they were experimenting through various implementation techniques by replicating an existing system imported from elsewhere, often creating a circle-of-repetition by duplication of efforts and over utilization of resources. As a result, a majority of the earlier implemented e-government systems in many countries could not see the light of success. Moreover, this failure of the system cascaded, especially in developing countries where funding is scarce, technology is inadequate, skill is low, policy is hazy, culture is eccentric and mindset is turbulent (Gupta & Jana, 2003; Brown, 2005; Kovačič, 2007; Choudrie, Wisel & Ghinea, 2009).

Furthermore, e-government has little impact in the absence of any effort or thrust at the national level that includes policy makers, government and non-government agencies, academics, researchers, entrepreneurs and individuals. Most of the success cases of e-government around the globe that has been incorporated in this casebook portray effective participation and sustained patronage from the government, the entrepreneurs, the civil society, the research sector, the development partner and the academia. This has also been observed that majority of the stakeholders within an accomplished e-government system become benefited from being within the system, not from being an outsider.

This casebook has tried to include researches, cases, and studies accommodating various e-government systems across the countries focusing inherent benefits of e-government within the system to improve the livelihood of the communities, people at large and individuals. Ranging from design, implementation and operation of e-government systems, this casebook has tried to provide analytical approach into the system through available techniques and methods. These incorporate benchmarking on implementations, ranking of the system, evaluation in terms of its usefulness, effectiveness and impact in the society (measuring short, medium, and long-term implications), and ultimate benefit (societal, entrepreneurial, public, edutainment, etc.) of the system in the overall improvement of the government system focusing grass roots e-governance.

REFERENCES

Accenture (2004). *eGovernment Leadership: High Performance, Maximum Value*, Accenture.

Bridges dot org (2003). *Provincial Government of the Western Cape Cape Gateway Project Evaluation*, A report of the Knowledge Economy & E-Government Branch of the Provincial Government of the Western Cape and bridges.org

Brown, D. (2005). Electronic government and public administration, *International Review of Administrative Sciences*, *71*(2), 241-254.

Choudrie, J., Wisel, J. & Ghinea, G. (2009). Evaluating the usuability of developing countries' e-government sites: a user perspective, *International Journal of Electronic Government*, *6*(3), 265-281.

Garson, D.G. (2006). *Public Information Technology and E-Governance*. Sudbury, MA: Jones and Bartlett Publishers

Gupta, M. P. & Jana, D. (2003). E-government evaluation: A framework and case study, *Government Information Quarterly*, 20, 365-387.

Katre, D. (2007). Indian e-Government Initiative: An Ideal Case for Universal Usability, India Scenario/ Article 5, *Journal of HCI Vistas*, available at http://www.hceye.org/UsabilityInsights/?p=21

Kovačič, A. (2007). Process-based knowledge management: Towards e-government in Slovenia, *Management*, *12*(1), 45-64.

Kunstelj, M. & Vintar, M. (2004). Evaluating the progress of e-government development: A critical analysis, *Information Polity 9*, 131–148.

O'Donnell, O. & Humphreys, P.C. (2003). *E-Government and the Decentralisation of Service Delivery*. CPMR Discussion Paper 25, Institute of Public Administration.

OECD (2001). *E-Government: Analysis Framework and Methodology*, PUMA (2001) 16/ANN/REV1, Organization for Economic Cooperation and development (OECD), Paris.

Paul, J. (2008). User-Centered Policy Evaluations of Section 508 of the Rehabilitation Act: Evaluating E-Government Web Sites for Accessibility for Persons With Disabilities, *E-Government News*, available at http://www.egovnews.org/?cat=4&paged=4

Scapin, D.L. (2009). *E-government HCI: a genuine research field?* A proceedings of DEGAS 2009: Workshop on Design and Evaluation of e-Government, Uppsala, Sweden, pp. 33-37.

Timonen, V., O'Donnell, O. & Humphreys, P.C. (2003). *E-Government and the Decentralisation of Service Delivery*, CPMR Discussion Paper 25, Institute of Public Administration, Dublin, Ireland.

Acknowledgment

The editor gladly acknowledges the persistent support and generous assistance from all authors, advisors and reviewers involved in the entire accumulation of manuscripts, review process, revision and finalization of the cases, without which the project could not have been satisfactorily completed. He would like to thank Nilsun Sariyer for her comprehensive revision of the manuscript, Tolga Demirbas for his relentless support in reviewing late submitted manuscript, and good old friends Kam Hou Vat and Abdul Raufu Ambali for their continuous support in providing quality manuscripts.

Special thanks go to the enthusiastic publishing team at IGI Global. Particularly to Elizabeth Ardner, and Joel Gamon for their continuous suggestions, enthusiastic supports, authentic feedbacks and committed co-operations for keeping the project on schedule, and to Mehdi Khosrow-Pour, Jan Travers and Kristin Klinger for their everlasting professional guidance. Finally, sincere thanks go to my family, friends and colleagues for their love and support throughout this period.

Hakikur Rahman, PhD
ICMS, Bangladesh

November 2009

Section 1
Foundation, Benchmarking and Evaluation

Chapter 1
Community Practices to Improve E-Governance at the Grass Roots

Hakikur Rahman
ICMS, Bangladesh

EXECUTIVE SUMMARY

Wide use of information technologies has lead governments across the globe to adopt the new nature of governance system for their citizens, businesses and within the government structure. Governance systems nowadays do not only enclave simply the dissemination of government regulations and directives to their stakeholders, but also target to improve their knowledge and capacity. At the threshold, by putting the information technologies as a thrust sector for many years and with well adopted e-governance framework, several countries have achieved remarkable success. However, many of them despite diversified efforts could not put into the track mainstreaming electronic format of the governance system. This research feel that to improve the governance system, inclusion of grass roots participants are necessary and nurturing of community practices targeting to raise their knowledge and skills through an adoptive e-governance framework would enhance the process. As a case study, it put forwards a case from UNDP, including hints on similar other cases.

BACKGROUND

This chapter, as a case study would like to put forward a pioneering programme of the United Nations Development Programme (UNDP) that acted as catalytic factor in many developing countries initiating from 1992. Many of projects under this programme, namely the sustainable development networking programme (SDNP) lead the country's information technology sector and eventually act as a positive contributor towards improvement of the government infrastructure. However, the theme of the chapter has been focused to a broader lens of community development approach that has been termed as community practice, which this chapter would like to showcase as an effective way to improve the grass roots e-governance.

DOI: 10.4018/978-1-61692-814-8.ch001

In doing so, the chapter has tried to define different facets of the title focusing utilization of information and communication technologies (ICTs) at the initial part of this section. Subsequently, it tries to involve different accepted methods of community practices that are being applied to improve the e-government structure at the outer peripheries of the government structure. To support the argument, it will put forward a framework for e-governance augmenting community practices leading to local level governance improvement. Furthermore, it will try to designate products, processes or services that surround the concurrent development actors or may direct the agencies and parties involved in this process. Finally, it will illustrate the case of SDNP Bangladesh (SDNBD) that existed during 1998-2006 as a project and later on transformed into a not-for-profit entity since January 2007. However, as an enhancer of argument or justification or simple exemplification, the chapter will enlighten its readers with similar projects and programmes that existed earlier in various formats or currently running in other countries enhancing the governance systems.

According to Shaffer & Anundsen (1993:10), a community is a dynamic entity that emerges when a group of people participate in common practices, depend on each other, identify themselves as part of something larger than the sum of their individual relationships, and commit themselves for a long term relationship to improve their well-being. This relates to another pertinent term that requires commitment from the community participant to be part of the development process of a nation, which is community development. Spergel (1987) referred to community development as a premeditated intervention into the social network among people and organizations to facilitate social problem solving and improve patterns of service delivery. This definition was updated by Harrison (1995:556) as the process of working with communities to help them recognize how they can improve community life and welfare both in the present and in the future. NASW (2006a; b; c) and Petter, Byrnes & Choi (2002) further emphasizes both the achievement of specific goals and the development of less tangible qualitative aspects of social life in a community, such as the improvement of their leadership capabilities, especially the ability to take adequate decision by their own.

Author would like to redefine the term, in association with the Wiki, as a community building one should consider approaches to be applied through community practices and basic academic disciplines should incorporate knowledge and ideas (through interactive interactions) of civic leaders, civil societies, community participants, professionals and researchers to improve various aspects of local communities. Community development seeks to empower individuals and groups of people by providing with necessary skills to prompt necessary changes in their own communities[1]. These skills could range from enhancement of civic knowledge, understanding of basic laws and governance system, validation of national identity (national consensus or voting), and knowledge on establishing small entrepreneurship to tax proclamation, land registration, vehicle registration or obtaining driving license, requesting national identity cards or certificate, birth or death certificate, loan acquisition, and so on.

In recent years, governments, and non-government agencies including development partners and research institutions are actively involved in promoting e-governance through utilization of information and communication technologies and using the diversified applications of ICTs in enhancing the livelihood activities at community level. However, in spite of placing ICT as high priority in many countries, much of the efforts to raise the magnitude of governance at the community level remain unattended. During the evolution of Internet in early nineties of the last century, many developing and under-developed countries were in high enthusiasm to include ICT in their national manifestos, and advocate about introducing ICTs in every aspect of the social process. A recent research[2] reveals that almost 840billions

USD annually spent around the globe for ICT for development purpose. Despite, all these efforts, in many countries ICT for Development initiatives have been failing in larger rates.

Author argues that, instead of involving the actual beneficiaries, i.e., the community participants, often development agencies and their partners try to implement their own ideas and philosophies to the community without being improving their mental capacities or their real necessities. Of course, food and shelter are the basic part and parcel of most of the disadvantaged communities, which are major element of a developing or transitional country. But, whenever they would feel the real urgency of governance system to be an effective tool in their livelihood, either now or very near future, and most importantly could reduce some economical burden or provide some economical gain, they would certainly welcome the entire system of development. Furthermore, when they would feel themselves as a part of this important development process, they would be eager to participate, not being remained aloof or bypass the system, as it is happening nowadays in many countries. These processes require introduction of the development sequences through community practices.

Community practices evolve from very early days of socialization when human beings adopted to live in socialized form of life by sharing a common geography, culture, economy, desire, objective, belief, resource, risk, and other numerous numbers of parameters affecting a common group of people living together[3]. Social pattern transforms through evolution, demand, and availability of resources. Subsequently, community practices changes to elevate the life pattern of each community. They may comprise of human service management, community development, policy advocacy[4], community foresting, community learning (basic laws of the country, tax payment, and civic rules); collaborative learning (pedagogy, and non-formal), community health and sanitation; ecosystem management; disaster preparedness; and other initiations to improve the life pattern of the community participants. The essence of this form of participatory approach is to include the practitioners (development agencies, international organizations, donor agencies, etc.), participants (government, citizen, civil society including all mentioned before), and pedagogists (academics and researchers) inclusively are the part of the participation and fit into the learning curve. One of the important components of the learning curve is to translate current knowledge into community practices (Tandon, et. al., 2007), and at the same time, these community practices could be utilized on the sustainable use of natural resources, community forest and biodiversity management (Saelee, 2002), life-long learning, skill development, micro-entrepreneurship, and healthcare (Saelee, 2002; Anderson, 2004; McIntyre, 2005; McDowell, Nagel, Williams & Canepa, 2005; Michael & Margaret, 2007; Rahman, 2006; 2007).

To improve e-governance at the outer periphery of the government structure, several channels already exist in almost all countries, including the traditional government structure. In terms of e-governance, many adopted dynamically developed e-governance framework, many replicated some established framework, or many just converted the traditional government transactions into electronic formats. Consequences are that only a handful of countries could achieve sequential gain from those e-governance frameworks, and majority of them are yet to pin-point the specific demand of the society to develop the eco-system of governance as a whole, nonetheless projects or programmes in some countries have already at failed state. This research would like to argue that, to promote e-governance at the grass roots several channels of learning sequences need to be adopted focusing community practices.

Channels of Learning Sequences

Education- As a base instrument to raise the platform of knowledge ecosystem of local community, education is the best channel. However, to rapidate the process of knowledge acquisition aiming at improved e-governance, the basic education system up to at least secondary level should incorporate knowledge about common civil rules and regulations, bio-diversity and ecosystem of environment, and management of basic livelihood systems, as such agriculture, food security, consumer commodity, common laws, practices and regulatory issues of a country. Furthermore, many countries have achieved successes in adopting mandatory secondary or pre-secondary education. Undergraduate syllabuses' would include curriculums not only leading to science, arts or technology, but also necessary technical skills and knowledge to be readily fit the learners to local industries and entrepreneurships. Utilization of ICTs can enhance the learning methods. Tertiary education system may be focused to specific channel of learning as per requirement of the community, or nation, or learner. At this junction, both community and learner would be synthesized according to the demand of the society (not leading to earning money, but to uplift the livelihood of the community).

In many countries, lack of a unified syllabus or curriculum has developed multiple channels of education systems, which are creating tremendous knowledge gaps among learners and this may lead to some form of uncontrollable situation from where there will no way out after 10 or 15 or 20 years of continuation of such multiple channels of education systems. Nations are losing hard earn local and foreign currencies; outcome of the education system is not directly benefiting the community or nation; like other commodities, education is also being adulterated by cheap middle men and farias; and creating enough confusion at the national level thus even creating a generation gap.

Capacity development- To nurture and sustain local community development sequences in tune of the governance system of that country, in addition to the traditional and or technical or vocational pedagogical channels, a separate channel needs to evolve through existing information infrastructure if not too late just waiting for a new layout of infrastructure that often seem too critical to design, establish and maintain, especially in developing and transitional economies. Capacity development initiatives can target subjects like homestead horticulture, or domestic cattle breeding, or automobile mechanics, or ready-made garments skills, or consumer electronics or basic ICT skills. One may wonder, already all these programs are running in their countries, but author argues that lack of creating a sustainable network among them utilizing ICTs many of them could not create necessary impact in their society instead of high class technology incorporation or abundance of funding during the establishment stage or lack of support from the highest statute in their countries.

Social network- Large scale access of mobile phone and rapidly increasing Internet penetrations failed in many countries to target the basic necessities of their communities in terms of producing some form of social network (targeting knowledge building), or creating value added services. Lacks of proper manipulations, providers of these services are misleading the community participants, especially the younger generation. Similar to age old radio network or FM stations or community radios, Internet based social network or mobile based community network could enhance the process of knowledge development and rapidify the e-governance system in a country rather than mere late night subsidy offerings.

Local e-governance network- Using the services of village centers, or knowledge centers, or tele-centers, or entities closer to the communities connected with ICT facility may promote a portal or an interactive web site (one or many, depending on availability, not complicating the acceptance of the local community, but leading to value added propositions) comprising the basic social infrastructural system transformed into a virtual format. In the longer run, like basic commodities of life, community people would feel this network as an essential element of their livelihood.

Framework of Community Practices

This research argues that, a comprehensive framework is desired at the national level emphasizing development at the local level incorporating community practices. The framework of community practice should aim to improve the knowledge capacity of the community participants and enhance their knowledge dimension so that they can make independent intelligent decisions to improve their livelihood surroundings leading to improved governance system. If, ICTs could be embodied within the system intermingling the service providers and the beneficiaries at an elevated platform of value addition, the system would be effective and sustainable.

Framework of community practices may form a four-dimensional circular cycle of emancipation. They would evolve within any of the existing dimension, fitting into the framework, and create metabolism within the process (with or without external catalyst) to expedite the process of improvement. Figure-1 illustrates the grass root e-governance improvement framework. Bi-directional extended threads are indication of processes that may oscillate between two stages targeting positive achievement, and the uni-directional arrows marks the sequential development of the whole system, but should swivel at each stage of the elevated platform of the knowledge communities. The system should act as a perpetual system, desiring increased emphasis of the previous stage at each consecutive stage. Author argues that, an improved e-governance system would always demand greater input from its preceding stage,

Figure 1. E-governance framework leading to community practices

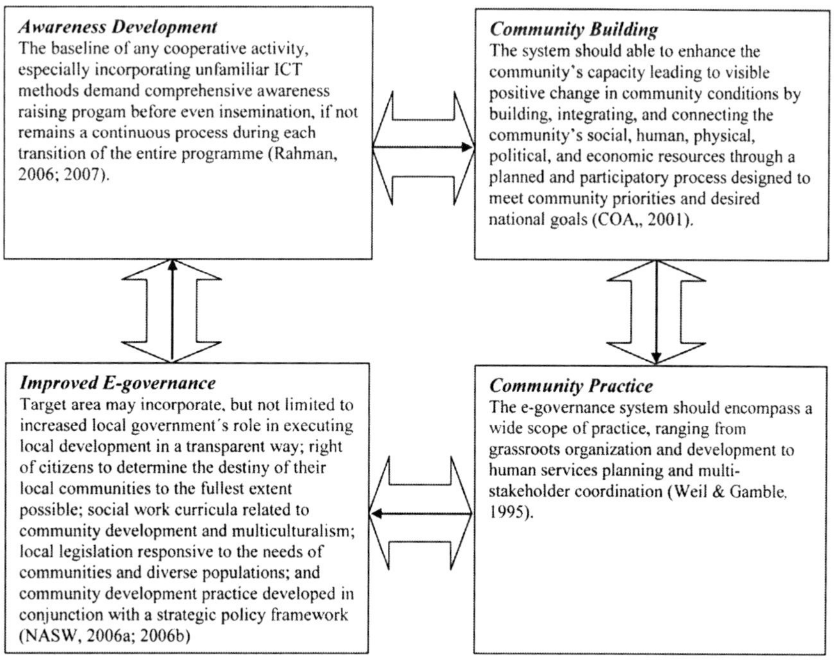

Context of the Framework

- Awareness development activities can be carried out in partnership with government agencies, non-government organizations and civil societies;
- Community development activities should incorporate available physical and logical infrastructures (information, social, or other form of networks);
- Community practices may follow social work curricula related to community development. Social work participants should be knowledgeable about the ways in which communities and populations with socioeconomic disadvantages can become more involved and competent in drawing on their strengths to solve problems and enhance the quality of their lives. Community developers should have a broad view of the community so that they can provide and develop local leadership and participate in the coordination of the multidisciplinary efforts incorporating a variety of community groups.
- The framework would promote legislation related to support the self-identified need of communities and strategies that directly engage community residents in leadership and service provision
- The framework would advocate the development and dissemination of best practices supporting open communications, intergroup dialogue, and expanded educational curricula that honor and reflect the strengths of diverse groups and encourage participation of these groups within their communities
- The framework would promote increased local government's role in executing functionaries at the local government level
- The right of citizens would determine the destiny of their local communities to the fullest extent possible
- Ctivities at local level should assist communities in gaining access to information and resources, develop local and participatory organizational mechanisms, and help citizens make socially responsible decisions and contributions
- Community development practice would be developed in conjunction with a strategic policy framework in which community participants may have effective contribution on both local and larger community context
- Knowledge workers can learn from their efforts in partnering with citizens from low-income, minority communities through community development activities, which address community concerns within positive and systemic strategies (nasw, 2006a; b; c).

and after a sequential run of a few rotations, the entire system would act on its own and rotate itself.

Contexts of SDNP

Acting in similar framework, the Sustainable Development Networking Programme (SDNP) was a revolutionary concept to promote community practices and sustainable development in small island countries and developing economies. Initiated by the United Nations Development Programme (UNDP) through a seed funding of around USD 4.7 millions, SDNP started establishing national hubs in about 15 countries during 1992-1996. By 2000, SDNP covers it's activities close to 80 countries to promote greater use of ICT for sustainable and human development (SDNP, 2004). There were about 14 in Africa; 7 in Asia; 9 in Eastern Europe; 2 in Middle East, 10 in Latin America; and 1 in South Pacific. This novel project was thought-provoking in those early days of information and communication technology evolution and enactment of another new concept, the sustainable development in many countries. It was a pragmatic step taken by the UNDP to promote grass root governance, and luckily the programme was taken in such a period when the whole world was thinking of promoting ICT for grass roots governance and sustainable development. As such, SDNP philosophy was nurtured at the WSSD[5] and WSIS[6]. Till date, much of those SDNP concepts are being carried out by major international forums that are involved in capacity development of the society as a whole, namely ITU[7], IGF[8].

SDNP, in most of the country of implementation, were the forerunner in terms of opening a new dimension of information dynamism in each country they started their journey. Ranging from providing simple secretarial services, information infrastructure development, skills development, and development of knowledge communities at the grass roots to advanced core information technological platforms like maintenance of root server, country code top level domain (ccTLD) servers, Internet exchange (IX), and so on.

SETTING THE STAGE

Concept of SDNP at the UNDP HQ

SDNP was launched by UNDP in May 1992, a month before the UN Conference on Environment and Development in Rio de Janeiro. The programme initiated about forty five country-level SDNP programmes and supported related feasibility studies in another thirty. It launched three sub-regional projects and provided managerial and technical support, including conceptual motivation to others. Over the years it was an advocate for the use of ICTs for sustainable development within UNDP itself and outside. Although new funding for the programme has not been secured at the global level after 2000, many SDNP projects continue to operate, and a significant legacy remains (Siochrú, 2002; SDNP, 2004).

At the United Nations Conference on Environment and Development (UNCED) in Rio de Janeiro, Brazil in June 1992, a global plan of action for sustainable development was endorsed by over 179 countries. This blueprint of action, more popularly known as AGENDA 21, emphasizes the importance of environmentally competent technologies, education, public awareness and training in achieving the goals of sustainable development. AGENDA 21 also recognizes the importance of capacity building, especially in developing countries in order that strategies for sustainable development could be implemented. Capacity building refers to cooperation among developing countries that encourages them to develop human and organizational resources to plan and implement sustainable development. At the Earth Summit, the UNDP was given the leading role within the UN development system for capacity building. CAPACITY 21, an action plan to assist developing countries formulate economic, social and environmental goals, plans, programs and policies that would lead to sustainable development became UNDP's response to this challenge (Siochrú, 2002; SDNP, 2004).

Originally called the *Sustainable Development Network* (SDN), it was later changed to *Sustainable Development Networking Programme*, reflecting the ongoing process of building consensus on the benefits of sharing information through the use of ICTs, and its design not as a single network but as many interlinked networks with gateways and linkages among them (Siochrú, 2002).

The objectives were to facilitate access to information for knowledge building leading to decision-making and encouraging the participation of various development actors such as civil society organizations (CSOs) in the development process. Originally conceived as a support mechanism for Agenda 21[9], the programme expended about USD 16 millions from a variety of sources inside and outside UNDP by 1998 (SDNP, 2004).

The focus was forward looking, in the sense that the goal is to extract lessons, and examine to what extent SDNP projects might in the future contribute to areas related to sustainable development and ICTs. As indicated earlier, the initial inspiration for the SDNP concept came during preparations for the 1992 Earth Summit, with the perception that many countries, especially poorer ones, lacking in reliable information base on sustainable development issues. However, the basic question was: How could countries take responsibility and be accountable implementing decisions at UNCED, in the absence of information needed to analyze and understand the current situation, and to monitor developments in the future? (SDNP, 2004).

Though conceptually mainstream, they were quite novel and exciting for UNDP at that time, but their combination into a single programme was a real challenge. The idea that information and access to it could play a critical role in decision-making; that networking and opening out to stakeholders to render the process and outcome of decisions on sustainable development in a more robust and effective way; and that ICTs and especially the Internet were tools that could revolutionize information and networking;

were also new to many countries, developed and developing. SDNP as a programme thus came lightly (but, adequately) equipped with strategies and concepts. Neither was it overburdened with institutional infrastructure and procedures (Siochrú, 2002; SDNP, 2004)

SDNP in other Countries

SDNP lasted in the main form during the period of 1992 to 2000 and reached close to 80 countries in efforts to promote extended use of ICTs for sustainable development and human capacity development. Presumably, the SDNP was one of the first global initiatives focused on bringing the benefits of ICTs to people in the developing world. A small team at UNDP HQ in New York managed the corporate programme, but the essence of the SDNP's activities took place in over 40 partner countries located around the world. The following table is compiled from a variety of sources, including documentation, interviews and Internet searches. It very briefly depicts the situation as of March 1, 2002 of all SDNP national and regional level projects (SDNP, 2004). During this research, available URLs were re-visited on June 10, 2009.

SDNP in Bangladesh

As stated in the Project Implementation Plan (PIP) of SDNP Bangladesh (SDNP, 2001), the SDNP is one of the concrete initiatives under the Global Agenda 21, specifically on Chapter 40 entitled "Information for Decision Making." In a sense, it is more than an information network. It embraces a whole spectrum of processes and events that ultimately contributes to the formulation and implementation of sustainable development strategies. In linking sources and users of information, the SDNP employs both face-to-face meetings, electronic and other means of communications. In this manner, the target population becomes more active for participating in the development processes.

The Government of Bangladesh put efforts to address these issues in collaboration with donors, policy initiators, NGOs and other advocacy groups. Among others the government approved the National Environment Management Action Plan (NEMAP) in 1996. NEMAP was in line with Agenda 21 and the Rio Earth Summit of 1992 (SDNP, 2003).

In 1997, as a follow-up to NEMAP, the Government also approved the UNDP assisted Sustainable Environment Management Programme (SEMP). There were five sub programmes under SEMP: Policy and Institutions, Participatory Eco-System Management, Community Based Environmental Sanitation, Awareness and Advocacy, and Training and Education. One of the strategies for promoting Awareness and Advocacy was enabling easy access to information and knowledge. To effectively implement such a strategy, the Sustainable Development Network (SDN) aimed to capitalize on the revolution in electronic communications technology and tried to provide a new set of tools to achieve sustainable human development through a sharing of vital information, experience and expertise both within the country and globally. The Bangladesh Institute of Development Studies (BIDS) was the implementing agency for two of the 26 components in SEMP - The Policy Analysis Studies which falls under the Policy and Institutions Sub-Programme, and the Sustainable Development Network (SDN, later given the name SDNP Bangladesh as other SDNPs across the globe) under the Awareness and Advocacy Sub-Programme (SDNP, 2001). After the funding was over in December 2006, SDNP Bangladesh became a not-for-profit Foundation, namely Sustainable Development Networking Foundation (SDNF).

CASE DESCRIPTION

With the advent of ICTs and the Internet, community practices inclined towards more virtual

Table 1. Summary table of sustainable development networking programme projects in various countries

Country	Began	Host	Website (spin-offs and comments in brackets)	Status (2002)	Revisit (2009)
Angola	1994	National University	http://www.angonet.org/ (www.ebonet.net)	Funding ended 1998. Project merged with ANGONET; Project staff created Ebonet	Site found live; acting as a repository for information on humanitarian NGOs and projects operating in Angola
Armenia	1996	UNDP	http://www.freenet.am/	Project 1999. Armenia Freenet part of the outcome.	Site found live; acting as an ISP
Bangladesh	1998	Research Center-BIDS/Government	http://www.sdnbd.org/	Funding continuing. Project still active with UNDP funded	Site found live; acting as a repository for information on sustainable development, acting as a Foundation
Benin	1996	Government	www.agentic.bj	Funding ended 1999. Transformed into government supported agency for IT promotion	The name server was unable to process this query
Bolivia	1993	Government Ministry of Sustainable Development	www.coord.rds.org.bo (closed)	Project closed in 1998, absorbed by government. Undertook Y2K project and Open Source, and ICT policy, including Dot Force focal point	Site found live; acting as a directory of web sites
Bulgaria	1996	Centre for Study of Democracy (NGO)	www.online.bg	Closed 2000. Training focus. Mainly ARC funded. Website now commercial Portal.	Site found live; acting as an ISP
Cameroon	1996	University	www.sdnp.undp.org/sdncmr	Funding ended 2001. Spun off as Schoolnet, independent from UNDP, active.	The requested URL was not found on this server.
Chad	1994	Research Center	closed	Project closed 2000. First ISP in Chad.	No URL
China	1995	Government	www.acca21.org.cn	Funding completed 2002. Current status uncertain	Site found live; found as the site of the Administrative Centre for China's Agenda 21
Colombia	1996	Local NGO/APC	www.rds.org.co	Active with UNDP CO support, new partnership with Development Gateway	The name server was unable to process this query
Costa Rica	1995	Research Center	http://www.rds.ucr.ac.cr/ Page not updated	SDNP support ended 1999. Development Observatory continues supported by University.	The name server was unable to process this query
Dominican Rep.	1998	Local NGO	www.rds.redid.org.do (inactive)	Project closed in 2000, no clear results	The name server was unable to process this query
El Salvador	1997	National Centre for Science & Technology	www.rds.org.sv (inactive)	Project closed in 1999, no clear results	The domain name does not exist
Estonia	1994	University	www.ciesin.ee (not updated – material archived)	Closed 1997. Regional Baltics, CIESIN partnership	Site found live; acting as an archive
Gabon	1996	Library, National Archives, Government of Gabon	www.primature.gouv.go or www.primature.gov.go	Closed 1998	The domain name does not exist

Continued on the following page

Table 1. continued

Country	Began	Host	Website (spin-offs and comments in brackets)	Status (2002)	Revisit (2009)
Guatemala	1995	University	www.rds.org.gt (inactive)	SDNP funding ended 1998. Content and training based. Project active, now an NGO Red de Desarrollo Sostenible (RDS-GT)	The domain name does not exist
Guinea		Isoc Guinee	http://www.snu-gn.org/CD-ENV/rddgn-ndx.htm	Inactive	The domain name is free for sale
Guyana	1998	UNDP	www.sdnp.org.gy	SDNP funding ended 2002. Recently founded an NGO called DevNet, with good prospects for the future.	Site found live; acting as a non-governmental non-profit organization
Haiti	1997	Government	www.rddh.org	SDNP funding ended 2000. Project active, now an NGO with UNDP CO support.	Site found live; providing various on-line services
Honduras	1993	Various	www.rds.org.hn	SDNP funding ended 1999. Successful NGO, starting large rural telecentre with IADB	The domain is free for sale
Hungary	1997	NGO (REC)	www.omikk.hu/sdnp (inactive)	Part of HP Donation, limited SDNP activity.	The name server was unable to process this query
India	1995	Government	www.sdnp.delhi.nic.in	SDNP funding ended 2001. Continuing, revised, with World Bank funding until mid 2003.	The domain name does not exist
Indonesia	1994	Government	www.sdn.or.id	Closed 1997. Limited results due to Government intervention. Web site now contains Open Source resources.	The domain name does not exist
Jamaica	1998	University	www.jsdnp.org.jm	SDNP funding ended 2002. Active, major activity in telecentres with some IADB funding	Site found live; acting as an NGO
Jordan	1998	University	www.sdnp.jo	Site not up to date although accessible.	Site found live; acting as an archive
Korea	1995	NGO (YMCA)	www.ksdn.or.kr (inactive 2001)	Closed 1998. Integrated into Korean APC node	The domain is free for sale
Kyrgyzstan	1997	NGO	www.ecology.elcat.kg (sporadic)	SDNP funding ended 1999; continues precariously on voluntary basis	The domain name does not exist
Latvia	1994	University	www.ciesin.ee	Regional Baltics, CIESIN partnership. Reference to the work undertaken before 1997 has been archived.	Site found live; acting as an archive
Lebanon	1996	Ministry of Env.	www.sdnp.org.lb (not updated)	Ended late 1999, active within Ministry	The name server was unable to process this query
Lithuania	1994	University	www.ciesen.ee (not accessible)	Part of regional Baltics project, CIESIN partnership	Site found live; acting as an archive
Malawi	1997	University	www.sdnp.org.mw	SDNP funding ended 2000. Active, self-sustaining ISP	Site found live; acting as a UNDP supported Malawi Government Programme

Continued on the following page

Table 1. continued

Country	Began	Host	Website (spin-offs and comments in brackets)	Status (2002)	Revisit (2009)
Mauritania	1998	Government	www.iiardd.mr in no more	Partnership with RBA IIA (no SDNP funding). Civil Society cyber café active. http://www.pnud.mr/cyberforum/index.html is an NGO e-forum that was developed as a result of the IIA/SDNP and is still active.	The name server was unable to process this query
Mexico	1996	Ministry of Environment	www.rds.org.mx (inactive)	SDNP funding ended 1999. Active, now a national NGO.	Site found live; acting as a directory service
Morocco	1994	Ministry of Environment	www.minenv.gov.ma (inactive)	Closed in 1997. Ministry took over the operation..	Site found live; acting as the site of the Ministry
Mozambique	1997	Ministry of Environment	www.sdnp.org.mz	Closed in 1999	The name server was unable to process this query
Nicaragua	1994	NGO	www.sdnnic.org.ni	Funding ended 1998. Active as national NGO, with ongoing funding difficulties.	The name server was unable to process this query
Pakistan	1993	IUCN Pakistan	www.sdnpk.org	SDNP funding ended 2001. Active, successfully changing gear. Associated with the Pakistan Development Gateway. Although it exists as a separate entity as well.	Site found live as a Fedora test page
Philippines	1993	Foundation	www.psdn.org.ph	Funding ended in 1998. Active, A foundation since its inception	Site found live; acting as a Foundation
Poland	1997	University	www.ciesin.ci.uw.edu.pl	SDNP was a junior partner in CIESEN; received HP Donation, limited SDNP work	The domain name does not exist
Romania	1997	Research Centre	www.sdnp.ro	Continuing until at least December 2004 with LA 21 funding.	Site found live; acting as the National Centre for Sustainable Development
South Pacific	1994	South Pacific Comm.	Never developed.	Closed after funding ended, little impact	No URL
Togo	1996	Chambre de Commerce, d'Agricultureet d'Industrie du Togo	www.rdd.tg (inaccessible)	Continues to be associated with the Chambre de Commerce but no further details available.	The name server was unable to process this query
Tunisia	1993	Ministry of Environment		Developed as intranet for Ministry Funded end 1997. Ministry executed.	No URL
Ukraine	1993	UNDP	freenet.kiev.ua (inactive)	FreeNet, associated with SDNP. Limited SDNP funding.	The name server was unable to process this query
SIDSNet	1996	UNDP	www.sidsnet.org	SDNP funding ended 1999. Moved to UNDESA in 2000, active. Now funded by the GEF	Site found live; acting as an archive

Note1: Websites were visited on January 09, 2004 (Adopted from SDNP, 2004) and re-visited on June 10, 2009

Note2: A few of those SDNPs are still alive serving communities in various forms, varying from non-profit, not-for-profit, foundation to commercial entities (shaded in Table-1) form of communication, rather than physical mode of communication. This chapter remained confined among community practices that seem beneficial to the community participants through effective utilization of ICTs, with special focus on knowledge development and e-governance at community level. For sake of comparison, it will cite a few other initiatives around the globe that are or were adopting community practices through ICTs, but as a case study the chapter will put forward information about SDNP Bangladesh. Like other countries, as initiated by the UNDP, the programme was one of the pioneers in adopting community practices to raise the standard of community participants in the country. Furthermore, the chapter will try to put forward a few future research hints for researchers acting in this field around the globe. The reason for choosing this case though it has been died out in 2006, is that SDNP in Bangladesh has acted as a pioneer in leading several strategies on ICT driven activities for knowledge acquisition at the community level, of which a few could be taken as success stories and perhaps, could even be replicated in other places of the country. This case will try to generate some illustrations from various reports and studies about its dilution, despite its tremendous potential to be a unique institution of excellence.

As mentioned earlier, unusually among SDNP projects globally, SDNP in Bangladesh from the outset was conceived an integral part of a much larger $26 million UNDP-supported initiative, the Sustainable Environment Management Programme (SEMP). This provenance accounts for its exceptionally large budget as compared to other SDNPs of around USD1.5 million, but also incurs some delays and ambiguities around its objectives (Siochrú, 2002).

SEMP[10] was a Programme of twenty six components, under the Ministry of Environment and Forest (MoEF). It follows on from the National Environment Management Plan (NEMAP) which ran from 1997 until 1999 and traces its linkage to Agenda 21 and the Rio Summit. SEMP components were organized into five sub programmes (mentioned earlier). It was quite decentralized in structure, the components being implemented by selected Sub-Implementing Agencies (SIAs). Most of these were autonomous entities, including statutory agencies, several NGOs, and even the World Bank. Built into this programme was a sub-programme component 4.5, "Awareness and Advocacy and Training and Education" which constitutes the basis for SDNP in Bangladesh (Lal, 1999; Siochrú, 2002).

The SDNP in Bangladesh comprised one component of SEMP under the Sub-Programme: Awareness and Advocacy, and the SIA responsible for it was the Bangladesh Institute of Development Studies (BIDS). BIDS is a highly-respected, influential and relatively impartial policy-oriented research organization, working across many disciplines of social science and human aspects. It has a major national information dissemination function through publications, library services, regular seminars and workshops. Mainly due to its central role in research and information dissemination made it a candidate to implement SDNP.

UNDP in Bangladesh floated the idea of SDNP Bangladesh as early as mid-1996, but initially it had not been taken up. A UNDP mission´s visit to SDNP in Pakistan had developed some ideas relating to ISP (Internet Service Provider) development. But by 1997 there were already about 20 ISPs operating in Bangladesh (though full internet services were available only in Dhaka and perhaps one to two other metropolitan cities) so that the Pakistan model (at that time SDNP Pakistan was the leading national ISP) would not easily slot into place. Moreover, at government level, there was also little initial interest in SDNP (Siochrú, 2002).

In early 1997, as SEMP appeared on the horizon, UNDP found a more welcoming context. It was promoted primarily as an 'internal' resource for SEMP, but always had its broader SDNP objectives alongside. Without the SDNP input, SEMP would undoubtedly have had a support component for interaction and dissemination, but it would probably have lacked the ICT dimension and the specific experience and approaches of SDNP (Siochrú, 2002; Zambrano, 2003; SDNP, 2004).

Development Goals

The objective of SDNP was to create an appropriate framework for achieving and facilitating exchange of information/knowledge, encouraging increased collaboration, communications and networking among development partners, academia, policy makers and the civil society at local, national and international level, in order to design and implement plans for sustainable development in Bangladesh (SDNP, 2001; 2003).

Immediate Objectives

As stated in the development goals, the main objective of the programme was to provide an ICT-based information, content and service network for Bangladesh that was open, inclusive and participatory so that an increasingly level playing field is created for all. Other broad objectives were to:

- help create conditions for civil society, the government, business and individuals to work, both together and separately towards facilitating quality and transparent governance through knowledge and information sharing;
- create an instrument for generation of public opinion on matters of developmental importance and facilitate the exchange of experiences and follow-up of civil society actions;
- facilitate social, economic, cultural and intellectual development of individuals and groups in society;
- facilitate the development of the private sector through e-commerce;
- facilitate proper development of a knowledge management system; and
- promote the Bengali culture and heritage (SDNP, 2003).

The programme had several specific objectives, though, as such, to achieve the broad objectives, the SDNP would:

- Design, develop, establish and continuously improve upon the web portal and its database;
- Provide access to information and resources through suitable means to end users for enhancing knowledge and experience;
- Create a common platform of information bench mark for shared materials, making dialogues, problem solving sessions with easy access and faster communication speed;
- Generate, design and disseminate data and information for utilization by the stakeholders;
- Provide links to ideas and success stories, best practice information about development activities and trends, funding sources, and commercial and research opportunities;
- Support the local government, community representatives and NGOs, particularly small ones in their development activities thus increasing transparency, speed of action and better governance (SDNP, 2003).

Management

The policy oversight was provided by a Steering Committee, chaired by Prof. Jamilur Reza Chowdhury (a renowned ICT expert in the country) and comprised of Secretary, Planning Division, Ministry of Planning; Secretary, Ministry of Post and Telecommunications; Resident Representative of UNDP, National Programme Director, SEMP; Director General, BIDS and representatives from NGOs, ISPs, journalists and social elites. The terms of reference of the Steering Committee is given in Box 1.

Initial Scenario

As it was conceived, the methodology for achieving those aims in a sustainable way, was to consider a model where SDNP would be a non-profit Internet service provider (ISP) having a central hub in Dhaka city at the Bangladesh Institute of Development Studies (BIDS), and five regional nodes in Chittagong, Khulna, Barisal, Sylhet, and Rajshahi involving a combination of systems including Local Area Networking, Wide Area Networking, and Microwave links. However, as both the technology and management of such network was unfamiliar in Bangladesh, and it was being established for the first time, by the suggestion of the Steering Committee, another regional node was included for Mymensingh. The reason was that by learning from the experience in running the Mymensingh regional node, operating other regional nodes that are far away from the head quarter would be easier. Moreover, there were tremendous demand of Internet based information network at the nearest periphery of the capital, Mymensingh, which is about 100Km away from the BDIS. Most importantly, the regional node was established in the largest agricultural university in the country, which obtained high appreciation from home and abroad[11]. Figure 2 shows the five regional nodes, including the Mymensingh node.

Initial concept of SDNP was like that, subscribers to the SDN would be given access to standard Internet services as well as to a database maintained by BIDS. The target subscribers would include Ministries of the Government of Bangladesh and other agencies implementing the various components of SEMP. They were allowed to contribute to the database, and/or through the SDN and have their websites, setup to disseminate information on their activities and achievements, hosted on the SDNP server. In addition the SDNP catered to other corporate users wishing to access the database and to standard Internet services, including national and regional press clubs, academic and research institutions, and public libraries (Lal, 1999).

Project implementation began in mid 1999. An inception workshop, an important step for SDNP

Box 1. Guideline for the formation of the Steering Committee

TERMS OF REFERENCEOFTHE SDNP STEERING COMMITTEE

"The SDNP Steering Committee is an integral part of the overall implementation process of the project. The role of the Steering Committee is to provide advice, direction and support to the SDNP Implementing Unit (SDNPIU) on an ongoing basis. The Committee will comprise IT specialists as well as representatives of the Government, of the SEMP partners, of the media, of academic/research institutions, of the private sector, and other stakeholders. The Steering Committee thus ensures stakeholder participation in the management and operation of the SDNP, without being directly responsible for any aspects of project implementation such as financial management.

The Committee will seek consensus on decisions, and where consensus is not possible, a majority vote will carry weight with any dissenting notes recorded in the minutes if so desired.

The Chairperson of the Committee will be selected from among the members and will be appointed for a period of one year. The Secretary of the Committee will be the SDNP Administrator from within BIDS. Quorum for a meeting of the Committee is 50 percent of membership and meetings will initially take place quarterly which may later be reduced to half-yearly if SDNP progresses satisfactorily. Extra-ordinary meetings may be called as and when necessary.

The Steering Committee will advise on:

- Plans, activities and achievements with the SDNP Coordinator;
- Long-term planning measures;
- Sustainable operation of the SDNP on a non-profit basis;
- Contents of database;
- Policy issues regarding operation of SDN;
- Resolving conflicts between SDNP users/members;
- Sensitizing and promoting actual and potential user groups;
- Any other relevant issues that may arise from time to time" (SDNP, 2001:40).

Figure 2. Six regional nodes of SDNP Bangladesh

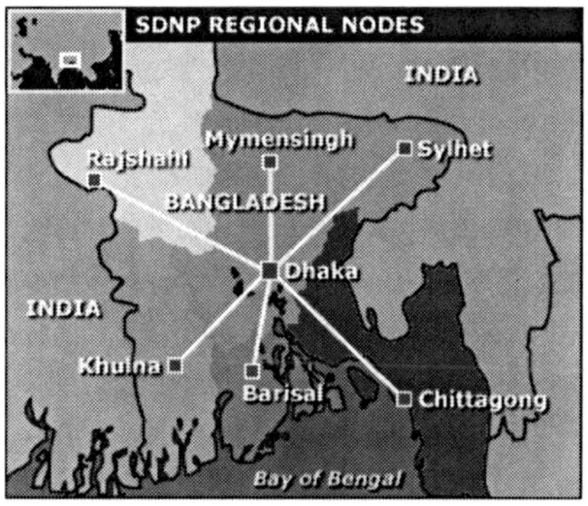

in Bangladesh to formally begin the process of concretizing SDNP, was held on July 4th 1999. Input from the stakeholders provided information on on-going initiatives by other sectors and focused on the conditions under which the project could be sustainable, whether or not the project should offer services free of charge (which the ISPs felt could undermine their own profitability), whether given the pace at which the Internet was proceeding to penetrate Bangladesh there should be a rethinking about the formation of the project, the ways in which the project could reach out to the poorest of the poor. The first SC meeting scheduled for the week of July 12th, 1999.

As per the project implementation plan (PIP), outlined by BIDS, over the next few months, the project was expected to:

- Determine connectivity solution and contract selected ISP;
- Recruit project staff;
- Train project and other BIDS staff;
- Procure necessary hardware and software;
- Prepare BIDS site and arrange communication systems and other necessary facilities such as electricity, a stand-by generator, UPS, etc.;
- Install and operationalise central hub in BIDS, including LAN, intranet, etc.;
- Develop database;
- Develop BIDS policy for SDN's usage by BIDS staff;
- Recast/revise budget with approval of UNDP and the Ministry of Environment;
- Operationalise desktop publication section for printing/publishing brochures/reports for information dissemination on SDN (Lal, 1999; SDNP, 1999).

TECHNOLOGY CONCERNS

The Methodology

The methodology for developing the SDN was to establish a non-profit ISP with the central hub in Dhaka city at the BIDS and six regional nodes throughout the country. Regional nodes would be established in Barisal, Chittagong, Khulna, Mymensingh, Rajshahi, and Sylhet through a combination of systems that include Local Area Networking, Wide Area Networking, Microwave links, and Online networking using VSAT.

Stakeholders would be given access to standard Internet services, web support and database services. The primary subscribers included Ministry of Environment and Forests, Ministries and other agencies that were implementing the various components of SEMP. Those agencies were also contributed to the database through the SDN, set up websites for better information dissemination to showcase their activities and achievements.

In addition the SDN was catering to other corporate users wishing to access the database, build web sites for them and avail standard Internet services. Such users included national and regional press clubs, academic and research institutions, and public libraries. Later on to promote community practices on ICT, SDNP extended its operation through multifarious activities, such as School Programme, Telemedicine, eLearning, Online Bloodbank, accessing server using cellular phone (long before it was commercialized) for email, news update and database search. To assist in the establishment of the SDN, UNDP provided BIDS with a starter kit comprising computer hardware and software, key databases, management and training tools, decision support tools, and other resources to meet individual needs and ensure long-term compatibility with SDNs operating in other developing countries. Later on SDNP acquire adequate hardware of information infrastructure to establish the most complex Internet based information network at that period in the country.

The Steering Committee provided advisory support to BIDS. The Committee comprised of ICT specialists as well as representatives of the Government, of the SEMP partners, of the media, of academic/research institutions, of the private sector, and other stakeholders, as depicted in Box 1 (SDNP, 1999).

PROJECT STRATEGY AND INSTITUTIONAL ARRANGEMENTS

Technological

The telecommunications sector in Bangladesh was characterized by a very low level of penetration, limited capability to meet the growing demand, low level of investment and old outdated systems and technologies necessitating reactive remedial measures. In order to develop a national sound telecommunication infrastructure to support the economy and welfare of the country by providing telecommunication facilities on demand, assuring satisfactory quality of service and ensuring value to the customers, a sound National Telecommunication Policy was essential. The strategic vision of the government was to facilitate Universal Telephone Service throughout the country and where there is a demand, all those value added services such as cellular mobile telephone paging, data service, access to Internet, voice mail and video conferencing- all at an affordable cost without compromising performance (SDNP, 2001).

SDNP emerges in Bangladesh throwing a challenge to provide networking support through IT media using the available infrastructure, which could at most meet a minor demand of that contemporary period. Lack of a defined national communication backbone similar to many other developing countries remained the prime factor among numerous inclusive constraints. SDNP aimed to develop a unique tool set at the national level for establishing communications network among development partners in the country capitalizing innovative methodologies and adoptive policies. The project also contributed in the national IT policy consensus by devoting knowledge, experience, expertise and collaboration.

The strategy of SDNP depended on building information infrastructure, institutional collaborations and strategic alliances with all the stakeholders as development partners. The outreach programme included the community at large and reached through not only the digital media, but also through other available means and technologies. The essence of SDNP was to offer the services to all linked organizations and extend the linkages by assisting in setting up multi-directional interactive communications.

The Technology strategy was divided in three criteria:

- **Base stations:** Establishment of the information infrastructure in main node, regional node, information centres, cyber centres, Public Access Centres, Press clubs, schools, libraries and other important places;

- **Organizational linkage:** Efforts were given to develop at least 100 active users at each nodal point of SDN. Beside SEMP components, SDN connected environment and forestry, agricultural, science and technology, water resources and similar activity related government, non-government, UN and international agencies to establish a digital information network;
- **Outreach programme:** By the extension of SDN's nationwide network, activities involved offering of
  - information dissemination processes through egroups, web sites and BBS[12];
  - web site design, development and hosting;
  - database access;
  - email and Internet connectivity;
  - UUCP connectivity;
  - Leased line connectivity;
  - WAP connectivity;
  - Training facility;
  - School Programme;
  - e-Health Programme;
  - Institutional Collaboration Programmes
  - Establishment of Cyber centres and Public Access Centres and
  - Other human resources development programmes (SDNP, 2001).

TECHNOLOGY COMPONENTS

The Pilot Phase Project of SDNP Bangladesh comprised of the following technology components (to provide readers and researchers the ground view of ICT project implementation in those days, author preferred to provide the direct quote from these two documents- Lal, 1999; SDNP, 2001) (See Box 2)

NETWORKS OF SDNP BANGLADESH

As stated in earlier section, after various modifications of implementation strategies, the Barisal regional node (due to some unforeseen reasons) was shifted to Dinajpur (most North-West part of the country, agriculture rich base and predominantly more community focus). Mymensingh node (which was established at the Bangladesh Agricultural University (BAU) about 100Km from BIDS) was further penetrated to Phulpur (22Km from BAU) in partnership with a local NGO engaged in community practices, and more further to Haluaghat (28Km from Phulpur) in partnership with one of the largest privately run library in the country. Khulna regional node at the South-West was further extended to Tala (20Km away from Satkhira where the node was established), in partnership with the Bangladesh Red Crescent Society, BDRCS (which gave the opportunity to serve the remotest Bay areas through various fishermen villages and BDRCS (see Figure 3). The Tala sub-node was surprisingly run by village women providing emergency and regular health care services to the nearby communities. The astounding fact was that in 2005, the Tala node provided health care services to community women in number more than the government run institute in that area.

In the North-east, the Sylhet regional node could not be established due to the local partner′s engagement with solely for-profit mode of operation, though the MoU was signed much earlier. However, experience sharing and technology sharing continued till the end of SDNP. Being a base of non-expatriate Bangladeshis', Sylhet region find various investors to establish their Internet based services in more attractive ways. SDNP′s initial non-profit entity refrained the programme to take various for-profit or not-for-profit ventures, though that was necessary for its sustainability.

Box 2. Technical set up of SDNBD at the initial stage of its pilot phase

i. Technical Setup- The Pilot Phase (PP) of the project is planned by keeping the 'Daughter nodes' of the SDNBD (with a "Mother Node" at BIDS). At a later stage, the PP will be moved to a nodal point and the setup will be duplicated there.

ii. The Servers- In the PP, there will be two servers. They will act as primary and secondary servers.

iii. The Primary server- This server will perform as the database server. Since the 'Daughter nodes' will only mirror the database from the 'Central server', the database server is not going to be a single server by itself. The same server will act as the authentication server for the users, electronic mail (e-mail) server and primary Domain Name System (DNS) server as well. In addition, it will be configured for World Wide Web server and newsgroup server (which will be served by the secondary server) so that in case of a failure of the secondary server, it can resume those services to the users.

iv. The Secondary server- The Secondary server will provide World Wide Web service, File Transfer Protocol (FTP) service, News group service and also act as the secondary DNS server. But this server will have a duplicate setup of the main server, so that in case of a failure of the primary server, this will act as the primary server until the primary server restores its operation for uninterrupted services. This server will also be connected to the data backup device.

v. Other Major Hardware- The other major hardware are the Terminal server, the Modem pool and the Local Area Network (LAN) Switch. The details are provided below.

vi. Terminal server- A Terminal server acts as an answering machine for the users connecting over phone lines using modems. Since most of the users will be connecting over phone lines, a Terminal server is required. All the ports of the Terminal server will be configured for dial-in. The users will get connected to the Terminal server from outside the BIDS by dial-up method and the Terminal server will connect them to the whole network. Until further modification of the central node's setup, the PP is going to be connected to the Internet through one of the ports of the Terminal server by dial-up to the ISP.

vii. The Modem pool- The Modem pool is nothing but a group of modems in a single box or chassis for better management. The Modems in the pool will be connected to the Terminal server. The dial-in phone lines will be connected to each of the modems in the pool.

viii. Local Area Network Switch- For a UTP cable based Ethernet network, a LAN Hub or a Switch is required. It's opted to use a Switch because it provides much better bandwidth utilization over a Hub by reducing collision and caching the hardware addresses of the network adapters in the servers.

ix. Software- The Operating System (OS) and the various server software used for the project has to be highly reliable and stable as well as well performed. That is why Linux has been selected as the Operating System. All other various server software that are required are available under Linux, a Unix platform. The added advantage of Linux is that it is completely free of cost. The other SDN projects are also using Linux for their servers all around the world. Using Linux will give the flexibility of configuring the system better suited to the SDNP targets.

x. Network Protocol- The Network protocol is going to be the Transmission Control Protocol/Internet Protocol (TCP/IP). TCP/IP is the standard protocol for the Internet. It is also the native network protocol for the selected OS, Linux. Using TCP/P will give the PP the option of connecting to the Internet and exchanging information without any major modification to the setup.

xi. Servers setup details- The servers (Primary, Secondary server and the Terminal Server) will be connected to the Switch, thus forming the server LAN. The Hub of the Local Area Network consisting the workstations will be connected to a port of the Switch.

xii. Software setup details- Both the primary and the secondary servers will run under Linux. To make the setup robust, both servers will be configured to run all common services.

xiii. Database server- The Primary server will run as the database server. At the PP stage not much have been done regarding the database and they are not been finalized yet. Rather at the primary stage, it will be acting as a dummy database server by offering accessibility through any web browser.

xiv. Authentication server- When someone will try to log in over phone lines, the Terminal server will have to verify that the person is indeed a valid user with appropriate access. The Terminal server does this by contacting the authentication server. The primary server will hold all the user accounts and passwords. Therefore, the authentication service will be running on the primary server. The authentication service for dial-in will be the standard Remote Authentication Dial In User Service (RADIUS). The primary server will run the RADIUS service. The secondary server will keep a duplicated copy of the user database in case it has to serve as the Authentication server.

xv. Electronic Mail server- The email server software is going to be sendmail, the Internet standard Mail Transport Agent (MTA). All Linux distribution comes with the sendmail software. However, sendmail only acts as the transport agent, in other words, a different service is required for the user to download their mails. The standard protocol for that is POP3. Both of these services will be running on the primary server, since the user accounts are going to be on that. The secondary server will also have these services configured.

xvi. Domain Name System server- In the network world based on TCP/IP, each computer (either a user or a server) is identified by a numeric address. This numeric address is known as the IP Address. But for human usability, all the machines are given a name as well. The name to IP address mapping is known as the Domain Name System (DNS). Both the primary and the secondary server will run the DNS service. The DNS server software going to be used is Berkeley internet Name Domain (BIND). BIND itself has the feature of running in primary and secondary mode, which is going to be deployed in the standard way in the servers.

xvii. World Wide Web server- The protocol used for the World Wide Web is Hyper Text Transfer Protocol (HTTP). The WWW or HTTP server we are going to use is Apache, the most used http server on the Internet. The Secondary server will run this service, but the primary server will be configured for it as well.

xviii. File Transfer Protocol server- A File Transfer Protocol (FTP) server acts as a server that has many files (could be information, could be programs) which the user can transfer (known as download) to his or her computer. The Secondary server will provide this service. That means, all the downloadable files will also reside on the Secondary server. The primary server will also have this service configured.

Continued on the following page

Box 2. continued

xix. Newsgroup server- A Newsgroup is a discussion group, where any user can post an article or respond to an article posted by someone else. The Newsgroup server going to be used is InterNetNews (INN). INN is the most used Newsgroup server software on the Internet and comes with Linux as well.

xx. The PP in Operation- When a user needs some information and accesses the servers over the phone line, this is what happens:

1. A user wants to access some information
2. He/She dials the PP dial-in number using his/her computer
3. The modems get connected
4. The Terminal server asks for the users credentials (i.e. login and password)
5. The Terminal server consults the Authentication server to verify that the credentials provided by the user is valid
6. If they are invalid, access is denied and the user is disconnected. If they are valid, connection to the Terminal server is allowed to establish, which makes the user connected to the whole Local Area Network.
7. The user starts the appropriate application software (a web browser or email software) to access his required information
8. The application package connects to the server and fetches the information
9. The user disconnects. The phone line is freed.

If the user is on a local workstation on the LAN, the process is different. Since the user is already on a connected computer (the workstation), it is assumed that he or she is an authenticated user. Therefore, no additional authentication is required, except in case of the service he wants to access requires it (for example, checking e-mail requires authentication in all cases).

xxi. Maintenance and Backup Schedule- During the normal operation of the servers, the major maintenance job is to take backup of the servers on a regular basis. We have selected to use DLT4000 tape drives, which can hold up to 2OGB of uncompressed (40GB compressed) data. Backup will be taken every other day to a new tape. The tapes will be received after 30 days, which means there are going to be 15 tapes, each holding the backup of the servers for the past 30 days at an interval of 2 days. The backup device will be connected to the secondary server. The Primary server will be backed up over the network and the secondary server will be backed up directly (Lal, 1999: Direct quote from http://www.sdnbd.org/mission_report.htm).

Along the South-East belt, Chittagong University, another renowned public university hosted the Chittagong regional node, and as Sylhet node could not be established, the hardware were utilized to established another unique interface across the Bay of Bengal, the sea-resort city, Cox's Bazar. Establishing, the Cox's Bazar regional node not only provided an interface between environment and calamity prone Bay areas, but also bought immense opportunity towards its sustenance through providing Internet based services to a private run university at Moheskhali (an isolated island, where SDNP also established one multi-purpose village information center), and sea-resorts, hotels and motels through a privately run Internet service provider. As stated, utilizing the dedicated services

Figure 3. Transformed regional nodes of SDNP

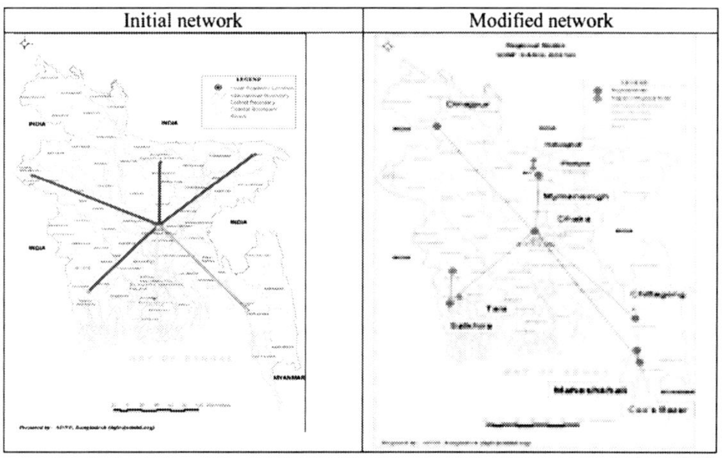

Figure 4. Southern portion of the country across Bay of Bengal

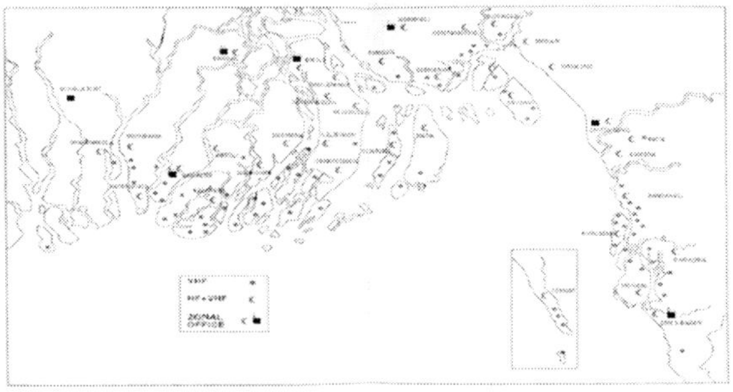

of BDRCS, the Southern belt of the country was taken under disaster management program (Figure 4). Even, many computers were donated to different fishermen villages under SDNP School Programme.

SDNP took the advantage of running weekly tele-medicine sessions utilizing this complex backbone of MCPC (Multi Channel Per Carrier) VSAT (see Figure 5), SCPC (Single Channel Per Carrier) VSAT, own established radio links (operating on free frequency of 2.4 and 3.6GHz), ADSL, and simple data cables. SDNP could provide its various services across the country through its multi-faceted clients and stakeholders. They varies from government high officials, to NGO workers (especially, at Phulpur and Satkhira), to journalists (at Dinajpur), to salt farmers in Moheskhali, to village women (at Tala), to students (at all stations), to patients (at all stations), and to fishermen across the Bay of Bengal. All of the community participants could obtain their respective services from all regional nodes, sub-nodes, and multi-purpose village information centers, but within parenthesis the activities at those particular areas are being emphasized.

In terms of establishing community based information center and cyber center where Internet services were be made available, SDNP was a forerunner in the country. Establishment of the first publicly available free cyber center at BIDS, and later on extension of the service to other parts of the city (see Figure 6) was a milestone for SDNP. Similarly, wherever the project went, it tried to made partnership with local communities, whether they were village women, or fishermen, or researchers or academics. While going to Mymensingh over Gazipur (a town of education and agricultural hub, see Figure 7), SDNP made part-

Figure 5. MCPC VSAT circuit of SDNP covering Chittagong, Dinajpur, and Satkhira regional nodes

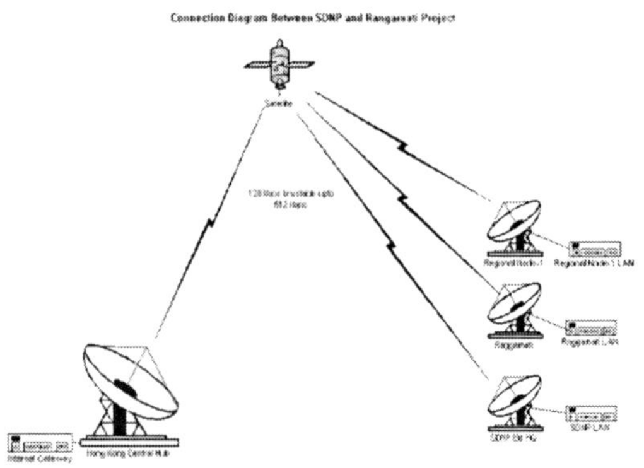

Figure 6. Several free cyber centers in Dhaka city

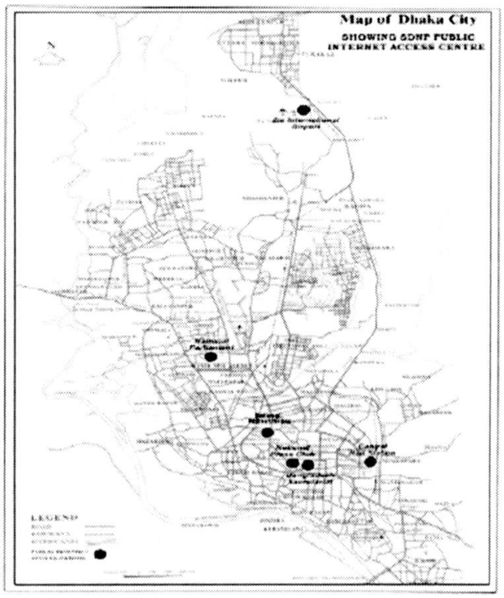

nership with Bangladesh Rice Research Institute (BRRI), and BIT (Bangladesh Institute of Technology) Dhaka (later on became, Dhaka University of Engineering and Technology, DUET). Moreover, Bangabandhu Sheikh Mujibur Rahman Agricultural University (BSMRAU) was purposely chosen as the repeater station for the radio relay towards Mymensingh. BSMRAU was a successful partner of SDNP Bangladesh. Furthermore, as another relay station at Bhaluka, the local rural electrification board of Bhaluka, REB Bhaluka was selected, as they were the successful rural electricity provider of the country, and deals with huge databases on energy distribution (see Figure 8).

Finally, to show some more community partnership of SDNBD, connectivity between the lone government high official training centre at Savar,

Figure 7. The Gazipur sub-node along the Mymensigh regional node

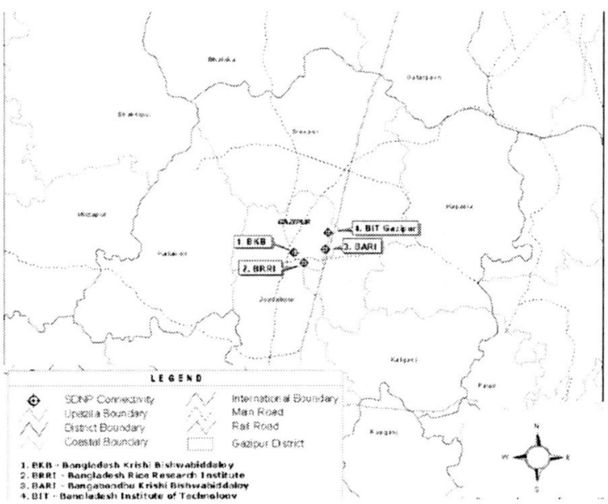

Figure 8. Radio link connectivity between BAU and SDNP at BIDS

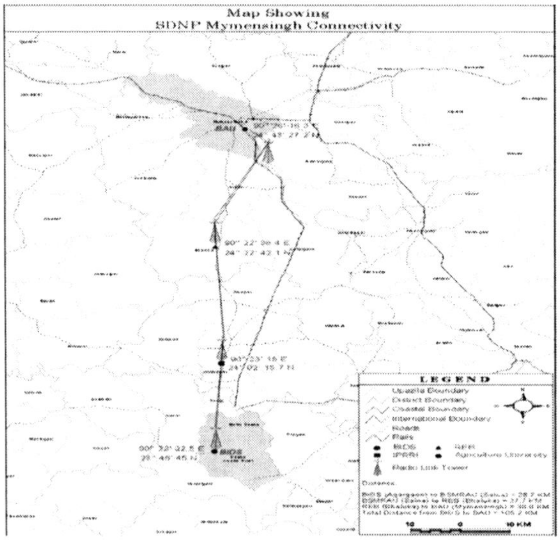

namely Bangladesh Public Administrative Training Centre (BPATC); connectivity between geographically dispersed database servers of SDNBD, but sequentially updated; and connectivity of Bangladesh Internet Exchange (BDIX), the lone Internet exchange at that period in the country are shown in Figures 9, 10, and 11 respectively.

MANAGEMENT AND ORGANIZATIONAL CONCERNS

As the project has already been closed since December 2006, the author would like to draw attention of concurrent researchers on the management and organizational issues, just quoting from various reports and investigations, rather not rephrasing any words or sentences. They were taken with the intention to enlighten researchers engaged in similar researches across the globe. (Box 3)

Global SDNP projects were developed in collaboration with the governments of the countries concerned, but did not always focus their operations on the government. CSOs were mainly the main beneficiaries (community participation was emphasized) along with other non-governmental stakeholders. The project in most, but not in all countries included a Steering Committee that brought together representatives of different stakeholder groups as advisors and partners with a stake in the SDNP project. A local management group was established, and a manager was sought, preferably with entrepreneurial skills and some understanding of local needs and of the potential of ICTs (SDNP, 2004). In this way, in terms of operational management, SDNP (globally and locally) established a unique pattern of community participation and community practices.

CURRENT CHALLENGES FACING THE ORGANIZATION

Challenges Faced at the SDNP HQ

Most of the projects of SDNP across countries faced various challenges, especially in terms of sustainability, after the completion of funding from UNDP. Sustainability involves a transition from the status of a donor-funded project guided by an initial set of prescribed objectives, to an entity

Figure 9. SDNP network connecting Bangladesh Public Administrative Training Center (BPATC) at Savar

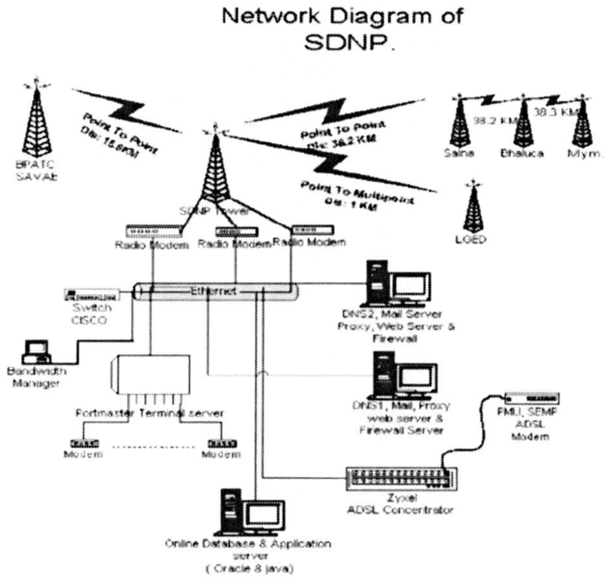

Figure 10. SDNP data bank located at various regional centers

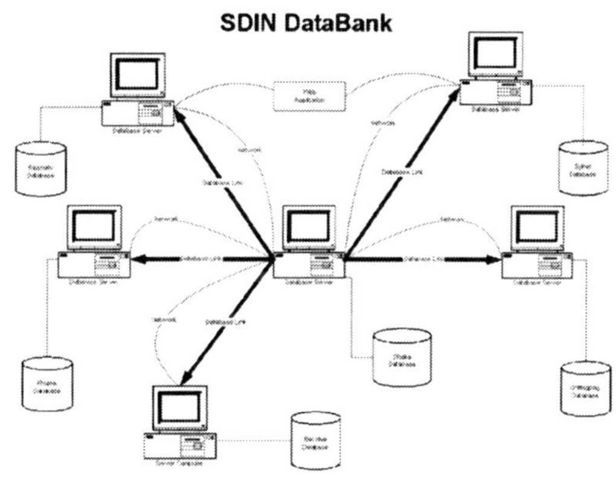

Figure 11. Bangladesh Internet Exchange

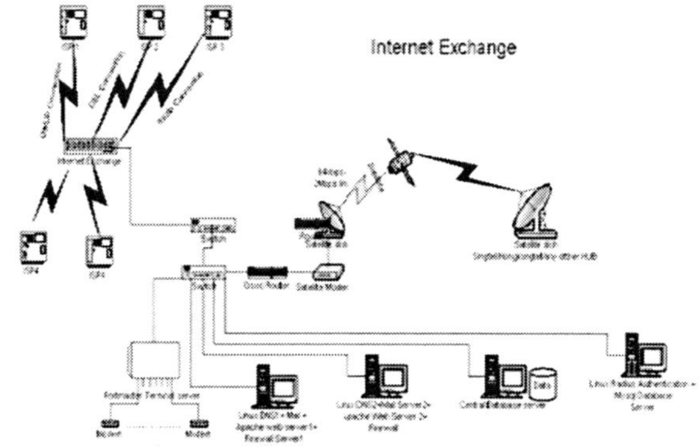

Box 3. Management concerns for the SDNP Bangladesh

"SDNP in Bangladesh did not from the beginning have a 'natural' home, as happened in some other countries. The idea did not originate with an organisation or entity that would later become the obvious candidate in which to house it. Rather, integrated as a component in a larger programme solely on the merits of the concept, an implementing agency had to be found, and SDNP had to be incorporated into this context or beneath its umbrella. BIDS was chosen because of its national reputation and national information generation and dissemination capacity and role.

However, it did take a little time for the more or less autonomous form of SDNP, housed within but not integrated within BIDS, to emerge, and this followed a number of discussions between BIDS and UNDP. The current institutional form and management structure were secured at the end of the first year with the appointment of the Project Coordinator.

The Project Director is also the Research Director of BIDS, and devotes part-time only to the Project – though in general his time commitment goes well beyond what is expected. The Project Coordinator is the full-time manager. The two work well together. The Project Director provides high level guidance and advice, often some ideas and contacts, and ensures a smooth and productive relationship with BIDS. SDNP has benefited from BIDS' good reputation.

The role of the Steering Committee is to provide "advice, direction and support", and is intended also to provide broad stakeholder input into the Project. It has met four times in the life of the Project so far *(till the report was written in 2002)*, first in mid 1999, and includes representatives of BIDS, UNDP, PMU, the Ministry of Posts and Telecommunications, IUCN Bangladesh, MoEF, IUCN, the ISP Forum, and the SDNP Coordinator (member-secretary). It has been chaired from the beginning by Professor Jamilur Choudury, the Vice Chancellor of BRAC University and a renowned ICT specialist in the country.

Though only four meetings have been held, it offers at least some link to major stakeholders including the MoEF, the PMU and UNDP. It also facilitates positive relations with non-SEMP stakeholders such as the ISP Forum (representing private ISPs) - although they have other occasions to interact. Meetings have given advice and, as far as can be ascertained, that advice has been acted upon.

The Project interacts more frequently with some individual members of the Steering

Committee on an informal basis, especially with the Chair. Professor Choudury is a highly experienced and respected professor from BRAC University, with a strong commitment to the Project and with a broad vision of its potential. His support continues to be an important element.

Overall then, the management oversight structure and functions reasonably well. It has allowed flexibility and not hindered progress. It has met and given advice which has largely been followed. And, as is often the case, it is at the personal level of commitment and caliber of individuals that the positive value has arisen, and here the Project is served well. Internal management is distinct.

SDNP has a total of 14 staff, with at present only the Project Coordinator (advised by the

Director) engaging in management activities *per se*. The SDNP team appears to be appropriately-qualified, very committed and highly motivated, and the technical quality and outputs of activities is high. The Coordinator is well-qualified and suited to the job, experienced and extremely committed. But he is personally responsible for a huge range of simultaneous tasks that are generated by the project's large, diverse and demanding portfolio.

The fact that delays resulted in the need to move concurrently on many fronts compounds the challenge. As a result, management is extremely stretched and cannot possibly handle all the demands currently upon it, no matter the level of commitment. Understandably, the highest priority is given to designing, launching and running the main activities.

This probably explains, at least in part, the relatively poor communication, in level and quality, between SDNP and the PMU and UNDP. Exacerbated by the accelerated rate of implementation, the result is that the UNDP and PMU appear to underestimate the potential and actual achievements of the SDNP Project; whilst SDNP is failing to report on its strategies and ideas and even successes.

A further contributory factor may be the dual origins of this Project. SDNP reports to the

PMU on both SEMP and non-SEMP related activities; but the PMU is understandably focused on SEMP. UNDP provided the original inspiration for many of the non-SEMP

SDNP activities, yet with its changing personnel and removed relationship, it cannot offer the continuity in direction. Thus the non-SEMP activities are somewhat out on a limb.

Perhaps the Steering Committee might have been expected to bring together the several objectives of SDNP into a more coherent whole. However, the first step would have been to identify the issue of the dual objectives, and the strains it causes internally within the Project and in relation to communications with major stakeholders. This was not done, but the question could be raised again now.

SDNP has not so far suffered materially from the relatively poor lines of communication.

However, as the SEMP Programme comes under review, it will be essential that all sides are communicating well and understand their challenges and achievements.

The PMU itself also seems to be under pressure in terms of its management and coordination burden. It appears to have made little effort to familiarise itself with non-SEMP activities of SDNP, or indeed to prioritise the networking and dissemination activities of SEMP to which SDNP is to act as the key partner.

This points to another area in which SDNP is not achieving as much as it might – serving the SEMP programme. This was already considered above, but the pressure on management, combined with poor communication with PMU, probably results in less creative energy on both sides being devoted to devising ways in which the SEMP programme can be better supported and disseminated through the use of ICTS and networking.

A third area receiving insufficient attention is around monitoring and evaluation of activities. This is not merely a question of learning abstract le ssons. It is about feeding into the ongoing management design of the activities, reporting on successes, and building for future sustainability. It also related to formulating and reformulating objectives and resources usage" (Siochrú, 2002:24-25).

with the capacity to support itself by attracting the necessary resources, capable of autonomous strategic thinking and flexible adaptation to a changing environment. In the best of circumstances it was a difficult transition to navigate since it demanded an inversion in approach. From being driven by concrete finite *goals*, sustainability means evolution towards a more abstract and ongoing *process*. From an initially secure (and hence ignored) resource base, it was to learn to tap into ongoing resources as a critical survival tactic. The skills required to implement a project were sometimes quite different, even contradictory to, those needed to build institutional sustainability. Thus, achieving sustainability comprised two parallel processes that sometimes came into tension. The task for project management at every level was to steer the process such that tension would be minimized, and the optimal balance was maintained during the lifetime of the project between capacities essential to effective project implementation and those essential to institution building and sustainability (SDNP, 2004).

The pressure to generate income, in itself, also raised tensions within Projects, and continued to, in terms of a tradeoff between maximizing income and keeping the focus firmly on development. For some, the issue became how much the project would have to forego its original mission on the grounds, in terms of financial survival, especially where there was doubt over the development value of the income-generating activity, as such the provision of conventional ISP services. But even an apparently effortless transition, moving from a project within a Ministry to a mainstreamed activity or programme was problematic. Although funding would be secured through mainstreaming, the challenge facing an SDNP in retaining a clear identity and a focus on the principles and *modus operandi wa*s probably only just beginning. This was not helped in many countries where governments could not, for legal reasons, allow SDNP as a UNDP funded project to adopt a cost-recovery strategy that might have helped to secure its identity and character. Maintaining a responsive and flexible approach to ongoing needs, innovating in a dynamic environment, remaining transparent and inclusive, and sustaining credibility and interaction with non-governmental stakeholders was difficult while operating within a government environment and without the corrective influence and support of external donor agencies. Much depended on whether the government understood the concept, the value it has placed on it, and the benefits it believed could be derived. This in turn was likely, initially at least, to rely on a few 'champions' to take it to secure moorings within the governmental complex, and on constructing a credible internal institutional context (SDNP, 2004).

Internally (including the Steering Committee), the transition referred to above meant that basic objectives would be reformulated in the light of the experience of the project, and the requirements of sustainability. On the business side, the development of Business Plans and management information systems was essential, but not enough. A psychological transition towards maturity and self-sustainability was often a critical part of that. And management and staff would take control and responsibility for the future of the project, changing the entire culture. This could involve a combination of income-generation, donor funding, government programme support and other elements. However, even if successful in terms of income generation, those models resulted in severe strains to the development approach or policy of SDNP. It demanded a constant balancing act between the incentive to maximize revenue generation, and the need to remain true to clear development goals and address currently marginalized groups (SDNP, 2004).

There were some constraints that negatively affected management, including;

- The combination of ICT, sustainable development and entrepreneurial experience required of coordinators was not always easy to find, sometimes causing significant delays in recruitment

- The short duration and uncertainty of some projects led to a high turnover. Some coordinators and other key staff understandably accepted offers from the private sector, once technical or managerial training provided by SDNP was finalized
- Occasionally, the Ministry or other agency in charge severely constrained the activities of the Coordinator and the project, leading to disillusionment, inaction and sometimes staff departure
- Projects varied in staff numbers from two or three up to fifteen or more, which generated different levels of complexity of management tasks. It is difficult to adjudicate on management effectiveness beyond considering results and achievement, but as a general rule, projects often had some difficulty with nonoperational management tasks. Thus developing Business Plans and Strategies, communicating results, monitoring and evaluating progress and other 'secondary' matters were sometimes less well implemented than the main project actions (SDNP, 2004).

Challenges Faced by SDNP Bangladesh

The main challenge of SDNBD was to keep track of the development processes in general and monitor development indicators and activities and their consequences in particular, and make these information freely available to all stakeholders including the Government, civil society, business community, professional and other organizations, development partners and the people at large (SDNP, 2001).

The reach and effectiveness of SDNBD was critically depended upon resolution of other challenges successfully. They were:

- *Technology*: Keeping track of modifications regarding innovations in the field of information technology and adapt them for implementation within the network;
- *Social*: An overriding consideration for SDNBD was that no strata in society should be debarred from information (free flow of information down to earth to reach the terminal community, is a precondition of e-governance). However, the social challenge was to create awareness among all social elements and remove as far as possible the digital divide within the country, target the potential beneficiaries through proper techniques to improve their access to information technology;
- *Manpower*: The original project profile lacked to focus on adequate manpower provisions and hence needed to be upgraded with additional manpower both at the central node and regional nodes, including Public Access Centres (PACs), or multi-purpose village information centers (MVICs);
- *Resources*: Other than manpower, logistics and resources were also need to be upgraded for continuous technological updating. Most of the equipment needed to be upgraded at three to five years of interval; and
- *Sustainability*: The most important aspect of the project was a pragmatic plan of sustenance for its continuity in future. A sustainability plan was needed to be developed and operationalized (SDNP, 2001; SDNP, 2004).

SOLUTIONS AND RECOMMENDATIONS

Several of the SDNPs had success in bringing affordable connectivity to many stakeholders and creating adequate local capacity (through community participation) to carry the effort on a sustainable basis; and furthermore, those were coupled with awareness promotion and skill development aimed at marginalized and more rural groups. SDNP fostered the introduction of Free/Open Source Software (FOSS), provided adequate governance mechanisms for the management of national Internet domain names and numbers, helped in the creation of national and regional Cisco Academies and contributed on a substantial basis to the emergence of e-governance networks that connected citizens and governments. Moreover, many of the technologies and applications were not readily available in developing counties and this favored the SDNP as an instrument of change that introduced new technologies and ways of doing things through utilization of ICTs (SDNP, 2004).

At the same time, even during the early days of Internet revolution, global SDNP guidelines could identify essential features of national level management and the institutional context, including a multi-stakeholder Steering Committee, and an independently appointed Project Coordinator. But recognizing that no single blueprint was possible or desirable, national stakeholders could steer this model in directions most suited to the local characteristics (adopted to local demand), building in these features as appropriate and thus enhancing the national 'ownership' and maintaining UNDP as a neutral facilitator. At the outset, the flexibility of the SDNP was essential to allow for adaptation to local specificities (SDNP, 2004). That assisted SDNPs to grow locally, and at the same time adopting global level technologies to the door step of extremely marginalized communities in their own ways, advocating community practices.

The SDNP Guidelines called for external recruitment and open competition in the selection of a Project Coordinator (National Project Coordinator, in most cases, as most of the projects were being implemented at national contexts), and this was insisted upon in every case. Open and public recruitment was the norm and the local media were used the medium for communicating employment opportunities at the SDNP. Selection criteria were established in several cases and selection was undertaken on the basis of an interview involving UNDP and representatives of the Steering Committee and of others as well, depending on the circumstances. In a number of SDNP projects, candidates were scouted for during the pre-feasibility study if possible. So some candidates were being already being courted before the establishment approval of an SDNP; in others recruitment took some time. There were a few cases where the Coordinator did not perform satisfactorily, and procedures were applied to remedy this situation. In overall, however, external recruitment was a success, and yet could be one of the fair selection process of recruitment at global level. Furthermore, SDNP projects were often perceived as exciting and rewarding jobs, which attracted high quality candidates who brought enthusiasm, commitment, entrepreneurial skills, experience and ability to the job. However, the quality and commitment of SDNP staffs and the Coordinator were absolutely critical to success. The level of commitment of some was such that even where financial sustainability was not achieved, staff members continued working for much lower remuneration or on a voluntary basis. In a few projects, delays and suspensions also left staff in part-time employment for lengthy periods during which departures were surprisingly few. Conversely, a few coordinators who never extended their employment horizon beyond the duration of funding significantly reduced prospects for sustainability (SDNP, 2004).

The SDNP Legacy

Within the context of UNDP's mainstreaming on ICT4D (ICT for Development), there was clearly a role for an expanded SDNP inspired or "*SDNP like*" activity aimed at enhancing the capacity of development actors to take advanage of ICTs, to be informed and to participate in the development process and in decision making as well as in government. They acted as catalytic factor in many countries in improving grass roots e-governance, if not initiated the process of e-governance in many countries. Indeed, the importance of ICTs as enablers of many of the essential ingredients of good governance combined with the need to build the capacity of governments and of other development actors to take advantage of these technologies and management practices are reasons to seriously consider supporting an ICT for Governance (or e-Governance) initiative or activity at UNDP (SDNP, 2003; SDNP, 2004).

The SDNP created many bridges between government and NGOs as mentioned above. In some cases, the Steering Committees were useful in bringing key decision makers together, people that would otherwise not meet. SDNP's experience in many countries of working closely with the government and especially with civil society organizations is a model upon which UNDP build as a way of delivering the benefits of ICTs in support of good governance. Given the agency's strong corporate experience as a result of the SDNP and other successful ICT for development initiatives, this would seem as a logical consideration. As a result, UNDP was in a very good position, given the expertise and corporate experience that the agency has acquired through the SDNP, to support endeavors to use appropriate ICTs and community participation practices in support of more transparent, inclusive and informed decision making within the government and in general across those involved institutional bases in support of human development (SDNP, 2004).

SDNP, more than most other development agencies, has a track record that UNDP could leverage to the benefit of the countries, development actors and other partners it worked with internationally.

One of many possible future directions that UNDP could move in, would be to work closely with governments and other development actors in pushing for a model of governance for development (in effect, e-governance) that uses ICTs at the best advantage in order to encourage greater participation, access to and exchange of information and knowledge in development decision making and foster similar activities. UNDP could be involved with other partners in documenting best practices of ICT use for managing the development process in a fashion consistent with the principles of human resource development. This could form the base for activities and/or a practice area that focuses on helping countries and development actors to apply appropriate ICTs and appropriate management practices in support of good governance and human development. This practice area could draw on the extensive corporate experience of UNDP and help apply the lessons learned as a result of over 10 years and several millions of dollars of work undertaken and experience gained by the SDNP (SDNP, 2004).

Sustainability of SDNBD

This research argues that despite being a leading national project in the country, and befitting through a win-win situation from all stakeholders involved within, and despite smooth transition from the project state to the formation of an independent autonomous entity, SDNBD struggled to survive along the context of the SDNP legacy. Though the good news is that several of the partners became self-sufficient through the capacity development initiatives of SDNBD (Bangladesh Agricultural University at Mymensingh, Chittagong University at Chittagong, Bangabandhu Sheikh Mujibur Rahman Agricultural University

Box 4. Sustainability of SDNBD

"The issue of SDNP Bangladesh's long-term sustainability, as in a number of other SDNPs, has been somewhat ambiguous. The original Programme Support Document (PSD) of August 1998 for SEMP talks of a 'Terminal report' to evaluate the project and draw lessons. But the first Project Implementation Plan in March 1999 proposes by Year 3 to "place major focus on making SDN financially sustainable..." and the UNDP mission there in July 1999 takes it for granted that sustainability is "a major concern for the implementing agency and UNDP" but points to the absence of plan. The July 2001 Project Implementation Plan argues that if the Project is given additional funding until the end of 2004, sustainability will be possible. A Section is devoted to the topic, under a page in length, noting that many of its activities can contribute to sustainability. It singles out services such as training, Website development, UUCP and other Internet services, and professional networking consultancy. The Steering Committee of July 23rd 2001 approved a 'sustainability plan', which it has to be said amounted to no more than a revised tariff sheet for e-mail, Web browsing, UUCP, Web hosting and leased line, and (proposed) WAP services.

At present, the project still lacks a coherent model of what sustainability might look like, what it means in terms of its development goals, and how it can be achieved. Ultimately, the prevarication and uncertainty probably comes back to a combination of having two masters, as well as the frantic level of activity imposed on the Project in an attempt to make up lost time. But some months back, both project management and the Steering Committee fully acknowledged the urgent need for a Business Plan to follow this evaluation that will address sustainability in a comprehensive manner.

Here, we make merely a few comments on the potential for sustainability evident in the various activities; as well as the avenues suggested by those interviewed. In the Recommendations at the end, we suggest a few first steps that could begin even before the business Plan is developed.

The following are relevant to a future sustainability plan and emerged in discussion with the various SDNP stakeholders:

- Most believe that SDNP has a future as an autonomous entity, a registered non-profit company with development goals. SDNP management would favour this.
- BIDS, whose status is as an implementing agency of a Project, would also be satisfied with this, and might consider prolonging its close association with the continued use of the space and transmission tower, in return for the provision of services. BIDS has benefited from the SDNP project, especially in building up its LAN and general ICT capacity. At this point, however, BIDS has reached a reasonable ICT capacity, and Internet services generally are less costly and more readily available than before.
- All the income generated by SDNP has been held by BIDS for the Project. There is a general will to utilise this towards sustainability
- The not inconsiderable bank of equipment in SDNP could also go forward as an asset, and UNDP would probably be happy to see it used to development ends. This would include the Regional nodes, infrastructure links, Community Access Centres, as well as the ISP technologies. Of course, as assets, these are rapidly decreasing with the pace of technological change.

The more important assets in terms of sustainability are somewhat less tangible:

- As noted, the team at SDNP is highly skilled and motivated, and works well together. But their institutional capacity goes beyond the sum of individual staff members. There can be few groups in Bangladesh with this combination of technological, applications, and content development capability, and surely none with a development orientation. Technical skills include: IT system design and specification; Open Source software development; content sourcing, analysis and processing; advanced online database and Portal design; Domain name maintenance; Web design and maintenance; ISP service provision; and training and capacity building. Management skills in terms of identifying opportunities, building partnerships, project design and implementation are particularly strong.
- SDNP has, as far as we could ascertain, already gained a reputation for work of integrity and efficiency, among educational circles, with the press, and with some agencies and NGOs. This can be built upon.
- Partnerships entered into represent a net cost to SDNP, and are likely to continue to do so (at least overall) until the end of the funded period. Where income is generated, there is no assumption that it should match the cost, since this is a development project funded by the UN. These partnerships, as outlined-earlier, have significant potential to support a sustainability plan through the contacts made, the experience gained, the reputation earned. But in addition, a few may seamlessly evolve in the short to medium term from a net cost to a net income earner, such as Financial Information Service (BFIS[13]) and the JOBS[14] initiatives.
- The Regional Nodes may also have significant potential for income generation, much of it as yet unrecognised and emerging when services are rolled out around the nodes.
- When SDNP is confronted with private sector competitors for some of its activities, it may retain a certain cost advantage. There is evidence that private sector consultants currently charge very high prices – SDNP as a non-profit could offer similar services for considerably less (notwithstanding issues of unfair competition, which must be guarded against.) Furthermore, government ministries and agencies may be more comfortable working with an organisation like SDNP in relation to the internal organisation, networking and dissemination of its information. Both these points were made during interviews with well-placed non-SDNP informants.
- Although income generation is bound to comprise at least part of a sustainability package, the demonstrable success of its current activities would place the project well to attract further international grant funding.

Finally, it may soon be an opportune time to seek work in the ICT area. In September 2002, the Government endorsed a national *Information and Communication Technology Policy*, which proclaims the intention of using ICTs "as the key driving element for social-economic development". It covers a huge range of topics, from infrastructure to regulation to education and training. Although it is as yet low on specifics, a number clearly could relate to SDNP.

For instance, objectives include:

- To "set up national databases that are reliable and easily accessible to all the people";
- "special allocations for ICT project implementation in the public sector"; and~
- There are proposals around extensive ICT education in public and private educational institutions, for the creation of an Internet-exchange, 'cyber kiosks' in Post Offices; the provision of ICT facilities to NGOs; and much more. SDNP is well placed to bid for or implement many of these, if and when these aspirations are translated into an Action Plan, budget lines and concrete projects (Siochrú, 2002:26-27).

at Salna, Bangladesh Internet Exchange at Dhaka, and the mother institute itself at Bangladesh Institute of Development Studies), many of the extremely essential components of SDNBD could not continue after the funding was exhausted. There remains, a big question of why, though along the day of inception, till the day of transition, SDNBD had all out support from all corners, including UNDP, the government and BIDS. This research feel that, a specific research may be carried out with restricted mandate to study the follow up actions, and that study will be learning instrument for many donor agencies and civil-society organizations who are still finding new ways of strategies to improve grass roots e-governance through community participation. Similar to above, this research would like to point out a few remarks from a report prepared during the final evaluation of SDNBD during 2002. The surprising fact is that majority of the text in Box 3 remained applicable to SDNBD´s future existence, even after the project run for over six years from the submission of the report (The project started with a funding assurance from UNDP at around 1.4million USD, later on half way, during 2001-2002, the project budget was being reduced to around 700,000USD, however, with support from the UNDP core ICT4D team and the government, and by the recommendation of another independent evaluation carried out during 2003, final funding of SDNBD raised to around 1.9million USD). The observations of SDNP (2004) report are included in Box 4.

CONCLUSION

In e-government programmes, access has been considered as an essential element to reach out the citizens, but greater facilitation, broadening the gateway of knowledge, deepening the openness of the community participant, and mostly increased community participation in national dialogues would remain challenge for community participated programmes (Pacific Council on International Policy, 2002).

Community informatics is an emerging field that incorporates the utilization of ICTs for community practice in order to improve the socioeconomic well-being of a community. As mentioned by Gurstien (2000), community informatics is the application of ICTs to enable community development processes and achieve community objectives, including overcoming "digital divides" both within and among communities. Furthermore, the pervasive nature of the Internet has brought ICTs to large numbers of people who have never used them before, especially community-based telecentres in developing countries have provided access to ICTs where there is very little likelihood of individual to own a personal computer (Songan, Hamid, Yeo, Gnaniah & Zen, 2004). Recently developed community practices across many countries involve multi-dimensional aspects in terms of raising the livelihood standards through various means of ICTs, and found to be effective in elevating the basic knowledge level of community participants, which in effect has enhancing e-government structures in those countries.

However, as detailed out in this case study, it is worthwhile to mention that despite efforts from all corners towards attaining positive achievement and sustenance, many programs and, or projects across the world failed (just failed due to lack of proper attention or fund or support: total failure), or could not produce the desired outcome (failed to create sufficient community participation to remain to be part of the community: partial failure), or could not able to mainstream ICT4D within the local social domain (failed to attract interest at the national scenario, though somehow surviving at the local level providing various services: semi-failure), or could not remain within the legacy of SDNP (with which the novel project was designed at the very early stage of information revolution: a failure but need to be termed). The last terms, which has not been defined in this research and perhaps, the other terms are very fragile in terms of providing sufficient background, ethics and impetus on the entire subject matter. As mentioned before, this sort of project failures demand intricate, thorough, transparent, and inclusive research so that similar other projects may take preventive measure, and reach towards sustainability. Otherwise, many billions of dollars are being entered in this sector globally, but without much visible outcome.

Talking about this specific project of UNDP in Bangladesh, this research is quoting the concluding paragraph from the report of Siochrú (2002:28), "Overall, this Project is ambitious, dynamic, capable and could potentially make a significant contribution to sustainable development, using ICTs, in Bangladesh. As SDNP Project's go, it is very well funded, but it expends these resources in a responsible and well directed manner. If anything, it risks taking on too much, to the extent that its management can barely stay on top of developments. The solution at this point is not to scale back on activities, but to redefine and refocus them, improve the monitoring and management information systems, provide additional management support, and design and implement a meaningful and robust sustainability plan". This research would like to look beyond horizon for a successful project in a sustainable way to reach out the people at large through community practices.

REFERENCES

Anderson, R. (2004). *Removing barriers, not creating them: Submission to the senate inquiry on the progress and future direction of life-long learning*. Canberra: Adult Learning Australia.

COA. (2001). "*COA's Standards and Self-Study Manual, 7th Edition, for Public Organizations*," by the Council on Accreditation of Services for Children and Families, 2001. Available from the Council on Accreditation of Services for Children and Families, Inc., 120 Wall St., 11th Floor, New York, New York, 10005, (212) 797-3000

Gurstein, M. (2000). *Community informatics: enabling communities with communication technologies*. Hershey, PA: Idea Group Publishing.

Harrison, D. D. (1995). Community development. In R. L. Edwards (Ed.-in-Chief), *Encyclopedia of social work* (19th ed., Vol. 1, pp. 555–562). Washington, DC: NASW Press.

Lal, R. (1999). *Mission Report: SDNP Bangladesh*. Available at http://www.sdnbd.org/mission_report.htm

McDowell, C.L., Nagel, A, Williams, S.M. & Canepa, C. (2005). Building knowledge from the practice of local communities. Volume 1(3): 30-40

McIntyre, J. (2005). Adult Learning and Australia's Ageing Population: A Policy Briefing Paper, Adult Learning Australia, Canberra, Retrieved 15/06/09 from http://www.artpages.com.au/johnmac/Age_learn_report.pdf

Michael, N., & Margaret, R. (2007, July). Creating Older Adults Technology Training Policies: Lessons from Community Practices . *Australian Journal of Adult Learning*, *47*(2), 308–324.

Murty, S. A. (2005, Spring). The Future of Rural Social Work . *Administration in Social Work*, *6*(1), 132–144.

NASW. (2006a). *National Association of Social Workers Policy Statements. National Association of Social Workers: 2006-2009*. Washington, D.C.: NASW Press.

NASW. (2006b). *Social work speaks. National Association of Social Workers*. Washington, D.C.: NASW Press.

NASW. (2006c). Community Development: The Community Development policy statement. In NASW's Social Work Speaks 2009-2012, Washington, DC: National Association of Social Workers, pp.56-60.

Pacific Council on International Policy. (2002). *Roadmap for E-Government in the Developing World: 10 Questions E-Government Leaders Should Ask Themselves*. CA, USA: Pacific Council on International Policy.

Petter, J., Byrnes, P., & Choi, D. (2002). Social Work Speaks: Community Development, *Policy statement approved by the NASW Delegate Assembly,* Washington, DC. *NASW Press, 2002*, 56–60.

Rahman, H. (2006). Empowerment of Marginal Communities through Information-Driven Learning. In Rahman, H. (2007) (Ed.). *Empowering Marginal Communities with Information Networking* Hershey, PA: Idea Group Publishing, 2007: 16-42

Rahman, H. (2007). Role of ICT in Socioeconomic Development and Pocerty Reduction. In Rahman, H. (2007) (Ed.). *Data Mining Applications for Empowering Knowledge Societies*.Hershey, PA:IGI Global, 2008: 180-219

Saelee, K. (2002). *Sustainable use of Biological Resources, Indigenous Peoples' Contributions to COP-8 of the* (pp. 227–243). CBD.

SDNP. (2001). *Project Implementation Plan: PIP,). Sustainable Development Networking Programme, Bangladesh, Version-D, 2001*. Available at www.sdnbd.org

SDNP. (2003). *Status Report of Sustainable Development Networking Programme (SDNP): Bangladesh Institute of Development Studies*, September 30, 2003. Available at www.sdnbd.org

SDNP. (2004) *Sustainable Development Networking Programme: Final Assessment,* Report of an independent external assessment, February, 2004. Available at www.sdnbd.org

Shaffer, C. R., & Anundsen, K. (1993). *Creating community anywhere.* New York: Tarcher/ Perigree.

Siochrú, S. Ó. (2002*). Sustainable Development Networking Programme, Bangladesh: Final Report*, December 2002. Available at www.sdnbd.org

Songan, P., Hamid, K. A., Yeo, A., Gnaniah, J., & Zen, H. (2004). Community Informatics: Challenges in Bridging the Digital Divide. In H.M. Khalid, H.M., M.G. Helander, M.G. & A.W. Yeo, A.W. (Eds.). *Work with Computing Systems 2004*, Kuala Lumpur: Damai Sciences.pp. 267-270

Spergel, I. A. (1987). Community development. In A. Minahan (Ed.-in-Chief), *Encyclopedia of social work* (18th ed., Vol. 1, pp. 299–308). Silver Spring, MD: NASW Press.

Tandon, et. al. (2007). Progress in Community Health Partnerships: Research, Education, and Action, Spring 2007 • vol 1.1, The Johns Hopkins University Press, pp.11-30 (1)

Weil, M. O., & Gamble, D. N. (1995). Community practice models. In R. L. Edwards (Ed.-in-Chief), *Encyclopedia of social work* (19th ed., Vol. 1, pp. 577–594). Washington, DC: NASW Press.

Zambrano, R. (2003). *Mission Report: SDNP Bangladesh.* 22 – 27 February 200. Available at www.sdnbd.org

ADDITIONAL READING

Amulya, J., & McDowell, C. (2003) *How Reflection Support Learning in Race and Democracy Work*. Available at http://crcp.mit.edu/documents/ReflSupportsLearning.pdf

Annie, E. Casey Foundation. (2007). *Making Connections: A neighborhood transformation family development initiative*. Available at http://aecf.org/initiatives/mc.

Aspen Round Table. (1995). *Voices from the field: Learning from the early work of comprehensive community initiatives*. Available at http://www.aspeninstitute.org/site/c.huLWJeMRKpH/b.612045/k.4BA8/Roundtable_on_Community_Change.htm

Bala, P., Harris, R. W., & Songan, P. (2003). E Bario project: In search of a methodology to provide access to information communication technologies for rural communities in Malaysia . In Marshall, S., Taylor, W., & Yu, X. (Eds.), *Using community informatics to transform regions* (pp. 115–131). Hershey, PA: Idea Group Publishing.

Bellefeuille, G., Hemingway, C., & Schmidt, G. (2004). Move to Community Governance fails again: Why can't the Liberals — or the NDP — get it right? *Perspectives, FALL*, *26*(3), 1–3.

Bellefeuille, G., & Hemingway, D. (2004). Transition to regional community governance: An opportunity to discover the partnership power of community. *Presented to the Circles of Influence: Building Capacity Through Partnership and Collaboration Conference*, May 9-12, 2004, Prince George, BC.

Bowen, G. L., Martin, J. A., Mancini, J. A., & Nelson, J. P. (2000). Community capacity: Antecedents and consequences. *Journal of Community Practice*, *8*(2), 1–21. doi:10.1300/J125v08n02_01

Castelloe, P., Watson, T., & White, C. (2001). *Participatory change: An integrative approach to community practice*. Asheville, NC: Center for Participatory Change.

Castelloe, P., Watson, T., & White, C. (2002). Participatory change: An integrative approach. *Journal of Community Practice*, *10*(4), 1–32.

Chaskin, R. J. (2001). Building community capacity: a definitional framework and case studies from a comprehensive community initiative. *Urban Affairs Review*, *36*(3), 291–323. doi:10.1177/10780870122184876

Coare, P., & Johnston, R. (2003). *Adult learning, citizenship and community voices: Exploring community-based practice*. Leicester, UK: National Institution of Adult Continuing Education.

Johnston, R. (2000). Community education and lifelong learning . In Field, J., & Leicester, M. (Eds.), *Life learning: Education across the lifespan* (pp. 12–28). London: Routledgefalmer.

Kubisch, A. C., Auspos, P., Brown, P., Chaskin, R., Fulbright-Anderson, K., & Hamilton, R. (2002). *Voices from the field II: Reflections on comprehensive community change*. Washington, DC: The Aspen Institute.

Organisation for Economic Cooperation and Development. (2001). *Devolution and Globalization: Implications for local decision makers*. Paris: OECD.

Rohe, W. M., Bratt, R. G., & Biswas, P. (2003). *Evolving challenges for community development corporations: The causes and impacts of failures, downsizings and mergers*. Chapel Hill: University of North Carolina.

KEY TERMS AND DEFINITIONS

E-Governance: This research would like to define e-governance as the action of electronic form of government system to improve the overall governance system of a country.

Grass Roots E-Governance: This terms may refer to elevated electronic form of governance at the local government structure in that country, so that the basic notion of governance system reaches out to the poorest of the poor, or the disadvantaged communities.

Community Practices: Activities, processes or performances conducted by government, academia and civil society at the local level of the government structure through collaborative approaches inclusive of the participation from the community people.

Community Building: Community practices in relationship to build communities in a homogeneous way for taking intelligent decision and contribute in community livelihood development.

Capacity Development: Human skill development through community practices for community building.

ENDNOTES

[1] http://en.wikipedia.org/wiki/Community_development

[2] http://ict4dblog.wordpress.com/

[3] Google definitions

[4] Wiki definitions

[5] World Summit on Sustainable Development (WSSD), available at http://www.un.org/events/wssd/

[6] World Summit on the Information Society (WSIS), available at http://www.itu.int/wsis/index.html

[7] International Telecommunication Union (ITU), http://www.itu.int/en/pages/default.aspx

[8] Internet Governance Forum (IGF), http://www.intgovforum.org/

[9] What is Adenda 21?

[10] [project: BGD/96/007/A/01/99]

[11] BBC Feature- Web without wires reaches out, Wednesday, 15 January, 2003, 11:58 GMT, available at http://news.bbc.co.uk/2/hi/technology/2660715.stm; BBC Feature- Wireless net strides Bangladesh, Sunday, 6 October, 2002, 11:28 GMT 12:28 UK, available at http://news.bbc.co.uk/2/hi/technology/2303431.stm; DANIDA´s Good ICT Practices Website, available at http://goodictpractices.dccd.cursum.net/client/default.aspx?CAID=218526 ; Communica-

Chapter 2

Citizen-Centric Service Dimensions of Indian Rural E-Governance Systems: An Evaluation

Harekrishna Misra
Institute of Rural Management Anand, India

EXECUTIVE SUMMARY

E-governance systems in India have witnessed prolific advancement over the years. India has strategically adopted e-governance as a part of its policy. In recent times each state has its own e-governance plan to deliver services as planned. National policy also aims to provide formalized services across the nation while recognizing the importance of state specific services. This approach includes various mission mode projects under national e-governance plan (NeGP). Manifestation of such approach has resulted in 100,000 common service centers (CSC) in rural areas. It is expected that rural citizens would find them useful and it may contribute for effective governance. In this chapter it is argued that such an initiative would be successful if rural citizens find these CSCs useful for their livelihood security. Various dimensions of this phenomenon are also examined through some cases in this chapter to understand their contributions to successful CSCs in India.

BACKGROUND

E-governance initiatives, despite acceptance to an extent in the form of e-government systems, have so far remained hype in many parts of the world. Failure stories abundantly reflect that such initiatives with development perspectives have not yielded encouraging results. Estimates indicate that 35 per cent are total failures, 50 per cent are partial failures, and 15 per cent are successes in developing and transitional countries. It is argued that e-governance initiatives are often on project mode and each project forms island for deliveries creating an overwhelming gap between project design and on-the-ground reality (known as design-reality gaps). This gap contributes to failures (Heeks 2003). Despite such discouraging outcomes, e-government initiatives in developing countries have evolved to a level of acceptance among government agencies and backend service

DOI: 10.4018/978-1-61692-814-8.ch002

provisioning organisations. Most countries are now in the phase of assessing the "impact" on issues related to "efficiency", "effectiveness", and "equity" since they have gone beyond the initial phases of addressing primary challenges of "digital divide", "setting up infrastructure", and "spreading awareness" for ICT use and delivering citizen-centric e-governance services. Most of the countries are now able to showcase their e-governance services and declare the "availability" of these services uninterrupted crossing the spatial challenges (Figure 1). E-governance systems in many countries have evolved to the level of maturity. However, usage of such services has been a challenge. E-governance systems have so far remained supply-driven in most countries and their actual use largely depends on the type of services rendered. E-government services are "mandatory" in nature and citizens are expected to use them. However, usage of many services which have development perspectives like income generation, health and education depends largely on the success of these services related to citizen needs. Though it is argued that readiness, availability, and uptake phases of e-governance systems are not contemporary anymore for evaluation of success in managing such projects, most of the developing countries still grapple with this phenomenon. There is still use divide, low latent demand, and sub-optimal usage of e-governance services (Misra & Hiremath 2009; Misra 2009).

Discussion on global e-governance systems suggests a clear direction to policy makers and implementers which calls for provisioning of converged and value added services to citizens with least cost, time, and effort. It is also evident that e-governance systems need to evolve to connected governance through establishment of robust infrastructure, backend integration with all stakeholders, and transforming the government itself through innovation and value addition (UN, 2008). Information indicates that connected governance is possible through phases (Heeks, 2006; Heeks & Molla, 2009; Archmann, 2008). It needs a concerted effort to graduate any e-government effort to connected governance. (Box 1)

Figure 1. Changing e-government issues over time

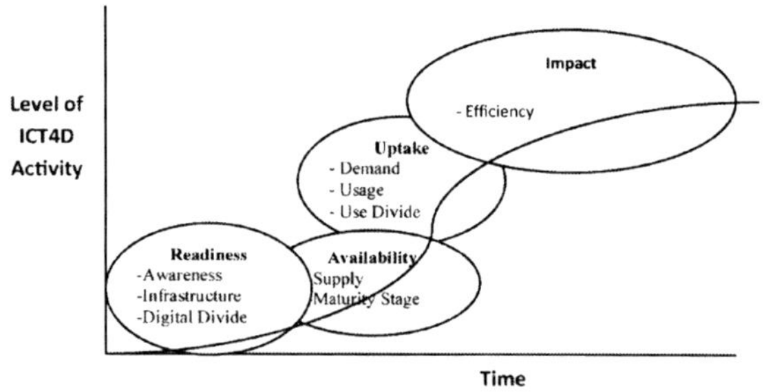

Box 1. Three critical considerations for establishment of connected governance (UN, 2008)

In order to establish ICT enabled connected governance, UN recognizes following three areas:

- **Infrastructure:** Creating an information infrastructure both within the public sector and across society at large, one based upon reliable and affordable Internet connectivity for citizens, businesses and all stakeholders in a given jurisdiction;
- **Integration:** Leveraging this new infrastructure within the public sector in order to better share information (internally and externally) and bundle, integrate, and deliver services through more efficient and citizen-centric governance models encompassing multiple delivery channels; and
- **Transformation:** Pursuing service innovation and e-government across a broader prism of community and democratic development through more networked governance patterns within government, across various government levels and amongst all sectors in a particular jurisdiction.

As shown in Figure 1 and Box 1, it is mandatory for any country to ensure its readiness in each stage before going to the next higher stage. In the context of Indian e-governance efforts, the situation is not different when compared to global e-governance scenarios, experiences, and trends. In India, foundation of e-governance was laid during 1954 when the Planning Commission introduced computers followed by setting up of the Department of Electronics (DOE) in 1970 and establishment of the National Informatics Centre in 1970 as a national agency to make available necessary infrastructure across all states to provide

Table 1. Indian e-governance genesis

Year	Mile-stones for E-Governance Efforts	Goal
1984	New Computer Policy	Spread of Computer Use
1986	Policy on Software Export, Development and Training	To promote Sectoral growth in ITeS, Business Process Outsourcing
1987	Setting up of NICNET, DISNIC	Setting up of IT infrastructure in Government Sector
1994	Policy on National Telecommunication (NTP 94)	To ensure better Tele-density, focus on Rural Telephony
1995	Launching of Internet; Spectrum Allocation and Release	Web Access and bandwidth allocation for use
1997	Establishment of Telecom. Regulatory Authority (TRAI)	To unbundle telecommunication services (last mile)
1998	National Task Force on IT	To formulate an IT policy document
1999	Creation of Ministry of IT	To oversee implementation of IT policy
1999	Policy on National Telecommunication (NTP 99)	To accelerate tele-density
2000	Formulation of IT Act	To provide legal status to use of IT in business, government, and governance systems
2000	Formulation of Communication Convergence Bill	Convergence of content, convergence of carriage, and convergence of Terminal
2000	Telecom Disputes Settlement and Appellate Tribunal (TDSAT)	Fair and transparent telecom. services
2000	Corporatization of DoT (formation of BSNL)	Unbundling of the telecommunication sector, private sector investments and managing USO
2004	Formulation of Broadband Policy	To implement broadband services in the last mile
2006	National E-Governance Plan (NeGP)	To formulate, plan, design, and deploy e-government solutions and establish citizen interfaces
2007	Mission 2007	To consider each village a knowledge centre

Adopted from (Misra & Hiremath, 2009).

required connectivity with the central government (Mishra 2007; Prabhu 2004; Planning Commission, 2001). The government's policies to encourage digital empowerment are presented in Table 1.

E-governance efforts globally have been challenged by plethora of socio-technical, cultural and economic issues (Riga Declaration,2006). In India, theses challenges are enormous because of the diverse nature of the issues concerning not only the socio-technical, cultural and economic dimensions but the rural citizens who constitute an integral part to contribute to the success of the e-governance efforts. Despite e-governance policies formulated and directed towards rural citizens, voluntary participation of rural citizens is yet to gain momentum. However, sporadic efforts are visible through pilot projects directed towards collaboration of rural citizens. Therefore, there is a considerable need to examine the influencing factors for ensuring participation of rural citizens in the national level effort for development. In this chapter, various dimensions influencing rural citizen participation are discussed aimed at fruitful delivery of e-governance services. In this chapter it is posited that demand driven information infrastructure needs to be developed for successful implementation of e-governance systems and especially demands of rural citizens need to be reflected adequately in the e-governance systems. In order to provide demand driven rural information infrastructure in India, it is argued that livelihood security based assessment of such information infrastructure would be beneficial.

This chapter verifies the dimensions of such demands and assesses the status of e-governance efforts undertaken in one of the districts in Gujarat state, India.

The organization of the chapter is as follows. The chapter provides a global perspective of e-governance initiatives, their rationale to adopt such strategies, challenges and opportunities faced during implementations of e-governance projects. It includes underpinnings of current global e-governance initiatives. It then presents the e-governance scenario and initiatives taken up in India and discusses the challenges faced for its effective implementation. Subsequently, focus on rural e-governance scenario, role ICT for development in the context of rural India are examined through a model. The model is aimed at interfacing demand and supply characteristics of information infrastructure and relating them to e-governance models deployed nationally. The chapter also examines the of a village information system (VIS) with livelihood perspectives which needs to be established before any ICT infrastructure is deployed. It is argued that VIS should aim to provide information and "services" on demand through "stakeholder-ownership oriented development" initiatives. In order to appreciate the applicability of the proposed framework, results obtained through a survey undertaken in a sample district in Gujarat are discussed. Finally, the chapter discusses observations and elaborates on the direction for further research.

E-GOVERNANCE ASSESSMENT IN INDIA: THE NEED

As discussed in Figure 1 (Heeks 2006) and as recognized by UN (UN 2008), infrastructure is a critical contributor to the success of "connected governance". E-governance efforts in a country strongly reflect the role and contributions of infrastructure in their policies, projects and implementation strategies. Infrastructural readiness is one of the concurrent evaluation criteria which have been set for the countries globally. There are various agencies involved in assessment exercises globally. In Table 2 a list of such agencies are presented. E-governance assessment frameworks have evolved with the intention to benchmark the e-government strategies, policies and provide an environment of learning from these ever dynamic processes. It is largely recognized that e-governance efforts are country specific, related to national level policies, socio-cultural systems and government systems. Though it is not easy to map all the success factors of e-governance efforts made in other countries to the Indian scenario, overall learning from them would help the country to improve upon.

While the number of agencies involved in the assessment process is not important, their approaches lead to the conclusion that the e-readiness exercises have their importance in any phase of deployment of e-governance. E-governance efforts are continuous and these efforts require concurrent evaluation to add value progressively. In the Indian context, the global e-readiness exercises provide an insight to various challenges that the country faces to set up and use infrastructure. India, being a developing country, experiences harsh realities of e-readiness attributes explained in Figure 1. However, in recent times last mile dimensions of digital divide is increasingly being addressed through various policies like tele-density increase, broadband penetration, establishment of common service centers, and state and centre sponsored content management through state- wide area network backbones (SWAN) under NeGP. A close look at the global IT report indicates that India needs to improve upon many other dimensions of e-governance including digital divide (Misra & Hiremath, 2009).

E-readiness assessment exercise is an implicit phenomenon for all nations and there is a mechanism to display the status of e-readiness

Table 2. Profile of e-readiness assessment agencies (Global)

Study	Focus
APEC (Asia Pacific Economic Cooperation)	E-Commerce Readiness
CIDIF (Centre International pour le Development de l'Inforoute en Francais)	Internet Service Market
EIU (Economist Intelligence Unit) with IBM	E-Business Readiness
IDC	Infrastructure
World Bank (KAM)	K-Economy
McConnell International (MI)	Infrastructure, Digital Economy, Education, and Government
MN (Metric Net)	E-Economy
MQ (Mosaic Group)	Internet
NRI (CID, Harvard)	Infrastructure, E-Society, Policies, Digital Economy, Education, and Government
CID (Centre for International Development)	Society
CIDCM (University of Maryland)	Qualitative Assessment based on past performance and current internet pervasiveness
World Telecommunication/ ICT Development Report; International Telecommunication Union (ITU)	Telecommunication; Measuring ICT for Social and Economic Development; Measuring ICT availability in Villages and Rural Areas (ITU, 2006a; ITU,2007b)
SIDA (Swedish International Development Cooperation Agency)	Mainly Strength, Weakness, Opportunity and Threat (SWOT) analysis of a Nation
USAID (US Agency for International Development)	Access, Government,
World Economic Forum; Global IT Report	E-Readiness
United Nations Development Programme	E-Governance
World Economic Forum	Global Competitiveness Report
Measurement of Information Society, ITU	ICT Opportunity Index
Economic and Social Commission for Asia and The Pacific (ES-CAP), UN	Regulations, Polices, Legal Framework Related to ICT; UN's Global E-Government Survey
United Nations Development Programme (UNDP)	ICT Indicators for Human Development; Democratic Governance Indicators

Compiled from (Budhiraja & Sachdeva,2009; Misra & Hiremath, 2009)

of each country in order to examine the progress and identify the areas of improvement. There are various components of e-readiness exercise and important among them are "infrastructure readiness", "individual readiness", "government readiness", and "political and regulatory readiness". In Figure 2 the e-readiness components in India vis-à-vis other countries are shown in a time line. It may be observed that infrastructure readiness needs considerable attention in India to achieve better e-governance service utilization. Other readiness indicators have shown appreciable improvements in global standards, despite diverse socio-economic ambience. Individual readiness, government readiness, and political and regulatory readiness indicators support the fact that awareness among stakeholders to accept ICT enabled services has increased. But as a nation, India has to traverse a long path to achieve all inclusive readiness in order to bring in overall development and appreciable use of e-governance services.

Figure 2. E-readiness indices of India

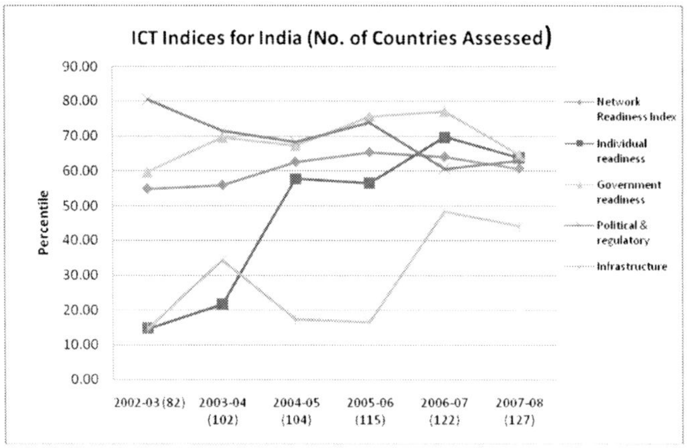

Figure 3. Tele Density in India

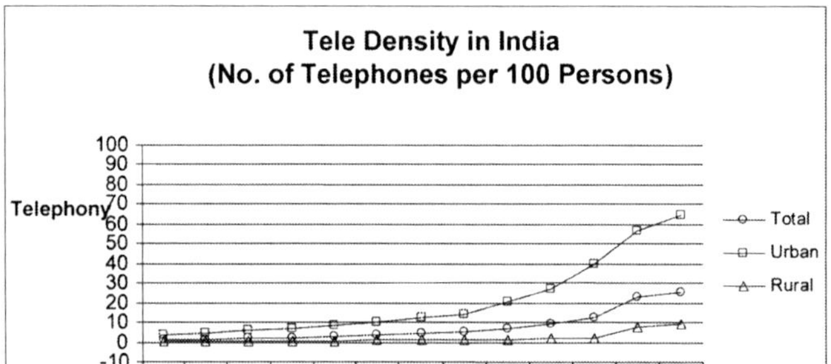

	1995-96	1996-97	1997-98	1998-99	1999-00	2000-01	2001-02	2002-03	2003-04	2004-05	2005-06	Sep' 07	Feb' 08
Total	1.28	1.56	1.94	2.33	2.86	3.58	4.29	5.11	7.02	8.95	12.7	23.2	25.3
Urban	3.95	4.76	5.78	6.87	8.23	10.4	12.2	14.3	20.8	26.9	39.5	56.9	64.5
Rural	0.29	0.34	0.43	0.52	0.68	0.93	1.21	1.49	1.57	1.73	1.86	7.3	9.03

Availability of Integrated E-Governance Infrastructure and Services

Availability of integrated infrastructure in a nation is reflection of its sound policy and implementation strategy. In India ICT initiatives and their convergence are integral parts of its policies. Various policies and Five Year Plans have elaborated the role of connectivity and possible road maps for converged approaches. The tenth and eleventh five year plan documents (Planning Commission 2001) provide a comprehensive approach towards achieving convergence in ICT infrastructure and content management with special emphasis on rural development. Some among them are convergence bill, broadband policy, NeGP with MMPs, and universal service obligation (USO).

As a strategic move, spread of basic telephony to all citizens has been part of India's sound infrastructure policy. Telephony has been a powerful mode of establishing the required connectivity among citizens. It has catalyzed the convergence of other stakeholders in the governance system which is involved in provisioning of user services. Telephony has also been instrumental in spread of Internet services and the Internet is the backbone of e-governance infrastructure today. Tele-density

Figure 4. Status of Internet and Telephony in India

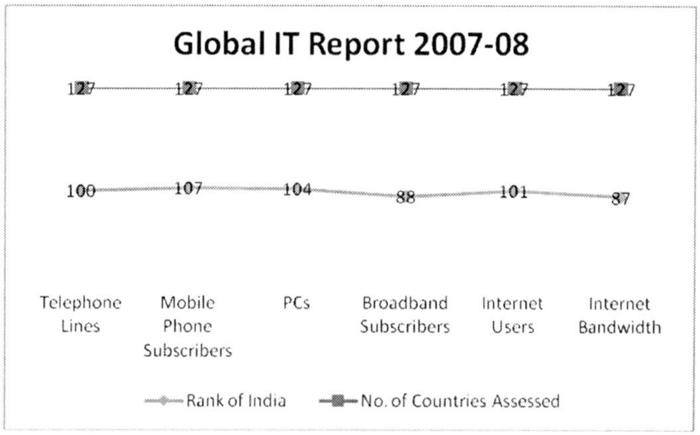

has been a globally accepted metric for understanding the spread of telephony because of such critical contribution. A comparative assessment of urban-rural tele-density in India is provided in Figure 3. However, the picture is far from satisfactory and there is a huge disparity in urban-rural tele-density despite policy level support.

Internet and telephone users in India are way below world figures. From Figure 4, it is evident that there is tremendous scope to improve upon the infrastructure as India's rank ranges between 87 and 107 among 127 countries assessed. As regards Internet users in India, it is estimated that 12 per cent of urban population are using the Internet whereas only 1.2 per cent of rural population is using the Internet (JuxtConsultIndia Online 2008).

Availability of services is another important dimension of e-governance systems. Conceptualization, design, development, and deployment of electronic services online are major responsibilities of content management. The Convergence Bill of India calls for convergence of content and convergence of carriage as national initiatives (Planning Commission 2001). Convergence of carriage calls for major changes in structures of the computer industry and more comprehensively the telecommunication and networking industry that are responsible for data communication and broadcasting of multi-media applications.

The National Task Force on IT and Software Development recommended in 1998 in addressing the last-mile connectivity problem. Convergence of content calls for efforts in e-government and e-governance, and provision of a single window service to the citizen. Another issue is to address the convergence of terminal in order to provide multilingual services on multimedia applications anywhere and anytime in India. Today there are various attempts made to provide the content in local languages including the operating system initiative of C-DAC named as the Bharat Operating System Solutions (BOSS). As regards service oriented contents, NeGP recognizes the scope for large-scale implementation of application under mission mode projects (MMPs) with emphasis on integrated services. Under NeGP, national level MMPs and state level MMPs are identified for implementation on scale-up mode as presented in Figure 5 (Ministry of Information Technology [MoIT] 2009a).

Every interested state government is now under a state wide area network (SWAN). Each state is now in the process of having state data centres under the NeGP policy. This endeavour is part of state readiness exercise which is adapted mostly from the global information technol-

Figure 5. MMPs under NeGP

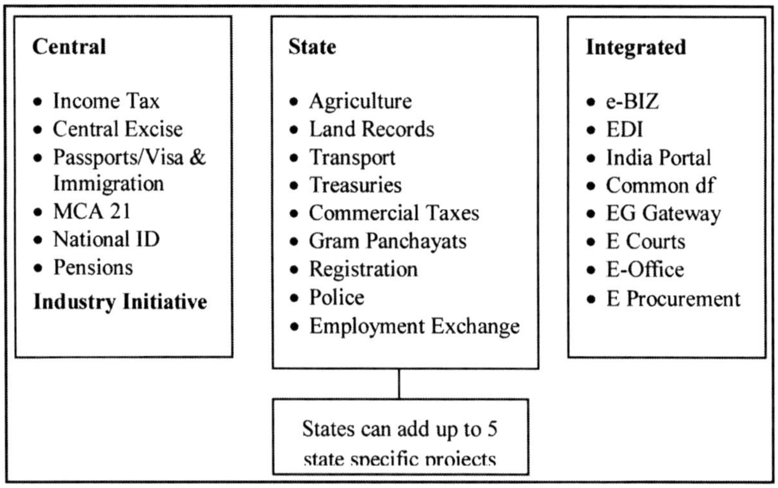

Figure 6. State e-readiness pyramid of the states

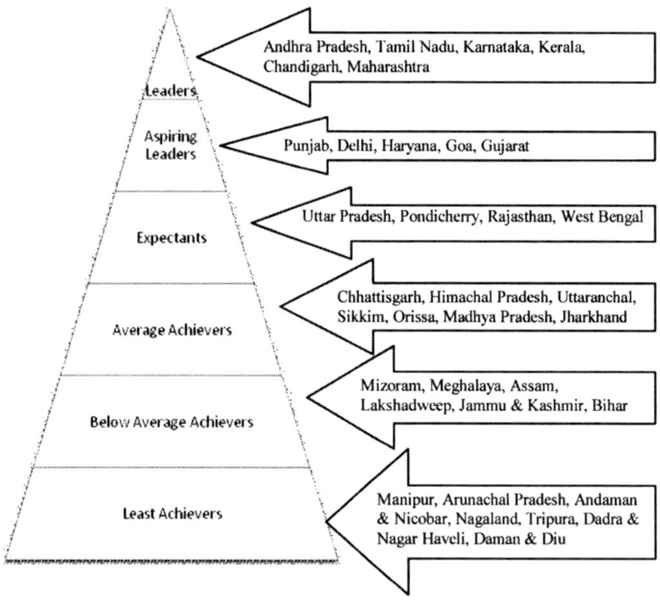

ogy report framework published annually by the World Economic Forum. This assessment commencing in 2003 has provided insight to the performance of states which are placed in six categories: Least Achievers (L1), Below Average Achievers (L2), Average Achievers (L3), Expectants (L4), Aspiring Leaders (L5), and Leaders (L6). The latest rankings of the participating states are given in Figure 6.

E-readiness for districts has been on the agenda of the e-governance policy in India. This readiness is essential to implement e-district services which are parts of the state level mission mode projects under NeGP. It envisages provisioning of services through CSCs planned to be made available in every sixth village across the country and these services include district administration and citizen- centric government services (MoIT 2009).

Uptake of E-Governance Services in India

It is quite evident that Indian efforts are in line with global e-governance scenarios and the Indian government is making all possible efforts to establish the e-governance infrastructure and provide converged services for the citizens. This supply mode of services has long lasting effect on the readiness of government systems and integration of backend services. As regards mission mode projects at the state and national levels, most of them are related to government systems and citizens would have no option but to accept them as made available to them. The real challenge, however, lies in assessing the net uptake of the services which largely depends on demand; usage and usage divide as shown in Figure 1. In the Indian context, these three dimensions of demand are quite relevant because of the digital divide. It is largely felt that the digital divide has now been converted to digital opportunities because of various policies/acts such as the Broadband Policy, NeGP, and RTI Act. There are many well documented challenges in India to maximize the uptake of services because of the diversity and disparities in the needs of rural-urban citizens. Despite many efforts, e-government services are yet to render the desired pro-citizen services and are mostly targeted towards internal efficiency (Bhatnagar 2006). Pro-poor services may be available through state and national MMPs in due course since the projects are in the phases of transition.

Impact of E-Governance Services in India

The current scenario e-governance efforts has provided the right platform to render effective services at the national and state levels through organized backbones, data centers, and MMPs. NeGP caters to the 100,000 CSCs and provides the platform for convergence of various services through the private-public-partnership (PPP) mode. There is a significant change in the way government systems are working now because of the impact of the information technology Act, and the RTI Act. MMPs alike NCA-21, Income Tax, and Railways have added the right impetus to citizen-acceptance of IT enabled services. Penetration of telephony (wire and wireless) has been phenomenal, triggering the right ambience for m-government (mobile government) applications. But the real challenges to improve upon the impacts are many. It is argued that mere provisioning personal computers, connectivity, and content do not correlate with actual use of services (Heeks et al. 2009). This situation is prevalent especially in rural areas.

NATIONAL E-GOVERNANCE PLAN IN INDIA: THE CASE

In the previous sections, e-governance efforts supporting the development process in developing countries are discussed. E-inclusion has been a critical consideration for global apex bodies such as UN, EU, UNDP, and ITU in provisioning of e-governance services to citizens (EU,2007). MDG efforts include ICT enabled services as one of the most critical indicators for understanding the success of goals set. It is also recognised that global e-governance efforts face challenges of infrastructure, integration, and transformation. There are many failures in implementing e-governance projects and some of the attributes leading to unsuccessful results are design-reality

Figure 7. NeGP Approach for Integration

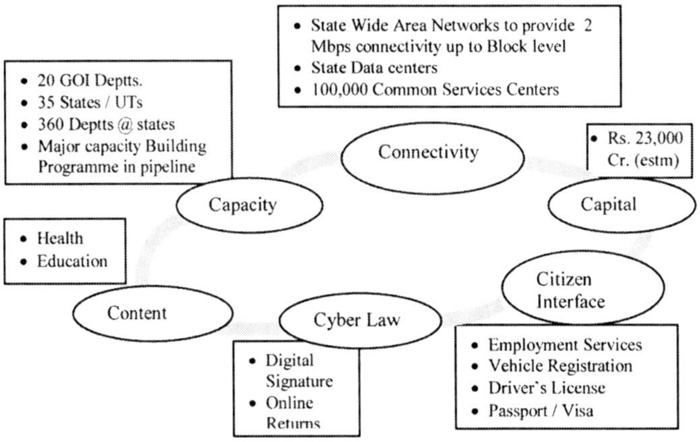

gaps, digital divides, supply-driven services and scanty usage of services.

In India, e-governance services have gone beyond the phases of incubation, prototyping and showcasing of standard software engineering processes. Despite sincere efforts, the services have remained supply driven and need to be transformed to a level of high use through creation of latent demand at village level. Along these lines, National e-Governance Plan (NeGP), has laid emphasis on deploying MMPs at state and central government levels and has provided the desired attention to integrate them so as to generate citizen-centric services on demand and to increase the latent demand. In Figure 7, the approach to integrate various services is presented.

In this integrated approach NeGP intends to provide a service grid through adequate connectivity, increased influx of capital with focused deliveries, increase in the capacity and capabilities of service provisioning agencies in the government, providing adequate content in local languages, establishing required policies and legal frameworks to encourage convergence of services and service providers, establish security standards, and channel the grid based services to citizens through an established channel of interface.

The citizen interface is the most critical element in the grid which largely influences the success of e-governance services. In this chapter, it is hypothesized that services supplied would meet their desired level of success through sustained use by end users. The study discusses the interface of NeGP services being planned, designed, and deployed with that of the latent demand and its influencing factors. The objective is to understand user-divides prevalent in rural areas in India since the success of e-governance efforts largely depends on their contributions to rural development indicators nationally and as per MDG imperatives. This study is largely a continuation of our work in the sample district in Gujarat in India (Misra & Hiremath, 2006). The study also posits that user-divides in rural India is intensely influenced by livelihood security metrics of the households. In this chapter, an attempt is made to explore the effects of livelihood metrics on the latent demand of the information and services network being deployed.

NeGP, in its phase of implementation and scale up recognizes the fact that CSCs should work on sustainable basis with public-private-partnerships (PPP). This approach calls for a sustainable demand from the rural citizens and this demand largely depends on usability, usefulness and usability of services. User interfaces and user orientation of

Figure 8. The Framework to Reflect Demand Influencers

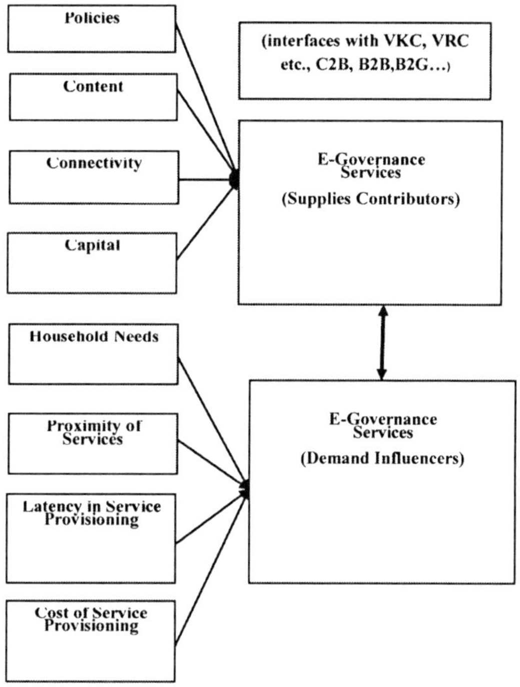

services have still remained a challenge for ICT planners, developers and implementers (Heeks et al., 2009; Misra, 2009). The situation is more complex in the Indian context where information infrastructure for ICT enabled governance systems grapple with development challenges. The challenges are not limited to "technology", but the "people" and the "processes". Specifically rural ICT enabled governance initiative face daunting task, not because it involves the rural infrastructure, but the complex process of involving the rural masses. These masses (the rural citizens), who lack access to basic livelihood opportunities, are oblivious of ICT initiatives. They continue to remain so because of poor reflections of their interests in such projects. Such apathy has contributed immensely to "poor user interfaces" which is termed as "citizen interfaces".

FRAMEWORK FOR ANALYSIS OF THE CASE

Considering the challenges in implementing e-governance services in Indian context, a framework is presented to reflect the contributors to the success of such endeavor (see Figure 8).

The framework suggests that success of e-governance services is dependent on the "demand" created locally in rural ambience in India (Misra, 2009). As discussed earlier, various agencies are engaged in extending services to rural citizens in villages/ Panchayats through entrepreneurship models. Thus there is a strong need for assessment of demand in the village/ Panchayat so that entrepreneurs engaged in providing the services earn their livelihood, make the service provisioning centre as an income generating avenue and establish the right linkage between service providing agencies and rural citizens.

The Influencers of Supply-Demand

The framework recognizes the need for a strong collaborative interface between "e-governance service- information supplies" and "e-governance service- Information demands". It is considered that e-governance centered information supplies are mostly contributed by policies, infrastructure for establishing connectivity, content developed for the purpose and capital invested in the process. These are mostly incubated, piloted and implemented within the framework of policies. The framework includes influencers discussed in the first method and uses them in the second method to understand the "supply-contributors" as shown in Figure 7. Readiness, availability, uptake and impacts are essentially influenced by policies, content, connectivity and capital which remain supply-driven. The framework suggests that parameters like e-readiness, availability of content, connectivity and capital would critically influence the uptakes and impact of e-governance services. However, the framework also considers the citizens' demand to be local, household specific. It also considers that "supply-demand interface" can be successful only when service is made available on demand, with better proximity at optimized cost and low latency. Suitable interface with information demands generated at the points of services is also necessary to build a sustainable and trustworthy relationship with the citizens. The citizens in general and rural citizens in India in particular, are influenced by the quality of services that are provided for better and sustained use. These influencers are household needs, proximity of services, latency in service provisioning and cost of services. The information supply mechanisms need to consider all these influencers well in advance and incorporate them in the supplies contributors discussed in the framework. In other words, policies, infrastructure for establishing connectivity, content developed for the purpose and capital invested in the process should recognize household needs, proximity of services, latency in service provisioning and cost of services. Besides, the services to be rendered need to recognize the intentions of citizen who look for support of agencies to have better infrastructure, income generation opportunities, and increased awareness etc.

The Framework for Impact Study

The village information system assumes a critical role in contributing to the national information services plan. Diversity in social, cultural, demographic, economic and infrastructural assets in a village influences the household livelihood security options and thus generates a unique scenario. Information economics principles has a far-reaching effect on VIS which argues that information is increasingly recognised as a capital and can add to the livelihood pentagon framework which has five faces of capital to assess the livelihood of a household: financial, human, natural, physical, and social. This information capital can be used for the advantages of citizens in developing countries to support livelihood options (Heeks et al. 2009; World Bank 1986). Box 2 explains these advantages.

Availability of information capital at the household level in developing countries can immensely influence local livelihood opportunities through information management at right time, at appropriate locations, and with right language interfaces. Therefore, it is important that information availability is measured through its proximity to the source and recipient, latency in extending information and its related services, decrease in the uncertainty in provisioning of information through integration, and ability of citizens to gain access to the information at affordable cost. The proposed framework aims to establish a synergy between the information provisioning agencies and citizens in the villages and map the services through these metrics. It is posited that VIS would assume this role in establishing the required synergy.

Box 2. Advantages of information capital for rural citizens in a developing country

- Information absence: key information that development actors need is not available.
- Information quality: key information that development actors need is available but of poor quality.
- Information uncertainty: key information that development actors need is available but its quality is uncertain.
- Information asymmetry: some development actors have access to key information that others lack.
- Information cost: key information can only be obtained at high cost (often a physical journey).

Source: (Heeks & Molla, 2009)

Methodologies

There are two aspects that the framework intends to address. First, the e-governance services-supplies are assessed. This is done through examination of two cases of e-governance efforts "NeGP" and "E-Gram" which are considered for scale up at national level and state level respectively. This assessment is based on the parameters explained in figure 7 under "e-governance services, supplies contributors". The objective is to understand the rigor of the deliveries based on information supplies of the suggested framework. Second, these two cases are examined with viewpoints of interfaces with information demand influencers.

Primary surveys are conducted in seven sample villages to understand the efficacy of these influencers. These sample villages are drawn from a particular district in the state where both E-Gram and NeGP projects are co-existing. These samples are mostly homogeneous, small and therefore, there is a limitation in generalization of the findings. Research method included a sampling plan to elicit responses of rural citizens with respect to their aspirations and the limitations these endeavours attempt to meet them. There are 284 respondents who participated in the interview and participatory rural appraisal (PRA) exercises in the village. In the interview method, random sampling was adopted to avoid bias. However, seven villages provided a cluster scenario for the researcher. As regards PRA exercise, each village had one and interested villagers were encouraged to participate (Misra & Hiremath, 2009).

Readiness would relate critically to local infrastructure and local sources for information retrieval and integration among these sources in order to encourage citizens to avail such services. Availability largely depends on the readiness of infrastructure and integrated services. Besides, it is also largely influenced by the cost factor. Increase in uptake would depend on availability of integrated services and low latency with focus on livelihood-centric services because it might build trust in the system. Impact assessment is also an important stage in the evolution since it measures the net effect of e-governance services. Latency and integrated services in a sustainable manner are expected to provide a larger impact. While all stages of evolution in e-governance services are expected to be largely influenced by the integrated information infrastructure, latency in availing and providing services are the next most important metric for successful evolution. Proximity and cost of information and services are considered important metrics; they are largely critical for the readiness, availability, and uptake stages of the evolution process.

Village Information System: The Critical Interface

Village Information System (VIS) is the core issue in this study. The research propositions are as follows:

1. VIS is expected to provide the desired interface with the citizens and supplied services for supporting their livelihood prospects in local conditions.
2. VIS is treated as "atomic" in order to establish the uniqueness of the demand that the concerned village would place on the service providing agencies to meet livelihood security based challenges at the household level.

It is argued that each village has uniqueness in raising demand on e-governance services. Each village is therefore, a unit of study. Each village provides an aggregated ambience based on household level demand to understand prioritised information requirements.

3. Proximity to information and service resources, latency, integrated information, and cost of services influence readiness, availability, uptake, and impact in provisioning e-governance services.

The research propositions demand a primary survey at the household level because of the premise that each household has uniqueness in placing its demand on the "orchestrated" information network available through the e-governance policy framework.

In this chapter, severity metrics are formed to support the measurements. Severity is presented as a term associated with difficulty/ importance attached to citizens' critical needs to support livelihood security. Severity metric depends on quantifiable parameters of the livelihood security profile of a household aggregated at the village level. This metric indicates the difficulty level of a household/village to get support from agencies for receiving information. In Table 3, this severity is explained for the purpose of benchmarking results that the proposed framework examines. These metrics are indicative of the perspectives of sample respondents who participated in the exercise. An assessment of these metrics indicates that rural citizens are not averse to payment for availing services provided desired services are rendered on demand and at a convenient place. Besides, the rural citizens are unanimous to argue that services need to be rendered as per their convenience and they also agree that service supplying agencies need to provided improved services keeping in view the rural citizen's livelihood centric requirements. It means a continuous innovation approach should be adopted for sustainability of services. Sample citizens also viewed that trust in the system would accrue if such an approach is taken in a concerted manner.

In the proposed framework, VIS metrics are posited to be the interfaces with the livelihood security oriented delivery systems for rural citizens. This delivery system needs to understand the ICT imperatives to provide livelihood-centric information. These metrics will be used to examine critically the processes and services available to citizens. In Table 4, VIS metrics are mapped to the four stages of evolution in e-governance services, readiness, availability, uptake, and impact. As per the sample respondents, influencers discussed in the framework have a varied impact in the interfaces of services that VIS could manage.

SOLUTIONS AND RECOMMENDATIONS

The framework is applied to understand two dimensions of e-governance services in India. The first one is to understand the supply contributors whereas the second addresses the demand influencers for the cases related to NeGP, and E-Gram services.

Result of the First Method

In this method e-readiness, availability, uptake and impact are examined to appreciate the efforts planned during development of information supplies and actual deliveries. In Table 5 the status is presented. It is noted that both the e-governance initiatives are backed by state and national level polices. These two initiatives are in growth stages and their infrastructure is readily available in the Panchayat/ for a group of villages. As regards uptakes, e-gram has better uptake because of local contents, state managed and controlled by Panchayats. NeGP services, on the other hand, are driven by national policies and are based on entrepreneurship model. Business models are

Table 3. Information severity metrics and benchmarks

Livelihood Security Profiling	Severity Metrics			Demand on VIS
	Description	**Range**	**Metric**	
Food Security	Sufficiency of Food	0-4months	+++ (Most Severe)	Very High
		5-8 months	++ (Severe)	High
		9-12 months	+ (Less Severe)	Important
	Income Generation Opportunities (Information Asymmetry)	Proper Sale Value Realization in the Village		
		> 80 per cent said Yes	+ (Less Severe)	Important
		<80 per cent>40 per cent	++ (Severe)	High
		<40 per cent	+++ (Most Severe)	Very High
		Distance Travelled for Sale		
		< 5 Km	+ (Less Severe)	Important
		> 5 < 10 Km	++ (Severe)	High
		> 10 Km	+++ (Most Severe)	Very High
		Availability of Work Opportunity in Village		
		> 80 per cent said Yes	+ (Less Severe)	Important
		<80 per cent>40 per cent	++ (Severe)	High
		<40 per cent	+++ (Most Severe)	Very High
		Household Asset Sold for Purchase of Food		
		> 80 per cent said Yes	+++ (Most Severe)	Very High
		<80 per cent>40 per cent said Yes	++ (Less Severe)	High
		< 40 per cent said Yes	+ (Severe)	Important
Health Security	Human	Accessible to Health Infrastructure		
		< 5 Km	+ (Less Severe)	Important
		> 5 < 10 Km	++ (Severe)	High
		> 10 Km	+++ (Most Severe)	Very High
		Availability of Health Services in the Village		
		> 80 per cent said Yes	+ (Less Severe)	Important
		<80 per cent>40 per cent	++ (Severe)	High
		<40 per cent	+++ (Most Severe)	Very High
		Availability of Immunization /Health Training Services in the Village		
		> 80 per cent said Yes	+ (Less Severe)	Important
		<80 per cent>40 per cent	++ (Severe)	High
		<40 per cent	+++ (Most Severe)	Very High
	Livestock	Availability of Livestock Support Services in the Village		
		> 80 per cent said Yes	+ (Less Severe)	Important
		<80 per cent>40 per cent	++ (Severe)	High
		<40 per cent	+++ (Most Severe)	Very High

continued on following page

Table 3. continued

Education Security	Formal Education Facility (Primary)			
	> 80 per cent said Yes	+ (Less Severe)	Important	Important
	<80 per cent>40 per cent	++ (Severe)	High	High
	<40 per cent	+++ (Most Severe)	Very High	Very High
	Access to Formal Education Facility (Primary)			
	< 5 Km	+ (Less Severe)	Important	Important
	> 5 < 10 Km	++ (Severe)	High	High
	> 10 Km	+++ (Most Severe)	Very High	Very High
	Formal Education Facility (Secondary)			
	> 80 per cent said Yes	+ (Less Severe)	Important	Important
	<80 per cent>40 per cent	++ (Severe)	High	High
	<40 per cent	+++ (Most Severe)	Very High	Very High
	Access to Formal Education Facility (Secondary)			
	< 5 Km	+ (Less Severe)	Important	Important
	> 5 < 10 Km	++ (Severe)	High	High
	> 10 Km	+++ (Most Severe)	Very High	Very High
	Formal Education Facility (Higher)			
	> 80 per cent said Yes	+ (Less Severe)	Important	Important
	<80 per cent>40 per cent	++ (Severe)	High	High
	<40 per cent	+++ (Most Severe)	Very High	Very High
	Access to Formal Education Facility (Higher)			
	< 5 Km	+ (Less Severe)	Important	Important
	> 5 < 10 Km	++ (Severe)	High	High
	> 10 Km	+++ (Most Severe)	Very High	Very High
Financial Security	Ability to meet Household Expenses			
	> 80 per cent said Yes	+ (Less Severe)	Important	Important
	<80 per cent>40 per cent	++ (Severe)	High	High
	<40 per cent	+++ (Most Severe)	Very High	Very High
	Availability of Credit/ Insurance Services			
	> 80 per cent said Yes	+ (Less Severe)	Important	Important
	<80 per cent>40 per cent	++ (Severe)	High	High
	<40 per cent	+++ (Most Severe)	Very High	Very High
	Access to Credit/ Insurance Services			
	< 5 Km	+ (Less Severe)	Important	Important
	> 5 < 10 Km	++ (Severe)	High	High
	> 10 Km	+++ (Most Severe)	Very High	Very High
	Savings Activities			
	> 80 per cent said Yes	+ (Less Severe)	Important	Important
	<80 per cent>40 per cent	++ (Severe)	High	High
	<40 per cent	+++ (Most Severe)	Very High	Very High

continued on following page

Table 3. continued

Social Security	Activities in Groups (Social)			
	> 80 per cent said Yes	+ (Less Severe)	Important	Important
	<80 per cent>40 per cent	++ (Severe)	High	High
	<40 per cent	+++ (Most Severe)	Very High	Very High
	Activities in Groups (Religious)			
	> 80 per cent said Yes	+ (Less Severe)	Important	Important
	<80 per cent>40 per cent	++ (Severe)	High	High
	<40 per cent	+++ (Most Severe)	Very High	Very High
	Activities in Groups (Community Organisations)			
	> 80 per cent said Yes	+ (Less Severe)	Important	Important
	<80 per cent>40 per cent	++ (Severe)	High	High
	<40 per cent	+++ (Most Severe)	Very High	Very High

Table 4. Relationship of VIS metrics with e-governance evolution

Stages of E-Governance Evolution	**VIS Metrics**			
	Proximity of Source of Information/ Services	**Latency in Availing Information/ Services**	**Requirement of Integrated Information**	**Cost of Services**
Readiness	+++	+	+++	+
Availability	+	+++	+++	+++
Uptake	+++	+++	+++	+
Impact	+	+++	+++	+

Highly Critical: +++ Important: +

Table 5. Assessment of supplies contributors

Parameters	**NeGP**	**E-Gram**
E-Readiness	CSCs are established; Connectivity is in place; Services are through entrepreneurs; MMPs are being introduced; State level integrations are being implemented.	E-Gram centers are established and connected to state Head Quarters; Services are through Panchayats; State controlled applications are in place.
Availability	Available for every six villages	E-Gram centers are in Panchayats (a group of villages)
Uptake	Growth stage and Uptake is minimal	Growth stage and uptake is minimal
Impact	Non-availability of integrated services lead to low impact	Non-availability of integrated services lead to low impact

integrated with e-governance objectives. Maturity of the services is yet to be assessed which could have been examined during pilots. There were no pilots for both these services. Digital divide issues are not visibly addressed since the uptake is minimal. Impacts are also not visible since most the citizens resort to conventional governance procedures.

In Table 6 the results obtained through primary survey are presented. These seven sample villages provide varying results in each of the assessment factors. Under e-readiness, it indicates that awareness and digital divide issues need immediate attention whereas infrastructure is adequately available in each sample village.

As regards availability, both supply and maturity issues are critically poised and they need to be addressed with due attention. Because of poor availability and moderate e-readiness, the uptake has been affected severely in terms of demand, usage and usage divides. Similarly, low impact has remained visibly dismal in terms of efficiency and effectiveness whereas equity has moderately improved. This is because of some increased inquisitiveness and acceptability among women, poor and children in the households.

Result of the Second Method

The second stage of the evaluation is to understand and capture influencers of information demands of the citizens. In Table 7 these influencers are discussed. The respondents were encouraged to contribute to the assessment based on their household needs, proximity of source or point of service, requirement of integrated services (single window service) and their cost.

Citizens' demands in Indian context are influenced by various factors. Some of them have been considered here for evaluation. It is considered important here that information on citizens' basic requirements need to be made available on demand, with least latency and at the village or nearby locations so that their opportunities to receive the desired services are adequately available at an affordable cost. Such a scenario needs appropriate integration of services, networking of service providing agency with ICT backbone.

In Table 8, results of the survey conducted on the influencers n the influencers considered for evaluation in seven sample villages are presented. In this evaluation process, information needs described in Table 3 are taken as the influencers in Table 8. This evaluation exercise indicates that in five out of seven sample villages, information needs for income generation opportunities is regarded as very critical and these services are poor. Health service related information is also poor in four out of seven sample villages which need adequate attention. As regards formal education related information, the services are adequately

Table 6. Assessment of e-governance efforts in villages

Assessment Factors	Factors	Sample Villages						
		1	2	3	4	5	6	7
E-Readiness	Awareness	++	+++	+++	+++	+++	+++	+++
	Infrastructure	+	+	+	+	+	+	+
	Digital Divide	+++	+++	+++	+++	+++	+++	+++
Availability	Supply	+++	+++	+++	+++	+++	+++	+++
	Maturity	+++	+++	+++	+++	+++	+++	+++
Uptake	Demand	+++	+++	+++	+++	+++	+++	+++
	Usage	+++	+++	+++	+++	+++	+++	+++
	Use Divide	+++	+++	+++	+++	+++	+++	+++
Impact	Efficiency	+++	+++	+++	+++	+++	+++	+++
	Effectiveness	+++	+++	+++	+++	+++	+++	+++
	Equity	++	++	++	++	++	++	++

+ -> quite adequate, ++ -> moderately adequate and +++ -> poor

Table 7. Understanding demand influencers

Demand Influencers				
Household Needs	**Proximity of Source of Information / Services**	**Latency in Availing Information / Services**	**Requirement of Integrated Information**	**Cost of Services**
Income Generating Opportunities	In the Village	In Hours	Full Integration	Free Information
Providing Information on Doctors, Interaction with Doctors, Receiving advice from Doctors	Doctor/ Agency in the vicinity of the Village	No Latency	Full Integration	May be Priced for Access to Information
Information on the Institutions and Courses	In the Village	No such Criticality	Full Integration	May be Priced for Access to Information
Information on demand on Appropriate skills	In the Village	No such Criticality	Full Integration	May be Priced for Access to Information

available in all sample villages whereas skill development related information is not adequately available.

Recommendations

The chapter intended to set an agenda to appreciate rural citizens' aspirations for sustaining their livelihoods and incorporate them in the e-governance services being rendered at the local level. It argued that a VIS needs to be developed to assess demand influencers and supply contributors at the village level so that right information and services are rendered locally. The case analysis through the framework substantiated the argument and suggested that e-gram and NeGP should provide the desired synergy by including the demand influencers.

The framework provided a tool to assess the village level demand for establishing the desired interfaces with NeGP services being supplied. Application of this framework for ample villages indicated that VIS metrics are different and are dependent on the livelihood centric demands. Such diversity in demand makes VIS more critical and dynamic. It is thus important that e-governance projects should capture desired demand and provide citizen centered services so as to ensure desired impact. This is more prevalent in Indian context. In this chapter, it was argued uptake and

Table 8. Understanding demand influencers

Information Demand Influencers	Sample Villages						
	1	2	3	4	5	6	7
Income Generating Opportunities	++	+++	+++	+	+++	+++	+++
Providing Information on Doctors, Interaction with Doctors, Receiving advice from Doctors	+	++	+++	+	+++	+++	+++
Information on the Institutions and Courses	++	++	++	++	++	++	++
Information on demand on Appropriate skills and vocational courses	++	+++	+++	+	+++	+++	+++

+ -> quite adequate, ++ -> moderately adequate and +++ -> poor impact are influenced by several citizen needs and especially these factors critically influence the success of e-governance services in Indian context. In India, e-governance services to be successful, rural citizens' needs are to be captured adequately and interfaced with e-governance service network being designed. Rural citizens' livelihood perspectives are important contributors to organize a sustainable interface between "e-governance service- information supplies" and "e-governance service- information demands".

This chapter focused on citizen interface in general and rural citizens in particular in Indian scenario and argued in favour of an interface with backend e-governance plan through an agile VIS. This VIS arguably concluded that rural citizens' would continuously access the services rendered by e-governance services if certain dimensions like proximity, latency, quality of services are taken care of and are related to their livelihood options. It concluded that mere supply of services through e-governance network would not sustain itself in the long run. Strategic planners need to take cognizance of the demands of rural citizens if overall development is to be assured in the context of rural India.

REFERENCES

Archmann, Sylvia & Kudlacek, Immanuel, (2008). Interoperability and the exchange of good practice cases. *European Journal of ePractice*, No 2 · February.

Bhatnagar, S. (2006), *Paving the Road towards Pro Poor e-Governance*, UNDP, APDIP, UNCRD Workshop Report, 26-27, Bangkok.

Budhiraja, Renu & Sameer Sachdeva (2009) *E-Readiness Assessment (India)*. Retrieved from:<unpan1.un.org/intradoc/groups/public/ documents APCITY/ UNPAN014673.pdf > accessed on March 2, 2009.

Riga Declaration, (2006). *Internet for all: EU ministers commit to an inclusive and barrier-free information society*, press release of June, IP/06/769.

Dutta, S., Lopez-Claros, A., & Mia, I. (2008). *The Global Information Technology Report.INSEAD*. New York: Oxford University Press.

EU, (2007). Inclusive e-Government: survey of status and baseline activities, European Commission, *DG Information Society and Media*, e-Government unit, December.

Heeks, R. (2006a). *Most E-Government Projects-for-Development Fail: How can Risk be Reduced?* Working Paper 14, IDPM, University of Manchester, UK.

Heeks, R., & Molla, A. (2009b). *Impact Assessment of ICT-for-Development Projects: A Compendium of Approaches*. Working Paper 36, IDPM, University of Manchester, UK.

ITU (2006a). World Telecommunication/ICT development Report 2006.

ITU. (2007b). *World Information Society Report*. Beyond WSIS.

Ministry of Information Technology. (2009). Retrieved from: http://www.mit.gov.in/default.aspx?id=832 accessed on 03.03.09.

Mishra, D.C. (2007). Sixty years of Development of E-Governance in India (1947-2007). *Are there Lessons for Developing Countries?,* ICEGOV2007, December 10-13, Macao, ACM978-1-59593-822-0/07/12.

Misra, H. K. (2009), *Managing Rural Citizen Interfaces in E-Governance Systems: A Study in Indian Context, ICEGOV2009*, November 10-13, 2009, Bogota, Colombia, Proceedings of ACM, pp.155-162

Misra, H. K. (2009). *Governance of Rural Information and Communication Technology: Opportunities and Challenges*. New Delhi: Academic Foundation.

Misra, H. K., & Hiremath, B. N. (2006). *Citizen-led Participatory E-Governance Initiatives: An Architectural Perspective*, IIM Lucknow . *Metamorphosis*, *5*(2), 133–148.

Misra, H. K., & Hiremath, B. N. (2009). *Livelihood Perspective of Rural Information Infrastructure and E-Governance Readiness in India: A Case Based Study*, IRMA Working Paper Series 215, IRMA, Anand, India.

Planning Commission. (2001). *Government of India, Report of The Working Group on Convergence and E-Governance for Tenth Five Year Plan* (2002-2007), New Delhi, November, p6-25.

UN. (2008). *UN E-Government Survey*. New York: From E-Government to Connected E-Governance.

ADDITIONAL READING

(2003a). *E-Readiness Assessment Report*. New Delhi: Department of Information Technology. Ministry of Communication and Information Technology. Government of India.

E-Readiness Assessment Report. (2004b). *Department of Information Technology. Ministry of Communication and Information Technology*. New Delhi: Government of India.

E-Readiness Assessment Report. (2006c). *Department of Information Technology, Ministry of Communication and Information Technology*. New Delhi: Government of India.

EU, (2007), Inclusive e-Government: survey of status and baseline activities. European Commission. *DG Information Society and Media, e-Government unit,* December.

European Commission, (2005). i2010 – A European Information Society for Growth and Employment, SEC (2005)717, 01.06.2005 COM(2005) 229 final, Brussels (BE)

Kochhar, S., & Dhanjal, G. (2005), Skoch e-governance Report Card 2005: From Governance to e-governance, Skoch Consultancy Services Pvt. Ltd., October, New Delhi.

Korten, D. C. (1980). Community Organisation and Rural Development: A Learning Process Approach. *Public Administration Review*, (Sept-Oct): 480–510. doi:10.2307/3110204

Levina, N., & Vaast, E. (2005). The Emergence of Boundary Spanning Competence in Practice: Implications for Implementation and Use Of Information Systems, MIS Quarterly, June, 29 (2), pp. 335-363.

Luftman J., (2000) Assessing business – IT alignment maturity. *Communications of the AIS*, 4, December.

Rao, T.P., Rao, Venkata, V., Bhatnagar, Subhas, and Satyanarayana, J, (2004), E-Governance Assessment Framework, EAF Ver-2.0, *Department of Information Technology, Ministry of Communication and Information Technology*, Governmnet of India, New Delhi, May.

Riley, T. B. (2003), *E-Governance Vs. E-Government*, I4D, November, 1-4, New Delhi.

Satyanarayana, J. (2004), *e-Government, the Science of the Possible*.(pp.8-22). New Delhi:Prentice-Hall of India.

Shah, T. (1997). *Design Issues in Catalising Peoples Institutions for Sustainable Development*. (IRMA, Unpublished).

Signore, O., Chesi, F., & Pallotti, M. (2005). E-Government: Challenges and Oppertunities. *XIX Annual Conference*, CMG-Italy, 7-9 June, Florence, Italy.

Subramanian, K., & Sachdeva, Sameer, (2003). Quantifying and assessing e-Governance, I4D, November, 1-4, New Delhi

UN. (2008). *UN E-Government Survey*. New York: From E-Government to Connected E-Governance.

UNDP. (2004). *ICT and Human Development: Towards Building a Composite Index for Asia, Realising the Millennium Development Goals*. ELSEVIER.

Venkatesh, V., Morris, M. G., Davis, G. B., & Davis, F. D. (2003). User acceptance of Information Technology: Toward a Unified View. *Management Information Systems Quarterly*, *27*(3), 425–478.

Ward, J., & Peppard, J. (2002). *Strategic Planning for Information Systems* (pp. 25–59). England: John Wiley and Sons, England.

Weill, P., & Broadbent, M. (1998). *Leveraging the Infrastructure: How Market Leaders Capitalise on Information Technology*. Boston: Harvard Business School Press.

World Bank. (1986). *Poverty and Hunger: Issues and Options for Food Security in Developing Countries*. A World Bank Policy Study. Washington, D.C.

KEY TERMS AND DEFINITIONS

E-Governance: Electronic form of citizen interfaces and citizen service delivery.

E-Government: Electronic form of back end and formalized services for citizens that bureaucracy provides.

Governance: Participation of citizens in availing services of government.

Government: Formalized bureaucracy for provisioning of citizen services.

Information: Processed data for the benefit of users or intended recipients.

Latency: Minimum delay in a system to render services.

Livelihood: Sustaining opportunity provided for having better living conditions.

Metrics: Measurement criteria for interpreting the result.

Proximity: the distance for the citizen to travel for availing the services.

Chapter 3
E-Government Policy: A Case Study of E-Filing System

Abdul Raufu Ambali
University Technology MARA, Malaysia

EXCUTIVE SUMMARY

One must admit that the emerging of faster delivery service required a faster mechanism of transaction between government and its people. But such transaction is not without issues that have to be addressed by the governments of the public sectors. The primary issues addresses by this chapter are the relationships between the perceived: security tightening, facilitating conditions, usefulness, eases of using e-filing system and users' retention. The second issue addresses by the chapter is differences in gender of the users with respect to factors that influence their state of retention. The findings of the study show a strong relationship between the predicting factors and user's intention to continuing using the system. The findings also show that the retention of users is highly affected by the differences in the gender of the users. This research would like to recommend that faster transaction mechanism between the government and the people enhances the e-governance system and in this context, this chapter is focusing on some potential implications of e-filing system of Malaysia.

ORGANIZATION BACKGROUND

Lembaga Hasil Dalam Negeri (LHDN) or the Inland Revenue Board of Malaysia is one of the potential agencies under the Ministry of Finance (MOF) in the country. The agency was established on 1st March 1996 and has been charged with collection of revenues in the country. It was established in accordance with the Inland Revenue Board of Malaysia Act 1995 and the Income Tax Act 1967 to enhance the quality and effectiveness of tax administration. The agency also act as an agent of the Government and provide services in administering, assessing, collecting and enforcing payment of income tax, petroleum income tax, real property gains tax, estate duty, stamp duties and any other taxes as may be agreed between the Government and the Board. The agency has also

DOI: 10.4018/978-1-61692-814-8.ch003

been charged to participate in or outside Malaysia in respect of matters relating to taxation and advice the government accordingly. It also extends its function by liaising with the appropriate Ministries and statutory bodies on taxation matters and acts as a collection agent for and or behalf of anybody on matters relating to the recovery of loans due for repayment under any written law.

Corporate Culture of IRBM

The Inland Revenue Board of Malaysia has been known to be the foremost tax administration agency and the best government income tax representative body in the Malaysia. The overall corporate culture of IRB can be envisaged from creation of a just, transparent and respectable tax management system. The vision of the board includes sensitivity to the welfare of its employees, career advancement opportunities for each employee and recognition of individual excellence. It is part of the Board's corporate culture to be committed towards excellence achievements and/or efficient client service provider. It also committed to a high degree of fairness of the country's tax system. IRB also focuses on continued improvements through development of appropriate skills and efficient workforce that is equipped with the high level of professionalism. Board vows to constantly upgrading income tax administration to become easier while simultaneously simplifying tax laws. The agent believes in offering fair and transparent service to people in the country at all time and always strive to encourage voluntary compliance of the taxpayers (see: www.hasil.gov.my).

Taxation Policy in Malaysia

Under the Malaysian tax policies, income tax is a fact of life and compulsory for resident that is due for its payment. However, Malaysian taxation policy is quite brightening and exciting for many reasons. *First* there is no capital gains-tax in the country. *Second*, there is no gift, inheritance nor estate taxes in Malaysia as well. *Third*, even the only capital gains tax in Malaysia related to the Real Property Gains Tax has been withdrawn for disposals made on 1 April 2007 (see: Budget Commentary & Tax Information 2009, PWC Tax Booklet 2007-2009).

Income tax in Malaysia is 'territorial' in nature because only income accruing in or derived from Malaysia is taxed. In other word, other form of incomes such as foreign remitted income into the country whether by resident or non-resident is exempted from taxation policy system. Generally speaking, there are several categories of income tax as described and delineated by section 4 of the Malaysian Income Tax Act, 1967. These categories include: gains or profits from business; income from employment; dividends interest and discounts; rents, royalties or premiums; pensions, annuities or other periodical payments; and gains or profits not falling under any of the above.

Manual Income Tax-Filing of Returns

Before the implementation of e-filing system in Malaysia, tax filing returns used to be done manually under a Self Assessment System (SAS). The taxpayer him/herself is responsible to correctly compute manually the amount assessable on a form and file the return to the Inland Revenue Board of Malaysia (IRBM). He or she then makes payment of any tax due and payable within the stipulated deadline to the respective IRBM's branches in the country. There are two categories of manual income tax returns forms. The first is employment income delineated as Form BE while the second is business income and/or other income form known as Form B. The due dates are usually 30th of June for business income tax purpose and 30th of April for non-business income tax every year.

Chargeable Income Tax

The chargeable income tax is described as tax residency. Individuals are regarded as tax resident if he or she is in Malaysia within certain periods of time. For example, an individual is a tax resident if he or she has spent at least 182 days in the country per year; or spent a period less than 182 days but the time spent is linked to another period following or preceding where he was present in Malaysia for 182 or more consecutive days. In addition, if a person has spent 90 days or more during the year and was present in Malaysia for at least 90 days in any 3 of the 4 immediate preceding years. The tax residential status of an individual citizen or non-citizen is important because it determines the rate of tax; it also determines if the person is entitled to personal relief and rebate and the income on which the person suppose to be taxed (see: see: Budget Commentary & Tax Information 2009, PWC Tax Booklet 2007-2009).

Joint Assessments

Following the amendment to Section 45(2) of the Income Tax Act, 1967 in Malaysia, a wife is automatically assessed separately on her income. However, the husband or the wife is given the opportunity to put in writing before 1 April every year if they want their income to be jointly assessed. In a situation where the spouse is not resident, this opportunity is applicable. In other words, spouse may decide only if he or she is a citizen or resident. Under the combined assessment, a spouse will be given a relief of RM3, 000 and a further RM3, 500 if the spouse is disabled. This is applicable if the spouse elects for joint assessment under his or her name, or the spouse has no source of income.

The chapter highlights some potential implications of the findings necessary for policy makers to achieve a successful e-filing system in the country. As reflected in the findings, it is imperative for all agencies' staff charged with e-government policy implementations to equip themselves with more sophisticated ICT tools to guide the users. The fact is that the gaps in IT infrastructure can affect people's intention (i.e., retention) to continue to use or not use the system provided by the government. Above all, the findings show that users must perceive the technology somehow useful, easy and friendly as well as security guaranteed.

In addition, the chapter also sheds light on the importance of ensuring technology readiness among the public users of the system in order to eliminate the external difficulties in terms of Internet access, ICT literacy among the public as these can also affect the user's retention. Finally, the chapter suggest that (i) more IT infrastructures and other incentives should be provided to encourage the public to use the system; (ii) effective program such as capacity building for the agency's staff that can facilitate readiness of the people to use the system is highly needed, if e-filing is to become a successful policy program. Thus, agency's staff must play effective roles to respond to the public perceptual complaints about the e-filing system and government must pay attention to gender differences in retention to use the system.

SETTING THE STAGE

E-Government and E-Filing System

The launching of Multimedia Super Corridor (MSC) in August 1996 by the Malaysian government was part of a major strategy to accelerate the country's entry into the Information Age. Thus e-government was introduced as one of the seven flagships of the MSC (Muhd Rais and Nazariah, 2003). In 1997, the Malaysian Government launched the Electronic Government initiative, generally known as e-Government, to reinvent itself to lead the country into the Information Age. E-government is one of the seven flagship applications introduced in MSC with the objectives of accelerating the growth of MSC, enhance national competitiveness and reduce digital divide (Ambali, 2009).

E-governments is about a process of reforming the way government works, shares information, delivers services to internal and external clients and specifically harnesses information technologies to transform its relations with citizens businesses and other arms of government. These technologies can serve a variety of ends and better delivery of government services to citizens. They can also be used to empower citizens through access to information or a more efficient government-citizen management (Bhatnagar, 2004).

Moreover, e-Government seeks to enhance the convenience, accessibility and quality of government's interactions with the public and businesses at large, (Shaidin). This would enable the government to be more responsive to the needs of its citizens. Hence, the principal aim of implementing e-government policy in various public sectors is to facilitate the effectiveness of government delivering services through electronic system and to create a strong relationship between government and its people at large. As such, several programs were launched by government to support the implementation of e-government, which includes e-filing system for taxpayers. In fact, e-filing is a reflection of government commitment to quality service delivery to people in the country.

Under the e-government flagship, seven main projects were identified to be the core of the e-government applications. The e-Government projects are Electronic Procurement (eProlehan), Project Monitoring System (PMS), Electronic Services Delivery (eServices), Human Resource Management Information System (HRMIS), Generic Office Environment (GOE), E-Syariah and Electronic Labour Exchange (ELX). Besides these seven main projects under e-government flagships, several government agencies has taken initiatives to introduced online services for the public, with aims to increase the ease and efficiency of public service to the people. Among them were Public Services Portal (myGovernment), e-Tanah, e-Consent, e-Filing, e-Local Government (e-PBT), e-Kehakiman, Custom Information System (SMK), Pensions Online Workflow Environment (POWER), and Training Information System (e-SILA) (Shaidin, 2007; Ambali, 2009).

Growing Population of Workforce and E-Filing Alternative

The data below shows that Malaysia labours force is increasing since 1980 until 2003. Although it seems decreased in 2003, but still achieves the level of above 8 million persons. In other words, it shows an increasing trend since 1985 to 2002. On the other hand, the unemployment rate recorded a lower percentage within the same periods as compared to 1980's as indicated in the Figure 1.

One important point to ponder from the increasing trend of workforce is the capability of the IRB officers to handle all income tax file returns manually with the growing population of such labour force today. As the population of those employed among the growing labour force is increasing, the number of tax payers is also expected to steadily rise (see: labour force graph above). According to the department of statistic in Malaysia (2008), the predicted number of the population that is expected to be within the age group of 25-55 year in 2010 is expected to rise to 12 million. This implies that the cost that would be borne by IRB for manually processing every individual tax file return form will be at an average figure of RM10 ringgit. The immediate implication of this is that the IRBM has to handle approximately 10 million employed citizens' tax returns every year manually.

Technology and Components Concerns for E-Filing System

E-filing implementation was introduced by a government agency called LHDN (Lembaga Hasil Dalam Negeri). It allows taxpayers to submit their income tax details online and is considered as an alternative to the usual manual paper submission

Figure 1. Labour force/unemployment Rate

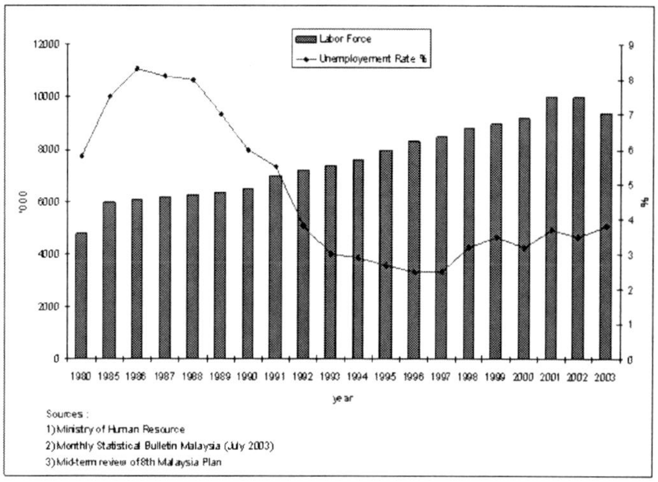

Graph source : Poon Wai Ching (2006); The development of Malaysia Economy, Prentice Hall

(i.e., BE or B forms). E-filing was first introduced in 2006 and has since undergone a progressive improvement with a more robust system promised to the users via Internet Explorer browsers technology. Today, the e-filing application is not only limited to Internet Explorer browsers like before; taxpayers can now also use other browsers like Firefox and Opera to reach LHDN wherever they are in the country. In terms of technology, a big picture of e-filing system in Malaysia is that it integrates tax preparation, tax filing and tax payment, which serves as a major advantage over traditional manual procedures. With the e-filing system, taxpayers and tax practitioners can file income tax returns electronically via the enabling technologies, rather than through mail or by physically visiting the tax offices. This is believed to make the art of tax filing returns easier by some users.

However, there has been some question of concerns on the authenticity of the transaction among the citizens and non-citizen taxpayers. In addition, the security loop holes have been discovered in the past but the Lembaga Hasil Dalam Negeri (LHDN) known as Internal Revenue Board (IRB) folks were very quick to address the issues and resolve them in a timely manner. Again, with the specter of the growing digital divide looming large, the significance of technology acceptance assumes paramount position in the roadmap towards e-government applications in public sector. Therefore, the implementation of e-government in any country would therefore require an environment that is very conducive to realize its potential for development. Ideally, an environment that is more 'e-ready', people are in general more comfortable with the new technologies and thus e-filing initiatives can be easily accepted and adopted.

Management and Organizational Concerns

From managerial and organizational perspectives, there were twofold concerns of implementing e-filing system by the charged agency LHDN. *First*, is for the agency to become more effective in the operational and processing tasks involving tax filing returns. For example, it has been realized that using manual system limits the ability to process tax files expeditiously and subsequently causing a lot of delay in income tax collections. In addition, given that the volume of taxpayers is increasingly risen up in the country, additional manpower and time are required to screen tax returns and enter the data manually into the system. Thus it is believed that implementation of e-filing system would significantly streamline the process, improve the accuracy of the tax returns and reduce transcribing error that characterized the manual base system. *Second* is to better serve the interest of the taxpayers by overcoming their difficulties in using paper base or manual system and to encourage voluntary compliance of the taxpayers in submitting their tax returns. Thus implementation of e-filing system serves as another additional channel for taxpayers to reach the agency. In other words, implementation of e-filing system is expected to provide greater convenience for taxpayers in the sense that it allows them to file their tax returns at anytime and from anywhere within the stipulated tax filing period.

CHALLENGES AND ISSUES IN THE LITERATURE

This section of the case examines the various challenges and issues pertaining to implementation of e-filing in Malaysia. The current challenges include how many and which segment of the population is using the system; perception of users towards it; perceived barriers, gender effect, age; security issue technology acceptance and readiness, perceived usefulness and ease as well as simplicity of the website of the service provider. This section covers both experience in Malaysia and elsewhere in the world with respect to theories and practices. This section begins with the challenges and/or issues can be found in practice and supported them with related theories in the literature.

Since 2006, both Malaysian and non-Malaysian citizens have been given the opportunity to choose either manual tax-filing or the internet-based called e-filing method of filing their tax-returns. However, the number of taxpayers using e-filing system is far below the expectation. According to an empirical report in newspaper, the user of e-filing in Malaysia only reached 448,742 users from 6.4 million taxpayers in the country (Izatun, 22/4/08, The Star). In an exploratory research conducted Ramayah et al (2006), the result has shown that many taxpayers did not use e-filing system to file their tax returns. One of the major issues identified in that study was related to *the 16-digit PIN number* that an e-filer must obtain directly from the income tax office. Furthermore challenges found include the queuing up at income office to get the PIN number; lack of step by step explanation on how to use the e-filing system as well as e-filers' skeptical of security and privacy of their personal data furnished in the online e-filing system. In terms of demographic effects the findings in Ramayah's study have shown that e-filers are "*predominantly female, aged 30-55 years old, married, Chinese with a bachelor or masters degree, earning more than RM 3000 per month and working in private sector*" *(p.4)*. However, access to computer and network facilities at home and at work was not a problem for both manual and online users in that study.

One obvious scenario is that though adoption of e-filing systems may seem to benefit taxpayers in many ways, however, the importance of understanding and influencing citizens' acceptance of this system is critical. The e-filing system may offer potential benefits to improve administrative commitments towards efficiency and quality of service delivery, but the benefits gained may be obstructed by tax users' unwillingness to accept and use the available electronic services for many reasons that worth to be researched.

Learning from the experience of overseas tax agencies, one may say that the move to embrace an e-filing system is not hassle free and is not well accepted by all parties in society. Thus, worldwide, tax users' resistance and under-utilization of the e-filing system remains a great concern and still plagues various tax agencies who are embracing electronic tax administration systems (see: ETAAC, 2002).

According to one survey on Success and Failure Rates of e-government policy in developing countries only 15% are successful, while 35% and 55% are total/partial respectively (eGovernment for Development; Heeks, 2003). The result of a survey conducted by H.D. Vest Financial Services, Inc, - a US largest provider of financial products and services delivered through tax professionals in 2000 - has shown that majority of Americans are comfortable with e-filing.

In fact the acceptance of e-filing has given rise to an increased comfort with web preparation and it seems that Americans are catching on to the e-filing system and more swiftly than expected. To substantiate this point, the report has shown that over half of the country says that they are very comfortable by e-filing their tax returns. Fifty-four percent of American taxpayers (65 million) say that they are comfortable filing their tax returns electronically, which is more than twice the number that actually e-filed their tax returns in the previous year (30 million).

An almost identical proportion expressed the same level of comfort in receiving their refunds electronically. Not surprisingly, younger Americans in particular are more likely to e-file their tax returns and receive refunds electronically than citizens aged 65 or older who are significantly less comfortable with e-filing system. The nation's elderly are also uncomfortable with receiving a refund electronically in spite of the fact that many have already been receiving direct deposit of their Social Security payments electronically. The study also found that men are much more willing than women to use the Internet for tax preparation and e-filing.

In Asia, Taiwan is an example of country practicing e-government services where the citizen has been using the e-filing system for their personal income tax. However, there is a clear difference in willingness between men and women e-filers in terms of its usefulness, cost saving, and the ease of use (Jen et al, 2006). Many other studies have also reported similar cases of this kind and pointed to several factors such as technology readiness of the people, perception of the public in terms of technology usefulness, ease of use, and security of their information provided online (James, 1987; Davis, 1989; Parasuraman, 2000; Parasuraman and Colby, 2001; and Yurcik and Sharma, 2004).

People's Acceptance of Technology and Readiness Theory

People's acceptance of e-filing is highly related to their level of technology readiness on the one hand, ease and usefulness of e-filing system as well as security and facilitating support on the other. Technology readiness is defined as people's propensity to embrace and use new technologies for accomplishing certain tasks. The people's propensity towards e-filing system has to do with their level of optimism, innovativeness, discomfort, and security tightening in the system. Parasuraman and Colby (2001) highlighted that technology readiness is an overall state of mind and not a measure of competency and has pointed to some important issues surrounding human aspects of technology readiness. First, technology readiness varies from one individual to another. Some people can be consumer of a technology, but some may seek technology actively, whilst others may need special help or coaxing depending on the level of their readiness. Second, technology readiness can be used to predict and explain people's responses towards new technologies. Empirical findings also indicate that technology readiness correlates with actual use and intention to use the technology-based products and services in varying degrees (Parasuraman and Colby, 2001). In addition, an individual with a higher level of technology readiness has higher usage intention and more experience in using the technology based products and services in varying degrees. Similarly, prior studies by Dabholkar (1994) and Mick and Fournier (1998) also demonstrated that people with more positive beliefs are more receptive and ready to use the various new technologies.

People's Perceived Usefulness of Technology, Security and Acceptance Theory

The perceived usefulness is a prospective user's subjective probability that using a specific application system will increase his or her job performance within an organizational context (Davis et al. 1989). As far back as 1989, Davis et al had developed a theoretical assumption relating to technology acceptance model (TAM) to explain the computer usage behaviour and had adopted the generic Fishbein and Ajzen's Theory of Reasoned Action (TRA) model to the domain of user acceptance of computer technology. The goal of TAM was to provide an explanation for the determinants of computer acceptance. He contends that this would generally capable of explaining behaviour across a broad range of end-users of computer technologies. In other words, TAM is usually used for explaining the relationship between usages [both self-reported and anticipated future usage] and perceived usefulness as well as perceived ease of use.

According to TAM, usage and acceptance of technology is a direct function of behavioural intention, which in turn a function of attitude toward actual usage. This will reflect feelings of favourableness or unfavourableness toward using any particular technology. The perceived usefulness will reflect the belief that using the technology will enhance performance. From such theoretical assumption, one may likely to conclude that behavioural intention of using, continuing to use, and actual usage of a any technological device for carrying out any transaction is determined jointly by perceived usefulness and perceived ease of use. In the same line of argument, Mathieson (1991); Adams, Nelson and Todd (1992); Segar and Grover (1993); Igbaria et al. (1995, & 1997); Ndubisi et al (2001); Jackson (1997); Ramayah et al. (2004) and Livari et al, (1997) had all shown that the three factors especially perceived usefulness and security have a direct influence on technology usage intention.

In addition, the Unified Theory of Acceptance and Use of Technology (UTAUT) by Venkatesh et al. (2003) have also been used to explain users' intention to use Information System and subsequent usage behaviour. The theory holds that four key constructs related to performance expectancy, effort expectancy, social influence, and facilitating conditions are direct determinants of usage intention and behaviour of the people. In UTAUT model, gender, age, experience, and voluntaries of use, are posited to moderate the impact of the four key constructs on usage intention and behaviour (see: Venkatesh et. al., 2003). The theory was developed through a review and consolidation of the constructs of eight models that earlier researchers had employed to explain Information Systems usage behaviour, such as theory of reasoned action; technology acceptance model; motivational model; theory of planned behaviour; a combined theory of planned behaviour/technology acceptance model; model of PC utilization; innovation diffusion theory; and the social cognitive theory. Subsequent validation of UTAUT in a longitudinal study found it to account for 70% of the variance in usage intention studied by Venkatesh et al, (2003).

As far as security issue is concerned it is obvious that people rarely worry about security in the physical world. Most of them, even while filing the paper-based tax returns, never bother to find out who is in charge of the post office where they will post their returns nor worry about the percentage accuracy of postage delivery services. But, when it comes to e-filing, people go out to extraordinary length to worry about the security of their information required in the system. The reason for such inconsistent behavior is that security violations in Internet-based systems have received much notoriety in the popular sections of press and mind of the people.

It is this perception of security in the online transactions that causes majority of the tax payer population to be reluctant to use this alternative medium of filing tax returns. People may perceive current facilities in electronic tax filing website not adequately secure and/or helpful. This may also lead to a general belief that electronic transaction are inherently insecure and that any hacker/geek, if he/she wants, can break into the computer system and can steal and misuse their confidential personal data information. Perhaps, it is this general paranoia that has gripped the public taxpayers.

In other words, electronic tax filing has been, without any doubt, gaining a lot of popularity in these days, but a lot of users go to this system and try to get a 'feel' of how to file electronically but poor navigability and sense of uncertainty about the functionality and security concerns for their sensitive information result in the users 'giving up' the idea of electronically filing tax returns in despair. Thus, even though these websites may initially attract a large number of people, the retention may be low.

In line with such view, Pfitzmann's work (2001) has shown that to perceive security and credibility of a website a person makes assessment of both trustworthiness to arrive at conclusion that the website is credible or not and to whether he/she should use it or not. If the user is able to feel that the system is well secured and trustworthy he/she will be able to put trust into the website and use it. One can easily argue that public users will have no doubt in trusting Malaysian federal and state government websites for providing information. However, users can still be sceptical in the manner the agency is going to transmit or store their personal information provided to them.

People's Perception of Ease and Simplicity of the Site

Another crucial issue related to users' perception, acceptance and usage of the e-filing system is the concern for simplicity of the site and availability of support. If the system matches the users' mental model and users can find it intuitive with nothing strange or unlikely happening, they feel more confident about the e-filing tax site. If they feel ease of using it and safe, they don't mind providing information about themselves. A sense that nothing is hidden or obscure on the e-filing tax website is a very important factor for the users to be able to perceive it as secure and trustworthy and have intention to continuing using it.

Thus the ease of use and users' feeling of control of the e-filing tax system would give them confidence about the system. Finally, a user's perception about genuineness of the tax web, authenticity and trustworthiness of the process of filing tax returns can also be enhanced if user feels ease about what he/she is doing when they are filing their tax returns. Thus, the users' awareness and experience also help enhance the users' retention dramatically.

To sum up, first people may have a positive view (optimistic) of e-filing and belief in the benefits of it in terms of time, cost efficiency and enhancement of their compliance. Second, they may be discomfort about it when they perceived themselves to be lack of control over technology and non confidence in using the new technology properly. Third is insecurity, which can lead to distrust of technology-based transactions and skepticism about its ability to work effectively for their needs.

CURRENT ISSUE EXAMINED IN THIS CHAPTER: A RETENTION PROBLEM

This section of the case study investigates the current challenges and issues in Malaysian e-filing system. The section seeks to confirm the relevance of some of the potential issues and challenges highlighted in the theoretical literature to Malaysian e-filing system with respect to users' retention and gender effect issues. As such this section of the chapter examines the user's perceptual retention and gender difference on the new electronic income-tax-paying or filing system in Malaysia, as an alternative to the traditional paper-base. The section begins with methodology and approach to the investigation. It then discusses the details of the finding about the new current challenge. Finally, it discusses the implications of the findings for the policy-makers with some recommendations for improvements.

Methodology and Approach to the Investigation of Retention Issue

The Design and Source of Data

The study is designed in a cross-sectional survey to obtain information from respondents over a period of time about their perceived usefulness, perceived security, facilitating condition, ease of using e-filing technology system to file their income tax returns and retention. Hence, the unit of analysis for the study is every individual taxpayer that has used the e-filing system and hoping to re-use it again. The study limits its scope to two geographical locations in Kuala Lumpur and Shah Alam for data collection.

A survey of questionnaire was distributed to participants and supported by unstructured interview for an in-depth investigation about the perceived ease, usefulness, security, facilitating conditions and retention for e-filing system. A sample size of 450 taxpayers was purposively and randomly chosen to participate in the study over a period of two months (March-April, 2009) of data collection. But, out of the 450 questionnaires distributed, only 302 were returned. Again, out of the 302 returned questionnaires only 300 were appropriately completed with valid information. The remaining 2 questionnaires were not used in the analysis due to too many omissions or non-completeness of the questions and more than two answers were chosen or ticked for some questions in the 2 questionnaires. As such they were dropped in the subsequence analysis.

Measurement and Instrumentation

Methodologically, the chapter employs a survey of the users of the new electronic system. The questionnaire covers the perceptual retention of the users to continue using e-filing system on the basis of the perceived level of security in using the e-filing system. The measurement of security variable embraces a lot of dimensions which include whether: use of e-filing may cause personal income tax information to be stolen or not; users do not consider it safe to give out bank account number through e-filing; users feel uneasy psychologically if they use e-filing; users do not think it is safe to use e-filing because of the privacy concerns; and overall, users find e-filing to be secured in preparing and filing tax returns. The rationale behind covering the perceived security is logical as it can affect the perceptual intentions (retention) of the users to use or continuing to use the system.

In addition, the survey questions also focus on the facilitating conditions/supports that are in place to encourage the users to use the system. For this variable the measurement includes availability of: the necessary resources such as computer and internet to use e-filing; the Internet knowledge of the users to use e-filing; a step by step guideline on how to use e-filing by the agency's staff; the easy of getting support when the users have problems, in using the e-filing, from the staff. The survey also went further to capture the ease of use of the e-filing system. The dimensions of this variable includes whether e-filing is: easy to learn; easy to master; easy to operate; has instructions that are easy to follow; easy for users to input and modify data; easy to use in general; clear and/or understandable to the users.

Above all, the survey items also cover another potential variable referred to as perceived usefulness. This variable is measured in different dimensions in terms of whether the system: enables users to accomplish the tasks more quickly; enhances effectiveness in preparing their income tax filing;

simplifies the process of filing income tax return; enables users to reduce error in their tax filing process; reduces communication and filing costs; and overall users find e-filing useful in preparing their income tax at large. Finally, the survey questions also look at the natural characteristic factor, such as gender, that can shape users' perceptions in using e-filing system as a moderating effect. All questionnaire items except demographic variables are measured on 5-point likert scale, 1= strongly disagree, 2 = disagree, 3 = undecided, 4 = agree, and 5 = strongly agree.

Goodness of Data

The goodness of data starts from consistency of the items with the concepts being measured in the survey. In other words, consistency indicates how well the items measuring a concept hang together as a set for any constructs and must be tested. Internal consistency and reliability of the survey instrument used was tested via Cronbach's alpha. Cronbach's alpha is computed in terms of the average inter-correlations among the items measuring the concepts.

The results confirm the suitability and validity of the designed survey instruments in this study with a value ranging from 0.8-0.9 and thus indicate the goodness of the items in the survey and their appropriateness (De Vaus, 2006). The Cronbach's alpha value exceeded the 0.7 standard proposed by Nunnaly (1978). The reliability coefficient values is categorized ranging from 0.6 acceptable to excellent (> 0.7) according to George and Mallery (2001) and hence the scale instrument is found to be adequate and well reliable in this study as indicated in Table 1.

Statistical Approach and Assumptions

At the inception of the OLS (ordinary least square) approach to this work, various assumptions such as normality of the data distribution, homoscedasticity and collinearity are examined and satisfied (see Aiken and West, 1991, Aguinis, 2004). Normality test is a prerequisite for any inferential statistical technique. As argued by Coakes and Dzidic (2006), there are a number of ways to explore this assumption graphically by histogram, stem and leaf plot, box-plot, normal probability plot. There are also a number of statistical methods to test such assumption which includes Kolmogrove-Smirnov with Lillifors significance level and Shapiro-Wilk as well as Skewness and Kurtosis.

Essentially, skewness and kurtosis are the two statistics used to summarize the shape of the distribution of the variables in this study. According to Hair et al (2006), the degree to which a distribution is asymmetrical is indicated by the skewness values whilst kurtosis meanwhile suggests the degree of flatness or peakness in data distribution relative to the shape of a normal distribution. Thus, Hair et al (2006) suggested that a normal distribution should occupy a range within an acceptable ± 2. In this study, the results for all items are well below such value ± 2 and thus indicate normality of the data distribution. In addition, other indicators of normality of data

Table 1. Internal consistency, validity and reliability of the survey instrument

Variable	Cronbach's Alpha	No of Items
Perceived usefulness	0.86	6
Perceived ease of use	0.91	7
Facilitating conditions	0.80	5
Users' retention	0.88	4
Perceived Risk/security	0.82	5

Table 2. Normality test

Variables	Skewness	Kurtosis	Kolmogrove Smirnov	Sig.
User's retention	-0.297	0.830	0.049	0.2000*
Perceived usefulness	0.321	0.013	0.065	0.2000*
Perceived ease of use	0.181	0.613	0.070	0.197*
Facilitating conditions	0.055	-0.106	0.027	0.2000*
Perceived security	-0.232	-0.086	0.052	0.2000*

*>0.05 alpha value

Table 3. Correlations among independent variables to examine collinearity assumption

	Perceived Usefulness	Perceived ease of use	Facilitating conditions	Security	Tolerance
Perceived usefulness	1				0.70
Perceived ease of use	0.422(**)	1			0.81
Facilitating conditions	0.353(**)	0.438(**)	1		0.75
Security	0.319(**)	0.391(**)	0.222(**)	1	0.80
N=300					

**Correlation is significant at the 0.01 level (2-tailed).

distribution for using inferential statistics as in this study are the Kolmogrove-Smirnov and Shapiro-Wilk with p-value > 0.05 (see Table 2)

Furthermore, the multi-collinearity assumption is examined through a partial correlation statistics between variables. The result in Table 3 shows an absence of collinearity among all independent variables. In fact a lower values of correlation (r) (Mallery, 2001) among independent variable, which range from 0.2 to 0.4, as well as tolerance values between 0.7 and 0.8 indicate absent of multi-collinearity problem.

Statistical procedures of realizing the objective of this study began with the use of mean and standard deviation to assess the level of users' perceived usefulness, security, facilitating conditions and ease of using e-filing system (independent variables). Then, the causal relation between the levels of users' perception and retention i.e., an intention to continue using e-filing to file their tax returns (dependent variable) was examined through OLS (Regression) analysis. As such, a causal relation equation was derived as follows:

(a) First order analysis:

Estimated Users' Retention: (UR) = $\alpha + \beta_1$ perceived usefulness + β_2 perceived ease of use + β_3 facilitating condition + β_4 security + error term……. Equation 1.

Where $\beta 1 - 4$ are the estimated coefficient values of the users' retention and a constant α.

This is used with entry method to see the overall effects of predictors, while controlling for all demographic variables.

(b) Second order analysis:

The likely question on which type of genders has retention for e-filing system should be addressed. That is, is male or female feeling that: e-filing is a useful alternative; is easy to use; facilitating conditions are well in place; is very secure or safe to use among the taxpayers? This

Table 4. Percentage level e-filing usage.

Usage of e-filing system usage	Frequency	% of e-filing
Yes	135	45
No	165	55

allows us to know specific intension to continuing using e-filing tool in relations to each of the predicting factors. As such, a block method was used to allow us to see the effect of each specific predictor, while controlling for all demographic variables except gender variable in order to test its moderating effect between each predictor and users' retention. The fact is that people by nature do not perceive and/or feel things in the same way.

Hence, new equations were generated for estimating the users' retention as follows:

UR = $\alpha + \beta_1$ perceived usefulness + β_2 gender + β_3 usefulness*gender....................Equation 2.

UR = $\alpha + \beta_1$ perceived ease of use + β_2 gender + β_3 ease of use*gender...................Equation 3.

UR = $\alpha + \beta_1$ perceived facilita-Condition + β_2 gender + β_3 facilita-Cond*gender......Equation 4.

UR = $\alpha + \beta_1$ perceived security + β_2 gender + β_3 security*gender.............................Equation 5.

Where usefulness*gender; ease of use*gender; facilita-Cond*gender and security*gender are the product terms in each respective equation.

To estimate a moderating effect, the equation must proceed from first order of each predictor to the second order, which involves a product term between the predictor and the moderator as can be seen in the equations 2 to 5 (see: Aguinis, 2004). The moderator in this study is coded with binary or a dummy coding system (effect order: male = 0 and female = 1). Finally, as mere statistical change in the value of R-square may not clearly show the effect with respect to each type of gender and therefore graphical moderating effect of gender is drawn to further shed lights on the effect.

The Findings of the Study

Level of Usage of E-Filing System in Filing Tax Returns

With reference to Table 4, the findings show that 45% (135) of respondents have used e-filing technology to file their tax returns, while a large number of respondents (55%) never use the e-filling services provided. In other words, it is a reflection that many still prefer to use their traditional manual to the new modern technology system!

Perceived Usefulness, Ease of Use, Facilitating Condition, Security Level of E-Filing System and Perceptual Retention of Users

On perceptual users' retention the research questions were measured on a 5-point likert scale to have a good sense of usage intention of e-filing system by taxpayers. The result shows that the level of respondents' retention is not very high but within moderate point (mean M= 3.23, std. Deviation SD= 0.62). This indicates that the majority of the respondents have moderate intentions of continuing using e-filing system. However, respondents have lower level of perceived security and safety about their personal data with mean 2.6 and std. deviation of 0.62.

In contrast, an examination of the result for perceived level of usefulness, ease of use and facilitating conditions in using e-filing system by respondents reflects a very high level except for security variable that below moderate (M= 4.58 SD= 0.57; M=4.43, SD=0.56; M=4.41, 0.54 and M=2.60, 0.63 respectively) as indicated in Table

Table 5. Descriptive statistics of predictors with users' perceptual retention

Variable Deviation	Minimum	Maximum	Mean	Std.
User's retention	1.20	4.00	3.23	0.62
Perceived usefulness	2.50	5.00	4.58	0.57
Perceived ease of use	2.17	5.00	4.43	0.56
Facilitating conditions	2.28	5.00	4.41	0.54
Perceived security	1.22	3.00	2.60	0.63
Valid N = 300				

Table 6. Estimated users' retention by predictors (first order effect)

Variables	Standarized Beta	t	Sig.
Perceived usefulness	0.529	6.310	0.000
Perceived ease of use	0.235	2.896	0.004
Facilitating conditions	0.123	2.144	0.034
Perceived security/risk	0.128	2.240	0.012
R^2=0.63**			
Adj R^2=0.62			

**$P<0.05$

5. A mere reflection on these results indicates that elements of perceived usefulness, ease of use and facilitating conditions for effective use of e-filing system could serve as driving forces that capture the taxpayers' retention or intentions to continue to use e-filing system to file their tax returns, since 2006 till the present time.

First Order Effect of Predictors on Users' Retention of E-Filing System

An examination of the results in Table 6 reflects that all the independent variables ranging from perceived usefulness to security or risk association are good predictors of users' retention for e-filing system in this study. In fact, as the results indicate, perceived usefulness is the most significant predicting factor that determine users' retention followed by perceived ease of use (Beta = 0.53, t = 6.3; and Beta = 0.24, t = 2.90) respectively. Facilitating condition and perceived security issue associated with the system (Beta = 0.12, t = 2.14; and 0.13, t = 2.24) are also good predictor of users' retention but on a lower rank compared to perceived usefulness and ease of using the e-filing system. Overall, as indicated by the result of the R-square, 62% of users' retention for e-filing system is explained by the whole predictors in our regression equation (1) put forward in this study.

Assessing the Moderating Effect of Gender

An examination of Table 7 gives a clear reflection on moderating effect of gender of users with respect to their relative perceived impact of each predictor against their intention to continuing using e-filing system. The effect is clearly shown through a change in R-square values when gender was used to moderate the relationship between each predicting factor and users' retention as indicated in model 1 and model 2 of the Table 7 respectively.

Table 7. Estimated users' retention by predictors and moderating effect of gender (2nd order effect)

	without gender	with effect of gender				
Variables	**Model 1 (R^2)**	**Model 2 (R^2)**	α	β_1	β_2	β_3
Perceived usefulness	48.7	49.5	-2.05	0.70	3.06	**-0.14**
Perceived ease of use	59.3	59.8	-1.94	0.72	2.74	**-0.11**
Facilitating conditions	21.5	22.1	4.22	0.11	0.02	**-0.03**
Perceived security/risk	68.3	68.6	-1.06	1.03	1.90	**-0.11**

Where β_1 is the estimated coefficient of UR due to each predictor. β_2 is the estimated coefficient of UR due to gender; and β_3 is the estimated coefficient of UR due to product term effect of gender*the respective predictor.

Thus, with moderating effect of gender there is a significant change from 48.7 to 49.5 for perceived usefulness. The same applies to perceived ease, facilitating condition and perceived security level from 59.3 to 59.8, 21.5 to 22.1 and 68.3 to 68.6 R-sq respectively.

However, these significant changes, due to moderating effect of gender (model 2), in the values of R-square may not be well appreciated in the sights of the readers for twofold reasons. First, it is ordinary minute figures to non-statisticians and therefore difficult to see the impact clearly. Second, these minute changes in R-square values again do not reflect the magnitude of such effect in relation to the type of gender of the users. Therefore, I have taken a one step further to show the impact of gender graphically to account for those two reasons that R-square values cannot be able to tackle and to provide answers to questions on gender differences among the users.

So by computation of the previous equations 2 to 5 with the substitutions of all parameters from Table 4.yielded the following moderating effect of gender of the users on the relationships between the predictors and the users' retention as the graphs illustrate.

Figure 2 (a), shows the moderating effect of gender between the perceived usefulness of e-filing and users' intention to continuing using the system to file their tax-returns. As clearly indicated by the graph, gender play a significant effect in intention to use e-filing. In fact, the result of this graphical representation of such effect shows that the degree of perceived usefulness of e-filing is higher for female e-filers than the male counterparts, wherein the slope of the female is quite steeper than the male, indicating a higher level of females' retention of e-filing system in relation to its perceived usefulness.

In addition, as indicated by the gradient of the slope, both genders have positively perceived the usefulness of e-filing system as enabler to file their tax returns as compared to traditional manual procedure or way. However, looking at perceived usefulness of e-filing system for female e-filers, the intention to continuing using the system (UR) ranges from 3.7 approximately to 4.5 as compared to male's retention level between 0. 7 and 1.6 as the graph indicates.

Just like perceived usefulness of e-filing system, the finding in Figure 2 (b) shows that female e-filers have high retention to continuing using the system as compared to male e-filers. In other words, as perceived ease of use of e-filing system increases so also the users' retention for both genders, but that of female is extremely higher, ranging from 3.2 to 4.0 as compared to male between 0.9 and 1.7 approximately. Interestingly, the estimated minimum retention (UR) for female is even higher than maximum retention for male users as can be clearly seen in the graph with about 2.3 values difference.

In terms of facilitating conditions and/or supports put in place to enhance the using of e-filing system by e-filers, the results in Figure 2 (c) shows an opposite trend to the way the gender perceived

Figure 2. (a) Moderating effect of gender by perceived usefulness of e-filing system. (b) Moderating effect of gender by perceived ease of use of e-filing. (c) Moderating effect of gender perceived by facilitating conditions. (d) Moderating effect of gender security tightening in e-filing.

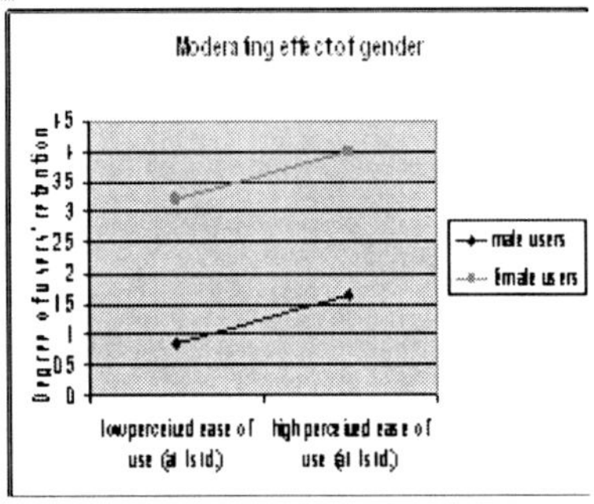

(a) Moderating effect of gender by perceived usefulness of e-filing system

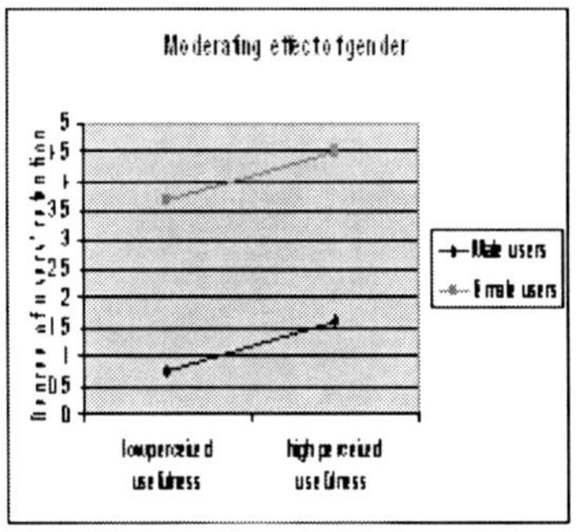

(b) Moderating effect of gender by perceived ease of use of e-filing

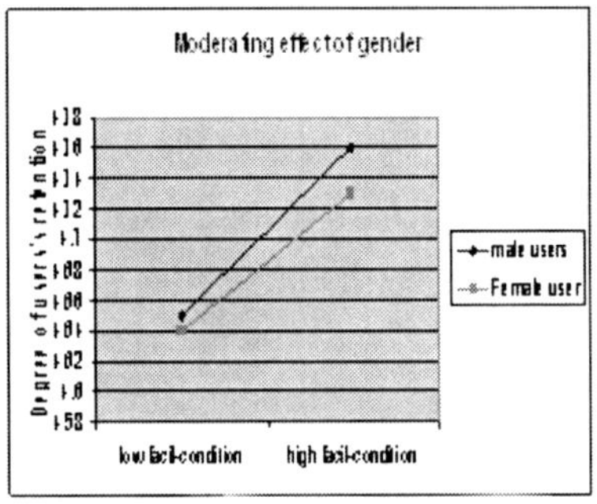

(c) Moderating effect of gender perceived by facilitating conditions

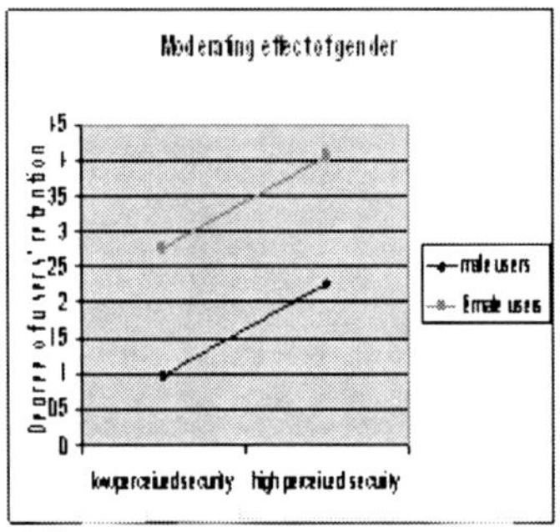

(d) Moderating effect of gender security tightening in e-filing

the first two variables (usefulness and ease of using the system), where the female e-filers have the highest degree of retention for using e-filing due to a highly perceived usefulness and ease of using the system. However, in the case of facilitating condition component, although both genders have positively perceived that there are a lot of facilitating conditions and supports, but the male e-filers' retention is slightly higher than the female counterparts as indicated by the graph. As the results indicate the lowest or minimum retention for both genders, regardless of their differences, ranges from 4.64, 4.65 to 4.73, 4.76 respectively when compared with perceived usefulness and ease of use component variables.

By looking at the graphical indicator (Figure 2 (d)) of the users' retention with respect to perceived security associated with using e-filing, both male and female are differ in retention as indicated by the gradient of the slopes. Just like all other predicting factors, both of the slopes for male and female e-filers are paralleled but unequally steepened. In other words, both genders of the users have the same impressions regarding the extent to which their personal data submitted online can be protected or saved from being exposed to unauthorized people who may likely take advantage of making use of their data wrongly within and outside the country.

However, for female users, the degree of their perceived security tightening in e-filing is higher as compared to their male counterpart users. Thus, the female' retention for e-filing system is much higher ranging from 2.7 to 4.1 as compared to the male e-filers with retention between 0.9 and 2.3 approximately. In other words, the higher the perceived security tightening and protection of their personal information, the higher their retention to continue using e-filing system in filing their tax returns. Overall, differences in gender perceptions about the usefulness; ease of use of e-filing; enough facilitating conditions/supports; and level of security have a significant effect on each type of users' gender. In other words, both genders do not have the same feeling for e-filing system in filing their tax returns.

DISCUSSION OF FINDINGS AND RECOMMENDATIONS

There is no doubt that in this era of fast moving world, better services from respective governments or agencies to their citizens are highly needed. Therefore, creating a fast, reliable and safe service should be the main priorities of any governments in the world. Thus, adapting technology into the public service delivery system is one of the ways to create fast reliable and safe services. In Malaysia, e-government flagship was launched to cater for these technological needs of its citizens under which e-filing system is becoming a popular method for the citizens to file their tax returns. However, one thing is to provide a technology system for people to speed up the service processes, but it is another thing for people to accept and perceived it as something useful, easy, convenient, and enhance their situation as compared to the manual form.

In relation to the findings of this study, one can obviously say that the overall level of the e-filing usage among taxpayers is still low, despite many campaign activities by LHDN to increase the level of e-filing usage in the country. This finding is very similar to the statistical reports on the usage record for the previous years and also in line with similar disappointing numbers of the e-filing users reported by Izatun (2008) in one of the local news paper as discussed the section on literature review of this study. However, such disappointing lower number of usage of e-filing system by taxpayers to file their income tax returns is not confined to Malaysia, but also to some other developed countries including USA as discussed in the literature.

Regarding the other crucial issues of security level, holding the gender of the users constant, a lower mean level of using e-filing system shows some elements of negative perceptions of the users, which may likely affect their retention and/or a continuing usage of e-filing system in the nearest futures. This equally shows that many taxpayers are still not satisfied with the e-filing service security. Hence, it implies that many of the participant taxpayers still have less trust in the system or agency in protecting their personal data. In the same line of argument a work conducted by Yurcik and Sharma (2004) has reinforced trustworthiness to be among the factors that influence the respondent perceptions on the online security. As far as security level is concerned in this study trustworthiness and security must achieve a reliable stage where federal government's web would not be questioned. It is true that taxpayers may have due respect for the federal or state government's website however; users can still be sceptical in the manner the information provided is going to be managed, transmitted or stored by the agency.

Since perceived ease of use is the degree to which a person expects the use of certain technology system be free of effort (Davis et al., 1989), there is a direct significant effect of perceived ease of such technological tool on users' retention as the finding of this study indicates and also ascertained by Hong et al., study in 2002. Thus, in general, if a technological tool is easy to use, it requires a less effort on the part of users thereby increasing the likelihood of its acceptance and usage (Teo, 2001). So as the result of this study shows that ease of use of e-filing is one of the key significant determinants of level of users' retention, the e-filing system should be made easy to use by the taxpayers in filing their tax returns.

With regards to facilitating conditions the finding of the study, apart from being a potential factor that challenge the users' retention, reflect how imperative is for all government agencies charged with e-government policy implementations to equip themselves with more sophisticated ICT skills in order to provide necessary guideline and support to the users. In other words any gaps in IT infrastructure can affect people's intention to use the system provided by the government. Such gap for example, may include the difficulty of Internet access, ICT literacy among the public, which can influence the public masses to use or neglect the system. Therefore, it is important to close the gaps by providing adequate IT infrastructure to encourage the public to use the system. Thus, it means there is a need for government to come out with better effective program for capacity building of the agency's staff and to ensure readiness of the people in society to use the system so that e-government implementation may realize its primary objectives in the country.

As far as perceived usefulness of e-filing is concerned, the findings in the chapter implied that it is a key influential and potential contributing factor of users' retention. Such a finding indicates that any technological devices provided in enhancing the service interface between the government and its citizens must be found useful, less complicated. Thus, e-filing system must be further seen to be more useful alternative, to the people, in terms of time and cost save as well as more convenience compared to manual; otherwise it wouldn't make any difference from the usual traditional manual system.

Finally, as the findings of the study show, there is a profound moderating effect of gender difference on the relationship between perceived usefulness, ease of use, facilitating conditions and security and users' intention to continue using the e-filing system. As the findings indicate, the female users have positively perceived a high usefulness of e-filing, ease of use and security level for e-filing and as such possessed a high retention level for the system. The male counterparts have the opposite of this perceptual feeling in all cases except for facilitating conditions variable. This result also confirms Ramayah's et al (2008) report where the e-filers are predominantly female with ratio 2 to 3 (see: Table 8).

In other words, it is a typical reflection of man's nature to be very rigid in mind and may not be easily convinced as compared to woman. Thus, there is a lot more to be done to convince and encourage more male taxpayers to use the new electronic system for tax returns. However, in some other parts of the world the finding is opposite. For example, the results of a survey conducted by H.D. Vest Financial Services show that most e-filing users in America are males.

Overall, there is a need for improvement in the implementation of the online e-filing to ensure that the system conform to the public e-filers' satisfaction as the result for users' retention only indicate moderate level. Perhaps, this might be due to the finding on security issues in e-filing system. It is argued that e-filing is associated with accountability of the government agencies in delivering quality services, while protecting detail data of the users.

Finally, e-filing must be seen and recognized as a means to promote electronic form of financial transaction as well as a value addition for enhancing the e-governance system of the country. Paying and e-filing income tax is a social responsibility of every citizen of a country; however, they must be impressed and encouraged to discharge such

Table 8. Profile of the respondents

Variables	Frequency	Percentage
Gender		
Male	120	40
Female	180	60
Age		
18-30	90	30
31-55	204	68
>55	6	2
Marital status		
Single	114	38
Married	186	62
Race		
Malay	60	20
Chinese	135	45
Indian	51	17
Others	54	18
Sectors		
Government	90	35
Private	195	65
Monthly Income		
RM2000-RM3000	54	18
RM3001-RM4000	84	28
>RM4000	162	54
Computer & Network Facilities at work		
Have no computer	39	13
Computer, no Internet	60	20
Computer & Internet	84	28
Dial up	66	22
Broadband	51	17

responsibility with the best and fast electronic devices.

REFERENCES

Adams, D. A., Nelson, R. R., & Todd, P. A. (1992). Perceived usefulness, ease of use and usage of information technology: A replication. *Management Information Systems Quarterly*, *6*(2), 227–247. doi:10.2307/249577

Aguini, H. (2004). *Regression analysis for categorical moderators*. New York: The Guilford Press.

Ajzen, I., & Fishbein, M. (1980). *Understanding attitudes and predicting social behaviour*. NJ: Practice-Hall.

Ambali, A. R. (2009). Digital divide and its implication on Malaysian e-government: Policy initiatives . In Hakikur, R. (Ed.), *Social and political implications of data mining: Knowledge management in e-government*. Hershey, PA: Information Science Reference (an imprint of IGI Global). doi:10.4018/978-1-60566-230-5.ch016

Bhatnagar, S. (2004). *E-Government: From vision to implementation – a practical guide with case studies*. London: Sage Publications Pvt. Ltd.

Coakes, J Sheridan and Steed Lyndall (2007). *SPSS version 16 for windows: Analysis without anguish,* Australia: Jon Wiley and Sons, Ltd.

Davis, F. D. (1989). Perceived usefulness, perceived ease of use, and user acceptance of information technology. *Management Information Systems Quarterly*, *13*(3), 319–340. doi:10.2307/249008

Davis, F. D., Bagozzi, R. D., & Warshaw, P. R. (1989). User acceptance of computer technology: A comparison of two theoretical models. *Management Science*, *35*(8), 982–1003. doi:10.1287/mnsc.35.8.982

ETAAC. (2002). *Electronic tax administration advisory committee (ETAAC)*. USA: Annual Report to Congress.

George, D., & Mallery, P. (2001). *SPSS for windows step by step: A simple guide and reference* (3rd ed.). Boston: Allyn and Bacon.

Hair, J. F., Black, W. C., Babin, B. J., Anderson, R. E., & Tatham, L. R. (2006). *Multivariate data analysis*. Upper Saddle River, NJ: Pearson Education International.

H.D. Vest Financial Services, Inc. (2000). Acceptance of e-filing gives rise to increased comfort with Web. *IRVING, Texas-BUSINESS WIRE*, March 22; also available at: http://www.icrsurvey.com/Study.aspx?f=hdvest.html [accessed on 2nd March 2009].

Heeks, R. (2003). *E-government for development: Causes of e-government success and failure, factor model*, IDPM, University of Manchester UK, available at: http://www.egov4dev.org/causesfactor.html [accessed on 2nd March 2009].

Hong, W., Thong, J. Y. L., Wong, W. M., & Tam, K. Y. (2002). Determination of user acceptance of digital libraries: An empirical examination of individual difference and system characteristic. *Journal of Management Information Systems*, *18*(3), 97–124.

Igbaria, M., Livari, J., & Marogahh, H. (1995). Why do individuals use computer technology: A finish case study . *Journal of International Management*, *29*, 227–238.

Igbaria, M., Zinatelli, N., Cragg, D., & Cavaye, A. (1997). Personal computing acceptance factors in small firms: A structural equation model. *Management Information Systems Quarterly*, *29*(3), 278–305.

Inland Revenue Board. Malaysia (IRBM), (2008). *The e-filing website*. [Online] available at: http://e-hasil.org.my/index/e-hasil.asp (accessed: 21 August 2009).

Izatun, S., (2008, April 22). Almost half a million taxpayers now using e-filing. *The Star.*

Jackson, C. M., Chow, S., & Leitch, R. A. (1997). Toward an understanding of the behavioural intention to use an information system. *Decision Sciences*, *28*(2), 357–389. doi:10.1111/j.1540-5915.1997.tb01315.x

Jen, R., F., Cheng, K. F., Wen, P. C. (2006). Acceptance of electronic tax filing: A study of taxpayer intentions. *Information & Management*, *43*(1), 109–126. doi:10.1016/j.im.2005.04.001

Karim, M. R. Nazariah A. K., (2003). *E-government in Malaysia*, Kuala Lumpur: Pelanduk Publications (M) Sdn. Bhd.

Livari, J., & Magid, I. (1997). Determinants of user participation: A finnish survey. *Behaviour & Information Technology*, *16*(2), 111–121. doi:10.1080/014492997119950

Mathieson, K. (1991). Predicting user intention: Comparing the technology acceptance model with the theory of planned behaviour. *Information Systems Research*, *12*(3), 173–191. doi:10.1287/isre.2.3.173

Ndubisi, N. D., Jantan, M., & Richerdson, S. (2001). Is the technology acceptance model valid for entrepreneurs? Model testing and examining usage determinants. *Asian Academy of Management Journal*, *6*(2), 31–54.

Nonnaly, J. C. (1978). *Psychometric theory*. New York: McGraw Hill.

Parasuraman, A. (2000). Technology readiness index (TRI): A multiple-item scale to measure readiness to embrace new technologies. *Journal of Service Research*, *2*(4), 307–320. doi:10.1177/109467050024001

Parasuraman, A., & Colby, C. L. (2001). *Techno-ready marketing: How and why your customers adopt technology*. New York: The Free Press.

Pfitzmann, A., & Wolf, G. (2000). Properties of protection goals and their integration into a user interface . *International Journal of Computer and Telecommunication*, *32*(6), 669–683.

Ramayah, T., Ramoo, V., Amlus, I., (2008). Profiling online and manual tax filers: Results from an exploratory study in Penang Malaysia. *Labuan e-Journal of Muamalat and Society*, 2, 1-8.

Segars, A. H., & Grover, V. (1993). Re-examining perceived ease of use and usefulness: A confirmatory factor analysis. *Management Information Systems Quarterly*, *17*(1), 517–725. doi:10.2307/249590

Sekaran, U. (2003). *Research methods for business: A skill building approach*. India: John Wiley & Son, Inc.

Shafie, S. (2007). E-government initiatives in Malaysia and the role of the national archives of Malaysia in digital records management, Conference paper on *"Development of E-Government and Digital Records Management"* at: *The 8th General Conference of* Teo, T.S. H., (2001). Demographic and motivation variable associated with internet usage activities. *Internet Research: Electronic Networking Application and Policy*, *1*(2), 125-137.

Vaus, D. (2006). *Analyzing social science data.* London: Sage Publications, Ltd. eGovernment for Development (eGov4Dev). Success and failure rates of egovernment in developing/transitional Countries: at: http://www.egov4dev.org/success/sfrates.shtml, [accessed on 20 Feb. 2009].

Venkatesh, V., Morris, M. G., Davis, G. B., & Davis, F. D. (2003). User acceptance of information technology: toward a unified view. *Management Information Systems Quarterly*, *27*(3), 425–478.

Yurcik, W., Sharma, A., & Doss, D. (2002). False impressions: contrasting perceptions of security as a major impediment to achieving survivable systems. *IEEE/CERT/SEI Fourth Information Survivability Workshop (ISW-2002)*, Canada: IEEE Computer Society Press, Vancouver, BC.

ADDITIONAL READING

James, G. J., (1987). *The ecological approach to visual perception*. New York: Lawrence Erlbaum Associates.

Kahan, S. (1998). Is Widespread E-filing Inevitable? *The Practical Accountant*, *31*(11), 22–29.

Kocakulah, M. C., & Grower, G. M. (2000). Modernizing the Bureaucracy: Government information systems and technology. *The National Public Accountant*, *45*(8), 24–25.

Lee, E. (2002). Merge, Acquire and Prosper [the Journal of Malaysian Institute of Accountants]. *Akauntan Nasional*, *15*(6), 12–17.

Legris, P., Ingham, J., & Collerette, P. (2003). Why Do People Use Information Technology? A Critical Review of the Technology Acceptance Model. *Information & Management*, *40*, 191–204. doi:10.1016/S0378-7206(01)00143-4

Lindsay, P. H., & Norman, D. A. (1977). *Human Information Processing* (2nd ed.). New York: Academic Press.

MIA. (2000), *Income Tax (Amendment Bill 2000)*, Malaysian Institute of Accountants (MIA), Circular No.20, November.

Mick, D. G., & Fournier, S. (1998). Paradoxes of Technology: Consumer cognisance, emotions and coping strategies . *The Journal of Consumer Research*, *25*(2), 123–143. doi:10.1086/209531

Newsberry, K. J., Reckers, P. M. J., & Wyndelts, R. W. (1993). An Examination of Tax Practitioner Decisions: The role of preparer sanction and framing effects associated with client condition . *Journal of Economic Psychology*, *14*(2), 439–452. doi:10.1016/0167-4870(93)90010-I

NTRS. (2000), *The 2000 National Technology Readiness Survey*, 8 March at http://www.technoreadymarketing.com

Nunnally, J. C. (1978). *Psychometric Theory*. New York: McGraw Hill.

Parasuraman, A., & Rockbridge Associates Inc. (1999). *Technology Readiness Index: Instructions for use in a survey*.

Rogers, E. M. (1995). *Diffusion of Innovations* (4th ed.). New York: The Free Press.

SGATAR. (2001), Creating a Paperless Environment in Tax Administration., Paper presented at the *31st Study Group on Asian Tax Administration and Research (SGATAR) Conference*, Kuala Lumpur, Malaysia.

Sheppard, B. H., Hartwick, J., & Warshaw, P. R. (1988). The Theory of Reasoned Action: A Meta-Analysis of Past Research with Recommendations for Modifications and Future Research . *The Journal of Consumer Research*, *15*(3), 325–343. doi:10.1086/209170

Zmud, R. W. (1979). Individual Difference and MIS Success: A review of the empirical literature. *Management Science*, *25*(10), 966–979. doi:10.1287/mnsc.25.10.966

KEY TERMS AND DEFINITIONS

E-Filing: The process of submitting your tax returns to the government agency through the Internet: using computers and tax preparation software.

E-Government: The use of information technology to enhance: service provision, digital democracy, and economic development of a country. This definition covers a broad definition of e-government and applies to all customers of local, sate and federal governments in a country, including all interactions and transactions between government and the public (G2P) or government and business (G2B); or government and other government agencies (G2G), and between government and its own employees (G2E). A definition of e-government is not complete until it embodied all of its stakeholders.

E-service: A broad definition for all services done through the Internet. In our definition: e-services include all e-commerce transactions such as online orders. It also includes any processing or applications that are obtainable through the Web and/or online.

Retention: A condition or an intention of retaining and reusing something. Therefore: in this chapter it is refers to intention of users to continuing re-using e-filing system as means of filing their tax returns to government agency.

Security: Generally the state of being and/or feeling secure. It includes freedom from fear: anxiety, danger, doubt, and sense of safety or certainty. Specifically in e-filing, it is the combination of user's data integrity and data confidentiality.

Tax: A sum of money required of a person or business group or company by the Government of a country to pay as contributions to support its source of revenues. Hence: is a government levies upon individual incomes or property or sales, etc. which are taxable within the domain of government.

Technology: Referred to devices which are purposefully designed to enhance information: production and services and the organization of human activities.

Users: Persons who make use of something. Therefore: someone who uses or employs something is referred to as a user. For example, people who are using e-filing system to file their income tax returns via online in this chapter are referred to users.

Chapter 4
Capacity Development Initiatives for Grass Roots Communities:
Two Cases

Hakikur Rahman
ICMS, Bangladesh

EXECUTIVE SUMMARY

The world has seen the unprecedented development of information and communications technologies (ICTs) and adoption of their diversified methods in elevating all forms of human endeavors. Even a few years back, it was fashionable to speak about the global village. In recent years, many countries have taken leading role in implementing innovative ICT products to accelerate their national developments, enhance their livelihoods, strengthened their national economies and improve their governance systems. This has been observed that those countries could reap the most benefits out of ICT strategies, which could penetrate at the lowest tier of their governance system. In this context, human development is an element of importance. This research emphasizes that cumulative human development through community approach would be the next level of knowledge dynamics across the world. It also argues that as much the country provides thrust on capacity development initiatives at the grass roots, it has more opportunity to reach at greater context of governance system. This chapter would like to focus on two cases, which penetrated the grass roots reaching out to the community level, act as catalyst to strengthen their national economy and government. Some features and perspectives of e-Sri Lanka and e-Korea are being discussed here to provide insight into these cases, so that researchers in developing and transitional economies could gain knowledge.

ORGANIZATION BACKGROUND

The twenty-first century predominately constitutes a information and knowledge-based society, where every country aspires to achieve its goal of social and economic development, including education, food security, health, environment, gender equity and cultural pluralism. However, the most important problem would remain as attaining and sustaining those goals. Therefore, every continent

DOI: 10.4018/978-1-61692-814-8.ch004

is concentrating in building its own Information Society, until a global village is formed.

However, in contrast to the developed countries that have been steadily capitalizing the rapid pace of information and communications technologies (ICTs), a large number of developing countries, particularly low-income countries are lagging behind in adapting these technologies and contributing to the information-divide or digital-divide, or more appropriately knowledge-divide (GITR, 2006; 2007). This is also true in case of rural villages where modern technologies are struggling to reach. The majority of people living in rural areas has neither access nor the means to obtain modern ICT because of their low economic position (Gunatunge & Karunanayake, 2004; Escudero-Pascual, 2008). They aggravate further when other hindrance parameters such as policies or politics, cultures or societies, regulations or regulators, promotions or motivations, and economic gain or status gain mingle up altogether.

The term 'global village' perhaps, coined by the United Nations Development Programme (UNDP) in 1998 (UNDP, 1998) with aspiration that everyone will be a full member of this village. With support from UN, ITU and others, IGF (IGF, 2008) coined another term, 'Internet for All', which could bring everyone on the planet under this future umbrella. But, author argues that both of these terms are over ambitious, despite their importance, and need to be nourished with total subsidized support from all corners to establish at least the information backbone in all countries, which is the most basic pre-requisite for carrying out those two slogans. Furthermore, he argues that with the shifting of focus of international organizations and donor agencies towards the development of information base knowledge society may lead to another form of divide within or among the country's in need. He would like to give one example from the Internet Governance Forum, which is the most effective and dynamic forum providing all out issue support for the development of the Internet. Focus of IGF has even shifted from openness, security, diversity, access (emphasizes the openness) (IGF, 2006); access, diversity, openness, security (emphasizes the access) (IGF, 2007); Reaching the Next Billion, Promoting Cyber-Security and Trust, Managing Critical Internet Resources, Emerging Issues: The Internet of Tomorrow- Innovation and the Evolution of the Internet (more pragmatic approach in reaching out for the grass roots, emphasizing perhaps the access) (IGF, 2008); Managing Critical Internet Resources, Security, Openness and Privacy, Access and Diversity, Internet Governance in the Light of WSIS Principles (emphasizes more on technology issues; access is there, but in diluted form (IGF, 2009).

The shift of focus or emphasizing of efforts or re-direction of resources are inevitable for any development programme, especially who are dealing with human development utilizing the novel techniques of ICTs. But, there remain several forms of gaps or laggings, in those countries who are not among the forerunners. Hence, in spite of putting all out painstaking efforts and resources, and even dedicated willingness, many set apart from being among the mainstream. There could be many failed projects, programmes or strategies, but this research scope would like to focus on two success cases of ICT strategies in two countries, who have taken lead in terms of providing e-government services at the grass roots.

This chapter as a continuation of research work in the perspective to reach the people at large, especially the marginalized and disadvantaged through utilization of ICT (for previous work, see the case portion of e-Sri Lanka from Islam, Murelli, Noronha & Rahman, 2006:338-351), would like to revisit a case, the e-Sri Lanka who has proved itself as a success case in South Asia, and in addition being familiar with the other project, e-Korea (through three consecutive visits to various project area in 2001, First Asia Internet Right Conference, Organized by Jinbonet and the Association for Progressive Communications, Seoul, South Korea; participant of a World

Bank and S. Korean Government e-government programme, 2002 and a visit under the Sustainable Development Networking Programme of Bangladesh, 2005), author would like to discuss a few policy issues of e-Korea. Main purpose is to follow up the e-Sri Lanka that was initiated in 2001 and officially launched in 2002 (Rainford, 2006), on the other hand, e-Korea project has been finalized in 2006-2007, and now it has been taken as a role model in many countries to roll out their e-governance systems.

SETTING THE STAGE

ICT undoubtedly brings profound changes to every community. It influences how the community knows and understands the world. It also changes working methods and the ways in which they communicate. At the same time, it affects how the community accesses and shares it with others and establishes information as an important source of power. But, despite advances in many aspects, yet pro-poor or for the grass roots people as per se, glitches are there (Heeks, 1999; 2002; 2009; Rahman, 2006; 2007; 2009). It has been broadly recognized, by acquiring the equipment and necessary skills to use information effectively, the poor and marginalized population can gain access to power, and the Internet can act as the tool to raise their skills and share knowledge based information among them. However, to avail the aggregated benefit from the information society, manifestation is not good enough, but to act rigorously in achieving the result. Two cases in this chapter are good examples in this regard.

Even though there have been increased global initiations to reduce digital divides, technology gap is expanding at the periphery. Digital Access Index (DAE), the ITU launched new index[1] which measures the overall ability of individuals in a country to access and use new ICTs. It has Sweden with the highest ranking of .85 (in a score of 1.00)[2] (with high competition at the top), while the bottom ranked ten countries could not achieve over 0.01 or 0.02 in this ranking[3]. The picture is not so gloomy in recent years, due to the innovation of cellular phones across the globe, but while comparing in contrast to the developed countries the margin is there. Economist Intelligence Unit (EIU, 2009) is carrying out another benchmarking index, called e-readiness ranking for many years. If one looks at the ranking for 2009, Denmark is at the top with 8.67 (ranked first in 2008 with score of 8.83, thus increasing the level of competition), while bottom 5 countries of 70 countries in the study could not score over 3.5[4].

One may argue about citation of those two indices, but author would reason that it will provide similar picture in other indices. However, as a manuscript in a casebook on e-governance issues, author would like to put forward the e-government readiness ranking that has been carried out by the UN (2008) for many years. Sweden is at the top with ranking of 0.9157 (shows tremendous competition among the top ranked countries with Denmark scoring 0.9134), with lowest scoring of 0.2110 in West African region. The promising fact is that bottom 35 countries among the top chosen 70 countries have ranked almost 0.5 (in a score of 1.0), which provides sufficient confidence and prospects of e-governance across the globe.

A NUA survey conducted in 2002 (NUA Internet Surveys, 2004) found that the number of users connected to the Net was about 605.60 million: World Total 605.60 million, Africa 6.31 million, Asia/Pacific 187.24 million, Europe 190.91 million, Middle East 5.12 million, Canada & USA 182.67 million, Latin America 33.35 million; and these figures raises to (Internet World Stats, 2009): World Total 1,733.99 million, Africa 67.37 million, Asia 738.25 million, Europe 418.03 million, Middle East 57.42 million, North America 252.91 million, Latin America/Caribbean 179.03 million, and Oceania/Australia 20.97 million.

There was a clear indication that Internet subscribers were rapidly increasing in Asia, Africa and pacific regions. Thereby, by taking pragmatic steps, many countries have brought their grass roots communities under ICT based development umbrella. Currently, with the highest growth rate on Internet in the Middle-East (2000-2009) 1,648.2%; followed by Africa 1,392.4%; Latin America/Caribbean 890.8%, Asia has the highest number of Internet users (42.6% of the world Internet user) (InternetWorldStats, 2009).

It is now proven fact that ICT can accelerate economic development through better manipulation of information usage at appropriate way, at appropriate form and at appropriate time. Availing this opportunity, many developing countries have made economic management their prime agenda and trying to overcome the problems of rural poverty, inequality, and environmental degradation (Bhatnagar, 2000). In those countries, it is observed that management of information system, such as on-line/off-line document management, electronic data exchange, file sharing, electronics groups, groupwares, blogs, moodles, mashups, open source software, and the Internet are leading to innovative planning and thereby becoming a means of empowering the communities through raising their knowledge (Bhatnagar, 2000; Kiangi & Tjipangandjara, 1996; Traunmuller & Lank, 1996; Gunatunge & Karunanayake, 2004; Rahman, 2006; 2008). Both the countries, in these two cases have adopted ICTs methods to promote their governance system and at the same time to gain economic benefit for their communities.

CASE DESCRIPTION

Sri Lanka

By definition of a person with age of 15 and over who can read and write, Sri Lanka's 90.7% of the total population are literate[5]. In 2008, the country had 246,000 Internet users, which gives 5.8% Internet penetration[6]. In 2008, Sri Lanka's position in the e-governance readiness index (UN, 2008) is 101 among 189 countries with index value of 0.4244 (in a score of unity), and in 2009, the country has the e-readiness ranking (EIU, 2009) of 63 among 70 countries with score of 3.85 (in the total score of 10). In comparison to the world leaders, these figures are low, but in comparison to the other countries in the South Asian region, they are significant (India scored 4.17 and Pakistan scored 3.50 in e-readiness ranking (EIU, 2009), while in terms of e-government readiness index, except Maldives- 0.4491, other countries are struggling to achieve a better ranking; India-0.3814, Pakistan-0.3164, Bangladesh-0.2936, Nepal-0.2725) (UN, 2008).

To achieve success in terms of promoting e-government services, three constituents are essential. They are Government, Citizens and Businesses (Davidrajuh, 2004). e-Sri Lanka enclave all three of them with clear vision, defined objectives, and transparent strategies, which help the country to achieve those rankings. Apparently, all those stakeholders also have the benefit out of the project, which has been described next.

E-Sri Lanka

Earlier version of this research (Islam, Murelli, Noronha & Rahman, 2006:pp. 338-351) provided the rationale, project description, selection process, implementation of pilot projects and programmes, including the vision and objectives of the project. To obtain an overview on strategic ICT implementations and analytical issues in a few other countries, readers may follow another consecutive research (Rahman, 2008). This research, as a continuation of the earlier versions, will try to provide new insight into the vision, objectives and strategies with critical assessments on e-Sri Lanka project.

The Vision

Use ICT to enhance education at the school and tertiary level, to increase the number and quality of high-level ICT professionals and to develop a computer-literate citizenry.

Note: The high literacy rate of Sri Lanka acted as an added catalyst to materialize this project including educated mass at the school and tertiary level. The former group raised the basic stronghold of ICT base in that country, and the later group carried out it further in terms of applying it for the benefit of the community through applied research.

Objectives

- To establish a multi-layered and multi-skilled pool of ICT trained staff at workforce, professional and managerial levels;
- To provide ICT education to students in schools throughout the country;
- To increase the number of undergraduates at university courses in ICT and provide higher-level training to university staff;
- To enhance the opportunities and incentives for improving English and ICT literacy; and
- To increase the supply of ICT professionals to the rest of the world and to encourage foreign ICT professionals to set up training institutes in Sri Lanka.

Note: To achieve national success in ICT projects, a multi-layered and multi-skilled pool of ICT professionals are pre-requisite. e-Sri Lanka intelligently could pinpoint that area and targeted to attain the same. Furthermore, emphasis was given to promote English skill and raise the local ICT professional´s to global standard.

To achieve these, the three-pronged strategy adopted:

- Firstly, in building an ICT skilled workforce and increasing the employability of school leavers with the help of the government, the private sector and academia to:
  - Facilitate the establishment of quality, affordable ICT skills enhancement programmes and recognized ICT qualifications, both at a foundation and a diploma level;
  - Facilitate the upgrading of the skills of trainers at IT training institutes, especially in the outstations; and
  - Improve the quality and availability of text books and course materials for IT training.
- Secondly, strengthening teaching in primary and secondary schools, tertiary education and universities, so that:
  - All school children would obtain basic ICT training and user-level skills through e-learning programmes;
  - The management of school IT centres be strengthened;
  - ICT could be introduced into national curricula; and
  - Schools could be connected to the Internet.
- Thirdly, strengthening management and professional skills in ICT industry by:
  - Organizational scholarship programmes for postgraduate/specialist qualifications;
  - Providing grants for short courses;
  - Assisting national conferences, seminars and study tours; and
  - Empowering the ICT industry to attain excellence by strengthening HR and promoting innovation (Islam, Murelli, Noronha & Rahman, 2006:pp. 338-351).

As benefits, e-Sri Lanka provided support to;

a) the government:
  - to empower civil servants with information and communication tools, to facilitate coordination across government agencies and increase com-

   petition and transparency in public procurement
  - to integrate marginalized regions and communities within an equitable resource distribution framework,
  - to facilitate effective decentralization and broadening of public participation in development policy formulation and program implementation,
  - to transform government services to become cost-effective and citizen-centred;

b) the entrepreneurs:
  - to revitalise Sri Lanka's main and traditional industries, like agriculture, tourism and apparel, so that the share of value-addition to the end product is increased, and to penetrate into new markets via internet-based sales channels
  - to emerge as a major transportation hub for air and sea cargo, by modernizing ports and by developing a modern trade net that dramatically reduces transaction costs for importers and exporters; and

c) the citizens:
  - to improve the delivery of public services and knowledge and education to all, and to make government (services, information, and overall government structure) accessible and accountable to the average citizen
  - to create a communication environment that allows optimal opportunities for all Sri Lankan citizens to participate fully in the global information economy, and for all citizens to support their economic, learning and personal needs
  - to facilitate inexpensive contact with families abroad via e-mail and voice over the Internet via Cyber Cafes in all towns (Davidrajuh, 2004).

South Korea

With the same definition of literacy given above, South Korea's 97.9% of the total population are literate[7]. ITU's 2008 (ITU ICT EYE[8]) statistics states that the country's Internet penetration rate is 76.5%, based on the number of Internet users. E-readiness ranking (EIU, 2009) is 19 among 70 countries with a score of 7.81(out of 10.00); and e-government readiness ranking (UNDP, 2008) is 6 among 189 countries with score of 0.8317 (index score is 1.00).

Having the same notion of incorporating the government, businesses and citizens, e-Korea played a successful role and the country progressed further as a key player in the global market through providing robust information infrastructure, promoting relevant industries, providing cybersecurity, and establishing international cooperation (see Figure 1). A few features of e-Korea Vision 2006 is being described next.

E-Korea Vision 2006

Rationale

The Korean government enacted the Framework Act on Informatization Promotion in August, 1995 (Framework); established the first Master Plan for Informatization Promotion in June, 1996 (Action Plan); and established a national organization for planning and implementation of the goals outlined in the Master Plan (Institutionalization). The plan presented 10 key projects for the realization of an advanced information society by the year 2010 (Definite deadline and specific tasks). In March, 1999, the government established Cyber Korea 21 as the blueprint for the new information society of the 21st century in order to overcome the Asian economic crisis and to transform the Korean economy into a knowledge-based one (dynamic adjustment of action plans according to nature and demand of the situation) utilizing an advanced information infrastructure.

Figure 1. Framework for e-Korea Vision 2006 (Adopted from Govt. of Korea, 2002)

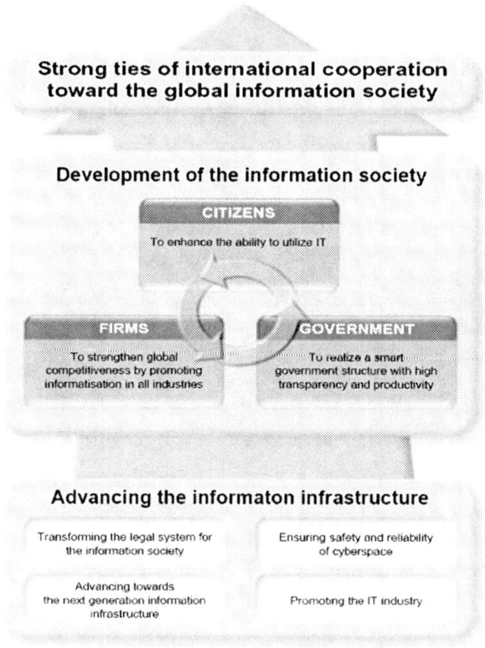

Main aims and objectives were to:

- reform legal and institutional systems and increase the capacity to utilize information technologies in all areas of society including the government, private companies and individuals in order to increase the positive effects of informatization
- strengthen the ability to respond rapidly to changes in the social environment caused by the rapid developments of information technologies; and
- stimulate national development through informatization efforts in order to resolve the national agenda such as strengthening our competitiveness in the global economy (Govt. of Korea, 2002).

Technology Concerns

High-speed telecommunications networks were constructed up to the village level to enable the citizens of Korea to have fast access to the broadband Internet services throughout the nation. As of the end of 2001, the number of Internet users totaled 24.38 million, where 7.81 million households had high-speed access to broadband Internet services. In addition to this, mobile telephony has become a basic telecommunication device for the general public. As of March, 2002, the number of mobile subscribers has reached 30.31 million, surpassing the 22.95 million fixed line subscribers (Govt. of Korea, 2002).

ICTs are extensively being utilized in economic or social activities including financial transactions and health administration. Financial institutions are utilizing ICTs to provide 24 hour electronic banking services. In 2002, there were about 11.31 million customers subscribed to Internet-based banking services, and the popularity of online financial transactions has risen dramatically. For example, 66.6% of the total monetary value of stock trades was handled on the Internet as of December 2001. As of December 2001, approximately 40,400 health care facilities have introduced EDI to health insurance to improve the efficiency in the health insurance administrative process (Govt. of Korea, 2002).

The IT industry has become an industry which increases the competitiveness of other industries and leads the growth of the Korean economy. Establishment of numerous IT ventures helped to create numerous professional jobs in the past few years. In addition, the industrialized sectors have benefited with an increase in productivity from the employment of the IT experts and specialists. As of December, 2001, the number of IT ventures reached 5,073 companies (44.5% of the total ventures). The number of IT workers increased from 1.01 million in 1997 to 1.16 million in 2001 (Govt. of Korea, 2002; 2003).

A Few Major Applications and Benefits

Informatization of the overall administrative processes in the government increased not only the administrative efficiency, but also established a solid foundation for the e-Government, such as:

- *Informatization of customs services* has shortened the processing time (for exports processing and services, from more than a day to less than 2 minutes; for imports processing and services, from more than 2 days to less than 2 and half hours), and has reduced logistic costs by at least 500 billion won a year; UNI-PASS of the Korea Customs Service (KCS, http://portal.customs.go.kr) is the world's first 100 percent electronic clearance portal system, which provides a one-stop PASS service by unifying all customs clearance procedures, including export/ import clearance, duty drawback, inbound/outbound passenger control, and tracking of bonded cargo;
- *Establishment of the electronic employment information system* has assisted 1.9 million people obtain jobs between 1999 and 2001 by providing comprehensive employment information regarding job openings, vocational training programs, and other related information;
- *Informatization of government procurement services* through the introduction of online services enhanced the productivity and transparency by reducing the time to process documents (from more than 2 days to less than 30 minutes) (Govt. of Korea, 2002; 2007).

e-Korea, also embraced the three prong approach which contained; promotion of national informatization, advancing the information infrastructure, and strengthening international cooperation for the Global Information Society. For easy reading and obtain a glimpse of the action plans along with the objectives in this aspect, a detail notes up to three levels of segregation are being provided in Appendix-1. However, the dynamic characteristics of the initiation are worth noted:

The government will establish and implement a yearly operational plan based on the Master Plan, e-Korea Vision 2006 each year. The Master Plan will be revised in response to the rapid environmental changes and technological developments of each year. The government will develop a detailed action plan in order to evaluate achievements semi-annually and report annually to the Informatization Promotion Committee. The realization of the global leader, e-Korea will be promoted through the systematic management of all issues and outcomes from each area, and cooperation will be strengthened between relevant government ministries and departments for the promotion of related businesses through the coordination of the Informatization Promotion Committee (Govt. of Korea, 2002:88).

Utilizing the benefits of ICTs on national economies on the ROK is fourfold; they have created:

- *New industries and economic sectors or sub-sectors* (e.g. the software industry, cellular phones, computers and peripherals),
- *New ways of doing business* (e.g. electronic commerce, globally distributed organizations, integrated supply chains),
- *New tasks and opportunities for government* (e.g. electronic government, privacy policy legislation, ICT industrial policy, security), and
- *New issues in economic and political development* (e.g. availability of information access, computer literacy, the digital divide) (Chadwick, 2005).

Thus, one can observe that the consequences of ICTs and the digital revolution on economic growth, social capital, and political development in a country goes far beyond the contribution of the ICT sector to national GDP. ICTs influence the efficiency and productivity of other economic processes as well, including the distribution of economic gains and basic services, and foremost, the transparency and accountability of the government (Chadwick, 2005). This research would like to thank the unnamed author(s) who has minutely compiled many aspects, issues, developments and policy formations of South Korea and preserved it in the APNG (Asia Pacific Networking Group) server. Some major aspects are being included in this research as Appendix-2, with intention that they will be extremely beneficial to new comers (even as a refreshment of doing things for others), who are looking forward to establish grass roots e-governance in their economies.

CURRENT CHALLENGES FACING THE ORGANIZATION

Overcoming the barriers toward empowering grass roots communities through information networking vary over places, localities, regions and times, which need to be addressed both horizontally and vertically. Literatures reviewed during earlier research with respect to policy formulation (Accascina, 1999; Gurstein, 2003; Keniston & Kumar, 2004; UNDP, 2001; World Bank, 2000; Bridges, 2004; OECD, 2004; G8DOT Force, 2001; DFID, 2001; ITU, 2003), found that contemporary trends tend to be biased against marginal populations. Literature review during the current research (Pascual, 2003; DRAP, 2003-2004; 2005-2006; 2007-2008; 2009-2010; NCA, 2003; UNDP, 2005; 2007), poise much better scenario in many countries, but still, there is a need for broad-based and equitable access to ICTs in areas consistent to the processes of decentralization, democratization, and mobilization of targeted population through policy reforms to achieve grass roots governance.

At the beginning of the information technology revolution governments in many of the developing countries, were not only slowly catching up with the new communication technologies, but also in a few cases adopted a negative view on the expansion of electronic network to the community level. At the same time, networking at the civil society level found to be increasingly challenging to national governments on many issues (Slim & Thompson, 1993). However, as NGO networking within and among countries of common peripheries, as well as, in many outreach programmes related to marginal people increased over time – mostly through the use of e-mail, e-groups, blogs, private sector TV, community radio and cell phones, their leverage vis-à-vis at the national government levels has also increased.

Generic challenges that e-government projects faces are how to expand the coverage to more agencies and regions; how to provide essential services in the rural areas; how to design projects to deliver economic value; how to enhance their impacts on increase in transparency and reduction of corruption; and foremost how to make those projects self-sustainable in the longer run.

Apart from the low awareness on ICT based programmes and their acceptance by the general community people, there were several challenges e-Sri Lanka project faced. One of them was the unstable and constantly changing political environment. In terms of implementation, ICTA faced various challenges to take the e-Sri Lanka Roadmap from what was essentially a comprehensive vision document and programme strategy, to a detailed plan of implementation, with actionable and fundable programmes and projects. Other challenges include, the process of ensuring ownership, role of key stakeholders and beneficiaries in the design and planning stages, to ensure equal opportunities for all to benefit, and to ensure that the introduction of ICT does not in any way diminish the social fabric, history and strong cultural traditions prevalent in the communities, but instead serve as a complement (Rainford, 2006; ICTA, 2005; 2009).

Despite high motivation and high absorptive capability of S. Korean people, e-Korea project had weakness of the resources gap and the institutional gap. In addition to these, there were disputes over the digitization initiatives, such as national electronic ID card, e-procurement, or electronic education system. The government in Korea as in other countries has also faced opposition from citizens and suffered setbacks in pursuing its ICT projects (UN, 2006; Suh & Chen, 2007).

SOLUTIONS AND RECOMMENDATIONS

The basic objective of human capacity development is to widen the range of people's choice and make development more participatory and democratic (UNDP, 1991). ICT can improve the knowledge and awareness of people by providing information about social and economic programmes, markets, employment opportunities, health, agriculture, education and learning, weather and disaster warning. These can be achieved only by being able to reach out at the lowest tier of the society or the governance level, and global agenda has accepted several ways of reaching out to them, such as establishing integrated knowledge centres/ information centres within the communities and integrating them to the nearest communication centre/ local centre/ regional centre to form comprehensive knowledge networks (Barton & Bear, 1999; Gunatunge & Karunanayake, 2004; Rahman, 2004).

ICT offers opportunities for individuals and communities in two ways; one as the information consumers and the other as the information generators. Through media convergence, ICTs can also build on and integrate the capacities of other media (e.g. cell phone, radio and television) to cover the people at large. These facilitate low-cost infrastructure development, easy access and fast distribution of information, which requires a distributed approach rather than a centralized one (Stillitoe, 1998). Moreover, there is a need for peoples' centered ICT institutions in the public and non-profit sectors to avail these opportunities. With that objective in mind this chapter recognized that key to the impact of ICTs is not the technology itself, but the networking and information exchange with particular emphasis on the information those grass roots people needs. This research while synthesizing those two projects implementing ICT strategies through various programmes and activities found that they eventually cover all the eight broad areas of MDG, including community mobilization, capacity building, information networking, ICT policy issues, sustainability, and ICT applications and research.

At the outset it is always felt about the necessity to promote a culture of information management and inclusion of new skills. Moreover, human and social capacity development through ICT aiming at empowering grass roots communities involve establishment of targeted, goal-oriented, horizontal and vertical linkages. Firstly, capacity development should be achieved through development at the individual level; secondly, bringing the individuals under a network; and finally, through congenial national, as well as, international policy support the whole initiative can be turned towards a result based outcome.

At the horizontal level, each individual should be brought under network of multi-faceted information blanket for creating a positive change in the marginal society as a whole. At the vertical level, adequate awareness raising programmes need to be initiated for decision makers, practitioners, researchers, academics and stakeholders on the investment assessment in ICT capacity building through formal and non-formal methods. This may include training of development workers incorporating ICTs in their activities with emphasis on training of rural women, youth, and deprived groups. With respect to content and its applications, it is observed that currently available and practiced networks have limited scope of empowering marginal communities as well as rural uplift. To make it applicable to the community beyond physical access to information, it has to be made timely, retrievable and easily applicable to a broad range of users, accessible in their own languages and consistent with their need and at the same time, demand driven. Top down approach of S. Korea in this aspect is worth mentioning.

To improvise these processes further, needs assessment for information flow in various network layers should be carried out periodically to enable feedback and widen participation in developing these information resources with user-specific, locally sensitive content and applications. This calls for piloting, monitoring, evaluating and documenting successful and unsuccessful applications of ICTs for the people at large. From these applications, models may be developed by providing guidelines for future strategic investments and replication of similar programmes in other places of the country. Both the cases adopted this form of localization and extended their networks at the horizontal level.

Adequate ICT education and capacity building programmes facilitate to form a coalition of stakeholders and organizational partners, in conjunction with national agencies, to develop policies for supporting the application of ICTs to empower peoples at large. Evidently, both the projects have taken such initiatives to reach out their entire population in various phases and trajectories.

To achieve the long-term benefit of ICT integration, ICT initiatives have to be self reliant and financially sustainable. However, this type of development process should proceed within a social accountability context and specific demand from deprived populations. A portion of revenue from telecommunications sector can be used to support the expansion of ICTs for marginal community as well as in rural areas. In turn, there is a need for integration of policies and extended investments to stimulate initial demand for reducing investment risks for rural ICTs. This could include, for example, enabling the potentiality of e-commerce for rural producers. S. Korea, by providing information infrastructure to the village level, has ensured e-commerce at the community level.

At the national level of ICT design, there is a need to develop strategies and action plans for rural areas by taking care of the differences in languages, culture, socio-economic conditions and infrastructure. This should be reflected in participatory need assessment and development of the technology itself. The forms of information content, including linkages to more conventional communication media such as rural radio can be thought of as development media. There is also a need to move away from centrally managed hub of information towards distributed repository system, which should not assume ownership of information resources that are generated by variety of providers. Both of the projects have adopted various strategies and plans to reach the entire population through education, learning, skill development initiatives, policy development, and mostly incorporation of various other agencies taking on a unified platform.

In this cyberspace context of developing countries, thanks to a mixture of adoption of innovations and of the national cultural values, as well as the co-operation among all the nations, which are creating a positive atmosphere for providing easy access to information and knowledge that can be used for the development of the country and eliminate the gap between the information rich and the information poor. However, this demands integration of available lower level information networks to form larger networks covering wider areas and regions opting updated locally generated contents. In this way, they create not only positive aspiration among the participants, but also, enhance their responsibilities and participation. Eventually these networks of network emerge as knowledge hubs for the entire community, region and country.

In conclusion it is imperative to recommend a coordinated network of access centres (efforts are there to establish village centres or knowledge centres in both the cases) acting as delivery nodes for community empowerment which in turn act as powerful resources at the national context (Robinson, 1998; Fouche, 1999). These access centres support grass roots communities and at the same time have their sustainability by providing accurate information about local needs, and facilitating cooperation and interaction among organizations, institutions and communities distributed throughout the country. They may be termed as information centres or knowledge centres or village centres whatever appropriate. But their rationale lies in shared-access models that allow provision of a wide range of services to more users at lower cost than commercial entities which are often out of financial reach of common people (Digital Dividend, 2003). Widespread rollout of these access centres, however, can be achieved only by mobilizing private sector entrepreneurship and investment (Wellenius, 2003), through appropriate national policies and favorable regulatory reforms. On the top, government subsidies for the period of survival act as catalytic agent to involve commercial entities and civil societies in establishing similar ventures.

Finally, looking into causes and effects along these cases it can be derived that, to address policy issues related to information management and access for need based information at community level, it is essential to improve not only the capacities of the out reach communities, but also, capacities of decision-makers and professionals.

REFERENCES

G8DOT Force (2001). *Digital Opportunities for All*: Meeting the Challenge Report of the Digital Opportunity Task Force (DOT Force) including a proposal for a Genoa Plan of Action, May 2001.

Accascina, G. (1999). *Keynote presentation, AP-DIP Regional Information technology Conference.* march 24-27, 1999, Kuala Lumpur, Malaysia.

Barton, C., & Bear, M. (1999). *Information and Communication Technologies: Are they the key to viable business development services for micro and small enterprises?* Report for USAID as part of the Micro enterprises Best Practices Project. March 1999 by Development Alternatives Inc, MD, USA.

Bhatnagar, S. (2000). Social implications of information and communication technology in developing countries: lessons from Asian success stories. *The Electronic Journal on Information Systems in Developing Countries* [Electronic version]. Available at http://www.unimas.my/fit/roger/EJISDC/EJISDC.htm

Bridges. (2004). *The Real Access / Real Impact framework for improving the way that ICT is used in development*, November 2004.

Chadwick, B. P. (2005). Information Technology Revolution in the Republic of Korea: Socio-Economic Development Issues and Policymaking Challenges . In Mansourov, A. Y. (Ed.), *Bytes and Bullets: Information Technology Revolution and National Security on the Korean Peninsula* (pp. 52–69). Honolulu, Hawaii: Asia-Pacific Center for Security Studies.

Davidrajuh, R. (2004). Planning e-government start-up: a case study on e-Sri Lanka . *Electronic Government, 1*(1), 92–106. doi:10.1504/EG.2004.004139

DFID. (2001). *Sustainable Livelihoods Guidance Sheets*, Department for Informational Development, 2001.

Digital Dividend. (2003). Retrieved June 08, 2003 from www.digitaldividend.org.

DRAP (2003-2004). *Digital Review of Asia Pacific2003/2004,* Orbicom, IDRC, UNDP-APDIP

DRAP (2005-2006). *Digital Review of Asia Pacific2005/2006,* Orbicom, IDRC, UNDP-APDIP

DRAP (2007-2008). *Digital Review of Asia Pacific 2007-2008,* Orbicom and the International Development Research Centre, SAGE Publications India Pvt Ltd

DRAP (2009-2010). *Digital Review of Asia Pacific 2009-2010,* Orbicom and the International Development Research Centre, SAGE Publications India Pvt Ltd

EIU. (2009). *E-readiness Ranking 2009: The usage imperative, a report from the Economist Intelligent Unit*, The Economist Intelligence Unit Limited, UK.

Escudero-Pascual, A. (2008). Tools and technologies for equitable access *Association for Progressive Communication (APC)* issue paper, www.apc.org

Fouche, B. (1999). *A Web-Based Agricultural System for South Africa. Feasibility Study - Part 1*. National Department of Agriculture March 1999. Unpublished document.

GITR. (2005). *Global Information Technology Report*. (2004-2005). World Economic Forum. Retrieved March 12, 2005 from www.weforum.org.

GITR. (2006). *Global Information Technology Report*. (2005-2006). World Economic Forum. Retrieved January 12, 2009 from www.weforum.org.

GITR. (2007). *Global Information Technology Report*. (2006-2007). World Economic Forum. Retrieved January 12, 2009 from www.weforum.org.

Govt. of Korea (2002). *e-Korea Vision 2006: The Third Master Plan for Informatization Promotion* (2002-2006), Ministry of Information and Communication, Government of the Republic of Korea

Govt. of Korea (2003). *To Enhance Efficiency and Transparency in the Public Procurement Sector by Utilizing the Government electronic Procurement System (GePS),* Government Procurement Experts Group, Phuket, Thailand, 15- 16 August 2003, 2003/SOMIII/GPEG/009 Agenda Item:7a, Asia-Pacific Economic Cooperation (APEC)

Govt. of Korea (2007). The best practice, UNI-PASS Korea customs service, *Korea e-Government Webzine, 6*, Ministry of Government Administration and Home Affairs (MOGAHA), Government of the Republic of Korea. Retrieved September 30, 2009 from http://www.idrc.ca/en/ev-140957-201-1-DO_TOPIC.html, (http://www.korea.go.kr/eng/Webzine/webzine.jsp?vol=200704&paper=services_01&no=1197878948443)

Gunatunge, R.S. & Karunanayake, M.M. (2004). *Information and Communication technologies for Enhancing Socio-economic Development at the Local Level in Sri Lanka: Issues, Challenges and Strategies*, a research report for Sida/SAREC Research Cooperation Project on Overcoming Regional Imbalances and Poverty, 2004.

Gunawardana, N., & Wattegama, C. (2004). Sri Lanka (chapter), in Digital Review of Asia Pacific, published by GKP.

Gurstein, M. (2003). Effective use: A community informatics strategy beyond the digital divide, *First Monday, 8*(12), December 2003.

Heeks, R. (1999). *Information and Communication Technologies, Poverty and Development.* Development Informatics: Working paper Series. Paper No 5, June 1995 Institute of Development Policy and Management. Published on the www: http://www.man.ac.uk/idpm

Heeks, R. (2002). Information systems and developing countries: failure, success and local improvisations. *The Information Society*, *18*(2), 101–112. doi:10.1080/01972240290075039

Heeks, R. (2009). The ICT4D 2.0 Manifesto: Where Next for ICTs and International Development? *Working Paper Series for Development Informatics Group, Institute for Development Policy and Management*. University of Manchester, Manchester, UK

ICTA. (2005). *Draft ICT Policy for the Government, Information and Communication Technology Agency of Sri Lanka*. Colombo, Sri Lanka: ICTA.

ICTA. (2009). *Information and Communication Technology Agency of Sri Lanka*, Retrieved November 05, 2009 from http://www.icta.lk/index.php/en/icta/739-e-sri-lanka-transforming-a-nation-through-ict

IGF. (2006). *First IGF Meeting*: Athens, Greece, http://www.intgovforum.org/cms/index.php/athensmeeting, Retrieved December 05, 2009

IGF. (2007). *Second IGF Meeting*: Rio de Janeiro, Brazil http://www.intgovforum.org/cms/index.php/secondmeeting, Retrieved December 05, 2009

IGF. (2008). *3rd Annual Internet Governance Forum (IGF)* at Hyderabad, India, http://www.intgovforum.org/cms/index.php/2008-igf-hyderabad, Retrieved December 05, 2009

IGF. (2009). *Fourth annual IGF Meeting in Sharm El Sheikh*, Egypt http://www.intgovforum.org/cms/index.php/the-meeting, Retrieved December 05, 2009

International Telecommunication Union (ITU) Report, 2003.

Internet Surveys, N. U. A. (2004). http://www.nua.ie/surveys/how_many_online, 2002 (last survey published on 2004)

Internet World Stats. (2009). World Internet Users and Population Stats, Miniwatts Marketing Group, available at http://internetworldstats.com/

Islam, M. A., Murelli, E., Noronha, F., & Rahman, H. (2006). Capacity Development Initiatives for Marginal Communities: A few case studies . In Rahman, H. (Ed.), *Empowering Marginal Communities with Information Networking* (pp. 318–351). Hershey, PA: Idea Group Inc.

Keniston, K., & Kumar, D. (Eds.). (2004). *Bridging the Digital Divide: Experience in India*. London: Sage Publications.

Kiangi, G.E. & Tjipangandjara (1996). Oppoetunities for information technology in enhancing socio-economic development of a developing country. In M. Odedra-Straub (Eds.), *Global Information technology and Socio-Economic Development*. Nashua:Ivy League Publishing, 73-81.

NCA. (2003). *Informatization: White Paper*, National Computerization Agency (NCA), Seoul, Rep. of Korea

OECD (2004). Organisation for Economic Co-operation and Development, *Annual Report*, 2004.

Pascual, P. J. (2003). *e-Government*, e-ASEAN Task Force, UNDP-APDIP, Malaysia

Rahman, H. (2004). Empowering Marginal Communities with Interactive Education Systems, Commonwealth Open Learning (COL). *3rd Pan-Commonwealth Forum on Open Learning* (PCF3), Dunedin, New Zealand, July 4-8, 2004.

Rahman, H. (2006). Empowerment of Marginal Communities Through Information Driven Learning . In Rahman, H. (Ed.), *Empowering Marginal Communities with Information Networking* (pp. 16–42). Hershey, PA: IDEA Group Publishing.

Rahman, H. (2007). Role of ICTs in Socioeconomic Development and Poverty Reduction . In Rahman, H. (Ed.), *Information and Communication Technologies for Economic and Regional Developments* (pp. 180–219). Hershey, PA: Idea Group Inc.

Rahman, H. (2008). An Overview on Strategic ICT Implementations Toward Developing Knowledge Societies . In Rahman, H. (Ed.), *Developing Successful ICT Strategies: Competitive Advantages in a Global Knowledge-Driven Society* (pp. 1–39). Hershey, PA: Information Science Reference.

Rahman, H. (2009). Local E-Government Management: A Wider Window of E-Governance . In Rahman, H. (Ed.), *Handbook of Research on E-Government Readiness for Information and Service Exchange: Utilizing Progressive Information Communication Technologies* (pp. 295–323). Hershey: Information Science Reference.

Rainford, S. (2006). *e-Sri Lanka: An Integrated Approach to e-Government Case Study, Asia Pacific Development Information Programme (APDIP),* Bangkok

Robinson, S. (1998). Telecentres in Mexico: The first phase. *Paper presented to the UNRISD Conference*.

Slim, H., & Thompson, P. (1993). *Listening for a Change: Oral History and Development*. London: Panos Publications.

Stillitoe, P. (1998). The Development of Indigenous Knowledge: A new applied anthropology. In *Current Anthropology,* 49 (2).223-253, April 1998.

Suh, J., & Chen, D. H. C. (2007). (Eds.). *Korea as a knowledge economy: evolutionary process and lessons learned*, The World Bank, Washington DC.

Traunmuller, R., & Lenk, K. (1996). *New public management and enabling technologies, advanced IT tools. Edward.* London: Chapman and Hall.

UN (2006). E-procurement, a joint publication of Economic and Social Commission for Asia and the Pacific (UNESCAP), Asian Development Bank (ADB) Institute, and Public Procurement Service of the Republic of Korea, United Nations publication

UN. (2008). United Nations e-Government Survey 2008: From e-Government to Connected Governance, UN, NY

UNDP. (1991). *Human Development Report. United nations Development Programme (UNDP)*. Oxford University Press.

UNDP. (1998). *Human Development Report*. UNDP, Rosemberg & Seller.

UNDP. (2001). *Human Development Report: Making New Technologies Work for Human Development*. UNDP.

UNDP. (2005). *Promoting ICT for Human Development in Asia: Realizing the Millennium Development Goals, Regional Human Development Report*. Elsevier.

UNDP. (2007). *e-Government Interoperability: Guide, UNDP*, Bangkok

Wellenius, B. (2003). Sustainable Telecenters, *Private Sector and Infrastructure Network*, World Bank, Note number 251, January 2003.

World Bank. (2000). *World Development Report 1999/2000*. Washington, DC: World Bank.

FURTHER READING

Asgarkhani, M. (2003), *A Strategic Framework for Electronic Government*, paper presented at 22nd IT Conference, Colombo, Sri Lanka. Available at http://www.cssl.lk/conferences/A%20Strategic%20Framework%20for%20Electronic%20Government_medi%20asgarkani%20letter%20size.doc

Backus, M. (2001). E-*governance and Developing Countries, Research Report – No3*, available at http://www.ftpiicd.org/files/research/reports/report3.pdf

Bhatnagar, S. (2004), *Enabling E-Government in Developing Countries: From Vision to-implementation*. available at www.worldbank.org/publicsector/egov/lweek/Bhatnagar.pdf

Carlos, A. P. B. (2003). *Government in the Information Age*. Colombo, Sri Lanka: National E-Government Conference.

Choudrie, J., & Weerakkody, V. (2004). Evaluating Global E-Government Initiatives: An Exploratory Study . In Gupta, M. P. (Ed.), *Towards E-Government –Management Challenge*. Tata McGraw Hill Publishing Company Ltd.

Davidrajhu, R. (2004). Planning e-government start-up: a case study on e-Sri Lanka. Electronic Government, 1, (1).

Government of Sri Lanka. (2003). *Policy on E-government*. May, Sri Lanka: Government of Sri Lanka.

Govt. of Korea (1999). *Cyber Korea 21: Korea's Vision for a Knowledge Based Information Society.* Ministry of Information and Communications, Seoul, ROK

Govt. of Korea (2002a). *Broadband in Korea: Korea Information Infrastructure,* National Computerization Agency, Ministry of Information and Communication Seoul, ROK

Govt. of Korea (2002b). *E-Government in Korea,* National Computerization Agency, MIC, Seoul, ROK

Govt. of Korea (2003). *White Paper: Internet Korea 2003,* National Computerization Agency, Ministry of Information and Communication, Seoul, ROK

Govt. of Korea (2004a). *The Realities of Informationization in the First Quarter of 2004,* public opinion survey, Ministry of Information and Communication and Korea Network Information Center, Seoul, ROK

Govt. of Korea (2004b). *The Road to US$20,000 GDP/capita: IT 8-3-9 Strategy,* Ministry of Information and Communication, Seoul, ROK

KAIT. (2001). *Research on the Trend of Major Information and Communication Items, Korea Association of Information and Telecommunication*. Seoul: ROK.

KAIT. (2002). *Survey on Current Trends in the IT Industry, Korea Association of Information and Telecommunication*. Seoul: ROK.

KAIT. (2003). *Information and Communication Industry Statistics Reports for 2000, 2001, 2002, and 2003, Korea Association of Information and Telecommunication*. Seoul: ROK.

Kelly, T., Grey, V., & Minges, M. (2003). *Broadband Korea: Internet Case Study*. Geneva: International Telecommunication Union.

Ki-seok, H. (2004). *Korea Wireless Services 2004-2008 Forecast and Analysis: 2003 Year-End Review,* IDC Korea, Seoul, ROK, available at http://www.idckorea.com/

Kim Deok-hyun. K. (2002). Telecom Industry Undergoes Revolutionary Change in Two Decades, *Korea Times*, Seoul

KISDI. (2002). *IT Industry Outlook of Korea 2002, Korea Information Society Development Institute*. Seoul: ROK.

KISDI. (2003). *IT Industry Outlook of Korea 2003, Korea Information Society Development Institute*. Seoul: ROK.

KISDI. (2004). *IT Industry Outlook of Korea 2004, Korea Information Strategy Development Institute*. Seoul: ROK.

Kumarawadu, P. (2003). Assessing and Benchmarking our Digital Readiness for e-Government: Moving towards e-Sri Lanka. *Paper presented at 22ndITConference*, Colombo, Sri Lanka, available at http://www.cssl.lk/conferences/360,1,Slide1

Madan, S. (2004). Evaluating the Development Impact of E-government Initiatives: An exploratory framework . In Gupta, M. P. (Ed.), *Towards E-Government – Management Challenges*. Tata McGraw Hill Publishing Company Ltd.

KEY TERMS AND DEFINITIONS

E-Government: Refers to the utilization of innovative information and communication technologies (ICTs) by governments as applied to the full range of government functionalities.

E-Governance: Is a network of organizations to include government, for-profit, not-for-profit, non-profit, civil societies, practitioners and private-sector entities

Local Government: The lowest level of formal state institutions, such as district-level officials or local, publicly accountable decision-making and service-delivery organizations constituted in accordance with national laws (such as in local elections). It is a city, county, parish, township, municipality, ward, borough, board, district, or other general purpose political (and or administrative) subdivision of a state.

Local E-Government: Could be seen as the improvement, effectiveness and efficiency of local government in leading and delivering services to people at large through the use of ICTs with a vision of central and local government working in partnership to deliver better outcomes for people and places, including real challenges for local government in terms of political and managerial leadership, thus enhancing citizen engagement and participation for better service delivery

Grass Roots E-Governance: Effective utilization of local e-government structures and capacity in establishing a reliable, efficient and transparent governance system reaching out to the grass roots communities leading to economic, social, political, cultural and technology gains.

ENDNOTES

1 http://www.itu.int/ITU-D/ict/dai/index.html

2 http://www.itu.int/ITU-D/ict/dai/high.html

3 http://www.itu.int/ITU-D/ict/dai/low.html

4 http://www.eiu.com/site_info.asp?info_name=ereadiness&page=noads&rf=0

5 https://www.cia.gov/library/publications/the-world-factbook/geos/ce.html

6 http://www.itu.int/ITU-D/icteye/Indicators/Indicators.aspx#

7 https://www.cia.gov/library/publications/the-world-factbook/geos/ks.html

8 http://www.itu.int/ITU-D/ICTEYE/Indicators/Indicators.aspx

APPENDIX 1: DETAIL OF THE THREE PRONGED STRATEGY, OBJECTIVES AND ACTION PLANS (ADOPTED FROM GOVT. OF KOREA, 2002)

Three prong approach of e-Korea Vision 2006, included objectives and policy plans for:

1. Promoting national informatization, which firstly, targeted to enhance the capacity by expanding opportunities brought by ICTs, with objectives to:
   - expand Internet usage to 90% of the overall population
   - connect schools to a world-class information infrastructure
   - raise the participation rate of the life-long learning system to the level of OECD member nations; and

   policy plans included, to:
   - Enhance the ability of utilizing information and communication technologies by all citizens, by:
     - *Strengthening IT education*
     - *Creating a more accessible information environment*
     - *Creating an "Information Welfare" system*
   - Establish a lifelong learning system, by:
     - *Creating an environment for online learning*
     - *Expanding opportunities for online lifelong learning*
   - Establish the e-work system, by
     - *Promoting online and mobile working*
     - *Strengthening IT job training for the unemployed*

   Secondly, targeted to promote industrial informatization by leading economic growth through the realization of a digital economy, with objectives to:
   - enhance productivity and competitiveness of the existing manufacturing and service industries through informatization
   - develop and upgrade B2B e-commerce
   - create a reliable online business environment; and

   policy plan included, to:
   - Expand the reach of information and communication technology to all industries, by
     - *Promoting informatization across industries*
     - *Promoting informatization of SMEs*
     - *Setting standards for efficient informatization of industries*
   - Advance B2B e-commerce, through
     - *Enhancing productivity and transparency through informatization of all business activities*
     - *Expanding B2B networks*
     - *Improving logistics and payments systems for promoting B2B e-commerce*
     - *Establishing an infrastructure for international e-trade*
   - Provide a safe and reliable online business environment, by
     - *Establishing an online trust management system*
     - *Protecting e-consumers*
     - *Protecting personal information involved in e-commerce; and*

Thirdly, aimed to promote informatization in the public sector by realizing a productive and transparent smart government, with objectives to:

- expand online services to all the civil affairs
- enhance speed and transparency of the public administration on a "mobile government" infrastructure
- upgrade digital public services; and

policy plans included, to:

- Expand and upgrade online civil services, by
  - *Expanding online civil services*
  - *Introducing customized digital civil services*
  - *Constructing a mobile government infrastructure*
  - *Establishing an electronic authentication system*
- Continue innovation in the public administration through informatization, through
  - *Strengthening the linkage between informatization and public administration reforms*
  - *Encouraging greater electronic participation by the general public*
  - *Promoting joint utilization of public information*
- Expand informatization efforts in the administration of public finance, and science and technology, by
  - *Promoting informatization in the public finance field*
  - *Promoting informatization in the industry, energy, science and technology fields*
  - *Promoting informatization of social overhead capital*
- Promote informatization of public services for social welfare and the environment, through
  - *Establishing an e-medical system*
  - *Diversifying information services on social welfare*
  - *Improving employment information services in response to the flexible labor market*
  - *Expanding information services for a clean and healthy environment*
- Upgrade information services in education and culture, by
  - *Improving administrative services in education*
  - *Expanding cultural information services to enhance quality of life*
  - *Strengthening national competitiveness through continuous expansion of knowledge and information resources*
- Enhance efficiency in the administration of foreign affairs, justice and social security through informatization, by
  - *Raising efficiency of foreign affairs and trade administration through informatization*
  - *Raising efficiency in the legal and criminal justice system*
  - *Building and managing an integrated information system for public safety*

2. Advancing the information infrastructure, which firstly, targeted to transform the legal system to establish the information society by adjusting the legal framework, with objectives to:

- create the legal foundation which reflects the characteristics of the information society
- redesign institutional mechanisms in accordance with technological progress; and

policy plans included, to:

- Adjust basic laws and institutional mechanisms to the information society
- Revise laws for the information society

Secondly, to ensure Safety and Reliability of Cyberspace by Strengthening the security of the information infrastructure with private and public sector cooperation, with objectives to:

- establish a partnership between the private and public sectors against acts of cyber terrorism
- ensure the systematic protection of the national information infrastructure; and

policy plans included, to:

- Implement preventative measures and establishing a response system against acts of cyber terrorism, by
    - *Establishing a cooperative partnership to prevent acts of cyber terrorism*
    - *Protecting critical government information*
- Develop information security technology and training new information security experts, through
    - *Developing information security technology in response to new technological trends*
    - *Promoting public awareness of information security and training new experts in information security technologies*
- Create a sound cyberspace

Thirdly, to advance towards the next generation telecommunications infrastructure by constructing a world-class next generation telecommunications infrastructure, with objectives to:

- expand the broadband telecommunications networks for the realization of universal access to the broadband internet with a minimum transmission speed of 1 Mbps by 2005
- distribute digital televisions to more than 50% of the total households in Korea until 2006; and

policy plans included, to:

- Upgrade high-speed telecommunications networks, by
    - *Upgrading backbone networks*
    - *Upgrading broadband subscriber networks*
    - *Upgrading KOREN (KOrea advanced REsearch Network)*
    - *Introducing QoS to broadband internet services*
- Advance the construction of the Next Generation Internet, through
    - *Promoting the Next Generation Internet and its applications*
    - *Improving user environment for wireless internet*
    - *Developing a next generation management system for IP addresses*
    - *Preparing for the convergence of fixed line and wireless telecommunications; and*

Fourthly, for strategic promotion of the IT industry by advancing them as a source of economic growth, with objectives to:

- develop core information technologies which enhance the competency of the Korean IT industry and become a source for job opportunities and future economic growth
- foster advanced IT experts and specialists with global competitiveness
- promote technology-intensive ventures as a driving force for all industries; and

policy plans included, to:

- Strengthen the core competency of the IT industry by developing strategic products
- Promote R&D for next generation IT, by
    - *Promoting research and development for a new leap*
    - *Upgrading the information infrastructure for R&D of next generation strategic technologies*

- Promoting interdisciplinary research in response to the convergence of technologies
- Improving the R&D planning and evaluation system
- Promoting standardization of IT for market initiatives

◦ Foster IT experts and professionals, through
- Fostering IT experts
- Supporting studying abroad programs and employing foreign experts and specialists
- Strengthening applied education programs
- Conducting institutional amendments for fostering IT experts
- Fostering researchers in basic science and interdisciplinary fields

◦ Foster technology intensive ventures, by
- Enhancing the efficiency of venture policies
- Creating a favorable environment to stimulate growth of IT ventures
- Providing a favorable business environment for the survival of venture companies

◦ Conduct institutional amendments for the software and digital contents industries, through
- Providing an institutional foundation for the competitiveness of the software industry
- Conducting institutional reforms for the development of the digital contents industry; and in the third sector

3. Strengthening international cooperation for the Global Information Society, which firstly, targeted to establish a business hub in the East Asian region by building an IT hub in East Asia, with objectives to:

◦ take a leading role in the world market by facilitating e-business in East Asia
◦ promote information culture as a mediator of cultural exchange; and

policy plans included, to:

◦ Lead the world market through cooperation in East Asia, by
- Establishing a system of economic cooperation in IT
- Establishing CDMA coalition in East Asia
- Strengthening cooperation to stimulate e-commerce activities in East Asia
- Strengthening cooperation for facilitating software industries in East Asia

◦ Globalize information culture in East Asia, through
- Building cooperative frameworks for information culture in East Asia
- Promoting exchanges in information culture in East Asia

Secondly, targeted to take the initiative in international cooperation by emerging as a leader in global informatization, with objectives to:

◦ lead global informatization efforts through the expansion of the IT infrastructure at a global level
◦ lead the establishment of global governance and standard-setting in the global arena; and

policy plans included, to:

◦ Play a leading role in international organizations
◦ Bridge the global digital divide
◦ Expand the international information infrastructure; and

Thirdly, to facilitate the advancement of IT companies to enter into the world market by attaining international competitiveness, with objectives to:

◦ attain IT export levels of $350 billion, a trade balance of $110 billion in the period beginning in 2002 to 2006

- promote 30 key IT items as world-class products; and

policy plans included, to:

- Promote leading sectors for advancing into the world market, by
    - Promoting key IT products
    - Advancing the software and contents industries into the overseas markets
- Establish support systems for the advance into overseas markets, through
    - Creating a foundation for advancement into the overseas market
    - Providing financial support for the advance into world markets
    - Diversifying IT Export Markets
    - Building an information system to facilitate IT exports

APPENDIX 2: INTERNET CHRONOLOGICAL TABLE OF KOREA (HTTP://WWW.APNG.ORG/MUSEUM/PPT/20050510-INTERNET_CHRONOLOGICAL_TABLE_OF_KOREA.DOC, RETRIEVED NOVEMBER 20, 2009)

▸ 1981	
Jan	• Main subjects of communication part for the 5th 5-year economic and social development plan for modernization of telecommunication (1982~1986): Fulfillment of communication demand, call automation, support of semi-conductor industry and promotion of radio waves utilization • Korea Institute of Science and Technology (KIST) and Korea Advanced Institute of Science (KAIS) merged into Korea Advanced Institute of Science and Technology (KAIST), integrating research and education (Divided again in June, 1989)
▸ 1982	
Mar	• Korea Data Communication Co. Ltd. was established as a private company handling data communication
Jul	• SDN (Sustainable Development Network), the first computer network and also the first Internet in Korea, was implemented via TCP/IP connection between the computers in Seoul National University and Institute of Electronics Technology
▸ 1983	
Jan	• The year of information industry's was proclaimed
Mar	• Comprehensive information industry promotion plan for semi-conductor industry and information industry (including training for experts and expansion of education on computer)
May	• Ministry of Science and Technology, established the plan for computerization of administration • Korea Information Industries Association was established (changed to Federation of Korea Information Industries)
Aug	• Framework Act on Telecommunications and Telecommunications Business Act established
Dec	• Information Industries Promotion Committee, reported the State Backbone Network Plan to the President
▸ 1984	
Mar	• Information Industries Promotion Committee was reorganized to State Backbone Network Coordination Committee
Nov	• Information Telecommunications Training Center (ITTC) was established, reorganized to Information Cultural Center (ICC) in 1988 and Korea Agency for Digital Opportunity and Promotion (KADO) in 2003
▸ 1985	
Mar	• Institute of Electronics Technology and Korea Institute of Telecommunications Technology were merged into Institute of Electronics and Telecommunications, which was reorganized into Electronics and Telecommunications Research Institute (ETRI) in 1997.
▸ 1986	
Mar	• Education and research network committee was established
Jul	• .kr domain was first registered
Dec	• Act on Computer Network Promotion established • Computer Programs Protection Act established
▸ 1987	
Jan	• National Computerization Agency founded
Feb	• Administrative computer network basic plan established
Jul	• Free import of personal computer
Nov	• National Computerization Agency, established the State Backbone Network Standardization Plan

▸ 1988	
Jan	• Korea Information Society Development Institute (formerly, Telecommunications Policy Institute) was established
Apr	• The first agricultural and fisher area computer training class was opened in Goheung, Jeonranam-do • The 1st Information Cultural Month event organized
Jun	• Korea Software Industry Association was established • Education and research network out of State Backbone Network were separated as education network (KREN) and research network (KREONet) • National Defense Computer Network Committee, established the national defense computer network basic plan
▸ 1989	
Jan	• Information Cultural Center (ICC) opened Information Cultural Promotion Center
Feb	• Federation of Korea Information Industries proclaimed 'Declaration of Information Society'
Jun	• Ministry of Education, decided the training program for computer with 16bit computers • Selected as ITU management executive country
Jul	• Ministry of Communications, opened communication lines
▸ 1990	
Jan	• home banking service started
May	• Research network (KREONet) implemented experimentally in Daedeok complex
Aug	• Seoul National University launched campus integrated network SUNNET
▸ 1991	
Jan	• Ministry of Home Affairs started resident registration computerization service
Mar	• Ministry of Commerce and Industry released DB promotion plan
Apr	• Ministry of Communications announced draft for regulation on computer network technology standard
May	• Korea PC Telecommunication founded • International packet exchange based data communication started
▸ 1992	
Feb	• ANC, established Korea Network Information Center (KNIC) • 2nd stage State Backbone Network Plan established
Dec	• Subscriber line optical cable first launched; Pacific ocean submarine cable launched
▸ 1993	
Jan	• KAIST, started operating KNIC
Apr	• National Computerization Agency, installed KOSInet
Jun	• Ministry of Government Administration, opened administration information network
▸ 1994	
Jan	• Act on the Protection of Personal Information Maintained by Public Agency was established
Mar	• Ministry of Communications announced basic plan for information super highway
May	• Information super highway committee was organized
Sep	• National Computerization Agency started KRNIC (formerly, KNIC) service
Dec	• Ministry of Communications is reorganized into Ministry of Information and Communication (absorbed the information related functions of Ministry of Science and Technology, Ministry of Commerce and Industry, and Bureau of Public Information)
▸ 1995	
Feb	• National Computerization Agency, opened Korea Internet Exchange Center (KIX), and started education network and research network interoperation centering on KRNIC • Established information super highway infrastructure implementation plan (by 2015)
Mar	• First Internet newspaper was published
Aug	• Information Communication Ethics Committee was organized

Sep	• Framework Act on Informationalization Promotion was established
Nov	• First Internet café 'Netscape' was opened • Computer technology lab in Daegu Univ. developed the first search engine "Kachine", which provided free search service
▸ 1996	
Jan	• Ministry of Information and Communication, implemented the first web site among the government authorities
Apr	• KT deployed information super-highway model network in Daedeok
May	• Korea Information Security Center organized (reorganized to Korea Information Security Agency in July, 2001)
Jun	• The first internet shopping mall 'Interpark" and "Lotte Internet Department Store" were opened in Korea • The world first cyber expo "Information Expo 96"
Jul	• LAN opened in Government Offices
Sep	• I-net published the first webzine 'Image (im@ge)'
Nov	• Consortium of CERT (CONCERT) founded
▸ 1997	
Jan	• Korea Internet Association (KRIA) founded
Feb	• Ministry of Information and Communication and Ministry of Labor, opened the remote occupational training system
May	• First Internet home trading service (HTS) started
Aug	• Korea Information Security Center, started online security check service
Oct	• Federation of Korea Information Industries, held the first presidential candidates' forum on information policy
Nov	• Ministry of Information and Communication, announced information security industry development plan
▸ 1998	
Jan	• Office for Government Policy Coordination, established comprehensive measures against Y2K problem • Seoul University Hospital started remote diagnosis service • Information and Communications University was opened
Apr	• National Computerization Agency, started the Y2K Support Center
May	• 2nd stage Information Super Highway Infrastructure Plan
Jun	• Ministry of Government Administration and Home Affairs opened the government representative homepage
Jul	• Korea Information Security Industry Association founded • Internet based government's civil petition service was started
Oct	• Korea IT Industry Promotion Agency was founded
Dec	• Ministry of Information and Communication, announced the plan for content class system in PC communication and Internet (introduced in May 1999)
▸ 1999	
Jan	• Institute of Information Technology Assessment was founded
Feb	• Ministry of Information and Communication, started paid Internet address registration system • Digital Signature Act was established • Framework Act on Electronic Commerce was established
Mar	• Cyber Korea 21 Vision was established
May	• Korea Education & Research Information Service was opened • Online community service launched
Jul	• Korea Information Security Center, opened digital signature authentication center
Aug	• IPv6 based Internet implementation technology was developed
Oct	• KRNIC was opened • KOREN, secured IPv6 addresses

▸ 2000	
Jan	• Recorded 10 million Internet users • KRNIC, established the domain name registration rules
Mar	• Recorded 1 million Information super highway subscribers • KRNIC, hold APNIC Conference in Seoul
Jun	• Ministry of Information and Communication, established 10 million people information education plan
Aug	• IPv6 forum Korea workshop
Nov	• KRNIC, announced Korean domain model service plan
Dec	• Korea Personal Information Security Association was founded • Recorded 19 million Internet users • Recorded 4 million Information super-highway users • KRNIC established agreement on wireless domain search service
▸ 2001	
Jan	• Information Communication Infrastructure Protection Act was established • KRNIC hold the AT LARGE workshop of ICANN
Feb	• First paid community portal service started • Next generation Internet infrastructure implementation plan was announced
Mar	• 5-year plan for information security technology development • Ministry of Education and Human Resources Development, started Internet ethics education • PC room associations integrated into Internet PC Culture Association
Apr	• Ministry of Information and Communication, established Internet broadcasting promotion plan • Korea recorded 1st place out of OECD member states in broadband Internet propagation rate • Ministry of Commerce, Industry and Energy, opened online intelligent education information network 'Edunet' • KRNIC, started receiving plural application of personal domains, and started 2 letter service
May	• Korea Wireless Internet Standardization Forum was founded • KRNIC, established the agreement with Korea Women's Development Institute for joint research to solve 'digital divide' of women
Jul	• Korea Information Cultural Center, dispatched 1st overseas internet young men service group
Aug	• KRNIC made agreement with Vietnam NIC for cooperation on internet
Oct	• Designated the cyber terror protection day (15th of each month) • OECD announced that Korea took the 1st place in Information Super Highway propagation rate • Recorded 24 million Internet users
Nov	• Korea Knowledge Portal service was started • Information Communication Ethics Committee, established the Cyber Defamation and Sexual Violence Mediation
Dec	• Personal Information Dispute Mediation Committee was founded • Recorded 10 million Internet banking subscribers
▸ 2002	
Jan	• kr Domain Mediation Committee was established • State URI basic plan for implementation of next generation infrastructure
Feb	• KT started NESPOT commercial service
Mar	• Act on Consumer Protection for Electronic Commerce was established • Ministry of Information and Communication founded CONCERT
Apr	• On-line stamp system service started • e-Korea Vision 2006 plan was fixed • Korea Information Cultural Center, opened Center for Internet Addiction Prevention and Counseling
Jul	• KRNIC, started Wireless Internet Access Number System (WINC) service.
Aug	• .kr domain name registration agent was selected • KRNIC and 3 mobile service providers, started real-time registration of WINC
Sep	• The world first next generation network access gateway was opened

Oct	• Korea's IPv4/IPv6 conversion technology was registered as the official document (RFC) of IETR • Recorded 10 million information super highway subscribers • World first commercialization of information superhighway media based home media service • KISA started the first wireless authentication service
Nov	• Korea e-Government was opened • National Education Information System (NEIS) was launched • Wireless Internet promotion plan was started • Online 3D game engine was developed in Korea • KRNIC reserved word domain name deregistration and registration
Dec	• KRNIC provides free WINC supplementary service
▸ 2003	
Jan	• Korea Information Cultural Center (ICC) was reorganized to Korea Agency for Digital Opportunity and Promotion (KADO)
Feb	• Internet based national tax notification system was started • Medium-small sized enterprise informationalization adverse effect prevention center was opened
Mar	• Registered seal impression computerization was started • mil.kr domain registration for military defense authorities
May	• KRNIC detained route DNS in Korea
▸ 2003	
Jun	• KRNIC started WINC based mobile brand service
Jul	• Yonsei University implemented the world first 'u-Campus'
Aug	• KRNIC received registration for Korean .kr domain name
Oct	• KRNIC started e number (ENUM) test service
▸ 2004	
Jan	• Act on Internet Address Resources was established
Jun	• Recorded 30 million Internet users
Jul	• KRNIC was reorganized into National Internet Development Agency of Korea (NIDA) • KR domain, registered the world first IPv6 name server address in the route DNS zone • Internet Address Policy Deliberation Committee was founded • Domain Name Mediation Committee was reorganized into Internet Address Dispute Resolution Committee
Sep	• Gyeongbuk Univ., operated the first Internet Control Center in Korea

Section 2

Operation, Management and Innovation

Chapter 5
The Information Management of Co-Located Emergency Response Rooms in The Netherlands

Kees Boersma
VU University Amsterdam, The Netherlands

Peter Groenewegen
VU University Amsterdam, The Netherlands

Pieter Wagenaar
VU University Amsterdam, The Netherlands

EXECUTIVE SUMMARY

This case is about the re-organization of the Dutch emergency response sector. It involves the diffusion and implementation of new communication and information technologies (ICTs), the introduction of safety regions and the establishment of co-located emergency response rooms (ERRs). The challenge for those organizations is to introduce the new technologies in such a way that they meet the demands of the people who have to work with them. The impact of the reorganization is illustrated by two embedded case studies: new ICTs in the safety-regions Hollands-Midden and Amsterdam-Amstelland. What the case shows is that the implementation of new ICTs in the Dutch safety-sector is not just a matter of technological skills, but of a mutual shaping of the ICTs and the organizations to enhance platform of e-governance, in this aspect the emergency response system serves as an important element. That is an important lesson for those responsible for the Dutch safety-regions, which are confronted with a new organizational and technological challenge: Netcentric Work.

DOI: 10.4018/978-1-61692-814-8.ch005

ORGANIZATION BACKGROUND

This case is about emergency response organizations in the civil safety-sector in the Netherlands. The organization and information management of emergency response systems is an emerging area of interest to academics, students and practitioners (Perry, 1995; 2003). The emergency response rooms (ERRs) are interesting public sector organizational arrangements. They conduct the intake of 911-calls (in North America) or 112 (in Europe) for help and relay them to the appropriate services and disciplines; the fire brigades, the ambulance services and the police. ERRs are organizations, which highly depend on advanced information and communication technology (ICT) systems. They may comprise of time-critical decision support systems to provide real time support to the people or communities at need, and recent trend of research in this aspect leads to incorporate intricate ICT methodologies in designing, operationalizing and maintaining these systems. They not only save peoples life, or support them in various formats, but also provide a continuous source of information and knowledge during normal period of their livelihood. In essence, this form of real-time decision support system forms a core component of e-government and elevates e-governance at the grass roots (Nelson, 2004). However, this chapter is illustrating two cases on emergency response room that are being used for emergency purposes.

The case presented in this chapter is not about e-governance in the way that it presents changing communication patterns between the government and the citizens, but rather about the way ICTs are implemented and used in governmental organizations – in our case emergency response rooms – and on how they influence the way people in these organizations work and share information with each other.

Since 9/11 and hurricane Katrina academic studies on safety and security have increased dramatically. Many different aspects of these have received attention. In some studies the gap between policy makers and operators is discussed (McConnell & Drennan, 2006); others deal with the new safety environment (Walter, 2003), or the use of training in the preparation for disasters (Perry, 2004). Yet, the organizational dimension has received far less attention. Usually, preparation for disasters is done in military fashion. Hierarchy predominates in predetermined responses to crises to be. Only, increasingly, awareness is rising of the use of emergent, networked forms of organization. These should supplement but not replace the existing hierarchies (Moynihan, 2008; Newburn, 2001). Central to these networked forms of emergency response according to some are ERRs (Perry, 1995; 2003). Unfortunately, there is a relative scarcity of literature on ERRs, let alone on ERR ITs (an exception is Schooley & Horan, 2007).

Emergency response rooms are not only responsible for the first reaction at the time of an incident or crisis but also for the quality of information and communication of the relief workers and professional services. ERRs are not stand-alone entities. They are – or are supposed to be – integrated organizations that work together at times of crisis whether they are man-made (e.g. terrorist attacks), natural (e.g. flooding or hurricanes) or incidents (e.g. a plane crash).

An interesting aspect of emergency response organizations is that they are hybrid organizations. They are not hybrid in the sense that they consist of various disciplines per se (they do), but hybrid because they partly exist on a continuous basis and partly on a temporal basis. They are 'emergent' organizations, since an important part of the emergency organization only comes into being and action during a crisis. To give an example, emergency response organizations are operational on a daily basis, but when a plane crashes emergency response organizations are 'scaled-up', that is, extra organizational layers including administrative bodies are added to the basis-organization. Up-scaling also means the involvement of representatives from other municipalities, disciplines or safety-regions. In case of up-scaling the *Regional Incident Procedures* (the Dutch abbreviation is 'GRIP') is the leading protocol. This up-scaling characteristically asks for mutual agreements between the disciplines involved about the operating procedures including mutual understanding of ICTs in-use, adequate information sharing practices facilitated by ICTs, and the responsibilities and roles of the actors involved.

SETTING THE STAGE

As becomes clear in the introduction of this chapter, emergency response organizations are not isolated organizations but interconnected with other organizations and actors who operate in the context of safety and security. In the Netherlands some major incidents have given rise to an intensive and political discussion about the way emergency response organizations and especially the ERRs, function. Incidents like the El Al Boeing 747 plane crash in Amsterdam in 1992, the explosion of a firework factory in the city of Enschede in 2000, the fire in a pub in Volendam in 2001, the fire in 2005 in a building close to Schiphol Amsterdam that housed asylum-seekers and, finally, the crash of a Turkish Airline Boeing close to Schiphol Amsterdam in 2009, have not only caused national traumas but have also lead to a discussion about the quality of the information sharing practices of the ERRs.

The question that was made explicit by investigators in evaluation reports was whether the ERRs were sufficiently equipped for their task. The main problem was not the quality of information sharing practices within one discipline (e.g. communication between members of the police-force), but the mismatches between the various disciplines (e.g. the communication between members of the police, the ambulances, and the fire-brigade). To be short, and as an example: in the case of the explosion in Enschede the emergency response rooms were not able to transfer the information about the development of the fire to the ambulance services (Commissie Onderzoek Vuurwerkramp 2001). The incidents caused three direct reactions in the Dutch emergency response sector.

Firstly, in order to cope with communication problems, the Dutch government already in 1995 decided to implement a single national communications network for the police, the fire brigades and the ambulances, which was called C2000 (communication 2000). C2000 was part of the comprehensive approach to safety and supports the communication between the reliefworkers in the field and the ERR's operators. Next to C2000 the ERRs were equipped with the emergency room software GMS. GMS is the Dutch abbreviation for Integrated Emergency Room Systems (see for details on C2000 and GMSGMSGMS: Groenewegen and Wagenaar, 2006). It is linked to the public emergency telephone number 112, to the communication system C2000, to radio and telephone systems, and to a Geographic Information System (GIS). The latter is an important database for the operators in this respect. It is software in which entities are spatially indexed and which is used for all kinds of policing (see: Snellen 2000).

GMS facilitates the actions of the ERR operators in the following way. After an emergency-call the operators use GMS to electronically follow and develop the story of an incident. The GMS software enables the operator to make time-lines, to store information from the relief workers in the field, to make a visual image of the incident on GIS and to follow the police cars, ambulances, and fire engines that are operational. GMS is also used as a device to store the data – and in a way it is also a surveillance system. Since it is an integrated system, GMS can also be used as a tool that enables information sharing practices. It is a crucial device for the ERR to function properly.

In the second place, the Dutch government decided to re-organize the civil safety-sector in the Netherlands by implementing 25 different safety-regions that together cover the whole country - most of them are operational since 2007. The safety-regions vary in scale and have their own characteristics but have the same responsibilities. Each and every safety-region must: integrate the administrations of the different disciplines, organize itself around a regional bureau that is responsible for emergency-response and the communication with the majors of the cities that are part of the safety-region, develop a risk-analysis of its region, and facilitate an emergency response room.

Finally, as part of the reorganization and the implementation of the safety-regions, the Dutch government decided to house the three disciplines' ERR-personnel at one site. Such a new ERR, which is a crucial part of the safety-region, is known as a 'co-location' or a 'co-located' ERR. The idea behind the co-location is that communication and information-sharing between the three disciplines will become easier. Working in a co-location enables the operators of the three disciplines to get to know each other, and each other's practices, procedures and ICT systems in-use.

CASE DESCRIPTION

This section will present two sub-cases: the integrated co-location of the emergency response room of the safety region HollandsMidden and the virtual co-location Amsterdam-Amstelland. The sub-case HollandsMidden makes clear that the implementation of new ICTs and the merger of the three disciplines was a heavy managerial burden for the responsible actors of the room. However, the three different disciplines have been able to mutually develop the ICTs in such a way that multi-disciplinary routines could be developed. The second sub-case is about the safety-region Amsterdam-Amstelland, which is the only safety-region in the Netherlands in which the three disciplines still are located in separate locations spread over the city. The three emergency response rooms each have their own emergency room systems and are – at the time of writing this case - only virtually co-located by means of webcams.

With regard to the technological components and the synopsis of its structure, the reader must understand that the specific characteristics of the ICT in-use can differ from ERR to ERR. That means that, in the cases below, the technology in-use will not be described in detail, but generalized and described. In general, any GMS in-use in a Dutch ERR must be seen a decision support system is used as a communication tool, for data storage and - via the archive - enables the evaluation of first responders. Next to C2000 and GIS, the IT can be attached to MobiPol and Enterprise Resource Systems. MobiPol is an application in a police-car with which the officer can communicate with the ERR-operators. It also enables the individual police-officer to get access to the GMS-content while being in the field.

An important element of GMS is data-storage. The content of the archive can be – on an abstract level, provide the ERR manager of information regarding the response time and the adequacy/quality of the communication between the responder and the citizen. The archive – in which the data of previous incidents is collected - is also used for a periodical, external review of the ERRs quality.

Sub-Case HollandsMidden: A Co-Location with Integrated ICTs

The implementation of the co-location of HollandsMidden, which is in full operation since 2007, was not a process without problems (see for details of this sub-case: Wagenaar et.al, 2009). First of all the management of the three existing emergency response rooms had to find ways to (re)organize the rooms and to find a well-equipped room that was big enough to house the three disciplines. The details of this process are outside the scope of this chapter. What is important to know is that eventually the co-location was realized: the new emergency response room was housed under the roof of the fire brigade but under the administrative responsibility of the police in Leiden, which is the main city in the safety-region HollandsMidden. Interesting is the way in which the ICTs – and most important the GMS – was used as a basis for integration. The integration of the ERRs of the fire brigade, the ambulance services and the police took place in different phases.

Firstly, the three disciplines were brought together under the same roof but without really integrating the different operating procedures and information sharing practices of the disciplines. Although the management of the co-located ERR felt the urgency of more multi-disciplinary work, the implementation of the new GMS was a heavy burden that took too much of the time of the management. Multi-disciplinary work in the first stage of the co-location thus was an illusion. Yet, in the second stage, the operators of the different disciplines within the ERR stared to understand each others' routines and work-procedures and – as a result - they actually started to collect information that was needed by the other disciplines without direct intervention of the management. Yet, there still were no multi-disciplinary procedures, and there were many misunderstandings of each others' work. For example in the case of a fire, the fire brigade is interested in the extent, development and putting out the fire itself, the emergency medical team is focused on saving possible victims, and the police wants to apprehend witnesses or perpetrators. These different routines made multidisciplinary communication difficult. Instead of using the GMS that was implemented to facilitate multi-disciplinary information sharing practices, for a long time the operators relied on the telephone to get into contact with the other disciplines. Part of the problem was the inadequate translation of the different work routines into GMS.

In the final stage of the co-location, however, the ERR's personnel started to develop interdisciplinary operating procedures. The ERR's operators came to appreciate and understand each other's work. At the same time they were able to translate this appreciation into new practices – also based on multi-disciplinary training – and adaptations of GMS. That means that the operators were able to change parts of GMS' information scripts so that certain information that is relevant for the other disciplines can be shared and other information can stay within one discipline. For example if the citizens' privacy is at stake, the operators of the ambulance services do not transfer that information from their GMS to that of the police. The new GMS is also extended by a so-called scratchpad on which on discipline can transfer the most crucial information about an incident to another discipline. However, the co-location enables them to orally exchange that information to the other discipline. We found that most of the crucial information was exchanged on an informal way: by walking to each others' desks the operators are able to quickly share information with the other disciplines.

What this sub-case illustrates is that the way the ERR of HollandsMidden functions nowadays is a result of a mutual shaping of ICT (GMS) and the organization (the co-location). Yet, the ERR still lacks embedded multi-disciplinary work routines and information sharing practices. And, as Stinchcomb and Ordaz have shown, the integration of different disciplines within one location is problematic from an organizational (cultural) point of view (Stinchcomb & Ordaz, 2007). Too often the disciplines have to be focused on their own work, have different work routines, and sometimes the law doesn't even allow them to exchange information. Also the formal terms of employment (e.g. the salary, pensions, etc.) are still subject for discussions within the ERR. The operators of the different disciplines now work closely together but are paid different. It is the local employees councils of the ERR in HollandsMidden that tries to find a solution for this problem. That means that whereas the benefit of fully integrated ERRs is not questioned, how the ICTs can facilitate multi-disciplinary work still is the question.

Sub-Case Amsterdam-Amstelland: A Virtual Co-Location with Loosely Coupled ICTs

The region Amsterdam-Amstelland is the only region in the Netherlands that still houses its ERRs in three different rooms. Amsterdam-Amstelland is a relatively small safety-region in which the city of Amsterdam is the main agglomeration (see for details of this sub-case: Boersma et.al, 2009). Interesting about this sub-case is that the three disciplines of this region are still housed in their own ERR at different locations in Amsterdam. And, in addition, the ICTs in-use are not (yet) electronically connected. The ERRs of the police and the fire-brigade each work with their own version of the Dutch standard GMS systems, but these differ slightly from each other. The ERR of the ambulance services does not work with GMS but with a system called 'MIOS', which it has developed itself. In the daily practice of the emergency response organization this means that the information is not shared via an integrated emergency response room system.

Because the emergency response systems are not interlinked with each other, most information is still exchanged through telephone. This makes it difficult for the operators of the various disciplines to come to a shared understanding of what exactly is going on during an incident. It can even happen that not all ERRs are aware an incident is taking place. Especially during the up-scaling GRIP-procedures of the emergency response rooms the exchange of information between emergency response rooms is insufficiently guaranteed. In the daily practice of the emergency response organization the information (as laid down in the systems) is usually not digitally shared real-time among the different ERRs, which can lead to simple miscommunications (for example about the exact location of an incident). Not coupling the systems is thus a huge disadvantage. Clearer agreements on communication between emergency response rooms are definitely required. Enabling operators to look into other emergency response rooms' information systems could prevent a few of the most elementary mistakes.

The question in this sub-case is whether a co-location with an integrated GMS can help the disciplines to communicate (better) with each other. The sub-case of HollandsMidden has taught that the implementation of a co-located ERR is complicated and the outcome of a mutual shaping of the ICTs in-use (especially GMS) and the organization. This mutual shaping is a situational matter and the failure and success depends highly on local circumstances and choices. A complicated factor is that the three Amsterdam ERRs operate in a very demanding area because of the population density, and therefore the operators work under constant pressure. A co-located ERR in the Amsterdam situation could also create a too large and too turbulent environment. Yet clearer agreements on communication between ERRs are definitely required.

CURRENT CHALLENGES FACING THE ORGANIZATION

As the two sub-cases show, in the process of ICT implementation both the organizational and the technological structures and systems are (re) interpreted and (re)defined. The selection of possible practices is a process that takes place in the context of daily routines and therefore, depends on situational circumstances. Only when an ICT is studied 'in use' can one understand the way an ICT, like in this case a GMS or a GIS, affects the organization and vice versa. That means that whenever new systems are introduced, subgroups of users decide the manner in which the system fits their purposes and work processes (Orlikowski, 2000). ICT in-use puts emphasis on the idea that actors, through working with it, reconfigure the information system where possible due to their needs. This can be seen as a mutual shaping (MacKenzie & Wajcman, 2002) of the technology and the organization of the ERR, which is an on ongoing process.

Many actors are involved in the mutual shaping of the ERRs and the ICTs in-use. It is important for the work of these people in the ERRs to create a culture of trust. The disciplines have to find a common ground for operating and communicating with each other. In order to facilitate information-sharing practices of a high quality, emergency response organizations are equipped with ICT tools of all kind. The challenge for the different disciplines is to find shared ICT routines. GMS, through standardization, was supposed to facilitate the communication between the different ERRs and the disciplines. Yet, thus far the ICTs in-use, like GMS, still has to prove that they can meet that goal. As long as the routines are not standardized and the ERR operators do not create multidisciplinary routines, this will continue to pose a constraint. Therefore the Dutch government, in cooperation with the civil safety-sector, is looking for new ways to cope with this problem.

The latest development in information management that tries to give a solution to the multidisciplinary information sharing problems is Netcentric Work (Von Lubitz et al., 2008; Houghton et al., 2008; Van Lier, 2009). Netcentric Work is an organizational principle based on the innovation of interactive internet-tools. These interactive tools – the so-called *web 2.0* technologies like Wiki's, Youtube and Blogs – enable the netcentric worker (in and outside the emergency response room) to collect real-time information about a certain incident from the professionals in the field and to add information about the operation in the systems. This information is supposed to be shared without the restraints of formal organization. The main idea behind Netcentric Work is netcentric warfare – a concept from the military that is suppose to enable the troops to create a 'common operational picture' at the time of an incident or action.

Important to consider is that Netcentric Work is based upon Geographic Information Systems (GIS), containing one map per discipline involved. Because the users of Netcentric Work can consult each others' GIS, it is expected that Netcentric Work can provide the operators with a view of the others disciplines' worlds, and help them to make sense of the work routines and information sharing patterns of the others. Although so far there is no formal decision about the implementation of Netcentric Work at the level of the safety-regions in the Netherlands, it is most likely that the emergency response sector will hook up with this international trend. When they actually do so, they will have used a new information system (instead of GMS) to solve the problem of organizational fragmentation and differences in sense making between disciplines. The challenge for those involved in the implementation and adaptation of Netcentric Work is to nurture the mutual shaping of the technology that comes with Netcentric Work and the organizations (in the Netherlands these are especially the 25 safety-regions) in which the new concept must be embedded. That implies also that one cannot solve organizational problems by simply implementing new technologies. As the cases have shown, these technologies are used in different and sometimes unintended ways. And maybe more important, these technologies only have a meaning when they are in-use. The idea that there is a one-for-all IT solution, therefore, is rather naïve.

SOLUTIONS AND RECOMMENDATIONS

The lack of really integrated systems in the ERRs certainly is a problem when it comes to smooth communication among the disciplines. Yet, as this chapter has tried to illustrate, it is not so much the ICTs per se, as it is the institutional and organizational arrangements that are the bottlenecks when it comes to the emergency response room in-action. That means that if future technicians and managers of governmental organizations such as emergency response rooms start thinking of the implementation of new technologies they should include organizational issues into account.

Authors would like to say that, although the emergency response rooms in the Netherlands do function well as stand-alone organizations, the ERRs as a whole in Amsterdam-Amstelland and, less so, in HollandsMidden, are still facing problems to fulfill their most important task: to coordinate the communication between the safety services at the time of a major incident. This contribution has made it clear that although the Dutch government invested a lot in the civil safety-sector, the communication between the emergency rooms of the three disciplines is not yet optimally organized. Shared information systems such as GMS and the planned implementation of Netcentric Work – as presented in this chapter - might prevent situations of misunderstanding and miscommunication, but must be mutually shaped with the organization in which they will be in-use. In the end, it are the users (the professionals of the ERRS) who have to work with the new ICTs – therefore their wishes should be taken seriously during the various stages of ICT-implementation. That is especially true when it comes to the implementation of netcentric work as a new promising technologies and way of work.

ERRs and their information systems might seem far removed from E-governance; especially if the latter is conceived as G2C relations. Yet, when one realizes that ERRs redirect citizen calls to emergency services, after having processed them, then their E-governance character becomes much more manifest. Interesting is how these relations are evolving under the influence of new tools like Twitter and Youtube. Nowadays, because news – and footage! - of disasters hits the afore-mentioned social media as fast as it reaches the ERRs emergency services are confronted with new questions. One of those is whether one should use information citizens have gathered. The other is how to respond to citizen concerns in a situation where the public information position has so drastically improved.

REFERENCES

Boersma, F. K., Groenewegen, P., & Wagenaar, P. (2009). Emergency Response Rooms in Action: an ethnographic case-study in Amsterdam. In Landgren, J., & Jul, S. (eds.)*Proceeding of the 6th International*ISCRAM*Conference (pp.1-8)*. Gothenburg, Sweden, May 2009.

Commissie Onderzoek Vuurwerkramp (Investigation Committee Fireworks-incident). (2001). *De Vuurwerkramp eindrapport*. DenHaag/Enschede.

Groenewegen, P., & Wagenaar, P. (2006). Managing emergent information systems: Towards understanding how public information systems come into being. *Information Polity, 11*, 135–148.

Houghton, R. J., Baber, C., Cowton, M., Walker, G. H., & Stanton, N. A. (2008). WESTT (workload, error, situational awareness, time and teamwork): an analytical prototyping system for command and control . *Cognition Technology and Work, 10*, 199–207. doi:10.1007/s10111-007-0098-4

MacKenzie, D., & Wajcman, J. (2002). *The Social Shaping of Technology*. Buckingham: Open University Press.

McConnell, A., & Drennan, L. (2006). Mission Impossible? Planning and Preparing for Crisis. *Journal of Contingencies and Crisis Management, 14*(2), 59–70. doi:10.1111/j.1468-5973.2006.00482.x

Moynihan, D. P. (2008). Combining structural forms in the search for policy tools: Incident command systems in US crisis management. *Governance - an International Journal of Policy and Administration, 21*(2), 205-229.

Nelson, G. B. (2004). *Real Time Decision Support: Creating a Flexible Architecture for Real Time Analytics, SUGI29*. Data Warehousing, Management and Quality.

Newburn, T. (2001). The Commodification of Policing: Security Networks in the late Modern City . *Urban Studies (Edinburgh, Scotland)*, *38*(5/6), 829–848. doi:10.1080/00420980123025

Orlikowski, W. J. (2000). Using Technology and Constituting Structures: A Practice Lens for Studying Technology in Organizations. *Organization Science*, *11*(4), 404–428. doi:10.1287/orsc.11.4.404.14600

Perry, R. W. (1995). The structure and function of community emergency operations centres . *Disaster Prevention and Management*, *4*(5), 37–41. doi:10.1108/09653569510100983

Perry, R. W. (2003). Emergency Operations Centres in an Era of Terrorism: Policy and Management Functions. *Journal of Contingencies and Crisis Management*, *11*(4), 151–159. doi:10.1111/j.0966-0879.2003.01104001.x

Perry, R. W. (2004). Disaster Exercise Outcomes for Professional Emergency Personnel and Citizen Volunteers. *Journal of Contingencies and Crisis Management*, *12*(2), 64–75. doi:10.1111/j.0966-0879.2004.00436.x

Snellen, I. Th. M. (2000). Territorializing governance and the state: Policy dimensions of Geographic Information Systems . *Information Infrastructure and Policy*, *6*, 131–138.

Stinchcomb, J. B., & Ordaz, F. (2007). The Integration of Two "Brotherhoods" into One Organizational Culture: A Psycho-social Perspective on Merging Police and Fire Services . *Public Organization Review*, *7*, 143–161. doi:10.1007/s11115-006-0026-8

Van Lier, A. F. (2009). *Luhmann ontmoet The Matrix. Uitwisselen en delen van informatie in netcentrische omgevingen*. Delft: Eburon Academic Publishers.

Von Lubitz, D.K.J.E., Beakley, J.E., & Patricelli, F. (2008). Disaster Management: The Structure, Function, and Significance of Network-Centric Operations, *Journal of Homeland Security and Emergency Management, 5*(2), article 42,1-24.

Wagenaar, P., Boersma, F. K., Groenewegen, P., & Niemandsverdriet, P. (2009). 'Implementing C2000 in the Dutch police region 'Hollands-Midden', for publication in: Meijer, A., Boersma, F.K., & Wagenaar, P. (eds). *ICTs, Citizens & Governance: After the Hype! Amsterdam: IOS Press series "Innovation and the Public Sector"*, 119-134.

Walter, P. (2003). Surveillance and Security: A Dodgy Relationship. *Journal of Contingencies and Crisis Management*, *11*(1), 19–24. doi:10.1111/1468-5973.1101004

ADDITIONAL READING

Cooper, M. (2000). Safety Management in the Emergency Response Services, *Risk Management. International Journal (Toronto, Ont.)*, *2*, 39–49.

Horan, T.A., McCabe, D., Burkjard, R., & Schooley, B. (2005). Performance Information Systems for Emergency Response: Field Examination and Simulation of End-To-End Rural Response Systems, *Journal of Homeland Security and Emergency Management, 2*(1), article 4.

Meijer, A., Boersma, F. K., & Wagenaar, P. (Eds.). (2009). ICTs, Citizens & Governance: After the Hype! *Innovation and the Public Sector*, 14. Amsterdam: IOS Press series

Mendonça, D., Jefferson, T., & Harrald, J. (2007). Collaborative adhocracies and Mix-and Match Technologies in Emergency Management. *Communications of the ACM, 50*(3), 45–49. doi:10.1145/1226736.1226764

Militello, L. G., Patterson, E. S., Bowman, L., & Wears, R. (2007). Information flow during crisis management: challenges to coordination in the emergency operations center . *Cognition Technology and Work, 9*, 25–31. doi:10.1007/s10111-006-0059-3

Rogers, E. M. (1983). *Diffusion of Innovations* (3rd ed.). New York: The Free Press.

Schooley, B. L., & Horan, T. A. (2007). Towards end-to-end government performance management: Case study of interorganizational information integration in emergency medical services (EMS) . *Government Information Quarterly, 24*, 755–784. doi:10.1016/j.giq.2007.04.001

Wallace, P. (2004). *The Internet in the Workplace. How New Technology is Transforming Work.* Cambridge: Cambridge University Press.

KEY TERMS AND DEFINITIONS

Emergency Response Room (ERR): Public sector organizational arrangement that conducts the intake of 911-calls (in North America) or 112 (in Europe) for help and relays them to the appropriate services and the disciplines involved in emergency work: the fire brigades, the ambulance services and the police and other professional workers like those of the Waterboards.

Co-Location: An ERR in which the disciplines are physically housed in one building [niet 'room'] in order to stimulate multi-disciplinary work routines and information-sharing practices among the operators of the different disciplines.

GMS: Standardized Emergency Response Room System facilitates the work of the operators in the ERR by offering an electronic platform to import and store the (communication) data used by the relief workers at the time of an incident.

GIS: Geographical Information System is software through which entities are spatially indexed on maps (e.g. Google Earth) and which, in safety and security sectors, is used for all kinds of policing.

Netcentric Work: An organizational principle based on the innovation of interactive internet-tools. These *web 2.0* technologies like Wiki's, Youtube and Blogs – enable the netcentric worker to collect real-time information about a certain incident from all kinds of sources to create a 'common operational picture'.

Mutual Shaping: The mutual shaping of technology and organization is the idea that the development of a certain technology never occurs in isolation but always in interaction with its environment (in this chapter the mutual shaping of the GMS and the ERR).

Chapter 6
Methods for Software Complexity and Development Effort Estimation and its Importance in the Area of ICT Governance

Zdeněk Struska
Deloitte Advisory, Czech Republic

Jiří Vaníček
Czech University of Life Sciences, Czech Republic

Martin Závodný
Czech University of Life Sciences, Czech Republic

EXECUTIVE SUMMARY

The area of applications development for government purposes can be characterized to be task specific. In this context, development projects are usually more complex and there are some differences in comparison with commercial projects. The mission of the proposed chapter is an explanation of methods of project complexity evaluation based on analogy, crisp and fuzzy expert estimation and measure models. The selected methods for aggregation of expert's estimations are also presented. Further the chapter introduces selected methods designed for complexity estimation. All the introduced methods are widely known except one that was designed by the lead author of the chapter. The method is called BORM Points and is developed for an IS project designed in BORM method (Business Object Relation Modeling). Each method is introduced first, then its step-by-step computation procedure is described and finally suggestion of software, which is supported method computation procedure. The results of the methods are in non-dimensional numbers and it is necessary to set up the relationship between complexity and effort, and introduces COCOMO model and its variants. Efforts are given about the implementation of this form of estimation approach in the area of ICT governance, especially at the grass roots e-governance.

DOI: 10.4018/978-1-61692-814-8.ch006

ORGANIZATION BACKGROUND

Early SW systems were often developed uncontrolled without consideration about costs of its development and implementation. For that reason the development was not finished timely or costs of system implementation exceeded original estimations. The proper estimations of costs were finally enabled by emerging of methodical approaches of system design. For public information systems is important the public funds were spent efficiently and the utility of public information systems for grass roots was as high as possible. The main specific of public information systems is a fact that they are primarily not created for the purpose of increasing of company's profit, but for the purpose of providing public services to citizens. They should simplify the contact between citizens and government.

This case summarises current knowledge related to effort estimations constructed in early phases of IS development project. These estimations enable to make decisions, wheatear to invest money in the project or not. The case contains knowledge, experience and results of researches of several authors, who are on a long-term basis involved in the area of effort estimations.

This case does not describe a particular solution in comparison with others. It follows one selected, but quite important problem "automation" of public administration, concretely cost estimation for information support of public administration's projects. It summarizes authors' experience from various projects, in which authors have participated as resolvers or submitters. Next authors' experience is from pedagogical work at the universities including cooperation with postdoctoral students. Finally it includes experience from international standardization on the level of standardization authority - ISO/IEC JTC1 (Join technical committee for Information technology) and its subcommittee SC7 (System and Software Engineering), where one of the authors has worked as a representative of Czechoslovakia and as a representative of Czech Republic since 1993. His main role is a coeditor of international standards.

Next authors' background consists of long experience with leading of project in the area of development of operation systems and base software for mainframe computers, then experience with public procurements and management of many government and public projects in the area of public administration and government, especially for Government office for public information systems of Czech Republic and later for Ministry of Informatics of Czech Republic.

Currently, authors' research activities are based on projects for Czech Ministry of Education: Grant No. MSM 6046070904 "Information and knowledge support of strategic control" and Grant No.2C06004 "Intelligent tools for content assessment of relevance of general and specialized data and knowledge resources".

SETTING THE STAGE

Why Should Complexity be Estimated?

If government wants to successfully develop the Information and Communication Technology (ICT) support, it has to accurately and appropriately react to citizen's needs and demands. Government representatives should try to optimize expenses of information systems (IS) including subsequent implementation and operation activities. The public sector is responsible for the effective usage of funds received from the taxpayers. They should, therefore, guarantee that benefits of the deployed IT surpass the related costs of system development - especially for software. Furthermore, government needs to determine objectively whether the price of work, which is demanded by external developers, corresponds to the labor consumed during the project realization. Therefore, it is vitally important to dispose of methods for work effort estimation and to have tools for applying those methods. This chapter addresses some methods for software (SW) development complexity and demanded work effort estimation.

The methods described in this chapter determine the costs of software development indirectly by means of complexity estimation. In this area it is very difficult to get accurate and timely values, because estimations are done in the early project phases of IS development, when the availability of relevant input data for the effort estimation is strictly limited.

The main benefit of the described methods and approaches is findings of cost estimation based on generally accepted procedures. It is possible to make the estimation more accurate in the later stages of the project. Improving the accuracy of the complexity estimation is important for project management, and for decision-making concerning whether to cancel the project if it does not comply with the expectations and planned results, and available resources.

An expert estimation is at present the generally predominant approach to estimation of IS development complexity. The role of the expert has key importance in this approach. These persons should be able to combine knowledge of similar projects, and on this basis give qualified estimations. This chapter also describes how to aggregate more expert statements regarding the same problem.

Besides this approach, some methods are based on a SW development model and measurement of attributes during different phases of project life-cycle. An important sign of these models is the fact that in the earlier phases of a project there are, fewer measurable inputs available, and less precise estimation of work effort and costs can be obtained. On the other hand, the question about starting SW development and preparing an appropriate budget must be resolved very early. Any belated decisions can be very costly. For this reason it is desirable to set the work effort estimation as soon as possible. Preferably it should be set immediately after the functionality analysis, based on the business needs. It is always necessary to rely on measurable inputs, which are available in given time. It is possible to refine these estimations in later project phases.

Development costs of information system are a part of all costs for entire solution. The total costs consist of costs of process re-engineering including organizational changes and training costs. All these additional costs could be higher than costs for IS development.

Specifics of E-Governance Environment

The area of e-government application has its own characteristics, and a company that decides for e-government applications has to take into consideration different circumstances than in standard projects. The main points that have a high impact in complexity estimation are the following:

- Political cycle;
- Change requirements and communication;
- Project team experience, motivation and capacity;
- End users knowledge;
- Interoperability and reusability; and
- Special security objectives.

These differences have influence on development life cycle of information system. During specification phase it is usually difficult to obtain the system requirements from public administration, because public clerks are usually conservatives and politics follow the short time horizon of their election period.

This situation implies higher demands on project team on the side of supplier, especially environment knowledge and qualification of business consultants. Furthermore, requirement gathering can be longer and more difficult and it increases the final effort.

Terminology

In this chapter terminology is used in compliance with international standard ISO/IEC 24765 – Systems and software engineering vocabulary.

As a suitable introduction, this research considers it appropriate to provide an explanation of some selected terms used in the following text.

Process is regarded as a set of interrelated or interacting activities, which transforms inputs into outputs. The result of the process is a *product*. Generally a product can be an artifact of the hardware or software, or the service, or some input of the further intermediate process (the raw material). *Software* artifact product is usually a complete set of computer programs, procedures and associated documentation and data, designed for delivery to a user, with the combination of services.

Software product development effort is regarded as the number of labor units required to complete a product for delivery. Usually it is expressed as staff hours (man hours), man-days, or man weeks, and depending on local conditions it is possible to re-calculate it into currency units.

CASE DESCRIPTION

The following chapter is divided into two parts. The first part clarifies the group of methods and approaches, whose main presumption for successful estimation of IS development complexity is participation of an expert, who makes the estimation on the basis of his knowledge and experience acquired from previous similar projects.

The second group tries to eliminate the influence of an expert on work effort estimation by use of more rigorous methods. These methods use, for the purpose of complexity calculation, approaches based on an analysis of internal and external relationships of IS, and an evaluation of characteristics of developed IS. These methods are built on measurable attributes of outputs of particular development processes.

ESTIMATIONS BASED ON THE ANALOGY AND EXPERT EVALUATION

Analogy

The most accurate and also less costly way to estimate work effort and possible time duration of a SW project is to find similar projects and use past experience regarding incurred implementation costs. Such knowledge can be ideally recovered from self-experience. For reusability of this knowledge, it is necessary for every company to ensure storage, evaluation and sharing of relevant data in an appropriate knowledge base. It is the basic condition fulfilled within "learning organizations". Thanks to these companies who can attain competitive advantage. Experience usable for future application can be received from previous successes, but even more from past failures.

It is more difficult to find an analogy outside the company - at competitors. It can be very difficult, because companies do not like to publish any figures about their own costs. They consider this information as a company's know-how, and part of its business secrets. Data obtained by unofficial and private sources can be untrustworthy. Data about costs are often published long after the date of their origin and therefore are not so valuable, because methodologies of SW development are changing very quickly.

When making estimations based on analogy it is important to take into consideration the following principles:

- It is necessary to check whether it is really being dealt with an analogical product. Not only is the area of the required product function important, but also other quality attributes. Authors recommend following the ISO/IEC quality model of software products, created within the SQuaRE project. This model is, and will be, incorporated into international standards ISO/

IEC 250xx. Besides functionality, which has commonly not been miss out, it is also important to notice other characteristics:

- Requirements for secure access to software and data,
- Requirements for collaboration with other software products,
- Requirements for failure-free operation of system,
- Requirements for easy system usage,
- Requirements for efficiency of system (time of response) and of other resources (e.g. memory),
- Requirements to easily change the product because of environment changes or further requests on development,
- Requirements for easy portability of product to another software or hardware environment.

However, higher or lower requirements for each of these characteristics can significantly influence costs. At the same time, increased requirements imply the estimation is multiplied by a number greater than 1, lower requirements are multiplied by a number less than 1. The list of requirements above is certainly not complete. Nevertheless it can help us to not forget and miss out any important requirement concerning the developed product, affected to necessary effort.

- The product requirements only are not fully satisfactory for the development effort estimation. It is also necessary to verify that SW development conditions are also similar. The authors of this chapter, believe that the conditions can be favorably divided into two groups:
  - Internal factors are connected with the development team and conditions in which the team works. The most important factor is the qualification of team members. Another important factor is motivation of each employee. If the project is similar to the past project realized by the team, the demanded work and time duration can be significantly reduced. This is possible because of the reusability of some components created in the past. Team instability - changing team members or utilization of part time employees - can negatively influence team efficiency.
  - External factors in the case of a product made-to-measure for the customer, comprise completeness of system requirements, time capacity of customer employees assigned to project, qualification and competency of customer employees - are they aim-oriented or will they be likely to block the project? Instability of requirements and frequent changes can also significantly increase project work consumption.

Firstly the both points of view (internal and external) should be separately compared by analogical projects and project, which effort is estimated. Internal and external multiplication factors are set up so that their sum should be equal to 1, in case when conditions are equal. If conditions of estimated project are simpler, the multiplication factor will be lower than 1. If multiplication factors are more complicated, the sum could be higher than 1. If known project effort is multiplied with both estimated multiplication factors, the result is estimation effort of planned project.

The general principle for setting up corrective factors is not to forget any important condition that could influence the work consumption. Every significant condition should be count ones but also only once, not repeatedly within several factors.

Expert Estimation

Companies with a short history and limited experience in relevant projects generally do not have enough data, necessary for making conclusions on the basis of the analogy method. In such cases it is possible to take advantage of the opinions of experts, who have sufficient experience. It is usually quite costly to get an expert's verdict. It is not, however, recommended to spare money on an expert at the expense of quality of estimation. Bad estimation causes higher cost of the project. On the other hand it does not make sense to spend money on corrections of cost estimation, which would bring only small benefits comparing to costs of additional expert estimation.

In the process of choosing an expert estimation, it is recommended to follow these principles:

- Estimation is not a negotiation. Ask only impartial people, who have no personal interest in the estimated aspects.
- Answers to questions cannot be "proposed"; otherwise you will not find any new information and will only reshuffle your own presuppositions. The expert should not have any information about what values the submitter of expertise expects. Psychologists confirm that an expert could be subconsciously influenced by such referential information (see Jorgensen & Sjoberg, 2004).
- Not all expert opinions have the same relevance. It is recommended to assess expert qualification and experience, and depending on the results to add the appropriate value to the expert's opinion.
- Modify expert estimations by your experience. In the long-term, compare the estimations of particular experts with the final results. Make corrective coefficients for particular experts. It is necessary to gross up the estimations of optimists, and reduce estimations of pessimists.

The more expert opinions one has, the more reliable the final estimation probably is. An aggregation of expert opinions is not simply solvable problem. It is necessary to take into consideration not only the aggregated opinion, but also to evaluate the variability of particular expert estimations. The agreement rate can be expressed as:

- Consensus of estimations - Based on Shannon's information theory, is in the work of (Taste & Wierman, 2007) a proposed principle for consensus value in interval <0. 1>, where value 1 expresses full consensus and 0 absolute dissention of opinions. Calculation of consensus provides very valuable information about how much it can rely on expert opinions. The closer to value 1 the result is, the more reliable the estimation could be received. The arithmetic mean is only one possible aggregation operator. This operator does not emphasize or suppress extreme expert opinions. All opinions have the same importance. Mostly it is useful to prefer consensus to some extreme expert opinions (extreme opinions can be fully or partially suppressed). Full suppression of extremes can be attained by elimination of the highest and lowest estimation or several highest and lowest estimations. Partial suppression of extreme influence can be achieved by usage of different aggregation operators.
- The median ensures absolute preference of consensus and elimination of extremes. The median is very suitable for aggregation of expert estimations in cases where it is necessary to avoid distortion because of extreme opinions, but do not want to fully eliminate them. By use of median, extremely high or low estimations are put into effect in the same way as any other estimation higher or lower than aggregated result. In the case where the value is estimated in ordinal scale type, only median

is the only possible aggregation, which has guaranteed empirical sense and does not depend on the choice of individual milestone points on the ordinal scale.

Fuzzy Estimations

All the previous consideration was based on the condition that the estimation of every expert is crisp, determined by one value, which the expert considers optimal. Better notions of possibilities, which can happen, can be received, when each expert is able and agreeable to share his own sense of doubt.

The two following approaches can be used for a representation of uncertainty:

The stochastic approach, which describes the ratio of cases connected to a particular event and all occurred cases and its limit, and the fuzzy approach describing uncertainty of the estimation. In the fuzzy approach uncertainty is represented by so called fuzzy sets. Uncertainty of a particular statement is considered as a measure of the membership of the given statement into the set of all true statements. This measure is referred to as a value of the set membership function. If it is sure that the element belongs to a fuzzy set, the membership function value is 1. If it is sure the item does not belong to the set, the value is 0. In the case of estimation uncertainty, the value is in the interval between 0 and 1. The closer the value is to 1, the higher is the certainty of result.

Fuzzy sets are suitable means for representation of uncertain knowledge. Within them it can be define different types of operations between sets. As an exceptional case they can be used for the representation of probability; the fuzzy approach seems to be more appropriate to this research's problem than the stochastic one. When working with expert estimations authors consider the use of standard fuzzy set operations as the most favorable. They predict that reasons of uncertainty of particular experts can be mutually dependent. It corresponds to a real situation better than if it would predict full independence of factors and use product operations with fuzzy sets, which correspond to composition of probability of independent events. Fuzzy logic corresponds to fuzzy sets and reflects uncertain reasoning and reasoning on uncertain conditions (Further information regarding fuzzy set is in (Vaníček at al., 2008), detailed definitions in (Hájek, 2000)).

For expressing uncertainty of quantitative estimations, such as costs or project time duration, it is more suitable to use fuzzy intervals and fuzzy numbers. They express quantitative estimation as well as estimation uncertainty of possible values in its surroundings.

Fuzzy intervals and fuzzy numbers are suitable instruments for expressing individual uncertainty of an expert during the process of numeric value estimation. They enable one to include both the best estimation and the possible dispersion and slope, with which certainty of value in the neighborhood of the best-estimated value. It is possible to generalize arithmetic operations between crisp numbers to the respective arithmetic operations for fuzzy intervals and fuzzy numbers. The results of that operation are again fuzzy intervals or fuzzy numbers (Hájek, 2000).

When aggregating fuzzy estimations (in the form of fuzzy intervals or fuzzy numbers), it is possible to follow the same principles as when aggregating estimations with crisp values. For the computational point of view it is recommend dividing the support of the fuzzy set into several small intervals and in each these intervals replace the membership function by the appropriate constant value (see Figure 1). Membership function submitted by expert is therefore replaced by a piece vise constant function.

Performing fuzzy interval and fuzzy number operations following introduced formulas is computationally more complex. Computer usage is necessary. Time complexity of each arithmetic operation increases according to the introduced formulas quadratically depending on the number of particular intervals, on which the support is

Figure 1. Replacement of membership function to of fuzzy number by piece vise constantly function

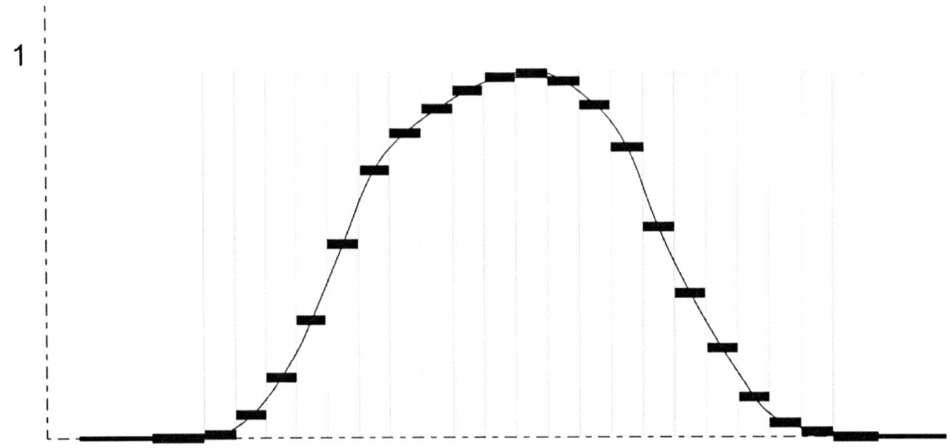

divided. In the case of an approximation pice vise constant function (such as is illustrated in Figure 1, and by usage of arithmetic fuzzy interval and fuzzy number operations, it can be proved that an increase of time complexity increases quadratically depending on the number of particular intervals, on which the support of the approximated membership function (fuzzy set) is divided.

Experience shows that for a suitable two-sided setting of constraint range for estimated value, it is in principle sufficient to have 10 – 100 partitioning intervals to ensure it is usually obtained results with satisfactory precision. Increase in computational complexity most highly by ten thousand amounts while it has relatively low number of expert estimations does not represent invincible problem for existing high-performance computer technology. On the other hand the process time is significantly extended when more detailed resolution is requested. Received estimations are trustworthier than in the case when experts are required to provide us with only one estimated value.

Further information regarding aggregation of crisp and fuzzy expert estimations can be found in (Vaníček, Vrana & Aly, 2009).

ESTIMATIONS BASED ON MODELS

Firstly it is necessary to mention one restriction of all of estimations based on a model that is a disadvantage of all commonly used approaches. The basis of this handicap is that the subjective estimations (e.g. evaluation "low – average – high") are given ordinal scale type numbers. The differences between two consequent scale levels may be not the same or may have not equal consequences.

It is generally not possible to prove that the results of this computation with ordinal values have an empirical relevance. The results of these methods are of course dependent on the values assigned to individual levels in the ordinal estimation scale. This proviso could be alleviated if the values for individual ordinal levels would be proportionate to effort. This requires practical evidence on the basis of long-term experience.

Function Points Analysis

IBM Function Points Analysis

The first type of this method was developed by A. Albrecht in the IBM laboratory in the middle of the 1970s, for complexity estimation of IS projects. It was officially published in 1983 (Albrecht & Gaffney, 1983) and the original version was developed for data processing software and mainframes. The IBM Function Points method has become a basis for the design of modifications of the Function Points Analysis described below.

It is generally known that complexity depends not only on functionality. These other factors could only be applied on function point method indirectly.

The system characteristics that are the input for the effort estimation consists of functions crossing IS borders to/from IS, the function could be split into two groups. The first group is known as transactional functions and the second as data functions. There are five items concerned according to Longstreet (Longstreet, 2007):

Data Functions

- **Internal Logical Files** (ILF): a user identifiable group of logically related data that resides entirely within the applications boundary and is maintained through external inputs.
- **External Interface Files** (EIF): a user identifiable group of logically related data that is used for reference purposes only. The data resides entirely outside the application and is maintained by another application. The external interface file is an internal logical file for another application.

Transactional Functions

- **External Inputs (EI)**: is an elementary process in which data crosses the boundary from outside to inside. This data may come from a data input screen or another application. The data may be used to maintain one or more internal logical files. The data can be either control information or business information. If the data is control information it does not have to update an internal logical file.
- **External Outputs (EO)**: an elementary process in which derived data passes across the boundary from inside to outside. Additionally, an EO may update an ILF. The data creates reports or output files sent to other applications. These reports and files are created from one or more internal logical files and external interface file.
- **External Inquiry (EQ)**: an elementary process with both input and output components that result in data retrieval from one or more internal logical files and external interface files. The input process does not update any Internal Logical Files, and the output side does not contain derived data.

IFPUG Function Points Analysis

The first method in a list of the presented modification methods Function Points is known as IFPUG Function Points (IFPUG = International Function Points Users Group). According to the group of authors (IFPUG 2002), who compiled IFPUG, it is the method based on an original concept of the FP method, which was projected in laboratories IBM in the 1970s. The method works like a device for the measurement of a functional value of commercial demands for application software, which is seen from the software user's viewpoint.

The method subsequently comprehends the functional value of the commercial requirements. From the user's view, a formal description of the commercial requirements for a created SW is done through the user's language.

The user's requirements have to be translated into a programming language in order to compile the projection of requirements into the final SW.

This approach based on IFPUG (IFPUG, 1999) implies that the more detailed parts of functionality, which have to be developed, stay hidden for users, for commercial reasons. The simple example is e.g. for a new user it isn't too important, whether the required functionality is ensured by utilization of one processor, or if is distributed on several reciprocally cooperating processors. The user can see only the final functionality and just one value without a view to implementing the next calculations. From this viewpoint the software functionality is, to a certain extent, below the application level unseen by "a standard user", and the next requirement to change it is ignored.

IFPUG Function Points Analysis divides (IFPUG, 2002) the measured IS or it's Functional User Requirement (FUR) into three elementary processes (inputs, outputs and requirements) and two data files (internal logical file and external interface files). Each component is classified by following ordinal scale:

Simple – Average – Complex

It then gets a number of function points according to its complexity depending on a number of data elements, format complexity, users, etc.

The complexity of a simple process depends on the number of data element types per component and the number of files processed. E.g. *simple, average, complex* have 4, 5 and 7 unadjusted function points (*UFP*), respectively.

On the other hand, the complexity of files depends not only on data element types but on record element types as well. E.g. if the rate of an internal logical file is *simple, average* or *complex*, should be equal to 7, 10 or 15 *UFP*, respectively. After totaling the values, the result should be the total *UFP* of software. The total *UFP* is then multiplied by the Value Adjusted Factor. The Value Adjusted Factor is defined by 14 technical and qualitative factors adjusting total function points.

Computation of IFPUG Function Points

A. Systems Characteristics

After the components have been classified as one of the five major components (EI's, EO's, EQ's,

Table 1. EI

Data elements type	**FTR's**		
	0 – 1	2	3 or more
1 – 4	Low	Low	Average
5 – 15	Low	Average	High
> 15	Average	High	High

Table 2. EO and EQ

Data element type	**FTR's**		
	0 – 1	2 – 3	> 3
1 – 5	Low	Low	Average
6 – 19	Low	Average	High
> 19	Average	High	High

Table 3. Values for transactions

Values	**Rating**		
	Low	**Average**	**High**
EO	4	5	7
EQ	3	4	6
EI	3	4	6

ILF's or EIF's), a ranking of low, average or high is assigned. For transactions (EI's, EO's, EQ's) the ranking is based upon the number of files updated or referenced (FTR's) and the number of data element types (DET's). For both ILF's and EIF's files the ranking is based upon record element types (RET's) and data element types (DET's). A record element type is a user recognizable subgroup of data elements within an ILF or EIF. A data element is each user recognizable field (Longstreet, 2007). See Table 1, Table 2, Table 3.

Like all components, EQ's are rated and scored. Basically, an EQ is rated (Low, Average or High) like an EO, but assigned a value like an EI. The rating is based upon the total number of unique (combined unique input and out sides) data elements (DET's) and the file types referenced (FTR's) (combined unique input and output sides).

Table 4. ILF and EIF (Longstreet, 2007)

RET'S	Data elements type		
	1 - 19	20 - 50	> 50
1	Low	Low	Average
2 – 5	Low	Average	High
> 5	Average	High	High

Table 5. Value for transactions (Longstreet, 2007)

Rating	Value	
	ILF	EIF
Low	7	5
Average	10	7
High	15	10

If the same FTR is used on the input and output side, then it is counted only one time. If the same DET is used on the input and output side, then it is only counted one time. For both ILF's and EIF's the number of record element types and the number of data element types are used to determine a ranking of low, average or high. A Record Element Type is a user recognizable subgroup of data elements within an ILF or EIF. A Data Element Type (DET) is a unique user recognizable, non-recursive field on an ILF or EIF (Longstreet, 2007). See Table 4, Table 5.

During a decision on the complexity of each component each category gets a particular value according to its rating (low, average or high) from previous tables. In the next step the number of components in each category are counted, then each number is multiplied by an assigned rating (e.g. for low rating of ILF is used 7), so the result is total value for each type of component. The totals of each component are then summed separately, and then together. Final result is the total number of *UFP*.

B. Value Adjusted Factor (VAF)

To get the value adjustment factor (VAF) it is necessary to

- Evaluate the 14 characteristics below. Each characteristic determines a degree of influence of characteristics in IS design. The evaluation is done on an ordinal scale from 0 (characteristic has no influence) to 5 (characteristic has crucial influence);
- Count values assigned to characteristics;
- Add the count of values to FP formula.

$$VAF = 0.65 + 0.01 \cdot \sum_{i=1}^{14} e_i;\ 0.65 \leq VAF \leq 1.35,$$

where e_i is evaluation of relevant characteristic.

The IFPUG has the following 14 characteristics (Longstreet, 2007):

1. Data communications – how many communication facilities are there to aid in the transfer or exchange of data with the application or another system?
2. Distributed data processing – how are distributed data and processing functions handled?
3. Performance – did the user require response time or throughput?
4. Heavily used configuration – how heavily used is the current hardware platform where the application will be executed?
5. Transaction rate – how frequently are transactions executed daily, weekly, monthly, etc.?
6. On-Line data entry – what percentage of the information is entered On-line?
7. End-user efficiency – was the application designed for end-user efficiency?
8. On-line update – how many ILF's are updated by On-line transactions?
9. Complex processing – does the application have extensive logical or mathematical processing?
10. Reusability – was the application developed to meet one or many user's needs?
11. Installation ease – how difficult is conversion and installation?

12. Operational ease – how effective and/or automated are start-up, back up, and recovery procedures?
13. Multiple sites – was the application specifically designed, developed, and supported to be installed at multiple sites for multiple organizations?
14. Facilitate change – was the application specifically designed, developed, and supported to facilitate change?

C. Total number of Function Points

To get the total number of function points the unadjusted number of Function Points and the value adjusted factor are multiplied

$FP\ (IFPUG) = VAF \cdot UFP.$

COSMICS: FFP

The next modification of original method IBM Function Points come from the Common Software Measurement International Consortium workshop, and is called COSMICS - FFP. It was projected by the authors of the method so that the method represents a concept that is based on so called "view of measurement " (MV), and it offers to the "measurer" a chance for choice. Firstly, it can be used for the measurement of functional format of the measuring viewpoint "a final user", as well as in case of measurement by method IFPUG Function Points. Secondly, it can be used for the measurement of the functional format from the viewpoint of a developing worker.

If a complexity is measured from a measuring viewpoint of "a final user", it can be, according to the authors of the method, a more difficult confrontation with complexity of other IS projects, creating a software by a different way with different technology. For example, if is a software of project *A* developed on a simple basis, while project *B* is developed on more difficult basis by various technologies, and project *C* requires work on a software under an application level. These differences are unseen from measurement view by the final users, and also they don't consider a measure of the size of these working outputs.

So, the COSMIC-FFP method makes use of a developer view instead, which indicates an extra value for each component of a multi-level architecture, and for each single level of multi-level software. These evaluative criteria could be more usable for understanding the function within development and for an evaluation of goals. The values of various measuring points of view should not be compared and also they should not be combined.

The next benefit of using a developer view in combination with COSMIC - FPP is, that all functions which are allocated (equally divided) within the frame of software, are embodied into the measured value.

A measured software or its FUR (Function-User Requirements) is divided according to a functional process in the COSMIC - FPP (ISO/IEC, 2003) method. This functional process is defined as a basic component of a set of user's functionally requirements, involving a unique coherent set of types of data movements (inputs, outputs, reading, logging), which are independently created. This function is activated by one or more types of starting instruction command, either directly IS or indirectly through an actor. The process ends, when everything is done which is required in the types of starting instruction.

The function types of processes are distributed into two type processors (inputs, outputs) or two types of data movements (reading and recording), each with anticipated connected volume of data operation. Inputs and outputs go across an interface between measured software and its users (those could be persons, next parts of software, e.g. some sensor, which communicates with the measured software). Reading moves data from hardware store into a field of measured software, whereas logging sends data an opposite way, which means that data stays on the opposite side of the working process. Each movement is rated by value of one *Cfsu* (COSMICS Functional size unit).

The volume of functional processes is the sum of its data movements, and the total IS size is the sum of all volumes of all processes. The simplest process has a volume 2 *Cfsu* (one input and one output or one record and one reading), but there is no upper limit.

"Back-Fire" Function Points Method

The "backfire" method for Function Points estimation is based on empirical relationships discovered to exist between source code and Function Points in all known languages. This method is based on tables of average values. It is useful for doing retrospective studies of projects completed long ago, and for easing the transition to Function Point measures for people who are familiar with lines-of-code measures.

For selected programming languages, the estimation of the number of lines of code per one Function Point is, according to (Miller & Williams, 2000):

- Assembler 320 LOC/FP
- C 128 LOC/FP
- COBOL 107 LOC/FP
- Ada 70 LOC/FP
- DB Languages 40 LOC/FP
- Object Oriented 29 LOC/FP
- Query Languages 25 LOC/FP
- Generators 16 LOC/FP

Software Tools for Function Points Analysis

A software tool, which enables automatic calculation of Functions Points, is called FP Recorder Lite v2.00. The software was designed by Chipsl (www.chipsl.com) and may be downloaded from their web pages. If the estimator uses the software, his result may be presented in graphical or table format.

Another tool is Function Point Workbench, produced by Charismatek (www.charismatek.com.au). The software is available in commercial and free applications.

These software tools have been chosen as examples from many others, which could improve the computation process. The tools are designed so that users only enter input values and the tool automatically generates the final total Function Points. The user doesn't need to know the FPA computation steps.

Feature Points Method

SPR Feature Points

In 1986, Software Productivity Research (SPR) developed an experimental method for applying Function Point logic to system software such as operating systems, telephone switching systems, and the like. To avoid confusion with the IBM Function Point method, this experimental alternative was called "SPR Feature Points." Since the initial results of using Feature Points have been favorable, the method has been experimentally applied to many kinds of software: systems software, embedded software, real time software, CAD, AI, and even MIS software (SPR, 2002).

Function Points was originally invented to solve the measurement problems of classical Management Information Systems (Jones, 2007). This MIS origin means that Function Points are not necessarily perceived as optimal for the following reasons:

- Real time software, such as missile defense systems;
- Systems software, such as operating systems;
- Embedded software, such as radar navigation packages;
- Communications software, such as telephone switching systems; and

- Process control software, such as refinery drivers.

When Function Points Analysis is applied to such systems, they of course generate counts. However, the counts appear to be misleading for software that is high in algorithmic complexity, but sparse in inputs and outputs. From both a psychological and practical vantage point, these kinds of systems software seem to require a counting method that is equivalent to Function Points, but sensitive to the difficulties brought on by high algorithmic complexity.

The SPR Feature Point metric is a superset of the IBM Function Point metric and introduces a parameter, and algorithms, in addition to the five standard Function Point parameters. The algorithms parameter is assigned a default weight of 3. The Feature Point method also reduces the empirical weights for Logical Data Files from IBM's average value of 10 down to an average value of 7. This reflects the somewhat reduced significance of logical files for systems software *vis a vis* information systems (SPR, 2002).

Computation of SPR Feature Points

The advantage of Feature Points is that the method counts the number of data or transactional functions, but it doesn't evaluate them on an ordinal scale (simple-average-complex). These presumptions evaluate the method faster and more easily than with Function Points Analysis.

A. Unadjusted Feature Points

An unadjusted number of Feature Points is based on the same approach as the previous methods. As by IFPUG Function Points the method counts transactional and data functions. The difference with IFPUG is the number of algorithms. The numbers of EI, EO, EQ, ILF, EIF and Algorithms are multiplied with their weights and then summed. The result is the total Unadjusted Feature Points.

The algorithm has the weight 3, the EI and EQ 4, the EO 5, the ILF and EIF 7.

B. Complexity factor and multiplier

In the next step it is necessary to answer two groups of questions. The first group is concerning with problem complexity and the second with data complexity.

Problem complexity?

- Simple algorithms and simple calculations.
- Simple algorithms and calculations.
- Algorithms and calculations of average complexity.
- Some difficult and complex algorithms.
- Many difficult algorithms and complex calculations.

Data complexity?

- Simple data with few variables.
- Numerous variables, but simple data relationship.
- Multiple file, fields, and data intersections.
- Complex file structures and data intersections.
- Very complex file structures and data intersections.

The two most characteristic questions for a designed IS are chosen after evaluation of all previous questions and their ordinal numbers are counted. According to it a relevant complexity multiplier is chosen from Table 6.

C. Total number of Feature Points

The result of multiplication of the unadjusted Feature Points and the complexity multiplier should be the total number of Feature Points:

$$FP(SPR) = FC \cdot CoM.$$

Table 6. Complexity multiplier (SPR, 2002)

Sum of Problem and Data complexity	Complexity Multiplier (CoM)
2	0.6
3	0.7
4	0.8
5	0.9
6	1
7	1.1
8	1.2
9	1.3
10	1.4

Software Tools for Feature Points

A tool for Feature Points is designed by SPR and is named SPR Knowledge Plan. The big advantage of the tool is its project database that contains more than 11,000 various projects. An estimator could compare his project results with results of other similar projects. It can be said that the tool combines Feature Points and analogy approaches.

Use Case Points

Concept of Method

The method was developed by Gustav Karner in 1993. The author was inspired by IBM Function Points that has been described above, and applied similar approaches with benefit.

The Use Case diagrams could be simply used for complexity estimations of software design and it's testing, according to Karner. The understandability of Use Case diagrams, their relationships and actors' roles is very important for UCP application.

Similarly to the initial IFPUG Function Points, the estimation is based on two inputs:

1. From the complexity of functionality requirements for the system. This is expressed by the number of actors and use cases and its complexity. The result is called "Unadjusted Use Case Points"
2. From the evaluation of conditions for the project realization – so-called correction factors. Two groups of conditions are proposed: The technical factor and the environment factor. If these conditions are conventional, these factors will be equal to one, and after multiplying by factors the effort will be preserved. In case of the favorable conditions the factors will be less then one and the resulting effort after multiplying will be less than the result from functional complexity. In the case of unfavorable conditions the factors will be greater than one and the effort increases. The recommended principle is to adjust each of two factors in the interval from 0.6 – 0.7 to 1.3 – 1.4. This range is of course a heuristic only, based on the author's opinion and expert's assessments. The authors of the chapter recommend adjusting the choice of factors, their weights and the range of their influence to the effort, depending on the individual experiences of the company or software development teams.

After multiplying the Unadjusted Use Case Points by the correction factors, the Adjusted Use Case Points are multiplied by the Productivity factor. This factor is of the different nature. It is not a correction factor, but represents the amount of effort necessary for the realization of Adjusted Use Case Point.

The computation procedure of UCP is, according to Karner (Karner, 1993), as follows:

- Unadjusted Use Case Points
  - Unadjusted actor weight (An actor specifies a role played by a user or any other system that interacts with the subject (OMG, 2007)). Unadjusted Use Case weight (A Use Case Diagram is a specialization of

Class Diagrams such that the classifiers shown are restricted to being either Actors or Use Cases (OMG, 2007)).

- Technical factor.
- Environment factor.
- Productivity factor.

Unadjusted Use Case Points (UUCP)

The chapter will describe and explain the method computation, step-by-step (Figure 2).

A. Unadjusted Actor Weights (UAW)

The UCP is based on a presumption that actors are external objects, which have a mutual relationship. The most common examples are end-users, other programs, data warehouses, etc. All actors should be described in project documentation by their Use Case.

Actors are divided into three categories

Simple – Average – Complex.

A simple actor – represents another system with a defined application programming interface.
An average actor – either another system that your system is interfacing to via a protocol or a text based user interface. Average actors interact with the system through some protocols (such as http, TCP/IP, etc.) or this type of actor could be a data store. These types of actors qualify as average since the results of test case runs might need to be verified manually by running SQL statements on the store, verifying timing information for the protocol transfer, etc.
A complex actor – person interacting via a graphical interface (end-users are often referred to as complex actors).

After determining the number of actors, you have to weight them. A simple user has a factor of 1, an average user has a factor of 2, and a complex user has a factor of 3. These are called weighting factors and the sum of these products gives the total unadjusted actor weights. So, the total *uaw* is calculated by counting the number of actors in each category, multiplying each total by its specified weighting factor, and then adding the products.

B. Unadjusted Use Case Weights (UUCW)

Definition of number of Use Case is the second step. The use cases should be assigned weights depending on the number of transactions and/or scenarios.

Transactions are defined as a basic set of activities that are performed all over or not at all. The categorization distinguished number of transactions in Use Case.

Right now the method weighs the use cases. First use cases are divided into following categories.

Simple – Average – Complex.

The basis of the categorization is how many transactions they contain, where a transaction is defined as an indivisible set of activities that are either performed entirely or not at all. For a simple user, the description is usually less than or equal to three transactions and the factor is 5. For an average user, the description is usually four to seven transactions, and the factor is 10. For the complex user, the description is usually greater than seven transactions and the factor is 15.

The unadjusted use case weights are calculated counting the number of use cases in each category, multiplying each category of use case with its weight, and adding them.

C. Unadjusted Use Case Points (uucp)

The unadjusted actor weights from the first step, and unadjusted use case weights (*uucw*) from the second step are counted to get unadjusted use case points (*uucp*).

$$uucp = uaw + uucw.$$

Figure 2. UCP computation scheme (Struska, 2006)

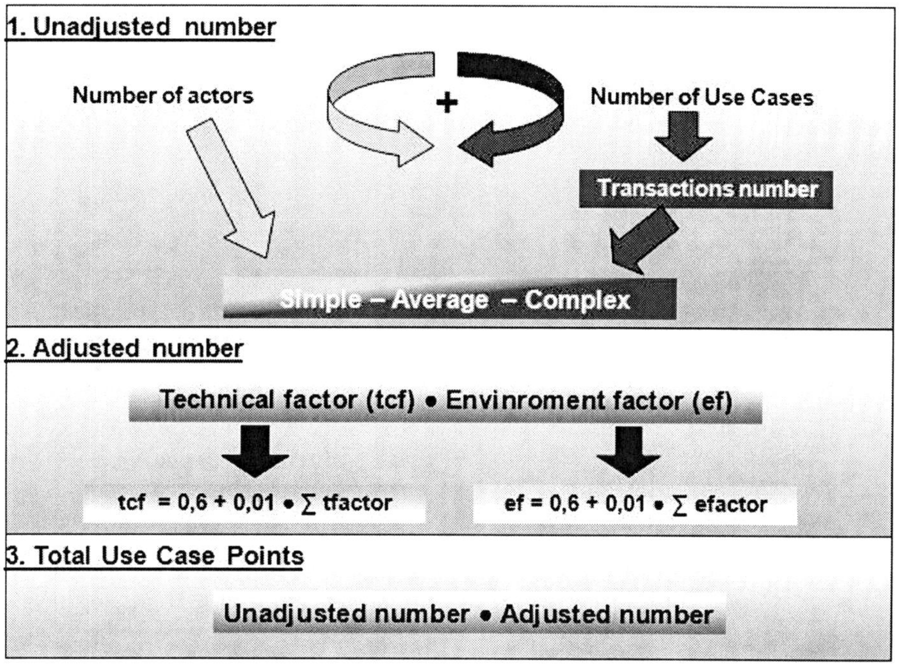

Technical Factor

It is necessary to count the technical factors to get the total number of complexity estimations. The technical factor represents technical characteristics of the designed IS. It consists of 13 sub-factors, which are evaluated on an ordinal scale from 0 to 5. If a sub-factor is zero, it means that sub-factor has no influence with the designed IS; a sub-factor with 5 has high influence with designed IS.

With the weight 2:

- Distributed system.
- Portable.

With the weight 1:

- Response time or throughput performance objectives.
- End user efficiency.
- Complex internal processing.
- Code must be reusable.
- Easy to change.
- Concurrent.
- Includes special security objectives.
- Provides direct access for third parties.
- Special user training facilities are required.

With the weight 0.5:

- Easy to install.
- Easy to use.

The technical complexity factor (*tcf*) is calculated by multiplying the value of each sub-factor by its weight, and then adding all these numbers to get the sum called the *tFactor*. This factor is calculated from the following formula

$$tcf = 0.6 + 0.01 \cdot tFactor; \; 0.65 \leq tcf \leq 1.35.$$

Environment Factor

Employees' experience and knowledge has an influence with complexity estimation as well.

An environment factor includes these facts. The evaluation procedure is same as for the technical factor. First 8 sub-factors are evaluated on a scale 0 – 5 (0 – sub-factors with no influence, 5 – the most crucial sub-factors).

With the weight 2:

- Stable requirements (e_6).

With the weight 1,5:

- Familiar with the project model that is used (e_1).

With the weight 1:

- Object-oriented experience (e_3).
- Motivation (e_5).

With the weight 0.5:

- Application experience (e_2).
- Lead analyst capability (e_4).

With the weight –1:

- Part time staff (e_7).
- Difficult programming language (e_8).

Every sub-factor need not be evaluated in every case, but it is important to choose these, which are most characteristic for evaluated, IS, they get the highest value – 5.

The environment complexity factor (*tcf*) is calculated by multiplying the value of each sub-factor by its weight, and then adding all these numbers to get the sum called the *eFactor*. The factor is calculated from the following formula

$$\boldsymbol{ecf = 1.4 - 0.03 \cdot eFactor;}\ 0.575 \leq ecf \leq 1.4.$$

Productivity Factor

The number of man-hours per one UCP is different according to dependences on various influences (experience of programmers, size of designed IS, etc.), it means that everybody could modify the factors in this model to work better in your own projects. The recommended value of productivity factor proposed by Karner (Karner, 1993) is twenty man-hours per one *aucp*. If estimators are not satisfied with Karner's number, they could use a simple rule which enables one to set up their own coefficients in intervals recommended for a project.

Karner defines the productivity factor between fifteen and thirty-six man-hours per one *aucp*. It is based on a simple presumption of factor productivity value, which is simply calculated from weights assigned to individual sub-factors of environment factor. The calculation provides individual numbers of productivity factor for a specific company.

The number of factors in the range e1 through e6 that are below 3 are counted and added to the number of factors in the range e7 through e8 that are above 3. If the total is 2 or less, the general idea is to use twenty staff hours per UCP. If the total is 3 or 4, use twenty-eight staff hours per UCP. If the number exceeds 5, it is usually recommended that changes should be made to the project so the number can be adjusted because, in this case, the risk is unacceptably high. Another possibility is to increase the number of staff hours to thirty-six per use case point.

Total UCP

All the method parts described above are used to get the total adjusted use case points (*aucp*), which is the result of multiplication of unadjusted number, technical and environment factors.

$$\boldsymbol{aucp = uucp \cdot tcf \cdot ecf.}$$

The result of the previous formula is a number. To get an effort *aucp* has to be multiplied with productivity factor (number of man-hour per one use case).

Effort = aucp·pf.

Software Tools for UCP

There are many tools, which enable automatic complexity estimation of UCP, for example Enterprise Architect, which has a toll called Project estimation. The software module enables automatic complexity estimation during IS analysis.

BORM Points Method

The proposed concept of BORM Points (BORMp) is based on the calculation of Use Case Points (Struska & Pergl, 2006). The Use Case Points is a method known worldwide, and is used for complexity estimation of information systems. Proposed BORM Points use some parts of Use Case Points which are useful for BORM methodology. See Figure 3.

The BORM method is oriented on the support of pure object-oriented programming languages and development environment software systems design which are, for example, the Smalltalk environment, and non-relational object databases. BORM is not only applicable for software design, but for requirement analysis of planned system and business process modeling.

The BORM method covers two levels of information system proposal – business analysis of IS and conceptual analysis of IS. Business analysis is concerned about current and future processes mapping that are described by functions, scenarios, architectures and business diagrams. Conceptual analysis reassumes on the results of business analysis so that it transforms a business model into programmers' submissions, which are described by objects and classes diagram, software objects diagram and software component diagram. Further reading can be found in (Knott, Merunka & Polák, 2003).

The new BORM Points parts are designed to eliminate some known disadvantages of Use Case Points. The authors of this chapter think that one of them is the small concentration of the Use Case Point method to the role of the customer during system development. The influence of customers and their requirements can essentially influence project complexity.

BORM points try to estimate the complexity on the basis of chosen components, which are characteristic for BORM. The calculation is divided into two independent parts. In the first step the number of participants and the number of business diagrams is counted. The second step consists of technical, environment and customer factors evaluation.

Business diagrams provide information about transactions between activities and states and about communication that are transmitted between engaged participants.

The proposed calculation of complexity estimation using BORMp is divided into two steps, to separate the unadjusted number that comes from the reality model and technical, environmental and customer factors that represent external influences on the system development.

The principle well proven in Use Case Point is used. The difference is in the number of factors that can correct the effort estimation calculated from functionality requirements only, which may raise or decrease the effort estimation, from two to three. The new view was added depending on the customer's role in the system development. Based on the author's experiences this role has a vital influence to the necessary effort and therefore has to be taken into account. The suggested computation diagram is similar to that in Use Case Points.

As in the previous method, it has to be mentioned that the choice of factors, their weights and the range of their influence to the effort, is based only on heuristic consideration. It is recommend-

Figure 3. BORMp computation scheme (Struska, 2006)

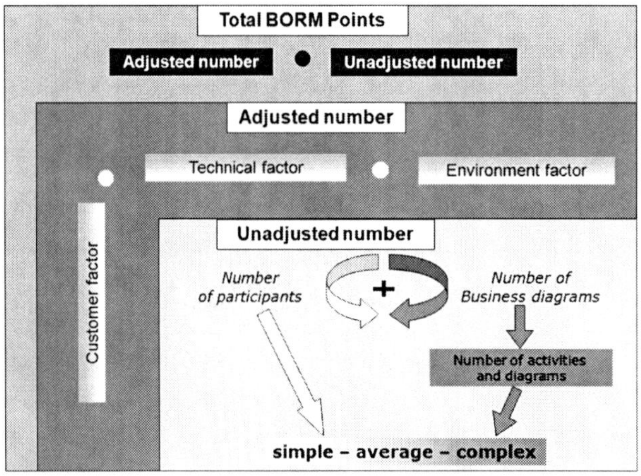

able to maintain the factor choice, it weights and range of its influence depending on the individual experiences of the company or software development teams.

The unadjusted number is computed in the first step. In the second step individual technical, environmental and customer factors are computed:

- Unadjusted part of BORM points
  - Number of participants
  - Number of business diagrams.
- Technical factor,
- Environment factor,
- Customer factor,
- Productivity factor.

Unadjusted BORMp Part

The first part divides the count in the next two parts, as was mentioned above. This separation represents a clear specification of number of participants and business diagrams. The unadjusted part is directly connected with designed information system.

A. Unadjusted Participant Weights: UPW
The participants are external objects that have some sort of relationship with the modeling system. They may be the system users, cooperating users, other software systems, etc. Participants should be described in the project documentation.

It is thus necessary to identify business diagrams related directly to the designed information system. Business diagrams get complexity weight according to their number of activities and/or transactions.

The business diagrams are divided into the following three categories:

Simple – Average – Complex.

A simple participant – systems with automated interface to the measured system (e.g. standard applications (or API)).
An average participant – systems (such as data warehouse) connected to the measured system by a protocol (e.g. TCP/IP) or through a user interface.
A complex participant – participants cooperating with the system through a manual interface (mostly final users).

After determining the number of participants, one has to weight them. A simple participant has a factor of 1, an average participant has a factor of 2, and a complex participant has a factor of 3.

These are called weighting factors and the sum of these products gives the total unadjusted actor weights. So, total *upw* is calculated counting the number of actors in each category, multiplying each total by its specified weighting factor, and then adding the products.

B. Unadjusted Business Diagram Weights: UBDW

The BORM method is used for a wide area of process mapping (including IT analysis). It is thus necessary to identify business diagrams related directly to the designed information system. Business diagrams get their complexity weight according to the number of activities and/or transactions.

Simple – Average – Complex.

The next criteria are the communication number between individual activities of participants, and the number of transactions between states and activities by all engaged participants in the business diagram at the same time. These two numbers are counted and used like the second evaluative factor with lower priority. In the situation where the communications are out of the interval, it is recommended to decide according to activities number.

The basis of the categorization is how many activities they contain, where an activity is defined as an indivisible set of activities, which are either performed entirely or not at all. For a simple user, the description is usually less than or equal to three transactions, and the factor is 5. For an average user, the description is usually four to seven transactions, and the factor is 10. For the complex user, the description is usually greater than seven transactions and the factor is 15.

C. Unadjusted Bump

Total unadjusted Bump is the sum of the unadjusted participant weight (*up*) and the unadjusted business diagram weight (*bud*) described above.

unadjusted BORMp (uBORMp) = upw + ubdw.

Adjusted BORMp Part

The adjusted part of BORMp revises the exact result provided by the unadjusted part. Adjusted factors are selected so that they should cover all influences that may have impact on the complexity of the developed IS.

The adjusted part consists of three factors. Two of them come from UCP and one factor is newly introduced. It was designed based on UCP analysis and identification of its weaknesses. The technical factor is completely shared with UCP and the environmental factor is partly modified. The new factor is the "Customer factor". The customer factor takes into consideration the influence of the customer on the project complexity. The customers usually have some sort of influence on the IS complexity and the aim of customer factor is to reflect this influence.

The BORMp is an original method, whose main developer is one of this chapter's authors. The following paragraphs introduce individual factors, their components, sub-factors, developed weights and coefficients.

A. Technical Factor

The technical factor consists of 13 sub-factors that specify the technical aspects of designed information system. The evaluation scale is 0 to 5. A sub-factor with no influence gets 0; the most crucial sub-factor gets 5.

It is important to carefully assign suitable weights to individual sub-factors according to their expected impact on the designed IS. The technical factor consists of the following sub-factors:

With the weight 2:

- Distributed system – complexity of distributed IS architecture (if IS runs on more computers).

- Portable – IS portability to other platforms and environments.

With the weight 1:

- Response time or throughput performance objectives – performance requirements factors.
- End user efficiency – how effective must the system be the response time or the tournament time for the user interaction,
- Complex internal processing – complexity of external processing.
- Code must be reusable – usability of the whole or part of code for programming of other applications or their parts.
- Easy to change – complexity level of the changes of the system.
- Concurrent – aspects of possible parallel development of individual system parts.
- Includes special security objectives – alignment to special security requirements.
- Provides direct access for third parties – level of third parties access support and related aspects.
- Special user training facilities are required – influence of special training needs.

With the weight 0.5:

- Easy to install – the system installation complexity.
- Easy to use – users' learnability and understandability.

BORMp introduces the same sub-factors of the technical factor as UCP. These sub-factors cover well the technical area of software development. The sub-factors with high impact on the project should be identified and evaluated with the highest weight. The assigned values (0-5) are multiplied with the sub-factor weights and then summed. The technical factor (*tFactor*) is computed this way; next it is used in the following formula – the technical complexity factor (*tcf*):

$\boldsymbol{tcf = 0.65 + 0.01 \cdot tFactor}$; $0.65 \leq tcf \leq 1.35$.

B. Environment Factor

The environment is understood in BORMp from the viewpoint of the supplier, and that is the reason why supplier's employee skills, used equipments or methods are evaluated in the software development project. These influences are covered by the environmental factor. The evaluation is the same as for the technical factor. Firstly 8 sub-factors are evaluated by weights from 0 to 5 (0 – no influence, 5 – the most considerable influence).

The environment factor contains following sub-factors and their definitions:

With the weight 1.5:

- Familiar with the development process – level of employee knowledge of the methodology used for project development.

With the weight 1:

- Object-oriented experience – employee knowledge of object-oriented environment.
- Motivation – level of motivation to complete the project in time and in costs.

With the weight 0.5:

- Application experience – level of employee knowledge of tools that are used for IS development (for modeling, developing, etc.).
- Lead analyst capability – capability of the lead analyst including the capacity that he can dedicate to the estimated project.

With the weight –1:

- Part-time staff – number of part-time employees working on the project.
- Difficult programming language – complexity of programming language(s).

The procedure is the same as in the case of the technical factor. The evaluated sub-factors with assigned values are multiplied with sub-factors weights and then summed to give the total environment factor (*eFactor*). This factor is used in the environmental complexity factor (*ecf*).

ecf*=1,3 – 0.02** · ***eFactor; $0.65 \leq ecf \leq 1.3$.

C. Customer Factor

Customer factor is a new view on the software development process incorporated in the BORMp estimation. Its aim is to reflect the impact of customer requirements to the project. As was mentioned above, uncoordinated customer requirements may significantly affect the efforts of information system development.

The procedure of the factor evaluation is the same as for the technical and the environmental factors. Six customer sub-factors are evaluated by the weights 0–5 (0 – no influence, 5 – the most considerable influence).

Customer factor has following sub-factors:
With the weight 2:

- Customer's project manager capacity – capacity, which the customer's project manager could dedicate to the project.
- Connection with existing IT projects – relation to other IS projects.

With the weight 1.5:

- Customer's project members' capacity – capacity, which the project team members could dedicate to the project.
- Complexity of replaced IS – in the case that the new system should replace an old one.

With the weight 1:

- Balance of requirements – customer ability to identify and communicate requirements and their expected changes.

With the weight 0.5:

- Knowledge of IS – level of IT knowledge of customer's project team.
- Knowledge of project organization – understanding of the project organization and time schedule.

The sub-factors values are multiplied by their weights and then summed. The result is the total customer factor (*cFactor*), which is used to determine the customer complexity factor (*ccf*):

ccf*=0.65 + 0.015** · ***cFactor; $0.65 \leq ccf \leq 1.37$.

Productivity factor

The productivity factor is an important input for methods of complexity estimation. It is a recommended number of man-hours per one BORM point depending on various influences (e.g. experience of project team, size of the developed IS, etc.).

The value of the productivity factor is set to 30 man-hours per one BORMp according to expert estimation. Because of the customer factor, the value is set higher than for UCP (20 man-hours per use-case).

Total BORMp

The above computed values are connected by one formula adjusted BORMp – *aBORMp* that counts the result of the adjusted BORMp. The formula consists of the unadjusted part (the participant and the business diagram numbers) and the technical, the environmental and the customer factor:

$$aBORMp = uBORMp \cdot tcf \cdot ecf \cdot ccf.$$

The complexity is now specified by a non-dimensional number, which is the result of the aBORMp formula. To get the actual effort it is necessary to multiply the adjusted BORMp by the productivity factor:

$$Effort = aBORMp \cdot pf.$$

RELATIONSHIP BETWEEN SOFTWARE COMPLEXITY AND DEVELOPMENT EFFORT: COCOMO MODEL AND ITS VARIANTS

The input of all kinds of function point methods is data, which is received as an output of analysis of the system life cycle stage. It is the phase, in which task specifications, solved within the project, are available. The specification deals with formalized requirements for product functionality. This data are part of documents, which are created in the specification. The specific names and content of documents, from which this data can be received, are varying depending on the methodology used for the development and the type of task being solved.

The output of all kinds of function point methods is in fact strictly speaking not directly the effort, but the volume of the final software. The volume is generally expressed as a "Modified number" of source code rows. Modification of this number represents inclusion of a range of different factors. It can significantly change the real number of physical source code rows. The example is contained in the following list with three such important factors. The enumeration is certainly not complete:

- Programming language or CASE tool, in which is implemented a code. Different programming languages environments may require a significantly different number of code rows for implementation of the same function.
- Algorithm complexity is measured by suitable parameters of flow graph (for example whether the imperative code is structured or not, using the McCabe flow graph measure, context analysis of the code, deepness of structured constructions nesting, etc.)
- Special requirements for other quality parameters of final software, for example increased requirement for reliability, data security, collaboration and compatibility with other software products, easy usability (intuitive user interface), efficiency (short response or low requirements of computer storage size), easy maintainability (changeability), portability to another software or hardware environment. It is recommended taking into consideration the requirements for particular quality parameters of software in compliance with International standards ISO/IEC 9126-1 and ISO/IEC 25000 and ISO/IEC 25010.

At the first sight this volume is expressed in modified numbers of code rows appropriate to the effort needed for its creation – effort of its realization, expressed in man-days, man-months or man-years of work of employees, and implicitly in costs of development, expressed in money units. The experience confirms that it is approximately applicable only to relatively small tasks, which can be assigned to one solver, who finishes the task in a short time. Most projects undertaken at present are large-scale and complex.

The work effort is not additive for large scale mutually interrelated systems. A double-size complex project requires more work effort than the sum of the efforts of two separate projects of the half size.

The reason is that, if one employee solves the large-scale project, the number of decisions he has to adopt increases non-linearly with the scale of project. Besides this, it also increases with the difficulty of every decision, because the solver has to take into consideration all other circumstances and aspects, which could depend on the project as a whole. Therefore every particular decision regarding some specific question is more and more difficult. If the task is divided into several smaller tasks and delegates these tasks to different employees or teams, then every particular task is more transparent, but on the other hand new supplementary tasks are emerging. Additional work effort must be spent on the interface definition between particular tasks, monitoring and division of testing phase into local testing and global testing phases. This additional effort depends on cohesion and coupling of partial modules and the number of relationships between them. The number of relationships grows quadratically with respect to the number of tasks, on the condition that every module is able to communicate with each other. In the case of hierarchical level architecture, this number grows linearly. In both cases, when assigning a large-scale task to one solver (team) or dividing a task into several smaller and transparent tasks, the work effort of the large-scale projects is increasing.

After some attempts to find the most trustworthy relationship between volume and work effort of software product development, it showed that this relationship is best described by the "COnstructive COst Model", which is also known by the abbreviation COCOMO (Boehm, 1981).

The first COCOMO formula says

$$E=a\cdot V^{\beta},$$

where E is effort expressed in man-days, V is volume expressed in thousands modified code rows and $a > 0$ a $b > 1$ are constants. This formula is not applicable for small software projects, which have less than a thousand source code rows. The dependency of effort on volume is linear. In the final work effort, the solution design is included based on requirements described in the tasks specification, software implementation and testing activities, until the software is released and deployed. The maintenance is not included. The effort of maintenance not only depends on the scale of the software, but also on the number of users and the frequency of change requests, as a result of subsequent requirements for further development of the product, and because of changes to the environment, in which the product is used.

The constant $b > 1$ ensures superadditivity of work effort in reference to volume. Its value determines the slope of work effort growth in large-scale projects. It depends on project parameters, but especially on the chosen design methodology and software realization. In the case of spontaneous software development, about fifty or sixty years ago, $b = 2$ was considered the theoretical value. Soon after was the value decreased to $b = 1.5$. Manager methods of software creation, and mainly object paradigm of software development, decreased this value. It is predicted the value will also decrease in future. Nowadays, an interval of $b \in <1.05; 1.2>$ is considered an appropriate value, depending on the type of software. An exception exists with projects with extreme requirements for time efficiency, reliability or security, for example, in the case of software used for cosmic flights, weapons system, etc.

The constant $a > 0$ determines the number of man-days needed for the design, implementation and testing of modified thousands rows of source code of small programs (up to one thousand rows). For well-managed teams, which use hard methodology of software development, the value of this constant is estimated as the interval $b \in <30; 55>$. The range is relatively large. It depends on the type of project (unique project, or type of project for which the solving team has sufficient experience), professional skills and experience of the team, and many other factors. In the long-term the best case is, when the software company watches the scales and costs of projects undertaken, and from the received experience continuously corrects the constants in the COCOMO formula.

The COCOMO model also makes available another very important estimation for software development planning. It is the estimation of minimum time, in which the software project can be undertaken at reasonable costs (at costs estimated by the first COCOMO formula). But the presumption of validity of this second COCOMO formula is that the necessary number of employees is available. This presumption cannot be easily attainable in real conditions. The estimation results come out from the fact that when a company has enough employees, the project time cannot increase linearly depending on task scale. However, it can never be constant. In each project some time exists which cannot be further reduced by adding another team capacity. Each attempt to shorten the project time leads to enormous growth of costs, and it is not further possible to get under some specific limitation even if it would be content with the waste of workforce.

The second COCOMO formula estimates the relationship between the volume of the software project V (again in modified thousand of source code rows) and the shortest "reasonable" time T_{opt} necessary for its realization (design, implementation and testing), expressed as a number of months. It has again (for $V \geq 1$) the formula:

$$T_{opt}=c \cdot V^d.$$

Nowadays the value of exponent d is estimated in interval $c \in$ <0.32; 0.38> and coefficient c in surroundings of value 2.5. The specific choice depends again on the type of project and the experience of individual team members. Dependency *Topt* on V is therefore always subadditive. It is an increasing function, which increases less slow then linear functions.

Increase of costs during attempts to reduce the realization time below the value *Topt* tries to estimate the "Putnam's principle", or the SLIM formula. They both can be referred to heuristics and are based on some practical experience more than on a serious theoretical foundation. They agree on the fact that the increase of cost while reducing time below the value *Topt* in relation to costs estimated on the basis of the first COCOMO formula, increase with power of fourth of ratio of shortened time to value *Topt.* It means that, by reducing the time by 10% the costs increase by half, and when reducing the time by 20% the costs increase three times. Further reduction of the time is entirely unrealistic.

In many COCOMO model variants used at present it is recommended to adjust the work effort estimation on the basis of factors which take into consideration some additional requirements for software product and circumstances, on which the software is realized. Each view of such a factor describes a requirement or circumstance that influences the work consumption. If the influence of this view is neutral, the factor will be 1. If the view makes the realization easier, the respective factor will be less than 1, and the resulting work effort will be lower after multiplying the value by the factor. On the contrary, if the respective view makes realization more difficult, the factor will be greater than 1 and the final work effort will be higher. The specific choice depends on what the significant influence has on work effort. While choosing factors it is necessary not to forget anything important, however be careful to ensure that every view was counted only once and not more. It is necessary to realize that if the input for COCOMO is the range determined on the basis of the realized product, the range of factors was included during recalculation of the existing number of source code rows to the modified number. Besides that, some views were taken into consideration during the choice of particular coefficient values *a, b, c, d,* in the COCOMO formulas within the given intervals.

If the development work effort was estimated in an early life cycle phase, after analysis and on the basis of document specification and by usage of some variant of function point method, the range of factors was taken into consideration within the volume estimation on the basis of appropriate inputs. During the estimation of development complexity, that means that the software volume is an even number of points, received on the basis of functional requirements, multiplied by factors, which already reflects many of these views. Double inclusion of the same item during a two-stage method to estimate work effort in the early life cycle is a frequent error.

Practical experience shows that COCOMO formula, which estimates the work effort on the basis of software volume, is relatively accurate. After tuning coefficient values, they provide estimations with deviation up to ±10%. If the estimation is made in the early phases of the lifecycle, it is necessary to combine this deviation with an error of appropriate variant of function point method.

Estimations of work effort, created on the basis of projection complexity of software volume by the help of more sophisticated formulas, do not provide better estimations. It can be confirmed not only by practical experience, but also theoretically. Both the projection complexity (volume in modified number of source code rows) and work effort (man-days, man-months, man-years, eventually cost on development in appropriate money unit) and also realization time (days, months, years) are measured in a ratio scale type. It can be proved by a mathematic sentence (Roberts, 1979), who stated that two ratio scale type measures μ a η of the same attribute x can be only in relationship

$$\eta(x)=\alpha\cdot\mu(x)^{\beta},$$

where $\alpha > 0$ and $\beta > 0$ are suitable real numbers. In case the scale and work effort are attributes of a product, where one attribute unambiguously depends on the second, it is already not reasonable to find their mutual dependency different to that shown by the COCOMO formulas. The only possibility to obtain a precise estimation is to find the most suitable values of a, b, c and d constants in these formulas.

CURRENT CHALLENGES FACING THE ORGANIZATION

It is vitally important to have on time the estimations of work effort and costs, which are related to software development. It significantly decreases the number of unsuccessful projects, which cannot be finished with satisfactory results, because there are no longer any available human and financial resources. Estimations enable timely cancellation of project, where it is predicted that costs of implementation surpasses potential project benefits. For all other projects estimations enable planning of human and financial resources needed for project realization. For made-to-measure software the cost estimation forms the main basis of price negotiation. This activity has to be concluded before the beginning of development. Every responsible company, which develops software, needs to deal with cost estimations. Data about estimation methods concerning their success rate is difficult to obtain. Companies, which develop software solutions, do not publish relevant data for obvious reasons. It considers them to be valuable know-how.

For these reasons the companies have to significantly rely on experience of their own experts specialized in particular phases of IS development. Expert knowledge is the most important part of human factors. The comparison of estimations and real costs on development enriches knowledge of company and causes the future estimations are more precise.

SOLUTIONS AND RECOMMENDATIONS

At present the estimation accuracy of software product development made immediately after finishing product requirements analysis is estimated on average at ±30%. Estimations with a deviation of ±15% are considered to be very successful. These positive results are attained mostly at experienced software houses, which apply hard-standardized methods of development. More detailed information is difficult to obtain because of the above-mentioned reasons.

For choice of a particular way to receive estimation, it is necessary to follow the principles below:

1. For each method it is necessary to have resources, tools and data inputs. It means while using analogy, on the other it is necessary to have a sufficient experience and knowledge base, which comprises previous projects solved by solver team. While using expert estimations, it is necessary to have enough qualified and independent solvers; while using estimations based on the model it utilizes outputs of the previous phase of software life cycle. It is not possible to construct high-quality estimations on the basis of untrustworthy data.
2. While using estimations on the basis of a model in the early phases of development that means after requirements analysis and definition of software requirements. Clear and preferably formalized inputs for estimation have to be available for defining the required functions. This input varies, depending on the methodology. The choice of appropriate variant of function point method depends on the method used for analysis.
3. The cost of estimation has to be appropriate to its intended use. It is not effective to spend money on further estimation corrections, which do not influence decision-making. Doing "estimations for estimation" should be avoided.

Although the error rate of estimations is not minor, it cannot be predicted that in the near future methods for significantly more precise estimations will become available. In the early phases of software life cycle, the estimation with its predicted accuracy is invaluable for management decision-making.

Correct estimations reduce the number of projects failure and enable save money on the IS development. It directly influences the amount of public expenses on system implementation and increase comfort for grass roots.

ACKNOWLEDGMENT

The authors wish to thank the Czech Ministry of Education for support of this work by the Grant No. MSM 6046070904 "Information and knowledge support of strategic control" and Grant No.2C06004 "Intelligent tools for content assessment of relevance of general and specialized data and knowledge resources".

REFERENCES

Albrecht, A. J. & Gaffney, J. E., Jr. (1983). Software Functions, Source Line of Code and Development Effort Prediction: A Software Science Validation. *IEEE Transactions on Software Engineering (TSE) 9*(6), London, United Kingdom: IEEE Computer Society.

Boehm, B. W. (1981). *Software Engineering Economics*. Englewood Cliffs, USA: Prentice Hall.

Fenton, N. E., & Pfleeger, S. K. (1998). *Software Metrics: A Rigorous and Practical Approach (Revised 2nd edition)*. New York: PWS Publishing Company.

Hájek, P. (2000). *Mathematics of Fuzy Logic.* Dordrecht, Niederlanden: Kluwer.

International Function Point Users Group. (1999). *Fucntion Pointss Counting Practices Manual – Release 4.1.* Wisconsin, USA: International Function Points Users.

International Function Points Users Group. (2002). *IT Measurement PractialAdvice from the Experts.* Reading, MA: Addison-Wesley.

ISO/IEC 19761 (2003). Information technology - Software measurement - Functional size measurement - Part 6: Guide for use of ISO/IEC 14143 series and related International Standards. JTC 1/SC 7. International standard.

ISO/IEC 24765 (2008). - Systems and software engineering vocabulary. International standard.

Jones, C. (2007). *Estimating Software Costs.* New York: McGraw-Hill.

Jorgensen, M., & Sjoberg, D. (2004): The Impact of Customer Expectation on Software Development Effort Estimates. *Simula Research Laboratory,* Retrieved June 20, 2005, from http://simula.no/research/engineering/publications/SE.4.Joergensen.2004.b/?searchterm=The%20Impact%20of%20Customer%20Expectation%20on%20Software%20Development%20Effort%20Estimates

Knott, R. P., Merunka, V., & Polák, J. (2000). Process Modeling for Object Oriented Analysis using BORM Object Behavioral Analysis, *Fourth International Conference on Requirements Engineering ICRE 2000.* (pp. 7 – 18), Chicago: Computer Society Press.

Longstreet, D. (2007). *Function Points Analysis Training Course,* Retrieved May 22, 2009, from http://www.softwaremetrics.com/Function%20Point%20Training%20Booklet%20New.pdf

OMG. (2007). *OMG Unified Modeling Language (OMG UML),* Superstructure, V2.1.2, 585-603. Retrieved April 1. 2008. from http://www.omg.org/docs/formal/07-11-02.pdf

Roberts, F. S. (1979). *Measurement Theory with Applications decisionmaking, Utility, and Social Sciences.* Reading, MA: Addison-Wesley Publishing Company.

Software Productivity Research – SPR. (2002). *Counting Rules for Function Points and Feature Points,* Retrieved January 3, 2005, from http://www.spr.com

Struska, Z. (2007). *The concept comparison of BORMp method with Use Case Points.* Paper presented at the International Conference on Software Engineering Theory and Practice (SETP-07). Orlando, USA.

Struska, Z., & Pergl, R. (2009). *BORM Points: Introduction and results of practical testing. Enterprise Information Systems.* Proceeding from ICEIS 2009, 590-599. Heidelberg, Germany: Springer Verlag.

Taste, W., J. & Wierman, M. J. (2007). Consensus and dissention: A measure of ordinal dispersion. *International Journal of Approximate Reasoning, 45,* 531–545. doi:10.1016/j.ijar.2006.06.024

FURTHER READING

Choppy, C. (2004). Improving Use-Case Based Requirements. *FASE – Fundamental Approaches to Software Engineering, 2002,* 244-261.

Edwards, R. (2007). Advantages of the COSMICS-FPP method. *IFPUG Bulletin.* Retrieved July 20, 2007, from www.cosmicson.com/advantagecs.asp

Garmus, D., & Herron, D. (2001). *Function Points analysis: measurement practices for successful software project.* Upper Saddle River, NJ: Addison Wesley.

Gottwald, S. (1993). *Fuzzy Sets and Fuzzy Logic*. Toulouse, Spain: Friedr. Vieweg & Sohn.

Gottwald, S. (1993). *Einführung in Fuzzy-Methoden*. Berlin: Academie Verlag.

Hájek, P. (2000). *Mathematics of Fuzzy Logic*. Dordrecht, Germany: Kluver.

Hoffman, D. (2000). *The darker side of metrics*. Software Quality Methods, LLC. Retrieved October 11, 2004, from www.softwarequalitymethods.com/papers/darkmets%paper.pdf.

ITpapers. (2003). *Quantitative Methods – Principles of Function Points*. Retrieved May 15, 2004 from www.itpapers.com.

Klir, G. J., & Yuan, B. (1995). *Fuzzy Sets and Fuzzy Logic. Theory and Applications*. New York: Prentice Hall.

Knott, R. P., Merunka, V., Polák, J. (2003). *The BORM methodology: a third-generation fully object-oriented methodology*. Knowledge-Based Systems 3(10). New York: Elsevier Science Publishing.

Kruse, R., Gebrhart, J., & Klawon, F. (1994). *Foundations of Fuzzy Systems*. San Francisco: J. Wiley.

Ligett, D. (2005). CALICO 7.0 *Calibration Software*. SoftStar Systems. Retrieved June12, 2006, from http://www.softstarsystems.com/calico.htm.

Ligett, D. (2005). COSTAR 7.0 *Calibration Software*. SoftStar Systems. Retrieved June 12, 2005, from http://www.softstarsystems.com/demo.htm.

Liu, L., & Roussev, B. (2005). *Management of the Object-Oriented Development Process*. Hershey, PA: Idea Group Publishing.

Lowen, R. (1995). *Fuzzy Logic*. Dordrecht, Germany: Kluwer.

McGibbon, T. (1997). *Modern Empirical Cost and Schedule Estimation Tools*. Retrieved August 20. 1997, from www.dacs.dtic.mil/tech/estimation/costtools.pdf.

Nguyen, H. T., & Walker, E. E. (2000). *A First course in Fuzzy Logic. London, United Kingdom, New York*. Washington, USA: Chapman & Hall/VRC, Boca Raton.

Rubin, D. M. (1998). *Uses of Use Cases. Methodologies and Practices – White Paper.* Softstar Research. Retrieved November 21, 2004, from http://itpapers.com/whitepaper.aspx?&kw=use+case+Points&sortby=date&docid=23877

Shriver, B., & Wegner, P. (1987). *Research Directions in OOP*. New York: MIT Press.

Smith, J. (1999). The estimation of Effort Based on Use Cases. *Rational Software Corporation.* Retrieved November 21, 2004, from http://www.bfpug.com.br/Artigos/UCP/Smith-The_Estimation_of_Effort_Based_on_Use_Cases.pdf.

Struska, Z. (2008). *Methods of complexity estimation for software development.* Unpublished doctoral dissertation, Faculty of Economics and Management, Czech University of Life Sciences in Prague, Czech Republic. (in Czech language).

Struska, Z., & Vaníček, J. (2007). Complexity Estimation of eGovernment applications development. *International Conference on Theory and Practice of Electronic Governance (ICEGOV) 2007*. Macao, China.

Turunen, E. (1999). *Mathematics Behind Fuzzy Logic*. Heidelberg, Germany: Phisica/Verlag.

Zimmermann, H. J. (1991). *Fuzzy Sets, Decision Making, and Expert Systems*. Deventer, Netherlands: Kluwer, B.V.

KEY TERMS AND DEFINITIONS

Complexity: The degree to which a system or component has a design or implementation that is difficult to understand and verify.

Complexity of Functionality: The weight allocated to a function on the basis of which a number of Function Points is assigned to the function.

Effort: Number of labor units required to complete a schedule activity or work breakdown structure component. Usually expressed as staff hours, staff days, or staff weeks.

E-Government: Information and communication technologies for providing and improving government services and interactions with citizens, businesses, and other parts of public administrations.

Expert Estimation: Systematic determination of the extent to which an entity meets its specified criteria or an action that assesses the value of something.

Function Points Analysis: A standard method for measuring software development and maintenance from the customer's point of view.

Measurement: The act of process of assigning of number or category to an entity to describe an attribute of that entity.

Project: Endeavor with defined start and finish dates undertaken to create a product or service in accordance with specified resources and requirements.

Product: Output of the software development activities (e.g., document, code, or model).

Chapter 7
The Adoption Process of Free & Open Source Software (FOSS) in Turkish Public Organizations

Mete Yildiz
Hacettepe University, Turkey

Mustafa Kemal Oktem
Hacettepe University, Turkey

Turksel Kaya Bensghir
Public Administration Institute for Turkey and the Middle East, Turkey

EXECUTIVE SUMMARY

Free and open source software (FOSS) has been increasingly used both in public and private organizations in order to contain costs, increase software transparency and reliability, and information security, among other reasons. This article identifies and examines the arguments and actors, who have promoted and opposed the use of FOSS in the Turkish public sector. It also analyzes how these actors organize the processes of adoption and presents the discourses that they used to affect the open source-related policy decisions. The methods used e-mail questionnaires directed to IT experts in government, academia, private sector and the media, together with the archival analysis of related documents. It is found that FOSS enhances e-government implementations being relatively secure than proprietary software, low cost, participative, scalable and easy to manage. The article concludes with the evaluation of the current level of FOSS use in Turkish government agencies, an explanation of the process of adoption by presenting a process model of FOSS adoption in Turkey that may be applied in other similar countries and different frames of analysis that shape the adoption process. In this vein, the main aim is to link FOSS to the e-government processes and ultimate aim is to link this manuscript to the grass roots e-governance improvement literature.

DOI: 10.4018/978-1-61692-814-8.ch007

BACKGROUND

The use of "free and open source software" (FOSS) has become an important information and communication technology (ICT)[1] policy issue in the world during the last decade. It is increasingly used in government agencies to contain costs, increase software transparency and reliability, strengthening national information security, among other reasons. The FOSS topic at first sight seems to be a technical matter, but upon closer inspection, it is realized that it has very important social, economic and political ramifications of both national and global scale, and especially so for developing countries such as Turkey.

The process of FOSS adoption in Turkish government agencies can be better understood by a process model, which is developed by the authors based on the findings of this study. The process model of FOSS adoption, presented in Appendix 3, can be used to analyze FOSS adoption in government, not only in Turkey, but in other similar countries as well. The direction of interaction among actors are shown mostly by two-sided arrows representing the fact that the model can be used to explain both top-down and bottom-up approaches to FOSS adoption. In addition to national-level actors, international ICT vendor firms and international organizations such as the World Bank, IMF and OECD are also presented as influential actors in the adoption process.

This chapter relates three important concepts: "Free and open source software" (FOSS), public administration (government agencies, their administration, finance and personel; as well as their relationship with the political system), and e-government (the provision of government information and services via the use of information and communication technologies, ICTs). To this end, the chapter aims to explain the conditions, under which the public administration system of Turkey can adopt FOSS as a way to plan and implement its e-government processes and outcomes. Critical in this process are the expectations of government agencies from FOSS in terms of being relatively secure than proprietary software, low cost, participative, scalable and easy to manage.

SETTING THE STAGE

This chapter presents the arguments for and against the use of FOSS in Turkish government agencies. The main research questions that the article aims to answer are; (i) To what extent have FOSS been adopted in the Turkish public sector? b) What are the various barriers jeopardizing the adoption of FOSS in Turkish public service organizations? and c) What can be done to avert the existence of the barriers? In order to answer these questions, FOSS use in various government agencies ranging from national government ministries to major local government units (metropolitan municipalities), from universities to independent regulatory agencies (such as Turkish Radio and Television Supreme Council (RTUK)) is examined in detail. The study also presents the arguments/ discourses that the policy actors use so as to affect the FOSS-related policy decisions. The chapter concludes with proposing a different frame of analysis of decision-making with regard to FOSS use, along with a process model of FOSS adoption which is developed by the authors, and the discussion of possible policy implications of using or neglecting FOSS use in government for Turkey and developing countries elsewhere.

Adoption and implementation of FOSS in governmment agencies in very important as this operating system provides a technically secure and reliable, economically sound and easy to use technical backbone that helps the implementation/ management of individual e-government projects at the grass roots.

CASE DESCRIPTION

Methodology

The methods used in this study are semi-structured in-depth interviews with ICT professionals, who are interested in or knowledgable about FOSS, by using open-ended questions and surveys sent to national government ministries and metropolitan municipalities about their FOSS use. The interview questions were e-mailed to 68 ICT professionals, who work in various government agencies, private sector technology firms, universities, civil society organizations that deal with technology issues, research facilities and the media. It must be noted that since most of the respondents of the e-mail interviews are direct or indirect members of the Linux Users Association (that will be introduced later), their answers may be slightly biased against proprietary software. The surveys are sent to 16 national level ministries and 16 metropolitan municipalities. However, only four of the ministries (25%) and three of the metropolitan municipalities (19%) answered the surveys. These limited answers largely confirm the findings from the interviews.

The findings from the e-mail interviews and surveys are triangulated with archival analysis of related documents such as national ICT strategy reports, as well as e-mail and telephone exchanges with one public and one private sector organization member who are kowledgeable about FOSS development in Turkey.

The interview and survey questions (see Appendix 1 and 2) were initially e-mailed to 10 ICT professionals/Turkish FOSS community members, the names of whom were initially taken from the Linux Users Association representatives as knowledgeable experts in this area. One question in the interview is asking the intervieweees who else to ask these questions to. In other words, the 10 original names were asked to provide the names of other ICT professionals/ Turkish FOSS community members, whom can be interviewed as well. Therefore, a "snowballing method" is used to increase the number of ICT professionals/ Turkish FOSS community members to e-mail the interview questions to. Between January 15th and 30th, 2008, interview questions were sent to 68 people via e-mail messages. 20 of them (29,4%) returned their detailed answers. Two of these 20 respondents answered the e-mailed questions through an ICT professionals e-mail list. In other words, few of the original receivers of the e-mail interview questions posted these questions on professional e-mail lists that they are members of and the two respondents mentioned above saw the questions on this e-mail list. Finally, one person (the 20th respondent) preferred to give his answers orally instead of sending them via e-mail.

Literature Review

This section summarizes the arguments for and against using FOSS, based on the literature. It is not meant to be a complete literature review of FOSS, but it aims to serve the purpose of introducing the reader to the main arguments regarding FOSS, as a conceptual introduction to the following sections of findings and discussion.

Some authors argue that open standards[2] should be a priority, since they can pave the way to achieve e-government objectives efficiently without wasting public money (Simon, 2005: 230). In order to integrate (physically and hopefully ethically) and advance government agencies 'into a flexible electronic service provider', 'consistent data exchange' standards are needed, and open standards are deemed as a check-point in 'moving toward seamless e-government services' (Simon, 2005: 231). Proprietary software and FOSS are differentiated both by their philosophies and by their development methodologies (Simon, 2005: 231) as summed up in Table 1.

As seen in Table 1; at first look, advantages of FOSS are "openness of a program's source code", "freedom of use to: view, share, modify", and "flexibility to customize software solutions".

Table 1. The development techniques of FOSS and proprietary software

FOSS	Proprietary Software
-Openness of a program's source code -Freedom of use to: View, share, modify -Maintenance is a challenge -Flexibility to customize software solutions -Designed to be modular, reuse of modules -Fast development, -Large scale collaboration, users can fix it -Sparks innovation, compatibility, interoperability -Coexistence with commercial applications -Technology advancement, flexibility of implementation	-Closed source technique conditions of use -Restricted by copyright -Sustainable business, continued investment –Intellectual property -Designed with a focus on integration -Products with better performance -Limited testing, reliable maintenance

Source: Adapted from Simon, 2005: 231-234.

Notions of openness, freedom and flexibility would have some implication: As democratic and socio-economic development is a concern for the international community, participation in administration, building trust in government through better access to information (7th Global Forum, 2006), achieving full potential of enhancement by contribution of all citizens are to mention a few priorities. For example, "principles of equal participation and self-government would require public interactions" (Denardis & Tam, 2007: 3). Although it is not for sure if it is the method of software production having more effective influence than method of public control; publicly accessible/ open technical standards would be an advantage provided that they facilitate to take a step forward to transparency of government and functioning of political processes such as 'property rights and access to knowledge' so that trust in government could be improved. In this sense, "controlling of technical standards has reflections on public interest as citizens are dependent on technology" (Denardis and Tam, 2007: 5).

Whether open standards would reduce ICT costs or not by "avoiding single vendor lock-in" and "not compelling to purchase a propriety product" is another issue to be explored; however, citizens would at least have 'a choice of products with which to access government documents' (Denardis & Tam, 2007: 23). Therefore, it has been recommended that "when available, free software solutions would be preferred" depending upon the 'interoperability framework compliance' including the open standards requirement: Brazilian government, for instance, more specifically categorizes open standards into; *adopted, recommended, in transition, under evaluation,future consideration* (Denardis and Tam, 2007: 24).

However, Mackenzie (2001: 541-542, 551) sees "open source software as more of an infrastructure than a tool for a new kind of commodification of computer products" and asks questions such as "better for whom, or better for what?" (Mackenzie, 2001: 545, 547, 550). His answer is although "commercial software is built for a consumer market"; a group of programmers or "hackers have built open source software for themselves and their own communities of practice in order to deepen their sense of ownership". In capitalism, values of openness and freedom in open source software also could be vulnerable to "commodification" (Mackenzie, 2001:552).

Once again, as mentioned in Table 1, FOSS, by having characteristics as being designed to be modular, reuse of modules, fast development, large scale collaboration, users fix, spark of innovation, compatibility, interoperability may call for "a nationalist and populist overtone" as could be seen in some open source software projects; nevertheless it could be a tool "to develop capability and create best-of-breed products offered over the Web" (Mary Ann Fisher in Applewhite,

2003: 89). As Simon (2005: 227-228) refers to a study by the e-Cology Corporation reporting that 'FOSS and open standards are inherently valuable, and in some 24 countries, open source is a good fit for ICT environments with respect to "data integration, IT architecture, standards compatibility, coexistence with commercial applications, technology advancement, flexibility of implementation". "Open standards are valuable as in the case of Internet (and its document standard Hypertext Markup Language: HTML)" (Simon, 2005: 228-229). Some major international companies and related systems integrators supply open-standard-enabled products and support to governments for an easy transition to the use of open source. And their position lessens hesitations and contributes to the credibility of open source (Applewhite 2003: 90).

Like Archimed shouting out (evreka!); social scientists' may find FOSS as an almost "perfect alternative" to proprietary software on the grounds of "voluntary contribution" (Gozukeles, 2006: 138), however, the issue has some other aspects to be considered such as "motivation, organization and community of projects, adoption by MIS organizations, economy, adoptive decision of end users (Ozaygen, 2005:11), innovation, diffusion, communication, social change" (Rogers, 1995 in Ozaygen, 2005).

Protecting intellectual property in software may even involve the definition of basic terms such as computer program and translation of a program, etc., and regulations may 'disturb competitive e-market system, prohibiting innovation, and limiting utilization of copyrighted material by bona fide parties' (Gunes, 2006: 31, 34-36). On the other side of the continuum, open source software takes place. Although it may not be a well-debated issue among scholars and practitioners of public administration in Turkey, in the literature there is a growing awareness on the FOSS and open standards use in government agencies "over the last two decades": It has been recorded that 'after Stallman founded the Free Software Foundation and provided the first copyright license in 1984, Linux operating system started to be used widely in 1992-1993, and combined with a free web server, challenging the existing propriety makers'. It is 'not deemed only as a technical preference, but as a philosophy', in addition to philosophy of software (Wood, 2006), "a part of an innocent traditional gift culture, and would be emerging as a new set of practices in ownership, political representation, norms, taboos, exchange ..." (Kelty, 2004: 499, 503, 506).

By reviewing the literature, one may think that this issue deserves attention otherwise public interest may well be at stake under the monopoly of the ICT sector. And "given governments' obligation to spend tax money wisely on software systems as costly powerful political tools, open source makes sense in the public sector", "because it is less expensive and it works" (Applewhite, 2003: 88, 89).

Schweik and English (2007) suggest that government agencies worldwide are using more FOSS and seeing it as a "development paradigm for software products developed either in public departments or by contractors"; and government agencies would imitate this work model of modularity and cooperation in other areas of their services. Their study further suggests that FOSS projects are more likely to be successful if additional programming support is added. They emphasize that the concern is the longer term support of these projects as outlined maintenance in Table 1. In spite of that, "FOSS market penetration is also high in the public sector: Europe is leading Asia and Latin America; and in the private sector medium and large sized firms are faster in adopting it; and almost two-thirds of open software written by individuals, 15% by firms and 20% by other institutions" (Ghosh, 2006: 9). FOSS increases the value of the ICT infrastructure, supports wider information ecosystem, and its voluntary dimension may bring some other potential up the surface with "similar collaborative models of creativity to harness the full power of active citizens in the information society" (Ghosh, 2006: 11). "Governments need to examine the relevance of open standards to maximize benefits to their citizens and business constituents by engaging outside services, consultants, non-government agencies, industry associations, and so on" (Simon, 2005). However, "current policies and practices may implicitly or explicitly favor proprietary software; governments should encourage FOSS innovation and R&D incentives, and public R&D funding and public software procurement should be competitive (Ghosh, 2006: 12).

Some analysts foresee that "government adoption of FOSS policy is a major driver for the ICT market, since public sector would benefit from the cost reductions" (News Report, 2007). Some other group of experts on the other hand, would argue that in the definition of free software, "liberty" matters not price (Free Software Foundation, 2004 in Hemphill, 2005: 486). Or on the contrary to the term "copyright", the term "copyleft" implies 'freedom to run, study, redistribute and improve the program and release those improvements to the public, so that the whole community benefits' (Hemphill, 2005: 486).

Open Source Initiative's definition based on the criterion of 'not charging a fee for redistribution of the particular software is the focus of public sector's worldwide interest' (Hemphill, 2005: 486). Hemphill (2005: 486-487) suggests that there is both 'commercial and noncommercial efforts to move public sector to use open source software, for example, Open Source Software Institute was formed in 2001 as 'an industry backed nonprofit organization to promote development and implementation of open source software solutions within US agencies and academic entities to ensure a more effective administration'.

As some authors suggest, "neither propriety software nor FOSS is a panacea. Both are necessary to continue improvements in IT". However, when and where open standards are valued, can FOSS provide "a superior development philosophy and technique" (Simon, 2005: 234-236) by interoperable, more flexible and secure solutions (?). Can public administrators 'select software on its merits based on functionality, performance, security, value and cost of ownership, if it is given the choice of commercial and noncommercial solutions? (Hemphill, 2005: 487).

In terms of "coexistence with commercial applications" and "technology advancement" (from the table1); we can relate basic assumptions. Hemphill (2005: 490) proposes that "as long as there is technical interoperability between and among software system models, the final beneficiary of software model diversity will be taxpayers and their representative governments". And if competition itself "by its nature" is good for public benefit, it is sure that FOSS at least offers an alternative option to proprietary software. 'The strengths and weaknesses of both of them needs to be explored and understood if policy decisions are to be made for applications in a rapidly changing environment of public administration and ICT marketplace' (Simon, 2005).

Simon (2005) claims that open source standards can 'support government agencies bargaining advantages over proprietary software vendors by establishing competition'. He also stresses that 'successful ICT operations and efficient services of government agencies require balancing ICT industry to not to rely solely on proprietary vendors, and governments must be able to determine whether proprietary software or FOSS is a better fit for particular public projects' (Simon, 2005: 236). Figures may indicate this trend. It has been reported that "public sector and government agencies around the world are adopting increasingly mature open-source products, with Australia at the front of the trend" (Bushell, 2007). Referring to a Gartner survey, Bushell highlights the need for "maturity in establishing FOSS policies in public-sector organizations...and covering aspects such as inventory, procurement, vendor assessment and selection, FOSS license risk assessment and management, liability limitation, and participation in FOSS communities". Being at 'a lower cost' argument becomes debatable if we take Gartner survey into consideration that is most of the software development and maintenance costs are "incurred in applications where most public-sector organizations still rely on legacy, custom-made development, or on enterprise or domain-specific packages, in which the risk of vendor lock-in is as high as in the more traditional areas of servers or desktop operating systems".

Having said that, we try to take a more stable standpoint by mentioning Hemphill (2005: 484) who proposes that governments should be sensitive on 'the encouragement of neutral standards, preferring neither open nor propriety license model of software development, open competition for research funding, and nondiscrimination in software procurement policies would result in the most effective and efficient decisions so that ICT sector continues to be an innovative force for society'. In this regard, the U.S. federal government also provides evidence by adopting a formal policy of neutrality in software acquisition, "that is, OSS/FS and proprietary software must be considered using the same criteria" (Office of Management and Budget (OMB) memorandum M-04-16 "Software Acquisition" of July 1, 2004): "Agency information technology (IT) and investment decision … policies are intentionally technology and vendor neutral, and to the maximum extent practicable, agency implementation should be similarly neutral".

However, another US example, the US Department of Defense takes aside to "the formal adoption, support and use of open licensed systems" to lower costs, improve the quality and the speed of the information system, and thinks that "open licensing can improve the morale and retention of staff and improve the ability to defend the nation" (Seiferth 2009). Whereas European Union focuses on economics-related FLOSS statistics by emphasizing that "FLOSS-related services could reach a 32% share of all IT services, and its share of the economy could reach 4% of European GDP by 2010." And more importantly, ""FLOSS would save industry over 36% in software R&D investment" (EU 2006).

UK Government is considering OSS solutions alongside proprietary ones in IT procurements and awarding contracts based on a *value for money* basis through its Office of Government Commerce (OGC) which is an independent office of HM Treasury, established to help Government deliver best value from its spendings (2002). In 2004, OGC reported that "adoption of Open Source, particularly for the desktop, requires investment in planning, training of users, development of skills for implementation and support, and detailed consideration of migration and interoperability issues" (Lettice 2004). Korea has also started migrating civil servants to Linux desktop (Cullen 2002).

Government of Malaysia launched *the Malaysian Public Sector OSS Master Plan* "to create and enhance value using OSS within the Public Sector ICT framework in providing efficient, secure and quality services" . The Open Source Competency Centre which is the single point of reference to guide, facilitate, coordinate and monitor implementation of OSS in the Public Sector is established. After having OSS awareness success, the OSS Master Plan accelerated adoption in 2007 for OSS usage throughout the whole Public Sector nation wide (Malaysian Public Sector Open Source Competency Centre (OSCC) 2009).

Introduction to the Turkish ICT Sector

ICT production is important for a country's present and future in terms of strategy, economics, politics, public values, norms, power relations, national security and defense, employment, added value production, etc. since these might be influenced by ICTs and at the same time assist in promoting e-governance. The Turkish case presents a dilemma in this sense. Turkey, as some experts point out, 'has almost no policy on this issue, as it is common for every field, only in Istanbul, there are 7000 firms operating in this field, causing a disorganization instead of quantum loops' (Başaran, 2007): For instance, comparing to India, whose ICT exports add up to an amount of US$10 billion, realized by human resources educated in ICTs, especially those more than 400,000 vocational school graduates; and although Turkey's ICT capacity is around US$1.5 billion, its ICT exports are only US$150 million. Including mobile phones, the Turkish ICT sector has a 7 billion US$ capacity, which is 0,5% of the world capacity. Turkey has no such policy of having ICT vocational schools to educate technicians yet. It is emphasized that the main profit is on the software side of the production process, since hardware's added value and profit margins are relative low, and only by mass production a firm would make money. The Turkish private sector has achieved some positive results by the support of *Scientific and Technological Research Council of Turkey* (TUBITAK), Ministry of Industry and Trade Small and Medium Industry Development Organization (KOSGEB) and Technology R&D Organizations (Teknoparks) only at a number of universities. However, all these do not seem to be enough.

Besides its big share in international competition, ICT has another dimension, i.e. national security. In order to have less dependency on foreign resources, Turkish public administration should use Turkish made software, and PARDUS is one of those operating systems based on Linux, mentioned below in detail. That brings us to university-industry cooperation, and it should be strategically planned in the long term to be able to act at a right speed in the right direction. There are some civil society organizations, namely the Informatics Association of Turkey (TBD), the Turkish Informatics Foundation (TBV), the Association of Turkish Information Entrepreneurs (TUBISAD), the Turkish Association of All Telecommunication Businessmen (TUTED), Software Industrialists Association (YASAD), Turkish Electronics Industrialists Association (TESİD), Free Telecommunication Administrators' Association (TELKODER), which aim to contribute to this sector in Turkey.

The Context of FOSS in Turkey

The use of FOSS by government agencies is a recently-popular public policy option that has been recommended by National Information Society Plans and Strategy Documents only for the past few years: Almost a decade ago, there was no mention of FOSS in the final report of the *Turkish National Information Infrastructure Master Plan* (TUENA, 1999). Four years later, the objective of "contemplating policies regarding the transformation of Turkey to a center of excellence in software development" in Action Number 2 was the only mention of software throughout the *e-Transformation Turkey Project Short Term Action Plan: 2003-2004* document, prepared by the State Planning Organization (SPO, 2003: 2). The first direct reference to FOSS in national strategy documents came two years later. The *e-Transformation Turkey Project 2005 Action Plan* explicitly stated in Action Number 7 that:

The applicability of open source software in government agencies will be analyzed as to cover its legal, administrative and financial aspects. Following this research, a pilot application will be launched in a public agency for implementing open source software (State Planning Organization, 2005: 4).

Interest in FOSS use in government was culminated when it is specifically mentioned in the "National Information Society Strategy" and "Action Plan" documents prepared by the State Planning Organization in 2006[3]. Item 74 of the Action Plan[4] prescribes the use of open source software in government. This action item also recommends the implementation of a pilot project in a government agency by early 2008, so as to assess the possible problems of and barriers to

FOSS use in Turkish government. This specific action is described as:

Pilot implementation will be undertaken at an agency to set an example for the use of open source software in the public, and the applicability analysis of the open source coded software will be developed according to the results of the pilot implementation (State Planning Organization, 2006b: 34).

In addition to national information society strategy documents, there are several threads of developments that need to be mentioned in order to provide an overall picture of the FOSS use in Turkish government agencies (for example, Cetin et al., 2006b). These FOSS initiatives are the national FOSS-based operating system named PARDUS, parts of the tOSSad (Towards Open Source Software Adoption and Dissemination) Project that pertain to Turkey, and most importantly, the Linux Users Association, a major force that promotes FOSS use as an active civil society organization, which has a diverse membership base.

First, PARDUS is a Linux-based national operating system based on open source software, which is being developed under the National Distribution Project in the *National Research Institute of Electronics and Cryptology* (UEAKE), an affiliate of the *Scientific and Technological Research Council of Turkey* (TUBITAK)[5]. The PARDUS project was initiated by the Prime Ministry of Turkey in 2003 as a response to the needs of national security and technological independence of the country. A project team was gathered in TUBITAK in 2004; and it produced the first version of PARDUS on CD in 2005. Later versions were subsequently produced in 2006 and 2007. As mentioned in the findings section, some government agencies are already using it as their operating system. Earlier versions of PARDUS were only distributed on CDs. Today, in addition to CDs, it can be downloaded online.

Second, tOSSad (Towards Open Source Software Adoption and Dissemination) is a pan-European project, aimed at promoting FOSS use in general and in government agencies in particular. Currently organizational members from 16 European countries including Turkey are contributing to the cause of increasing awareness and use of FOSS throughout Europe. This project is one of coordination, networking and synergy among individual national-level FOSS communities by providing a common platform[6]. A recent tOSSad report (2007:9) that aims to capture the perceptions of middle and high level public administrators around Europe on FOSS emphasized risk aversion of bureaucrats, as well as FOSS product quality, availability of support, expertise and documentation, total cost of ownership, vendor lock-in, political influence, administrative attitudes, productivity and training costs as important factors that affect the decision to switch to FOSS or not.

Finally, Linux Users Association[7] is the major policy community that works for increasing awareness and use of FOSS in Turkey. The Association was established as the informal Linux Users Group in 1995, and evolved into its current status in 2000. It promotes the use of open source software in government through organizing conferences, training seminars, special panels, and preparing online and traditional newsletters. The individual, organizational and national level FOSS promoters, who are mentioned in the FOSS adoption process model presented below are mostly members of this associaiton.

Parallel to the ideas of the Linux Users Association, year 2005 witnessed the emergence of the "Open Source Platform", a civil society umbrella organization that aims to explain and promote FOSS. In a written statement signed by 800 FOSS enthusiasts, including 50 organizations, 350 academicians and 150 ICT professionals, the Platform members emphasized the importance of FOSS in Turkey's national development. In addition to educational activities, the platform members pledged to go to courts if necessary, in order to prevent the violation of competition rules in Turkey in favor of proprietary software (BT Dunyasi, 2005).

In addition to these organizations and general developments, there are very few master's and doctoral theses prepared in universities, which examine the overall reception of FOSS in Turkey: According to Gozukeles (2006: 138-143), IT professionals in Turkey are not quite used to FOSS knowledge-sharing business models; and programmers (or hackers in some cases) do not necessarily contribute to and support all FOSS models. They are more 'inclined to social motivations, nationalism (project specific), technically challenging tasks, they lack monetary motivations compared to their European counterparts; some consider proprietary software complimentary, hackers and firms "reinforce each other"; and above all, TUBITAK as an governmental scientific organization, which was successful in transforming its "Uludag project" (PARDUS) into public vision, as a well received and supported project.

Erdogan, in his master's thesis that examined the use of FOSS in the Turkish Central Bank, argued that the main reason of using FOSS in the Central Bank was the experience of ITC staff in FOSS. The other reasons were security, continuity of services and cost reduction (Erdogan, 2007: 57). Erdogan pointed out the the main problems faced in adoption process of FOSS in the same organization as resistance of staff towards FOSS, complications of current software programs produced with closed source into open source programs, and difficulties in transforming documents having macros and cryptical documents (Erdogan, 2007: 63).

Finally, in a study surveying a public university's position against FOSS, Ozaygen (2005: 11) has also identified "being of help to social environment" as an inclination value; 'from the standpoint of adopters, lack of ease of use, lack of support in Turkish, and non-user-friendliness were important issues'. According to the above mentioned study (Ozaygen, 2005: 13):

Use of FOSS is in its early stage, with appropriate policies such as live CDs enabling trialability and observability that help adoption process, the percentage and accessibility would rise, decreasing the cost of software usage in long run; moreover, this public university could serve as a model for deciding migration strategies for other institutions in Turkey, if followed-up by research on the diffusion of innovation theory.

FINDINGS: CURRENT CHALLENGES

This section presents the main findings regarding the extent of FOSS use in Turkish government agencies, arguments and counterarguments for FOSS use in government, policy actors that support and prevent FOSS adoption, and the various environmental factors that shape the adoption processes. First, the answers from the interviewees suggested that using FOSS in servers (Web site design, e-mail and database systems, etc.) is much more common than its use on desktops by individual users in Turkish government agencies. The limited answers to surveys, however, showed the opposite direction. That is, the respondent organizations argued that desktop use is much more common than that of servers.

The government agencies the use of FOSS is most well-known by the respondents are the Turkish Republic Central Bank, various public universities, TUBITAK, and the Ministry of National Defense's ASAL (The Military Draft Management) unit. Other less well-known uses of FOSS are found in the Turkish National Health Information System, Turkish Radio Television Agency, the monitoring unit of Turkish Radio and Television Supreme Council (RTUK), General Directorate of Security and Gendarme.

The respondents listed the major advantages of using FOSS in government as paying no licensing fees, greater national information security, high customizability, being free from vendor lock-in, ability to create and/or promote a national ICT sector. Minor advantages are listed as the code being examined and proofread by many, having less legal (software copyright-related) problems, and getting free and fast technical support from e-mail groups.

The major disadvantages in the process of switching to FOSS as an organization are seen as the lack of information and vision of the political and organizational decision-makers, perception of insufficient technical support, education and documentation on FOSS, fears from the cost of software migration, and not being able to have a definite expert ICT organization (like an ICT vendor firm) to turn to in case of need and/or emergencies. Minor disadvantages are listed as (perceived) higher frequency of updates, lack of technical experts on FOSS, the lack of education in universities on FOSS and the lack of a clear business-model based on FOSS.

The policy actors which support FOSS in Turkey are listed as international ICT firms such as IBM, Oracle and SUN as a part of their competition with Microsoft Corporation; local ICT, education and consulting firms such as Labris, Portakal and Eteration; and the FOSS policy community mainly but not exclusively represented by people and groups in and around the Linux Users Association. The policy actors that potentially prevent FOSS use are seen as international ICT firms such as the Microsoft Corporation, Symantec and their international and local solution partners. Alternative to this dichotomous view, a few different ways of perceiving this picture are presented in the discussion and conclusion section.

The respondents also emphasized the importance of some variables in understanding the adoption of FOSS in Turkish government organizations: These factors can be listed as the lack of clear and consistent political support for FOSS and a corresponding national strategy, the risk-aversion of managerial and technical staff in government organizations, the level of enforcement in software copyright in Turkey (stricter enforcement may force users the real cost of proprietary software ownership, which in turn can be an incentive for FOSS use), impact of software migration on the organizational status-quo and power structures (the need to learn new things and update expert knowledge of technical systems), and finally, some cultural factors such as the undervaluation of a free product as people may think that "if it is free, it should not be of good quality". All of these factors and their impact on the adoption of FOSS in Turkish government organizations are analyzed in detail in the discussion and conclusion section.

DISCUSSION: SOLUTIONS AND RECOMMENDATIONS

This study takes a preliminary look at the arguments and counter-arguments of using FOSS in Turkish government agencies, the policy actors, who use these arguments in Turkey as an initial step to define the decision-making environment that surrounds a model of the FOSS adoption process. We have tried to provide a consice model of adoption process based on our outcomes during this study (see Appendix 3 for the model presented).

In this section, the repercussions of the findings as solutions and recommendations are presented in three subsections: In the first subsection, general implications of the findings are discussed. In the second section, a model of FOSS adoption in Turkey based on the findings is presented. In the final section, alternative ways and categories of making sense of FOSS adoption in Turkey and elsewhere in the developing countries are discussed.

The findings of this study suggest that the most serious barrier that limits FOSS adoption in Turkish government agencies is the lack of a detailed national strategy and accompanying political support for FOSS. The efforts of civil society organizations such as the Linux Users Association seems to have produced results of limited success. There are indeed government agencies such as the Turkish Republic Central

Bank, various public universities, TUBITAK, TODAIE (Yerelnet Project), and the Ministry of National Defense's ASAL unit, which actively use FOSS. However, the bottom-up approach to FOSS adoption does not seem to persuade enough government agencies to adopt FOSS in order to each a critical mass that would initiate wide-spread change which would accompany a government-wide FOSS adoption process. Instead of a bottom-up adoption process supported by users, a top-down adoption decision made by top-level politicians may work better within the Turkish context. Such an initiative by the high level political and bureaucratic decision-makers, and long-term, unwavering support and commitment to FOSS by the politicians is the only force that would eliminate the risk-adverse behaviors of ICT managers in government agencies.

There are contradicting positions regarding FOSS in different parts of the Turkish government today. On the one hand, the PARDUS operating system is being developed by an autonomous government agency (TUBITAK) and it is used by some other government agencies. On the other hand, some other government agencies such as the Ministry of National Education, make agreements with Microsoft[8]. This Ministry employs almost 700,000 people and the impact of these kind of agreements on the process and pace of FOSS adoption may be disastrous. It must also be noted, however, that in addition to the Microsoft Corporation, there are many international vendor firms such as the IBM, Oracle, Sybase, Symantec, Checkpoint and CA, as well as numerous Turkish software firms that sell proprietary software to the government. While making an agreement with the Microsoft Corporation, the Ministry of National Education also partnered with IBM-Turk to open a "Public Sector Linux Proficiency Center" (BTHaber, 2007), a move which can be explained by the mixed environment arguments regarding different frames of analysis presented below.

Secondly, the migration issue is one of great importance for the government agencies which plan to use FOSS. ICT managers from both ministries and metropolitan municipalities, who answered our questions regarding FOSS voiced their concerns about the risks of software migration. The costs and risks associated with software migration are understandably worrying risk-adverse public administrators. These costs and risks, however, can be minimized by carefully planning every aspectof the migration process. A detailed study by Cetin et al. (2006a) analyzes and explains this complicated process for public administrators in great detail.

The process of FOSS adoption in Turkish govenment agencies can be better understood by a process model, which is developed based on the findings of this study. The process model of FOSS adoption, presented in Appendix 3, can be used to analyze FOSS adoption in government, not only in Turkey, but in other similar countries as well. The direction of interaction among actors are shown mostly by two-sided arrows representing the fact that the model can be used to explain both top-down and bottom-up approaches to FOSS adoption. In addition to national-level actors, international ICT vendor firms and international organizations such as the World Bank, IMF and OECD are also presented as influential actors in the adoption process.

The first part of the model presents an initial three-step pre-adoption process which takes part before beginning to use FOSS at individual, organizational or national level (which are the fourth, fifth and sixth steps of the same process). The first pre-adoption step is "not being aware of what FOSS is". The second pre-adoption step is "being aware of FOSS, but not using it or using it in a limited way". The third pre-adoption step is "being FOSS-aware and become a user of FOSS". At this point of the model, although awareness of and ability to use FOSS are present, motivation to use it is still largely absent.

It is at this exact point that the presence of FOSS promoters is critical at individual, organizational and national levels in order to increase the motivation to use FOSS. Some of these people (whom we call "promoters") are in places of bureaucratic and/or network power, while some of them are not. Their common trait is their enthusiasm to promote the use of FOSS. They try to promote FOSS use by various methods, such as persuading the top-management in their organization or elsewhere, initiating projects that would promote and use FOSS, organizing conferences and training seminars, publishing books, periodicals and reports, etc. There are FOSS promoters at individual, organizational and national levels of influence. FOSS promoters who come from different backgrounds may emphasize different advantages of FOSS use. For example, while the managers may emphasize the cost-reduction advantage, technical experts may use the security and flexibility arguments for persuasion.

In addition to the FOSS promoters, some technology firms such as IBM and HP are supporting FOSS use in government as a part of their strategy of competition with other international ICT companies such as the Microsoft Corporation. The model recognizes the critical importance of these organizations as potential promoters and preventers of FOSS adoption.

FOSS adoption in different types of Turkish government agencies are explained in the model by using three main categories. First, FOSS adoption in universities and research institutions such as TUBITAK can be seen as "innovation-driven adoptions" since these organizations are expected to be on the cutting edge of the technology and lead other government agencies as pioneers in the use of emerging technologies. Second, FOSS adoption in the Central Bank of Turkey and the Ministry of National Defense can be attributed to "security-driven adoption", since national information security concerns are of prime importance in these two cases. Third, "promotion of national ICT sector-driven adoption" category explains the motivation to use FOSS as a strategic tool of supporting the development of Turkish ICT companies that are/will produce FOSS-based products and services.

The effective use of the proposed model necessitates the understanding of the political and economic environment in which the model exists. Here we propose several "frames of analysis" to understanding the macro environment that the FOSS adoption or non-adoption decisions are being made: The difference between FOSS and proprietary software is not as black and white as it is assumed. As of 2010, there are many shades of gray in the picture as well. In other words, there are alternative ways of perceiving the old dichotomy between FOSS and proprietary software. A few different models of perception are presented below in Table 2.

One way of perceiving the adoption of FOSS is to explain the context as one of competition between two models of ownership. According to this frame of analysis, FOSS and proprietary software are on different ends of a dichotomous system and these two sub-systems are accepted as being mutually exclusive. Szczepanska, Bergquist and Ljundberg (2005: 438-442) explain this "us vesus them mentality" as the "intelligent

Table 2. Alternative frames of analysis as ways of making Sense of FOSS Adoption

Frame of Analysis	FOSS Adoption as...
1	competition between two models of ownership
2	competition between two business models
3	competition among multiple models of making business
4	reflection of competition between major global political forces
5	an overall strategy of the global ICT sector to sell ICTs to the "next billion"

and able FOSS community and the enemy, the evil empire" discourse. The perception seems to be mutual, since the 2006 Annual Report of the Microsoft Corporation (2006: 16) states that "in recent years certain "open source" software business models have evolved into a growing challenge to our license-based software model".

Such a discourse of rivalry may benefit government decision-makers: Taking advantage of this competitive frame of analysis, public administrators in government agencies may use the possibility to switch to FOSS as a threat against proprietary software firms and their solution partners to reduce prices and manage service quality.

A second way to make sense of the context as a frame of analysis of competition between two models of making business. According to this second frame of analysis, international ICT vendor firms such as IBM and HP, which lost their competitive edge against the Microsoft Corporation in the ICT sector support FOSS in order to use it as a strategic tool to remain competitive. Therefore, their support is not based on the principle of FOSS being a better software category. Instead, FOSS provides a "window of opportunity", a strategic business tool for these firms to remain competitive in the market in the long-run.

A third frame of analysis is one of competition among multiple models of making business. The dichotomy of open or closed source code is no longer meaningful since there are additional categories: First, the Microsoft Corporation has been agreeing to open its source code to many governments such as Russia, China and Turkey, which have special security concerns since 2001 (Parloff, 2004: 43). Secondly, there are now commercial firms such as RedHat, Novell, MySQL AB and Ubuntu, which are making money from FOSS not via licensing fees, but by providing services like technical support and updates (Cetin et al., 2006a: 8, 11-15). Third, after a decision by the European Union Court of First Instance on October 22, 2007, the Microsoft Corporation agreed to allow the access of the necessary information by the open-source developers for reasons of interoperability (The Economist, 2007). Fourth, the Microsoft Corporation has been collaborating with its longtime rival Novell in developing solutions for interoperability in a mixed environment since 2006 (Network Security Journal, 2007; Novell Annual Report, 2007: 5, 14; Microsoft Annual Report, 2007: 10). The parties signed "A Business Collaboration Agreement, a Technical Collaboration Agreement, and a Patent Cooperation Agreement" in November 2006 (Novell Annual Report, 2007: 91). Finally, the Microsoft Corporation itself is researching open source software in its Open Source Software Lab and by promoting the Codeplex portal[9], which is "an online community portal for developers to innovate and actively participate in collaborative software development projects" (Network Security Journal, 2007).

A fourth frame of analysis is one of competition between major global political forces, such as the US, the European Union, China, and Russia. Since most of the proprietary software firms are of US origin, major global political players use FOSS as a strategic tool for their information security. Policies of the EU, China and Brasil can be seen from this viewpoint (Parloff, 2004).

A fifth and final way is to perceive all these as an overall strategy of the global ICT sector to sell hardware, software and technical support to the developing countries. These people are called the "next billion" ICT users (Miller, 2002; Upbin, 2007) people who have not been consuming technological products as much as the "first one billion" people, who live in the industrialized nations of North America, Western Europe and South/Southeast Asia. Nicholas Negroponte's *One Laptop Per Child* (OLPC) Project's "100-dollar-laptop" idea (Anderson, 2006; Rapoza, 2007) can be regarded within the same framework.

The process model of FOSS adoption proposed in this study can be understood in different ways taking into account different alternative frames of analysis proposed above. In order to examine the adoption process of FOSS in Turkish government agencies and those of similar countries, all alternative frames of analysis may add value to the quality of the adoption/non-adoption decision-making and planning. Governments should be cautious in making macro-level decisions that would lead to any kind of "lock-in", before fully analyzing the sustainability of the mixed environments. An incremental model of planning and decision-making can be advocated to government decision-makers, in which they can analyze the subsequent development of the different alternative frames of analysis and their final outcome.

The implementation of FOSS may play a very important role in creating and maintaining grass roots e-governance in general and in improving the performances of individual e-government projects, in particular. A technically secure and dependable, low-cost, easy-to-maintain and manage operating system will add value to the technical development of government agencies and the country in general.

REFERENCES

Anderson, H. (2006). OLPC and Unintended Consequences. *New World (New Orleans, La.), 23*(29), 33.

Applewhite, A. (2003). Should Governments Go Open Source. *IEEE Software, X(Y)* 88-93.

Basaran, B. (2007). We do not have a National IT Policy. *Cumhuriyet Strategy*, *176*, 6–7.

BTHaber. (2007). *MEB'de Linux Yetkinlik Merkezi* (A Linux Proficiency Center in the Ministry of National Education), Retrieved March 1, 2008, from http://www.bthaber.com.tr/haber.phtml?yazi_id=460000804

Bushell, S. (2007). Public Sector Warms to Open Source, *CIO*, 08.24.2007, Retrieved October 22, 2007, from http://www.cio.com.au/index.php/id;1234886256

Cetin, G., Ozel, B., Tasci, K., Koksal, M. A., Basar, N., Ayata, R., et al. (2006b). *Acik Kaynak Kodlu Yazilimlarin İdari, Mali ve Hukuki Boyutlari* (Administrative, Financial and Legal Aspects of OSS). Retrieved February 15, 2008, from http://www.kdep7.org.tr/kamuda-akko-yazilimlar.pdf

Cetin, G., Tasci, K., Ayata, R., Yılmaz, O., Gulum, T., Sehitoglu, O. T., et al. (2006a). *Goc Plani Hazirlanmasi ve Uygulanmasi* (Preparation and Implementation of a Migration Plan). Retrieved February 15, 2008, from http://www.kdep7.org.tr/goc_kilavuzu.pdf

Codeplex (2008). *Codeplex FAQ*, Retrieved February 13, 2008, from http://www.codeplex.com/

Cullen, D. (2002). Korea migrates 120K civil servants to Linux desktop, *The Register,* January 14, 2002, Retrieved September 7, 2009, from http://www.theregister.co.uk/2002/01/14/korea_migrates_120k_civil_servants/.

Denardis, L., & Tam, E. (2007). *Open Documents and Democracy: A Political Basis for Open Document Standards*. Yale Information Society Project White Paper, Retrieved February 8, 2008, from http://isp.law.yale.edu

Dunyasi, B. T. (2005). *Türkiye'nin Kurtuluşu Açık Kaynak Kodlarında* (Turkey's Salvation Depends on FOSS), Retrieved March 1, 2008, from http://www.btdunyasi.net/index.php?module=news&news_id=863&cat_id=4

Economist (2007). Microsoft Concedes Defeat. *The Economist*. October 27, 2007, Retrieved February 15, 2008, from http://www.economist.com

Erdogan, N. (2006). *Kamu Yönetiminde Açık Kaynak Kodlu Yazılım Alternatifi: T.C Merkez Bankası Örneği* (The FOSS Alternative in Public Administration: The Case of the Turkish Central Bank), Unpublished Master's Dissertation, Ankara: The Institute of Public Administration for Turkey and the Middle East.

EU. (2006, November). *Study on the: Economic impact of open source software on innovation and the competitiveness of the Information and Communication Technologies (ICT) sector in the EU.* November 20, 2006, Retrieved September 7, 2009, from http://ec.europa.eu/enterprise/ict/poicy/doc/2006-11-20-flossimpact.pdf.

Ghosh, R. A. (2006). *Economic Impact of FLOSS on Innovation and Competitiveness of the EU ICT Sector. Study on the Open Source Software, Information and Communication Technologies Sector in the EU, Final Report.* MERIT.

Gozukeles, I. I. (2006). *Free and Open Source Software in Turkey*, Unpublished Master's Thesis, Middle East Technical University.

Gunes, I. (2006). *Bilgisayar Programlarının Korunması Hakkındaki 91/250 Sayılı AB Yönergesi ve 5846 Sayılı Kanun'un İlgili Hükümlerinin Karşılaştırılması (European Directive Numbered 91/250 on Protecting Computer Programs and Comparing the Turkish Law No. 5846), Terazi Aylık Hukuk Dergisi, 6, February* (pp. 30–37). Ankara: Seçkin Publishing House.

Hemphill, T. A. (2005). Government Technology Acquisition Policy: The Case of Proprietary Versus Open Source Software. *Technology & Society.*, *25*(6), 484–490.

Kelty, C. (2004). Social Thought and Commentary: Culture's Open Sources: Software, Copyright, and Cultural Critique. *Anthropological Quarterly*. George Washington Institute for Ethnographic Research, 499-506.

Lettice, J. (2004). Open Source ready for prime time in UK.gov, says OGC, *The Register.* October 28, 2004, Retrieved September 7, 2009 form http://www.theregister.co.uk/2004/10/28/ogc_oss_pilot_report/.

Mackenzie, A. (2001). Open Source Software: When is a Tool? What is a Commodity. *Science as Culture*, *10*(4), 541–552. doi:10.1080/09505430120093621

Malaysian Public Sector Open Source Competency Centre (OSCC). (2009). *Accelerated Adoption for Malaysian Public Sector Open Source Software (OSS) Program.* Retrieved September 8, 2009, from http://www.oscc.org.my/.

Microsoft Corporation. (2006). *Microsoft Corporation Annual Report 2006.* Retrieved March 1, 2008, from http://www.microsoft.com/MS_2006_AnnualReport.doc

Microsoft Corporation. (2007). *Microsoft Corporation Annual Report 2007.* Retrieved on March 1, 2008, from http://www.microsoft.com/MS_2007_AnnualReport.doc

Miller, M. J. (2002). Beyond the Box: Driving the Next Billion. *PC Magazine*, *21*(15), 7.

Network Security Journal. (2007). *Microsoft Opens Its Arms to Open Source*, Retrieved February 16, 2008, from http://www.networksecurityjournal.com/features/microsoft-open-source-lab/.

News Report (2007). South Africa Adopts Open Source Software Policy. November 1.

Novell (2007). *Novell 2007 Annual Report.* Retrieved March 1, 2008, from http://www.novell.com/novell_annualreport_2007.pdf

Office of Government Commerce (OGC). (2002). *Policy on the use of Open Source Software.* July 2002, Retrieved September 7, 2009, from http://www.ogc.gov.uk/index.asp?docid=2190#finalreport.

Office of Management and Budget (OMB). (2004) *memorandum M-04-16 "Software Acquisition"* of July 1, 2004 Retrieved September 7, 2009, from http://www.dwheeler.com/oss_fs_why.html.

Ozaygen, A. L. (2005). *Diffusion of Free/Open Source Software as Innovation: A Case Study of METU*, METU STPS-Working Paper, October 25, 2005.

Parloff, R. (2004). Redmond's Open Door Policy. *Fortune*, *150*(8), 43–44.

Rapoza, J. (2007). OLPC Remains Laudable. *eWeek*. 24(35), 64.

Rogers, E. (1995). *Diffusion of Innovations*. New York: The Free Press.

Schweik, C. M., & English, R. C. (2007, November). Brook's Versus Linus' Law: An Empirical Test of Open Source Projects. *Paper presented at the Association for Public Policy Analysis and Management Conference,* Washington D.C.

Seiferth, C. Justin (2009). *Open Source and These United States*. Retrieved September 7, 2009, from http://skyscraper.fortunecity.com/mondo/841/documents/99-184.html.

Seventh Global Forum. (2006). *On Reinventing Government*. Retrieved February 3, 2006, from http://www.7thglobalforum.org

Simon, K. D. (2005). The Value of Open Standards and Open-Source Software in Government Environments. *IBM Systems Journal*, *44*(2), 227–238. doi:10.1147/sj.442.0227

State Planning Organization. (2003). *e-Transformation Turkey Project Short term Action, Plan: 2003-2004*. Retrieved February 15, 2008, from http://www.bilgitoplumu.gov.tr/eng/docs

State Planning Organization. (2005). *e-Transformation Turkey Project 2005 Action Plan*. Retrieved February 15, 2008, from http://www.bilgitoplumu.gov.tr/eng/docs

State Planning Organization. (2006a). *Turkish Information Society Strategy (2006-2010)*. Retrieved February 15, 2008, from http://www.bilgitoplumu.gov.tr/eng/docs/Information_Society_Strategy.pdf

State Planning Organization. (2006b). *Turkish Information Society Strategy (2006-2010)*. Retrieved Feb. 15, 2008, from http://www.bilgitoplumu.gov.tr/eng/docs/ Action_Plan.pdf

Szczepanska, A. M., Bergquist, M., & Ljundberg, J. (2005). High noon at OS corral: Duels and shoot-outs in open source discourse . In Feller, J. (Eds.), *Perspectives on Free and Open Source Software* (pp. 431–446). Cambridge, Mass.: The MIT Press.

tOSSad (2007). *Current Status of FOSS: D18, Version 2.3*. Retrieved February 13, 2008, from http://www.tOSSd.org

Upbin, B. (2007). The Next Billion. *Forbes*, *180*(10), 48–56.

Wood, L. (2006). *Philosophy of Software*. 1-5, Retrieved January 20, 2008, from http://www.q-d.com

Yildiz, M. 2004. *Peeking into the Black Box of E-government Policy-making: The Case of Turkey*. Unpublished doctoral dissertation, Indiana University-Bloomington.

ADDITIONAL READING

Avgerou, C. (2003). The link between ICT and economic growth in the discourse of development. In M. Korpela, R. Montealegre, & A. Poulymenakou (Eds.). *Proceedings of the International Federation of Information Processing*, IFIP 9.4 and 8.2 Joint Conference on Organizational Information Systems in the Context of Globalization (pp. 373–386). Dordrecht, The Netherlands: Kluwer.

Avgerou, C., & Walsham, G. (Eds.). (2000). *Information technology in context: Implementing systems in the developing world*. Brookfield, VT: Ashgate Publishing.

Blumler Jay, G., & Coleman, S. *Realizing Democracy Online: A civic Commons in Cyberspace*, IPPR / Citizens Online Research Publications No.2, March 2001, http://www.ippr.org.uk/publications/covers/Realising%20Democracy%20 Online%20-%20in%20.pdf

Brewer, E., Demmer, M., Du, B., Ho, M., Kam, M., & Nedevschi, S. (2005, June). The Case for Technology in Developing Regions. *Computer*, *38*(6), 25–38. .doi:10.1109/MC.2005.204

Burgelman, J.-C., & Clements, B. IPTS, *"A New Paradigm for eGovernment Services"*, IPTS Report, Issue October 2003, http://www.jrc.es/home/report/english/articles/vol78/ICT1E786.htm

Cassell, M. (2007). *Adoption and Implementation of Open Source Software by Four European Cities*. Unpublished Conference Papers, Midwestern Political Science Association; 2007 Annual Meeting, p 1-31.

Castells, M. (1996). *The rise of the network society*. Boston, Oxford: Blackwell.

Castells, M. (2000). Globalization in the network. *Prometheus Journal*, *4*, 109–123.

Cattaneo, G. Databank Consulting (Italy), *Building eGovernment: European Regions alternative strategies*, April 2004, http://www.databank.it/star/index_2.html

Centeno, C., van Bavel, R., & Burgelman, J. C. (August 2004) "eGovernment in the EU in the next decade" eGov_Vision&KeyChallenges_final_Aug2004.doc *FINAL DRAFT, Retrieved September9, 2009, from*http://fiste.jrc.ec.europa.eu/download/eGov_VisionKeyChallenges_Final_Draft_Aug2004_v1.pdf.

Coleman, S., & Gøtze, J. *Bowling together: Online Public Engagement in Policy Deliberation*, 2001, http://bowlingtogether.net

EIPA (European Institute of Public Administration). 2003, *eGovernment in Europe: The State of Affairs*, 2003, http://www.eipa.nl

Escobar, A. (1995). *Encountering development: The making and unmaking of the Third World*. Princeton, NJ: Princeton University Press.

European Commission. Communication. (n.d.). *The Role of eGovernment for Europe's Future*, COM(2003)567 of 26 Sep 2003, http://europa.eu.int/eurlex/en/com/cnc/2003/com2003_0567en01.pdf

Geoff Walsham & Sundeep Sahay. (2006) Research on Information Systems in DevelopingCountries: Current Landscape and Future Prospects. *Information Technology for Development, 12* (1) 7–24 (2006) Published online in Wiley InterScience (www.interscience.wiley.com).

Glaser, B. G., & Strauss, A. L. (1967). *The discovery of grounded theory: Strategies for qualitative research*. London: Weidenfeld & Nicholson.

Gurstein, M., & Harris, R. (Eds.). (2001). Telecentres, community informatics and development: What do we know now? *Electronic Journal of Information Systems in Developing Countries*, 4, V4R1-V4R5.

Heeks, R. (2002). Information systems and developing countries: Failure, success, and local improvisations. *The Information Society*, *18*(2), 101–112. doi:10.1080/01972240290075039

ISTAG, IST Advisory Group. *Ambient Intelligence: from vision to reality – For participation - in society & business*, Sep 2003, http://www.cordis.lu/ist/istag-reports.htm

King, J. L., Gurbaxani, V., Kraemer, K. L., McFarlan, F. W., Raman, K. S., & Yap, C. S. (1994). Institutional factors in information technology innovation. *Information Systems Research*, *5*(2), 136–169. doi:10.1287/isre.5.2.139

Madon, S. (2000). The internet and socio-economic development: Exploring the interaction. *Information Technology & People*, *13*(2), 85–101. doi:10.1108/09593840010339835

Maldonado, Edgar,(n.d.). *IT policies for development: A framework to analyze Open Source Initiatives in the Bolivarian Republic of Venezuela*, Retrieved September 10, 2009, form http://www.cspo.org/igscdocs/Edgar%20Maldonado.pdf.

Matt Asay. (n.d.). *Open source gains while proprietary software declines*. Retrieved September, 10, 2009, form http://news.cnet.com/8301-13505_3-10223005-16.html.

Millard, J. Danish Technological Institute,(n.d.). *"ePublic services in Europe: past, present and future"*, Research findings and new challenges, Final Paper, September 2003, ftp://ftp.cordis.lu/pub/ist/docs/epublic-services.pdf

Millard, J., Iversen J.S., Danish Technological Institute & Kubicek, H., Westholm, H., Cimander, R., University of Bremen, *"Reorganisation of Government Back Offices for Better Electronic Public Services – European Good Practices (Back-office*

Mursu, A., Lyytinen, K., Soriyan, H. A., & Korpela, M. (2003). Identifying software project risks in Nigeria: An international comparative study. *European Journal of Information Systems*, *12*(3), 182–194. doi:10.1057/palgrave.ejis.3000462

OECD, 2003, *eGovernment Imperative*, 2003

OECD. 2003a, *The eGovernment imperative: main findings*, Policy Brief, March 2003, www.oecd.org/publications/Pol_brief

OECD. 2003b, *The learning government: Introduction and draft results of the survey of knowledge management practices in Ministries / Departments / Agencies of Central Government*, 27th Session of the Public Management Committee, 3-4th April 2003, Paris, March 2003.

OECD. 2003c, Checklist for eGovernment Leaders, Policy Brief, September 2003, www.oecd.org/publications/Pol_brief

Orlikowski, W. J. (1993). CASE tools as organizational change: Investigating incremental and radical changes in systems development. *Management Information Systems Quarterly*, *17*(3), 309–340. doi:10.2307/249774

Orlikowski, W. J., & Barley, S. R. (2001). Technology and institutions: What can research on information technology and research on organizations learn from each other? *Management Information Systems Quarterly*, *25*(2), 145–165. doi:10.2307/3250927

Orlikowski, W. J., & Baroudi, J. J. (1991). Studying information technology in organizations: Research approaches and assumptions. *Information Systems Research*, *2*(1), 1–28. doi:10.1287/isre.2.1.1

reorganisation)", Report to the European Commission, January 2004, http://europa.eu.int/information_society/programmes/egov_rd/documentation/text_en.htm

Sahay, S., & Walsham, G. (1995). Information technology in developing countries: A need for theory building. *Information Technology for Development*, *6*(3/4), 111–124. doi:10.1080/02681102.1995.9525264

Sen, A. (1999). *Development as freedom*. Oxford, New York: Oxford University Press.

Silva, L. (2002). Outsourcing as an improvisation: A case study in Latin America. *The Information Society*, *18*(2), 129–138. doi:10.1080/01972240290075057

Silva, L., & Backhouse, J. (2003). The circuits of power framework for studying power in institutionalization of information systems. *Journal of the AIS*, *4*(6), 294–336.

United Nations, Department of Economic and Social Affairs, *World Public Sector Report 2003: eGovernment at the Crossroads*, 2003

Walsham, G. (2001). *Making a world of difference: IT in a global context.* Chichester, New York: Wiley.

Walsham, G. (2002). Cross-cultural software production and use: A structurational analysis. *Management Information Systems Quarterly*, *26*(4), 359–380. doi:10.2307/4132313

KEY TERMS AND DEFINITIONS

Free and Open Source Software: Software, the source code of which is open for examination, distribution and development. It is assumed to have the characteristics of being designed to be modular, reuse of modules, fast development, large scale collaboration, users fix, spark of innovation, compatibility and interoperability.

Proprietary Software: Software, the source code of which is closed to viewing and unlicensed distribution, and the ownership of which belongs to a person or legal entity.

Information System Investment Decision Process Model: The model that explains the total impact of and the interaction among the variables that affect the process of making a decision regarding an information system`s selection and or upgrade.

E-Governance: The inclusion process of all related societal actors (citizens, businesses and non-governemntal organizations, supranational organizations, etc.) in the provision of government information and services by the help of information and communication technologies.

ENDNOTES

1. The use of "information and communication technology" (ICT) is a deliberate choice over using "information technology" (IT). How the information is used for communication among various stakeholders in government operations is as important as how information is collected, stored and shared among government agencies (Yildiz, 2004:3).
2. It should be noted that open standards are different from open source software and they can be found both in FOSS and proprietary software environments.
3. These documents can be found at the Web site of the State Planning Organization's Department of Information Society: http://www.bilgitoplumu.gov.tr
4. http://www.bilgitoplumu.gov.tr/eng/docs/Action_Plan.pdf
5. For more information, visit: http://www.uekae.tubitak.gov.tr/home.do?ot=10&lang=en
6. For more information, visit: http://www.tossad.org/
7. For more information, visit: http://www.lkd.org.tr/about.us.php
8. For more detail, see: http://www.microsoft.com/turkiye/mslife/sayi29/editorden.mspx. The "Partners in Learning" agreement was signed by the Microsoft Corporation and the Turkish Ministry of National Education in May 2004.
9. For further information, visit: http://www.codeplex.com/

APPENDIX 1: INTERVIEW QUESTIONS

1. Which government agencies use free and open source software in Turkey?

2. What are the arguments for free and open source software use in Turkey?

3. Which actors use the arguments for free and open source software use?

4. What are the arguments against free and open source software use in Turkey?

5. Which actors use the arguments against free and open source software use?

6. Would you recommend me to interview any other persons or get in touch with any other organizations?

7. Any further comments?

Appendix 2: FOSS Use in Ministries and Metropolitan Municipalities in Turkey Survey Questions (Sent by e-mail to IT Department Heads of all 16 National Government Ministries & 16 Metropolitan Municipalities, Follow up by Telephone Calls)

1. Is Free and Open Source Software (FOSS) used in the government ageny that you work in? If yes, Please mark the level of use on the table below.

a. () We use FOSS

b. () We do not use FOSS

Application	High Level	Mid-Level	Low Level
Desktop			
Operating System			
E-mail			
Firewall			
Web Server			
Document Server			
Other: Please specify			

2. Did you have a migration strategy when you switched to FOSS?

() Yes

() No

3. If you did have a migration strategy, which of the following steps did you follow?

() Preparation of the hardware inventory

() Preparation of the software inventory

() Preparation of the applications inventory

() Planning of migration prcess education

4. Which of the following FOSS-based software and platforms are used in your agency?

Software/Platform	Present in the Ageny		Being Used in the Agency	
	Yes	No	Desktop	Server
Pardus				
Apache				
Debian				
Free/Open BSD				
PERL /PHP/C/C++				
Open office				
Mozilla				
Firefox				
Linux				
Red Hat				
Suse/Open Suse/ Novell				
MySQL/PostgreSQL				
Other (Please specify)				

5. Are any of the following reasons present for using FOSS?

Reason for FOSS Use	Yes	No	Do not know
Organizational Preference			
Government Mandate			
Tax Subsidy			
Other (Please specify)			

6. Please select the position on the statements below that best reflects your views regarding the advantages of FOSS use in government agencies:

	1	2	3	4	5
Customization/Elasticity					
Organizational Security					
Natonal Data Security					
Cost (Total Cost of Ownership)					
Ability to Change Code					
Support of Innovation					
Other (Please specify)					

(1=Completely agree; 2=Partly agree; 3=Not sure; 4= Partly disagree; 5= Completely disagree)

7. Please select the position on the statements below that best reflects your views regarding the disadvantages of FOSS use in government agencies:

	1	2	3	4	5
Lack of FOSS experts					
Lack of technical support					
Cost of technological transformation					
Incompatibility between current applications and FOSS					
Unwillingness/reservations of the Management					
Lack of hardware					
Cost of extra hardware					
High cost of (re)education					
Other (Please specify)					

(1=Completely agree; 2=Partly agree; 3=Not sure; 4= Partly disagree; 5= Completely disagree)

8. What is the percentage of your organization's software or technical budget that is used for FOSS?

Less than 10%	%10-%30	%30-%50	More than 50%

Chapter 8
Using Web Sites to Improve Fiscal Transparency:
The Case of Turkish Municipalities

Tolga Demirbaş
Uludag University, Turkey

EXECUTIVE SUMMARY

Fiscal transparency today is considered as an essential element of both good governance and e-governance. Therefore, in the new public management and budgeting reforms made by governments, it is clearly observed that fiscal transparency is one of the key elements. E-government technologies and especially the internet are supportive to the efforts on the part of governments offering unprecedented opportunities to public administrations enabling the dissemination of fiscal information and improving the e-governance system. In Turkey, where there is the tradition of Continental Europe, the reforms made through new laws in early 2000 contain various legal and institutional regulations to improve fiscal transparency and encourage the public administrators to use websites in an attempt to enhance fiscal transparency. This chapter, within the context of evaluating the endeavors in question, examines the websites of municipalities in Turkey in terms of fiscal transparency and eventually presents some suggestions for the improvement of the e-governance system.

INTRODUCTION

E-governance, the latest trend in the governance process, can be defined as using information and communication technologies (ICTs) to improve the delivery of information and services, encourage the public to participate in the decision-making process and make the government more accountable, transparent and efficient (Prabhu, 2005; Palvia & Sharma, 2007). While e-governance is a concept beyond a government website only in the Internet (Backus, 2001), it is also an interactive network that brings the public, non-governmental organizations (NGOs), businesses and other units in the community together with the government on the plane of ICT. Therefore, it encapsulates new policy formulation models, new forms of citizenship, new power and relationship patterns, new options for

DOI: 10.4018/978-1-61692-814-8.ch008

economic development and new ways in order to bring the public together with the political process (Chandra, 2003). Briefly, e-governance is the use of ICTs to strengthen good governance describing a significant transformation.

The realization of the benefits expected from the e-governance system and the ability of the government, an important agent in this system, to be able to improve its capacity to meet the needs of the public (Shiang, 2008), depends on the generation of sufficient and intelligible information by the agents in the system and especially by the government and on the easy access of this information by the agents. In other words, the efficiency of e-governance system is directly related to "transparency".

ICTs and especially the Internet offer policy makers and administrators unprecedented opportunities in order to strengthen transparency, a fundamental element of e-governance (Justice, Melitski, & Smith, 2006). However, some high costs have had to be paid globally for raising awareness for those opportunities. Towards the end of the last century, the financial crises that broke out because the fiscal information produced by governments was not standard, clear and comparative, had a negative impact on many countries and led to some serious economic and social costs. Therefore, fiscal transparency has started to occupy an indispensable place on the reform agendas of international financial organizations and states. Almost all governments have made some important technical reforms in order to improve paper-based transparency and have encouraged the dissemination of fiscal information produced via the Internet. Thus, public administrations have started to use the Internet more to take the opportunity of making their fiscal information more accessible, reaching more and more people simultaneously in an economical way (Wescott, Pizarro, & Schiavo-Campo, 2000).

In addition to this research, there have been a very few studies on how efficiently the public administrations use the Internet to increase fiscal transparency and it has been found that majority of the existing studies have been limited to developed countries. Therefore, Turkey, with its Continental European Tradition and still maintaining its accession talks with the European Union (EU), is an important subject of study to carry out in this sense. After the financial crises that followed early in the year 2000, some vital reforms were made in Turkey in order to improve the fiscal transparency of the state. Many legislations and regulations passed within the framework of the reforms in question have prescribed the preparation of comprehensive documents and reports inclusive of fiscal information of public administrations. Moreover, the new legal regulations encourage the publication of those relevant documents on internet sites and thus aim to contribute to the effectiveness of a local e-governance system. For this reason, this chapter, in the context of the latest developments, aims to measure to what extent the municipalities in Turkey use the Internet to disseminate fiscal information on their websites, focus on some of the variables explicating the results of these measurements, and thus present some important suggestions in an attempt to improve the local e-governance system at the grass roots.

In this framework, this chapter briefly explicates the concept and significance of fiscal transparency at first and emphasizes the part websites play in the improvement of fiscal transparency. Thereafter, what follow is the reforms made in Turkey in order to improve fiscal transparency and the regulations made in an attempt to disseminate fiscal information in the Internet. In the case part of the study, the websites of 207 municipalities in Turkey are evaluated using a fiscal transparency index. After the analysis of some of the variables capable of explicating the success of the municipalities, various problems hindering the use of websites in order to strengthen fiscal transparency of the municipalities are highlighted. In the final section, some suggested solutions for the improvement of the e-governance system are discussed.

THE CONCEPT OF FISCAL TRANSPARENCY AND ITS SIGNIFICANCE

Fiscal transparency is defined as generating reliable, comprehensive, timely, understandable and internationally comparable information regarding the accounts and operations of the government and making it as accessible as possible (Kopits & Craig, 1998). Fiscal transparency is regarded as a fundamental norm in public fiscal administration (Schick, 1999) since it allows the public to see and assess to what extent public institutions use fiscal resources (Premchand, 2002); it helps the administrators ensure fiscal discipline (Bushman & Smith, 2003) and enables the prevention of corruption through the curtailment of powers of public workers (Klitgaard, 1998). The financial crises that occurred at the end of the 1990s in Latin America and Asia generating significant macro global economic instabilities caused fiscal transparency to become internationally more important. The studies carried out revealed the extent of the importance of the lack of fiscal transparency such as the insufficiency of information regarding the accounts and operations of the governments, and the hidden obligations not visible in the accounts, in the deepening of the fiscal crises in question (Parry, 2007). Therefore, the International Monetary Fund (IMF) in an effort to ensure fiscal stability on a global scale, developed the Code of Good Practices on Fiscal Transparency (1998) in an attempt to make the fiscal information produced by governments more reliable and comparable. Today, whether and to what extent countries comply with those standards is announced in the national assessment reports of the IMF (IMF, 2007). After IMF developed these standards, a similar enterprise was started by the Organisation for Economic Co-operation and Development in 1999 (OECD, 2000) and the World Bank today provides governments with technical and financial assistance in an attempt to enhance fiscal transparency. The fact that fiscal transparency has gained international importance has increased the pressures on governments to make their fiscal systems more transparent and fiscal transparency has become one of the cornerstones of the public finance management reforms in almost every country.

Fiscal transparency is regarded as an indispensable reform element for the new public management (NPM) movement postulating the information problems between the principal and agent as a reference point (Kettl, 2005). Accordingly, public administrations are in possession of knowledge of how resources can be used effectively. However, the strict control and procedures on the administrators and financial resources fail to provide the necessary encouragement. Therefore, the NPM reforms, based on reliability, allow administrators some flexibility. This flexibility is also supported by the tools that will enable public administrators to be more accountable for the results (Kettl, 1997). One of the most prominent tools is the creation and announcement of comprehensible information about the operations of public administrations which is accessible by the public for evaluation (Bovaird, 2003). As has been seen so far, both the international financial institutions and the new conception of public administration regard fiscal transparency as an important tool. Therefore, the pressure on public administrations and administrators to improve fiscal transparency is gradually increasing.

The most effective tool which increases the pressure on public administrators and also offers them important opportunities to enhance the level of transparency is the advance in information technology and use of the Internet. In a world where internet use is spreading rapidly, any public administration without a website will be judged negatively by citizens. This demand forces change upon the structures of public administrations which have been traditionally self-enclosed refusing to share information with the public. Therefore, it is possible to argue that the most important function of e-government in general and the internet specifically is to make government more transparent.

THE ROLE AND IMPORTANCE OF THE WEB SITES IN IMPROVING FISCAL TRANSPARENCY

Governments have been adopting reforms, especially since the 1990s, in an attempt to improve fiscal transparency, which has been proved to have key importance for both the global economy and global citizens. However, many of the tools used in these reforms enable complex and detailed information produced mostly for experts. To give an example, medium term budgets, performance reports of up to thousands of pages, a comprehensive classification of expenditure according to international standards, all enhance fiscal transparency for experts in this field but are very difficult to understand for the average citizen who has no detailed technical knowledge of budget and financial management issues. In this respect, the internet enables public administrators to submit fiscal information related to budget and accounting processes for public in a comprehensible form. Thus, it becomes possible for citizens who are most certainly not as knowledgeable as a budget expert to be informed about the process and, therefore, paves the way for the strengthening of public accountability (Justice et al., 2006).

Citizens may be reluctant to take part in the decision-making process of the government. Attending meetings, producing formal feedback and filling out questionnaires on public services may require time commitment and cost for citizens, which they may be unwilling to give (Hoo, 2002). Since the production of information via the internet has the quality of being a public good in terms of political economy, it has important potential to overcome those difficulties. The production of information by public administration via websites is a public good that has the qualities of relative nonexcludability and nonrivalness. Everyone has access to the information posted on the website and the access of one user mostly does not impede the access of another user (Weare, Musso, & Hale, 1999). Thus, it becomes possible for the citizens who are unwilling due to the intensity of the everyday life and can not afford to access the information to have quicker, more economical, easier access to this information 24/7 (Justice et al., 2006; Heeks, 2000). Above and beyond, since the internet allows a citizen to access the fiscal information of more than one public administration quickly, there is the opportunity to make a comparison between the administrations. Therefore, the public has the opportunity to compare and interpret the information such as budget figures and annual accounts of more than one public administration, and can eventually produce new information based on the information obtained (Justice et al., 2006).

Civil servants, on the other hand, who are faced with time pressure from the daily tasks of government, may regard contact with the public and proactive cooperation with them as an unnecessary and unwelcome burden (Hoo, 2002). It has even been stated that some civil servants may be so unwilling to share information with the public that they impede the intensive demand for government information (Heeks, 2000). This contributes to the disappointment of citizens who have spent time and money trying to access information. Websites help to remove this obstacle between the public administration and citizens. As PC ownership and internet usage increase, there is a greater demand for the spread of information from public administrations via websites, and administrations without a website or those that do not operate properly are negatively assessed (Hoo, 2002).

The key role that websites play in enhancing fiscal transparency has also attracted the attention of international financial institutions. Therefore, both the IMF and the OECD crucially lay emphasis on the fact that public administrations publish information and documents on fiscal transparency on the internet free of charge (OECD, 2000; IMF, 2007).

THE EFFORTS TO IMPROVE FISCAL TRANSPARENCY IN TURKEY AND THE INTERNET

The Republic of Turkey, founded in 1923 upon the collapse of the Ottoman Empire, is a unitary state that functions as a bridge between Asia and Europe and whose 70-million population is mostly composed of young people. The fiscal transactions of the government and public administrations in Turkey were for a long time subjected to the general accounting law which were adopted from France in 1927. Since it was an important goal in the early years of the Republic not to pave the way for financial corruption, the tradition of Continental Europe was adopted, where all expenditure of the administration was centrally controlled. This tradition proved to be very successful during the period concerned (Bayar, 2003). However, after this period, in order to be able to operate freely, some institutions were formed that were not subjected to the strict limitations and parliamentary control of the general accounting law. Revolving capital enterprises, extra budgetary funds, foundations and associations are examples of such institutions in Turkey. The fact that there was no proper reporting system regarding institutions that were extrabudgetary damaged the public's right to obtain information and the accountability of government. Besides, similar to other developing countries, the treasury guarantees were not directly reflected in the budget, operational losses of state banks and state economic enterprises became areas of expenditure whose cost was not known and that had not been budgeted for. All these developments caused the total size of public expenditure in Turkey to be unknown and, therefore, there was unaccountability of a significant amount of expenditure (State Planning Organization, 2000).

This state of affairs, which significantly damages fiscal transparency, was not properly questioned until the last ten years. This had been due to the fact that budget and government's accounts required some expertise and was boring to the public, there were a few non-governmental organizations that were equipped to inform the public about these issues, there was little awareness of questioning how and where taxes paid by the public were spent and an unwillingness on the part of politicians and bureaucrats to reveal the true financial situation of the government. The problem of transparency in public finance management in Turkey came to the forefront after two critical financial crises that occurred in November 2000 and in February 2001. The on-time unpaid operational losses of the state banks, since they did not appear in the public accounts, played an important role in these crises and eventually resulted in a debt of about 40 billion dollars, and debt being taken over by the government (Emil & Yılmaz, 2004).

Having been awarded EU candidate status at the 1999 Helsinki summit, Turkey started, after the two crises mentioned, to deliver the commitments she had made to the EU and within this framework, strengthen her fiscal transparency. In addition, the IMF and the World Bank provided financial aid to Turkey on condition that Turkey improved her fiscal transparency. Therefore, a new public financial law that was in line with the requirements of the new century was drafted. Thanks to the influence of some external institutions and then later approved by the Turkish Parliament. The most important feature of the Public Financial Management and Control Law (PFMCL), all provisions of which came into effect in early 2006, made public administrations and their administrators more accountable for their operations and guaranteed "fiscal transparency" as its fundamental insurance. The new law differed from the previous one in that it acknowledged fiscal transparency both as a main goal of public financial management and as a basic principle of budgeting (Article 1 & 13). In addition, the law includes many significant institutional arrangements. Accordingly,

- preparing three-year budgets (Article 17 & 18),
- making strategic plans (Article 9),
- preparing annual performance programs (Article 9),
- preparing annual activity reports (Article 41),
- publishing the six-monthly budget execution results mid year (Article 30),
- informing taxpayers of their rights and obligations (Article 36/d),
- being clear about the tasks, powers and responsibilities (Article 7/a),
- preparing the financial statistics in line with the standards and publishing them regularly (Article 52 & 53),
- imposing fines on administrative officials who fail to submit them to the Ministry of Finance (Article 53),
- public access to the reports (Article 7/b),

are among the important recent changes introduced by this law in terms of producing fiscal information and sharing it with the public.

Another development supportive of enhanced transparency in fiscal administration in Turkey is the right to information law that came into force in 2004. This law legally secured the right of every citizen to acquire information and ensured "the information acquisition units" to be established, and thanks to a specific regulation (The Regulation on the Procedures, 2004) made within this framework. This regulation also encouraged the institutions and organization to prepare informative and instructive brochures and publications about their organizational structures, tasks and services, and required annual activity reports together with the budgetary reports to be made available for public scrutiny (Article 6).

As is seen, some important legal changes have been made in Turkey in recent years in an attempt to enhance fiscal transparency and strengthen citizens' rights to obtain information. These changes can be regarded as significant steps toward changing the self-enclosed structure of the government previously unwilling to share information. One common important feature of the laws concerned is the increase in the responsibilities of public administrations and their administrators in terms of producing information and making it available to the public. The PFMCA remarks that public institutions are responsible for making the necessary arrangements to ensure fiscal transparency and taking the necessary measures, and all these points are under the scrutiny of the Ministry of Finance (Article 7). The right to information law confirms these remarks as follows:

The institutions and organizations are obliged to take the necessary administrative and technical measures in an attempt to make all kinds of documents apart from those indicated in the Law available for the use of those demanding it and finalizing the applications for obtaining information in a quick and correct manner (The Right to Information Law, 2004, Article 5).

The internet, the most effective tool of information sharing today, is in a position to become the most efficient instrument for public administrators in Turkey to use in order to improve fiscal transparency. The regulation related to the right to information law (The Regulation on the Procedures, 2004) based on this particular fact imposed the condition that public institutions with no web page should set up their own websites and institutional e-mail addresses by 24th of June, 2004 (Temporary Article 4). According to the regulation, it is compulsory for the relevant e-mail addresses and application forms for obtaining information to be posted on their websites (Article 6 & 10). For the right of obtaining information to be used effectively and to decrease the workload stemming from those applications, the regulation also encourages budgetary documents and statistics as well as information about tasks and services to be made available to the public on their websites (Article 6 & 7). Although it is optional to publish all this information on the internet, a regulation of PFMCA (The Regulation on Activity Reports, 2006) has made it compulsory for the annual activity reports of the public administrations to be posted on their websites. This compulsion is regarded as an important revolution in order for the local community to assess the activities and operations of public administrations.

THE EFFORTS OF THE MUNICIPALITIES IN TURKEY TO SPREAD FISCAL INFORMATION OVER THE INTERNET: AN EMPIRICAL STUDY

Methodology

Public administrations in Turkey, within the tradition of Continental Europe, are held responsible, in terms of the producing and spreading of fiscal information, for taking the necessary measures in accordance with the provisions in law, and are encouraged to disseminate the fiscal information through their websites. The aim of this study is reveal to what extent the public administrations in question make use of their websites for this purpose and offers some solution suggestions for the quality of e-governance system. The municipalities in Turkey, despite the centralized structure of the government, are among the most expedient local governments that are relatively very close to the public and powerful units. Especially in recent years, some arrangements have been made in order to increase the financial resources of municipalities and the service provision capacities of these administrations have been strengthened within the framework of "fiscal decentralization". The other reason why municipalities have been dealt with in this study is that the municipalities have gradually begun to perceive that "the internet" is an important window opening into the local community. While the internet was introduced in Turkey for the first time in 1993, there were only 30 municipalities with a website in March 1999 (Yıldız, 1999). This number rose to 92 in June 2000 (Bensghir, 2000) and to 1298 in September 2008 (Naralan, 2008). This trend is very positive for local e-governance in Turkey.

In this study, in order to be able to understand how effectively the municipalities use websites as a tool to enhance fiscal transparency, a total of 219 municipalities with a population of 50 000 and over have been examined[1]. The main reason for this is that the laws in Turkey made it an obligation for these municipalities to prepare a strategic plan (Municipality Law, Article 41). The strategic plan, an essential document for the efficient management of resources, is an administrative tool that determines the mid-term objectives and targets of the administrations linking them to the resources. The fact that the municipalities concerned have the competence to be able to use this tool also provides them with an important source of motivation to strengthen fiscal transparency.

In this study, in order to measure the degree of the municipalities' use of their websites for the purposes of fiscal transparency, a fiscal transparency index (FTI) has been used. Since there is no index with a general validity in the field of local governments which can be used for this purpose, Pérez, Hernández, & Bolívar (2005), Pérez, Bolívar, & Hernández (2008) and Justice et al. (2006) have been used extensively to establish the index used in this study. Accordingly, FTI is composed of three categories:

The first category is based on the fact that the basic documents (and reports) legally obligatory to be prepared by the municipalities and containing fiscal information be available for public scrutiny. It is noteworthy to remember that this is an issue significantly emphasized by both the PFMCA and the IMF. Within this framework, a measure has been set as to whether four basic documents are available to view and/or download from their websites. These documents are the strategic plan, the annual performance program, the original budget (or a comprehensive summary) and the annual activity report.

Even though the fact that the documents in the first category are available on the website can be regarded as an indication of fiscal transparency, it may not essentially reflect the reality. There may not be crucial information available in these documents, or a municipality may choose to publish some fiscal information on its website without publishing these documents. Therefore, the second category of the index is related to the content and characteristics of the information available both in the documents concerned and, apart from those documents, on the website of the municipality. In this context, the four important characteristics found in the definition of fiscal transparency have been established as four separate criteria. These are, possessing complete information about the current and past activities of the municipality (comprehensiveness); the characteristics of fiscal information being comparable across the past years and administrations (comparability); the characteristics of fiscal information being understandable and clear to the public (comprehensibility) and finally, the characteristics of fiscal information being published in periods of less than a year (timeliness) when they are out (IMF, 2007).

The third category of the index is related to the design and user-friendliness of the website. The ease of accessing fiscal information, presentation of the data in different formats to the user, availability of choice of accessing fiscal information in a foreign language (English) and availability of various ways for users to contact the municipality about fiscal information have been established as the criteria of this group.

The criteria and sub-criteria together with their categories are shown in Table 1. In this study, all the categories were weighted based on a total of 24 points. Therefore, the total of 12 criteria available in the three categories gives us the fiscal transparency index (FTI):

$$FTI = DOCUMENT - INFO$$
$$= \frac{1}{4}\sum_{i=1}^{4} Vi + CONTENT - CHARACT = \frac{1}{4}\sum_{i=5}^{8} Vi + NAV - DES = \frac{1}{4}\sum_{i=9}^{12} Vi$$

In this equation, the *Vi*'s are the values obtained by each criterion as a result of examining municipality websites. The *Vi* value takes values of 2 and 0 based on the documents available on the municipality's website (document-info), content and characteristics of the information (content-charact) and the design of the website and its user-friendliness (nav-des). While the totality of high index scores illustrate that municipalities use their websites in order to enhance fiscal transparency, the low scores describe the exact opposite situation.

FTI ranks the municipalities in terms of online fiscal transparency, but it does not reveal the factors effective in this sequencing. Specially, political economy and diffusion literature show the variables that can be effective in a municipality spreading information through its website as in the following (Weare et al., 1999): population size, the number of internet users, per capita income, municipality size, the level of fiscal capacity, the rate of political participation and the number of social elites. Unfortunately, in this study, due to lack of data, it is not possible to analyze all the variables in question for all the municipalities. Therefore, in this study, the effect of the variables of population size, political participation, per capita income, education and municipal expenditures on the level of fiscal transparency of the 66 municipalities in the FTI is analyzed. In this study, multivariate linear regression analysis is to be used. The specification of the model is as follows:

$$FTI = \alpha_0 + \beta_1(PolPar) + \beta_2(PerCI)$$
$$+\beta_3(MunExp) + \beta_4(Edu) + \beta_5(MunPop) + \varepsilon_i$$

Table 1. Fiscal transparency index for Turkish municipalities

Measures			*Score*
A.	**The Basic Documents being available for Public Scrutiny and accessible (DOCUMENT-INFO)**		**8**
	1. The updated strategic plan is available on the website.		2
	2. There is the current (2009) performance program or the original budget / its comprehensive summary on the website.		2
	3. The current activity report (2008) is available on the website.		2
	4. Any one or more of the past documents (those indicated in A1, A2 and A3) are available.		2
B.	**The Content and Characteristics of the Information Available on the Web Site and in The Basic Documents (CONTENT-CHARACT)**		**8**
	5. Comprehensive information		2
		a. Resource allocations in line with aims and objectives are available	0,33
		b. Budget expenditures together with types	0,33
		c. Budget revenues together with types	0,33
		d. Projections for two years following the budget (multi-year budget)	0,33
		e. Budgetary results	0,33
		f. Balance sheet	0,33
	6. Understandable information		2
		a. There is a citizens' guide to explain the main features of the budget	0,66
		b. Tasks, powers and responsibilities are explicated	0,66
		c. Percentages and graphics are provided together with interpretations	0,66
	7. Comparable information		2
		a. The user has a chance to compare the fiscal data with each other	1
		b. Data of at least three years old are comparatively available on the website or in the fiscal document	1
	8. Timely information		2
		a. Three-monthly (quarterly) data are periodically published	1
		b. Six-monthly data are periodically published	1
C.	**Navigation and Design of the Web Site (NAV-DES)**		**8**
	9. Ease of Accessing the Data		2
		a. There is a special part on the website allowing access to most of the fiscal information and very easy to notice	1
		b. Searching within the website is possible	0,50
		c. A site map is available	0,50
	10. Ease of Data Management		2
		a. Format: html	0,50
		b. Format: pdf or doc	0,50
		c. Format: xls	1
	11. Ease of Use within International Context		2
		a. Fiscal information in English on the website is available	2
	12. Interaction with the User		2
		a. E-mail addresses and legal on-line application documents of the information acquisition unit is available	0,66
		b. Apart from the information acquisition unit and webmaster, e-mail addresses / telephone numbers for requesting fiscal information and enquiry is available	0,66
		c. It is possible for taxpayers to have access to their personal obligations (such as debt inquiry, paying tax)	0,66

Source: The index in this table was established by the author based on Pérez, Hernández, & Bolívar (2005), Pérez, Bolívar, & Hernández (2008) and Justice et al. (2006).

The fiscal transparency index (FTI) in the model is the dependent variable. The five independent variables respectively are, the rate of political (or electoral) participation (PolPar), per capita income in the municipality (PerCI), municipality expenditure (MunExp), the percentage of those in the municipality population over 23 years of age with a university degree (Edu) and the municipality population (MunPop). ε_i refers to a random error term'.

Findings and Discussion

In order to determine to what extent the municipalities in Turkey use their websites to enhance fiscal transparency, initially the websites of 219 municipalities were examined in July 2009[2]. Of these, 12 were excluded from this examination since they did not have a website or their existing websites did not operate properly. The websites of the remaining 207 municipalities were subjected to content analysis in terms of the criteria specified in the FTI and the results were recorded. To achieve greater clarity, the index scores were converted into percentages.

The FTI results indicate that the index scores of the 207 municipality websites in Turkey are on average 23.84%. Perez et al. (2008), who examined the websites of 65 municipalities in Spain, found this percentage as 14.36%[3] and the authors described this percentage as quite low. Therefore, it is possible to indicate that the average of the index is high for a developing country like Turkey. According to the index, the 5 municipalities meeting the criteria the most are; Çanakkale municipality (83.83%), Istanbul metropolitan municipality (78.25%), Konak municipality (72%), Mersin metropolitan municipality (69.92%) and Kocaeli metropolitan municipality (69.33%). It is an interesting result that the Çanakkale municipality with its population of 66 000 people outstripped 16 metropolitan municipalities. The municipalities that failed to meet the criteria are Merzifon, Gemlik, Ergani, Siverek, Esenyurt and Atakum municipalities.

According to the first category of the index indicating whether the basic documents containing fiscal information are available on the website, the performance of the municipalities is 26.45%. The number of municipalities that never published any of the documents in question on their websites is only 12. The remaining 195 municipalities published at least one of the basic documents on their websites. It is believed that the legal changes made in Turkey have had an important contribution to the performance achieved.

The second category of the index regarding the content and characteristics of the fiscal information showed a value of 20.18%. Based on this value, it is possible to say that the municipalities, when compared to their publishing of the fiscal documents on their websites, are less successful in achieving information quality. One of the interesting points in this category is the fact that the majority of the municipalities (69%) published their tasks, powers and responsibilities on their websites as required by fiscal transparency. Many municipalities publish the relevant laws in this issue on their websites. Apart from these, for most of the basic fiscal documents mentioned above, there are some relevant parts. Another interesting point in this category is the accessibility and availability of the budget practice results in 44% of the municipalities. It is observed that the basic fiscal documents have a role to play in this issue. Contrary to these successful ones, there are also some issues that should be available in those fiscal documents, but the municipalities fail to provide. For instance, while the percentage of the municipalities whose strategic plan can be accessed on their website was 29%, the percentage of the municipalities that provided resource allocation related to the necessary objectives in the plan (and in the performance program) was lower (14%). This shows that some of the municipalities were short of the capacity in preparing a strategic

Table 2. Spearman correlation matrix of independent variables (n=66)

	1 PolPar	2 PerCI	3 MunExp	4 Edu	5 MunPop
1 PolPar	1				
2 PerCI	0.35	1			
3 MunExp	-0.11	0.47	1		
4 Edu	0.04	0.66	0.52	1	
5 MunPop	-0.26	0.28	0.79	0.40	1

plan. Çetinkaya (2008), who drew attention to this particular issue, indicated that the administrations lacked both staff and knowledge in this area (p.248). In this category of the index, only the Istanbul metropolitan municipality published a guide document explicating the municipality's budget process on its website.

In the third and last category of the index, the success rate of the municipalities was 24.89%. In this part, the criterion where the municipalities were most successful was interaction with the users (62.1%). Due to the influence of the right to information law, in 70.5% of the municipalities, it is possible to reach the e-mail addresses and application forms related to information acquisition. In addition, the percentage of access to the staff in the municipalities via e-mail and telephone from whom fiscal information could be requested was 61.4% and the percentage of the taxpayers who could access their personal financial information was 55.8%. Another interesting point in the third category is the fact that the fiscal information on the websites of the municipalities was placed under headings that were not easy to find or difficult to notice. For instance, some municipalities such as Nazilli municipality, Kuşadası municipality and Alanya municipality presented the information related to their budgets to their local communities under the link of council decisions. Interestingly, in Fatsa municipality, the performance program of the municipality was published in the "online services" section on its website. Nevertheless, in 52% of the municipalities, it is possible to make a "site search" and 27% of them have a site map. The most important factor that reduces the performance level of the municipalities in the third category is the criterion of presenting fiscal information in English. Out of the municipalities examined, only Kocaeli municipality could meet this criterion. Finally, most of the information and documents (42%) published by the municipalities were in pdf or doc format. The percentage of xls format, which facilitates analysis, is only 1.9%.

Clearly, FTI shows the degrees of the municipalities' fiscal transparency on the web. Nevertheless, it requires a separate analysis to work out why some municipalities have obtained high scores and others low scores. Therefore, in order to test some of the variables by which one can explicate the FTI in this study, the model author specified in the methodology section has been used. There has been an important data problem regarding local governments in Turkey. In this model, the rates of political participation and municipal expenditures are based on the 2004 data of the Turkish Statistical Institute. The population information on the basis of municipalities for the year 2004 have been estimated by the author (through the interpolation technique). Due to insufficiency of data, for the figure of the income per capita, the data of the year 2001 and for the percentage of those with a university degree, the data of the year 2000 were used. Those data are appropriate for only 66 municipalities out of 207.

The Spearman correlations of the independent variables are found as following table:

The highest correlations were found between municipal population and municipal expenditure

(0.79), education and per capita income (0.66). The approach was to use all available data. So, at first author chose to omit only the municipal population variable that has the highest correlation with municipal expenditure from the model. Thus, in the estimation process this research used all four variables (political participation, per capita income, municipal expenditure and education). Several regression models were estimated. Finally, the following regression model results were found to be appropriate.

$\hat{FTI}$ = - 1.21 + 0.001 PerCI + 0.533 Edu + 0.09 PolPar + 0.03 MunExp

T (- 0.13) (1.840) (1.529) (0.097) (1.903)

Sig. (0.071)* (0.132) (0.923) (0.062)*

$R^2 = 0.324$

$\check{R}^2 = 0.279$

$F = 7.299$

$P = 0.000$

The estimation above shows that per capita income and municipal expenditure are statistically significant at 10% level (See the significances marketed with *). Although these two variables are statistically significant, political participation and education are not. The coefficients of two significant variable signs were all found as expected (positively). The coefficient of determination was found to be 0.324. This value shows that the 32% change of the FTI was explained with the four independent variables that were used above. The significance of F statistic was found to be 0.000. This value shows that the variables fit well to the model. When author look at the estimation results, it was seen that the impact of the variables of per capita income and municipal expenditure on the transparency index is quite low (0.1% and 0.3% respectively).

According to these findings, the significance of the variable of per capita income seems to be compatible with the literature of e-government in general. For instance, Weare et al. (1999) found that as the welfare of the local community in 454 cities in California increased, website adoption increased as well. The articles of Musso, Weare, & Hale (2000), Huang (2006), Hoo (2002) and La Porte, Demchak, De Jong (2002) demonstrate that the variable of income had an impact on the quality of a website and its design. Although the variable in question in Turkey seems to have a little impact on the spread of fiscal information by municipalities on their websites, it is rather difficult to test how this impact operates. This is because the relevant literature claims that those individuals with high income will make more demands regarding e-government (La Porte et al., 2002), thus the public administrations will make more effort to meet this demand (Weare et al., 1999). Insufficiency of data on the basis of municipalities regarding internet users in Turkey makes it difficult to test this claim.

The variable of municipal expenditure is an important indicator of municipality size. The fact that one municipality can spend more in comparison to another one is an indication of its (purchasing) power. As this power increases, the likelihood of making more e-government investment may also increase (La Porte et al., 2002). The fact that this study found a positive impact, though little, (0.3%) of the municipal expenditure on fiscal transparency on the web is supportive of this argument. However, it is not yet known how much e-government investment is made by municipalities in Turkey.

Theoretically, university graduates are expected to be more interested in the fiscal information of local governments. Nonetheless, in addition to those in the literature who found positive relationships between the level of education and e-government adoption like Huang (2006), there are also studies that found no positive relationship (Pérez et al., 2008). According to a survey in Turkey, university graduates are at the top amongst internet users (Turkish Statistical Institute, 2009). Therefore, the finding that the level of education had no positive impact on transparency is incompatible with the existing theory.

Municipalities that are units of local governments are the essence of democracy; the rate of participation to municipality elections, on the other hand, is an important indication of the level of democracy and transparency. This study, contrary to the expectations, found that political participation had no impact on the dissemination of municipalities' fiscal information on their websites. This particular state of affairs can be regarded as the result of a governmental tradition that has continued until the present day from the time of the Ottoman Empire. On the other hand, this centralized governmental tradition also plays an important role in municipalities in Turkey spreading the fiscal information on the web as we have seen in this chapter.

CURRENT CHALLENGES

In Turkey, just like in other countries, various obstacles negatively affect the municipalities' efforts in the dissemination of fiscal information on their websites. It is vitally important to reveal these obstacles in terms of the improvement of local e-governance.

The Problem of Leadership and Coordination

Since Turkey has the tradition of Continental Europe, "legislative framework" comes to have a primary significance in public administration reforms. Thus, the legislations passed in recent years have encouraged the municipalities and other public administrations to set up a website and disseminate their fiscal information and have become partially successful in this. However, it is vitally important for these legislative frameworks to be accomplished within the context of detailed plans and a strong institutional structure. Unfortunately, it is clearly observed that there has not been sufficient progress for planning, organizing, implementing and monitoring the efforts enabling e-transformation of the local governments in Turkey. Although a document of "information society strategy (2006-2010)" that displays a medium and long term strategy and targets aimed at enabling a transformation into an information society has been prepared with a participatory approach, this strategy has not yet been implemented at the local level. In this strategy document, it is stated that the Ministry of Interior, General Directorate for Local Authorities is responsible for the coordination between local governments, for sharing the technology in similar technology applications together with ensuring efficiency in investments and for monitoring and assessing the applications (State Planning Organization, 2006a). Also, in the action plan prepared based on the relevant strategy document, it is proposed that the measurement of performance in the provision of local services is carried out by the collective efforts of the State Planning Organization, local governments and the relevant NGOs under the supervision of the same General Directorate (State Planning Organization, 2006b). All the same, as was stated in the evaluation report in relation to the action plan dated March 2009, it is clearly seen that no action has yet been taken with regards to the activities in question (State Planning Organization, 2009).

Funding Problems

Funding issues are the main problems negatively affecting the entrepreneurship efforts of the public administrations. As has been mentioned before, municipalities in Turkey are local administrative units that are closest to the public and the most powerful in comparison to other local administration units. Some legislative regulations have recently been made in an attempt to increase the revenues of municipalities and efforts have also been exerted to enhance their service provision capacities. Nevertheless, the proportion of the expenditure made by the municipalities with regards to Gross Domestic Product (GDP) is approximately 3.2% (Ministry of Finance, 2009) and the municipalities in Turkey fall behind those in the EU. Moreover, almost half of the revenues of the municipalities are constituted by the funds transferred from the central government (Ministry of Finance, 2006), thus negatively affecting their fiscal autonomy. This condition, certainly, constitutes a huge obstacle especially for small-sized municipalities to start their e-governance initiatives and to be able to employ qualified personnel. In fact, the results of a survey conducted by Turkish Statistical Institute in 2005 revealed that the most important problems encountered by municipalities while providing services on the web are respectively lack of qualified personnel and the high cost of hardware and software programs (Turkish Statistical Institute, 2006).

Digital Divide

Digital divide is an important problem in terms of e-governance in Turkey as is the case in many other developing countries. According to the results of ICT Usage Survey on Households and Individuals done in April 2009, only 30% of households in Turkey had access to the Internet (Turkish Statistical Institute, 2009). This percentage is on average 60% in European Union countries (Eurostat, 2009). Moreover, the Internet usage percentages of individuals in the age group 16 to 74 are respectively 48.6% in males and 28.0% in females. Similar differences exist in rural and urban areas as well (Turkish Statistical Institute, 2009). These limitations result in not all the citizens being able to make full use of the websites of the municipalities and being unable to deliver their democratic requests and demands on the web. This condition, without a doubt, may negatively impact the municipalities' motivation to disseminate information on the web.

The Level of Public Interest in Fiscal Information

The interest of the local communities in fiscal information is one of the most important elements determining the dissemination of fiscal information via the website of a municipality. The citizens in Turkey, as is the case in many other countries, find issues related to government budgeting and financial management complex and boring in general, and do not show enough interest in them. In fact, according to a survey, the percentage of citizens in Turkey using the internet for the purpose of obtaining information from public institutions is 23.5% and is an indication of the lack of interest in question (Turkish Statistical Institute, 2007). In the research part of this study, the fact that the university graduates who constitute the group of people using the internet the most in Turkey did not make any significant contribution to the online fiscal transparency level of municipalities can be interpreted as the result of this lack of interest in fiscal information. The fact that there is an insufficient number of NGOs that will encourage the public in the pursuit of transparency informing them about financial issues and the tradition of centralized state are among the most important reasons behind the lack of interest in fiscal information. As a natural result of all these reasons, it is clearly observed that accountability of the municipalities to the public is not strong enough.

SOLUTIONS AND RECOMMENDATIONS

The pursuit of the municipalities in Turkey to reach the public and pay attention to what they have to say via the internet generally proceeds by means of their own efforts away from a clear vision. Therefore, a strong vision and strategy have to be urgently developed by central government and put into effect in a decided manner. The General Directorate for Local Authorities has to play a more active part in this issue. There are many steps that can be taken under the leadership of this Directorate. Developing some standards for municipalities for setting up websites and online transparency and measuring and publishing the performance of the municipalities in disseminating fiscal information via the web can be among the first of these steps to be taken. Such an approach may encourage municipalities to compete with one another, enabling them to enhance their performances.

It is necessary to strengthen the technological capacities and human resources of Turkish municipalities in order to support them to disseminate their fiscal information on the web at an institutional level. The most viable long term strategy on this issue is to enhance the individual revenues of the municipalities, thus strengthening their autonomy. However, since small-sized municipalities suffer more from such problems, it can be a short and medium term solution that they be supported by a fund to be set up by central government.

Public participation in the processes of administration and budget in local administrations is a crucial tool in meeting the demands of local needs and strengthening transparency. Therefore, encouraging "participatory budgeting" and efforts of "e-democracy" to be accomplished by the participation of the municipality, public and NGOs at the local level can be a viable approach in terms of improving the local e-governance system. Indeed, the fact that the municipality of Çanakkale occupying the first place on the transparency index developed in the research part of this study is the municipality which commenced the application of the very first participatory budget (Benyamor, 2007) supports this hypothesis. The city councils that have developed as a model of governance throughout the process of Local Agenda 21 in Turkey appear as ideal structures in terms of municipalities preparing a participatory budget and drawing the attention of the public and NGOs to fiscal issues (Economic Policy Research Foundation of Turkey, 2007). The functioning of this process also supported by the medium of the Internet can make crucial contributions to the improvement of transparency and e-governance.

Municipalities, just as is the case with other public institutions, do not have the motivation to adapt to the technological developments either, unlike private sector institutions. Problems such as digital divide and lack of technical capacity decrease this motivation even further. However, municipalities should remember that they are not in a position to choose their own citizens and that accessing information is a basic right of all citizens (Beckette-Camaratta, 2002). Therefore, it is vitally important that the administrators in municipalities be more sensitive to the dissemination of information via websites, making use of the existing resources and possibilities more efficiently. The familiarity of the administrators in municipalities with the technology and their occupations may play a part in this sensitivity.

CONCLUSION

This study, for the first time, comprehensively examined the websites of municipalities in Turkey in terms of transparency and rated 207 municipalities based on their performance. Accordingly, it was found that the level of municipalities improving their fiscal transparency through their websites was quite high (23.84% on average) for a developing country like Turkey. Given the fact that only 30 municipalities in Turkey in 1999 had billboard-type websites that were not updated regularly (Yıldız, 1999), it is possible to say that the municipalities have gone a long way in the last ten years. Without a doubt, in reaching this particular level today, the new laws that have both motivated the municipal administrators and imposed some obligations via some of their clauses have made a huge contribution. Therefore, it is possible to say that "the approach of law" in general is successful in Turkey, which has the tradition of Continental Europe. All the same, there is still a long way to go for the municipalities in terms of fiscal transparency. Under the leadership of a strong political and administrative command, the steps to be taken in this issue by the participation of the public, NGOs, the private sector and other agents are sure to enhance the quality of e-governance at the grass roots.

REFERENCES

Backus, M. (2001). *E-Governance in Developing Countries*. (Research Brief No 1). Retrieved October 21, 2009, from International Institute of Communication & Development: http://www.ftpiicd.org/files/research/briefs/brief1.pdf

Bayar, D. (2003). Kamu Mali Yönetimi ve Kontrol Kanunu Ne Getir(m)iyor? [What does Public Financial Management and Control Law Yield (or not)?]. *Maliye Dergisi*, *144*, 47–62.

Beckette-Camaratta, J. (2002, October). *Assessing E-Budgeting in US Local Governments: A Case Study*, Paper presented at the Korean Association For Public Administration Conference, Seoul, S. Korea.

Bensghir, T. K. (2000). Web'deki Belediyelerimiz: Bursa Büyükşehir Belediyesi [Our Municipalities on the Web: Bursa Metropolitan Municipality]. *Çağdaş Yerel Yönetimler, 9*(4), 106-118.

Benyamor, G. (2007, April 10). Türkiye'nin İlk Katılımcı Bütçesi Çanakkale Belediyesinden [First Participatory Budget in Turkey from Çanakkale Municipality]. *Hürriyet Gazetesi*. Retrieved October 22, 2009, from http://hurarsiv.hurriyet.com.tr/goster/haber.aspx?id=6300902&yazarid=20

Bovaird, T. (2003). The Changing Context of Public Policy . In Bovarid, T., & Löffler, E. (Eds.), *Public Management and Governance* (pp. 13–23). London: Routledge.

Bushman, R. M., & Smith, A. J. (2003). Transparency, Financial Accounting Information, and Corporate Governance. *Federal Reserve Bank of New York Economic Policy Review*, *9*(1), 65–87.

Çetinkaya, Ö. (2008). Kamu İdarelerinde Hazırlanan Stratejik Planlarda Mevzuata Aykırı Oluşan Durumlar [Legal Problems Related to Strategic Plans of Public Administrations]. *Yaklaşım*, *16*(192), 244–248.

Chandra, R. (2003). *Information Technology in 21st Century: Ethics and Governance of the Internet*. Delhi: Kalpaz Publications.

Economic Policy Research Foundation of Turkey. (2007). *İyi Yönetişim İçin Örnek Bir Model: Katılımcı Bütçeleme* [A Representative model for Good: Participatory Budgeting]. Yönetişim Etütleri Programı, Ankara. Retrieved October 21, 2009, from http://www.tepav.org.tr

Emil, M. F., & Yılmaz, H. H. (2004). *Mali Saydamlık İzleme Raporu* [Fiscal Transparency Monitoring Report]. Ankara: TESEV.

Eurostat (2009). *Households who have Internet access at home*. Retrieved October 21, 2009, from Eurostat database: http://epp.eurostat.ec.europa.eu

Heeks, R. (2000). Government Data: Understanding the Barriers to Citizen Access and Use. *iGovernment Working Paper Series (Paper No 10)*, Manchester: Institute for Development Policy and Management.

Hoo, A. T. K. (2002). Reinventing Local Governments and the E-Government Initiative . *Public Administration Review*, *62*(4), 434–444. doi:10.1111/0033-3352.00197

Huang, Z. (2006). E-Government Practices at Local Levels: An Analysis of U.S. Counties' Websites. *Issues in Information Systems*, *7*(2), 165–170.

International Monetary Fund. (2007). *Manual on Fiscal Transparency*. Washington, D.C.: Fiscal Affairs Department.

Justice, J. B., Melitski, J., & Smith, D. L. (2006). E-Government as an Instrument of Fiscal Accountability and Responsiveness: Do the Best Practitioners Employ the Best Practices? *American Review of Public Administration*, *36*(3), 301–322. doi:10.1177/0275074005283797

Kettl, D. F. (1997). The Global Revolution in Public Management: Driving Themes, Missing Links . *Journal of Public Policy Analysis and Management*, *16*(3), 446–462. doi:10.1002/(SICI)1520-6688(199722)16:3<446::AID-PAM5>3.0.CO;2-H

Kettl, D. F. (2005). *The Global Public Management Revolution*. Washington, D.C.: Brookings Institution.

Kickert, W. (2007). Public Management Reforms in Countries with a Napoleonic State Model: France, Italy and Spain . In Pollitt, C., van Thiel, S., & Homburg, V. (Eds.), *New Public Management in Europe: Adaptation and Alternatives* (pp. 26–51). Great Britain: Palgrave MacMillan.

Klitgaard, R. (1998). International Cooperation Against Corruption . *Finance & Development*, *35*(1), 3–6.

Kopits, G., & Craig, J. (1998). *Transparency in Government Operations*. Occasional Paper, IMF, Washington D.C.

La Porte, T. M., Demchak, C. C., & De Jong, M. (2002). Democracy and Bureaucracy in the Age of the Web: Emprical Findings and Theoretical Speculations . *Administration & Society*, *34*, 411–446. doi:10.1177/0095399702034004004

Law, M. *Laws of Turkish Republic*, No 5447 of 2005. Retrieved October 21, 2009, from http://www.tbmm.gov.tr

Ministry of Finance. (2006). *Belediyeler Seçilmiş Mali Büyüklükler*. [Municipal Fiscal Accounts]. Ankara. Retrieved October 21, 2009, from http://www.muhasebat.gov.tr

Ministry of Finance. (2009). *Kamu Hesapları Bülteni* [Public Accounts Report]. Ankara. Retrieved October 21, 2009, from http://www.muhasebat.gov.tr

Musso, J., Weare, C., & Hale, M. (2000). Designing Web Technologies for Local Governance Reform: Good Management or Good Democracy? *Political Communication*, *17*, 1–19. doi:10.1080/105846000198486

Naralan, A. (2008). Belediyelerin Resmi İnternet Sitesi Sahipliği ile Siyasi Partiler ve Nüfus Arasındaki İlişki [Relations among website ownership of municipalities, population and political parties]. *Cumhuriyet Üniversitesi İktisadi ve İdari Bilimler Fakültesi Dergisi*, *9*(2), 63–77.

OECD. (2000). *OECD Best Practices for Budget Transparency*. Public Management Service Public Management Committee.

Palvia, S. C. J., & Sharma, S. S. S. (2007). *E-Government and E-Governance: Definitions/Domain Framework and Status around the World*. Paper presented at the Fifth International Conference on E-Governance, Hyderabad, India. Retrieved October 21, 2009, from http://www.iceg.net/2007/books/1/1_369.pdf

Parry, T. (2007). *The Role of Fiscal Transparency in Sustaining Growth and Stability in Latin America*, Working Paper (Paper No WP/07/220), IMF, Washington D.C.

Pérez, C. C., Bolívar, M. P. R., & Hernández, A. M. L. (2008). e-Government process and incentives for online public financial information. *Online Information Review*, *32*(3), 379–400. doi:10.1108/14684520810889682

Pérez, C. C., Hernández, A. M. L., & Bolívar, M. P. R. (2005). Citizens' Access to on-line governmental financial information: Practices in the European Union countries. *Government Information Quarterly*, *22*, 258–276. doi:10.1016/j.giq.2005.02.002

Prabhu, C. S. R. (2005). *E-Governance: Concepts and Case Studies*. Delhi: Prentice Hall of India Private Limited.

Premchand, A. (2002). Fiscal Transparency and Accountability: Idea and Reality . In *United Nations. Globalization and new challenges of public finance: Financial management, transparency and accountability*. New York: Department of Economic and Social Affairs.

Public Financial Management and Control Law. *Laws of Turkish Republic*, No 5018 of 2003. Retrieved October 21, 2009, from http://www.tbmm.gov.tr

Regulation on Activity Reports of Public Administrations. *Regulations of Turkish Republic*, No 26111 of 2006. Retrieved October 21, 2009, from http://www.bumko.gov.tr

Regulation on the Procedures and the Methods Related to Implementation of the Right to Information Law. *Regulations of Turkish Republic*, No 25445 of 2004. Retrieved October 21, 2009, from http://www.mevzuat.gov.tr

Right to Information Law. *Laws of Turkish Republic*, No 4982 of 2003. Retrieved October 21, 2009, from http://www.tbmm.gov.tr

Schick, A. (1999). *A Contemporary Approach to Public Expenditure Management. World Bank Institute: Governance*. Regulation, and Finance Division.

Shiang, J. (2008). *Change and Adaptation of Stakeholder Relationships in e-Governance*. Paper presented at Fourth International Conference on e-Government, Melbourne, Australia. Retrieved October 21, 2009, from http://web.thu.edu.tw/jshiang/www/iceg2008.pdf

(2000). *State Planning Organization*. Ankara: Kamu Mali Yönetiminin Yeniden Yapılandırılması ve Mali Saydamlık Özel İhtisas Komisyonu Raporu. [The Special Experts Commission Report on Reinventing Public Financial Management and Fiscal Transparency]

State Planning Organization. (2006a). *Bilgi Toplumu Stratejisi (2006-2010)* (Pub. No. 2699). [Information Society Strategy], Ankara.

(2006b). *State Planning Organization* (pp. 2006–2010). Ankara: Bilgi Toplumu Stratejisi Eylem Planı. [The Action Plan for Information Society Strategy]

State Planning Organization. (2009). *Bilgi Toplumu Stratejisi Eylem Planı (2006-2010) Değerlendirme Raporu 3* [Evaluation Report 3 of the Information Society Strategy Action Plan (2006-2010)], Ankara.

Turkish Statistical Institute. (2006, January). 2005 Yılı Belediye Web Hizmetleri Araştırması, [Municipality Web Services Survey 2005], *Haber Bülteni*. Retrieved October 21, 2009, from http://www.tuik.gov.tr

Turkish Statistical Institute. (2007, August). 2007 Yılı Hanehalkı Bilişim Teknolojileri Kullanım Araştırması Revize Sonuçları [Revised Results of the Information and Communication Technology Usage Survey on Households and Individuals 2007]. Retrieved October 22, 2009, from http://www.tuik.gov.tr

Turkish Statistical Institute. (2009, August). 2009 Yılı Hanehalkı Bilişim Teknolojileri Kullanım Araştırması Sonuçları, [The results of 2009 Information and Communication Technology Usage Survey on Households and Individuals], *Haber Bülteni*. Retrieved October 21, 2009, from http://www.tuik.gov.tr

Weare, C., Musso, J. A., & Hale, M. L. (1999). Electronic Democracy and the Diffusion of Municipal Web Pages in California. *Administration & Society*, *31*(1), 3–27. doi:10.1177/00953999400935475

Wescott, C., Pizarro, M., & Schiavo-Campo, S. (2000). The Role of Information and Communication Technology in Improving Public Administration In S. Schiavo-Campo & P. Sundaram (Eds.), *To Serve And To Preserve: Improving Public Administration In A Competitive World* (pp. 673-701). Retrieved October 21, 2009, from http://www.adb.org/documents/manuals/serve_and_preserve

Yıldız, M. (1999). Yerel Yönetimde Yeni Bir Katılım Kanalı Internet: ABD'de ve Türkiye'de Elektronik Bilgi Ağları [A New Way to Participation in Local Government (Internet): Electronic Information Networks in USA and Turkey]. *Çağdaş Yerel Yönetimler, 8*(4), 144-156.

ADDITIONAL READING

Armstrong, E. (2005). *Integrity, Transparency and Accountability in Public Administration: Recent Trends, Regional and International Developments and Emerging Issues*. United Nations: Economic & Social Affairs.

Bolívar, M. P. R., Pérez, C. C., & Hernández, A. M. L. (2007). E-government and public financial reporting - The case of Spanish regional governments. *American Review of Public Administration*, *37*(2), 142–177. doi:10.1177/0275074006293193

Brito, J. (2008). Improving Government Transparency Online. *Public Management*, *37*(1), 22–26.

Bushman, R. M., Piotroski, J. D., & Smith, A. J. (2004). What determines corporate transparency? *Journal of Accounting Research*, *42*(2), 207–252. doi:10.1111/j.1475-679X.2004.00136.x

Cheng, R. H. (1992). An Empirical-Analysis of Theories on Factors Influencing State Government Accounting Disclosure. *Journal of Accounting and Public Policy*, *11*(1), 1–42. doi:10.1016/0278-4254(92)90013-N

Cuillier, D., & Piotrowski, S. J. (2009). Internet information-seeking and its relation to support for access to government records. *Government Information Quarterly*, *26*(3), 441–449. doi:10.1016/j.giq.2009.03.001

Gutierrez-Nieto, B., Fuertes-Callen, Y., & Serrano-Cinca, C. (2008). Internet reporting in microfinance institutions. *Online Information Review*, *32*(3), 425–436. doi:10.1108/14684520810889709

Kelton, A. S., & Yang, Y. W. (2008). The impact of corporate governance on Internet financial reporting. *Journal of Accounting and Public Policy*, *27*(1), 62–87. doi:10.1016/j.jaccpubpol.2007.11.001

Norris, D. F., & Moon, M. J. (2005). Advancing E-Government at the Grassroots: Tortoise or Hare? *Public Administration Review*, *65*(1), 64–75. doi:10.1111/j.1540-6210.2005.00431.x

OECD. (2007). *OECD e-Government Studies: Turkey*. Paris: OECD.

Ogurlu, Y. (2007). e-Government applications and its effects on public service in Turkey. In D. Remenyi (Ed.), *7th European Conference on E-Government, Proceedings* (pp. 395-404). England.

Pallot, J. (2001). Transparency in Local Government: Antipodean Initiatives. *European Accounting Review*, *10*(3), 645–660.

Pina, V., Torres, L., & Royo, S. (2007). Are ICTs improving transparency and accountability in the EU regional and local governments? An empirical study. *Public Administration*, *85*(2), 449–472. doi:10.1111/j.1467-9299.2007.00654.x

Pina, V., Torres, L., & Royo, S. (2008, October). *e-Government Evolution in EU Local Governments: A Comparative Perspective*, Paper presented at the Fourth International Conference on E-Government, Melbourne, Australia.

Piotrowski, S. J., & Van Ryzin, G. G. (2007). Citizen attitudes toward transparency in local government. *American Review of Public Administration*, *37*(3), 306–323. doi:10.1177/0275074006296777

Relly, J. E., & Sabharwal, M. (2009). Perceptions of transparency of government policymaking: A cross-national study. *Government Information Quarterly*, *26*(1), 148–157. doi:10.1016/j.giq.2008.04.002

Roy, J. (2008). Service, Security, Transparency, and Trust: Government Online or Governance Renewal in Canada? In Norris, D. (Ed.), *E-Government Research: Policy and Management* (pp. 314–335). New York: IGI Publishing.

Serrano-Cinca, C., Rueda-Tomas, M., & Portillo-Tarragona, P. (2009). Factors influencing e-disclosure in local public administrations. *Environment and Planning. C, Government & Policy*, *27*(2), 355–378. doi:10.1068/c07116r

Serrano-Cinca, C., Rueda-Tomás, M., & Portillo-Tarragona, P. (2009). Determinants of e-government extension. *Online Information Review*, *33*(3), 476–498. doi:10.1108/14684520910969916

Shakespeare, T. (2008, October 15). Information, Information, Information: Improving Access to Information for Local Areas. *Localis,* Research Notes 2. Retrieved July 18, 2009, from http://www.localis.org.uk/article/122/Information-Information-Information.htm

Stanforth, C. (2006). Analysing eGovernment Implementation in Developing Countries Using Actor-Network Theory. iGovernment Working Paper Series (Paper No 17), Manchester: Institute for Development Policy and Management.

Vishwanath, T., & Kaufmann, D. (2001). Toward Transparency: New Approaches and Their Application to Financial Markets. *The World Bank Research Observer*, *16*(1), 41–57. doi:10.1093/wbro/16.1.41

Welch, E. W., Hinnant, C. C., & Moon, M. J. (2005). Linking citizen satisfaction with e-government and trust in government . *Journal of Public Administration: Research and Theory*, *15*(3), 371–391. doi:10.1093/jopart/mui021

West, D. M. (2004). E-Government and the Transformation of Service Delivery and Citizen Attitudes. *Public Administration Review*, *64*(1), 15–27. doi:10.1111/j.1540-6210.2004.00343.x

KEY TERMS AND DEFINITIONS

Annual Activity Report: This is a report comprehensively demonstrating especially the past one-year activities of the public agencies comparatively, together with the targets and the agency is obliged to publish it on its website.

Continental European Tradition: This is a hierarchical and centralist tradition of public administration in which administrative law strongly governs the acts of public agencies (Kickert, 2007).

Fiscal Information: Information available in such documents and reports as the budget and annual activity report; also information related to the accounts and operations of the government and the other public administrative units.

Fiscal Transparency Index (FTI): This is an index with a maximum of 24 scores demonstrating the usage performance for the municipalities to improve their websites' fiscal transparency.

Fiscal Transparency: The accounts and operations of the government and the other public administrative units are to be made accessible to the general public, and they are clear and comprehensible.

New Public Management: This is a reform movement that grants authority and responsibility to administrators so that the public administrations can operate more efficiently and deal with the public on an interactive basis, which leads to greater transparency and accountability.

Performance Program: This is an annual document prepared by a public administration according to a strategic plan and basically demonstrating the performance targets, resource allocations and fiscal information.

Strategic Plan: This is a document demonstrating the vision, mission, quantitative and qualitative objectives of the public agencies; it is also a fundamental element of strategic management.

ENDNOTES

1. The number of municipalities with a population of 50 000 and over has been calculated based on the 2007 census. According to the latest regulations, the number of the municipalities in Turkey is 3209.
2. The website addresses of the municipalities were searched in the following addresses http://www.devletana.com, http://www.yerelnet.org.tr and the following search engine http://www.google.com.

Chapter 9
Şikayet Çöz:
A Proposal for E-Governance

Nilsun Sariyer
Çanakkale Onsekiz Mart University, Turkey

EXECUTIVE SUMMARY

This study aims to discuss how an NGO should have its place in e-governance model. Particularly, instead of structuring a complaint office in each state unit, process of a non-governmental organization's handling complaints have been evaluated. The aim is to demonstrate technological and administrative changes occurred in an NGO on its path from public to state in e-governance understanding by good will of a person and the activities of an NGO as public voice have been studied within the e-governance understanding. Actually this NGO shows the move from society to state and forms an example of total quality management by the technological and managerial changes occurred in its structure. This chapter is focused on a project, 'Sikayetimiz.com', which is an e-complaint on-line model providing various support services to the people at large in Turkey, discussed about its transformation stages leading to this format, put forward some important managerial and organizational issues including operational challenges.

ORGANIZATION BACKGROUND

Although governance can be referred to as a more developed phase of participative democracy, it has various definitions. Governance is positioned as "mutual management" or "management interaction". From this point of view, it is closely related to the development of autonomy and self management. Organization and management approach which dominated public administration in the past left its place productivity management approach which have targets such as total quality and customer satisfaction and which is based on participation of employees and stake holders. Besides services of public sector are seen as "services" which should be improved in quality. In this respect development of information and communication technologies increased the circulation capability of

DOI: 10.4018/978-1-61692-814-8.ch009

economic activities through global networks and facilitated a process which provides individuals with an option to obtain information and enrich their communication abilities and participate in the management process.

This process has led governments' position themselves as institutions that provide citizens with quality services as part of management understanding. This positioning has become more suitable target to achieve through information and communication technologies which played a key role in the global development. In this respect development of information and communication technologies especially the global communication network called as "Internet" have helped rise of a new model which improves governance process, increase the effectiveness and productivity of public administration and provide new opportunities for participative and effective democracy. The name of this model is e-governance. Definition of e-governance include relations among state sector and public, state sector and sectors related to economic activities, non-profit organizations called as third sector and non-governmental organizations (Durna & Özel, 2008). Non-governmental organizations (NGO) are institutions through which individuals come together to pursue shared goals, they disagree on how to classify these actors and their actions (Lewis & Wallace, 2000: Vakil, 1997) and on how to identify core questions to systematically study them (Johnson & Prakash, 2007). Non-governmental organizations aim for the participation of citizens into the e-governance framework.

E-governance must be responsive to the needs of citizens (Chen, Huang & Hsiao, 2002). Citizen participation is a means to reveal their collective preference to ensure that citizens' needs are appropriately matched by government services and the service quality is satisfactory (Osborne & Gaebler, 1992). Among citizens' participation initiatives employed by local governments in western democracies, the citizen complaints mechanism such as ombudsman in Europe is one of the most common practices (Cadeddu, 2004). In developing countries, the establishment of complaint line is considered cost (Chen, Huang & Hsiao, 2002). For this reason, it is not contained within e-government or e-governance. Whereas complaints handling increase emphasis of customer relationship management for public sectors (Hewson Consulting Group, 2002). Complaints system provides an opportunity for every segment of society to access the government easily. If the citizen conveys his complaint easily and quickly, the government will be informed of the problems more quickly (Chen, Huang & Hsiao, 2006). Actually a complaint basically indicates words of displeasure in verbal or written communication (Barlow & Moller, 1996). Customer complaints demonstrate dissatisfaction of customers implying that the service or goods provided do not meet their expectations. In fact, a customer complaint also implies that something is wrong (Stauss, 2002). Most customers buy a product or service and pay some amount of money. In return, they expect to get a value (functional, social, emotional etc.). They make a complaint when they are not satisfied.

In principle, a complaint is an indication of displeasure of a participant or stakeholder and it could be expressed ins. In the era of information technology, this has taken the opportunity of expressing the same in electronic format, which may be termed as e-complaint. The essence is that not to express someone's displeasure or dissatisfaction over a service or a requisition, but it is a new form of inclusiveness. Stakeholders can raise their voices, easily in participatory way and remotely. They are the part of the system, if appropriately their complaints are being dealt with and this would form a dynamic platform of communication to improve any service delivery system, which in turn could be a major reservoir of knowledge of a community in which the system belongs. This could raise the standard of operation, quality of service and at the same time due to the inclusiveness ambiances among the stakeholders, the system has a better chance to be sustainable.

While applying this form of e-complaint system within the e-government structure, naturally this sort of communicative (rather interactive) measure would lead to better governance and create a robust model of performance for the people at large (Gilad, 2001; ISDR-UN, 2003; Glantz, 2004; EWC III, 2006; Dokas & Ireland, 2007).

In today's high technology environment, e-complaint is quite a beneficial way for customers, businesses and government as it is easy to access and simple to use. However, there is not a complaint handling service or line in Turkey in which citizens can address their complaints. While local governments try to solve their problems through their own lines, there is no complaint line in e-government site of the state (Timur & Sarıyer, 2004). Actually state shows a complex nature in e-governance implementations (Bastan & Gökbunar, 2004). In this case citizens express their complaints reporting to the state and private sector through a web site which provide them with solutions. The web site which is proposed in this study to have a place in Turkey's e-governance network was established in 2001 as "Sikayetimiz.com".

It is as an e-complaint line to let consumers express their complaints easily and quickly. It defines itself as a non-governmental organization (NGOs). Based on volunteerism, the site's aim is to publicize complaints and direct businesses towards solving their customers' complaints.

"sikayetimiz.com" was founded by a doctor of medicine named Ömer Deveci. Deveci also became a partner in a clinic started by his friends. New regulations were started by the state to let private sector provide health services within the scope of "transformation in health sector" in 2001 in Turkey. Like many other doctors Deveci chose to do his own business and be self employed. The clinic was in a district of Ankara where people above middle income lived. Clinic was furnished classy, comfortable and attractive. Employees were friendly. However, state hospitals, privately owned hospitals and the polyclinics give good service completely in Ankara which is the capital in Turkey and which is the most crowded city in Turkey with migrants who want to live in the city as it is called the heart of Turkey. Deveci, internal diseases specialist, thought to make a difference for the polyclinic. He suggested his friends that they should give more importance to their clients' complaints. Because he had noticed positive relationships between doctors and patients as a result of the "customer relations management" course he had in Faculty of Medicine where he was trained for his career. Although he did not approved it to much, he let head of nurses to put a complaint box they called "let's put out our grievances box (in Turkish dertleşelim)", which helped express their complaints.

Doctor Deveci was surprised to see that patients chose to make their complaints through the box instead of talking face to face. He started to spend some of his time to read the complaints and he found many of the complaints, which came out of the box, right. He also noted the complaints which were dealt with on the board that he placed on top of the box. After these incidents, he noticed that the satisfaction level of clients rose and the employees behaved towards clients more kindly. He asked the staff to gather feedback from the patients and their companies. He also warned the staff to listen to complaints in every meeting held with the staff. The feedback obtained was always indicating that the clinic was a good one.

Therefore, Deveci asked the staff to gather complaints rather than the compliments since customer complaints were the main source of information which showed interruptions in the clinic. Security guard Hasan informed Doctor Deveci one day that someone commented on the clinic and said that the combi boiler could be seen behind the glass door and that the clinic was like a hardware seller. Doctor Deveci immediately gave his decision and asked for the paint of the glass door. He also thought that the very same person who made the complaint should see the final situation of the door to the clinic when he returned from shopping. To him, by overcoming this problem, not only did they prevent complaints from other people but also they satisfied a potential consumer. That they management of the clinic and the staff discussed that they ought to do everything to meet customer needs to gain customer satisfaction and that patients' demands should be paid attention (http://www.sikayetvar.com). Doctor Deveci said "when a patient in the radiology section asked for a cloth hanger we immediately provided him within ten minutes". A cloth hanger was a need and it was best known by the patients themselves. Moreover they provided bags for patients whose arm was plaster casted. They even gave the patient a lift to his house. In a short time the clinic became known in the city. Even patients from the European side of the city visited the clinic. Deveci said "we had patients from the well known families of Ankara. They even have patients who would not leave the clinic even if asked to leave". Doctor Deveci thinks it is because of dealing with complaints. Customers, who noticed that their complaints were dealt with and hesitated to talk, started to tell things that they were disturbed. This situation not only showed that people were taken care of but also increased the quality of the services. The main purpose here is to prevent complaints and satisfy clients as well as listening to the problems from the first hand and solve them. Doctor Deveci thought that there were other patients who hesitated to express their complaints. For this reason, he started to think about gathering complaints on the internet where no one saw anyone; people feel more comfortable and express themselves a lot easier.

Doctor Deveci also notices that he was aware of problematic situations in daily life. For instance a hole in front of the clinic caused by infrastructure efforts would cause trouble for cars though it could be dealt with by quite a little sum of money. It was not clear who to complaint in order to get it fixed. Moreover, in order to make a complaint one had to spare some time and needed to go to place where complaints are made which was difficult in a city such as Ankara. Verbal complaints were ignored. Moreover a lot of paperwork was required in order to make a complaint such as writing a petition, confirmation of petition and following the procedure. Although Doctor Deveci made his complaint accordingly the hole could not be fixed in one month. Complaints and the procedures especially those against the state should be made simpler. But how? The answer to this question is "sikayetimiz.com" (it means our complaint). The hole on the road caused the foundation of the internet site "Turkey's complaint line".

SETTING THE STAGE

The web site showed technological and administrative improvements each time it changed its name. Therefore, the progress and name changes have also been given in the study.

"sikayetimiz.com"

"sikayetimiz.com" is an Internet based e-complaint site aiming at dealing with consumer problems. There were four employees when it was first established. Employees work on volunteer basis. Two of the employees are barristers and support the site when there is a problem related to complaints. The main issue in the site is providing easy and fast access to the site so that complaints can be made this way too. The foundation purpose of the site is also complaints. The site has been designed accordingly. The consumer sends his complaints to the site and site expects the complaint to be dealt with by the business through media and public pressure groups. "sikayetimiz.com" adapts the philosophy that "consumer is the king" in every issue. In the first year when it was established no one visited the site except for the consumers who had made a complaint. Besides consumers businesses hadn't heard of the Internet site then. Because the site had not made any advertisement or announcement since it had no financial support. Doctor Deveci's patient in the clinic was usually directed to the site. Except from them, other consumers could reach the site if they conducted a search on the search engine and noticed the site.

Design of the internet site is too simple (Figure 1). Customer sends an e-mail to the site about his complaint. Employees of the site read the e-mail and if it does not include any abusive language then the e-mail is placed on the site without a change. Most of the businesses did not respond to the complaints since they did not know about the site then. Actually the idea that the businesses would deal with complaints as a result of public pressure groups was not successful. The owners of the site started to solve problem legally. However if a claim is made then some money were to be demanded by the consumer to open a file. So it caused a conflict that the site became a lawyer's office rather than an Internet site. Also, it was against the philosophy of the site that was fast and easy complaint. Moreover employees witnessed various issues. For instance, lawyer Murat Kaya, one of the employees of the site, noticed that some of the consumers exploited them. For instance, a consumers who claimed that an unknown matter came out of ayran applied to the site for compensation. Lawyer Kaya, concluded as a result of his research that the consumer himself put the matter into the ayran himself. In another incident, a consumer claimed that a lady who was a film artist and a singer thought herself as Jennifer Lopez and disturbed the consumer that the consumer wanted to sue the lady for compensation. Another consumer wrote a complaint saying that his fiancée dumped him because of the low coverage of GSM operator and he wanted to sue against the operator. These exploitations and compensation demands exhausted the lawyers of the site.

As can be seen in Figure 1, the web site has been designed very simple. The form acceptance page has been designed by using available script page with simple html forms rather than any graphics infrastructure. Once forms are obtained, they are published on the html page after the manual evaluation. Any database or interactive server has not been used. Open source software has been preferred. Employees are composed of volunteers rather than professionals. Personal computers are used as a server.

Figure 1. "sikayetimiz.com" Web Site (toolbar is not included)

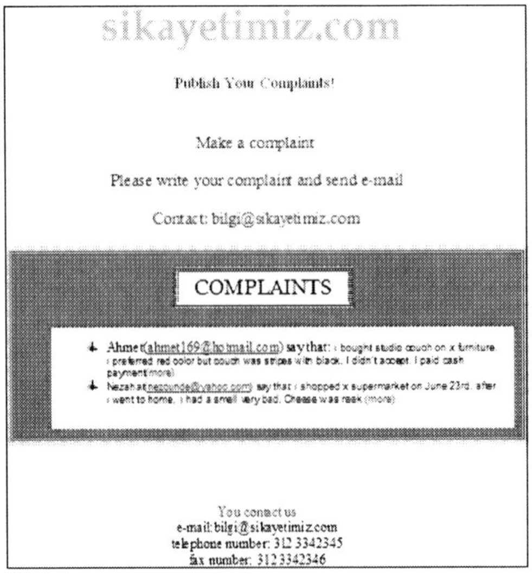

From "sikayetimiz.com" to "sikayetcoz.com"

By the end of 2002 the site had received complaints of over 2000 and could deal with only 65 of them. Most of the complaints solved were related to health. Doctor Deveci and his employees evaluated the situation as unsuccessful and attempted to understand reasons lied beneath this failure that the site was no different than other ordinary sites. They started holding meetings and tape recorded each meeting.

Deveci evaluated the results of meetings as follows:

The first reason of the failure was that most of the consumers and businesses did not know about the site. Consumers wrote their complaints to the site but the businesses did not know about it. Information given by the site employees to the business about the complaint does not increase the attention given to the complaints. Besides, most of the businesses shut the phone gently by saying that they had their own customer complaint line and to apply there.

Second reason was that the site was very similar to the other sites. There were two complaints line on the internet: first one was complaint lines of the businesses and secondly complaint lines that operated in relation with the consumer rights associations. Most of the complaint lines of businesses did not operate very efficiently. They were only there to demonstrate that the business had a complaint line. Those that were in relation with consumer rights were mostly consumer oriented. Most of the incidents were dealt with from the point of consumers. Consumers were always right.

However, it was seen in "sikayetimiz.com" site example that consumers were not always right and they sometimes told the incidents partly or changed them. Those sites that are in relation with the consumer rights regarded businesses always wrong. Consumer rights courts indicated that writing a petition was a right of the consumer. "sikayetimiz.com" had to be different. Therefore complaints should also be evaluated from the point of businesses as well. In order to do this the system of the site had to be changed.

Following long discussions, Doctor Deveci and the staff decided to architect a system that assisted in gathering consumers and businesses to the same platform. Having customer complaints were the main purpose of the businesses. First of all it was an opportunity to see the failures of the goods or services they provided. If the consumer notified the business for his complaint first then it could be solved before the majority heard and when everyone heard about the complaint then the business would come up with the explanation of how it solved the consumer's specific complaint. "sikayetimiz.com" should be a platform where the consumers and businesses met. They called this platform as "solution platform".

The platform was thought to function as follows; complaints from the consumers should be sent to the businesses as quick as possible and the businesses should be expected to solve the problem. If the businesses did not deal with the problem then the site stepped in. Moreover, businesses could also become members of the site and they could be given an opportunity to publish the complaints that they had dealt with. This platform also meant to change the philosophy of the site. The site should be in equal distance to the consumer, producer or the seller businesses. Therefore it would become different than the ordinary complaint lines on the Internet.

Third reason for the failure was identified as the name of the site. First person plural suffix in the word "sikayeti*miz*.com" put the site below the rank in the internet search engines list. Therefore the consumers chose the very first complaint lines instead of the site and also to be unaware of the site. The site started to use "sikayetçoz.com" in 2002 in which first person plural was omitted.

The site applied its new system and the new name and gave advertisements in the search engines. 15 visitors were recorded in 2003 and 650 businesses registered. Over 10.000 complaints were also dealt with. Because the number of complaints increased in 2004 number of employees reached 8. The number of businesses registered to site that year was 750. Over 21.000 complaints were also dealt with the same year. The site formed a law office within in its scope and complaints were dealt with a more legal approach. The barristers in the office were volunteers.

The new system included a button called make a complaint (Figure 2). When the button gets a hit, a complaint was sent to the site. Then the complaint was sent to the related business by the staff of the site. Then the complaint was sent to the related business by the staff of the site. In this designed web page, php scripts - simple and available resources – are used rather than simple html codes.

Businesses mostly solve the problem. However if the problem was not solved then the business was asked to give an alternative solution. If the consumer returned back to the site saying that the complaint was not dealt with then the law office appeared on the scene. Yet, if the consumer did not give his contact details except for the e-mail address then the procedure delayed for a while. Because most of the consumers were mentally relax when they made a complaint and were not interested in the result of complaint. In this case the site assumed that the complaint was not dealt with and the time spent by the site staff and the business was regarded as time loss. These time losses were important since the site got between 500-600 complaints everyday then. Because of this reason, the site owners decided to develop the system in 2006.

From "sikayetcoz.com" to "şikayetçöz.com"

In order to form the solution platform and respond to the complaints made through e-complaint line, Deveci and his team decided that not only the businesses but also the consumers became member of the site. The site explained its mission as "first address of anyone who is in search of quality" and decided that in order to reach quality standard, consumers became members to make a complaint. It was a tough decision for the site since some consumers would give up making a complaint because of the membership condition. However, there had been thousands of consumers whose complaint were dealt with but could not be informed. The site facilitated the membership procedure so that everyone could become mem-

Figure 2. "sikayetcoz.com" Web Site (toolbar is not included)

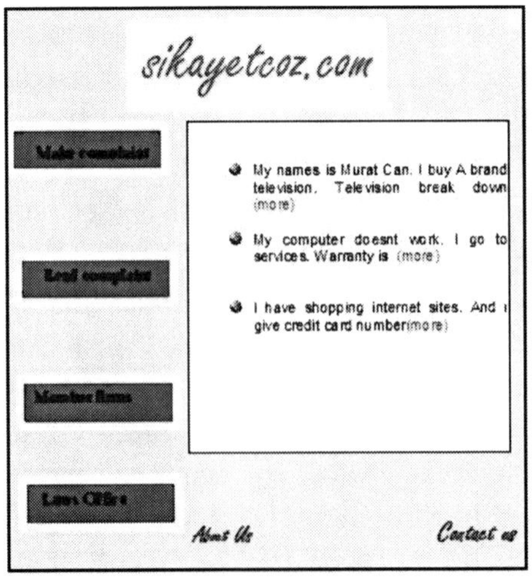

bers very easily. The consumer who became a member could make a complaint when he clicked on the complaint button. The complaints were read by the site staff first. This stage was called as "complaint publication process" and required careful attention. Redactors read and corrected the spelling mistakes and the barristers searched for criminal evidences of the complaints.

The aim of the site was to inform businesses about the problems of consumers. Therefore the staff paid attention to eliminate abusive words. Besides the aim of the site was not to expose businesses by verbal injury. The complaint was finally sent to the businesses after it turned into a format that informed about a problem. Businesses could see the complaint and the contact details of the consumer who made the complaint so that they could correspond with them. After the business solved the problem and confirmed it then it was published on the site as solved complaints.

There was also a "read a complaint button". If the consumer demanded, he could search for a specific brand or product to see whether or not it had complaints in the past. In addition it could see the complaints based on a sort list by businesses as well as products. Moreover, the consumers could also got a reference number for each complaints that they were interested in so that they could have an idea on the similar complaints of consumers. Another button added to the site was "solved complaints" in 2006. This part of the site included the complaints that were sent to the businesses platforms and that were dealt by the businesses (Figure 3).

The reason for upgrading the web page is that the number of complaints is more than expected. The administration has upgraded it in order to publish new solution platform on the new web page. Besides this, hosting has been provided through a professional hosting firm rather than personal pages. It has been preferred to use mysql database and apache server that provides interactive service. A new and developed algorithm has been designed for the site. It has gained an easier

Figure 3. "ŞikayetÇöz.com" Web Site (toolbar is not included)

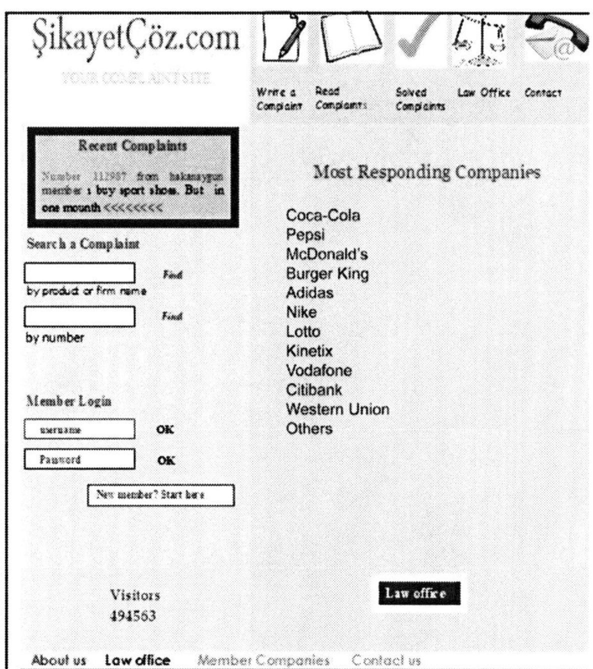

and user friendly configuration by including membership system. A faster and easier method has been provided with the help of categorizing the complaints. Graphic programs have been benefited in order to improve visual quality. Users are provided to reach the solved complaints and they are informed as to what to do in similar situations. In addition, a counter that shows the number of visitors to the site has been added to the home page. Firms that find solutions to complaints at most have been declared on the home page.

Another spotlighting part of the site is the platform of member businesses. This platform included the member businesses and consumers could see the related complaints when they clicked on the logos of the businesses (Figure 4). Those complaints that were dealt with were included on the platform with a smile face. This platform eliminated the prejudgments of the consumers. Because it let the businesses publish complaints explicitly so that they showed that they were complaint friendly.

When it became possible to use Turkish letters on the site, the site transformed its name into "ŞikayetÇöz.com" in 2006 so that the site became harmonized with Turkish writing rules and Turkish letters. Many of the citizens of Turkey chose sites with Turkish characters. Particularly mixed use of Turkish and English were criticized. The former two internet names of the site were directed to this new address. Thus the site gave advertisements by using the name change and the condition of membership in its system. Especially e-newspaper and banners were used.

30.000 complaints were dealt with and 900 businesses became members of the site in the year 2006. 55.000 complaints were dealt with in 2007 and the number of member consumers was 20.000. The number of member businesses reached to 1200 in 2007. This number increased to 2000 in 2008. The same year, the number of member consumers exceeded 250.000. The site

Figure 4. Solution Platform of "ŞikayetÇöz.com" Web Site

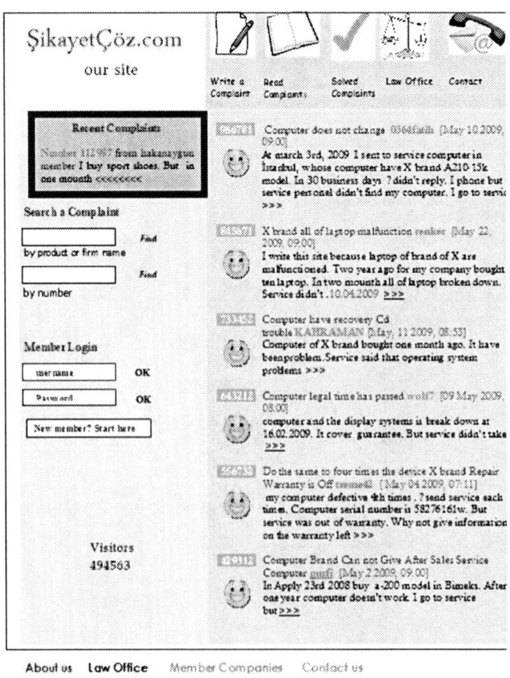

receives around 1000-1500 complaints everyday. The number of complaints that was dealt with exceeded 190.000. The number of daily visitors of the site is around 5000-7000. This web site has been resolved 214.960 complaints on September 2009 (http:/www.sikayetvar.com).

Doctor Deveci states that the number of the complaints boomed and they can not deal with them after 2009 Global Financial Crisis. The number of staff has reached 15. However, dealing with complaints is a slow process since each complaint is evaluated by redactors and the law office. Recently the number of consumers who states that his complaint is published has increased. Moreover, the site's office is not enough anymore and they are looking for a new place to settle. However it is quite difficult for an NGO whose funds are limited. Deveci stresses that their funds are limited to membership payments of businesses and they are thinking of selling data base that their members have formed. Besides they also think that accepting advertisement from the member businesses for the site (www.SikayetVar.com).

As can be seen in Table 1, the web site sikayetimiz.com developing later as sikayetcoz and lastly ŞikayetÇöz.com has shown development from the first stage. The web site has been solving the problems between customers and businesses by making novelties day by day. It comes into prominence as a site for customers to collect information about the business. The time when sikayetimiz.com was set up, none of the businesses were dealing with the customers' complaints – and then it became a site that many companies want to take part in. Besides this, the site has had the customers learn to complain when they come across a problem. Every segment of society has learned to apply to the contact center when they have problems with the products they bought. It also became a reference for the customers to consult about the brand before buying anything. Many customers who have realized that it is easy to complain and the process of solving the complaint is quick have learned that the complaints mechanism is necessary. Becoming widespread in the society, complainability is important for the customer to seek his right and talk about his problems. Dealing with the complaints and solving them at this stage, e-governance should be regarded as information gathering center.

Table 1. Summarizing of ŞikayetÇöz.com From The Beginning

Transformation improvements	sikayetimiz.com	Sikayetcoz.com	ŞikayetÇöz.com
Acquisition	market penetration	market awareness	market domination
Response of businesses	not interest	take cognizance of it	trying to solve problems
Feedback to complaints	rarely	generally	quite often
Customer satisfaction	little	medium	pleasant
Customer trust	none	medium	confidential
Response speed to customer	low	medium	quickly
Number of Member Companies	none	less	too many
Consumer awareness	none	less	too many
Visitors' characteristic	only have complaints	only have complaints	everyone have and haven't complaint
Staff number	little	little	little

CURRENT CHALLENGES FACING THE ORGANIZATION

One of the tasks and services of the state to its citizens is to handle their complaints. In this regard, state should put forward a managerial approach that interacts with the citizens. This management model should be more extensive and aim to increase quality of public services. In this sense, it is suggested that solution platform formed by "www.Sikayetçöz.com" should not be two-sided but multi-sided including customer (citizen in e-governance approach), private sector and state (state includes state institutions and other third sector establishments). Thus, citizens are provided with a chance to establish communication with the administration without a time constraint as in the cases of e-finance, e-tax and e-citizenship. Citizens can access to e-governance system by a citizenship id number and can express their complaint. Citizens' problems will be solved through e-complaint governance approach in the solution platform and the citizens will be informed.

This system can be formed by supporting current technology in "www.ŞikayetÇöz.com" web page and the system bears importance for customer satisfaction for both private and state sector. Certainly privacy is a basis in the process as in e-government's and state guarantee in storing and protecting data is important for citizens and institutions. This site is thought to have a positive effect in motivating public voice for complaints instead of keeping silent as most of the customers tend to keep quiet. In addition, the site will place customers in a position where they can ensure flawless production of the sectors. In this way, both citizen satisfaction and societal welfare of the community will improve.

SOLUTIONS AND RECOMMENDATIONS

'New public administration trend', a new concept that defines contemporary trends in public administration in recent years, and 'good governance' concepts have brought forward citizen oriented and effective service offerings concepts. In this regard, some fundamental changes have occurred in delivering public services in the last quarter of the 20th century. These changes have reflected on the state reform packages into the daily life. Good governance concept includes accountability, transparency, citizen orientation, participation of citizens into decision making and service offerings. Effective implementation of these concepts into daily life and e-governance approach has caused extensive use of information and communication tools in offering public services. Yet, the law on this issue stress development and handling of the issue from both demand and supply sides. For this reason, the law not only regulates e-state projects and their monitoring but also regulates establishment and development of knowledge society services, their general monitoring and policies towards strengthening demand side. Thus, the law also aims to strengthen demand towards e-government services and while doing this gives place to general provisions on increasing public trust and main principles of some basic knowledge society services.

"ŞikayetÇöz.com" is a successful site which upgrades itself all the time in its own field. It has been a technology efficient site since its foundation in 2001. However the site has some imperfections. For instance, when statistical information about the number of the complaints received by the businesses, number of the complaints that were dealt with, duration of the complaints process are added to the site it will have a more professional nature. Besides, products and brands which receive the most complaints could be stressed on the site. Yet, it is a site where consumers and businesses negotiate before a legal claim is made that makes the site significant with its approach. Therefore it is considered as a site where complaints are forwarded when there is one, like emergency number, telephone number query service, fire brigade or the police, consumers prefer to click on the "ŞikayetÇöz.com" on the Internet when it is required.

Established first as a fast and easy way of forwarding complaints, the site has become the Turkey's complaint line. It is an address of trust and reference for most consumers. However, the site has been trying to find solutions to deal with increased number of complaints received. Should they increase the number of staff? Establish a call center or robot systems that will automatically forward complaints to businesses? Moreover, should the founder of this NGO site, Dr Deveci though a good administrator and an entrepreneur, leave his place to a professional manager?

Actually "ŞikayetÇöz.com" sample is a good case in a way that has changed the understanding of businesses about complaints. Because the site has changed organizational cultures of businesses from a negative approach towards to complaints to a more positive approach that considers complaints as an opportunity to satisfy consumers. They have turned complaints into an instrument that satisfies consumers, an instrument that should not be concealed but that should be dealt with.

This research feels that, this web site could be included into e-governance system in Turkey. Moreover, inclusion of the site into the system would eliminate problems related to management and technology. Besides, inclusion of the site into the system would be the sign of a radical transformation from e-government into e-governance in Turkey and in the world. Turkey's e-government structure is suitable for this project.

E-government efforts are conducted in each state institutions own structure. E-finance, e-citizen and e-tax can be given as examples. It is seen that projects related to e-government have the same structural formation. For instance, MERNIS, a project developed related to citizen ids by the Census Bureau, is a project which is prepared after a long time and based on citizen id number and census. The project does not bring together e-government.

There are still problems encountered by other institutions of the state in their use of citizen ids. When Turkey's e-government site is examined, it can be seen that unrelated ministries have been put together (http://www.turkiye.gov.tr). Moreover, e-government site where citizens process their issues is not an official site. Above mentioned sites and links related to e-government have been combined together and used as a site preferred by the cizitens (http://e-devlet.com). This discontinuity puts forward that there is a need for a reform in Turkey about e-government and as an e-complaint line in the sense of customer satisfaction www.şikayetçöz.com web site can be included in this new formation. Because draft version of the law states on e-complaint issue suitable to sub-title of 'common e-government service' (a service, its elements and required technical infrastructure which are not assigned to a single state institution, a service, its elements and required technical infrastructure which include task area of several state institutions and a service, its elements and required technical infrastructure which should be performed from a central single point for the benefit of other state institutions) (T.C. Başbakanlık, 2009).

Thus satisfaction of citizens can be met through a technology supported by the state and a citizen number. Use of an NGO for this issue instead of using its own e-complaint line will not create problems for the state's e-governance and would help state transform into a new management understanding which could contribute to the participation of third parties into the process.

The handled website ŞikayetÇöz.com has shown a successful tendency as a civil society organization.

However, it should be aimed to reach all citizens by including e-complaint system in the e-governance understanding. In this respect, gathering the complaints fast and easily from the base can be provided by facilitating people's access to the central government. This is important for sure for the state. Citizens will have the opportunity to learn the problems and solve them by finding solutions. If the citizens are convinced that their complaints will be resolved by conveying them easily and fast, their participation will be pretty much. In fact, the e-complaint module included in the e-governance will be the voice of the public from the lower class to upper class. It will be a chance for the people especially who have problems in reaching the central government.

REFERENCES

Barlow, J., & Moller, C. (1996). *A complaint is a gift*. San Francisco: Berrett: Koehler Publishers Inc.

Başbakanlık, T. C. (7.8.2009). E-government and information society draft laws. Retrieved September 10, 2009, http://www.acikkod.org/2009/08/14/e-devlet-ve-bilgi-toplumu-kanun-tasarisi-taslagi/

Baştan, S., & Gökbunar, R. (2004). New developments related to e-government in the provision of public services: Towards an integrated e-government system. *Dokuz Eylül University Journal of Economics and Business Administration Faculty*, *19*(1), 71–89.

Cadeddu, S. (2004). The proceeding of the European ombudsman. *Law and Contemporary Problems*, *68*, 161–180.

Chen, D., Huang, T., & Hsiao, N. (2002). Citizen participation, e-government, and public management: a case of Taipei city mayor's e-mail box, International Symposium of Digital Divide and Digital Opportunity, nccuir.lib.nccu.edu.tw/bitstream/140.119/10761/1/6_02.pd

Chen, D., Huang, T., & Hsiao, N. (2006). Reinventing government through on-line citizen involvement in the developing world: a case study of taipei city mayor's e-mail box in Taiwan. *Public Administration and Development*, *26*, 409–423. doi:10.1002/pad.415

Dokas, I. M., & Ireland, C. (2007). Ontology to support knowledge representation and risk analysis for the development of early warning system in solid waste management operations. a *Proceedings of the International Symposium on Environmental Software Systems (ISESS)*, Crowne Plaza Hotel, Prague, Czech Republic.

Durna, U., & Özel, M. (2008). Information Transformation in the Managerial Approach –E (Local) Government. *Mustafa Kemal University Journal of Social Sciences Institute*, *5*(10), 1–32.

EWC III. (2006). *Developing early warning systems: A checklist, Third International Conference on Early Warning*. 27-29 March 2006, Bonn, Germany, Retrieved October 15, 2009 from http://www.ewc3.org/upload/downloads/checklist.final_pdf.pdf

Gilad, B. (2001). *The Next Step in the Evolution of Competitive Intelligence*. Cambridge, MA: Academy of Competitive Intelligence.

Glantz, H. M. (2004). Usable science 8: Early warning systems: Do and don'ts, Report of Workshop 20-23 October 2003, Shanghai, China. Available on line at http://www.ccb.ucar.edu/warning/report.pdf

Hewson Consulting Group. (2002). CRM in the public sector. Hewson Group. http://www.marketresearch.com/vendors/viewvendor.asp?vendorid=2623&g=1

ISDR-UN. (2003). *International Strategy for Disaster Reduction, Terminology: Basic terms of disaster risk reduction*. Retrieved October 15, 2009 from http://www.unisdr.org/eng/library/lib-terminologyeng%20home.htm

Johnson, E., & Prakash, A. (2007). NGO Research program: a collective action perspective. *Policy Sciences*, *40*, 221–240. doi:10.1007/s11077-007-9043-x

Lewis, D., & Wallace, T. (2000). *New roles and relevance: development NGOs and the challenge of change*. Bloomfields, CT: Kumarian Press.

Osborne, D., & Gaebler, T. (1992). *Reinventing government how the entrepreneurial spirit is transforming the public sector*. London: Addison-Wesley Publishing Co.

Retrieved April 17, 2009, from http://www.sikayetim.com/

Retrieved April 21, 2009, from http://www.sikayetiniz.com/

Retrieved April 21, 2009, from http://www.SikayetVar.com/

Retrieved July 20, 2009, from http://www.turkiye.gov.tr

Retrieved July 23, 2009, from http://e-devlet.com

Stauss, B. (2002). The dimensions of complain satisfaction: process and outcome complaint satisfaction versus cold fact and warm act complaint satisfaction. *Managing Service Quality*, *12*(3), 173. doi:10.1108/09604520210429240

Timur, N., & Sariyer, N. (2004). Complaint collecting methods for tools of customer satisfaction – A case of automotive agents in Kayseri. [Abstract]. *Erciyes University Journal of Social Sciences Institute*, *17*(2), 9–32.

Vakil, A. C. (1997). Confronting the classification problem: toward a taxonomy of NGOs. *World Development*, *25*, 2057–2070. doi:10.1016/S0305-750X(97)00098-3

ADDITIONAL READING

Barlow, J., & Moller, C. (1996). *A complaint is a gift*. San Francisco: Berrett: Koehler Publishers, Inc.

Chu, P.Y., Yeh S.C., & Chuang M.C. (2008). Reengineering municipality citizen electronic complaint system through citizen relationship. *Electronic Government, an International Journal*, *5*(3), 299-309.

Crie, D. (2003). Consumers' complaint behaviour. Taxonomy, typology and determinants: towards a unified ontology. *Journal of Database Marketing & Customer Strategy Management*, *11*(1), 60–79. doi:10.1057/palgrave.dbm.3240206

Fornell, C., & Westbrook, R. A. (1984). The vicious circle of consumer complaints. *Journal of Marketing*, *48*(3), 68–78. doi:10.2307/1251330

Homburg, C., & Andreas, F. (2005). How organizational complaint handling drives customer loyalty: An analysis of the mechanistic and the organic approach. *Journal of Marketing*, *69*(3), 95–114. doi:10.1509/jmkg.69.3.95.66367

Jagdip, S. (1990). A typology of consumer dissatisfaction response styles. *Journal of Retailing*, *66*(1), 309–311.

Johnston, R., & Mehra, S. (2002). Best-practice complaint management. *The Academy of Management Executive*, *16*(4), 145–154.

Kim, C., Kim, S., Im, S., & Shin, C. (2003). The effect of attitude and perception on consumer complaint intentions. *Journal of Consumer Marketing*, *20*(4), 352–371. doi:10.1108/07363760310483702

Lapré, M. A., & Tsikriktsis, N. (2006). Organizational learning curves for customer dissatisfaction: heterogeneity across airlines. *Management Science*, *52*(3), 352–366. doi:10.1287/mnsc.1050.0462

Luo, X., & Homburg, C. (2008). Satisfaction, complaint, and the stock value gap. *Journal of Marketing*, *72*(4), 29–43. doi:10.1509/jmkg.72.4.29

Matzler, K., Hinterhuber, H. H., Bailom, F., & Sauerwein, E. (1996). How to delight your customers. *Journal of Product and Brand Management*, *5*(2), 6–18. doi:10.1108/10610429610119469

Mcconnell, A., & Drennan, L. (2006). Mission impossible? Planning and preparing for crisis. *Journal of Contingencies and Crisis Management*, *14*(2), 59–70. doi:10.1111/j.1468-5973.2006.00482.x

Nel, D., Athron, T., Pitt, L. F., & Ewing, M. T. (2000). Customer evaluations of service complaint experiences in the public sector. *Journal of Nonprofit & Public Sector Marketing*, *7*(3), 3–31. doi:10.1300/J054v07n03_02

Shea, L., Enghagen, L., & Khullar, A. (2005). Internet diffusion of an e-complaint. *Journal of Travel & Tourism Marketing*, *17*(2), 145–165. doi:10.1300/J073v17n02_12

Snyder, P., Hall, M., Robertson, J., Jasinski, T., & Miller, J. S. (2006). Ethical rationality: a strategic approach to organizational crisis. *Journal of Business Ethics*, *63*(4), 372–383. doi:10.1007/s10551-005-3328-9

Stauss, B. (2002). The dimensions of complain satisfaction: process and outcome complaint satisfaction versus cold fact and warm act complaint satisfaction. *Managing Service Quality*, *12*(3), 173. doi:10.1108/09604520210429240

Strauss, J., & Hill, D. J. (2001). Consumer complaints by e-mail: an exploratory investigation of corporate responses and customer reaction. *Journal of Interactive Marketing*, *15*(1), 63–73. doi:10.1002/1520-6653(200124)15:1<63::AID-DIR1004>3.0.CO;2-C

Tyrrell, B., & Woods, R. (2005). Lessons to be learned from the service recovery literature. *Journal of Travel & Tourism Marketing*, *17*(2), 183–190. doi:10.1300/J073v17n02_14

Wang, J., Hutchins, H. M., & Garavan, T. N. (2009). Exploring the strategic role of human resource development in organizational crisis management. *Human Resource Development Review*, *8*(1), 22–53. doi:10.1177/1534484308330018

Wilson, J. R. (1999). *Word-Of-Mouth Marketing Over The Long Run*. New York: John Wiley.

KEY TERMS AND DEFINITIONS

Complaint Handling: is a means that businesses have developed for dissatisfaction consumers. These consumers come directly to businesses by methods.

Complaint Solution Platform: is internet platform where the consumers and businesses met. Consumers sent complaints to the businesses as quick as possible and the businesses solve the problem.

Complaint: is indicating displeasure words, writing, complaining, and jeremiad.

Customer complaints: demonstrate dissatisfaction of customers implying that the service or goods provided do not meet their expectations.

Dissatisfaction: customer is unhappy person because he buys the product or service paid the money but he don't get the worth of one's money.

E-complaint: is complaint manner, which aims at dealing with consumer problems by Internet space.

E-governance: is related state sector, public sector and non profit organization. It is aimed that citizens' are participated state management very well.

Total Quality Management: is a contemporary participative management process towards continuous development and improvement of all organizational processes and creating employee and customer loyalty.

Chapter 10
Conceiving Community Knowledge Records as E-Governance Concerns in Wired Healthcare Provision

Kam Hou Vat
University of Macau, Macau

EXECUTIVE SUMMARY

This article investigates the potential of community knowledge records (CKRs) in the electronic transformation for healthcare provision in Macau. Of specific interest is the electronic governance (e-governance) context to examine the various information and communications technologies (ICTs) for personalized healthcare support, such as the electronic health (or e-health) records (EHR). From a governance perspective, the installation of ICT-based e-health support must begin with the healthcare concerns of citizens. The challenge is to identify the organizational context of e-health provision, lying in the realm of e-governance, and referring mainly to the decisions that define expectations, enable empowerment, and verify performance of the systems involved. The goal of this chapter is to explore the context of citizens' e-health provision, including the EHRs considered as the digital records of personal medical history, accumulated from cradle to death. Elaborated are the issues of privacy that must be rendered in proper perspective where e-governance is to install a trustworthy electronic system of healthcare administration. The discussion around the e-governance concerns of any attempt to install e-health services based on the legitimate use of personal EHRs, should provide a sense-making perspective to interpret the e-health challenge of the contemporary knowledge society.

DOI: 10.4018/978-1-61692-814-8.ch010

ORGANIZATION BACKGROUND

With the expanded possibilities created by the emergent digital economy (Miller, 2009; Tapscott, 1997), the topic of computing in public administration is gaining increasing attention in today's Macau (http://www.gov.mo/) which is visible from the series of electronic government (e-government) projects available at this URL site http://www.emacao.egov.iist.unu.edu/index.php/emacao/projects. Obviously, following the trend of many a wired government around the globe (O'Looney, 2002), Macau is actively incorporating computer applications into public sector strategies for improving the efficiency, effectiveness, responsiveness and accountability of her governance.

Indeed, the e-Macau initiative as a major e-government transformation undertaken by the Macau Government comes in different stages. The first phase called the e-Macau Project, which commenced in July 2004 and ended in June 2006, focused on survey and assessment of 44 governmental units to establish the state of e-government readiness in the government as a whole. It included extensive training of public officers in technical and, to a lesser extent, managerial aspects of e-government. Specifically, this first phase also aimed at providing to information technology (IT) officers, with the required experience and know-how on large-scale development of electronic public services through training and various prototyping projects on public services of related interest (Macau, 2008).

Outputs from the first phase of the project include a series of policy recommendations to guide the development of e-government in Macau, and consequently the design of the next phase of the e-Macau initiative. We are witnessing many a public officer's increasing involvement both in the details of administration of information and communication technologies (ICTs) and in the orchestration of technology policy development in the local government, better called the *Macau SAR (Special Administrative Region) Government*. For example, realizing the development of e-health records (Moller & Vosegaard, 2008; Garets & Davis, 2006) as an important constituent of the e-government's healthcare system, many an SAR official have already expressed the use of e-health records must be considered as one of the long-term e-governance concerns in Macau.

In fact, the case of e-health record has often been considered as a specific instance of community knowledge record (CKR) (Kahn & Sheshardri, 2008; Gropper, 2007; Hartnell-Young, 2006; Handzic, 2003), carrying important populace details for the governance body to make timely decisions to better serve the needs of her citizens, such as the provision of suitable healthcare for different age groups across different geographical regions.

In order for governments to evolve their planning for citizenry healthcare in a way conducive to the buildup of proper e-health records, organizational, managerial, and inter-organizational structures, supports, staffing, training, practices, cultures, boundaries and policies will need to be considered. It is a challenge in governance rooted in radical changes in available technologies as well as the potential transformations in management practices, ownership rights, and the distribution and arrangement of political power (Jepsen & Jepsen, 2008; Liu, 2007; Malkia & Savolainen, 2004; Lanvin, 2003). As public managers in Macau's healthcare sector conceive their wired involvement over the coming decade, they will need to keep in mind such a challenge, and think deeply about how their policy making can contribute to the development of more effective and efficient public health services for the almost half a million people living in the SAR.

SETTING THE STAGE

It has been recounted in the literature (Landsbergen & Wolken, 1998) that governments are often unaware of what they know because their systems cannot talk with one another. This fits timely into the context of a wired government (O'Looney, 2002, p3) where connections are supposed to have been made among disparate pieces of information so as to form new insights and new levels of efficiency. The aim of the e-Macau project (http://www.emacao.egov.iist.unu.edu/index.php/emacao/program) is to raise the maturity of e-government in Macau through a well-planned framework of initiatives to further improve the application of IT by the Macau SAR Government and its constituent units, focusing on inter-unit, government-wide initiatives spanning technical, managerial, organizational and human aspects of technology use in the public sector.

This echoes with the fact that technology, like the wires in a computer, enables connections but does not ensure that they will be made. Only people and organizations can do that. In light of this, the use of the term "wired" by O'Looney (2002), more properly should refer to both the technical linkages that allow connections and to the features of the organization and environment that lead people to use the technology to actually make connections.

Accordingly, as governments become more wired, the people in and around government will know more and communicate what they know more effectively. Public managers, staff and ordinary citizens will then be able to use information and communication systems more effectively to know more and to know who to talk to about what. So far, the impact of Macau's e-government initiatives has continued to be felt by government units in terms of their increased technical capability in implementing e-government services and their understanding of the major organizational and management issues involved in e-government implementation.

According to a recent study conducted by the iCentre (http://icentre.manetic.org) of Manetic – Macau New Technologies Incubator Center (http://www.manetic.org) on Macau's overall e-government development status using the stages of e-government evolution model suggested in the United Nation's E-Government Survey 2008 (p.16):

- Stage I – Emerging: A government's online presence is mainly comprised of a Web page and/or an official Website; links to ministries or departments of education, health, social welfare, labor and finance may or may not exist. Much of the information is static and there is little interaction with citizens.
- Stage II – Enhanced: Governments provide more information on public policy and governance. They have created links to archived information that is easily accessible to citizens, as for instance, documents, forms, reports, laws and regulations, and newsletters.
- Stage III – Interactive: Governments deliver online services such as downloadable forms for tax payments and applications for license renewals. In addition, the beginnings of an interactive portal or Website with services to enhance the convenience of citizens are evident.
- Stage IV – Transactional: Governments begin to transform themselves by introducing two-way interactions between citizen and government. It includes options for paying taxes, applying for identity cards, birth certificates, passports and license renewals, as well as other similar government-to-citizen interactions, and allows the citizen to access these services online 24/7. All transactions are conducted online.
- Stage V – Connected: Governments transform themselves into a connected entity that responds to the needs of its citizens by developing an integrated back office infrastructure. This is the most sophisticated level of online e-government initiatives and is characterized by:

1. Horizontal connections (among government agencies)
2. Vertical connections (central and local government agencies)
3. Infrastructure connections (interoperability issues)
4. Connections between governments and citizens
5. Connections among stakeholders (government, private sector, academic institutions, NGOs and civil society)

It is found that the majority of Macau SAR Government units' Web presence is at Stage III – Interactive, which includes 47 governmental units and occupies about 72% in total (Ip, 2009). These units are from the category of Economy and Finance, Social Affairs and Culture, Transport and Public Works. There is no doubt that the SAR Government has been working hard to cope with the e-government challenges. Connected government is the trend of the world, and the finding shows Macau is still far from its destination. It is expected that there are many big challenges ahead in the electronic transformation of Macau's governance operations, including setting up frameworks, standards, guidelines and enhancing the infrastructure of various government departments. Yet, the greatest challenges foreseen in Macau's route to a connected government lie behind all the legacy systems used in many departments where process re-engineering in both the intra- and inter-governmental units are expected together with a change of mindsets and skills of the people involved.

Interestingly, as O'Looney (2002) points out, becoming wired requires a focus on organizational innovation – not just computer gadgetry; instead, in the process of becoming wired, governments will often change in a number of ways. Firstly, they generally employ a common network that cuts across hierarchies and organizational divisions so as to share, mine, analyze and act on large repositories of information. Secondly, because they employ high-speed processors within these networks, the sharing, mining, and analyzing takes place at unprecedented rates of speed. Thirdly, wired governments typically combine sensor, analytic, simulation and networking technology with new operational concepts to enable a dramatically improved sense of reality. Interpretively, they use technologies to model political, economic, operational and social realities.

In today's Macau, traditional barriers to communication and exchange between governmental units have been incrementally lowered mainly due to the interaction among public officers from different units cooperating on the same projects in a learning environment created as part of the e-Macau initiative. With increasingly accurate models and information, public managers in wired governments are expected to respond to changing conditions in dramatically improved ways. In line with the vision of Macau's e-government initiative, newly recruited trainees are now serving as champions and focal points at their respective units for e-government projects, and assisting in interfacing with other units on e-government issues.

Yet another striking impact of the initiative is the emergence of a self-learning culture in government. This is evidenced by the numerous seminars and conference events organized by various governmental units after the first phase of the initiative. Consequently, the wiring in "wired governments" should comprise those things that enable public managers to use ICTs to create new forms of organizational interaction and to manage the governmental units effectively. It is expected that wired governments should apply resources for greatest effect by using real-time information coupled with flexible and highly skilled personnel, research-based approaches, customized communications and command-and-control connectivity to spin decisions loops rapidly enough that mistakes are rendered short-lived, success are timely reproduced, and services are provided satisfactorily.

Hence, becoming wired implies that connections and paths of communications between government and citizens will change. Boundaries among governing units will change. The nature and effectiveness of managerial control will change, and the knowledge base, both tacit and explicit, on which public managers make decisions will change. In brief, as we switch the physical connections in a bricks-and-mortar government to the wired connections in its clicks-and-mortar counterpart, the neural and cultural networks that human beings have depended on for years to organize work will also be transformed or may need to be changed, too.

The Potential of Community Knowledge Records

The idea behind the community knowledge records (CKRs) is a derivative of two terms: "community" and "knowledge record". Traditionally, a "community" has been defined as a group of interacting people living in a common location. The word is also used to refer to a group that is organized around common values and social cohesion within a shared geographical location, generally in social units larger than a household.

Meanwhile, the word "knowledge record" refers to any kind of recording that is created and kept as something of value. There is currently no universally agreed definition of the word "knowledge"; rather, knowledge is often interpreted in terms of the relationships between data and information.

Hence, a community knowledge record is considered as something of value to the community to be referenced by the governance body for timely decision making. Indeed, the installation of CKRs is to support the e-governance initiative in citizen relationship management (CRM) (O'Looney, 2002, p.96), which relies on ICTs to help public managers and workers understand in a timely manner such things as: the size and scope of current citizen concerns; the speed and direction of emerging concerns; the breakdown of concerns among different constituencies; the underlying causes of concerns among different groups.

With this information, public managers should be able to respond in a timely and appropriate manner to citizens' calls. Basically, a CRM system will enable public service employees who receive communications from citizens to access substantial amounts of information about the citizen that already exist in one or more computer databases while the communication is being received. A sophisticated CKR-based CRM system is also expected to assist the public manager in analyzing concerns (problems or complaints) by type, locality, or other attributes of interest based on the integration of the system with the response and work processes in the related governmental units.

Namely, the CRM system should not just record data about the concern, but should also record data about when the units responded to the call, when the response was completed, which department(s) and personnel were involved in the response, what the government's response was, and how much it costs. More expectantly, by integrating CRM with office automation technology, the system should be able to generate a customized letter or automated e-mail response to the citizen by merging information from database files related to the call or the issue of concern with the word processing or e-mail application.

The Idea of Personalized e-Health Records

The idea of the e-health record as a specific instance of the community knowledge records implies the use of information and communication technologies (ICTs) to improve or enable an individual's healthcare (Spil & Schuring, 2005; Bashshur, 2002; Maia, Wangeneheim, & Nobre, 2006). It broadens the scope of healthcare delivery; citizens are put in the center of services offered by information systems often via the Internet. Indeed, healthcare is one of the industries that are currently fast adopting ICT into their daily use (Kart, Moser

& Melliar-Smith, 2008). Personalized e-health records (PHRs) (Moller & Vosegaard, 2008) have become the major concern of healthcare information management these days.

Yet, even in an age of electronic record keeping and communication, many an existing healthcare industry is still found tied to paper documents that are easily mislaid, often illegible, and easy to forge. In fact, patient data is seldom efficiently organized even within one organization, and when patient data is needed in applications covering several organizations, the situation becomes even more complicated. There is the indication that when multiple healthcare professionals and facilities are involved in providing healthcare for a patient, the healthcare services provided are not often coordinated. Nonetheless, countries that have centralized healthcare systems such as the UK have made considerable progress toward electronic medical records and prescriptions (Kart, Moser, & Melliar-Smith, 2008), including patient access to them.

Despite concerns about security and privacy, such systems provide increased accuracy and efficiency, better communication among healthcare professionals, and reduced risk of prescription errors. Traditionally, a physician writes a prescription on paper and gives it to the patient. The patient carries the prescription to the pharmacy, waits in line to hand the prescription to the pharmacist, who then fills the prescription. The pharmacist might be unable to read the physician's handwriting; the patient could modify or forge the prescription; or the physician might be unaware of medications prescribed by other physicians.

These and other problems indicate the need to improve the quality of healthcare, ease access to healthcare information, and reduce the cost of delivering healthcare. Undoubtedly, with the installation of personalized e-health record (PHRs), representing a patient-centric, longitudinal view of data collected from various source systems, the picture of providing accessible healthcare becomes promising.

For example, the Danish e-health record (EHR) system (Moller & Vosegaard, 2008) is a central patient record publishing system to which all regional hospitals upload extracts of relevant patient data on a regular schedule (nightly). Authorized healthcare professionals can browse the data through a dedicated user interface or extract it for analytical purposes. In other words, every citizen is given a PHR guarded by his or her unique citizen identifier. This PHR carries the longitudinal details of any healthcare incidents including the prescription of medicine by registered healthcare professionals (physician with a unique identifier issued by the government). Authorized professionals are allowed to browse the PHR for relevant information. In Denmark, a healthcare professional's access to a patient's health information is regulated by parameters such as the professional's type of authorization (doctor, nurse, dentist, pharmacist, and others), whether the information is related to a current health problem, whether the professional takes part in the patient's treatment, and whether the patient has consented to passing the information to the professional in question.

More importantly, in Denmark and other countries, patients have the right to give detailed directions about how their health information should be distributed and they can decide that certain information should not be shared or that only certain doctors can access specific parts of their records. Actually, this arrangement of access security is typical in the development of community knowledge records. There must be regulations to allow the owners of the records to set default access rights for some of the data, and customized access rights for others considered as sensitive data. Yet, when it comes to PHRs, the Danish operating philosophy takes into account that no patient should die because a system blocks access to vital data. In Denmark, the EHR system takes the approach that authorized healthcare professionals are allowed to look up any patient registered in the system, but they are prompted for a self-declaration of the rule according to which access to the patient's health information should be granted.

The fact that they retrieved this information will be logged in the system along with this declaration. The patient can monitor the log by personally signing up to be notified by email when new events are logged. In fact, it has been found (Suomi, 2005) that health professionals seem more reluctant to use the Internet and e-health systems in physician-patient communication owing to the power and responsibility issues of decisions.

The Essence of Citizen Relationship Management (CRM) in e-Governance

Today, the connotation behind the "e" transformation of governance is an important policy issue and surely one that will influence how governments and citizens will interact in the coming decade (Oliver & Sanders, 2004). Clearly, the Internet and the information technologies have the potential to fundamentally change how society is governed and what role citizens come to play in that important process (Garson, 2007). Still, as the "e" prefix becomes affixed to more and more aspects of governance and government operations, it is helpful to clarify the differences between governance and government, and the implications behind their "e" counterparts.

According to Kettl (2002), government is an institutional superstructure that society uses to translate politics into policies and legislation. Governance is the outcome of the interaction of government, the public service, and citizens throughout the political process, policy development, program design, and service delivery. Put it simply, we might say that governments are specialized institutions that contribute to governance.

As for the meanings of their "e" counterparts, Riley (2001) provides a useful description for e-governance: In its simplest sense, e-governance is about the use of emerging information and communication technologies (ICTs) to facilitate the processes of government and public administration. It is about providing citizens with the ability to choose the manner in which they wish to interact with their governments. And it is about the choices governments make about how ICT will be deployed to support citizen choices.

The term e-government, in many instances, is associated with the migration of government information and services to an online delivery platform, the so-called electronic service delivery (White, 2007; Andersen, 2004; Curtin, Sommer, & Vis-Sommer, 2003; McIver & Elmagarmid, 2002; Heeks, 2001). This is currently demonstrated by many a government especially in developed countries to migrate many of their government services to electronic portals.

Indeed, there is little doubt that the Internet and ICTs have helped create the transformative pressures that will dramatically influence the ways in which governments are organized and operated. The transformation of governance structures and processes, enabled by technology, will be embedded in new modes of information exchange, perhaps, more integrated and distributive approaches to operations and service delivery, and a more open and participatory system of policy making. By capitalizing on the Internet revolution, governments can create new channels of communication and new methods for participation via e-government. It is foreseeable that the changing environment, coupled with citizen and business demands, would continue to encourage government involvement in e-government initiatives and related uses of ICTs.

The idea of citizen relationship management is to enable the governance body to better serve her citizens through the introduction of reliable processes and procedures for interaction with these citizens. The context of citizen relationship management in the public sector is similar to that of customer relationship management in the private sector. In the private sector, CRM is an information industry term (searchCRM.com, http://searchcrm.techtarget.com/) for methodologies, software, and usually Internet capabilities that help an enterprise manage customer relationships in an organized way.

For example, an enterprise might build a database about its customers that describe relationships in sufficient detail so that management, salespeople, people providing service, and mostly the customer could do such things as: directly access information, match customer needs with product plans and offerings, remind customers of service requirements, and know what other products a customer have purchased. Indeed, the major areas of CRM – be it in the public or private sectors – mostly focus on service automated processes, personal information gathering and processing, as well as self-services. It attempts to integrate and automate the various customer/citizen serving processes within a company or a governing body.

In the context of e-governance for citizen participation, it is often suggested that the CRM activities should include the following mechanisms (Wiig, 2004; O'Looney, 2002):

- Create a virtual conference space where citizens are invited to collaborate and communicate with local government staff responsible for heeding citizen concerns at least once a week using such ICT devices as Wiki-based conversational forum. The forum could provide an opportunity for citizens and staff to strategize about trends and developments that could impact government electronic services. Each month the public manager in charge of strategic planning is expected to synthesize the best ideas aired in the virtual forum and presents them in the form of governmental blogs to the citizens as well as to any council or commission.
- Create an online database of citizen concerns and complaints on e-government services as well as that of citizen and staff solutions to common e-governance issues, ordered by variables such as department, work process, district, and timestamp of filing. It is expected that such a database is made searchable and available to staff across all departments (or jurisdiction boundaries). Each month the public manager in charge of strategic planning is expected to synthesize a summary report from the database for effective governance performance improvement.
- Create searchable repositories of time-stamped minutes of meetings, e-mail, documents, notes on conversations, and others – that is, of everything that goes into a decision or the design of a process or service in e-government issues – so that everyone in the government unit concerned can be updated on the issues and can get a sense of the total context in which decisions have been or have to be made.
- Create an online database of expertise which should include information on experts among personnel within government, citizen experts, consultants within the community, and experts from regional or national organizations. It is also expected that such a database must have the ability to provide feedback from government units that have used particular experts or consulting firms.
- Create cross-department knowledge groups that are charged with identifying best cross-cutting e-government practices and setting standards in these areas. It is expected that these groups should create center-of-excellence Web sites that provide online resources as well as skills training for the rest of local government staff.
- Create a feedback mechanism close to the e-government service context. An example is to install kiosks in multiple sites, including sites where citizens would normally be receiving services (such as outpatient clinics from government hospitals). These

kiosks would provide an alternative way to register service when staff is not available as well as a way for citizens to register their level of satisfaction with the services they receive. In this way, citizens standing in line for services can choose to provide information on service satisfaction while they are involved in receiving the service. This on-site feedback mechanism should help ensure that the information is timely and not lost due to decisions to just forget about a particular instance of inadequate e-government service.

CASE DESCRIPTION

Citizen healthcare has always been the concern of the Macau SAR Government since its installation in 1999 when it was returned to China by the Portuguese. The latest program launched in 2009 is the Healthcare Subsidy Scheme, an experimental subsidy program for medical services, through which the SAR Government aims to share with the public the economic outcomes of social development, and alleviate their living burdens. The specific objectives of this scheme based on the officially released information (http://www.vs.gov.mo/cv2/provider_main_2.htm?lang=en) include the following: 1) to promote family medicine concept and draw public attention to personal healthcare; 2) to strengthen the cooperation between private healthcare services providers and public healthcare market, and make full use of medical resources available in the community; and 3) to improve the overall level of the medical services in Macau and diversify the healthcare services in the field. Presumably, this is a potential application to be transformed into another e-government service if its impact turned out to be positive.

Macau's Healthcare Subsidy Scheme 2009

Under the healthcare subsidy scheme of 2009 (commencing in June 2009), each Macau permanent resident is considered as the eligible beneficiary entitled to receive a total of ten healthcare vouchers with personalized identification, each amounting to fifty patacas (MOP50.00) in face value. Namely, a subsidy of MOP500.00 is granted to each permanent resident of Macau, to be consumed in any of the eligible private healthcare units in Macau, which include physicians, traditional Chinese medicine practitioners or herbalists, dentists or odontologists, therapists and healthcare premises that have registered with the Health Bureau of the Macau SAR Government, but are not already subsidized by other Government schemes.

Meanwhile, the use of the healthcare vouchers is monitored by the following regulations:

- Vouchers should be used by August 31, 2010.
- The legitimate use of a voucher can be transferred to the beneficiary's spouse, lineal blood ascendants or descendants within direct kinship (i.e., parents or children), provided that the recipient is also holder of the Macau SAR Permanent Identity Card. To transfer the right of use, the beneficiary should complete the declaration of transfer on the reverse side of the voucher to signify the transfer action.
- When receiving the voucher(s) as payment, the enrolled private healthcare unit should perform the following:
    1. Check the identification information of the voucher user (patient) with his or her identity card;
    2. Check whether the declaration of transfer on the reverse side of the voucher is completed, in case the patient is not the registered beneficiary of the voucher(s)

used for payment. In such cases, the private healthcare units should pay attention to the user's name, identity card number, his or her relationship with the beneficiary of the voucher, and the date of transfer. Special attention should also be paid to ensure that the declaration of transfer is properly signed by the designated beneficiary;

3. Check the authenticity of the voucher(s) with the government-provided ultraviolet detector by checking with the visible emblem of the SAR Government and a hidden anti-counterfeit logo visible only under ultraviolet;
4. Turn down a beneficiary when he or she wishes to overpay the medical service with voucher(s) and have the surplus returned in cash, and should advise the patient to underpay and cover the difference in cash instead;
5. Issue a payment receipt (standard M/7 form) and mark on it the number of vouchers used for the payment;
6. Complete the obverse side of the voucher(s) with the name of the voucher user, the serial number of the payment receipt (M/7 form), and the date of use;
7. Ensure the patient affix the same signature as shown on his or her Macau SAR Permanent Resident Identity Card;
8. Affix an initial signature and a seal of the Service Provider's company stamp on the obverse side of the voucher(s) used for payment;

- The private healthcare unit should keep safe the vouchers received and the M/7 form duplicates or receipt stubs, in order to complete the reimbursement of the vouchers; the last date for reimbursement application is set as September 30, 2010.

The data security and privacy issues behind the implementation of this healthcare subsidy scheme involve the following:

- Voucher contains personal data of the beneficiary and the voucher user. Private healthcare units should treat the vouchers received as confidential information.
- Private healthcare units should properly keep the vouchers received in a safe place, presumably locked to prevent haphazard access.
- Private healthcare units should keep patients' treatment records for authorities' random inspection.
- Private healthcare units and its employees should not disclose any of the personal data on the vouchers exposed to them, or use the personal data for any other purposes. Personal data should be kept confidential with all necessary measures.

The e-Governance Concerns in e-Health Services

Meanwhile, in light of the healthcare development in Macau in the past decade, the Health Bureau (http://www.ssm.gov.mo/design/home_e_fs.htm) of the Macau SAR Government has also observed that effective and timely communication among patients, physicians, nurses, pharmacists, and other medical professionals is vital to proper healthcare provision. It is also understood that communication mechanisms that are based largely on paper records including prescriptions, are inefficient and unreliable (Kart, Moser & Melliar-Smith, 2008).

Yet, in an age of electronic record keeping and communication, connectivity can be undermined by the type of network infrastructure and citizen access. These are closely related but distinct areas of concerns. Networks must exist before citizens can access any e-health system, but this says little about the type of network, its capacity or its ability to serve desired purposes. Today, we have many different levels of access to a digital network. The amount of access (or bandwidth) determines the quality of service, and to a certain extent, the service type (e.g., video demands higher bandwidth). If governments decide to go digital to provide e-health services, they will be obliged to establish some level of universal service. A key policy question will be how to determine that level within an ever-changing technological environment. Also, when it comes to citizen and public employees' network access to the healthcare records, the context of network management regimes and architectures must be well conceived.

Management regimes define questions of when, where, how, to whom, using what software, with whose permission, for how long, and others in the context of accessing the necessary healthcare information. Network architectures embed these and other rules and policies into the management of any healthcare information system (HIS) itself. Indeed, each form of HIS architecture can have a different impact on the type, style, frequency, duration and content of citizen-to-citizen, citizen-to-government, government-to-citizen, public employee-to-government and business-to-government interactions. A poorly designed HIS architecture can limit or create an imbalance in each or all of these interactions, thereby limiting online healthcare provision.

Yet, the ease with which people are able to contact and communicate with others is essential if online communications (connectivity) are to be broadly encouraged. Unfortunately, there can potentially be conflict between the two values: privacy and connectivity. That is, we can ensure greater privacy by putting limits on connectivity (e.g., making it hard to find someone's e-mail address) or ensure greater connectivity by limiting privacy. Ideally, in the context of e-health system implementation, we would be able to discover public policies that would maximize these two public goods as much as possible.

Example e-Health Services in Action

The e-health services selected for discussion here is attributed to (Kart, Moser, & Melliar-Smith, 2008), who developed a distributed healthcare system for use by physicians, nurses, pharmacists, and other professionals, as well as by patients and medical devices used to monitor patients. The discussion hereby focuses on the design philosophy of a healthcare system, with two essential modules of services for elucidation: the clinic module and the pharmacy module.

- *The Philosophy of Service-Oriented Architecture (SOA)*

  The e-health system is designed based on the SOA philosophy, which is aimed to provide the opportunity for diverse systems to interoperate without requiring the use of a particular kind of computer system. This is made possible with the introduction of open standards such as XML and SOAP. SOA, an architecture in which the building blocks are services, supports diverse processing efficiently, enables cross-platform communication, and adapts dynamically to meet changing needs. It not only encompasses the services from a technology perspective but also takes into account the policies and practices that govern service provision and consumption. For healthcare in particular, SOA through incorporating specific healthcare standards (http://healthit.ahrq.gov/) is empowered to enable interoperability by encoding healthcare information using one or more generally agreed upon representations such as the Health Level 7 code (http://www.hl7.org/) to improve the quality of healthcare delivered to patients.

- *The Clinic Module*

  The clinic module supports routine activities of physicians and nurses at the clinic by keeping such information as appointments for a specific day or week, the patients that the physician has examined, and notes related to the patients. The software application for the clinic module renders two interfaces: the Web server interface, and the Web service interface. The former is designed for human user who can access the healthcare services from a Web browser. The latter is designed for software applications and devices to communicate with the clinic module. A physician or nurse can use the Web server interface to access the clinic module from a desktop or notebook computer or a PDA (portable digital assistant), and the patient can use the Web server interface to request appointments with the physician for specific time and date. The Web server is designed to use a Web service to access healthcare data.

Typically, a physician can use a PDA to enter and retrieve information about the patient during or after an appointment and to access the information when needed. The PDA can communicate with a desktop or server using a wireless connection. During the appointment, the clinic module would send prescriptions from the physician to the pharmacy over the Internet using the pharmacy Web service. To locate the pharmacy closest to the patient's home or the physician's office, the clinic Web service sends a Web service query to a Web service registry, where pharmacies offering such services have registered. Communication between the physician and the pharmacy occurs after the physician received a response from the registry.

To ensure accuracy, the physician must confirm the prescribed medication and its dosage upon entry because such information is critical to the patient's life. It is expected that integration with pharmaceutical applications or Web services that warn of interactions between medications can further improve the provided service's accuracy.

- *The Pharmacy Module*

  The pharmacy module provides services to the pharmacist and devices at the pharmacy. It keeps a record of the patient's prescriptions for reference and updates prescription status as the pharmacist fills them. This module also has both a Web server and a Web service interfaces. The Web server interface is typically used by the pharmacist to view prescriptions as the pharmacy receives them from physicians. The patient can use the same interface to determine whether a prescription has been filled and is ready for pick up or delivery. The Web service interface provides access for applications deployed at the pharmacy. The clinic module sends prescriptions from the physician to the pharmacy over the Internet using the pharmacy Web service. The Web service verifies the physician's identity, and also checks the patient's insurance (or payment status) before processing the prescription. It is expected that removing human intervention from communication between the physician and pharmacist and maintaining information electronically reduces the possibility of human error.

Typically, the Web server interface to the pharmacy module allows the pharmacist to monitor incoming prescriptions, update their status, and inform the physician and the patient about the status of the patient's prescriptions. The pharmacist can also query the pharmacy module to obtain the status of prescriptions, the records for a particular patient, and other information, with query results shown as a list for the pharmacist to view.

CURRENT CHALLENGES FACING THE ORGANIZATION

A major problem in Macau's healthcare today is that communication between the physician and the patient typically exists only within the physician's office. Once the patient leaves the clinic, communication is very limited. Yet, monitoring the recovery progress is essential to proper healthcare (CQHCA, 2000). This problem is even more contextualized for patients hospitalized. It is expected that a distributed e-health system can help solve this conundrum. Medical monitoring devices worn by patient, and frequent electronic communication between the patient and a nurse in charge of recovery care, can ensure that the prescribed treatment is being followed and that the patient is making good progress.

This e-health context can actually be extended to other healthcare professionals, including medical technicians who perform and report tests and analyses requested by physicians. Besides, the e-health system could also be interfaced to other applications that provide information on medications and dosages and warn of interactions between medications. Furthermore, the same system could also be interfaced to drug-delivery devices that prompt and monitor the regular and timely consumption of medications.

In fact, given the progress of technology over the years, many advanced features have become available for e-health system; they are sometimes called *telemedicine* in the literature (Yang, Takahashi, & Fei, 2007; Yajiong & Huigang, 2007). Today, most telemedicine projects focus on teleconsultation between a doctor and his or her patient, or on teleconferencing between two or more doctors analyzing a complex case. It is expected that e-health system in the telemedicine context (Wallauer, Macedo, Andrade, & Wangenheim, 2008) could reduce the costs for patient transport to specialized centers, provide for better source examination control, and promote significant improvement in patient care because it provides faster diagnosis and takes less time to generate a patient medical record. When it comes to personalized e-health records, the advantages of becoming wired are most evident in the management and operation of governments.

In particular, public sector organizations that are responsible for delivering e-health services can use ICT to deliver these services with relatively fewer staff. Moreover, as the number of healthcare units (private or public) needing coordination or the number of medical professionals or personnel entering a healthcare system increases, the communication, standardization and connectivity advantages of getting wired become more evident. Indeed, becoming wired is about shared awareness among dispersed staff empowered to change their behavior in order to achieve the desired impact, and who have to use the technology to increase the pace of operations in healthcare services.

Remarks of Continuing Concerns in Wired Healthcare

The promise of wired government (and so electronic healthcare provision) is that government will be more responsive, coordinated, efficient, effective and accountable. These attributes, rather than the wire that connects people and machines, represent the strategic goals of the government. Nonetheless, using ICT to increase these attributes requires that there first be clear objectives or measures for the attainment of these and other strategic goals. In the context of the discussion presented so far, one example objective is to build up the community knowledge records (CKRs) targeting the needs of citizen healthcare for subsequent e-health provision.

It is believed that simply becoming wired may not help governments in any strategic way unless governments have some strategy in mind. Namely, one of the important missions for any healthcare information system (HIS) must be positioned to gather data related to the concerns of citizen healthcare, and systematically organize the same with enough measures to balance privacy and connectivity before they are made available as important attributes in the CKRs for e-governance decision-making.

The truism that any healthcare system could support strategic goals should never be forgotten in the rush to be on the leading edge of technology. Forgetting this maxim, public managers often support the construction of information technology systems that make things out-of-focus, and sometimes waste resources.

Information systems are actually more than hardware; they are interlocking sets of personnel, skills, organizational forms, norms and processes. As such, HIS systems represent the epitome of rationalization. Most technical systems are designed for a single purpose, such as e-health, and they allow one to accomplish a complex task quickly and efficiently.

Still, the problem with the vast majority of technical systems is that even as they do a particular thing right, they can make it more difficult to identify the right (strategic) thing to do. This paradox exists not only because there not being enough resources to do *Activity A* because they were spent doing *Activity B*, but because systems by their nature pull attention in a particular direction.

Oftentimes, in building a system for one purpose, there is less time to study and plan to do another thing. In the context of e-health system, it is often the case that the finely specified routines for doing one thing or the expertise or technology needed to do that thing can get in the way of performing well other functions such as building up the necessary community knowledge records for providing long-term e-health services to citizens.

SOLUTIONS AND RECOMMENDATIONS

Becoming a wired organization (such as wired government, or wired e-health system) is a grand goal, but not necessarily a strategic one. There is no one wired organization; rather, there are many wired organizations. It is useful to identify a range of systems from coherent to incoherent. Some wired organizations are coherent in the sense that all the key parts, including the architecture and the displays of the technologies, the norms of the people staffing the organization, the organizational policies and processes, and the funding, incentives and performance measures, all promote the same goal.

Such a coherent system will be desirable, especially when the function being systematized through technology is a routine one and one that does not involve much discretion. Hence, the rationalization of the process that a coherent technology offers is generally commendable.

Nonetheless, wiring can also lead to incoherence. In such a case, one part of the system, for example, the culture of the staff or the incentive system or the organizational routines, may be at odds with the technologies being introduced or with another part of the system. Incoherent systems can create fissures in an organization. In government, such incoherence will typically lead to greater than average inefficiency, large staff turnover, ditched technology, and high levels of duplicated or unused technology investment.

Low-performing governments typically had systems that could not talk with each other and that could not grow to handle tasks. The expectation that governments can grow a system across functions assumes both a level of consistency across governmental functions and a level of software sophistication that traditionally have not existed.

However, the emergency of government information system strategic planning, on the one hand, and knowledge management applications, on the other, may change this situation. This is also the context of our discussion in this chapter: the design of healthcare information system supported by community knowledge records for citizen healthcare must be viewed as the strategic objectives behind the government's wiring efforts to provide electronic healthcare services to her people to ensure emergence of e-governance at the grass roots.

REFERENCES

Andersen, K. V. (2004). *E-government and public sector process rebuilding (PPR): Dilettantes, wheelbarrows, and diamonds*. Boston, MA: Kluwer Academic Publishers.

Bashshur, R. L. (2002). Telemedicine and health care. *Telemedicine Journal and e-Health*, *8*(1), 5–12. doi:10.1089/15305620252933365

Coe, A. (2004). Transforming government and governance for the 21st century: A conceptual framework . In Oliver, E. L., & Sanders, L. (Eds.), *E-government reconsidered: Renewal of governance for the knowledge age* (pp. 3–21). Saskatoon, Canada: Saskatchewan Institute of Public Policy.

Coleman, S. (2000). *Strong representation: Engaging citizens in a digital age*. Governance in the Digital Economy, Hansard Society.

CQHCA. (2000). *Committee on the Quality of Health Care in America, Institute of Medicine. Crossing the quality chasm: A new health system for the 21st century*. US: National Academy Press.

Curtin, G. G., Sommer, M. W., & Vis-Sommer, V. (2003). *The world of e-government*. Philadelphia, PA: The Haworth Press, Inc.

Eifert, M., & Puschel, J. O. (2004). *National electronic government: Comparing governance structures in multi-layer administrations*. New York: Routledge.

Garets, d. & Davis, M. (2006). Electronic medical records vs. electronic health records: Yes, there is a difference. Technical Report, *Healthcare Information Management Systems Society,* 2006JAN26.

Garson, G. D. (2007). *Modern public information technology systems: Issues and challenges*. Hershey, PA: IGI Publishing.

Gropper, A. (2007). Private health records and the health URL: A patient-centered care team approach to health information management. *Patient Safety and Quality Healthcare*, *4*(3), 28–32.

Handzic, M. (2003). Empowering society through knowledge records . In Wimmer, M. A. (Ed.), *Knowledge management in electronic government* (pp. 262–267). Berlin: Springer. doi:10.1007/3-540-44836-5_27

Hartnell-Young, E. (2006). ePortfolios for knowledge and learning. In A. Jafari & C. Kaufman (Eds.), *Handbook of reseach on ePortfolios* (pp. 125-134). Hershey, PA: Idea Group Reference.

Heeks, R. (2001). *Reinventing government in the information age: International practice in IT-enabled public sector reform*. London: Routledge.

Ip, F. (2009). The road of Macau eGovernment and challenges. *Macau ICT*, *1*(September), 38–41.

Jepsen, T., & Jepsen, M. (2008). Health IT: A roundtable discussion with healthcare information technology executives. *IEEE IT Professional*, *10*(2), 53–55. doi:10.1109/MITP.2008.27

Kahn, S., & Sheshardri, V. (2008). Medical record privacy and security in a digital environment. *IEEE IT Professional*, *10*(2), 46–52. doi:10.1109/MITP.2008.34

Kart, F., Moser, L. E., & Melliar-Smith, P. M. (2008). Building a distributed e-Healthcare system using SOA. *IEEE IT Professional*, *10*(2), 24–30. doi:10.1109/MITP.2008.22

Kettl, D. F. (2002). *The transformation of governance: Public administration for twenty-first century America*. Baltimore, MD: John Hopkins University Press.

Landsbergen, D., & Wolken, G. (1998). *Eliminating legal and policy barriers to interoperable government systems. Phase 1: Policy Barriers. August 12*. Washington, DC: Intergovernmental Enterprise Panel, Office of Information Resources Management, Department of Veterans Affairs.

Lanvin, B. (2003). Leaders and facilitators: The new roles of governments in digital economy. *Global Information Technology Report 2002-2003*. Oxford: Oxford University Press.

Liu, S. (2007). Enabling electronic healthcare information exchange. *IEEE IT Professional*, *9*(6), 17–23. doi:10.1109/MITP.2007.108

Macau (2008). http://www.icegov2008.icegov.org/icegov/events/invitedSession/session2

Maia, R. S., von Wangenheim, A., & Bobre, L. F. (2006). A statewide telemedicine network for public health in Brazil. *Proceedings of the 19th IEEE International Symposium in Computer-Based Medical Systems* (pp. 495-500). IEEE Computer Society Press.

Malkia, M., & Savolainen, R. (2004). eTransformation in government, politics and society: Conceptual framework and introduction. In M. Malkia, A. Anttiroiko, & R. Savolainen (Eds.), *eTransformation in governance: New directions in government and politics* (pp.1-21). Hershey, PA: Idea Group Publishing.

McIver, W. J. Jr, & Elmagarmid, A. K. (2002). *Advances in digital government: Technology, human factors, and policy*. Boston, MA: Kluwer Academic Publishers. doi:10.1007/b116295

Miller, M. (2009). *Cloud computing: Web-based applications that change the way you work and collaborate online*. Indianapolis, Indiana: Que Publishing.

Moller, J. E., & Vosegaard, H. (2008). Experiences with electronic health records. *IEEE IT Professional*, *10*(2), 19–23. doi:10.1109/MITP.2008.25

O'Looney, J. A. (2002). *Wiring governments: Challenges and possibilities for public managers*. London: Quorum Books.

Oliver, E. L., & Sanders, L. (2004). *E-government reconsidered: Renewal of governance for the knowledge age*. Saskatoon, Canada: Saskatchewan Institute of Public Policy.

Osborne, D., & Gaebler, T. (1992). *Reinventing government: How entrepreneurial spirit is transforming the public sector*. Reading, MA: Addison-Wesley.

Paquet, G. (1999). *Governance through social learning*. Ottawa: University of Ottawa Press.

Paquet, G., & Roy, J. (1998). Governance in Canada: Competition, cooperation in business-government-society relations. *Version VI* (Ottawa: University of Ottawa, Fall): 229-230.

Riley, T. B. (2001). Electronic governance: Living and working in the wired world. Commonwealth Centre for Electronic Governance, August. (http://www.electronicgov.net/pubs/research_papers/index.shtml).

Riley, T. B. (2003). E-government vs E-governance: Examining the differences in a changing public sector climate. *International Tracking Survey Report* (No. 4). Commonwealth Centre for Electronic Governance (http://www.electronicgov.net).

Rosell, S. A. (1999). *Renewing governance: Governing by learning in the information age*. Toronto: Oxford University Press.

Rosenfeld, S., Kiss, S., & Siler, S. (2007). *Privacy, security, and the regional health information organization*. California Healthcare Foundation.

Spil, Ton A.M., & Schuring, R.W. (2005). *E-Health systems diffusion and use: The innovation, the user and the USE IT model*. Hershey, PA: Idea Group Publishing.

Suomi, R. (2005). Introducing electronic patient records to hospitals: Innovation adoption paths . In Ton, A. M. (Ed.), *Spil & Roel W. Schuring, E-Health systems diffusion and use: The innovation, the user and the USE IT model* (pp. 129–146). Hershey, PA: Idea Group Publishing.

Tapscott, D. (1997). *The digital economy: Promise and peril in the age of networked intelligence*. New York: McGraw Hill.

Wallauer, J., Macedo, D., Andrade, R., & von Wangenheim, A. (2008). Building a national telemedicine network. *IEEE IT Professional*, *10*(2), 12–17. doi:10.1109/MITP.2008.23

White, J. D. (2007). *Managing information in the public sector*. New York: M.E. Sharpe.

Wiig, K. (2004). *People-focused knowledge management: How effective decision making leads to corporate success*. Amsterdam: Elsevier.

Wimmer, M. A. (2003). *Knowledge management in electronic government*. New York: Springer. doi:10.1007/3-540-44836-5

Yajiong, X., & Huigang, L. (2007). Analysis of telemedicine diffusion: The case of China. *IEEE Transactions on Information Technology in Biomedicine*, *11*(2), 231–233. doi:10.1109/TITB.2006.879599

Yang, X., Takahashi, D., & Fei, H. (2007). Telemedicine usage and potentials. *Proceedings of Wireless Communications and Networking Conference* (pp. 2736-2740). IEEE Computer Society Press.

ADDITIONAL READING

Ancarani, A. (2005). Towards quality e-service in the public sector: The evolution of web sites in the local public service sector. *Managing Service Quality*, *15*(1), 6–23. Available at http://www.emeraldinsight.com/0960-4529.htm. doi:10.1108/09604520510575236

Andersen, K. V. (2004). *E-government and public sector process rebuilding (PPR): Dilettantes, wheelbarrows, and diamonds*. Boston, MA: Kluwer Academic Publishers.

Ciborra, C. (2005). Interpreting e-government and development: Efficiency, transparency or governance at a distance? *Information Technology & People*, *18*(3), 260–279. Available at http://emeraldinsight.com/0959-3845.htm. doi:10.1108/09593840510615879

Coe, A. (2004). Transforming government and governance for the 21st century: A conceptual framework . In Oliver, E. L., & Sanders, L. (Eds.), *E-government reconsidered: Renewal of governance for the knowledge age* (pp. 3–21). Saskatoon, Canada: Saskatchewan Institute of Public Policy.

Curtin, G. G., Sommer, M. W., & Vis-Sommer, V. (2003). *The world of e-government*. Philadelphia, PA: The Haworth Press, Inc.

Davison, R. M., Wagner, C., & Ma, C. K. (2005). From government to e-government: A transition model. *Information Technology & People*, *18*(3), 280–299. Available at http://emeraldinsight.com/0959-3845.htm. doi:10.1108/09593840510615888

Deakins, E., & Dillon, S. M. (2002). E-government in New Zealand. *International Journal of Public Sector Management*, *15*(5), 375–398. doi:10.1108/09513550210435728

Garson, G. D. (2007). *Modern public information technology systems: Issues and challenges*. Hershey, PA: IGI Publishing.

Handzic, M. (2003). Empowering society through knowledge records . In Wimmer, M. A. (Ed.), *Knowledge management in electronic government* (pp. 262–267). Berlin: Springer. doi:10.1007/3-540-44836-5_27

Heeks, R. (2001). *Reinventing government in the information age: International practice in IT-enabled public sector reform*. London: Routledge.

Jepsen, T., & Jepsen, M. (2008). Health IT: A roundtable discussion with healthcare information technology executives. *IEEE IT Professional*, *10*(2), 53–55. doi:10.1109/MITP.2008.27

Kahn, S., & Sheshardri, V. (2008). Medical record privacy and security in a digital environment. *IEEE IT Professional*, *10*(2), 46–52. doi:10.1109/MITP.2008.34

Kart, F., Moser, L. E., & Melliar-Smith, P. M. (2008). Building a distributed e-Healthcare system using SOA. *IEEE IT Professional*, *10*(2), 24–30. doi:10.1109/MITP.2008.22

Kettl, D. F. (2002). *The transformation of governance: Public administration for twenty-first century America*. Baltimore, MD: John Hopkins University Press.

Liu, S. (2007). Enabling electronic healthcare information exchange. *IEEE IT Professional*, *9*(6), 17–23. doi:10.1109/MITP.2007.108

Moller, J. E., & Vosegaard, H. (2008). Experiences with electronic health records. *IEEE IT Professional*, *10*(2), 19–23. doi:10.1109/MITP.2008.25

O'Looney, J. A. (2002). *Wiring governments: Challenges and possibilities for public managers*. London: Quorum Books.

Oliver, E. L., & Sanders, L. (2004). *E-government reconsidered: Renewal of governance for the knowledge age*. Saskatoon, Canada: Saskatchewan Institute of Public Policy.

Saxena, K. B. C. (2005). Towards excellence in e-governance. *International Journal of Public Sector Management*, *18*(6), 498–513. Available at http://www.emeraldinsight.com/0951-3558.htm. doi:10.1108/09513550510616733

The 2008 International Conference on Theory and Practice of Electronic Governance (ICEGOV, 2008DEC(1-4), Cairo, Egypt). Available at http://www.icegov2008.icegov.org/icegov

The 2nd International Conference on Methodologies, Technologies and Tools enabling e-Government, (MeTTeG, 2008SEP(25-26), Ionian University in Corfu, Greece). Available at http://www.access2democracy.org/news/metteg-the-2nd-international-conference-methodologies-technologies-and-tools-enabling-e-governm

Thompson, D. V., & Rust, R. T. (2005). The business value of e-government for small firms. *International Journal of Service Industry Management*, *16*(4), 385–407. Available at http://www.emeraldinsight.com/0956-4233.htm. doi:10.1108/09564230510614022

(United Nations, 2008). *UN e-Government Survey 2008: From e-government to connected governance*. Last retrieved on 2009SEP10 at http://unpan1.un.org/intradoc/groups/public/documents/UN/UNPAN028607.pdf

Wagner, C., Cheung, K., Lee, F., & Ip, R. (2003). Enhancing E-government in developing countries: Managing knowledge through virtual communities. *The Electronic Journal on Information Systems in Developing Countries, 14* (4), 1-20. Available at http://www.ejisdc.org

White, J. D. (2007). *Managing information in the public sector*. New York: M.E. Sharpe.

KEY TERMS AND DEFINITIONS

Community Knowledge Records: Information of value to the community to be referenced by the governance body for timely decision making.

Healthcare: The prevention, treatment, and management of illness and the preservation of mental health through the services offered by the medical, nursing, and allied health professions. Healthcare embraces all the goods and services designed to promote health, including preventive, curative and palliative interventions, whether directed to individuals or to populations. The organized provision of such services may constitute a health care system, which can include specific governmental organizations such as, in the UK, the National Health Service.

Healthcare Information System: An information system designed to support the information exchange of healthcare-related information.

e-Health System: An electronic system designed to support the provision of healthcare.

e-Governance: The use of emerging information and communication technologies (ICT) to facilitate the processes of government and public administration.

Electronic Health (e-Health) Record: A personalized record keeping tracking of the longitudinal details of health treatment including diseases encountered and recovered, and any major experiences of hospitalization.

Wired Government: Also known as the digital government, undergoing the electronic transformation of public services and administration offered by the governance body.

Section 3
Knowledge Management and Research

Chapter 11
Promoting E-Governance Through Capacity Development for the Global Environment:
UNEP's Training Strategy in Integrated Environmental Assessment (IEA)

Jim Perry
International Institute for Sustainable Development, Canada

Leslie Paas
International Institute for Sustainable Development, Canada

Maria Eugenia Arreola
United Nations Environment Programme, Kenya

Elena Santer
United Nations Environment Programme, Kenya

Nalini Sharma
United Nations Environment Programme, Kenya

Johara Bellali
United Nations Environment Programme, Kenya

EXECUTIVE SUMMARY

Solving the world's great crises and taking advantage of the world's greatest opportunities requires innovation and capacity. E-governance uses Information & Communication Technologies (ICT) to broaden participation and make problem solving more effective. Environmental issues represent some of the world's greatest crises and most significant opportunities. The United Nations Environment Programme (UNEP) is a global leader in tackling such issues. UNEP's Global Environmental Outlook (GEO) relies on contributions from many experts from all regions of the world. Because capacity development is critical to UNEP's ability to fulfill its mandate, UNEP collaborated with the International Institute for Sustainable Development (IISD) to commission more than 50 experts to develop training resources for

DOI: 10.4018/978-1-61692-814-8.ch011

integrated environmental assessment and reporting at the sub-global level. These resources were adapted to an eLearning format, significantly broadening their utility and reach. All materials are organized onto the Moodle Learning Management System and use a facilitated interaction model. The eLearning curriculum and approach has been peer reviewed and pilot tested. This research has further developed a blended learning, Train-the-Multipliers program to train facilitators. This eLearning implementation has clearly demonstrated potential and is advancing e-governance at global, regional, national and sub-national levels in the area of environmental assessment and reporting. Although UNEP's position as a strong proponent of global environmental governance is unique, the detailed approach described for the eLearning programme is generic and therefore, would be a useful model for others who wish to develop eLearning curricula.

UNEP'S GLOBAL ROLE IN ELEARNING FOR ENVIRONMENTAL POLICY AND MANAGEMENT

It is widely recognized that effective use of ICTs can advance e-governance through promoting greater inclusivity and involvement (White, 2005). Capacity building for governments and decision-makers is also a key aspect of advancing e-governance. This chapter presents the strategy developed by the Department of Early Warning (DEWA) of the United Nations Environment Program (UNEP) for using ICTs in building capacity for Integrated Environmental Assessment. UNEP plays a strong role in promoting global governance of environmental resources through its several efforts, including training decision-makers, researchers and key actors at global, regional, national and sub-national (local) levels to manage, monitor and influence decision-making regarding natural resources. One of the ways it does this is through its Global Environment Outlook series-called GEO, which aims to keep under review the state of the world's environment, identify emerging issues that require international attention and provide options for policy making and action planning. Each GEO product is created through a methodology called "integrated environmental assessment (IEA)" – a consultative, participatory, capacity-development process and series of reports that analyses environmental change, causes and impacts of those changes, and policy responses. Its IEA training program started as workshop-based training materials used a delivery strategy called the *IEA Training Manual*. Quickly it was recognized by leveraging UNEP's ICTs, this training strategy for global environmental assessment and monitoring could be greatly expanded.

This chapter describes how UNEP came to develop its ICT strategy for promoting capacity building for global environmental governance. It begins with a brief background on UNEP, its mandate and recent reform process which brought greater focus on capacity building for managing the global environment. It describes the division responsible for this Programme of Work, and the chain of events which resulted in strategic use of ICTs, which in turn led UNEP to play a more active role in promoting e-governance. It gives a brief history of the need for and development of the IEA training materials, and how that culminated in creation of a community platform and an eLearning programme. The last section focuses on the eLearning approach, including instructional design, pedagogical methodology, platform and general characteristics, and how that serves as material relevant for teaching with this case.

ORGANIZATION BACKGROUND

The United Nations Environment Programme (UNEP) is the United Nations (UN) system's designated entity for addressing environmental issues at the global and regional level. Its mandate is to coordinate development of environmental policy consensus by keeping the global environment under review and bringing emerging issues to the attention of governments and the international community for action.

UNEP's mission is *to provide leadership and encourage partnership in caring for the environment by inspiring, informing, and enabling nations and peoples to improve their quality of life without compromising that of future generations (Online document,* http://www.unep.org/Documents.Multilingual/Default.asp?DocumentID=43*)*

UNEP is the voice for the environment in the UN system. It is an advocate, educator, catalyst and facilitator, promoting informed decision making about interaction between the planet's natural assets and sustainable development. The organization works with many partners, including UN entities, international organizations, national governments, non-governmental organizations, business, industry, the media and civil society. UNEP's work includes:

- assessing global, regional and national environmental conditions and trends,
- developing international and national environmental agreements and legal instruments,
- strengthening institutions for integrated management of the environment,
- integrating economic development and environmental protection,
- facilitating transfer of knowledge and technology for sustainable development, and
- encouraging new partnerships and approaches within civil society and the private sector.

UNEP's Reform Process

A number of recent developments have combined to make the 2005-2015 decade a significant period of review, reengineering and transition for UNEP and for UNEP's Division of Early Warning and Assessment (DEWA). Key developments which have had a significant bearing on the working modalities of UNEP and DEWA include the:

- UN Reform process leading to the call for delivering as One UN at country level,
- UNEP Medium Term Strategy 2010-2013,
- Strategic Framework 2010-2011, and
- Bali Strategic Plan for Technology Support and Capacity Building, and related decisions of UNEP's Governing Council.

The impetus for "delivering as One UN" came from the UN Reform process and a new environment for international assistance, which called for more coherent and coordinated work by the UN to increase effectiveness. In practical terms, where it has been adopted, the "One UN" system should have one leader, one program, one budget and where appropriate, one office per country. In aiming for greater aid effectiveness, the UN specifies that the following eight principles guide its assistance within country:

- alignment with national priorities,
- focus in areas where the UN has a comparative advantage,
- measurable support with clear accountabilities,
- human rights-based approach,
- gender equity,
- environmental sustainability,
- results-based management, and
- capacity development.

The Medium Term Strategy (MTS) 2010-2013 was a result of the twenty-fourth session of the Governing Council (GC) which called for a strategy "… with a clearly defined vision, objectives, priorities, impact measures and robust mechanism for review by Governments, for approval by the Governing Council at its twenty-fifth session" (UNEP 2007a). The proposed MTS presented to the Tenth Special Session of the General Council/Global Ministerial Environment

Forum (GC/GMEF) (UNEP 2007b) in February 2008, proposed that UNEP focus on delivery of its mandate by exercising environmental leadership in six cross-cutting thematic priority areas: climate change, disasters and conflicts, ecosystem management, environmental governance, harmful substances and hazardous waste, and resource efficiency – sustainable consumption and production.

The Strategic Framework (SF or Biennial Programme Plan) is the principal policy directive of the United Nations, and is proposed by the Secretary General and approved by the General Assembly. Within the UN, UNEP has responsibility for Programme 11: Environment, which in turn forms the basis of UNEP's biennial Programme of Work (POW). The POW is proposed by the Executive Director and initially approved by the GC/GMEF, and subsequently by the General Assembly. For SF 2010-2011, the new structure of six priority thematic areas outlined in the MTS (UNEP 2007b) forms the basis of subprograms which are no longer the domain of any one Division but are coordinated across UNEP by a Lead Division, with all Divisions contributing toward achieving the objective of each subprogram.

The Bali Strategic Plan (BSP) for Technology Support and Capacity Building, adopted by the GC in 2005, calls upon UNEP to reinforce its engagement in developing countries and countries in transition in the fields of technology support and capacity-building where UNEP has demonstrated comparative advantage and expertise. UNEP engagement at country level is based on national and regional priorities and takes into account obligations of national governments in respect to international agreements. To that end, the Plan recommends that UNEP play a substantial role in the UN Development Group (www.undg.org) framework and in particular, enhance its collaboration with the United Nations Development Programme (UNDP). Regional offices as well are being strengthened to facilitate effective support for implementation of the Plan at national, subregional and regional levels.

UNEP's Programme of Work (POW)

UNEP's Programme of Work (POW) to promote and facilitate sound environmental management for sustainable development is implemented by eight divisions:

- Early Warning and Assessment (DEWA),
- Environmental Policy Implementation (DEPI),
- Technology, Industry and Economics (DTIE),
- Regional Cooperation (DRC),
- Environmental Law and Conventions (DELC),
- Communications and Public Information (DCPI), and
- Global Environment Facility (GEF) coordination.

The Integrated Environmental Assessment eLearning programme is conducted through the Division of Early Warning and Assessment (DEWA). The mission of DEWA is to provide the world community with improved access to meaningful environmental data and information, and to help increase capacity of governments to use environmental information for decision making and action planning for sustainable human development.

DEWA monitors, analyses and reports on the state of the global environment; assess global and regional environmental tends; and provides early warning of emerging environmental threats. DEWA conducts its work through five sections at headquarters in Nairobi and six regional offices (www.unep.org/DEWA), and maintains an office at the UNEP World Conservation Monitoring Centre (http://www.unep-wcmc.org/) in Cambridge, UK.

The Division works closely with a large number of partners and collaborating centers in all regions of the world and has established functional networks for data, information, assessment, and capacity development.

Early Warning

Most people think of early warning in terms of immediate and short-term concerns such as major weather events (e.g., hurricanes, cyclones, tornadoes), climatic variation (e.g., *El Niño* events, droughts), or geo-physical events like earthquakes and tidal waves. These immediate and often unpredictable events require specific measuring and advisory systems. National and international organizations focus on early warning for these events. UNEP/DEWA supports these organizations and is directly involved in partnerships designed to ensure timely delivery of data and information on such natural hazards. However, DEWA's primary focus is on identifying issues which take much longer to develop and might better be identified as "emerging environmental threats." DEWA's key activities are guided by recognition that the environment is a key ingredient of development and there is a significant need to provide early warning on longer-term and cumulative environmental threats.

Environmental Assessment

DEWA undertakes, supports and is a partner in a number of environmental assessments with different thematic and geographic coverage. Environmental assessments are key vehicles for promoting interaction between science processes and various stages of the policy and decision-making cycle. They underpin decision-making by UNEP GC, multilateral environmental agreements, regional ministerial environmental forums, the private sector and national and local authorities.

Credible environmental information is essential for strategic policy making for sustainable development. The wide range of global, regional and national assessments being conducted was recognized by the UNEP GC in 1995, when it requested a new, global, integrated reporting series. In response, UNEP developed the Global Environment Outlook (GEO) process, a biennial (now quadrennial) reporting series filling a global need. GEO is a consultative, participatory, capacity-development process and series of reports that analyses environmental change, causes and impacts, and policy responses. The reports provide information for decision making at global and sub-global levels. The GEO series aims to keep under review the state of the world's environment, identify emerging issues that require international attention and provide options for policy making and action planning.

The main aim of GEO is to support environmental management and policy setting through integrated assessment of the state of the environment, analyzing environmental trends and their driving forces, current policies and emerging issues, and scenarios of possible futures. Four comprehensive GEO reports have been published to date (1997, 1999, 2002, 2007), based on information supplied by a global network of collaborating centers, individual experts and specialized institutions with a broad range of disciplinary and geographical expertise. GEO V is in initial stages of development and will be published in 2011.

Capacity Development in Integrated Environmental Assessment

Capacity development is a key element of the GEO process. Training activities carried out by UNEP and its partners since the late nineties contribute to wider adoption and mainstreaming of Integrated Environmental Assessment (IEA) methods and practices. In 2000, UNEP and the International Institute for Sustainable Development (IISD), a UNEP Collaborating Centre, jointly published a training manual that served as the basis for many training activities and as a basis for developing other regionalized training curricula (Pinter *et al.* 2000).

Since publication of the first GEO report in 1997, the GEO approach has been adopted by an increasing number of organizations at regional, national and sub-national levels. The *Capacity Building for Integrated Environmental Assessment and Reporting Training Manual* (Pinter *et al.* 2000) draws together the growing body of experience gained through those initiatives.

There emerged a need to update the first *IEA Training Manual* for a number of reasons, including evolution of GEO/IEA methods, a need for more detailed and more easily customizable information on the environment and its interaction with human well-being, and a need to increase effectiveness of capacity development. A 2004 meeting of the GEO Capacity Building Working Group discussed criteria for more effective capacity development efforts. These criteria, along with additional guidance from UNEP and the GEO Capacity Building Working Group inspired development of the current *Integrated Environmental Assessment Training Manual*.

For the purposes of this paper, the authors define IEA as the process of producing and communicating future-oriented, policy-relevant information on key interactions between the natural environment and human society. IEA integrates social (Davos 1977) and biophysical (Harremoes 1998) components of decision making. The methodology underlying IEA has been pioneered and championed by the GEO process and its contributors. Realizing the potential of IEAs to improve governance and decision making not only requires effective assessment tools, but also meaningful engagement with audiences through a participatory assessment process. The duality of processes and products is an essential feature of the GEO approach to IEA. The team has pilot tested the Integrated Environmental Assessment training in workshops at the global and regional level. Comments that were received from workshop participants led to a final version of the manual, available at http://www.unep.org/ieacp.

The purpose of the *IEA Training Manual* is to help build capacity for integrated environmental assessment and reporting at the sub-global level. Integrated environmental assessment requires continuous learning and improvement. Ideally, an integrated assessment is not a one-off exercise but an ongoing element of environmental and sustainable development governance. Only through reflection and continual growth can real learning take place. Successful users of the *IEA Training Manual* will:

1. understand the rationale for undertaking forward-looking, integrated environmental assessment using UNEP's GEO approach;
2. understand the importance of having a mandate for an IEA, options for its governance structure and participatory process, and be able to construct an impact strategy for an assessment;
3. be familiar with the conceptual and methodological aspects of carrying out the assessment, including analysis of environmental trends and policies and study of policy options in the context of forward-looking scenarios;
4. be capable of organizing the process for producing physical and electronic outputs from an IEA; and
5. have the knowledge and skills necessary to establish a monitoring and evaluation process focused on the IEA itself as part of a continuous learning process to improve assessment.

Integrated environmental assessments can play several roles in governance. For example, they can:

- help realize past successes and failures and their underlying causes,
- improve our understanding of the connections between environment and human well-being and anchor policy making in facts on the ground,

- increase awareness of interactions among the many global and local forces of environmental change and facilitate cross-scale coordination, and
- build capacity to recognize the challenges ahead and help articulate key environmental targets and policy options to achieve them.

While capacity can be strengthened through training exercises, true capacity will emerge through the process and practice of actually conducting an IEA. The practitioner community is already large; it has been built through the comprehensive GEO process, its many sub-global applications and other related assessment initiatives. UNEP DEWA, along with its other partners in IEA capacity development, continues to support a network of practitioners within which we share experiences and learn together.

SETTING THE STAGE

When the concept of GEO was first introduced by UNEP in 1995, it was a pioneering and very ambitious idea – matching the scale and complexity of the problems UNEP was designed to tackle. The GEO approach had clear roots in areas such as state of the environment (SoE) reporting and environmental assessment but the *combination* of various factors in one package made it genuinely new and innovative. Some of these factors included covering all areas of the world with regional differentiation, addressing all major environmental themes, and combining retrospective and forward looking analyses. The approach also called not only for information on the state of the environment, but also an analysis of how the environment is shaped by policy decisions and practices, and how it may change in the future depending on the decisions that would be taken. .

The fact that this approach had not previously been attempted at the global or even the sub-global scale with the exception of a few partial examples was not lost on the designers of the approach at UNEP and its partners. GEO has always been seen both as a product or rather a series of products, and as a process. The lead product is clearly the main GEO report, but emphasizing process is also a must. Conducting the assessment through a global network of UNEP DEWA regional offices and Collaborating Centers (CC) is an *essential* part of the design, both to provide relevant expertise (from thematic and regional perspectives) and to empower development of centers for applying the methodology more broadly.

Considering the novelty and complexity of the method and the need for a global network of distributed partners to carry out the assessment, it was obvious from the beginning that capacity gaps would need to be addressed. Capacity needs were diverse, reflecting the diversity of Collaborating Centres. Some CCs were well-established, internationally respected organizations such as the US-based World Resources Institute (WRI) or the Netherland's National Institute for Public Health and the Environment (ealth and the Enviropnemnt (RIVM), with expertise directly relevant for producing integrated outlooks. However, there were regions and sub-regions that had no institutions perfectly matching the task. In those cases, the Collaborating Centre involved had to learn through participation in the process. 'Learning by doing' has become a commonly used term in the GEO process, representing a basic need and a compromise. It allows involvement of regional institutions that bring familiarity with the issues and necessary connections to policymakers and the public, while requiring global the project leaders to ensure consistently high quality assessment content.

From the point of view of the global GEO process, one of the core materials that has served a capacity development function is the 'GEO production guidelines'. Developed with increasing detail and refinement as the global GEO approach evolved and always carrying a practical angle, their purpose is to provide common methodologies to develop regionally relevant content in situations ranging from small Asia-Pacific, island developing states to continental North America. The guidelines were introduced in plenary at global GEO production meetings and were used later in regional processes. They were not developed as training materials *per se*, but as a proxy they did serve a training /capacity development purpose.

The need for developing detailed training materials dedicated to the GEO approach formally emerged at a GEO meeting in Brasilia, where IISD as a Canadian CC was asked to coordinate preparation of a training kit covering all key aspects of the GEO methodology. The initial intent was for training materials to target mostly those participants in the GEO process who had the most limited capacity. Developed initially as a set of PowerPoint slides, the kit was pilot tested in a West Asia regional workshop in Manama, Bahrain. That initial effort has evolved significantly to become the *IEA Training Manual.*

The training approach GEO adopted reflects a mixed design, combining several didactic elements in the interest of leaving participants not only with a clear sense of core IEA concepts but also taking them through exercises and case studies to explore the subject and construct their own knowledge through exploration and interaction with others. The active elements of the program reflect the principles of active learning (Bonwell and Eison 1991). Perhaps more importantly, they also reflect the fact that all of the authors of these materials were experienced practitioners in environmental assessment and reporting, familiar not only with academically interesting details but also practical issues that had to be addressed on a daily basis when setting up and running an assessment process with clear deadlines, limited budgets and complex political expectations.

The initial GEO Training Manual was published in English in 1998, and was followed by a second edition (Pinter *et al.* 2000) that was translated into all official UN languages (i.e., French, Spanish, Arabic, Chinese, Russian). Other training products included Power Point slides and additional software tools where appropriate (e.g., the scenario section referred to the PoleStar model of the Telus Institute and included building a simple systems dynamics model that required Stella™). The Training Manual was a stand-alone kit covering a 5-day session that took participants through the technical and the institutional / managerial aspects of an assessment. A five day training program was of maximum length, given the type of audience expected to attend; at that scale, many details of the assessment approach could only be addressed in an introductory way.

With the organization of a large number of regional training workshops – usually by UNEP DEWA regional offices, and often in collaboration with GEO CCs – it became increasingly clear that there was a growing audience beyond those directly involved in GEO assessments either at the global or regional level. Countries conducting legislatively required state of the environment reporting with forward looking elements found the approach useful. From the early part of the new century, individual country reports following the GEO style started to be published. In the meantime, the global GEO approach itself evolved, and the 2000 version of the training manual no longer reflected all actual GEO details and needs.

Recognizing the increasing importance of capacity development as an essential component of the GEO process, UNEP established a Capacity Building Working Group (CBWG) with a mandate to provide overall advice and guidance for capacity development related to assessment and reporting. At a Geneva meeting, the CBWG identified a set of core criteria that characterize effective training for preparing GEO style integrated outlooks. The same meeting also concluded that new developments in GEO methods and the needs of the audience overtook the content and approach of the 2000 version of the GEO Training Manual. A small Manual Design Group was established to implement the general direction provided by the CBWG by scoping out the next generation of training materials. The new materials were to be rooted in the GEO approach, but were to clearly target the needs of countries and other sub-global entities interested in undertaking integrated environmental assessments. The basic premises of the Design Group were as follows:

- **More in-depth and up-to-date content** They detailed a need to cover certain substantive or process related subjects in significantly greater detail.
- **Modular design** They preferred a modular design so that audiences could be selective in choosing the most relevant content for their needs. They also realized that with expanding content, the possibility of organizing training sessions that go through the full content would probably not be feasible.
- **Active learning** They specified that the new materials should continue using the proven approach of the earlier manual, combining elements of different teaching styles such as short lectures, case studies, exercises and discussion.
- **Regionalization** They expected that materials would be customized with regional content, adopting core concepts and methods, but illustrating them through regional case studies and concepts.
- **Continuous learning and evolution** They felt that the materials should not be static; with the continuous improvement of GEO and IEA methods, the training materials would need periodic revisions. It was seen as particularly important to capture experience with the materials in training workshops and make use of this information in future updates.

In contrast to the 2000 version of the Training Manual, the *IEA Training Manual* was to be prepared by an extended group of lead and co-authors. The design group came up with an eight-module structure and guidance for authors. Eight author groups were established, involving about 40 authors in total from around the world. Many of the authors had direct experience in GEO and/or other global assessments such as the Interagency Panel on Climate Change (IPCC) or the Millennium Ecosystem Assessment (IMA) as well as assessment and reporting processes at the regional, national or ecosystem level, all of which were directly relevant for this exercise. Besides the modules themselves, an Instructor Guidance document was developed to help trainers prepare for and maximize the success of their sessions.

All eight modules were completed, subject to extensive peer review and finalized in 2006. The *IEA Training Manual* was launched in May, 2007 at a joint workshop of The Integrated Assessment Society (TIAS) and the International Water Association (IWA) in Washington, DC and later in 2007 at UNEP Headquarters in Nairobi, Kenya. In recognition of the fact that the modules will continue to evolve, the document has not been released in official hard copy, but all materials, including Power Point slides are made available free of charge in electronic form.

In implementing this training package, the UNEP regions play a key role. As per original plans, regions have begun customization of the modules. It remains important to maintain a clear mechanism for assisting the regions in meeting costs associated with sustaining capacity development and the skills needed to deliver IEA programming. For example, if a region desires to offer training, the structure allows an informed decision about who bears the costs and if there should be a cost to the individual who enrolls. Furthermore, within UNEP's divisions and extending to other UN organizations like UN-HABITAT and joint UNDP-UNEP poverty initiatives, there has been a clear demand for DEWA's Capacity Development Branch training materials and expertise. The trainings and trainers networks respond to a wider need found in programs across the organization.

The IEA Community Platform (CP)

As part of UNEP's development of eLearning, a Community Platform was developed to host eLearning materials and support for use of those materials. In this effort, a blended learning approach was adopted; blended learning is a hybrid usage of computer-based learning and face-to-face instruction (White, 2005). Through that approach, the Platform facilitates effective exchange of information and experiences, linking practitioners of integrated environmental assessment with scientific and technical experts in the relevant fields. It promotes the sharing of best practices, development of new knowledge on IEA and helps strengthen our network of trained trainers who assist in delivering the IEA training materials.

The platform emerged from a train-the-trainer (ToT) event organized in Nairobi in 2007, designed to broaden the global pool of qualified trainers. This event was followed by a series of regional ToT events. GRID-Arendal, in collaboration with UNEP DEWA and IISD developed the Platform to better serve this growing IEA trainer community The Platform provides access to qualified IEA trainers, all training materials in electronic format, and helps capture experiences with the training materials related to specific sections of the various Modules. It also houses a case study bank, now being populated with examples gathered through training workshops around the world.

The Platform's main aims include:

- share, test and improve successful practices,
- assist in finding solutions for daily problems,
- encourage collaboration among experts,
- facilitate faster learning, and achievement of higher knowledge levels,
- facilitate identification of experts for GEO type assessments among regions and for IEA training, and
- assist in development of new knowledge (e.g., IEA for Climate Change, for Resource Efficiency)

The training materials housed on the Platform are intended to be used in a face-to-face (F2F) workshop approach. Participants of F2F training sessions are encouraged to use the Platform in preparation for their session, for interaction post-workshop and for managing assessment processes. Because the Platform contains such a wealth of resources, it encourages practitioners to regard it as a preferred source of information, to contribute to it and refine it and to share changes with the rest of the community.

One lesson learned from this IEA ToT workshop in Geneva (Nov '08) is that, activity levels on the Platform will be sporadic and will be primarily related to a specific training event and/or assessment. That does not decrease its effectiveness as a capacity building resource.

Recently, the CDB began development of a thematic focus in which the IEA framework will be used to assess Climate Change, Water and Health, Vulnerability and other issues. This research team is now developing modules on Assessing vulnerability and on Adaptation to climate change at the national level, Climate change at the city level, Guidelines on water vulnerability, Climate change impact on water resources and an IEA Health module. All these materials will be freely available through the Platform, and eventually included in the eLearning modality, described below:

Developing an E-Learning *IEA Training Programme*

Discussions about development of an eLearning version of the *IEA Training Manual* started within the framework of a web-based platform called MENTOR (Marketplace for ENvironmental Training and Online Resources).

MENTOR provides access to quality-assured environmental resources (e.g., guidelines, methodologies, tools); structured training courses, as face-to-face, eLearning modules and CD-based versions of training modules; trainers' networks; and communities of practice in response to UNEP's Bali Strategic Plan and the six priority areas of UNEP's Medium Term Strategy (MTS) (UNEP 2007b). Led by UNEP's inter-divisional team, MENTOR coordinates and delivers training services to support internal and external capacity development needs. The platform consists of i) hardware and software; ii) knowledge (e.g., common tools and access to information), and iii) a common interface.

In the long term, MENTOR components will include:

- a quality assured collection of training resources (e.g., guidelines, methodologies, tools, manuals) for each of UNEP's six priority areas,
- multilingual, structured, training packages for each of the six priority areas,
- a Community of Practice (COP) that will facilitate effective exchange of information and experiences, transfer of best practices, collaboration among experts, and development of new knowledge for each of the six priority areas,
- a network of trained trainers that can assist in delivering any range of training packages for each of the six priority areas,
- a system for coordinating training opportunities (both offline and online) for each of the six priority areas, and
- a monitoring and evaluation component.

In sum, MENTOR helps UNEP to deliver its capacity development products and services in a coherent and integrated way by taking full advantage of modern ICTs by maximizing awareness of environment and sustainable development. In the long term, this will assist governments and other stakeholders in incorporating and mainstreaming environmental sustainability in national development and planning processes. For example, a further effort currently underway by the DEWA's CDB team is strengthening south-south cooperation through virtual meetings to provide an opportunity for intra-regional collaboration.

CASE DESCRIPTION

Basic Concept, Approach and Structure of the E-Learning *IEA Training Programme*

Currently, terms such as distributed learning, virtual learning, online learning, e-learning, open learning, and distance education are all being used interchangeably, although they may refer to applications and approaches that differ in widely in target audience and pedagogical/ administrative structure and combinations of learning tools provided (Paas & Creech, 2008). The IEA Programme understands eLearning as delivery of training materials over the Internet, in a facilitated, scheduled manner, as opposed to simply providing materials for anyone download, as in the IEA Community Platform.

Although the *IEA Training Manual* was not originally explicitly developed for eLearning, it was felt that with strategically directed efforts, the conversion could be made. eLearning was not envisioned to be a full replacement for other types of training /capacity development efforts but rather an important complementary tool available to make faster and deeper progress toward improving ways information on the environment and its interaction with human well-being was used in decision making. The research team saw this as a clear step toward e-governance for the global environment.

UNEP's IEA eLearning programme currently consists of eight modules, based on the objectives and content of the original *IEA Training Manual* which vary in length from 30 – 50 printed pages. The team made only slight modifications to the content of the original IEA material; in contrast, the learning activities, originally conceived for F2F offering, were completely restructured for eLearning, including creation of appropriate strategies for engaging learners at a distance.

There are two common approaches to carrying out online activities: synchronous (participants have to be online at the same time) and asynchronous (participants do not have to be online at the same time.) The IEA eLearning programme primarily uses an asynchronous approach, a choice that recognizes our global audience, dispersed among the world's time zones. A limited number of IEA training sessions are delivered synchronously, but those are principally regional (e.g., Elluminate is being used by the UNEP Latin American and Caribbean regional office to deliver some IEA training). These sessions use the F2F training activities rather than the eLearning modality as described here. A further decision was made is that the asynchronous approach is facilitated and scheduled; although participants do not need to be online synchronously, they are required to interact with other participants and the facilitator following a daily timetable of activities.

In the F2F delivery mode, each module requires between three and sixteen hours, over the course of one to several days, usually with several modules delivered together in a training program. In the eLearning mode, each of the eight modules is available as a separate online course varying in length from ten to forty-eight hours, designed to be completed over a period of 10 days to four weeks. The daily workload of readings and activities during the training varies from 1-3 hours. Courses can be taken individually or in specific "curriculum packages". The technological components, pedagogical underpinnings, instructional design model as well as technological and management concerns of this approach are detailed next.

Technology Components

All IEA eLearning modules are hosted on UNEP's web based platform MENTOR (www.mentor.org, described above), and organized onto the Moodle Learning Management System (LMS). Moodle was selected as the LMS after a critical review and benchmarking exercise comparing three open source LMSs: ATutor™, Claroline™ and Moodle™. ATutor is a web-based, LMS designed to maximize accessibility and adaptability. The authors felt that the ways ATutor manages content made course creation more difficult. Also, course elements could not be bookmarked. As developers, the team found it difficult to extend ATutor's functionalities, and only ATutor's internal database could be used for authentication. The LMS Claroline™ was initiated in 2000 at the Catholic University of Louvain (Belgium). We found usability problems with Claroline; the back button cannot be used reliably, not all course elements can be bookmarked, and documents are not protected against unauthorized access. Also, it was felt that the documentation (e.g., for administrators) was not user-friendly and customization options were limited.

DEWA chose Moodle because it has a user-friendly interface, making it easy to understand and easy to get started quickly. One can set up a simple course (i.e., content pages, forum, and quizzes) relatively quickly, yet Moodle offers a wide range of more advanced activities (e.g., Wiki, assignments, glossary, survey, lessons). Even with these advanced options, Moodle's interface remains clean, uncluttered and pleasant to use. Further, Moodle is currently one of the most widely-used, open-source, LMSs in the world. Moodle was created in 2002 and now is available in 75 languages and used in over 140 countries. Moodle is provided freely under the GNU Public License (Guardian 2008), can be installed on any web server with a php interpreter and fully supports using mySQL or postgreSQL databases.

It also recognized that Moodle did not solve all design issues equally.For example, most Moodle tools and blocks were created for academic programs that involve grading. The target audience of this LMS is not motivated by grading and has different motivation for participation than do the users for whom the platform was originally conceived. Also, although Moodle's creators argue it is based on social constructivism, it offers little support for group activities such as sharing student work or peer reviews, and offers no specific help in strengthening networking activities among participants. These types of tools would perhaps best be custom-made on a proprietary system, but at a significant expense. However, the Moodle user community is quite active (see forums on www.moodle.org) resulting in an ever-evolving pool of tools and shared practices.

Pedagogical Underpinnings

UNEP's Integrated Environmental Assessment eLearning adaptation closely follows the content and active learning approach of the original *IEA training manual*. It also draws from two well-established pedagogical approaches which are common in both F2F and online learning (i.e., Instructionism and Social Constructivism). Many online activities are also now engaging a new approach called Connectivism, a "learning theory for the digital age" (Siemens, 2005). Each of these approaches are described below, and the description is accompanied with corresponding examples of the types of learning activities and modes of content presentation.

- **Instructionism,** or the behaviourist/objectivist approach sees learning as a process where an expert or instructor presents knowledge and instructs learners on use of that knowledge. The strength of the instructionist approach is its potential to present knowledge in a delimited, measured and organized manner. Instructionism has been the backbone of most formal education for many years; most participants find this format familiar. However, this approach used alone does not sufficiently promote complex problem solving abilities, creative thinking or other abilities required in context of modern society (Bates, 1995; Harasim *et. al*., 1995; Tiffin & Rajasingham, 1995; World Bank, 2003). Components of UNEP's IEA eLearning program that reflect this approach include text and video with expert instruction on a specific topic, self tests on a module´s content, and step-by-step instructions for activities.
- The **social constructivism** approach holds that knowledge is not something that can be instructed; it must be *constructed* internally by each learner through personal, practical experiences, and by sharing understanding with others. This approach emphasizes peer learning; teachers act as facilitators rather than knowledge experts. Its strength lies in helping learners to develop pro-active and critical thinking, and learning how to understand other's perspectives -better preparing the learner for complex problem solving. The Moodle LMS (http://docs.Moodle.org/en/Philosophy) was designed to support social constructivism learning. This includes having participants think about and share personal experiences or knowledge on the topic at hand (e.g., sustainability problems and solutions); creating shared understanding in group learning activities; and using forum, chat, and wiki tools.
- **Connectivism** is a new approach that places emphasis on using Information and Communication Technologies (ICTs) as a central way to tap into new ways of thinking and knowledge generation that are continuously evolving in society. According to Siemens (2005), "Currency (accurate, up-

> to-date knowledge) is the intent of all connectivist learning". Facilitating continual learning requires nurturing and maintaining connections. Thus, knowledge lies in networks; "the network is the learning". A learner exponentially improves his/her own learning by plugging into an existing network. Furthermore, connectivism holds that knowledge may reside in, or be off-loaded into non-human appliances (e.g., networks, databases). Thus, know-how and know-what is supplemented with *know-where* (understanding where to find knowledge). The strength of this approach is that facilitates learners understanding of how to network with peers and where to find important information and tools useful to their own continual learning (White, 2005; Seely-Brown, 2002).

The connectivist philosophy fits well with the design and intent of UNEP's IEA capacity development materials. Components of eLearning adaptation conducive to connectivism include: a) participants from diverse locations around the world and diverse experiential backgrounds are encouraged to network, as well as read about and comment on fellow participants' products; b) principal learning activities are geared toward knowledge and resource sharing (e.g., all online modules include a resource database which links to pertinent information sources related to the topic at hand), and c) the eLearning program gives an impetus for participants to learn, teaching them to be pro-active and resourceful in looking for learning to manage their knowledge and use ICT-based knowledge tools (e.g. Google Earth; image editing software; spreadsheet programs). For each module, facilitators and participants are able to add further resources, as well as offer anecdotal experiences as part of the course interaction. Each new cohort of participants is able to consider these resources and add new ones. By creating a constantly growing data base, this activity ensures that each group of participants contributes to a learning resource for the next cohort. In this training model, participants′ foreknowledge is seen as valuable, and contributions each participant makes while carrying out learning activities become part of the content from which fellow learners can learn.

Polls, self-tests and course evaluation questionnaires are used to capture information (e.g., participants' opinions, ideas, previous experience with eLearning, self-test results on content) with the objective of helping participants determine their level of knowledge and take responsibility for filling their own learning gaps, as well as providing tools for discovering relationships between participants' previous knowledge and learning in this experience. These all serve as assessment and evaluation components – from helping participants and facilitators assess participants′ previous knowledge, to gauging progress, to providing a summative evaluation at the end of each module. This constant improvement through evaluation is also a central component of the instructional design model adopted for this project, as described below.

Instructional Design Model

Instructional Design (ID) refers to the systematic translation of general pedagogical principles into educational content, activities and tools. It provides a framework within which program designers ensure they are meeting their educational goals. ID's main tasks are to determine what outcomes are desired, and to plan and implement tools and activities leading to these outcomes. DEWA's IEA eLearning program is governed by an ID model called Rapid Prototyping (RP) (http://www.e-Learningguru.com/articles/art2_1.htm, http://it.coe.uga.edu/studio/seminars/paperplanes.html). RP, based on prototyping principles of software engineering, is being increasingly used in eLearning and computer-based instructional design. RP holds that, like designing any kind of software, the best way to determine the type of learning activities, content and procedures appropriate for a training program using electronic media is through rapid turn-over of design, development and evaluation (Figure 1). "A crucial part of the prototyping process is the utilization of the design with potential learners" (Tripp and Bichelmeyer, 1990, p. 37).

Traditional ID is a linear process which typically calls for extensive needs analysis and planning before any development and significant testing, and review before use of the product with a target audience. It is argued that traditional ID models are not efficient or realistic for designing learning based on electronic media because of the extremely short implementation schedules, tight budgets and ambiguity surrounding exactly what an electronic product should be at its outset. RP has emerged as a viable solution designed to quickly tap into users' needs and realities in order to create the most appropriate product. As a result, RP allows the creation of products more in line with users' needs and results in savings in development costs and time. It is also driven by demand for different outputs and learning approaches. Participants in eLearning come from different cognitive and cultural backgrounds and simply by the fact that they share their experience, they consolidate their knowledge and become actors in the learning experience shared between them and their fellow participants. As such, this method increases expression of the diversity of learning approaches.

Central to the RP model is the concept that evaluation is a continuous process happening at each step of the way. The IEA eLearning program carefully applies two types of evaluation: formative (i.e., process, evaluation of program activities as they happen) and summative (i.e., outcomes, success of a program at the end). Formative evaluation occurs within each module through self-tests, polls, facilitator feedback on activities and peer evaluations. Summative evaluation is carried out with course evaluation questionnaires completed by participants, peer reviews and pilot runs of each module, as well as frequent meetings with program organizers, content experts and developers in order to ensure the program continues to meet its objectives.

UNEP DEWA conducted extensive analysis of IEA training needs in general (not specifically for an eLearning version). Although eLearning obviously opens up other, new possibilities beyond changing the mode of delivery, the eLearning adaptation was built on this understanding of who the audience is, what they need and how they learn. The IEA eLearning program applies the RP model as follows:

Figure 1.

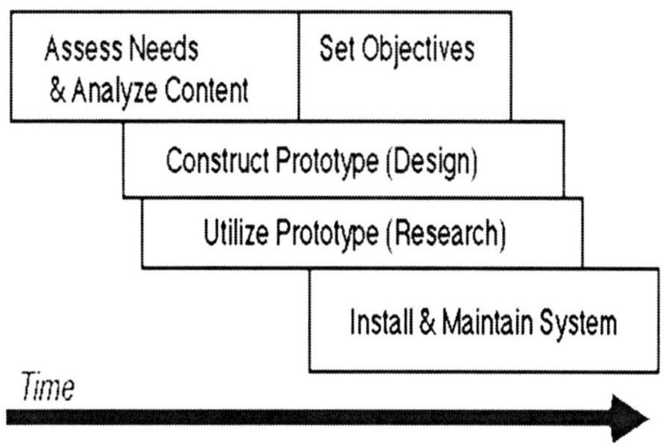

- **Assess needs** A needs analysis was conducted by UNEP in which it was determined that development of an eLearning modality for the IEA training would offer economies of scale and the possibility to avoid extensive time away from the office in order to learn about conducting IEA.
- **Analyze content** UNEP, together with IISD, developed and ran a pilot test on an eLearning version of one of the eight modules. A select group of target users (facilitators and participants) contributed to its testing and improvement. These target users were based in all five UNEP regions and brought together a wealth of expertise. The pilot run was highly successful, with evaluation results validating design of learning activities and delivery strategy. Participants made suggestions for improvement, and those were implemented.
- **Set objectives** It was then agreed that all eight modules of the *IEA training manual* should be adapted/ converted to eLearning
- **Construct and utilize prototype** Following the pilot run, a further four modules were developed based on the structure of the first module. These four modules were peer reviewed and corrections/ improvements were implemented.
- **Development** The eLearning variants of the final four modules were developed following the same process (i.e., content adaptation, peer review, pilot test).
- **Install and maintain system** Technical staff from UNEP also participated in the review and testing by upgrading some of the Moodle tools and running tests on a separate server.

It is important to us to view the IEA eLearning program as a permanent work-in-progress; changing as Internet tools evolve and users contribute suggestions for further improvement. This philosophy is consistent with the original intent of the designers of the *IEA Training Manual* who chose a modular format that can readily incorporate changes in IEA concepts and methods. Some fields relevant to IEA (e.g., data and indicators, integrated assessment of trends and policies, vulnerability and adaptation assessment, use of GIS or scenario tools) are evolving rapidly. Continuous improvement is built into all aspects of the eLearning program and tools from inception. Likewise, the content of all modules is routinely updated and grows through efforts such as participants' course work, experiences and comments, as well as demands for new content areas.

This research also recognizes that reorganization of some content will be necessary in the future as the modules evolve. This could include new schemes for indexing, cross-referencing, archiving, or new content sections. In parallel, the research is committed to ensuring that the technology components remain appropriate as new developments emerge in the area of eLearning. This may involve updating applications within Moodle (e.g., improved interactive tools such as blog, chat or survey applications, or new Moodle applications as they become available). This growth also may involve changing the overall LMS if appropriate, and/or incorporating more synchronous delivery modalities such as desktop videoconferencing.

Elements Common to All Modules

Although each module of this eLearning program has its own specific content, learning activities and content path, some common elements are available to participants among all modules at all times. These include organization and use of Moodle tools and blocks (e.g., activity calendar, participant profile, participant list, access to Moodle's communication tools such as chat and email) (Figure 2). Another common element is the organizational scheme of course materials and activities. Major content sections are organized into links containing 1-3 screens of text/images. In

Figure 2.

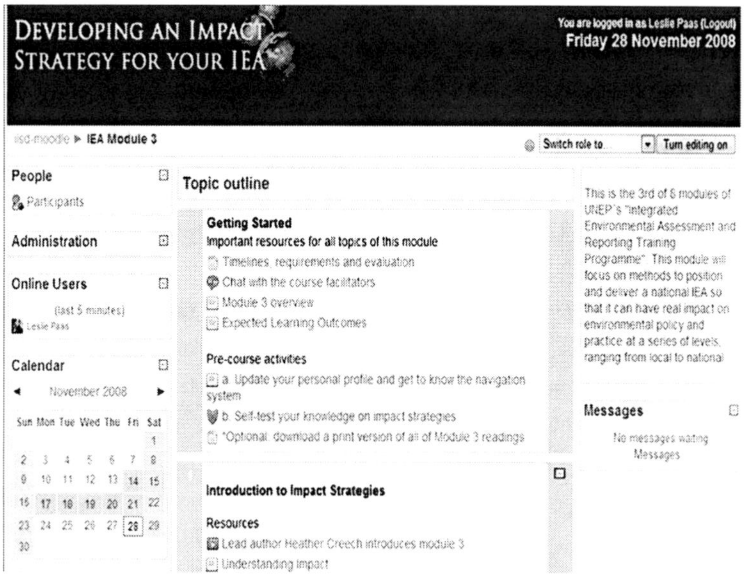

turn, the entire content of each module is available for download in PDF format, allowing access to all resources and learning activities at the click of a mouse. Each module begins with a unit called "Getting Started", which contains an overview of the module outlining its learning objectives, main activities, timelines and requirements for successful completion (c.f., central column, Figure 2). The next topic is an introduction, which addresses content of that specific module but does not deal with logistics. All content parallels the organizational structure of the *IEA Training Manual.*

A third common element is administrative structure, including participant registration, evaluation and distribution of a course-completion certificate. Participant performance is evaluated only on a pass/fail basis, based on completion of all required course activities. Motivation for learning is regarded to be intrinsic; each learner is an adult enrolled in the program because of his/her perceived need to acquire knowledge in this area. Within each module, evaluations are conducted by participants themselves via self-tests. An online evaluation form is completed at the end of each module to assess effectiveness of the learning model. Facilitators provide feedback to participants on each of the learning activities. Participants who have completed all activities are emailed a printable certificate.

The Moodle LMS provides tools for monitoring participant activities, including displaying reports according to course, date, participant, or specific activity/content (e.g., item most viewed by participants, participation in activities by student), allowing the facilitator to monitor individual and collective performance. The encouragement and stimulation by the facilitators and the built-in peer review process give participants deadlines for interaction with fellow participants, encouraging their engagement. Self-tests, polls and questionnaires also present opportunities for monitoring. This latter information helps the facilitator assess participants´ previous knowledge of the content (via self-test), as well as helping participants gauge their own knowledge in relation to that of their peers (via polls). A final evaluation is included in each module, allowing facilitators to see where improvement in activities is required. Monitoring/

evaluation examples from our modules are shown in Figures 3-5).

Another common element among all modules is facilitation. Each course module involves between 10 and 20 participants. Two facilitators are involved in each course. Although their work overlaps, one facilitator is a content guide, specialized in one or more areas directly relevant to IEA. The second is specialized in eLearning and provides technical/procedural support. Facilitation is an important component of making participants feel valued and stimulated. It provides the human interaction that is used in the instructionist style but brings it a step further by fostering the active ingredient of learning.

Elements Specific to Individual Modules

Each module in the *IEA Training Manual* has specific content and activities. Thus, for each module, the first step in developing the eLearning variant is to analyze the content path of the module, deciding how it can best be carried out online (e.g., do any changes need to be made such as adding new graphics, or making adjustments to the activities?). Not all workshop-based activities are appropriate for, or can be efficiently conducted online. For example, it may be appropriate in a F2F setting to conduct a 30-minute brainstorming session in plenary in which 20 participants offer ideas and debate the ideas of others. The same amount of interaction would take much longer in an asynchronous learning environment, would be tedious and would have a low probability that ideas would emerge in the same way. In contrast, online environments provide functionalities that may be difficult to accomplish in F2F settings. For example, peer review of activities can be more reflective, data rich activities can be generated through use of outside data searches. The peer review is a very important and interactive process that stimulates reflection on someone else's perspective and experience, and allows the chance to compare and challenge the participant's fist perception. It promotes double-loop learning from a group's perspective. Participant polls can easily record, update and display opinions and ideas of an entire group and can provide interesting and varied debate on the outcome of the polls.

Delivery and Content

The IEA eLearning program is designed to be carried out completely online. The exact delivery method of an individual eLearning offering varies among participant groups (e.g., some groups will take all modules, others will not; there may be a F2F component at some point in the program for specific groups). The strength of the approach is that it is flexible to the demands of a group, especially if a specific output is expected from the eLearning. An example of the latter is production of "environment and climate change outlooks" which are a set of nationally owned reports. Having a common objective among offerings increases sustainability of the networks created through the Community of Practice and the use of the eLearning materials.

The eight IEA eLearning modules require significant investment of time and energy to understand thoroughly. A few individuals have responsibilities and interests that allow them to invest the resources necessary to complete all modules. Most people however, have interests and/or time available to complete only the subset of the materials that more closely represents their interests and needs. Therefore, the team has designed several different curricular packages (i.e., subsets of the eight modules) to address needs of specific target audiences. The length, number of modules and schedules of these curriculum packages vary according to specific needs.

As previously indicated, the eLearning program was adopted from the F2F offerings and follows the specifications and peculiarities of each module. In general, each hour of workshop interaction is equivalent to three online hours nested

Figure 3.

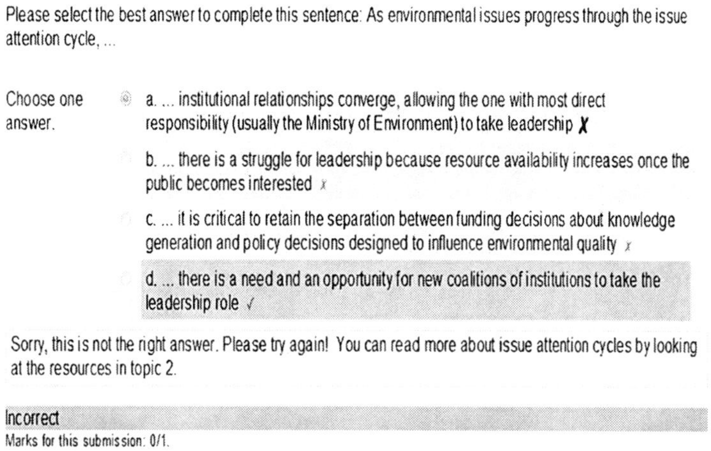

Figure 4.

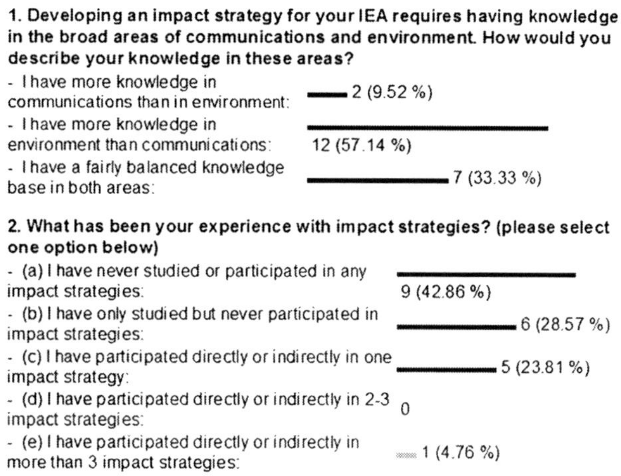

Figure 5.

within a day of asynchronous activity. ELearning participants have access to all readings and most activities in advance, but daily interaction is required and some activities depend upon the interaction of others. Thus, online activities and content maintain a linear format. Figure 6 briefly describes the main training elements used in the modules, contrasting how each learning element is conducted in a F2F setting and how it is conducted in the eLearning program.

Learning Activities

As in the F2F modality, specific learning activities vary among the modules. For example, Opinion-based discussions and brainstorming sessions are converted to polls online. Most small group discussions from the workshop setting are removed in the eLearning version, allowing the interaction to focus activities where eLearning can be most effective. Moodle´s forum, database and wiki are the main interactive tools; participants use these for their primary interaction around the main content elements. For group work, participants are divided into groups of 3-5, each group collectively building some product as specified in the module. Figure 7 describes how F2F activities have been converted to online activities in the modules.

Facilitators' Activities, Administrative Support and Course Evaluation

Interaction between facilitators and participants is mainly asynchronous, with the exception of "office hours" in which facilitators are available in chat mode during specific times or opportunities for participants to organize their own chat or VOIP sessions in order to complete group activities. Figure 8 compares facilitators' activities, administrative support and course evaluation in the ELearning and F2F modalities.

Figure 6.

Training element	Face-to-face (F2F)	eLearning
Delivery	Trainer-led F2F workshops administered to 20-50 participants (usually ~35). Time required for a module ranges from 3 to 16 hours	Asynchronous, linear and self-paced (but not self-directed) activities with set deadlines, guided by a facilitator, with extra technical support. Total amount of participants ≤ 20. Time required is approximately three hours for each workshop hour. Participants do 1.5 – 2.5 hours of online activities/readings per day.
Content	Resource book with explanations organized into sections	Upload module content as it is organized in the book, separated into sections with hyperlinks to move among sections. Give emphasis to the section that contains the content central to the given module
	Power Point slides to guide learning	Power Point slides used in the workshops can be uploaded and made available as an extra resource in the module. Videos and flash files of facilitators or content authors presenting the content can also be recorded and made available
	Case studies	Text descriptions of the case, with selected photos and direct links to resources, as well as external links (e.g., websites, YouTube videos) relevant to a case study
	Static list of additional references for consultations	Start with same list in the references, updated with links to web-based resources, as well as documents/PDFs stored in Moodle's library following suggestions from participants and/or trainers

Management and Organizational Concerns

Background

UNEP is conducting significant capacity development activities. Traditional F2F workshops benefit from personal interaction, but do not have the economies of scale, ways of knowing, and sharing that are available new, state-of-the-art technologies. In addition, most F2F training is based on traditional approaches (e.g., a range of hard copy materials) and has not always involved keeping systematic records of training activities and their impacts.

UNEP's reform has generated the need to approach training and capacity development in a more corporate and strategic way to increase accessibility for and service to UNEP clients. As a result, re-focused technology support and capacity development activities are more responsive to the growing needs of a wide range of user groups involved in environmental management in all regions of the world.

DEWA's Capacity Development Branch (CDB) designs and implements training for IEA and supports the extensive IEA community. CDB chose to engage in eLearning, especially in the context of IEA to:

- advance the successful IEA capacity development by using new technologies that serve remote clients. For example, web-based programs and courses allow UNEP clients access to training regardless of location,
- use ICTs to improve training activities. Alternative learning styles, self-paced tutorials, competency assessments, and identification of gaps in requisite knowledge are examples of learner-centered opportunities empowered by information technology,
- customize eLearning content to special interests expressed by regions, cultural specificities and/or languages,
- be cost-effective by reducing travel time and expense. For example, Pacific islands are eager to access online training and communities of practices because the cost

Figure 7.

Training element	Face-to-face (F2F) modality	
Learning Activities	Personal introductions (participants say their name in plenary and give a brief verbal bio).	Encourage networking and camaraderie among peers by having all participants fill out their bios online. This also provides valuable information to facilitators, in creation of groups.
	Small group and plenary discussions on content sections (e.g., questions from the module) and sharing ideas, information gathered, personal experiences, and incoming knowledge with other participants in small group discussions.	Questions are converted to polls in which participants engage after reading content sections. The facilitator makes a comment in the forum on results of the polls and identifies an interesting result for discussion. Participants are able to freely comment on poll results. Discussion time is somewhat limited, in order to allocate more time to constructing group products. Tools: Moodle poll (called "choice") and Moodle forum
	Before the course, participants are asked to individually gather information relevant to some learning activity.	Participants individually conduct online searches and upload ≤3 links and/or descriptions of information sources found, making the resources available to all participants. Tool: wiki or database

Figure 8.

Training element	Face-to-face (F2F) modality	eLearning program
Facilitator's Activities	Gives Power Point presentations, guides discussions and answers questions as they arise	Answers any content-related questions by email; may be available synchronously during "office hours" on Moodle's chat Tools: Moodle email, Moodle chat
	Gives feedback to participant groups on their impact strategies.	Checks product each participant has uploaded, makes suggestions for improvement, and finally gives a pass/fail status. In most cases, peer-review is involved. Participant groups are encouraged to "rate" or make comments on products produced by a peer. Tool: Moodle's commenting tool
Administrative support	Participant registration, course launching, course date determinations.	At the outset of the program, participants are sent an email with registration details. Tool: Moodle messages
Evaluation/assessment and course completion	Participants engage in the workshop and are given a course completion certificate on the last day. Formative and summative evaluations are trainer-specific.	Participants must engage in all activities as stipulated, by given date. The trainer indicates pass/fail of each participant. Administrative staff emails the course completion certificate to each successful participant. Tools. Self-tests serve as formative evaluation, a post-course survey serves as the summative evaluation

to bring participants to a central place is prohibitively expensive. ELearning enables us to allocate more funds to training and fewer to logistics, especially when participants are widely spread around the world. Further, participants can take as many courses as often as they need. Online courses are less expensive to produce and the principal cost of their offering is facilitation,

- achieve greater outreach (e.g., mainstreaming eLearning and blended learning into other training activities),
- obtain greater flexibility. Participants can choose from a variety of interactive, self-paced courses, can take advantage of an extensive reference library, and can contribute to the knowledge pool available to future participants,
- enable effective, inter- and intra-regional cooperation to allow participants from all around the world to share experiences on IEA and/or SoE reporting processes.

Sustaining DEWA's IEA Capacity Development Program

Central to success of this program is impact assessment, a program to monitor results and identify outcomes where increased capacity can be objectively demonstrated. In support of impact assessment, the team has established a long term strategy for implementing and sustaining the program. That strategy includes pre-established objectives that can be met within a specific time frame and can be measured and evaluated (Perry *et al.* 2009).

IEA F2F training workshops are led by trainers who have been involved in ToT workshops or otherwise have developed the skills and experience appropriate for such training. Ideally, they also have direct experience with IEAs, through GEO and/or other sub-global assessment processes. To date, ToT workshops have been delivered by trainers and/or facilitators selected from the global assessment and training community. Individuals have been recruited on an *ad hoc* basis, based on familiarity with GEO, with other forms of IEA, or with other individuals or institutions involved with GEO processes (e.g., contractors, regional centers). A sustainable approach to capacity development requires that capacity development be ambitious and involve multiple capacity development modalities, working over long periods of time with specific priority regions or countries.

It has become apparent we need to expand our ToT efforts to include all modalities of program delivery (e.g., F2F workshops, asynchronous eLearning, and synchronous eLearning via desktop conferencing). Toward that end, we now include a section entitled "How to Facilitate eLearning" in all our eLearning training materials.

Technology Concerns

A learning approach which relies on ICTs must consider at least three important factors: *access, acceptance,* and *appropriateness,* all in direct relation to its audience.

Access To ensure that the IEA eLearning program's target audience is indeed able to access all required materials, all participants must have access to adequate computer and Internet resources. Participants may access the IEA materials from home, through their employer, or any computer connected to the Internet (e.g., library or cybercafé). All required course components have been designed to be accessible with an Internet connection of as low as 56 kbps, although we recommend a connection speed of at least 256 kbps.

Acceptance In the design phase, the question was asked, "How open will our target audience be toward eLearning?" Authors also assumed that because eLearning has become a fairly widely distributed learning modality, many but not all potential participants would be amenable to the approach. Some members of our target audience do not have much experience with eLearning, do not understand it properly, and/or have had a negative experience which led to apprehensions or reservations. They designed the modules with specific attention to the apprehensive user (e.g., providing very basic access instructions and a practical guide to Moodle). Furthermore, each activity includes step-by-step instructions; any uncertainties participants may have can be resolved by chatting with either the content tutor or technical tutor during office hours, or sending an email at any time.

Appropriateness The team conducted an initial needs-assessment to determine if eLearning was a suitable delivery mode for the IEA training materials. They found it to be appropriate for the target audience because it allows participants to upgrade their skills by working from their home or professional location. This represents a significant economy in terms travel and accommodation expenses normally involved with F2F settings. However, "appropriateness" goes further than a decision about delivery mode; after the eLearning mode was embraced, the team analyzed LMSs and chose Moodle. Once that decision was made, the concern shifted to specific applications that were viewed as most appropriate considering our users' technological limitations. For example, videos require too much bandwidth to justify their use as a basis for important content but they are a useful way to allow original content authors to provide a more personal introduction to each module. Likewise, certain Moodle applications are too complex or too simple for the learning objectives of specific activities.

CURRENT CHALLENGES FACING THE ORGANIZATION

Bandwidth and Other Technological Constraints

MENTOR and the IEA Community Platform are hosted at UNEP Headquarters, Nairobi, which currently has relatively low bandwidth. UNEP has established a mirror site in its Geneva office to provide better access to UNEP's services globally. However, both MENTOR and the Community Platform are customized solutions for DEWA CDB and are based on the Microsoft .NET Framework technology which incorporates open source software. UNEP security concerns preclude running open access solutions on the Geneva mirror. Thus, access speeds to these platforms remain low. A high-speed cable is scheduled to be installed in Nairobi in the near future, although there are uncertainties about the precise timeframe. Although the IEA eLearning materials and the IEA Community Platform currently are structured to accommodate low bandwidth participants, it is important to find a long term solution in which both products are on a high speed network.

For long term success, a high speed installation should be implemented as soon as any given application has been tested and is ready for participation. That installation should provide reasonable access speed independent of the number of participants simultaneously accessing the site. If problems such as bandwidth limitation or other technological constrains (e.g., faults in content or functionalities that may have been missed during testing period) persist, that could lead to user frustration, significantly affecting motivation and enthusiasm of participants and reducing the value of the resources.

Connection Among MENTOR, eLearning Efforts and the IEA Community Platform

As mentioned above, both IEA eLearning and the IEA Community Platform incorporate the social constructivist approach in which knowledge is constructed internally by each learner through personal, practical experiences, as well as by sharing understanding with others. Participants in the eLearning course and the Platform would benefit if there was a clear connection between the two products. For example, results of individual and group eLearning exercises and poll questions could contribute to the IEA case study bank, becoming available for use by the broader community. At the same time, alumni of eLearning courses could become members of the Platform. They could then use the Platform to interact and obtain support during application of the knowledge and skills obtained during their eLearning experience. Ensuring that Platform members can access the eLearning modules and use them during capacity development activities could provide additional motivation for trainers and practitioners to actively participate in networking and to share experiences. DEWA CDB plans to evaluate potential benefits of establishing more clear linkages between the two products and recognizes the need to find a cost efficient, technical and managerial solution for maintaining such linkages. In this context, the biggest challenge will be establishing a smooth transition of eLearners to the Platform at the end of a given course to ensure they are empowered to stay in touch, feel appreciated and do not confuse the purpose and services of the two products.

Training the Multipliers

Current ToT (Train the Trainers) Activities

Currently, IEA ToT activities are based on the *IEA Training Manual*. The principal aim of the ToT effort is to enable selected trainers to use the *Manual* in a F2F environment. During training, participants strengthen their own knowledge of IEA and improve their ability to build others' capacities and/or develop multi-level IEA applications or non-GEO assessments. To achieve these objectives, ToT workshops utilize active learning in which future trainers are invited to participate in three ways:

- as a trainee, learning the *IEA Training Manual* content,
- as a trainer who will provide training to others, and
- as an IEA or other assessment practitioner.

For a number of years, DEWA CDB has conducted annual IEA ToT workshops at the global and regional levels. ToT workshops typically require 2-5 days and involve 15-20 participants; they are designed to provide content-related knowledge and to increase training skills. Our experience has been that extra attention is given to some parts of the IEA content and insufficient attention to other parts, often the most complicated parts (e.g., the IEA Scientific Framework, Policy Analysis or Scenarios). Also, development of specific training skills is often under-addressed. This disparity is a function of the limited time investment customarily associated with these workshops, and the workshop setting itself.

A Re-Envisioned Train the Multipliers (ToM) Structure

The research team has developed a Train the Multipliers (ToM) skill development structure for our eLearning programme. They initially hosted a global training which provides blended interaction between designers and first order participants. All participants are invited to complete the modules in an eLearning setting. During the F2F workshop, limited time is devoted to clarification of topics which were studied online; the overall focus of the workshop is on the pedagogical aspects of training (e.g., training techniques, presentation skills and group dynamics). That first order group is then commissioned to offering regional training to second order participants in a multiplier effect. The latter (the second order participants) then become the principal and growing core of facilitators for eLearning courses.

The ToM design is adaptive, based on the team's day-to-day experience till-date. It is clear that a blended approach to training is attractive, careful attention should be paid to the users and their modalities. Motivation, prior eLearning experience, technical capacities and skills of the participants, as well as support from the facilitators all should be considered in advance and addressed in design of ToM learning activities.

Definition and Management of Adequately Trained Facilitators

A successful eLearning course requires strong facilitation and administration to provide sufficient support and motivation to participants. In order to ensure sustainability of the IEA eLearning efforts, DEWA's CDB believes it is crucial to develop an adequate structure for selection, training and support of eLearning facilitators. Facilitation of eLearning sessions requires different skill than does facilitation in a F2F setting. An eLearning facilitator must be intimately familiar with the content knowledge and have strong pedagogical skills but also must understand the process of distance teaching and the related tools and means. He/she needs online communication skills and must be a fluent written and oral communicator (in English in the first adaptation). In some cases, facilitators also must be able to support students who have inadequate technological knowledge. In order to address the needs of a global audience, CDB is building a pool of eLearning facilitators that reflects the diversity of the audience. Ideally, this structure will allow partnerships between two or more facilitators, one specializing in content and the other in eLearning.

The team is still refining design of the eLearning ToM and the trainers' network. For example, there is a need to clarify minimum criteria (e.g., bandwidth, hardware, experience, content knowledge), for more guidance for instructors on "How to Facilitate Online Learning" for each of the Modules, for design and implementation of special training on eLearning pedagogy and technology, and for establishment of a Community of Practice for eLearning facilitators. Further, there must be a commitment to provide the funding and human resources required for basic support of the eLearning curriculum and for a 'help desk for eLearning facilitators' to address day-to-day technical, pedagogical and administrative questions.

Another challenge which eLearning programs should consider from the very beginning is that of keeping trained facilitators motivated and active. ELearning requires significantly more time for communication with students than does a F2F setting, and that occurs over a longer time period. Facilitators may be motivated early on by the novelty of running eLearning courses, a chance to adopt new technology and acquire new skills. At a later stage, their enthusiasm could be reduced by the lack of novelty and high time demands. Attention to motivation and professional growth within the facilitator pool will be resources wisely invested.

Ensuring Motivation of Participants

Due to the nature of its mandate, UNEP's training courses are provided free of charge. Because eLearning does not have the traditional motivating factors which affect participants at F2F trainings, some people may place a low value on access to free eLearning. That might reduce their effort to learn the content and participate in course activities. Many eLearning activities are interactive, designed as group discussions or group exercises. The presence of unmotivated or inactive participants complicates the learning process for others and makes facilitation difficult.

Administrative strategies that were used to increase participant motivation include creating apparent scarcity by requiring admission applications, thus boosting the perceived value of the education; rewarding participants with UNEP Certificates of Completion at the end of the course; providing access to the IEA Community Platform with the possibility to become a certified trainer if they complete the course successfully; and rewarding the best students with the opportunity to participate in F2F activities elsewhere in the IEA community. It is important to identify and use pedagogical strategies that ensure a critical number of active participants in each exercise. In some cases, it may be appropriate to design alternative group exercises which encourage individualistic learners to pursue their learning individually.

Sustaining the Effort

The IEA eLearning effort has been designed and implemented by UNEP DEWA. It is identified as a free good, accessible to the global community. That decision, however, carries responsibilities and potential liabilities. UNEP maintains the eLearning materials on its Nairobi server. Institutionally, it inherits the responsibility to consider maintenance and updates, both to software and content. Although the materials are freely accessible, access includes the caveat that all users must notify UNEP for tracking and data collection about use and utility. All IEA eLearning materials have embedded logos of both UNEP and IISD, the two institutions that developed the materials; this ensures some level of attribution. The eLearning materials are developed with a facilitated interaction instructional design. Any offering that follows that design (as certified by the facilitator) is eligible to offer its participants a Certificate of Completion issued by UNEP if so desired. The materials also are freely accessible for perusal by individuals, in a non-facilitated mode. However, such use does not qualify as facilitated interaction and does not qualify for a Certificate of Completion.

SOLUTIONS AND RECOMMENDATIONS

With the launch of an ambitious eLearning program to develop IEA capacity at the sub-global level, UNEP and its partners have embarked on a journey that promises greater efficiencies and effectiveness of capacity development. At the same time, they have added a new modality that creates its own challenges that need to be recognized and systematically tackled in order to help realize eLearning's potential. Some of those challenges are strategic and need high level solutions, while others are more specific and require technological responses. In this final part of the chapter, authors would like to identify a few key challenges that need to be tackled and proposed a way forward.

Strategic Direction for IEA eLearning

The current phase of the IEA eLearning work was initiated at a time when both UNEP's and DEWA's approach to eLearning was under development; to some extent, that remains true over the entire UN system. It is vitally important that IEA eLearning fit within the broader, strategic directions of DEWA, UNEP and UN-wide eLearning. Further, it must remain philosophically consistent with UNEP's capacity development strategy. Those goals will only be met through strategic communication and interaction within and among UN programs. Furthermore, capacity development and related training activities are not conducted in isolation. Training requests must be vetted through regional and or/country offices, and approved on the basis of well understood criteria (e.g., if the country or region is embarking on an IEA process and report and if capacity development and training will be an integral part of the process).

Embedding eLearning into Broader Capacity Development

ELearning is only one way, although an increasingly important way of increasing IEA knowledge capacity. One need to understand how eLearning works with other forms of capacity development, including F2F training, exchange programs or assistance with learning by doing. For example, this research team is implementing blended learning in their ToM work. In that case, they involve future trainers in eLearning activities delivered at a distance, meet in a F2F setting, then monitor and support their individualized delivery of remote eLearning.

Sustaining the Momentum

In the history of multilateral institutions, there are many examples of expensive and sophisticated materials being developed and forgotten before being put to their intended use. Maintaining momentum is often difficult and certainly not cost free. In order for qualified trainers to run electronic or F2F sessions, they need a mandate, time and resources in addition to the tools to engage relevant sub-global audiences. UNEP can do a lot in terms of outreach and marketing to ensure that potential audiences for, and participants in eLearning know about the program and articulate their needs either nationally or to other donors so that sessions with a practical orientation can be organized. The Community Platform is one vehicle that will assist in meeting this goal. Another important aspect that is developing momentum is the One UN concept, which increases communication and collaboration among UN agencies.

Technical Design

ELearning is a technology-heavy field that is influenced by constant changes in things ranging from available band-width to computer hardware and software. Both UNEP and its partners recognize the need to monitor new and emerging technologies and be ready to make necessary, perhaps fundamental modifications to the design. In the interest of efficiency, those changes may best coincide with a thorough review and revision of the basic content of the modules (including those designed for F2F sessions). Although that will occur sometime in the future, it is important to recognize the need, plan for a careful review, and budget for significant modification if necessary.

Access to ICT

Recently, UNEP conducted a survey among national environment authorities and ministries in developing countries, trying to assess their technological capacities. One of the findings was that not all clients had adequate Internet access (e.g., limited bandwidth) and some even did not have access to computers. This has a direct bearing to this eLearning program because if UNEP's clients do not have access to ICTs, the impact of eLearning program will be hampered. UNEP is responding to these findings by partnering with development agencies like UNDP to ensure that environmental authorities and ministries have access to, and gain the relevant skills for use of modern ICT.

Cross-Regional Coordination

The IEA modules, and by necessity their eLearning versions, are constantly being customized and refined by either DEWA regional offices or outside partners who are producing regional variations. It will be essential to coordinate this development work to ensure that structural and substantive attributes of the core IEA modules are protected. At the same time, regionalization needs to be encouraged because it helps increase the modules' relevance to regional audiences. Effective regionalization will best be advanced through careful and consistent communication within DEWA, as well as among UNEP branches and among UN agencies.

CONCLUSIONS

This eLearning effort has advanced the development and use of Integrated Environmental Assessment (IEA) by making the skills and knowledge of the field more readily accessible to a global audience. These materials specifically employ eLearning concepts and tools to advance e-governance at the grass roots level. Any person can now readily access all UNEP IEA eLearning materials; facilitators (either trained by UNEP or others) can design and offer the eLearning materials in a facilitated interaction mode, and may offer any subset of the eight modules. This offers opportunities ranging from a 7-day overview of IEA (Module 1) to a very thorough, 12-15 week experience covering all eight modules. Additional modules under consideration for eLearning include water vulnerability and climate change, among others. This advancement in access, skill and knowledge encourages grass roots efforts (e.g., citizens, NGOs) to engage in environmental assessment, to become knowledgeable about and to question the decisions made by political leaders as they consider environmental decisions.

REFERENCES

Bates, A. W. (1995). *Technology, Open Learning and Distance Education*. London: Routledge.

Bonwell, C., & Eison, J. (1991). *Active learning: Creating excitement in the classroom AEHE-ERIC Higher Education Report No.1*. Jossey-Bass, Washington, D.C.

Community Platform, I. E. A. Retrieved from http://gcp.aspen.grida.no/ (Accessed 26 May 2009)

Davos, C. A. (1977). Toward an integrated environmental assessment within a social context. *Journal of Environmental Management*, *5*(3), 297–305.

Global Environmental Outlook. Retrieved from http://www.unep.org/geo/ (Accessed 26 May 2009)

Guradian (2008). Moodle nudges forward. *The Guardian* January 8, 2008 http://education.guardian.co.uk/link/story/0,2236721,00.html Accessed 29 May, 2009

Harasim, L., & Hiltz, S. R. L Teles, M Turoff (1995). *Learning Networks, A field guide to teaching and learning online* In Harremoes, P (1998), The challenge of managing water and material balances in relation to eutrophication *Water Science and Technology* 37(3),9-17. MIT Press Cambridge, MA

Paas, L., & Creech, H. (2008). Current Uses and Trends in ICTs supporting Education for Sustainable Development. Winnipeg: IISD http:www.iisd.org

Perry, J, L Paas, L Pinter, N Sharma, J Belali, M Eugenia-Arreola, E Santer (2009). *Sustaining the IEA capacity building network Draft manuscript prepared for IISD and UNEP Nairobi.*

Pintér, L., Zahedi, K., & Cressman, D. (2000). *Capacity building for integrated environmental assessment and reporting training manual* Winnipeg: IISD for UNEP http://www.iisd.org/pdf/geo_manual_2.pdf

Seely-Brown, J 2002 GROWING UP DIGITAL: How the web changes work, education, and the ways people learn *United States Distance Learning Association USDLA Journal* 16(2): http://www.usdla.org/html/journal/FEB02_Issue/article01.html Accessed 26 May 2009

Siemens, G. (2005). Connectivism: A learning theory for the digital age . *International Journal of Instructional Technology & Distance Learning*, *2*(1). http://www.itdl.org/Journal/Jan_05/article01.htm and http://www.connectivism.ca/about.html Accessed 26 May 2009.

Tiffin, J., & Rajasingham, L. (1995). *Search of the Virtual Class*. London: Routledge. doi:10.4324/9780203291184

Tripp, S., & Bichelmeyer, B. (1990). Rapid prototyping: An alternative instructional design strategy . *Educational Technology Research and Development*, *38*(1), 31–44. doi:10.1007/BF02298246

UNEP, (2007a). Environment fund budgets: proposed biennial programme and support budget for 2008 - 2009: Report of the Executive Director (UNEP/GC/24/9)

UNEP, (2007b). Proposed Medium-Term Strategy 2010–2013 (UNEP/GCSS.X/8)

White, G. (2005). Beyond the horseless carriage: Harnessing the potential of ICT in education and training *Education.au limited*http://www.educationau.edu.au/jahia/webdav/site/myjahiasite/shared/papers/horseless_carriages_GW.pdf Accessed 26 May 2009

ADDITIONAL READING

Aston, M. (2002). *The development and use of indicators to measure the impact of ICT use in education in the United Kingdom and other European countries. Developing Performance Indicators for ICT in Education, UNESCO Institute For Information Technology* (pp. 62–73). IITE.

Benito, R. M., Camara, M. E., Losada, J. C., Arranz, F. J., & Seidel, L. (2007). *Using Moodle and Flash animations in an interactive learning environment for introductory physics in engineering. E-activities: networking the world-proceedings of the 6th WSEAS international conference on e-activities* (pp. 275–278). Electrical and Computer Engineering Series.

Bradley, M. E., Thom, L. R., Hayes, J., & Hay, C. (2008). Ask and you will receive: how question type influences quantity and quality of online questions. *British Journal of Educational Technology*, *39*(5), 888–900. doi:10.1111/j.1467-8535.2007.00804.x

Bull, G. (2006). Collaboration in a WEB 2.0 environment. *Learning & Leading with Technology* ISTE (International Society for Technology in Education) April

Chang, T. Y., & Chen, Y. T. (2009). Cooperative learning in eLearning: A peer assessment of student centered (*sic*) using fuzzy preferences. *Expert Systems with Applications*, *36*(4), 8342–8349. doi:10.1016/j.eswa.2008.10.050

Delfino, M, D Persico (2007). Online or face-to-face? Experimenting with different techniques in teacher training. *Journal of Computer Assisted Learning* 23(5), 351-365 2009.

Donavanat, B. W. (2009). The new, modern practice of adult education: Online instruction in a continuing professional education setting. *Adult Education Quarterly*, *59*(3), 227–245. doi:10.1177/0741713609331546

EDU CAUSE and NEW MEDIA. (2007). *The Horizon Report 2007 Edition.* The New Media Consortium and the EDU CAUSE learning initiative http://www.nmc.org/pdf/2007_Horizon_Report.pdf Accessed 26 May 2009

Ellis, R. A., Goodyear, P., Prosser, M., & O'Hara, A. (2006). How and what university students learn through online and face-to-face discussion: conceptions, intentions and approaches. *Journal of Computer Assisted Learning*, *22*(4), 244–256. doi:10.1111/j.1365-2729.2006.00173.x

Grossman, R. W. (1994). Encouraging critical thinking using the case study method and cooperative learning techniques. *Journal on Excellence in College Teaching*, *5*(1), 7–20.

Hioc-Bozic, N., Mornar, V., & Boticki, I. (2009). A blended learning approach to course design and implementation. *IEEE Transactions on Education*, *52*(1), 19–30. doi:10.1109/TE.2007.914945

Hull, D. M., & Saxon, T. F. (2009). Negotiation of meaning and co-construction of knowledge: An experimental analysis of asynchronous online instruction. *Computers & Education*, *52*(3), 624–639. doi:10.1016/j.compedu.2008.11.005

IMS. (2003). IMS Learning design best practice and implementation guide IMS Global Learning Consortium, Inc http://www.imsglobal.org/learningdesign/ldv1p0/imsld_bestv1p0.html Accessed 26 May 2009

Isaila, N. (2009). E-Learning-A modern way for employees' training. *Metalurgica International*, *14*, 97–100.

Keller, J. (2008). First principles of motivation to learn and e3-learning. *Distance Education*, *29*(2), 175–185. doi:10.1080/01587910802154970

Lamb, B. (2007). Dr Mashup or Why educators should learn to stop worrying and love the remix . *EDUCAUSE Review*, *42*(4), 12–25. http://www.educause.edu/EDUCAUSE+Review/EDUCAUSEReviewMagazineVolume42/DrMashuporWhyEducatorsShouldLe/161747 Accessed 26 May 2009.

Lanham, E., & Zuou, W. (2003). Cultural issues in online learning-is blended learning a possible solution? *International Journal of Computer Processing of Oriental Languages*, *6*(4), 275–292. doi:10.1142/S0219427903000930

Lustigova, Z., Lustig, F., Mechlova, E., & Malcik, M. (2009). A new eLearning strategy for cognition of the real world in reaching and learning science. *New Educational Review*, *17*(1), 305–317.

Marty, W. (2009). The blended classroom revolution. *Technology and Learning*, *29*(8), 28–32.

Moore, M. G., & Kearsley, G. (1996). *Distance Education: a system view*. Wadsworth Publishing Company Florence KY.

Payne, A. M., Stephenson, J. E., Morris, W. B., Tempest, H. G., Mileham, A., & Griffin, D. K. (2009). The use of an eLearning constructivist solution in workplace learning . *International Journal of Industrial Ergonomics*, *39*(3), 548–553. doi:10.1016/j.ergon.2008.10.019

Pearson, J., & Trinidad, S. (2005). OLES: an instrument for refining the design or eLearning environments . *Journal of Computer Assisted Learning*, *21*(6), 396–404. doi:10.1111/j.1365-2729.2005.00146.x

Seely-Brown, J., & Adler, R. P. (2008). Minds on fire: Open education, the long tail, and learning 2.0. *EDUCAUSE Review*, *43*(1). http://www.educause.edu/ir/library/pdf/ERM0811.pdf Accessed 26 May 2009.

Sendag, S., & Ferhan Odabasi, H. (2009). Effects of an online problem based course on content knowledge acquisition and critical thinking skills. *Computers & Education*, *53*(1), 132–141. doi:10.1016/j.compedu.2009.01.008

World Bank. (2003). *Lifelong learning for a global knowledge economy*. Washington, D. C.: The World Bank.

Zhu, C., Valcke, M., & Schellens, T. (2009). Cultural differences in the perception of a social constructionist eLearning environment. *British Journal of Educational Technology*, *40*(1), 164–168. doi:10.1111/j.1467-8535.2008.00879.x

Zsolt, T., & Istvan, B. (2008). Constructivism in creating learning environments and the Moodle system. *Informacios Tarsadalom*, *8*(3), 41.

KEY TERMS AND DEFINITIONS

Bali Strategic Plan (BSP) (formally the: "Bali Strategic Plan for Technology Support and Capacity building" 2004) is a leading capacity building and sustainable development document for the UN system. The Plan strives to enhance national participation and compliance with international environmental law and policies, increased capacity for negotiations, access to technology, gender equality, public private partnerships and collaboration among UN agencies. It provides cross cutting issues and thematic areas to guide international environmental governance.

Community Platform: is a meeting place on the Internet for people who share common interests and needs.

Environmental Sustainability: is the result of improving the quality of human life while living within the carrying capacity of supporting eco-systems.

Gender Equality: and **Gender Equity** are closely related. Gender equality is achieved when men and women have equal roles in society (e.g., equal pay for equal work, equal political power). Gender equity represents the policies and decisions that lead toward gender equality.

Governing Council (GC): The UNEP Governing Council is the principal oversight making body for the United Nations Environmental Programme. The GC has 58 elected members who serve four-year terms (http://www.unep.org/resources/gov/overview.asp).

Learning Management Systems (LMSs): are software packages that automate the administration of training. The LMS registers users, tracks courses in a catalog, records data from learners; and provides reports to management.

Moodle: is a free and open source eLearning software platform designed to help educators create online courses with opportunities for rich interaction.

United Nations Development Programme: (UNDP) is the UN's global development network, an organization advocating for change and connecting countries to knowledge, experience and resources to help people build a better life (http://www.undp.org/about/).

United Nations Environment Programme: (UNEP) is the voice for the environment in the UN system. Its coordinates development of environmental policy consensus by keeping the global environment under review and bringing emerging issues to the attention of governments and the international community for action (http://www.unep.org).

Chapter 12
The Characteristics, Responsibilities and Future of Chief Information Officers in the Public Sector

Rachel Lawry
Deakin University, Australia

Dianne Waddell
Deakin University, Australia

Mohini Singh
RMIT University, Australia

EXECUTIVE SUMMARY

This chapter presents a model which depicts the critical factors and assists in understanding the demands and effectiveness of Chief Information Officers (CIO) in public sector organisations. The chapter explores the literature on public sector CIO addressing personal and professional characteristics. It also reviews the literature pertaining to the responsibilities and career advancement and future directions in Government departments. The authors adopt a qualitative methodology by which semi-structured interviews are conducted with CIO representatives from a State Government in Australia. From collation of the interview results, utilising a 'mind mapping' strategy, the chapter identifies a model that adequately reflects the critical factors required for a public sector CIO. The chapter concludes that there are certain unique characteristics and responsibilities that a public sector CIO must possess yet a private sector CIO does not require. The chapter also acknowledges the importance of outlining a future direction of the role; something which is neglected by the literature.

INTRODUCTION

With an increased dependence by governments on Information Technology for internal management, delivery of services to citizens and meeting the demands of the digital environment, the importance of the CIO role in this sector has become prominent. The CIO role within the public sector is still at a formative stage whereas in the private

DOI: 10.4018/978-1-61692-814-8.ch012

sector it is well developed. The aim of this chapter is to understand the demands on CIOs in government and what characteristics are indicative of their effectiveness. The intention of this study is to compare the data gathered in an extensive literature review with information gleaned from practitioners. It is then possible to develop a model which bridges the gap between public and private sector experiences. This chapter is founded on the premise that one cannot fully execute a role, particularly an executive role, without fully recognising the fundamentals of what the role is designed to do. With the main role of the public sector being service delivery, it is expected that there needs to be clarity on the characteristics and responsibilities of the CIO role along with a shared vision for the roles future development in order for those in the CIO position to contribute the greatest value to the public sectors bottom line.

In the following sections we discuss the background to this research, a review of extant literature, a discussion of the public sector context, research methodology, findings and implications for the important yet emerging role of the CIOs in the public sector.

BACKGROUND

The need for the CIO role arose out of the 1970s information technology (IT) revolution. This era saw increased investment in information technology systems (ITS). There was also an increasing awareness of competitors using information and its associated technology to gain a unique competitive advantage in an increasingly global marketplace (Porter & Millar 1985). Executives could no longer view IT as an add-on to the business, but rather a function that required equal strategic importance and consideration to that of finance, human resources, operations and marketing.

The CIO was first coined by Synott & Gruber in 1981 as the "senior executive responsible for establishing corporate information policy, standards, and management control over all information resources" (p. 66). Since the coining of the term in the early 1980s, private sector enterprises have been successfully implementing the role within their organisational structures. They have reaped the benefits of the new executive who manages the unique organisational asset of information for near twenty years. In contrast, the public sector had only established the CIO role in the early 2000s.

Australian government, at both Federal and State levels, is considered to be 'leading the pack' with regard to establishing credibility and authority for the CIO´s role (Bushell 2006). Interestingly, Australia's first Whole-of-Government (WoG) CIO was not appointed until June 2005 (Nairn MP 2005). Victoria was the first Australian State Government to appoint a CIO, but it did not do so until 2003 (Department of Premier and Cabinet 2006). The Victorian Government has also endured a turnover in the WoG CIO position for two out of the three years of its establishment (Department of Premier and Cabinet 2006). This is a significant turnover rate for a position that is still in its infancy stages of development. The situation within the Victorian Government is not confined to the state of Victoria or even Australia, but is evident of issues surrounding the implementation of the CIO role within the public sector worldwide.

The situation highlighted above signifies a twenty-year gap between the establishment of the CIO role within the private and public sectors. It is clear that the CIO role is significantly more developed and ingrained within the private sector. In the public sector it is still within the formative stages of development.

LITERATURE REVIEW

The literature surrounding this issue is substantial, however the models have only been established in the last twenty years and the amount of available literature reflects such a time frame. Also, the chapter explores the contextual issue (private and public sector), and its impact on the CIO. In this area, the literature is more limited.

Existing Models of CIO Effectiveness

The literature describes many models which attempt to measure the effectiveness and success of CIOs in organisations. Feeny, Edwards & Simpson (1992) presented one of the first well-conceptualised models in the literature, which aimed to observe the relationship between the CEO and CIO in order to determine the components of a successful two-way relationship. Later, Earl and Feeny (1995) conducted a review of research studies they had previously conducted. As an outcome of this review, the authors identified several common areas that outlined where the CIO added value to an organisation. Earl and Feeny's (1995) model is somewhat similar to that presented by Feeny *et al* in 1992, but does make up, unconvincingly however, for the discounting of proactively planning for the future. They have addressed the concept of proactive planning by incorporating a 'shared vision for IT'. While this is still a limited representation, they are at least acknowledging that without planning for IT in the organisation's future they would suffer greatly in terms of total value added by the CIO.

One of the only Australian focused research papers (Pervan, 1998) focussed on key information system management issues as they are perceived by CEOs and CIOs. The aim was to identify if there existed any commonalities in the importance levels of the issues. The results of the study indicated there was some agreement between CEOs and CIOs on certain IS/IT issues. Just as equally however, there were distinct differences, "particularly in relation to the quality and effectiveness of systems and processes and also how CIOs perceive the IT knowledge of the CEOs" (Pervan, 1998: 95). While this study differs from the previous two models presented by Feeny *et al.* (1992), and Earl and Feeny (1995) in the respect that it does not present concrete components that can be tested, it does present issues that are real and prevailing, and could be argued to provide a greater representation of future expectations.

Melarkode, From-Poulsen & Warnakulasuriya (2004) focused on how CIOs can deliver agility within the organisation through the utilisation of IT. Discussion in the paper included an analysis of the old role of the CIO and how this has transformed into a new role. Their comparison of the old and new CIO role is similar to Pervan's (1998) study in that it presents contentious issues related to the CIO role that have evolved over time. They argue that the CIO is uniquely positioned within organisations where "they increasingly have the opportunity to participate in corporate and business strategy planning and work across business units in identifying opportunities to improve value via IT" (Melarkode et al., 2004: 46). The model presented by Melarkode et al. (2004) also ties in closely with the value added framework presented by Earl and Feeny (1995), particularly through the emphasis on value creation. Similar to the model presented by Melarkode et al. (2004), Capella (2006) presented a model depicting the dual role of the CIO. Capella's (2006) model establishes the importance of quickly establishing a vision for the role due to the evolving nature of CIO responsibilities and IT.

As evident from both the literature discussed on the role characteristics, responsibilities, future, and from the models found in the available literature, there are certain commonalities. By isolating the recurring themes regarding components to assist success in the CIO role, this study will be able to amalgamate the models and literature to formulate a holistic model for use in studying the public sector CIOs. However, to fully address the problem of this research study, an insight into the development of the CIO in the private and public sector is crucial. This will serve to provide context to this chapter and aid understanding of the issues at hand.

Context: Public vs. Private

There is a detailed history regarding how the private and public sectors are characterised, and there are many varied opinions concerning the similarities and differences between the two sectors. In order to understand this chapter, it is important to not only comprehend the components of the CIO, but to recognise and realise how and possibly why the role has evolved differently in the private and public sector.

The private sector is made up of small, medium and large-scale organisations where ownership is held either by an individual or a group of entrepreneurs, more commonly referred to as shareholders (Budhwar and Boyne 2004). As a result of the ownership of private sector organisations, the funding for the organisation within the private sector comes directly from one of two sources: fees paid directly by the customer purchasing a good or service, or from shares purchased by shareholders in listed companies which signifies claim to part ownership and a share of profits. As such there is no claim for public funds in order for the business to operate. The control within the private sector lies in the economy, or market forces (Boyne 2002). Accordingly, the ability to perform, operate and succeed are constrained or imposed by market forces, such as barriers to entering new markets, exchange rates, interest rate fluctuations and the like.

The Australian Bureau of Statistics (1998) defines the public sector as "enterprises which the Commonwealth Government, State/Territory and local Governments, separately or jointly have control over. It includes local Government authorities and all Government departments, agencies and authorities created by, or reporting to, the Commonwealth Parliament and State Parliaments" (p.1). When defining the public sector, the same three points of difference used above to define the private sector can be referred to in the same vain. Public sector agencies are owned, funded and controlled collectively by members of political communities at different levels of government (Budhwar & Boyne 2004). Funding within the public sector is generated by taxes, where citizens at the Local, State and Federal level pay taxes to the Government in return for essential services (Boyne 2002). Where market forces control the private sector, the public sector is subject to the imposition of political forces and the follow-through of political systems (Schneider & Vaught 1993), such as changes of political party leaderships.

Although the two sectors differ inherently in terms of ownership, funding and control, a considerable amount of similarities exist. In essence, both the private and public sectors function similarly with regards to management (Schneider & Vaught 1993). For example, whether or not one is operating in the private or public sector, management still consists of establishing an organisational purpose, developing objectives, planning, managing and motivating the human resources, and controlling the organisation's performance both internally and externally (Schneider & Vaught, 1993; Budhwar & Boyne, 2004).

While the actual process of management is similar between the two sectors, the conditions and constraints under which the management processes are conducted is where the differences between the private and public sector lie (Schneider & Vaught, 1993), for instance, time perspectives, performance measurement, media relations, authority, legal constraints, and personnel constraints. There are three *internal* characteristics of the public sector however, that serve as clear points of difference:

- More Bureaucracy: greater amount of formal procedures for decision making, and are less flexible and more risk-averse than their private sector counterparts (Bozeman & Kingsley, 1998; Farnham & Horton, 1996),
- More Red Tape: implies that the public sector operates with an unnecessary and

counter-productive amount of rules, and relies more on rules and processes rather than results and outcomes (Boyne, 2002), and

- Lower Managerial Autonomy: the public sector allows managers less freedom to react as they see fit to circumstances when they arise, which is exemplified by public managers' discretion over human resource issues which generally involves complex and time consuming processes to follow in hiring, firing and promotion, that, as a preferred alternative, is generally avoided (Baldwin, 1987; Boyne, 2002). <-APA

In considering the above definitions of the private and public sector, it is clear that private sector organisations operate on the basis of filling a need or want for a product or service where they are compensated by fees or shares. On the other hand, the public sector provides products and services as an obligation to taxes paid to them by the citizens they serve. From these definitions it is appropriate to assume that the management of IS in either private or public organisations is both multidimensional and complex (Loukis and Tsouma 2002). Furthermore, the public sector plays a primary role in the life and economy of its citizens at local, state and federal levels. Despite the similarities between the two sectors, the three internal characteristics of the public sector – bureaucracy, red tape and autonomy – serve as possible impediments to the productivity and effectiveness of the CIOs role and responsibilities, namely, ICT project execution and investment.

The literature up until this point with regards to CIOs has been heavily focused on private sector studies. There have been very few studies conducted where the management of IT and IS issues has been raised in a public sector context. It is clear that more research is necessary in this area due to the critical role the public sector plays in the economic and social life of all countries, and also the growing realisation, reliance and importance of ICT on public sector productivity and effectiveness (Loukis & Tsouma 2002).

From the above discussion, it is clear that there is a striking difference between the development of literature from the private and public sector. The private sector has a twenty-year advantage over the public sector with regards to role evolution, and it appears that the advantage extends to development in academic literature too. The literature available regarding CIOs has made one faux pas clear: the CIO is not a position that is exclusive to the private sector. The CIO is not an executive position that discriminates between organisations with regards to importance; regardless of being small or large in size, domestic or international in scope, or private or public sector based, the CIO is a critical executive.

There are no models to date that have been specifically developed for the public sector, nor is there cohesion surrounding the personal and professional characteristics, list of responsibilities and method for proactively planning the future for public sector CIOs. Yet it is evident through the discussion on the components of the CIO and the difference between public and private sector literature, that this is an increasingly crucial role. Moreover, the position within the public sector is so new that it is impossible to claim if the role is a success or failure. As a consequence of this, those that are establishing the position in Government bodies today will no doubt have a lasting impact on how the role will be seen by the public sector in the future. The early success will reinforce the CIO role for the future years to come, whereas high-profile fails will weaken the CIO outlook (Fabris 1998). By combining the key points from the discussion on the CIO function, and the CIOs context within the public sector, an adapted model can be devised. This model takes the key findings from the personal and professional characteristics, responsibilities and future of the CIO, and places them within the public sector context. This model will be confirmed or amended through the responses from the interviews with CIOs from the

Figure 1. Model for measuring CIO in public sector from the literature

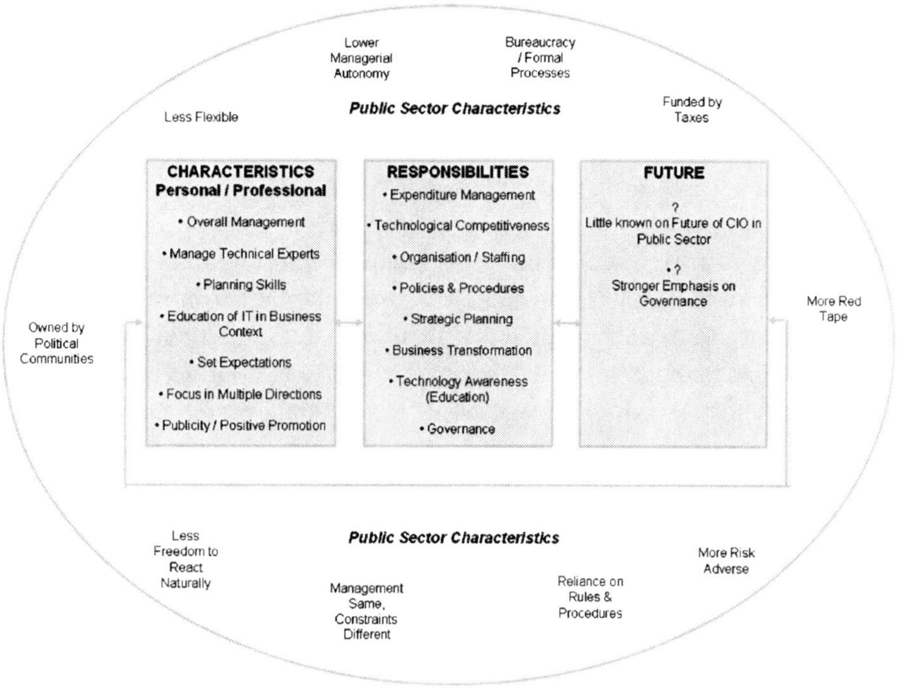

Victorian Government. Figure 1 below represents the amalgamation of the literature thus far.

METHODOLOGY

In order to compare current practice with existing literature a qualitative research approach was adopted. The major reason why this method was selected revolves around the inadequacy of quantitative methods when pursing an exploratory research approach. Qualitative research methods have also made a resurgence in studies of Information Technology (IT), Information Systems (IS) and Information Communication Technology (ICT) in academic literature. There has been a general shift in IT, IS and ICT issues from the technical side to the managerial side, and the methods by which these areas are studied has accommodated this shift in focus are also changing from statistical methods of analysis to qualitative methods (Myers 1997).

Ten semi-structured interviews took place with individuals from the Victorian Government, Australia, who hold the CIO title or perform the CIO function. An interview agenda was created and was emailed to the participants prior to the interview taking place to alert them to the topics for discussion. The interview agenda was devised to provoke discussion on six areas:

- Participant's educational background and work history;
- Current perception of their position;
- Perception of the role within Government;
- Predictions for the future direction of the role within Government;
- Personal future career goals or direction; and
- Critical success factors deemed important to their role.

Each area covered in the agenda was aimed at collating the data deemed necessary to translate into information for the purpose of answering the research questions. Ten interviews are regarded as saturation point, whereby adequate new information was collected from a range of areas within the Victorian Government so as to represent a diverse range of valid opinions.

In order to aid analysis of the codes isolated from the interview transcripts, Mind Maps were established for each of the participants' interview results. A Mind Map helps to organise, generate and present ideas in a simple and visual way; in essence, it is a graphical depiction designed to abstract the thinking process for an individual. Mind Maps assisted in dividing the topics and issues into smaller parts to help convey concepts to others in a clear and attractive method. The ConceptDraw MINDMAP program was employed for use in this research study to generate the Mind Maps.

After creating a Mind Map for each individual participant, a holistic Mind Map was constructed that represents an overview of the topics and issues discussed. The individual Mind Maps and the holistic Mind Map are used to aid discussion of the results as they highlight those topics and issues of greatest concern to the participants at this point in time. The Mind Maps were then integrated into the pre-existing model gleaned from the literature to present a new model which incorporates all facets identified by the interviewees.

RESEARCH FINDINGS AND DISCUSSION

The individual mind maps offered a clear and concise depiction of the topics and issues discussed by the individual participants. Each mind map varied in the topics and issues discussed, and also varied in depth and breadth of discussion. Some of the mind maps were limited in responses, whereas other cases appeared more varied in the responses. This is not a direct reflection on the individual respondent, their position, their experience or their knowledge on the subjects. It is merely the result of discussing a unique topic with ten very unique and individual people who have CIO responsibilities. It is natural in qualitative research to attract a wide variety of responses and patterns in responses.

While on their own the individual mind maps tell an interesting story, it is when they are amalgamated from ten individual mind maps into one holistic mind map, that they are most valuable and provide the most information. Figure 2 is a diagrammatic representation of the amalgamated model of the ten interviews into one mind map. It shows the twenty-two topics discussed by the ten participants of this study. Each topic was discussed in many different contexts and some commanded more discussion or attention than others.

As can be observed from the Mind Map (Figure 2), there were twenty-two major topics identified by CIO practitioners. Some topics demanded more attention than others, and this research can conclude that the most frequently discussed topics are the ones that represent the truest picture of the CIO in the public sector at this point in time. By synthesising the topics discussed, authors identified the seven major topics of this research study to be: the unique role of the CIO; impact of IT; Funding / Investment Management; Governance; Shared Services; Stakeholders; and Outsourcing /Contracting. These seven major topics reflect the issues of most concern to those currently fulfilling the position of the CIO within the Victorian Government, and can be used to generalise on the situation of the CIO in the public sector. Each of the seven topics is discussed below with regards to their importance and their link with the established literature of the public sector CIO.

The Unique Role of the CIO

The CIO role within the public sector is still within the early stages of formation and is being defined

Figure 2. Holistic participant mind map

within the changing perception of the role from technical guru to strategist. While it is theoretically understood that there is a distinction between the CIO and the IT Manager, where the CIO sits on the strategic side of IT and the IT Manager deals with the operations of IT, there still exists the belief that the position of some Departmental CIOs is just the renaming of the IT Managers. There are also some cases where the IT Manager is actually doing the CIO role, yet lacks the official title. It is evident that there is no clear idea of what the CIO does, and there is little available literature that acknowledges the public sector as having difficulty with implementing the role and establishing the role's difference to that of the several other IT positions that exist within Government.

The literature clearly identifies the CIO as a strategic business partner that should be situated within the CEO circle of executives. The CIOs within the various Departments of the VPS sit at different levels within the Departmental structures, and, therefore, the intended function of the role as a strategic business partner is diluted. An additional consequence of the structure of the CIO within the VPS Departments is that those in the CIO position believe that outside their office, there are very few external groups who know what the CIO is and what the office of the CIO deals with. If the role was situated at its intended level, perhaps such a situation would not occur and clarity over the role could begin to form. The literature also acknowledges that the CIO must have a strong relationship with the other senior executive positions such as the CFO and the CEO. Due to the lack of clarity surrounding the role and the CIOs structure within the Departments across Government, it is no wonder that many CIOs lack a strong relationship with the executive roles within Government, and, therefore, lack the impact they could have in promoting the value added by their role. What the literature fails to acknowledge is that the structure of Government is unlike that of a private enterprise. Therefore, the equal of a CEO or CFO is the Premier or Department of Treasury and Finance respectively, and access to such positions is filtered by Secretaries and their Deputies. The Victorian Government has sought a way to rectify part of this issue by creating the Office of the CIO (OCIO) at a WoG level; however, there is no clear reporting line from the Departmental CIOs to the OCIO and, therefore, the value that could be added by this central body is missing.

The literature acknowledges several personal and professional characteristics required by the individual filling the CIO position, however there are a few characteristics that the literature fails to recognise as important, and this is most likely due to the literature being private sector dominated. There are six key characteristics of the CIO role that are missing from the literature and from the synthesised literature model presented earlier, yet are evident in this study. They are: knowledge of the workings of Government; trustworthiness, a focus on the clients' needs, empathetic side, strategic thinker, and patience.

There is considerable discussion in the literature on what responsibilities constitute the domain of the CIO, however there are a few responsibilities that are not recognised in the literature. This is most likely due to the focus on the private sector throughout the majority of the literature. There are six key areas of the CIOs responsibility that the literature fails to adequately acknowledge yet they are evident through the findings of this study: centralising IT under the CIO function, providing advice, reducing duplication and exploiting common capabilities, service delivery, managing risk, and managing outsourcing agreements.

The Impact of IT

Apart from the Polanksy, Inuganti and Wiggins (2004) study, there were very few studies that recognised IT at the top of the CIO's priority list. As previously discussed, the CIO is an executive management position; however at the core of their management is information, communication and technology. While the literature acknowledges that the CIO must have a hand in IT strategy development and the management of IT projects, the literature does not acknowledge sufficiently the challenge of identifying the value of IT in the public sector. Many of the CIOs struggle within an environment that must be transparent and accountable to the public and are constantly battling to prove that the reputation of IT projects as a consumption rather than a production of money is actually a false reputation.

The CIOs from the public sector should only support business projects rather than IT projects, as this is one way of getting around the mindset of those outside the CIO office that IT projects are doomed to fail. In fact, there should be no IT projects developed without them being linked to a business solution. Creating IT procedures for IT's sake is a waste of money and time, and the reason why duplication of processes generally occurs. Through linking IT with a business outcome, the role of IT then becomes the enabler of a business initiative, and the benefits realised are business focused rather than IT focused. This point lacks emphasis in the literature, and needs to be recognised as a core characteristic of the role: being able to work with a business view and a WoG perspective.

As previously mentioned, some of the literature does acknowledge the role of IT in the CIOs job; however, it is generally focused on the technology side of IT and fails to acknowledge that information also plays a large part. The CIO must not only deal with technology, but also information, and be responsible for the diffusion of information throughout Government. The CIO is responsible for making sure the right information is available at the right time and is provided under the appropriate security measures. This is a missing component of the role in the literature available at present. While technology is the tool by which information is diffused, it is the CIOs job to ensure that the processes by which the information is collated, the channels by which information is transported, and the security procedures that ensure the information is safe, are established in accordance with Departmental and Government rules.

Funding/Investment Management

The literature acknowledges that a large part of the CIOs role is ensuring cost effectiveness and increasing value for money (Earl & Feeny 1995). As a result, investment management is key area of the CIO function, which is being realised in reality, not just in theory. Given the previous discussion on the IT component of the CIO role and the battle over changing perceptions on IT, it is understandable why investment management has grown in significance for the CIO and has become the true essence of the role. As with any executive managerial position, dealing with finances is crucial, and this is no exception with the CIO, as without full understanding of the money around the function there is little chance that any outcomes would be produced.

As the literature is predominately private sector focused, there is a large gap with regards to the CIO attaining funding in the public sector. One of the fundamental differences between the private and public sectors is the bureaucracy, processes and red tape that government departments face when obtaining funding. Many of the troubles faced by the CIOs in the public sector are that the time frames and procedures that need to be met strain getting the projects off the ground. This links very closely with the issues discussed in the previous two sections on the CIO and IT, as without the strong relationship with other executive members, without proving the value is added, and without changing the external mindsets of IT as a waste of money, attaining funding is near impossible. Similarly to the discussion on IT and with regards to developing business projects rather than IT projects, CIOs in the public sector must ensure that the business unit attains the funding for the business project, and that the CIO is only commissioned to source the way in which ICT can assist the overall outcome of the business initiative.

Governance

Governance is a critical part of the CIO role in the Government sector that is little acknowledged within the available literature. Some of the literature acknowledged that governance would become a core part of the role in the future (Bushell, 2006), but much of the literature – mostly likely due to the focus of the literature on the private sector – failed to acknowledge its ingrained importance in the role (Boyne, 2002). This is particularly true of the CIO in the public sector, as the major stakeholders are the citizens at large who dictate the public sectors need for transparency and accountability.

The key aspect of governance that relates to the CIO in the public sector is its link with project planning. The stereotype of IT projects failing and wasting money was not founded on false details. The public sector has experienced the consequences of poor project planning such as projects being under prepared, projects not meeting requirements, projects not producing intended benefits, and in some extreme cases, project failure. It is, therefore, the case that the governance structures set up in Government are predominately focused on project planning. The planning stage of a project is the most crucial stage as it outlines the intended outcome, the investment structure, and the benefits to be received. As can be concluded, this critical stage is linked heavily with investment management previously discussed, and aids in promoting the positive aspects of ICT. As there are no pure IT projects, planning for the project must be conducted in partnership with the business unit from which the initiative originates, and must be communicated in business terms.

Shared Services Centre

The Shared Services Centre (SSC) is a Victorian Government initiative to create an internal service provider so common applications and infrastructures can be joined together to service the whole rather than the individual Departments. The SSC at present joins four Departments together so that common and basic ICT functions can be carried out essentially once for four. The available literature implies that the CIO should reduce duplication and promote consolidation of processes; however, the literature fails to recognise how important this function is in the public sector.

Due to the long establishment of Government and its 'silo structure', there exists the challenge of dealing with duplicated processes and archaic systems. Due to poor planning, there are little checks in place to ensure that a new investment with the aim of solving an identified problem, is not just a re-investment in a new system that performs the same function as the one already operational. The SSC aims to address this characteristic of the public sector by joining together four Departments with similar economies of scale so that common systems and processes can be handled by an internal service provider, and then the remaining strategic functions can be handled individually to suit the needs and goals of the Departments. It exploits the commonalities that exist between Departments so that for example, common licensing agreements can be bought just once, instead of four times for four Departments which all come from the same State Government.

Stakeholders

The importance of delivery to and working with key stakeholders is a key function of the public sector and is an area that is not adequately explored within the available literature on this topic. The key function of the public sector is service delivery and their key stakeholder is the community and citizens at large. In the case of the Victorian Government, it is the Victorian citizens who are heavily invested in the actions of the Victorian Government. For this reason the Government must be held accountable for their actions and must be transparent in their activities. The private sector is short of this requirement as their fundamental concern is return on investment and, therefore, what needs to be reported to key stakeholders is much more tangible. Consequently, stakeholder management is a key part of the public sector CIOs role and at the same time plays a key part in project planning, as stakeholder identification must be considered.

Apart from the stakeholder who reaps the end benefits of Government initiatives, there are other stakeholders within Government whom the CIO must report to and have interaction with. It is through stakeholder reporting lines that projects and initiatives being worked on by individual Departments can be shared and talked about, so that opportunities for collaboration can be explored. Key internal stakeholders of the CIO include other Departmental CIOs, IT Directors, Chief Technology Officer, Secretaries, and Deputy Secretaries. By interacting and sharing with these key internal stakeholders, clarity and consistency in the service provided by the CIO can be achieved. It is also an avenue for promoting the benefits of the CIO and for increasing the profile of the CIO to assume the position of strategic business partner; its rightful position.

Outsourcing/Contracting

The role of outsourcing and contracting is a topic overlooked by the available literature, and this could be due to the fact that the literature is centred on private sector studies that do not deal with external service providers to the same extent that the Government relies upon them. As the public sector cannot compete with the IT salaries that the private sector provides and, therefore, cannot recruit the skills and expertise needed to deal with the projects on the level the Government runs, they compensate by outsourcing non core activities or by employing contractors.

There are two key issues with this situation. Firstly the Government has not established the required skill base for the CIO to be a successful office, and secondly, the cost of outsourcing and contracting is most likely equal to costs associated with increasing the salary structure of Government to recognise the price of IT professionals. The benefits, however, of outsourcing non core activities is that it leaves the Departmental CIOs time to deal with strategic issues, and outsourcing agreements are secured by contractual arrangements thus securing the job be done as utmost priority. The benefit observed by contractors is that they have more enthusiasm and passion for the tasks at hand, and are experts in their field, thus the public sector benefits from their contributions and experience. A challenge with recruiting into the public sector is that many of the IT professionals that do fit within the prescribed Victorian Public Service remuneration structure lack the experience and maturity of dealing with large business projects that have core ICT components. Also, external "wanna-be" IT professionals discard the public sector as a viable workplace, thinking they do not offer the same type and range of jobs that the private sector does. This is entirely unfounded as the public sector deals in a range of areas – indicated by the range of different Departments – and the scale of the projects ranges from the small to the very large.

Managing outsourcing agreements and contractors have become a key area of the CIOs responsibilities. It is an area that has been forced upon the CIO due to the structure of Government and the competitiveness of the private marketplace, and initiatives such as the SSC are internal Government initiatives to move away from a strong reliance on external service providers. While the benefits of using external service providers cannot be discounted, the extent to which they are employed within the public sector needs reviewing and possible restructuring so that the most effective value for money can be achieved.

The seven major topics that were isolated from the research are indicative of the concerns of CIOs in the public sector. Through discussing the CIO, IT, Funding/Investment Management, Governance, Shared Services, Stakeholders, and Outsourcing/Contracting, it became clear that there were aspects of each topic that failed to be acknowledged adequately in the available literature. The common cause for their abandonment in the literature is that the literature is predominately founded on private sector studies. The following figure outlines the key findings from the previous discussion and is an improved representation of the CIO in the public sector from that provided from the literature. Figure 3 recognises the major findings of the study and also rectifies the shortcomings of the current literature on the CIO in the public sector.

IMPLICATIONS FOR CIO MANAGERS

From the findings of this study, in particular the model developed to outline the critical factors required of a CIO in the public sector, there are certain implications that can be identified. There exists a clear need for clarity and consistency on the CIO role and the situation of the role within the public sector. There also exists a need for distinction between the CIO role and the many other IT management positions within Government. A consistent position description endorsed by the Office of the CIO (OCIO) would assist in achieving this consistency and clarity. Clear reporting, sharing and communicating lines should also be established between the OCIO and the Departmental CIOs to aid clarification of the role and to also provide support for those Departmental CIOs who are new to the role and are embedding it in the public sector for the first time.

This chapter also highlights the need for public sector CIOs to be aware when reading academic literature and industry publications, that they are generally private sector focused and they, therefore, do not acknowledge adequately that there are some components of the CIO role that require more focus in the public sector. Comparing private

Figure 3. Model of the CIO in the public sector

sector based literature to the role of the CIO in the public sector would only foster annoyance and frustration. The role can be just as effective and efficient as it is in the private sector, as long as those in the public sector recognise there are certain areas of the role that require more attention than it would in the private marketplace.

Furthermore, CIOs in the public sector need to be more creative and proactive in dealing with the policies and procedures of Government. It became clear through discussion with interviewees that the challenges of the role generally originate in the characteristics of the public sector. While these characteristics are intrinsic in the working environment of the CIO, the CIO can still be creative in how to work within policy and procedure constraints of Government. There is a sense of tradition in Government, and there are some policies and procedures that require removal, and their removal will only occur if the existence of such policies and procedures is challenged. The CIO, who is in a position of change and evolution, is the perfect role to champion such transformation and can provide substitute policies that are more flexible and accommodating to the types of projects and initiatives that the CIO deals with.

CONCLUSION

This chapter is qualitative and exploratory in nature. The topic took an under-researched area, the CIO in the public sector, and employed qualitative techniques to gather information from CIOs in the public sector arena to shed a brighter spotlight on the struggles surrounding the role. The overall value of this research is that the gap in the literature regarding the public sector CIO has been bridged. The plight of the public sector CIO has been addressed to adequately examine the personal and professional characteristics of the role, the responsibilities that befall the CIO, and the future direction of the role. Through analysis of these areas, through the combining of theory and reality, and through critical discussion on the results of this study, clarity and consistency on the role in the public sector has been acquired, and can continue to be acquired.

REFERENCES

Australian Bureau of Statistics. (1998). *Paid Work: Public Sector Employment*. Canberra: ABS.

Baldwin, N. (1987). Public versus private: not that different, not that consequential. *Public Personnel Management*, *16*, 181–193.

Boyne, G. (2002). Public and Private Management: What's the Difference? *Journal of Management Studies* 39(1),0022-2380.

Bozeman, B., & Kingsley, G. (1998). Risk culture in public and private organisations. *Public Administration Review*, *58*, 109–118. doi:10.2307/976358

Budhwar, P., & Boyne, G. (2004). Human resource management in the Indian public and private sectors: an empirical comparison. *International Journal of Human Resource Management*, *15*(2), 346–370. doi:10.1080/0958519032000158554

Bushell, S. (2006). *Government CIO Role Still Developing, But Australia Ahead of Pack.* http://www.cio.com/index.php?id=401118652&eid=-601.

Capella, J. (2006). The CIO's First 100 Days. *Optimize*, *5*(3), 46–51.

Department of Premier and Cabinet 2006. *About the Office of the Chief Information Officer.* http://www.dpc.vic.gov.au/

Earl, M., & Feeny, D. (1995). Is Your CIO Adding Value. *The McKinsey Quarterly*, *2*, 144–161.

Fabris, P. 1998. *Odd Ducks No More.* http://www.cio.com/archive/111598/index.html

Farnham, D., & Horton, S. (1996). Managing public and private organisations . In Farnham, D., & Horton, S. (Eds.), *Managing The New Public Service*. London: Macmillan.

Feeny, D., Edwards, B., & Simpson, K. (1992). Understanding the CEO/CIO Relationship. *Management Information Systems Quarterly*, *16*(4), 439–448. doi:10.2307/249730

Loukis, E., & Tsouma, N. (2002). Critical issues of information systems management in the Greek public sector. *The International Journal of Government and Democracy in the Information Age.*, *17*(1), 65–83.

Melarkode, A., From-Poulson, M., & Warnakulasuriya, S. (2004). Delivering agility through IT. *Business Strategy Review.*, *15*(3), 45–50. doi:10.1111/j.0955-6419.2004.00327.x

Myers, M. (1997). Qualitative research in information systems. *Management Information Systems Quarterly*, *21*(2), 241–242. doi:10.2307/249422

Nairn, M. P. G. (2005). *New Australian Government Chief Information Officer.* Media Release. Senator the Hon Eric Abetz. Special Minister of State. Australia.

Pervan, G. (1998). How chief executive officers in large organisations view the management of their information systems. *Journal of Information Technology*, *13*, 95–109. doi:10.1080/026839698344882

Polanksy, M., Inuganti, T., & Wiggins, S. (2004). The 21st Century CIO. *Business Strategy Review.*, *15*(2), 29–33. doi:10.1111/j.0955-6419.2004.00310.x

Porter, M., & Millar, V. (1985). How information gives you competitive advantage. *Harvard Business Review*, *63*(4), 149–174.

Schneider, D., & Vaught, B. (1993). A comparison of job satisfaction between public and private sector managers. *Public Administration Quarterly.*, *17*(1), 68–83.

Synnott, W., & Gruber, W. (1981). *Information Resource Management: Opportunities and Strategies for the 1980s.* New York: John Wiley & Sons.

ADDITIONAL READING

Anonymous, . (2000). Gartner Predicts "Zero-Budget" CIO. *Information Management Journal*, *36*(4), 8.

Highbarger, J. (1998). What's the proper role for the CIO? *Management Review*, *77*(3), 53–54.

Holmes, A. (2005). *Where there's a person, there's a problem*. Retrieved March 16th 2009, from http://www.cio.com/archive/040105/index.html.

Kost, J. (2005). *Government CIO position continues to mature*. Retrieved March 30th 2009, from http://www.gartner.com.

Mayor, T. (2003). *From private to public*. Retrieved March 16th 2009, from http://www.cio.com/archive/050103/index.html.

McDonald, M. P., & Blosch, M. (2003). *CIO Credibility: Proven Practices from the Public Sector*. Retrieved March 30th 2009, from http://www.gartner.com.

McDonald, M. P., & Tucker, C. (2004). *Making Time: The Office of the CIO*. Retrieved March 30th 2009, from http://www.gartner.com.

Passino, J. H. Jr, & Severance, D. G. (1988). The changing role of the Chief Information Officer. *Planning Review*, *16*(5), 38–42.

Remenyi, D., Grant, K. A., & Pather, S. (2005). The chameleon: a metaphor for the Chief Information Officer. *Journal of General Management*, *30*(3), 1–11.

Rockart, J. F., Ball, L., & Bullen, C. V. (1982). Future Role of the Information Systems Executive. *Management Information Systems Quarterly*, *6*(4), 1–14. doi:10.2307/248989

Stephens, C. S., Ledbetter, W. N., Mitra, A., & Ford, F. N. (1992). Executive or functional manager? The nature of the CIO's job. *Management Information Systems Quarterly*, *16*(4), 449–467. doi:10.2307/249731

Varon, E. 2000, *Uncle Sam Wants You*. Retrieved March 16th 2009, from http://www.cio.com/archive/080100/index.html.

Chapter 13
Vision Impairment and Electronic Government

Reima Suomi
Turku School of Economics, Finland

Irene Krebs
Brandenburgische Technische Universität, Germany

EXECUTIVE SUMMARY

Vision impaired are in a distinctive disadvantage when using computer screens based on visual presentation of data. Their situation becomes increasingly critical, as most society services, including issues such as eCommerce, eBusiness, eHealth, and eGovernment go on-line. Yet modern technologies can too offer solutions to their problems, both at hardware and software level, and often with reasonable cost. Effective ICT can open up new communication channels and functionalities for say totally blind people, that would not have been available for them otherwise. General sensitivity for this issue, and especially sensitivity among designers of governmental e-services must be developed. eGovernment is an especially demanding activity area as it comes to all sorts of imparities (not just vision impairment), as governmental services are often in a monopoly service delivery situation: citizen have to use them and there is often no other alternative. The issue binds it to the wider discussion on digital divide, where vision impairment is one cause for digital divide, and often very devastating, especially if still combined with other sources of digital divide.

ORGANIZATION BACKGROUND

Vision impairment is vision loss (of a person) to such a degree as to qualify as a handicap through a significant limitation of visual capability (Arditi & Rosenthal, 1998). It is a form of disability. Countries around the globe are acting to promote e-governance, so that people with disability are increasingly able to get access to information on the Internet. However, it is always a difficult commitment for many countries to reach the whole community (AHRC, 2009), and majority of the websites in the education, cultural and business sectors are still inaccessible to people with vision impairment. (HKBU, 2006).

DOI: 10.4018/978-1-61692-814-8.ch013

Currently, there is less than 6% percent of printed material that is accessible for those citizens who are vision impaired or have other print disabilities. Moreover, people with vision impairment report frustration that they must continually request that government documents are presented online in multiple formats apart from PDF such as RTF, MS Word, and HTML (ACCAN, 2009; BSI, 2006). The system should be able to consider the needs of people with disabilities, such as providing alternative keyboard navigation, animated displays, color and contrast setting, and other means of making the system usable to people with vision impairment (Govt. of US, 2007). In addition to these blind, deafblind and vision-impaired people have particular needs. Skill development programmes must not be designed solely for people who can see and read standard print, and who can use software without altering its on-screen appearance or using adaptive technology. (NZ Foundation, 2009; EATT Project, 2003). Foremost, there sould be studies to identify factors accounting for why some states or countries are more responsive than other states or countries to the needs of people with disabilities in their use of e-government (Rubaii-Barrett & Wise, 2008).

In this context, digital divide could be termed as the inequality in assessing services of the information society (Brodie, Flournoy et al. 2000; Compaine 2001; Norris 2001; Siochrú, Girard et al. 2002; Akhter 2003), and one form of digital divide is caused by vision impairment, that can take several forms from total blindness to minor shortcomings say in colour recognition. The number of people with visual impairment worldwide in 2002 was in excess of 161 million, of whom about 37 million were blind (Resnikoff, Pascolini et al. 2004).

The case is discussing governmental support for vision impairment in two well-developed countries, Germany and Finland. It is well clear that the problems might be totally different in less-developed countries, in which vision impairment can too be even more a severe problem; especially the area of e-Government is looking at. By e-Government this research means the delivery of governmental services to citizen through electronic means, mainly the Internet. In this perspective, parts of the government activities are; providing the needed regulation and legislation for both public and private organizations to deliver good services for vision impaired through electronic means; and delivering robust and well-designed government services to citizen with vision impairment. If the government fails in providing these services, pressure to serve citizen with vision impairment materializes strongly in other service channels.

SETTING OF THE STAGE

Vision Impairment

Equality of citizen is a central value in modern societies. In reality, the equality is of course eroded by many factors. Most permeating factors causing inequality are of course permanent physical capabilities of individuals. Alongside conditions such as deafness, dumbness, inability to move normally because of missing limbs etc. or failures in the neural system, vision impairment, at its worst form totally blindness, is a key source of inequality. The term often used in this connection is vision impairment.

In worldwide statistics vision impairment officially touches upon 160 million people (Resnikoff et al., 2004), but in reality the figure is most likely much bigger. The amount of totally blind people is expected to be around 37 million (Resnikoff et al., 2004).

The most common causes of blindness around the world are (World Health Organisation, 2009):

- cataracts (47.8%),
- glaucoma (12.3%),
- uveitis (10.2%),

Table 1 Vision impairment in Germany and Finland, some statistics from 2007 (combined from (Ojamo, 2008) and (Bertram, 2005)

Aspect	Germany	Finland
Total population	82,3 Mio	5,3 Mio
Vision impaired people total*, percent of total population	1.000 000; 1,34	80 000; 1,5
Totally blind people*, percent of total population	160 000; 0,2	10 000; 0,19

- age-related macular degeneration (AMD) (8.7%),
- trachoma (3.6%),
- corneal opacity (5.1%), and
- diabetic retinopathy (4.8%).

In this chapter, authors discuss the activities public authorities need to take when assisting vision impaired people, especially in the field of eGovernment. In Table-1 they have provided some basic vision impairment statistics from those two case countries, Finland and Germany. These countries were selected to be the sample countries in this research of piloting character, as the authors are from these countries and have access to documentation at the local language. Of course it must be noted that the two countries are very much alike, and drawing conclusions based on this discussion to less developed countries is not possible.

One form of visual impairment is that of colour blindness. Colour blindness can for example harm the interpretation of maps and other visual information sources. There is nowadays a tool called vizcheck (http://www.vischeck.com), which can be used to study the colour schemes of web portals. The study by showed that there were no major shortcomings as it comes to colour use in the studied governmental www-pages (Choudrie, Ghinea, & Weerakkody, 2004). Other automated tools to evaluate the user friendliness of www-sites as it comes to visual impairment are Dottie and Usability Enforcer (Becker, 2004).

e-Government

eGovernment is usually presented as using IT to (Grönlund, 2002):

- Provide easy access to government information and services for citizens and businesses
- Increase the quality of services, by such things as increased speed, completeness and process efficiency
- Give citizens opportunities to participate in the democratic process.

eGovernment is a generic term meaning all electronic contacts between citizens and their government. It is divided into two main areas: first, eDemocracy, catering for democratic processes in government, and secondly, eAdministration, containing many applications such as health care (eHealth), taxation, public procurement and police operations.

Silcock (2001) defines eGovernment as follows: "*...the use of technology to enhance the access to delivery of government services to benefit citizens, business partners and employees.*" Banerjee & Chau (Banerjee & Chau, 2004) provide the following illustration of the fast development of eGovernment: in 1996, less than 50 official government homepages could be found on the World Wide Web. In 2001, it was estimated that globally there were well over 50 000 official government websites. Of the 190 UN Member States, 169 were providing some degree of information and services on-line.

In the US, the State eGovernment strategy delivers the following summary of proceedings in the field: "*Federal information technology spending in the United States will exceed $48 billion in 2002 and $52 billion in 2003 ... a good portion of current federal IT spending is devoted to Internet*

Initiatives, yielding over 35 million web pages online at over 22,000 web sites."

Goverment and thus eGovernment activities take place at different levels: munipality, area, state/nation, federal and international. Yet the national level is often a natural level to study, as many important decisions, such as most of regulation and legislation. Different public-private partnerships are easily blurring the boundaries of eGoverment, as well as the tendency of public administration to work increasingly in a business way, approaching practices of eBusiness. The third sector adopting different responsibilies from the public authorities if further mixing the cards. A national government cannot always take the lead in eGovernment. As (Jarvenpaa, Tiller, & Simons, 2003) put it: *"The role of government varies, and at times it reverses from its typical stance in public choice as a supplier of regulation to being a customer of regulation."*

SUPPORT FOR VISION IMPAIRED PEOPLE

In this section we study what the Finnish and German authorities have made to support vision impaired people.

Finland

In Finland a person is entitled to help equipments based on vision impairment, when the vision of his/her better eye is after best available glass correction less than 0,3, or the total vision scope of both eyes is less than 60 grades, or the total invalidated defined in her/his case is at least 50% because of blindness.

As other health care services too, health care services are organized by individual municipalities. The government sets the regulation and laws for handicapped people. There is little disease-specific legislation, but rather general government guidance. This leads to a situation in which the real services individual get can vary a lot between different municipalities.

By law services without co-payment from vision impaired people are definition of the need for help equipment, tuning of the needed equipment, use education, follow-up and needed maintenance. Devices are given to the vision impaired either for use of for ownership, depending on the case and policy of the municipality.

Eyeglasses are of course the basic device for most vision impaired. Being as standard and wide-scale service, it is covered with a complicated and detailed legislation. We do not dwell into the details of providing eyeglasses for vision impaired people in Finland.

Help equipment is provided at two levels: Municipal health centers provide standard devices, such as white sticks, audio devices and audio enhancements to mobile phones. Luckily, such programs most often nowadays are a standard part of mobile phone operating and user interface systems. Municipal health centers are not allowed to refund any acquisitions vision impaired people have made themselves.

Central hospitals cater for expensive and non-standard devices for vision impaired people. These items might be special devices for reading normal paper-based text or extra lenses that are attached to normal televisions. Many of these devices however have to do with normal personal computers, to which non-standard extensions for vision impaired people can be given. These are items such as:

- scanner
- speech synthesizer
- Braille displays
- special software for helping reading the screen contents

An expensive item decided upon by the central hospital is the need for a guide dog.

In Finland, 10 special journals distributed in point writing are provided.

Germany

Hardly for any other group the paradigm shift in Germany in institutions and authorities for social care is so important than for people with disabilities. Not any action of the authoritarian state as well as a patronized and super coordinated care by institutions shall determine the everyday life, but self-determination, participation and equality must be focused more and more. This can be a step toward greater transparency and openness in dealing with disabled people, especially with visually impaired and blind people. Dignity, equality and participating are key concepts of human living together in Germany.

About ten percent of the German population has a handicap which complicates the access to computer and Internet. These include blind, impaired, deaf / hard of hearing, physically and motor-driven disabled persons, mentally and psychically disabled persons as well as intellectually disabled and people with learning difficulties. But also elder people and people with a temporary handicap often find barriers on the Internet which complicate the use for them. Just for these target groups the Internet illustrates an ideal platform to take part in the modern information society. And, however, not only differs the availability of technical preconditions for each of these persons as a user (e. g. browser versions or input devices), but there are also individual needs that should be taken into consideration with the programming of a web page.

A big part of the barriers towards the access to the Internet can be overcome thanks to modern technology and program-technical capabilities. However, the implementation often fails according to the fact, that this is widely unknown. The German Act on Equality for People with Disabilities here refers in § 4 as following: „Free of barriers are (…) systems of the data processing, acoustic and visual sources of information and communication facilities as well as other living spaces if they are accessible and usable to handicapped people in the general usual way, without special difficulty and basically without foreign help and support“ (ibid.) At present, many cities and municipalities work at the launching of „Guiding Principles and Participation Action Plans“ as well as resulting legal recommendations in this sense.

The use of e-health and information and communication technologies (ITK) in the public health sector has been recognized and particularly great hope regarding process optimization and saving is set on the voluntary application of the electronic health card.

The use of the electronic health card (obligatory applications "Transfer of insurance data" as well as "Electronic prescription transport") is highly appreciated in the study on health economy and e-health in Germany. The highest benefit is seen in the storage of emergency data and medicine documentation (Wegweiser GmbH Berlin, 2007).

The German National Ministry of Research has announced a major funding program for ambient assisted living (AAL). There are 16 million people in Germany now who are older than 65. In the year 2050 there will be 23 million. This means that with increasing age people's eye sight will continuously deteriorate. For this reason, €125m will be invested in 17 AAL projects over the next year. The goal is to develop IT-solutions that help elderly and chronically ill people to stay in their own flat or house as long as possible.

In Germany develop a lot of towns and villages, policy guidelines and local strategies, and out of it resultant list of recommendations in this spirit.

In Germany, some special journals distributed in point writing are provided, e.g. Electronic Journal of e-Government, eGovernment computing, Sonderpädagogik, eHealth International.

CURRENT CHALLENGES FACING THE ORGANIZATION

Governmental service provision is increasingly turning into electronic channels, under the phenomenon of eGovernment. This means that services have to be well designed and state-of-the art in the way that they are self-explaining without or with minimal human intervention. This creates challenges as such, but especially for services meant for impaired – say vision impaired – people. Governmental agencies are in a big pressure, as they should be good examples even for other actors in cyberspace – such as private companies.

SOLUTIONS AND RECOMMENDATIONS

Technical means to provide eGovernment and other services through the web to vision impaired are already on the market, and the selection of tools is increasing all the time. Yet market scan necessitates resources, and some tools might need financial resources in an amount becoming critical even for big organizations. A mostly important issue is in government as well as in private sector sensitivity to the needs of impaired people. Services can be well designed for vision impaired people, but first the wake-up to this issue must take place, and then the organizations must strengthen their service orientation even towards the vision impaired citizen.

Overcoming the handicap and digital divide caused by vision impairment necessitates actions at many levels, so even in the case of eGovernment. Many technological solutions are already there, and they are so powerful that they can crucially help even totally blind people However, technology is yet not used to its full extend, and awareness and availability of different solutions can vary considerably between different population groups.

Designers of eGovernment services have to be especially sensitive to different impairment, including vision impairment, as their services affect everyone in the society, and are often obligatory for citizen to use. Making these services available through well-designed web-interfaces is at their own interest too, because ignoring the design on good web-services will manifest itself in pressure in other, often more expensive and inefficient, delivery channels.

REFERENCES

ACCAN. (2009). *Submission to Government 2.0 Taskforce Secretariat, Australian Communications Consumer Action Network*. Australia: ACCAN.

AHRC. (2009). *Web accessibility and Government 2.0 Australian Human Rights Commission submission to the Government 2.0 Taskforce – Towards Government 2.0 an issues paper*, www.humanrights.gov.au

Akhter, S. H. (2003). Digital divide and purchase intention: Why demographic psychology matters. *Journal of Economic Psychology*, *24*(3), 321–327. doi:10.1016/S0167-4870(02)00171-X

Ambient Assisted Living Programme, A. A. L. (2009). Retrieved from http://www.aal-europe.eu/about-aal, March 23th 2009.

Arditi, A., & Rosenthal, B. (1998). Developing an objective definition of visual impairment. *In Vision '96: Proceedings of the International Low Vision Conference* (pp. 331-334). Madrid, Spain: ONCE

Banerjee, P., & Chau, P. Y. K. (2004). An evaluative framework for analysing e-government convergence capability in developing countries. *Electronic Government*, *1*(1), 29–48. doi:10.1504/EG.2004.004135

Becker, S. A. (2004). E-Government Visual Accessibility for Older Adult Users. *Social Science Computer Review*, *22*(1), 11–23. doi:10.1177/0894439303259876

Bertram, B. (2005). *Blindheit und Sehbehinderung in Deutschland: Ursachen und Häufigkeiten. Der Augenarzt, 6*. Dezember.

Brodie, M., & Flournoy, R. E. (2000). Health information, the Internet, and the digital divide. *Health Affairs*, *19*(6), 255–266. doi:10.1377/hlthaff.19.6.255

BSI. (2006). *Guide to good practice in commissioning accessible websites. British Standards Institution*. UK: BSI.

Choudrie, J., Ghinea, G., & Weerakkody, V. (2004). Evaluating Global e-Government Sites: A View using Web Diagnostic Tools. *Electronic . Journal of E-Government*, *2*(2), 105–114.

Compaine, B. M. (Ed.). (2001). *The Digital Divide: Facing a Crisis or Creating a Myth?*Cambridge, MA: MIT Press.

EATT Project. (2003). *Equal Access to Technology Training*. UK: UK LITERATURE REVIEW, Royal National Institute of the Blind.

Foundation, N. Z. (2009). *Digital Strategy 2.0 Submission - Royal New Zealand Foundation of the Blind,* Auckland, New Zealand

Govt. of US (2007). FY 2007 Report to Congress on Implementation of The E-Government Act of 2002, Office of Management and Budget, Government of the USA.

Grönlund, Å. (2002). Electronic Government - Efficiency, Service Quality, and Democracy . In Grönlund, Å. (Ed.), *Electronic Government: Design, Applications and Management* (p. 62). Hershey, PA: Idea Group Publishing.

HKBU. (2006). *HKBU's Views & Comment On The Digital 21 Strategy 2007*. Hong Kong: The Hong Kong Blind Union.

Jarvenpaa, S., Tiller, E. H., & Simons, R. (2003). Regulation and the Internet: Public Choice Insights for Business Organizations. *California Management Review*, *46*(1), 72–85.

Norris, P. (2001). *Digital Divide: Civic Engagement, Information Poverty, and the Internet Wordwide*. Cambridge: Cambridge University Press.

Ojamo, M. (2008). *The Finnish register of visual impairment. Annual statistics 2007*: National research and development centre for welfare and health in Finland and the Finnish federation of the visually impaired.

Resnikoff, S., Pascolini, D., Etya'ale, D., Kocur, I., Pararajasegaram, R., & Pokharel, G. P. (2004). Global data on visual impairment in the year 2002. *Bulletin of the World Health Organization*, *82*, 844–851.

Rubaii-Barrett, N., & Wise, L. R. (2008). Disability Access and E-Government: An Empirical Analysis of State Practices . *Journal of Disability Policy Studies*, *19*(1), 52–64. doi:10.1177/1044207307311533

Silcock, R. (2001). What is e-government. *Parliamentary Affairs*, *54*, 88–91. doi:10.1093/pa/54.1.88

Siochrú, S. Ó., & Girard, B. (2002). *Global media governance. A beginner's guide*. Lanham, Rowman & Littlefield Publishers.

Wegweiser Gmb, H. Berlin. (2007). *Monitoring eHealth & Gesundheitswirtschaft 2007/2008*.

World Health Organisation. (2009). *Causes of blindness and visual impairment*. Retrieved 14.4.2009, 2009, from http://www.who.int/blindness/causes/en/

ADDITIONAL READING

Becker, S. (2005). E-government usability for older adults. *Communications of the ACM*, *48*(2), 104. doi:10.1145/1042091.1042127

Buch, H., Vinding, T., la Cour, M., Appleyard, M., Jensen, G., & Vesti Nielsen, N. (2004). Prevalence and causes of visual impairment and blindness among 9980 Scandinavian adults The Copenhagen City Eye Study. *Ophthalmology*, *111*(1), 53–61. doi:10.1016/j.ophtha.2003.05.010

Bundrick, M., Goette, T., Humphries, S., & Young, D. (2006). An Examination of Web Site Accessibility Issues. *Communications of the IIMA*, *6*(2), 9–18.

Choudrie, J., Ghinea, G., & Weerakkody, V. (2004). Evaluating global e-government sites: a view using web diagnostic tools. *Electronic . Journal of E-Government*, *2*(2), 105–114.

Congdon, N., Friedman, D., & Lietman, T. (2003). Important causes of visual impairment in the world today. *Journal of the American Medical Association*, *290*(15), 2057. doi:10.1001/jama.290.15.2057

D'Allura, T. (2002). Enhancing the social interaction skills of preschoolers with visual impairments. [JVIB]. *Journal of Visual Impairment & Blindness*, *96*(08).

Dandona, L., & Dandona, R. (2006). What is the global burden of visual impairment. *BMC Medicine*, *4*(6), 1741–7015.

Jackson, W., Taylor, R., Palmatier, A., Elliott, T., & Elliott, J. (1998). Negotiating the reality of visual impairment: Hope, coping, and functional ability. *Journal of Clinical Psychology in Medical Settings*, *5*(2), 173–185. doi:10.1023/A:1026259115029

Kocur, I., & Resnikoff, S. (2002). Visual impairment and blindness in Europe and their prevention. *The British Journal of Ophthalmology*, *86*(7), 716. doi:10.1136/bjo.86.7.716

Rahmat, L., Yaakop, S., Mara, U., Tamil, E., & Idna, M. (2006). *The Experiences of Blind & Visually Impaired Users with the Malaysian Government Ministries Website.* Paper presented at the Conference on Social Science and ICT.

Reinhardt, J. (1996). The importance of friendship and family support in adaptation to chronic vision impairment. *JOURNALS OF GERONTOLOGY SERIES B*, *51*, 268–278.

Rubaii-Barrett, N., & Wise, L. (2008). Disability access and e-government: An empirical analysis of state practices. *Journal of Disability Policy Studies*, *19*(1), 52. doi:10.1177/1044207307311533

Šimonová, S. (2005). *E-government and approaches of e-inclusion.* Paper presented at the Proceedings of the 5th WSEAS International Conference on Applied Informatics and Communications table of contents.

Šimonová, S. (2006). E-inclusion and disabled-people-friendly web. *Scientific Papers of the University of Pardubice Series D*, 164–168.

Tielsch, J., Sommer, A., Katz, J., Quigley, H., & Ezrine, S. (1991). Socioeconomic status and visual impairment among urban Americans. *Archives of Ophthalmology*, *109*(5), 637.

Wang, J., Mitchell, P., Smith, W., Cumming, R., & Attebo, K. (1999). Impact of visual impairment on use of community support services by elderly persons: the Blue Mountains Eye Study. *Investigative Ophthalmology & Visual Science*, *40*(1), 12.

Weih, L., Hassell, J., & Keeffe, J. (2002). Assessment of the impact of vision impairment. *Investigative Ophthalmology & Visual Science*, *43*(4), 927.

West, S., Rubin, G., Broman, A., Munoz, B., Bandeen-Roche, K., & Turano, K. (2002). How does visual impairment affect performance on tasks of everyday life?: The SEE Project. *Archives of Ophthalmology*, *120*(6), 774.

Wood, J., & Troutbeck, R. (1994). Effect of visual impairment on driving. *Human Factors: The Journal of the Human Factors and Ergonomics Society*, *36*(3), 476–487.

KEY TERMS AND DEFINITIONS

Act on Equality for People with Disabilities: in German Behindertengleichstellungsgesetz (BGG), is a German Federal law from year 2006. The purpose of this law is to abolish and prevent any discrimination against persons with disabilities, to ensure their equal participation in social activities and to enable them to lead a normal life.

Ambient Assisted Living: (AAL): includes methods, concepts, (electronic) systems, devices as well as services that are providing unobtrusive support for daily life based on context and the situation of the assisted person.

Braille Display: is a computer input/output device supporting the Braille system. The Braille system is a leading method used by blind people to read and write.

Colour Blindness: means limited capability to differentiate between different colours, as to what can be expected from a similar individual or cohort.

eGovernment: refers to the usage of modern information and communication technologies to enhance the scope of communication and to make it more efficient between authorities and citizens, for mutual benefit.

Speech Synthesizer: is a software component that turns written text in digital form into speech. Typical user options are for example male/female voice. Speech synthesizers should too be adapted to different languages.

Vision Impairment: refers to a condition of an individual or group, where the individual's or groups seeing capability is less than what can be expected from a similar individual or cohort.

Chapter 14
A Citizen-Centric Platform to Support Networking in the Area of E-Democracy

Francesco Molinari
ALTEC S.A. Thessaloniki, Greece

Christopher Wills
Kingston University, UK

Adamantios Koumpis
ALTEC S.A. Thessaloniki, Greece

Vasiliki Moumtzi
ALTEC S.A. Thessaloniki, Greece

EXECUTIVE SUMMARY

This chapter describes experiences acquired during the research work conducted as part of the European Project Tell Me (www.tellmeproject.eu). The project envisaged to support the pan-European creation of Living Labs as new forms of cooperation between government, enterprises, citizens and academia for a successful transfer of e-Government, e-Democracy and e-Services state-of-the art applications, solutions, know-how and best practices. In this chapter the authors explore the potential of providing an existing system (DEMOS) allowing moderated and goal-oriented discourses between citizens and policy makers to become parts of open-ended ventures on the creation of collaborative networks for Electronic Democracy. This work would also recommend that this form of support network elevates e-Democracy of a country and thus improves e-governance systems at the grass roots.

ORGANIZATION AND TECHNOLOGICAL BACKGROUND

After the "Helsinki Manifesto" (2006) put the "human-centric way" at the very centre of the measures needed "for turning the Lisbon Strategy (2000) into a living reality", the topic of competitiveness and innovation in Europe has been enriched of a further dimension, namely, co-creative collaboration with the forthcoming users of the developing products and services.

DOI: 10.4018/978-1-61692-814-8.ch014

This is especially useful in the field of (private and Government) e-Services, where the people can be considered as "twice" beneficiaries, namely of public services as such – impacting per se on their lives and businesses – and of ICT based or supported services, where the question becomes to which extent this novel user-centric approach can improve customization (if not "tailoring") to individual needs and requirements.

Some "champions" of this new dimension of innovation belong to the so-called ENoLL – European Network of Living Labs. In a purely business perspective, a Living Lab can be seen as a service providing organization in the topic of R&D and innovation, based on the "co-creation" concept, which focuses on people in their daily living environments as active, if not decisive, contributors to products and services design, development and testing.

In spite of a limited evidence on the known experiences – most of which could count on a significant external funding - it can be affirmed that the cost of building up and maintaining a Living Lab from scratch (i.e. deploying the communication and collaboration infrastructure, gathering and orchestrating the community of users, carrying out the requested evaluation services) can be substantial, thus preventing a long-term impact into the regional innovation systems.

Here is where the Tell Me project initiative starts up. Through the adaptation of a service already operational in Germany and other European Countries, originally thought for the animation of democratic discussions and participative public opinion formation at local and regional level, establishes a solution for the networking and interaction of Living Lab trials participants during the development and implementation of innovative projects. More specifically, the Tell Me objectives were to investigate the administrative viability of the service on a European scale and to identify the conditions for future, pan-European deployment of the service under a juridical and a financial perspective.

The service is based on an existing ICT infrastructure for moderated and goal-oriented discourses involving citizens and political institutions as well as project developers and investors, at national and European level.

The users who tested the service during the pilot phase of the Tell Me project fall into two categories:

a. Living Lab 'Owners' (as their staff validated the services from the technical and administrative point of view and assess their viability and usability);
b. Living Lab 'Members' (Public Administrations, Citizens, Enterprises, Non Profit Organisations, who are the ultimate beneficiaries of these services), mostly operating in the same territorial areas, but also coming from different cities/countries. After each trial/pilot, the results were analyzed with a view to mapping the most relevant application areas and to replicating the service in one or more additional Living Labs in order to align the service to the national regulations (if any) and activate cross-fertilization among the Living Labs through the exchange of *best practices* at European level.

In light of the above, the main purpose of this work is to provide a Trans-European service integrated with a proven methodology that can enable a co-creative user driven e-Democracy service development. Most important is the fact that the service can "link together" the different stakeholders in order to let them work more efficiently, establishing an intimate communication channel between participants in a region. Besides, what is crucial is to increase the availability of easier-to-use e-Government applications that have been validated in advance through online interaction with the potential users. This will potentially enlarge the scope for public sector innovation in Europe.

The aim is to establish what users (the local public) expect from e-Government, e-Democracy and e-Services applications and to explore the cross-fertilization advantages of a "co-design/co-creation approach" using e-Democracy-like tools to plan, communicate and evaluate technologies, ideas, solutions and applications by moderated discourses.

Information and communication technologies and the Internet have great significance in a service-based economy. Just as service is not clearly defined in the literature, so too is the term e-Service. Rust & Lemon (2001) consider that the term is used in general to denote transactions in which information is the primary value exchanged. Gronroos et al. (2000) claim that e-Service is any product or service that is exchanged over the Internet. Others restrict their scope on services that are delivered electronically (Javalgi et al. 2004) or over electronic networks (Rust & Kannan, 2003). In Tell Me, the focus is on any type of (web) service that can be found or exchanged via the Internet.

The Internet tends to shift bargaining power to end consumers in their transactions with businesses (Porter, 2001) because it allows the end consumer to get in contact directly with a great number of producers. On the other hand, the concepts of "mass customisation" (Gilmore & Pine 2000), "one-to-one marketing" (Peppers et al., 1999) and "long tail economics" (Anderson, 2006) are based on the premise that, with the support of information technologies, business firms are able to target each consumer separately, personalise their services and disseminate them efficiently.

This is taken into account in the Tell Me framework. The framework supports both 'one-to-one' and 'many-to-many' marketing and dialogues within a social network, which enable the consumer to communicate with providers and other consumers able and willing to meet a need.

In order to design this network of consumers and providers, ideas can be gleaned from current business networks and ecosystems. In the literature we can find different kinds of business networks, such as business constellations (Normann & Ramirez, 1993), extended enterprises (Prahalad & Ramaswamy, 2003), value nets (Bovet & Martha, 2000), virtual enterprises (Sawhney & Parikh, 2001; Walters & Lancaster, 1999), strategic networks (Jarillo, 1988) and business ecosystems (Moore, 1996; Iansity & Levien, 2004). The concept of business ecosystem is a metaphor that steps forward the movement towards symbiotic and co-evolutionary business networks.

Although Tell Me allows user-defined services as well, in the case of business services, the Tell Me framework's network takes the form of a business and consumer ecosystem. Here, the role of the customer is of prime importance. Therefore, the network is crafted to respond to his/her special needs and where these needs cannot be met the social network would rise to fill this gap. This would also be of use in cases where the services sought are not related to business services, but rather of a voluntary nature.

The OASIS Group defines Service Oriented Architecture (SOA) as a powerful framework for matching needs and capabilities and for combining capabilities to address those needs (OASIS, 2006). Services in SOA are defined in a similar way to the definition of service in the business world that is as deeds performed by the service provider for the benefit of the service client. Consequently, from a conceptual point of view, SOA could be used to provide the technological foundations that are required for the empowerment of consumers in the selection, composition and consumption of products or services in electronic markets.

The services' world is discussing issues more closely related to providing Software as a Service (SaaS) components and how we can handle issues relating to security and transactions in web services. Security, the first of these issues, allows for secure usage of services regardless of the underlying platform and provides specifications (like WS-Security - Rosenberg & Remy (2004)) and languages (SAML – OASIS (2009)) for secure services. Additionally proposals for supporting transactions in web services have already been implemented, like the WS-AtomicTransaction - OASIS (2009)). Finally, the Software as a Service (SaaS) model promises to deliver "all" existing software that we use daily on our computers as services in the near future – this idea is now slowly emerging and it's being exploited in this project.

From an operational point of view, a SOA can be implemented with the use of Web Services. The basic Web Services model endorses three roles (service requestor, service provider and service registry) and three operations (publish, find and bind). Web Services follow the "find, bind and invoke" paradigm, where a service requestor performs dynamic service search by querying the service registry for a service; if the service exists, the registry provides the requestor with contact details for the service.

Such an operational model is clearly consumer-oriented and could support consumer-oriented value creation. The service requestor recognizes some need, searches for solutions, makes the selection, invokes the service and composes it with other services in his own context, in order to create value for him. Through a social network, other users can assist the service requestor in the composition and provide feedback.

Composition can be implemented with the use of mash-up technologies. Mash-ups are a new kind of data intensive and data integration applications which are based on the fusion of heterogeneous data sources that provide a public set of APIs. Depending on the API either a more traditional server based content generation process is followed or a client side scripting language or applet is used to mash-up the content. Most of the available mash-ups rely on the first solution and use the browser side technologies to produce an aesthetically pleasing result for the user. A technology or better an application model that characterizes mash-ups is AJAX (Asynchronous Javascript and XML) Lauriat (2007). AJAX has revolutionized the way web applications behave and provide a more robust and fulfilling user experience.

Other technologies involved in developing and supporting mash-ups include web services related protocols like SOAP (W3C, 2009) and REST Tyagi (2006). SOAP is the basic message exchange protocol used by services (including of course services used in the mash-ups) to communicate with each other. On the other hand REST provides a simple protocol for web services that supports only basic functions (like POST, PUT, DELETE, etc) but its simplicity makes it a prime candidate for mash-ups since it allows the easy fusion of different data sources.

An important issue in the mash-ups is the interoperability among the different data sources. This is addressed by the use of semantic web technologies like RDF/S based ontologies and RDFa (W3C, 2009) based annotations. That way data and their meaning can be seamlessly exchanged among the different sources and can carry their real meaning along. Mash-ups can be used as the main integration point for semantically described data bringing closer the concepts of Semantic Web and Web 2.0 by providing the best of both worlds.

Composition of services through mash-ups is also a consumer-oriented approach, as the consumer decides which services to mash-up and in which way in order to create value for him/herself and the community at large.

It must also be mentioned however that most existing research on Service-Oriented Architectures focuses on software services which are seen as software components providing access to "real" services (for example a software service for travel booking provides access to the actually service for travelling) (Pistore et al., 2009). In addition, software services are used, but not necessarily owned (in the sense of being able to customize them according to needs) by consumers (NESSI, 2006). This leads to the needs to define Service Level Agreements where appropriate (e.g. in chargeback mechanisms) as software services are not used exclusively by their producers.

In this project, we recognize the importance of technical considerations (e.g. Service Level Agreements) for business services. However, we also aim to provide a more user-friendly approach to services, trying to contribute towards viewing the Internet as an enabler of "real" services aimed towards the end consumer, instead of pure "software" services created by the provider of these e-Services.

As has been mentioned, there are two levels of users in the system, and for each of those different requirements (to be confirmed during the project) are foreseen to be essential:

- For the citizens (plain users), they may want to access services, and therefore issues such as Service Level Agreements, Quality of Service, chargeback according to different service models are still important. These considerations point to looking at the technical aspects of web services, therefore we are still looking at services from a "software" point of view.
- For institutional / public users, "real-world" considerations of services are of importance. It is for these reasons that some key assets relating to services must be defined with which the user (citizen) is able to construct / mash-up / configure services. Following the paradigm by Pistore et al. (2009), these assets (which can be enablers or constraints) are:
    1. Time, representing the temporal relation of the activities of the user, as well as conflicts and overlaps between these activities.
    2. Location, representing the (current and perspective) location of the user, the availability of (real-world) services in these locations, as well as the necessity of moving or travelling to use these services.
    3. Social relations (representing other parties such as family, friends, colleagues) involved in the user activities.
    4. Money and other values, representing costs and assets involved in the user activities.

NEEDS FOR E-DEMOCRACY AND CITIZEN PARTICIPATION

The field of e-Democracy in Europe has been developed by different players on the European, national and local level over the course of the last years.

On the European level the different organisations (EuroParl, EC etc.) have tested and implemented a series of e-Democracy programmes and initiatives to support the development of the field: The European Commission funded ca. 20 Information Society Technology projects with more than 30 million euro and many of the sixth Framework Programme projects support the field of e-Democracy (Chrissafis and Rohen, 2010). One major step forward to implementing "contribute to easing mobility of European citizens within the Internal Market, making European Citizenship a reality, supporting them as active citizens through innovative government services and through participation" (IST policy, 2004) on the European level is the Interactive Policy Making (IPM) project. The system has been put into place "to facilitate the stakeholders' consultation process by the use of easy-to-use and straightforward online questionnaires, making it easier both for respondents to participate and for **policy** makers to analyze the results" (Interactive Policy Making, 2007).

The Council of Europe supported the general development by the set up of the ad hoc Committee on E-Democracy of the Council of Europe (CAHDE, 2006). The goal of CAHDE is among others to "examine developments on e-democracy/e-participation at European and international level"; to "develop proposals for the Forum for the Future of Democracy as to how it could embrace issues of e-democracy". The recommendations on *e-Democracy* developed by CAHDE were finalized by the end of 2008 and will certainly help to convince policy makers in the 47 member states to support the field of e-Democracy.

Summing up, beyond the small list of examples given in this text there are many different *e-Democracy* projects already in place or planned on the European, national and local level and the count is still growing. This hints at a larger market potential lying ahead for electronic democracy in Europe, or as Stephen Coleman (2003) puts it: "Politicians are beginning to realize that connecting directly with the citizens they represent can lead to better **policy**-making and legislation, informed by public experience and expertise; a new kind of relationship between government and governed, based upon politicians' listening, learning and sharing ideas as well as steering and aggregating; and the reward of enhanced public confidence in democratic institutions and the renewed legitimacy of governance."

In this context, as indicated in the (OECD, 2001a) report: "A key challenge will be to make the transition from area wide (metropolitan) technical structures to area wide (metropolitan) political structures which empower citizens by addressing the 'democratic deficit' and thereby improve the effectiveness of policies at the local level. This implies central government building community **policy** frameworks, but leaving policy content largely in the hands of local actors".

"Achieving such a transition will involve a cultural change towards a people centre local democracy, not imposed from above, but achieved through strong community policy frameworks in which citizens are empowered to decide the changes they want to see.

This will require a more transparent and accountable decision-making process in which citizens are more fully informed and involved. Key elements of cultural change and improving the policy framework include: modernizing voting procedures, developing new leadership skills among the local political elites, encouraging new forms of participation, and ensuring that area-based approaches are linked to mainstream policy, are properly evaluated, and involve a long-term commitment by local government."

Identifying the "right" structures for local actors to participate may, however, present several difficulties. Municipalities are often both too big and too small to perform democratically. On the one hand, the gigantism of some contemporary metropolises tends to "alienate" the citizen who is far from decision-making centers. On the other hand, sub-national government may be too small to solve some problems that extend beyond its administrative boundaries, such as air pollution and traffic congestion.

Combined with the difficulty of encouraging a new sense of belonging and people's identification with topics of mutual concern is the additional problem of ensuring that the solutions allowing greater participation are not achieved at the cost of the socially and economically excluded. Making a transition to more effective forms of governance is, thus, not just a question of changing institutions, but crucially of moving to a political culture that is centered on the interests of people.

As indicated in another report (OECD, 2001b): "Engaging citizens is a sound investment in public policy-making. As these new relationships have evolved and matured, local governments have increasingly recognized their reliance upon the active contribution of citizens in making better decisions and achieving policy objectives. In this perspective, strengthening government relations with citizens may be seen as a sound investment in tapping new sources of policy-relevant ideas, information and resources for implementation".

Among the driving forces that have led governments to strengthen their relations with citizens, are the needs to:

Table 1. Types of local Government-Citizen interaction

Stage of policy making	*Information*	*Consultation*	*Active participation*
Formulation (Agenda Setting)	• White Papers, policy documents • Legislative programmes • Draft laws and regulations	• Large-scale opinion surveys • Use of discussion groups or citizens' panels • Invitation of comments on draft legislation	• Submission of alternative draft laws or policy proposals • Public dialogue on policy issues and options
Implementation	• New policy or regulations and their provisions	• Use of focus groups to develop secondary legislation	• Partnership with Civil Society Organisations to disseminate information on compliance with new laws
Evaluation	• Public notice of evaluation exercises and opportunities to participate	• Inclusion of stakeholders in reviews of government evaluation programmes and results	• Independent evaluation conducted by Civil Society Organisations

- Improve the quality of policy, by allowing governments to tap wider sources of information, perspectives, and potential solutions in order to meet the challenges of policy-making under conditions of increasing complexity, policy interdependence and time pressures.
- Meet the challenges of the emerging information society, to prepare for greater and faster interactions with citizens and ensure better knowledge management.
- Integrate public input into the policy-making process, in order to meet citizens' expectations that their voices be heard, and their views be considered, in decision-making by government.
- Respond to calls for greater government transparency and accountability, as public and media scrutiny of government actions increases and standards in public life are codified and raised.
- Strengthen public trust in government and reverse the steady erosion of voter turnout in elections, falling membership in political parties and surveys showing declining confidence in key public institutions.

Three types of local Government-Citizen interaction might be present all along the *policy life cycle* – see Table 1 (adapted from OECD, 2001b).

The major contribution of the citizens' involvement into the public action is to make better decisions and achieve in a consensual way **policy** objectives. In this perspective a local government has to adjust public action by a continuous evaluation of objective and results along the *policy life cycle*. Table 2 (adapted from QUALEG, 2004) includes the dynamically adjusted actions along the policy life cycle.

Table 2. Dynamically adjusted actions along the policy life cycle

Stage of policy making	*Continuous objectives evaluation*	*Continuous results evaluation*	*Continuous actions readjustment*
Formulation (Agenda setting)	- Understand the citizen needs	- Proposal or action plan presentation to the citizens	- Change of objectives formulation and key indicators
Implementation	- Continuous actions adaptation to the citizen's solicited or unsolicited feed back	- Continuous measurement of quantitative or qualitative action's results	- Continuous change of the qualitative indicators in order to action evaluation
Evaluation	- Collect the qualitative and quantitative citizen feedback and reconfigure the objectives	- Collect the qualitative and quantitative results and reconfigure the means	- Reformulate a new action plan for the next cycle

The "ideal" process of designing, implementing and evaluating public (e-)Services should come as a specific instance of the above scheme. However, what happens in reality – as noted, among others, by Følstad et al. (2007) – is that an insufficient care is given to users' involvement, in three respects:

a. to introduce and gain experience with resource-effective methods from the multitude of user groups and stakeholders relevant in the development of e-Government systems and services;
b. to manage evolving goal structures for public e-Services, where the goals of different users are reflected;
c. to give proper attention to the administrative and/or legislative reforms needed to align the new services to the underlying institutional and organizational framework.

DESCRIPTION OF THE SERVICE

Currently the DEMOS platform facilitates large-scale e-participation and on-line deliberation projects. This flexible framework supports integration of nearly every discourse process model currently used by on-line moderators. The DEMOS platform transcends the common approach of structuring user contributions (e.g. articles) in hierarchical and inflexible "threads". Instead, every contribution is deemed as equal; its position in e.g. listings of articles depends on meta information attributed to each article, for example the number of votes, hits, or comments. The moderators (as well as the users) may choose and combine these pieces of meta information to generate specific "views" (i.e. filtered and sorted lists of articles).

Together with innovative capabilities to structure discourses on a time-line and to integrate a huge variety of voting and rating mechanisms, the DEMOS system fosters goal-oriented on-line deliberations. Most features of the system are easily switched on and off by the moderators in the administration backend, for example the option to comment on any contribution may be turned off for the whole system but turned on for one specific view.

However, the main strength of the system emerges from the user interaction; e.g. users are allowed to create links between articles or assign articles to a specific position on a map which results in visually stunning cluster effects. Furthermore, the content is effortlessly available, due to compliance with the relevant accessibility and syndication standards.

DEMOS goes beyond the usual Internet chat or discussion forums to provide a powerful and integrated toolset with the following, configurable and customizable state-of-the-art features for supporting large-scale public participation in political discourses on the Web:

- support for a wide range of types of discourses, from not moderated, ad hoc discussions and to complex moderated, structured and goal-directed deliberations differentiated user roles and access rights
- modes for communication and feedback (direct/indirect, public/protected) supporting a variety of types of user interaction
- support for analyzing and visualizing the results of surveys, including sorting and aggregating quantitative data and qualitative semantic content (free answers, comments and statements)
- participative "bottom up" specification of issues, construction of questionnaires, and selection of experts
- conflict resolution strategies allowing differentiated outcomes (convergence, consensus, divergence, "rational dissent")
- support for self-organization and subgroup formation, with different levels of aggregation and distribution

These features have presented various technical challenges to the software developers, including:

- assuring scalability, to maintain process coherence and coordination in the face of a large numbers of participants
- providing powerful and convenient administration features for moderators and mediators, especially for structuring and dynamically restructuring large scale participative discourses
- using surveying, rating and voting to help discussions progress and to enhance conclusiveness of debates
- supporting procedures, similar to "rules of order", for essential parts of the participation process.

Apart from Living Labs, the DEMOS system has been adapted and specialized either to the needs and demands of informal and formal processes especially public administrations are promoting themselves or even obliged to perform as well as several e- services.

Tell Me services have been identified and built upon the DEMOS system and shifted to solution-oriented services in order to include a focused potential final users' analysis.

METHODOLOGY

Within this research, we built and populated the targeted experiential service according to the following steps of a Living Lab's configuration process:

1. Contextualization
2. Selection
3. Concretization
4. Implementation
5. Feedback

Step 1. Contextualization

Contextualization means a prior exploration of the technological and social challenges implied by the technology or service under investigation. Applicable methods are, consequently:

- a technological scan, giving an overview of current and future technologies but also to map the specific functionalities and characteristics related to them;
- a (state-of-the-art) study in order to determine the socio-economic implications of the research focus (framework as well as topic).

The contextualization phase is the starting point for the preparation of a Tell Me Living Lab trial. Within this phase all important decisions on topic selection, process structure, user to be involved and evaluation issues have to be made.

The Tell Me Living Labs can be adapted to the following application fields:

- urban and regional planning (UP)
- e-Services (E-S)
- product innovation / product development (PI)
- participative decisions on policies, projects or budget planning (BP)
- idea development (ID)

These fields require using different tools and the adaptation of different evaluation criteria. For this reason it is important to draw a clear picture of the test application / service / technology and to focus on the crucial research question.

To achieve this, so-called technological scans can be performed to provide an overview of current and future technologies but also to map the specific functionalities and related characteristics. State-of-the-art studies can additionally determine the socio-economic implications of the topic under consideration.

The selection of topics to be discussed and processed in the context of the Tell Me Living Lab process have to be defined carefully and the particular context should be explored in detail. All following phases and activities and the configuration of the DEMOS system are depending on this first decision about the issue to be debated.

It is left to the individual testbeds of the Tell Me project to clarify these aspects in more detail. Within the Contextualization Phase, five different tasks are specified:

a. Development of goals, quality standards and evaluation methods
b. Adaptation of DEMOS process and technology
c. Preparation of background information
d. User selection
e. Administration and moderation

Step 2. Selection

The Selection phase includes the identification of potential users or user groups, by means of non probabilistic or purposeful sampling. Useful criteria are, for instance:

- the maximum variation of underlying phenomenon (e.g. education or age);
- the search for a significant variation of observations (e.g. selective or criterion sampling)
- the theoretical variation of relevant concepts (according to some preexisting study).

The scope of participation has to be clarified in advance in order to avoid disappointments. The topic must be specified as well as the groups of people that have to be involved. It is particularly recommended to write a list of daily activities to monitor the progress in this area.

The following issues have to be tackled with in advance:

- Exploration of the user groups to be involved, e.g. experts, interest groups, members of authority etc.
- Investigation of already existing networks which can be directly addressed by the discussion
- Invitation of users to participate
- Preparation of a strategy and local activities in order to make people aware of the Tell Me Living Lab and motivate them to participate in advance and during the ongoing process.

The following Concretization phase is based on the assumptions made here at this stage.

Step 3. Concretization

Concretization means a thorough description of the current characteristics, everyday behavior and perceptions of the selected test users regarding the research focus. In this initial measurement phase we look at the specific user characteristics (socio-demographic and economic) as well their relation towards the introduced technology or service. The methodology used depends on the size of the test panel: for instance, a quantitative survey can be integrated, depending on the sample scale, by qualitative interviews. 'Initial' means that measurement of the sample is made before a technology or service is introduced or before the test panel becomes active in the Living Lab; it thus enables to perform a second measurement and a full evaluation at the end of the project.

This phase is intended to mainly cope with the user registration. DEMOS offers a registration mode that is adaptable to the needs of the trails. The registration process and the underlying threshold (low/high) have to be defined. It must be made clear which data are requested for the registration process, which information is mandatory or optional for registration. Table 3 includes an example of registration checklist. Examples for optional data:

Table 3. Checklist registration

Tasks	*Specification*
Define set of registration information	• Necessary for all Tell Me Living Labs • More and specialized questions for target group related issues like UP, E-S
Distinguish between mandatory and optional information	• Necessary for all Tell Me Living Labs
Define registration threshold	• Necessary for all Tell Me Living Labs • Lower for ID

- full name
- gender
- age
- town
- district
- education
- occupation

Examples for the different thresholds are:

- Very low: Within the registration process the user has to choose a login name and a password. No information else is mandatory or proved.
- Medium: Within the registration process, the user has to choose a login name and a valid email address. The mail is sent to the given address to validate the request.
- High: Just pre-invited users are able to register to the process.

User Rights are related to forum access, writing / reading and change documents, upload content etc. Typically, three different types of users are to be distinguished:

- moderators and administrators have all rights (read / write, access to all forums / wikis /documents etc., can change the content on the platform DEMOS)
- normal users have restricted rights (access to public forums, right to read and write, access to wikis)
- special or expert users have restricted rights (access to public and expert forums, right to read and write)

In order to gather information about current characteristics and every day life behavior of the users and their perceptions regarding the research focus, an initial online-survey was conducted. The participants who registered to the platform were actively motivated to take part in that survey.

Step 4. Implementation

Implementation is actually the behavioral validation and operationally running test phase of the Living Lab from a user-oriented and ethnographic viewpoint. Two major research methods are mostly used in literature (e.g. Pierson and Lievens 2005):

- direct analysis, using remote data collection techniques and strategies (like technological monitoring) and software logging tools (if applicable) on the device level (e.g. pda, mobile phone or digital television) as well as on the platform/network level;
- indirect analysis, based on (thematically organized) focus groups, in-depth interviews and self-reporting techniques like diaries, all being applied to investigate the meaning and motivation for behavior.

The following description specifies the 3 different stages of the DEMOS process with respect to their outcome and the moderator's intervention strategies. Due to the specification made within the Contextualization Phase, closed forums, polls, user diaries have to be put in place.

4.1. Implementation Stage 1

The purpose of the first stage is to initiate and facilitate the discussion, to generate different viewpoints and collect a widespread collection of opinions and statements and finally to identify the central and most important (sub) topics of the general subject matter. The stage concludes by splitting up the main forum into different thematic sub forums dedicated to the most central issues in Stage 2.

The moderators have to analyze and cluster the free text contributions in order to find out the issues most participants seem to be interested in. Additionally, the moderators have to summarize the discussion during the course of the first stage following a specific procedure. These summaries consist of content and progress related parts and highlight and profile emerging lines of conflict. The first stage finally results in a set of proposed sub topics that can be more intensively discussed in separate discussion forums in the next phase. Since this procedure is relying on interpretations of the individual postings as well as of the entire discussion, the result may not exactly meet the preferences of the participants. At this point the survey method might come into play in order to evaluate whether or not the proposed sub forums meet the demands of the community and, if necessary, to generate ideas on how to revise the list of sub topics.

4.2. Implementation Stage 2

In the second stage a limited number (~3) of sub forums are offered on the basis of the poll results. This phase is meant to intensively discuss the chosen topics among smaller discussion groups in thematic sub forums and to work out ascertained and feasible solution strategies.

In this stage specific aspects can intensively be discussed in smaller groups of interested participants, while the main forum still catches those participants who want to discuss the topic on a more general level. Again the moderators summarize the developing debate on a regular basis and at the same time try to tease out and manage emerging conflicts. They clarify how and to what extent people are agreeing or disagreeing and at the same time try to reduce the distance between diverging positions by deliberation.

In order to generate concrete results or possible solution strategies, the moderators invite the participants to fix their ideas in so called "wikis". Wikis are documents that can be developed collaboratively by different participants on the Internet. If the moderators foresee that a concrete idea is emerging, they will open a wiki that the participants can jointly work out or adapt to the discussion going on in the forum. At the end of this phase the sub forums and the wiki documents will be closed again. The participants can still read the content but not revise it any more. Finally, the moderators will close this phase with a summary of what was discussed so far and an outlook about what will happen in the last phase.

4.3. Implementation Stage 3

The third stage reintegrates the sub forums into the still existing main forum by transferring the summaries (wikis) and related survey results. Here the participants have the opportunity to see the particular sub topic as part of the general subject matter and a 'big picture' will emerge. Participants have the last chance to comment on the main topic and the assembled results of the sub forums. The community is asked to rate the sub topics in terms of importance for the main goal that the DEMOS process was intentionally set up for. The final result is a condensed document depicting both the results of a dynamic discussion and the importance given to its different aspects in the view of its participants.

Stage 3 intends to drive the single discussions again towards a wider perspective and highlight the interrelations of the different aspects. The moderators have to keep track of the discussion and help the participants to finally scrutinize the results of the discussion and the wikis. By the help of the rating system, users can rank the different ideas (wikis) which were developed in the second stage with regard to their quality and feasibility for the underlying discussion topic.

In cooperation with the users, the moderators work out the final summary of the discourse and its detailed results.

Step 5. Feedback

The Feedback phase consists of two research steps:

1. an ex post measurement based on the same techniques of the initial measurement, to check if there is any evolution in the users perception and attitude towards the introduced technology or service, to assess changes over time in everyday life in relation to technology use and to detect transitions of usage over time.
2. a set of technological recommendations from the analysis of data, gathered during the previous implementation phase. This outcome of the feedback phase can be used as the starting point for a new research cycle within the Living Lab; in this way the iterative feature of our research cycle can be made operational.

In the Tell Me project there are three different layers of feedback that have to be taken into account:

1. ex-post measurement: conduct and analyze a final online survey. At the end of the Living Lab process a final survey has to be conducted, analyzed and compared with the results of initial survey. The aim is to track a change of attitudes and opinions in the course of the Living Lab process. . The result of this comparison should be cross checked with the discussion.
2. analysis of the contributions: if necessary, a thematic analysis within the feedback phase of a Tell Me Living Lab should provide an in-depth analysis of the content by
    a. analyzing the argumentation process in forums
    b. analyzing user diaries especially for PI
    c. in-depth comparison of the different proposals UP, BP, ID especially with regard to users agreement / disagreement
    d. analyzing changes between different version of the same wiki
3. evaluation of the quality of outcomes: to assess the quality of the outcomes it is important to keep in mind the goals of the Tell Me Living Lab process.

EVIDENCE FROM A PRACTICAL CASE STUDY: THE TUSCANY REGION'S LIVING LAB

Case studies are generally regarded as particularly useful in depicting a *holistic portrayal of a experiences and results* regarding the application or implementation of a new concept or program as in the case of the Tell Me services. Though case studies are used to organize a wide range of information about a case and then analyze the contents by seeking patterns and themes in the data, and by further analysis through cross comparison with other cases. The case study's unique strength is its ability to deal with a full variety of evidence such as documents, interviews and observations. The multiple perspectives, methods and observations in the studies also provide a strategy of triangulation to add rigor, breadth and depth to the investigation.

The simple fact that what people say and what people do is not necessarily the same thing is also taken into consideration through observation and cross checking with the perspectives of others involved in various transactions in different settings. Evidence from the case studies highlighted many instances of the disparity between the language used to articulate the desire to collaborate and the organizational reality of how decision-making is exercised in implementing the practice. However, sufficient evidence has been collected that supports the efficacies of using the Tell Me service as a collaboration infrastructure for carrying out processes that are communications-intensive and exhibit a high degree of complexity as the result of the involvement of many actors and shareholders.

The Regional Government of Tuscany in the late 2007 published the Law no. 69 on "Rules on the promotion of participation in the development of regional and local policies" also known as 'law on participation' (See Figure 1).

That law is an innovative tool for encourage and disseminate new ways and methods of participation, through the construction of new participatory institutions, new processes and shared rules to discuss any size issues within a community and to assess possible solutions through dialogue and confrontation, within a defined time.

The trial was dedicated to evaluate the citizenship knowledge of the law and their comments and expectation about the law.

Contextualization

In the Tuscany land there is a community network whose name is PAAS (Access Points to the e-Services, see http://www.e.toscana.it/paas/). The 270 nodes are spread across the whole Tuscany region and at present have more than 32.000 subscribers. The network is a valuable result of an e-Inclusion initiative of the Regional Government of Tuscany.

The PAAS-LL has been built with the focus of e Participation, e Government and e Services, but, taking in account the importance of the law, the trial addressed only the e Participation theme.

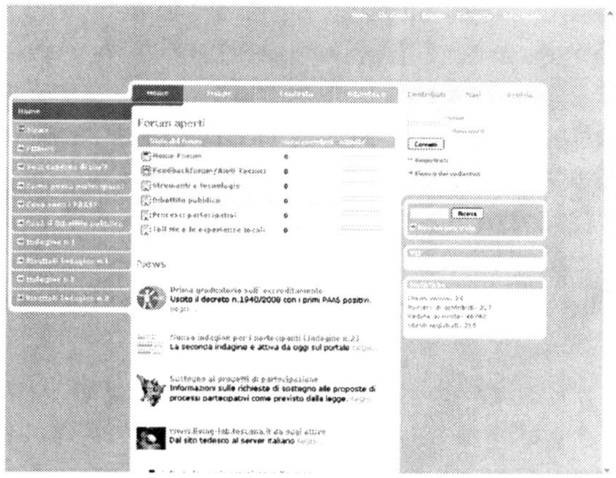

Figure 1. Home of Living-Lab.toscana.it (adopted from Tell Me project trial website http://www.living-lab.toscana.it/)

The target group of the trial were the citizens of all 10 Provinces of Tuscany, with age between 18 and 80 and therefore all the PAAS subscribers were considered in that group.

By means of a call for proposal, 20 PAAS nodes were selected using criteria like geographic coverage (2 every Province), knowledge and experience about participation and social networks of every single node manager. This choice has been taken in order to have a simpler management of the trial and to include the more motivated node-owners.

In the following the four different areas of contextualization phase are detailed, as stated in D4.1 "Operational Methodology" of Tell Me.

Development of Goals, Quality Standards and Evaluation Methods

During the initial phase of the trial, the discussion subject was about the Tuscany Regional Law no. 69/2007:_"participation gives the chance of a new active citizenship". The trial's main goal was a debate about the law's effectiveness and citizen's expectations.

Trial evaluation criteria were the number of participants registered on the platform, the number of contributions in the forum and the degree of satisfaction of the Regional Government of Tuscany Directorate. The latter was responsible for the Participation Law publishing. Based on the above. Table 4 includes the corresponding trial's Contextualization phase checklist.

Adaptation of DEMOS Process and Configuration of the DEMOS Platform

The adaptation of DEMOS has been carried out in two different phases.

The first phase has been used in order to learn the platform functions and complete the Italian translation of menus and windows. During the second phase the platform has been customized and settled for the trial (see Table 5).

Selection

The new regional law on participation affected all the citizenship of Tuscany and hence all the PAAS subscribers and visitors were interested by our survey. It has to be considered also that the goal of the trial was to highlight the powerfulness of e-Participation when used within a well-organized Community Network, just like a Living-Lab.

Therefore, all the PAAS-LL node maintainers were instructed to invite all their own subscribers over 18 years old to participate to survey. The people selected were a good sample of Tuscany citizenship because of the presence in the Living Lab of two PAAS nodes for every Province. In the following Table 6, the sample composition considering age, sex, and education is shown.

Concretization

In order to give to all the participants to the trial all the tools and information to understand the innovation of the web 2.0 and social networking platform, during the month before the pilot itself a public discussion was started providing insights

Table 4. Checklist of contextualization phase

Tasks	Specification	Checked y/n
Definition of type of Tell Me Living Lab (UP, E-S, PI, BP, ID)	• Explain the purpose of the Tell Me Living Lab • Explain main research focus • Define evaluation standards	yes yes yes

Table 5. Checklist of DEMOS adaptation

Tasks	Specification	Checked y/n
Translation	• Translation of information material • Translation of advertising material • Translation of system and process description • Provide translation possibilities during the process	Yes
Layout specification	• Necessary for all types of Tell Me Living Labs • Logo integrated? • Typo correct? • Phrases and sentences integrated? • Wording correct? • Color scheme correct?	Yes Yes Yes Yes Yes

Table 6. Checklist of selection phase

Tasks	Specification	Checked y/n
Define user groups	• Necessary for all types of Tell Me Living Labs especially for E-S and UP	Yes
Define communication channels	• Necessary for all types of Tell Me Living Labs • Define communication channels and marketing strategies for each target group separately	Yes
Invitation to participate	• Necessary for all types of Tell Me Living Labs • Plan invitation waves for each target group during the whole process • Develop a schedule for invitations and reminders of participating	Yes Yes

on the different ways to support debates within a network community. As a result of this, all the subscribers and visitors could start the trial with a full awareness of what they were going for and hence endorse their trust on the survey goals.

Furthermore, in order to let every subscriber to take part to the initial online survey, all of them were registered to the DEMOS platform as debate participants and therefore they got used to consider themselves as a member of the coming trial (see Table 7).

Table 7. Checklist of concretization phase

Tasks	Specification	Checked y/n
Define user groups	• Necessary for all Tell Me Living Labs	Yes, not relevant
Define access rights for user groups	• Necessary for all Tell Me Living Labs	Yes
Define user profiles in DEMOS for invited guests / experts	• Necessary for all Tell Me Living Labs	Yes
Conduct initial online survey	• Necessary for all Tell Me Living Labs	Yes

Implementation

The implementation phase duration was one month. The debates were divided in 5 different forums, two of them with the main topic of participation law and participative process, while the other topics were to support the discussion on web 2.0 tools, Tell Me project, and user assistance. At the end of the 23 days of trial there were 215 registered subscribers that produced 227 contributions, having the amazing number of 11047 hits, which means that the DEMOS platform was visited by subscribers of all PAAS nodes, not by PAAS-LL members only (see Table 8).

Table 8. Checklist of implementation phase

Tasks	Explanation	Checked y/n
Moderation	• Summarize topics • Report on rule violation • Comment on discussion process • Provide hand-over on shift change	Yes Yes Yes Yes
News announcement	• Produce daily news due current development • Report on events and summarize them • Produce news in advance • Report from the discussion	Yes Yes Yes Yes
Open wikis	• Name and implement subforums • Provide first structure for the wikis	Yes Yes
Edit final document	• Add user polls and rankings to this final document • Include results from starting / final questionnaire	Yes Yes

Feedback

In order to collect feedback from users, two questionnaires were prepared. One questionnaire was sent to the entire registered user community in order to get their feedback, while the other questionnaire was prepared for collecting qualitative feedback from the PAAS-LL maintainers and moderators. The summarized results are presented in the following (see Table 9).

Table 9. Checklist of feedback phase

Tasks	Explanation	Checked y/n
Final survey	• Conduct a final survey and compare results with initial survey	Yes
Thematic analysis (main method: content analysis)	• Argumentation process in forums, necessary for all types of Tell Me Living Labs • Proposal comparison, especially for UP, BP, ID	Yes Yes
Evaluation of quality outcome (main method: content analysis, quantitative research)	• Quantitative Research to evaluate user profile (especially for UP, E-S, BP) • Content analysis to value the quality of the ideas, suggestions, arguments etc, necessary for all types of Tell Me Living Labs	Yes Yes

BENEFITS AND CHALLENGES AHEAD

The Tell Me framework brings about a subjective richness to bear on decision-making (policy) problems faced by Public Administration. This richness implies that the Tell Me service, through a more conscious attention and deliberate experimentation and adoption of the real world users, offers the following benefits:

Improved functioning of Living Labs (set up in local e-governance systems): With Tell Me, a basic infrastructure (integrated with a methodology) is provided to "link together" the different stakeholders in order to let them work more efficiently. Equally important is that Tell Me establishes an intimate communication channel between the participants in a Living Lab. This communication service is the first step towards the provision of user centered and customized e-Services.

Co-creative e-Government: Another benefit of the Tell Me service is to develop trust between the people and stakeholders in a region; this is the first step to enable a co-creative user driven e-Government service development.

Improved quality of public services: It should be kept in mind that the main area of public interest for the project is related to online service provision to citizens by European public administration. Tell Me enables on one hand, improved staff efficiency in listening to the customers and on the other hand, more citizens/customers oriented and "socially accepted" e-Services.

Easily available e-Government applications: Another benefit for the community will be the availability of easier-to-use e-Government applications that have been validated in advance through online interaction with the potential users. This potentially enlarges the scope for public sector innovation in Europe.

Improved efficiency/effectiveness of the validation process: Outside and beyond the public sector, a number of additional benefits can be experienced by the repeated use of the Tell Me methodology in the private sector context as well.

According to the "Helsinki Manifesto" issued on 20th November 2006, a further dimension, namely, co-creative collaboration with the forthcoming users of the developing products and services, can enhance the outcomes of competitiveness and innovation in Europe. The most important impact to citizens is its usefulness in the field of (private and Government) e-Services. As a result, the framework of Tell Me networking can be an extremely beneficial toolset to bring together regional and industrial stakeholders with citizen academia and researchers.

Besides, it is obvious to us that citizens and community members fully engaged in a Living Lab develop a positive feeling for local authorities, both intuitively and through learning by playing; they can also e.g. gain a better understanding of the scope and limits of budgetary planning and of other specifications of policy-making. The users of the Tell Me platform learn what it means to implement political "dreams" against a background of limited resources and spending limits imposed by law. The complexity of the budget planner varies according to the degree to which the user goes deeply into the subject – from a smart game to a level verging on reality.

In that respect, any sustainable solution would require to:

- Communicate the scope and limits of local authority budget-setting in an intelligent and innovative way.
- Use the tool to explain the meaning of individual budget items.
- Let the public participate in making important decisions.
- Identify citizens' desires and priorities at an early stage.
- Generate acceptance for budget consolidation.
- Create more transparency – and thus more local democracy.
- Integrate the planner in the political process: create opportunities for discussion.

Conversely, municipality and regional representatives can use Tell Me to acquire information about the desires, preferences and needs of their citizens, being enabled to create opportunities for debating about future avenues for development or new projects.

CONCLUSION AND NEXT STEPS

Tell Me is a European project, which focuses on the design of transnational public services built on ICT in e-Government related areas. We aimed at demonstrating the pilot implementation and exploring the market potential of what was originally presented as a (joint) methodology and toolset for the configuration and the pan-European deployment of Living Labs in the areas of e-Government, e-Democracy and e-Services. As a result, the existing and upcoming best practices in such domains have been considered as a first market segment for our service since the beginning of the project. This chapter documents the steps ahead made by the Tell Me partners in the market validation of such a complex service during the 1st project year.

A Living Lab is a real-life environment, managed by a business/citizens/government partnership, which enables users to take an active part in the research, development and innovation process. Products and services are developed in a person-centric and co-creative way, based on continuous feedback from users to developers. As an open innovation platform, it creates an environment where users are confronted with ideas, concepts and prototypes or demonstrators of technology since the early stages of the research, development and innovation process, not only at its end, like in more classical field trials or product testing approaches.

The intuition behind the Tell Me project has been to replicate an existing service (DEMOS) - originally thought for the animation of democratic discussions and participative public opinion formation at local and regional level - and adapt it to the networking and repeated interaction of participants during the development and implementation of Living Lab trials. After a first phase where the Tell Me consortium focused into the preparation of five regional Living Lab trials in the domains of e-Government, e-Services and e-Participation, the second phase has been based on the most important findings derived from market analysis, project dissemination and the collection of the trials results, to build up a first draft of business plan for the consortium as a whole.

At a higher level, our analysis has focused on the understanding of the Tell Me service "portfolio" composition: i.e., what are the services making up the Tell Me suite?

In fact, a first piece of evidence has been that the DEMOS system – though very effective in allowing moderated and goal-oriented discourses between citizens and policy makers, as well as trial managers, developers and other stakeholders, at national and European level - simply adds up to a plethora of existing ICT solutions that are already operational at Living Lab level. It was then necessary to prepare an overview of the actual strengths and weaknesses of the service to lay the proper foundations for a good marketing action.

A second piece of evidence relates to the fact that, until now, very few Living Labs are actually operating in the areas of e-Government, e-Participation and e-Democracy. This can be seen as a promising market scope, at the only condition that it should not hide the good or best practices that are already operating in these domains, though not (or not explicitly) under the Living Labs "umbrella". In that respect, what we thought was missing from our original approach is a deeper consideration of the original traits being born and brought up in the context of public administration and participatory policy making.

ACKNOWLEDGMENT

Our thanks to the European Commission for partially funding the Tell Me project and the architect of the Tell Me ideas and vision, Mr Rolf Luehrs.

DEMOS was a research project funded by the European Commission (http://www.demos-project.org/). Tell Me is an eTEN Project, running as part of the European Union's Framework Programme 6 for Research in Information Society Technologies, aiming towards 'e-Government'. Official project Web site: http://www.tellmeproject.eu

REFERENCES

W3C (2009). *RDF Annotations (RDFa),* Retrieved from http://www.w3.org/TR/xhtml-rdfa-primer/ on 22/10/2009.

W3C (2009). *RDF Schema (RDFS)*. Retrieved from http://www.w3.org/TR/rdf-schema/ on 22/10/2009.

W3C (2009). *Resource Description Framework (RDF*). Retrieved from http://www.w3.org/RDF/ on 22/10/2009.

W3C (2009). *Simple Object Access Protocol (SOAP)* Retrieved from http://www.w3.org/TR/soap/ on 22/10/2009.

Ad hoc Committee on E-Democracy of the Council of Europe (CAHDE) (2006). Introduction to the Ad Hoc Committee on E-democracy (CAHDE). Retrieved from http://www.coe.int/t/e/integrated_projects/democracy/02_activities/002_e-democracy/00%20Intro%20CAHDE_en.asp

Anderson, C. (2006). *The Long Tail: Why the Future of Business is Selling Less of More*. New York: Hyperion.

Anttiroiko, A.-V. (2003). Building strong e-democracy: the role of technology in developing democracy for the information age. *Communications of the ACM*, *46*(9).

Bovet, D., & Martha, J. (2000). Value nets: reinventing the rusty supply chain for competitive advantage. *Strategy and Leadership*, *28*(4), 21–26. doi:10.1108/10878570010378654

Boyd, D., & Ellison, N. B. (2007). *Social Network Sites: Definition*. History, and Scholarship.

Cardoso, J., & Sheth Amit, P. (Eds.). (2006). *Semantic Web services, Processes and applications*. Springer. doi:10.1007/978-0-387-34685-4

Chrissafis, T., & Rohen, M. (2010). European eParticipation developments: from ad hoc experiences towards mass scale engagement. *eJournal of eDemocracy and Open Government (JeDEM)*. Special Issue in collaboration with PEP-NET: Sustainable eParticipation. ENoLL, The European Network of Living Labs – http://www.openlivinglabs.eu/

Gilmore, J. H., & Pine, B. J. (2000). *Markets of One: Creating Customer-Unique Value through Mass Customization*. Boston: Harvard Business School Press.

Grönroos, C. (2000). Service management: A management focus for service competition . *International Journal of Service Industry Management*, *1*(1), 6–14.

Iansiti, M., & Levienm, R. (2004). *The Keystone Advantage: What the New Dynamics of Business Ecosystems Mean for Strategy, Innovation and Sustainability*. Boston: Harvard Business School Press.

Interactive Policy Making Online Consultations website (2007). *Report on Interactive Policy Making* (http://ec.europa.eu/yourvoice/ipm/index_en.htm) IST policy on the objective of ICT research for innovative Government website (2004). (http://cordis.europa.eu/ist/so/govt/home.html) IST-507767 – QUALEG (2004). Deliverable 4.1 "Marketing Research"

Jarillo, J. C. (1988). On Strategic Networks . *Strategic Management Journal*, *9*(1), 31–41. doi:10.1002/smj.4250090104

Lauriat Shawn, M. (2007). *AJAX Advanced Ajax: Architecture and Best Practices* (1st ed.). Upper Saddle River, NJ: Prentice Hall PTR.

Luehrs, R., & Molinari, F. (2007). Participation in the Law-Making Process: The LexiPation Approach, *Proceedings of the University of Camerino's conference on "Methodologies, Technologies and Tools enabling e-Government" (MeTTeG07).*

Maglio, P., & Spohrer, J. (2008). Fundamentals of service science . *Journal of the Academy of Marketing Science*, *36*, 18–20. doi:10.1007/s11747-007-0058-9

Moore, J. F. (1996). *The Death of Competition: Leadership and Strategy in the Age of Business Ecosystems*. Winchester, UK: J. Wiley & Sons.

NESSI. (2006). *Strategic Research Agenda* (*Vol. 1*). Framing the Future of the Service.

Normann, R., & Ramirez, R. (1993). From value chain to value constellation: designing interactive strategy . *Harvard Business Review*, *71*(4), 65–77.

O'Hear, S. (2006). Web's second phase puts users in control, Tuesday June 20 2006, The Guardian Education. Retrieved from http://education.guardian.co.uk/elearning/story/0,1801086,00.html on 21 November 2008.

OASIS. (2006). *Reference Model for Service Oriented Architecture 1.0*. Retrieved from http://www.oasis-open.org/committees/ tc_home.php?wg_abbrev=soa-rm, August 2006.

OASIS. (2009). Business Process Execution Language v 2.0. Retrieved from http://docs.oasis-open.org/wsbpel/2.0/OS/wsbpel-v2.0-OS.html on 22/10/2009.

OASIS. (2009). Security Assertion Markup Language (SAML). Retrieved from http://www.oasis-open.org/committees/tc_home.php?wg_abbrev=security on 22/10/2009.

OASIS. (2009). Web Services Atomic Transaction (WS-AtomicTransaction). Retrieved from http://docs.oasis-open.org/ws-tx/wsat/2006/06 on 22/10/2009.

OECD. (2001a). *Cities for Citizens: Improving Metropolitan Governance* (pp. 39–43). Paris: OECD Publications.

OECD. (2001b). *Citizens as Partners: Information, Communication and public Participation in Policy Making* (pp. 20–22). Paris: OECD Publications.

Pierson, J., & Lievens, B. (2005). Configuring Living Labs for a 'thick' Understanding of Innovation. *Proceedings of EPIC Conference*, 114-127.

Pistore, M., Traverso, P., Paolucci, M., & Wagner, M. (2009). From Software Services to a Future Internet of Services . In Tselentis, G. (Eds.), *Towards the Future Internet*. IOS Press.

Prahalad, C. K., & Ramaswamy, V. (2000). Co-opting customer competence . *Harvard Business Review*, *78*(1), 79–87.

Prahalad, C. K., & Ramaswamy, V. (2003). The new frontier of experience innovation . *Sloan Management Review*, *44*(4), 12–18.

Prahalad, C. K., & Ramaswamy, V. (2004). *The Future of Competition: Co-Creating Unique Value with Customers*, New York: Harvard Business School Press, ISBN 978-1578519538.

Rosenberg, J., & Remy, D. (2004). *Securing Web Services with WS-Security: Demystifying WS-Security*. WS-Policy, SAML, XML Signature, and XML Encryption, Pearson Higher Education.

Rust, R. T., & Kannan, P. K. (2003). E-Service: A New Paradigm for Business in the Electronic Environment. *Communications of the ACM*, *46*(6), 37–42. doi:10.1145/777313.777336

Rust, R. T., & Lemon, K. N. (2001). E-Service and the Consumer . *International Journal of Electronic Commerce*, *5*(3), 85–101.

Sawhney, M., Balasubramanian, S., & Krishnan, V. V. (2003). Creating growth with services . *Sloan Management Review*, *45*(2), 34–44.

Sawhney, M., & Parikh, D. (2001). Where value lives in a networked world . *Harvard Business Review*, *79*(1), 79–90.

Shirky, C. (2003). Social Software: A New Generation of Tools. *Esther Dyson's Monthly Report* (10).

Strategy, L. Lisbon European Council 23 and 24 March 2000 Presidency Conclusions (2000). Retrieved from http://www.europarl.europa.eu/summits/lis1_en.htm

The Helsinki Manifesto. (2006). http://elivinglab.org/files/Helsinki_Manifesto_201106.pdf

Tyagi, S. (2006). RESTful Web Services. Retrieved from http://java.sun.com/developer/technicalArticles/WebServices/restful/ on 22/10/2009.

Walters, D., & Lancaster, G. (1999). Value and information: concepts and issues for management. *Management Decision*, *37*(8), 643–656. doi:10.1108/00251749910291613

KEY TERMS AND DEFINITIONS

Best Practice: One technique, method, process, activity, incentive or reward which is considered to be the most efficient and effective in delivering a particular outcome among the other already existing solutions is called best practice. Undoubtedly, the desired outcome can be achieved with fewer problems after a series of proper processes, checks, and testing. Even if the processes are continuously improved, a best practice is considered as a business buzzword used to describe the "methodology" and the standards for the development in cases of multiple organizations related to management, policy, and especially software systems.

Citizen-Centric: After the "Helsinki Manifesto" (2006) put the "human-centric way" at the very centre of the measures needed "for turning the Lisbon Strategy (2000) into a living reality", citizen-centric is meant to denote any approach related with or focused to the co-creative collaboration with the forthcoming users of products and / or services under development. This is especially useful in the field of (private and Government) e-Services, where the people can be considered as "twice" beneficiaries, namely of public services as such – impacting per se on their lives and businesses – and of ICT based or supported services, where the question becomes to which extent this novel user-centric approach can improve customization (if not "tailoring") to individual needs and requirements.

e-Democracy: Direct democracy tries to find the solution to the democracy deficit from the quantity of direct citizen participation in decision-making. E-democracy comes from the combination of the words "electronic" and "democracy". In particular it includes the use of electronic communications technologies such as the Internet in enhancing democratic processes within a democratic republic, representative democracy or any other democratic model. It is a political development still in its infancy, as well as the subject of much debate and activity within government, civic-oriented groups and societies around the world.

Policy Life Cycle: It normally includes three stages, namely *formulation* (agenda setting), *implementation* and *evaluation.*

Policy: Typically, the term policy is used to describe a deliberate plan of action to monitor and moderate decisions and achieve rational outcome(s). Governments, private sector organizations, groups and individuals can be referred to by using the term policy. Besides, the term policy is appropriate when it refers to the process of taking crucial decisions, including the recognition of several different alternatives such as programs or spending priorities, and finally the selection of the basic ones according to the impact they have. Policies are considered as management, political, financial, and administrative mechanisms that meet their explicit goals.

Compilation of References

(2000). *State Planning Organization*. Ankara: Kamu Mali Yönetiminin Yeniden Yapılandırılması ve Mali Saydamlık Özel İhtisas Komisyonu Raporu. [The Special Experts Commission Report on Reinventing Public Financial Management and Fiscal Transparency]

(2006b). *State Planning Organization* (pp. 2006–2010). Ankara: Bilgi Toplumu Stratejisi Eylem Planı. [The Action Plan for Information Society Strategy]

ACCAN. (2009). *Submission to Government 2.0 Taskforce Secretariat, Australian Communications Consumer Action Network*. Australia: ACCAN.

Accascina, G. (1999). *Keynote presentation, APDIP Regional Information technology Conference*. march 24-27, 1999, Kuala Lumpur, Malaysia.

Ad hoc Committee on E-Democracy of the Council of Europe (CAHDE) (2006). Introduction to the Ad Hoc Committee on E-democracy (CAHDE). Retrieved from http://www.coe.int/t/e/integrated_projects/democracy/02_activities/002_e-democracy/00%20Intro%20CAHDE_en.asp

Adams, D. A., Nelson, R. R., & Todd, P. A. (1992). Perceived usefulness, ease of use and usage of information technology: A replication. *Management Information Systems Quarterly*, *6*(2), 227–247. doi:10.2307/249577

Aguini, H. (2004). *Regression analysis for categorical moderators*. New York: The Guilford Press.

AHRC. (2009). *Web accessibility and Government 2.0 Australian Human Rights Commission submission to the Government 2.0 Taskforce – Towards Government 2.0 an issues paper*, www.humanrights.gov.au

Ajzen, I., & Fishbein, M. (1980). *Understanding attitudes and predicting social behaviour*. NJ: Practice-Hall.

Akhter, S. H. (2003). Digital divide and purchase intention: Why demographic psychology matters. *Journal of Economic Psychology*, *24*(3), 321–327. doi:10.1016/S0167-4870(02)00171-X

Albrecht, A. J. & Gaffney, J. E., Jr. (1983). Software Functions, Source Line of Code and Development Effort Prediction: A Software Science Validation. *IEEE Transactions on Software Engineering (TSE)* *9*(6), London, United Kingdom: IEEE Computer Society.

Ambali, A. R. (2009). Digital divide and its implication on Malaysian e-government: Policy initiatives. In R. Hakikur (Ed.), *Social and political implications of data mining: Knowledge management in e-government*. Hershey, PA: Information Science Reference (an imprint of IGI Global). doi:10.4018/978-1-60566-230-5.ch016

Ambient Assisted Living Programme, A. A. L. (2009). Retrieved from http://www.aal-europe.eu/about-aal, March 23th 2009.

Andersen, K. V. (2004). *E-government and public sector process rebuilding (PPR): Dilettantes, wheelbarrows, and diamonds*. Boston, MA: Kluwer Academic Publishers.

Anderson, C. (2006). *The Long Tail: Why the Future of Business is Selling Less of More*. New York: Hyperion.

Anderson, H. (2006). OLPC and Unintended Consequences. *New World (New Orleans, La.)*, *23*(29), 33.

Anderson, R. (2004). *Removing barriers, not creating them: Submission to the senate inquiry on the progress and future direction of life-long learning.* Canberra: Adult Learning Australia.

Anttiroiko, A.-V. (2003). Building strong e-democracy: the role of technology in developing democracy for the information age. *Communications of the ACM, 46*(9).

Applewhite, A. (2003). Should Governments Go Open Source. *IEEE Software, X(Y)* 88-93.

Archmann, Sylvia & Kudlacek, Immanuel, (2008). Interoperability and the exchange of good practice cases. *European Journal of ePractice*, No 2 · February.

Arditi, A., & Rosenthal, B. (1998). Developing an objective definition of visual impairment. *In Vision '96: Proceedings of the International Low Vision Conference* (pp. 331-334). Madrid, Spain: ONCE

Australian Bureau of Statistics. (1998). *Paid Work: Public Sector Employment.* Canberra: ABS.

Backus, M. (2001). *E-Governance in Developing Countries.* (Research Brief No 1). Retrieved October 21, 2009, from International Institute of Communication & Development: http://www.ftpiicd.org/files/research/briefs/brief1.pdf

Baldwin, N. (1987). Public versus private: not that different, not that consequential. *Public Personnel Management, 16*, 181–193.

Banerjee, P., & Chau, P. Y. K. (2004). An evaluative framework for analysing e-government convergence capability in developing countries. *Electronic Government, 1*(1), 29–48. doi:10.1504/EG.2004.004135

Barlow, J., & Moller, C. (1996). *A complaint is a gift.* San Francisco: Berrett: Koehler Publishers Inc.

Barton, C., & Bear, M. (1999). *Information and Communication Technologies: Are they the key to viable business development services for micro and small enterprises?* Report for USAID as part of the Micro enterprises Best Practices Project. March 1999 by Development Alternatives Inc, MD, USA.

Basaran, B. (2007). We do not have a National IT Policy. *Cumhuriyet Strategy, 176*, 6–7.

Başbakanlık, T. C. (7.8.2009). E-government and information society draft laws. Retrieved September 10, 2009, http://www.acikkod.org/2009/08/14/e-devlet-ve-bilgi-toplumu-kanun-tasarisi-taslagi/

Bashshur, R. L. (2002). Telemedicine and health care. *Telemedicine Journal and e-Health, 8*(1), 5–12. PubMed doi:10.1089/15305620252933365

Baştan, S., & Gökbunar, R. (2004). New developments related to e-government in the provision of public services: Towards an integrated e-government system. *Dokuz Eylül University Journal of Economics and Business Administration Faculty, 19*(1), 71–89.

Bates, A. W. (1995). *Technology, Open Learning and Distance Education.* London: Routledge.

Bayar, D. (2003). Kamu Mali Yönetimi ve Kontrol Kanunu Ne Getir(m)iyor? [What does Public Financial Management and Control Law Yield (or not)?]. *Maliye Dergisi, 144*, 47–62.

Becker, S. A. (2004). E-Government Visual Accessibility for Older Adult Users. *Social Science Computer Review, 22*(1), 11–23. doi:10.1177/0894439303259876

Beckette-Camaratta, J. (2002, October). *Assessing E-Budgeting in US Local Governments: A Case Study*, Paper presented at the Korean Association For Public Administration Conference, Seoul, S. Korea.

Bensghir, T. K. (2000). Web'deki Belediyelerimiz: Bursa Büyükşehir Belediyesi [Our Municipalities on the Web: Bursa Metropolitan Municipality]. Çağdaş Yerel Yönetimler, 9(4), 106-118.

Benyamor, G. (2007, April 10). Türkiye'nin İlk Katılımcı Bütçesi Çanakkale Belediyesinden [First Participatory Budget in Turkey from Çanakkale Municipality]. *Hürriyet Gazetesi.* Retrieved October 22, 2009, from http://hurarsiv.hurriyet.com.tr/goster/haber.aspx?id=6300902&yazarid=20

Bertram, B. (2005). *Blindheit und Sehbehinderung in Deutschland: Ursachen und Häufigkeiten. Der Augenarzt, 6*. Dezember.

Bhatnagar, S. (2000). Social implications of information and communication technology in developing countries: lessons from Asian success stories. *The Electronic Journal on Information Systems in Developing Countries* [Electronic version]. Available at http://www.unimas.my/fit/roger/EJISDC/EJISDC.htm

Bhatnagar, S. (2004). *E-Government: From vision to implementation – a practical guide with case studies*. London: Sage Publications Pvt. Ltd.

Bhatnagar, S. (2006), *Paving the Road towards Pro Poore-Governance*, UNDP, APDIP, UNCRD Workshop Report, 26-27, Bangkok.

Boehm, B. W. (1981). *Software Engineering Economics*. Englewood Cliffs, USA: Prentice Hall.

Boersma, F. K., Groenewegen, P., & Wagenaar, P. (2009). Emergency Response Rooms in Action: an ethnographic case-study in Amsterdam. In Landgren, J., & Jul, S. (eds.) *Proceeding of the 6th International* ISCRAM *Conference (pp.1-8)*. Gothenburg, Sweden, May 2009.

Bonwell, C., & Eison, J. (1991). *Active learning: Creating excitement in the classroom AEHE-ERIC Higher Education Report No.1*. Jossey-Bass, Washington, D.C.

Bovaird, T. (2003). The Changing Context of Public Policy. In T. Bovarid & E. Löffler (Eds.), *Public Management and Governance* (pp. 13–23). London: Routledge.

Bovet, D., & Martha, J. (2000). Value nets: reinventing the rusty supply chain for competitive advantage. *Strategy and Leadership*, *28*(4), 21–26. doi:10.1108/10878570010378654

Boyd, D., & Ellison, N. B. (2007). *Social Network Sites: Definition*. History, and Scholarship.

Boyne, G. (2002). Public and Private Management: What's the Difference? *Journal of Management Studies* 39(1),0022-2380.

Bozeman, B., & Kingsley, G. (1998). Risk culture in public and private organisations. *Public Administration Review*, *58*, 109–118. doi:10.2307/976358

Bridges. (2004). *The Real Access / Real Impact framework for improving the way that ICT is used in development*, November 2004.

Brodie, M., Flournoy, R. E., et al. (2000). Health information, the Internet, and the digital divide. *Health Affairs*, *19*(6), 255–266. PubMed doi:10.1377/hlthaff.19.6.255

BSI. (2006). *Guide to good practice in commissioning accessible websites. British Standards Institution*. UK: BSI.

BTHaber. (2007). *MEB'de Linux Yetkinlik Merkezi* (A Linux Proficiency Center in the Ministry of National Education), Retrieved March 1, 2008, from http://www.bthaber.com.tr/haber.phtml?yazi_id=460000804

Budhiraja, Renu & Sameer Sachdeva (2009) *E-Readiness Assessment (India)*. Retrieved from:<unpan1.un.org/intradoc/groups/public/ documents APCITY/UNPAN014673.pdf> accessed on March 2, 2009.

Budhwar, P., & Boyne, G. (2004). Human resource management in the Indian public and private sectors: an empirical comparison. *International Journal of Human Resource Management*, *15*(2), 346–370. doi:10.1080/0958519032000158554

Bushell, S. (2006). *Government CIO Role Still Developing, But Australia Ahead of Pack*. http://www.cio.com/index.php?id=401118652&eid=-601.

Bushell, S. (2007). Public Sector Warms to Open Source, *CIO*, 08.24.2007, Retrieved October 22, 2007, from http://www.cio.com.au/index.php/id;1234886256

Bushman, R. M., & Smith, A. J. (2003). Transparency, Financial Accounting Information, and Corporate Governance. *Federal Reserve Bank of New York Economic Policy Review*, *9*(1), 65–87.

Cadeddu, S. (2004). The proceeding of the European ombudsman. *Law and Contemporary Problems*, *68*, 161–180.

Capella, J. (2006). The CIO's First 100 Days. *Optimize*, *5*(3), 46–51.

Cardoso, J., & Sheth Amit, P. (Eds.). (2006). *Semantic Web services, Processes and applications*. Springer. doi:10.1007/978-0-387-34685-4

Cetin, G., Ozel, B., Tasci, K., Koksal, M. A., Basar, N., Ayata, R., et al. (2006b). *Acik Kaynak Kodlu Yazilimlarin İdari, Mali ve Hukuki Boyutlari* (Administrative, Financial and Legal Aspects of OSS). Retrieved February 15, 2008, from http://www.kdep7.org.tr/kamuda-akko-yazilimlar.pdf

Cetin, G., Tasci, K., Ayata, R., Yılmaz, O., Gulum, T., Sehitoglu, O. T., et al. (2006a). *Goc Plani Hazirlanmasi ve Uygulanmasi* (Preparation and Implementation of a Migration Plan). Retrieved February 15, 2008, from http://www.kdep7.org.tr/goc_kilavuzu.pdf

Çetinkaya, Ö. (2008). Kamu İdarelerinde Hazırlanan Stratejik Planlarda Mevzuata Aykırı Oluşan Durumlar [Legal Problems Related to Strategic Plans of Public Administrations]. *Yaklaşım*, *16*(192), 244–248.

Chadwick, B. P. (2005). Information Technology Revolution in the Republic of Korea: Socio-Economic Development Issues and Policymaking Challenges. In A. Y. Mansourov (Ed.), *Bytes and Bullets: Information Technology Revolution and National Security on the Korean Peninsula* (pp. 52–69). Honolulu, Hawaii: Asia-Pacific Center for Security Studies.

Chandra, R. (2003). *Information Technology in 21st Century: Ethics and Governance of the Internet*. Delhi: Kalpaz Publications.

Chen, D., Huang, T., & Hsiao, N. (2002). Citizen participation, e-government, and public management: a case of Taipei city mayor's e-mail box, International Symposium of Digital Divide and Digital Opportunity, nccuir.lib.nccu.edu.tw/bitstream/140.119/10761/1/6_02.pd

Chen, D., Huang, T., & Hsiao, N. (2006). Reinventing government through on-line citizen involvement in the developing world: a case study of taipei city mayor's e-mail box in Taiwan. *Public Administration and Development*, *26*, 409–423. doi:10.1002/pad.415

Choudrie, J., Ghinea, G., & Weerakkody, V. (2004). Evaluating Global e-Government Sites: A View using Web Diagnostic Tools. *Electronic. Journal of E-Government*, *2*(2), 105–114.

Chrissafis, T., & Rohen, M. (2010). European eParticipation developments: from ad hoc experiences towards mass scale engagement. *eJournal of eDemocracy and Open Government (JeDEM)*. Special Issue in collaboration with PEP-NET: Sustainable eParticipation. ENoLL, The European Network of Living Labs – http://www.openlivinglabs.eu/

COA. (2001). "*COA's Standards and Self-Study Manual, 7th Edition, for Public Organizations*," by the Council on Accreditation of Services for Children and Families, 2001. Available from the Council on Accreditation of Services for Children and Families, Inc., 120 Wall St., 11th Floor, New York, New York, 10005, (212) 797-3000

Coakes, J Sheridan and Steed Lyndall (2007). *SPSS version 16 for windows: Analysis without anguish*, Australia: Jon Wiley and Sons, Ltd.

Codeplex (2008). *Codeplex FAQ*, Retrieved February 13, 2008, from http://www.codeplex.com/

Coe, A. (2004). Transforming government and governance for the 21st century: A conceptual framework. In E. L. Oliver & L. Sanders (Eds.), *E-government reconsidered: Renewal of governance for the knowledge age* (pp. 3–21). Saskatoon, Canada: Saskatchewan Institute of Public Policy.

Coleman, S. (2000). *Strong representation: Engaging citizens in a digital age*. Governance in the Digital Economy, Hansard Society.

Commissie Onderzoek Vuurwerkramp (Investigation Committee Fireworks-incident). (2001). *De Vuurwerkramp eindrapport*. DenHaag/Enschede.

Community Platform, I. E. A. Retrieved from http://gcp.aspen.grida.no/ (Accessed 26 May 2009)

Compaine, B. M. (Ed.). (2001). *The Digital Divide: Facing a Crisis or Creating a Myth?* Cambridge, MA: MIT Press.

CQHCA. (2000). *Committee on the Quality of Health Care in America, Institute of Medicine. Crossing the quality chasm: A new health system for the 21st century.* US: National Academy Press.

Cullen, D. (2002). Korea migrates 120K civil servants to Linux desktop, *The Register,*January 14, 2002, Retrieved September 7, 2009, from http://www.theregister.co.uk/2002/01/14/korea_migrates_120k_civil_servants/.

Curtin, G. G., Sommer, M. W., & Vis-Sommer, V. (2003). *The world of e-government.* Philadelphia, PA: The Haworth Press, Inc.

Davidrajuh, R. (2004). Planning e-government start-up: a case study on e-Sri Lanka. *Electronic Government, 1*(1), 92–106. doi:10.1504/EG.2004.004139

Davis, F. D. (1989). Perceived usefulness, perceived ease of use, and user acceptance of information technology. *Management Information Systems Quarterly, 13*(3), 319–340. doi:10.2307/249008

Davis, F. D., Bagozzi, R. D., & Warshaw, P. R. (1989). User acceptance of computer technology: A comparison of two theoretical models. *Management Science, 35*(8), 982–1003. doi:10.1287/mnsc.35.8.982

Davos, C. A. (1977). Toward an integrated environmental assessment within a social context. *Journal of Environmental Management, 5*(3), 297–305.

Denardis, L., & Tam, E. (2007). *Open Documents and Democracy: A Political Basis for Open Document Standards.* Yale Information Society Project White Paper, Retrieved February 8, 2008, from http://isp.law.yale.edu

Department of Premier and Cabinet 2006. *About the Office of the Chief Information Officer.* http://www.dpc.vic.gov.au/

DFID. (2001). *Sustainable Livelihoods Guidance Sheets,* Department for Informational Development, 2001.

Digital Dividend. (2003). Retrieved June 08, 2003 from www.digitaldividend.org.

Dokas, I. M., & Ireland, C. (2007). Ontology to support knowledge representation and risk analysis for the development of early warning system in solid waste management operations. a *Proceedings of the International Symposium on Environmental Software Systems (ISESS),* Crowne Plaza Hotel, Prague, Czech Republic.

DRAP (2003-2004). *Digital Review of Asia Pacific 2003/2004,* Orbicom, IDRC, UNDP-APDIP

DRAP (2005-2006). *Digital Review of Asia Pacific 2005/2006,* Orbicom, IDRC, UNDP-APDIP

DRAP (2007-2008). *Digital Review of Asia Pacific 2007-2008,* Orbicom and the International Development Research Centre, SAGE Publications India Pvt Ltd

DRAP (2009-2010). *Digital Review of Asia Pacific 2009-2010,* Orbicom and the International Development Research Centre, SAGE Publications India Pvt Ltd

Dunyasi, B. T. (2005). *Türkiye'nin Kurtuluşu Açık Kaynak Kodlarında* (Turkey's Salvation Depends on FOSS), Retrieved March 1, 2008, from http://www.btdunyasi.net/index.php?module=news&news_id=863&cat_id=4

Durna, U., & Özel, M. (2008). Information Transformation in the Managerial Approach –E (Local) Government. *Mustafa Kemal University Journal of Social Sciences Institute, 5*(10), 1–32.

Dutta, S., Lopez-Claros, A., & Mia, I. (2008). *The Global Information Technology Report.INSEAD.* New York: Oxford University Press.

Earl, M., & Feeny, D. (1995). Is Your CIO Adding Value. *The McKinsey Quarterly, 2,* 144–161.

EATT Project. (2003). *Equal Access to Technology Training.* UK: UK LITERATURE REVIEW, Royal National Institute of the Blind.

Economic Policy Research Foundation of Turkey. (2007). İyi Yönetişim İçin Örnek Bir Model: Katılımcı Bütçeleme [A Representative model for Good: Participatory Budgeting]. Yönetişim Etütleri Programı, Ankara. Retrieved October 21, 2009, from http://www.tepav.org.tr

Economist (2007). Microsoft Concedes Defeat. *The Economist*. October 27, 2007, Retrieved February 15, 2008, from http://www.economist.com

Eifert, M., & Puschel, J. O. (2004). *National electronic government: Comparing governance structures in multi-layer administrations*. New York: Routledge.

EIU. (2009). *E-readiness Ranking 2009: The usage imperative, a report from the Economist Intelligent Unit*, The Economist Intelligence Unit Limited, UK.

Emil, M. F., & Yılmaz, H. H. (2004). *Mali Saydamlık İzleme Raporu* [Fiscal Transparency Monitoring Report]. Ankara: TESEV.

Erdogan, N. (2006). *Kamu Yönetiminde Açık Kaynak Kodlu Yazılım Alternatifi: T.C Merkez Bankası Örneği* (The FOSS Alternative in Public Administration: The Case of the Turkish Central Bank), Unpublished Master's Dissertation, Ankara: The Institute of Public Administration for Turkey and the Middle East.

Escudero-Pascual, A. (2008). Tools and technologies for equitable access *Association for Progressive Communication (APC)* issue paper, www.apc.org

ETAAC. (2002). *Electronic tax administration advisory committee (ETAAC)*. USA: Annual Report to Congress.

EU, (2007). Inclusive e-Government: survey of status and baseline activities, European Commission, *DG Information Society and Media*, e-Government unit, December.

EU. (2006, November). *Study on the: Economic impact of open source software on innovation and the competitiveness of the Information and Communication Technologies (ICT) sector in the EU.* November 20, 2006, Retrieved September 7, 2009, from http://ec.europa.eu/enterprise/ict/poicy/doc/2006-11-20-flossimpact.pdf.

Eurostat (2009). *Households who have Internet access at home*. Retrieved October 21, 2009, from Eurostat database: http://epp.eurostat.ec.europa.eu

EWC III. (2006). *Developing early warning systems: A checklist, Third International Conference on Early Warning*. 27-29 March 2006, Bonn, Germany, Retrieved October 15, 2009 from http://www.ewc3.org/upload/downloads/checklist.final_pdf.pdf

Fabris, P. 1998. *Odd Ducks No More*. http://www.cio.com/archive/111598/index.html

Farnham, D., & Horton, S. (1996). Managing public and private organisations. In D. Farnham & S. Horton (Eds.), *Managing The New Public Service*. London: Macmillan.

Feeny, D., Edwards, B., & Simpson, K. (1992). Understanding the CEO/CIO Relationship. *Management Information Systems Quarterly*, *16*(4), 439–448. doi:10.2307/249730

Fenton, N. E., & Pfleeger, S. K. (1998). *Software Metrics: A Rigorous and Practical Approach* (*Revised 2nd edition*). New York: PWS Publishing Company.

Fouche, B. (1999). *A Web-Based Agricultural System for South Africa. Feasibility Study - Part 1*. National Department of Agriculture March 1999. Unpublished document.

Foundation, N. Z. (2009). *Digital Strategy 2.0 Submission - Royal New Zealand Foundation of the Blind*, Auckland, New Zealand

G8DOT Force (2001). *Digital Opportunities for All*: Meeting the Challenge Report of the Digital Opportunity Task Force (DOT Force) including a proposal for a Genoa Plan of Action, May 2001.

Garets, d. & Davis, M. (2006). Electronic medical records vs. electronic health records: Yes, there is a difference. Technical Report, *Healthcare Information Management Systems Society*, 2006JAN26.

Garson, G. D. (2007). *Modern public information technology systems: Issues and challenges*. Hershey, PA: IGI Publishing.

George, D., & Mallery, P. (2001). *SPSS for windows step by step: A simple guide and reference* (3rd ed.). Boston: Allyn and Bacon.

Ghosh, R. A. (2006). *Economic Impact of FLOSS on Innovation and Competitiveness of the EU ICT Sector. Study on the Open Source Software, Information and Communication Technologies Sector in the EU, Final Report*. MERIT.

Gilad, B. (2001). *The Next Step in the Evolution of Competitive Intelligence*. Cambridge, MA: Academy of Competitive Intelligence.

Gilmore, J. H., & Pine, B. J. (2000). *Markets of One: Creating Customer-Unique Value through Mass Customization*. Boston: Harvard Business School Press.

GITR. (2005). *Global Information Technology Report*. (2004-2005). World Economic Forum. Retrieved March 12, 2005 from www.weforum.org.

GITR. (2006). *Global Information Technology Report*. (2005-2006). World Economic Forum. Retrieved January 12, 2009 from www.weforum.org.

GITR. (2007). *Global Information Technology Report*. (2006-2007). World Economic Forum. Retrieved January 12, 2009 from www.weforum.org.

Glantz, H. M. (2004). Usable science 8: Early warning systems: Do and don'ts, Report of Workshop 20-23 October 2003, Shanghai, China. Available on line at http://www.ccb.ucar.edu/warning/report.pdf

Global Environmental Outlook. Retrieved from http://www.unep.org/geo/ (Accessed 26 May 2009)

Govt. of Korea (2002). *e-Korea Vision 2006: The Third Master Plan for Informatization Promotion* (2002-2006), Ministry of Information and Communication, Government of the Republic of Korea

Govt. of Korea (2003). *To Enhance Efficiency and Transparency in the Public Procurement Sector by Utilizing the Government electronic Procurement System (GePS),* Government Procurement Experts Group, Phuket, Thailand, 15- 16 August 2003, 2003/SOMIII/GPEG/009 Agenda Item:7a, Asia-Pacific Economic Cooperation (APEC)

Govt. of Korea (2007). The best practice, UNI-PASS Korea customs service, *Korea e-Government Webzine, 6*, Ministry of Government Administration and Home Affairs (MOGAHA), Government of the Republic of Korea. Retrieved September 30, 2009 from http://www.idrc.ca/en/ev-140957-201-1-DO_TOPIC.html, (http://www.korea.go.kr/eng/Webzine/webzine.jsp?vol=200704&paper=services_01&no=1197878948443)

Govt. of US (2007). FY 2007 Report to Congress on Implementation of The E-Government Act of 2002, Office of Management and Budget, Government of the USA.

Gozukeles, I. I. (2006). *Free and Open Source Software in Turkey*, Unpublished Master's Thesis, Middle East Technical University.

Groenewegen, P., & Wagenaar, P. (2006). Managing emergent information systems: Towards understanding how public information systems come into being. *Information Polity, 11*, 135–148.

Grönlund, Å. (2002). Electronic Government - Efficiency, Service Quality, and Democracy. In Å. Grönlund (Ed.), *Electronic Government: Design, Applications and Management* (p. 62). Hershey, PA: Idea Group Publishing.

Grönroos, C. (2000). Service management: A management focus for service competition. *International Journal of Service Industry Management, 1*(1), 6–14.

Gropper, A. (2007). Private health records and the health URL: A patient-centered care team approach to health information management. *Patient Safety and Quality Healthcare, 4*(3), 28–32.

Gunatunge, R.S. & Karunanayake, M.M. (2004). *Information and Communication technologies for Enhancing Socio-economic Development at the Local Level in Sri Lanka: Issues, Challenges and Strategies*, a research report for Sida/SAREC Research Cooperation Project on Overcoming Regional Imbalances and Poverty, 2004.

Gunawardana, N., & Wattegama, C. (2004). Sri Lanka (chapter), in Digital Review of Asia Pacific, published by GKP.

Gunes, I. (2006). *Bilgisayar Programlarının Korunması Hakkındaki 91/250 Sayılı AB Yönergesi ve 5846 Sayılı Kanun'un İlgili Hükümlerinin Karşılaştırılması (European Directive Numbered 91/250 on Protecting Computer Programs and Comparing the Turkish Law No. 5846), Terazi Aylık Hukuk Dergisi, 6, February* (pp. 30–37). Ankara: Seçkin Publishing House.

Guradian (2008). Moodle nudges forward. *The Guardian* January 8, 2008 http://education.guardian.co.uk/link/story/0,2236721,00.html Accessed 29 May, 2009

Gurstein, M. (2000). *Community informatics: enabling communities with communication technologies*. Hershey, PA: Idea Group Publishing.

Gurstein, M. (2003). Effective use: A community informatics strategy beyond the digital divide, *First Monday, 8*(12), December 2003.

H.D. Vest Financial Services, Inc. (2000). Acceptance of e-filing gives rise to increased comfort with Web. *IRVING, Texas-BUSINESS WIRE*, March 22; also available at: http://www.icrsurvey.com/Study.aspx?f=hdvest.html [accessed on 2nd March 2009].

Hair, J. F., Black, W. C., Babin, B. J., Anderson, R. E., & Tatham, L. R. (2006). *Multivariate data analysis*. Upper Saddle River, NJ: Pearson Education International.

Hájek, P. (2000). *Mathematics ofFuzy Logic*. Dordrecht, Niederlanden: Kluwer.

Handzic, M. (2003). Empowering society through knowledge records. In M. A. Wimmer (Ed.), *Knowledge management in electronic government* (pp. 262–267). Berlin: Springer. doi:10.1007/3-540-44836-5_27

Harasim, L., & Hiltz, S. R. L Teles, M Turoff (1995). *Learning Networks, A field guide to teaching and learning online* In Harremoes, P (1998), The challenge of managing water and material balances in relation to eutrophication *Water Science and Technology* 37(3),9-17. MIT Press Cambridge, MA

Harrison, D. D. (1995). Community development. In R. L. Edwards (Ed.-in-Chief), *Encyclopedia of social work* (19th ed., Vol. 1, pp. 555–562). Washington, DC: NASW Press

Hartnell-Young, E. (2006). ePortfolios for knowledge and learning. In A. Jafari & C. Kaufman (Eds.), *Handbook of reseach on ePortfolios* (pp. 125-134). Hershey, PA: Idea Group Reference.

Heeks, R. (1999). *Information and Communication Technologies, Poverty and Development*. Development Informatics: Working paper Series. Paper No 5, June 1995 Institute of Development Policy and Management. Published on the www: http://www.man.ac.uk/idpm

Heeks, R. (2000). Government Data: Understanding the Barriers to Citizen Access and Use. *iGovernment Working Paper Series (Paper No 10),* Manchester: Institute for Development Policy and Management.

Heeks, R. (2001). *Reinventing government in the information age: International practice in IT-enabled public sector reform*. London: Routledge.

Heeks, R. (2002). Information systems and developing countries: failure, success and local improvisations. *The Information Society, 18*(2), 101–112. doi:10.1080/01972240290075039

Heeks, R. (2003). *E-government for development: Causes of e-government success and failure, factor model*, IDPM, University of Manchester UK, available at: http://www.egov4dev.org/causesfactor.html [accessed on 2nd March 2009].

Heeks, R. (2006a). *Most E-Government Projects-for-Development Fail: How can Risk be Reduced?* Working Paper 14, IDPM, University of Manchester, UK.

Heeks, R. (2009). The ICT4D 2.0 Manifesto: Where Next for ICTs and International Development? *Working Paper Series for Development Informatics Group, Institute for Development Policy and Management*. University of Manchester, Manchester, UK

Heeks, R., & Molla, A. (2009b). *Impact Assessment of ICT-for-Development Projects: A Compendium of Approaches*. Working Paper 36,IDPM, University of Manchester, UK.

Hemphill, T. A. (2005). Government Technology Acquisition Policy: The Case of Proprietary Versus Open Source Software. *Technology & Society., 25*(6), 484–490.

Hewson Consulting Group. (2002). CRM in the public sector. Hewson Group. http://www.marketresearch.com/vendors/viewvendor.asp?vendorid=2623&g=1

HKBU. (2006). *HKBU's Views & Comment On The Digital 21 Strategy 2007*. Hong Kong: The Hong Kong Blind Union.

Hong, W., Thong, J. Y. L., Wong, W. M., & Tam, K. Y. (2002). Determination of user acceptance of digital libraries: An empirical examination of individual difference and system characteristic. *Journal of Management Information Systems*, *18*(3), 97–124.

Hoo, A. T. K. (2002). Reinventing Local Governments and the E-Government Initiative. *Public Administration Review*, *62*(4), 434–444. doi:10.1111/0033-3352.00197

Houghton, R. J., Baber, C., Cowton, M., Walker, G. H., & Stanton, N. A. (2008). WESTT (workload, error, situational awareness, time and teamwork): an analytical prototyping system for command and control. *Cognition Technology and Work*, *10*, 199–207. doi:10.1007/s10111-007-0098-4

Huang, Z. (2006). E-Government Practices at Local Levels: An Analysis of U.S. Counties' Websites. *Issues in Information Systems*, *7*(2), 165–170.

Iansiti, M., & Levienm, R. (2004). *The Keystone Advantage: What the New Dynamics of Business Ecosystems Mean for Strategy, Innovation and Sustainability*. Boston: Harvard Business School Press.

ICTA. (2005). *Draft ICT Policy for the Government, Information and Communication Technology Agency of Sri Lanka*. Colombo, Sri Lanka: ICTA.

ICTA. **(online document, 2009).** ***Information and Communication Technology Agency of Sri Lanka*****,** Retrieved November 05, 2009 from http://www.icta.lk/index.php/en/icta/739-e-sri-lanka-transforming-a-nation-through-ict

Igbaria, M., Livari, J., & Marogahh, H. (1995). Why do individuals use computer technology: A finish case study. *Journal of International Management*, *29*, 227–238.

Igbaria, M., Zinatelli, N., Cragg, D., & Cavaye, A. (1997). Personal computing acceptance factors in small firms: A structural equation model. *Management Information Systems Quarterly*, *29*(3), 278–305.

IGF. (2006). *First IGF Meeting*: Athens, Greece, http://www.intgovforum.org/cms/index.php/athensmeeting, Retrieved December 05, 2009

IGF. (2007). *Second IGF Meeting*: Rio de Janeiro, Brazil http://www.intgovforum.org/cms/index.php/second-meeting, Retrieved December 05, 2009

IGF. (2008). *3rd Annual Internet Governance Forum (IGF)* at Hyderabad, India, http://www.intgovforum.org/cms/index.php/2008-igf-hyderabad, Retrieved December 05, 2009

IGF. (2009). *Fourth annual IGF Meeting in Sharm El Sheikh*, Egypt http://www.intgovforum.org/cms/index.php/the-meeting, Retrieved December 05, 2009

Inland Revenue Board. Malaysia (IRBM), (2008). *The e-filing website*. [Online] available at: http://e-hasil.org.my/index/e-hasil.asp (accessed: 21 August 2009).

Interactive Policy Making Online Consultations website (2007). *Report on Interactive Policy Making* (http://ec.europa.eu/yourvoice/ipm/index_en.htm) IST policy on the objective of ICT research for innovative Government website (2004). (http://cordis.europa.eu/ist/so/govt/home.html) IST-507767 – QUALEG (2004). Deliverable 4.1 "Marketing Research"

International Function Point Users Group. (1999). *Fucntion Pointss Counting Practices Manual – Release 4.1*. Wisconsin, USA: International Function Points User.

International Function Points Users Group. (2002). *IT Measurement Practial Advice from the Experts*. Reading, MA: Addison-Wesley.

International Monetary Fund. (2007). *Manual on Fiscal Transparency*. Washington, D.C.: Fiscal Affairs Department.

International Telecommunication Union (ITU) Report, 2003.

Internet Surveys, N. U. A. (2004). http://www.nua.ie/surveys/how_many_online, 2002 (last survey published on 2004)

Internet World Stats. (2009). World Internet Users and Population Stats, Miniwatts Marketing Group, available at http://internetworldstats.com/

Ip, F. (2009). The road of Macau eGovernment and challenges. *Macau ICT, 1*(September), 38–41.

ISDR-UN. (2003). *International Strategy for Disaster Reduction, Terminology: Basic terms of disaster risk reduction.* Retrieved October 15, 2009 from http://www.unisdr.org/eng/library/lib-terminologyeng%20home.htm

Islam, M. A., Murelli, E., Noronha, F., & Rahman, H. (2006). Capacity Development Initiatives for Marginal Communities: A few case studies. In H. Rahman (Ed.), *Empowering Marginal Communities with Information Networking* (pp. 318–351). Hershey, PA: Idea Group Inc.

ISO/IEC 19761 (2003). Information technology - Software measurement - Functional size measurement - Part 6: Guide for use of ISO/IEC 14143 series and related International Standards. JTC 1/SC 7. International standard.

ISO/IEC 24765 (2008). - Systems and software engineering vocabulary. International standard.

ITU (2006a). World Telecommunication/ICT development Report 2006.

ITU. (2007b). *World Information Society Report.* Beyond WSIS.

Izatun, S., (2008, April 22). Almost half a million taxpayers now using e-filing. *The Star.*

Jackson, C. M., Chow, S., & Leitch, R. A. (1997). Toward an understanding of the behavioural intention to use an information system. *Decision Sciences, 28*(2), 357–389. doi:10.1111/j.1540-5915.1997.tb01315.x

Jarillo, J. C. (1988). On Strategic Networks. *Strategic Management Journal, 9*(1), 31–41. doi:10.1002/smj.4250090104

Jarvenpaa, S., Tiller, E. H., & Simons, R. (2003). Regulation and the Internet: Public Choice Insights for Business Organizations. *California Management Review, 46*(1), 72–85.

Jen, R., F., Cheng, K. F., Wen, P. C. (2006). Acceptance of electronic tax filing: A study of taxpayer intentions. *Information & Management, 43*(1), 109–126. doi:10.1016/j.im.2005.04.001

Jepsen, T., & Jepsen, M. (2008). Health IT: A roundtable discussion with healthcare information technology executives. *IEEE IT Professional, 10*(2), 53–55. doi:10.1109/MITP.2008.27

Johnson, E., & Prakash, A. (2007). NGO Research program: a collective action perspective. *Policy Sciences, 40*, 221–240. doi:10.1007/s11077-007-9043-x

Jones, C. (2007). *Estimating Software Costs.* New York: McGraw-Hill.

Jorgensen, M., & Sjoberg, D. (2004): The Impact of Customer Expectation on Software Development Effort Estimates. *Simula Research Laboratory*, Retrieved June 20, 2005, from http://simula.no/research/engineering/publications/SE.4.Joergensen.2004.b/?searchterm=The%20Impact%20of%20Customer%20Expectation%20on%20Software%20Development%20Effort%20Estimates

Justice, J. B., Melitski, J., & Smith, D. L. (2006). E-Government as an Instrument of Fiscal Accountability and Responsiveness: Do the Best Practitioners Employ the Best Practices? *American Review of Public Administration, 36*(3), 301–322. doi:10.1177/0275074005283797

Kahn, S., & Sheshardri, V. (2008). Medical record privacy and security in a digital environment. *IEEE IT Professional, 10*(2), 46–52. doi:10.1109/MITP.2008.34

Karim, M. R. Nazariah A. K., (2003). *E-government in Malaysia*, Kuala Lumpur: Pelanduk Publications (M) Sdn. Bhd.

Kart, F., Moser, L. E., & Melliar-Smith, P. M. (2008). Building a distributed e-Healthcare system using SOA. *IEEE IT Professional, 10*(2), 24–30. doi:10.1109/MITP.2008.22

Kelty, C. (2004). Social Thought and Commentary: Culture's Open Sources: Software, Copyright, and Cultural Critique. *Anthropological Quarterly.* George Washington Institute for Ethnographic Research, 499-506.

Keniston, K., & Kumar, D. (Eds.). (2004). *Bridging the Digital Divide: Experience in India.* London: Sage Publications.

Kettl, D. F. (1997). The Global Revolution in Public Management: Driving Themes, Missing Links. *Journal of Public Policy Analysis and Management*, *16*(3), 446–462. doi:10.1002/(SICI)1520-6688(199722)16:3<446::AID-PAM5>3.0.CO;2-H

Kettl, D. F. (2002). *The transformation of governance: Public administration for twenty-first century America.* Baltimore, MD: John Hopkins University Press.

Kettl, D. F. (2005). *The Global Public Management Revolution*. Washington, D.C.: Brookings Institution.

Kiangi, G.E. & Tjipangandjara (1996). Oppoetunities for information technology in enhancing socio-economic development of a developing country. In M. Odedra-Straub (Eds.), *Global Information technology and Socio-Economic Development.* Nashua:Ivy League Publishing, 73-81.

Kickert, W. (2007). Public Management Reforms in Countries with a Napoleonic State Model: France, Italy and Spain. In C. Pollitt, S. van Thiel, & V. Homburg (Eds.), *New Public Management in Europe: Adaptation and Alternatives* (pp. 26–51). Great Britain: Palgrave MacMillan.

Klitgaard, R. (1998). International Cooperation Against Corruption. *Finance & Development*, *35*(1), 3–6.

Knott, R. P., Merunka, V., & Polák, J. (2000). Process Modeling for Object Oriented Analysis using BORM Object Behavioral Analysis, *Fourth International Conference on Requirements Engineering ICRE 2000.* (pp. 7 – 18), Chicago: Computer Society Press.

Kopits, G., & Craig, J. (1998). *Transparency in Government Operations.* Occasional Paper, IMF, Washington D.C.

La Porte, T. M., Demchak, C. C., & De Jong, M. (2002). Democracy and Bureaucracy in the Age of the Web: Emprical Findings and Theoretical Speculations. *Administration & Society*, *34*, 411–446. doi:10.1177/0095399702034004004

Lal, R. (1999). *Mission Report: SDNP Bangladesh.* Available at http://www.sdnbd.org/mission_report.htm

Landsbergen, D., & Wolken, G. (1998). *Eliminating legal and policy barriers to interoperable government systems. Phase 1: Policy Barriers. August 12.* Washington, DC: Intergovernmental Enterprise Panel, Office of Information Resources Management, Department of Veterans Affairs.

Lanvin, B. (2003). Leaders and facilitators: The new roles of governments in digital economy. *Global Information Technology Report 2002-2003.* Oxford: Oxford University Press.

Lauriat Shawn, M. (2007). *AJAX Advanced Ajax: Architecture and Best Practices* (1st ed.). Upper Saddle River, NJ: Prentice Hall PTR.

Law, M. *Laws of Turkish Republic*, No 5447 of 2005. Retrieved October 21, 2009, from http://www.tbmm.gov.tr

Lettice, J. (2004). Open Source ready for prime time in UK.gov, says OGC, *The Register.* October 28, 2004, Retrieved September 7, 2009 form http://www.theregister.co.uk/2004/10/28/ogc_oss_pilot_report/.

Lewis, D., & Wallace, T. (2000). *New roles and relevance: development NGOs and the challenge of change.* Bloomfields, CT: Kumarian Press.

Liu, S. (2007). Enabling electronic healthcare information exchange. *IEEE IT Professional*, *9*(6), 17–23. doi:10.1109/MITP.2007.108

Livari, J., & Magid, I. (1997). Determinants of user participation: A finnish survey. *Behaviour & Information Technology*, *16*(2), 111–121. doi:10.1080/014492997119950

Longstreet, D. (2007). *Function Points Analysis Training Course*, Retrieved May 22, 2009, from http://www.softwaremetrics.com/Function%20Point%20Training%20Booklet%20New.pdf>

Loukis, E., & Tsouma, N. (2002). Critical issues of information systems management in the Greek public sector. *The International Journal of Government and Democracy in the Information Age.*, *17*(1), 65–83.

Luehrs, R., & Molinari, F. (2007). Participation in the Law-Making Process: The LexiPation Approach, *Proceedings of the University of Camerino's conference on "Methodologies, Technologies and Tools enabling e-Government" (MeTTeG07).*

Macau (2008). http://www.icegov2008.icegov.org/icegov/events/invitedSession/session2

Mackenzie, A. (2001). Open Source Software: When is a Tool? What is a Commodity. *Science as Culture, 10*(4), 541–552. doi:10.1080/09505430120093621

MacKenzie, D., & Wajcman, J. (2002). *The Social Shaping of Technology.* Buckingham: Open University Press.

Maglio, P., & Spohrer, J. (2008). Fundamentals of service science. *Journal of the Academy of Marketing Science, 36*, 18–20. doi:10.1007/s11747-007-0058-9

Maia, R. S., von Wangenheim, A., & Bobre, L. F. (2006). A statewide telemedicine network for public health in Brazil. *Proceedings of the 19th IEEE International Symposium in Computer-Based Medical Systems* (pp. 495-500). IEEE Computer Society Press.

Malaysian Public Sector Open Source Competency Centre (OSCC). (2009). *Accelerated Adoption for Malaysian Public Sector Open Source Software (OSS) Program.* Retrieved September 8, 2009, from http://www.oscc.org.my/.

Malkia, M., & Savolainen, R. (2004). eTransformation in government, politics and society: Conceptual framework and introduction. In M. Malkia, A. Anttiroiko, & R. Savolainen (Eds.), *eTransformation in governance: New directions in government and politics* (pp.1-21). Hershey, PA: Idea Group Publishing.

Mathieson, K. (1991). Predicting user intention: Comparing the technology acceptance model with the theory of planned behaviour. *Information Systems Research, 12*(3), 173–191. doi:10.1287/isre.2.3.173

McConnell, A., & Drennan, L. (2006). Mission Impossible? Planning and Preparing for Crisis. *Journal of Contingencies and Crisis Management, 14*(2), 59–70. doi:10.1111/j.1468-5973.2006.00482.x

McDowell, C.L., Nagel, A, Williams, S.M. & Canepa, C. (2005). Building knowledge from the practice of local communities. Volume 1(3): 30-40

McIntyre, J. (2005). Adult Learning and Australia's Ageing Population: A Policy Briefing Paper, Adult Learning Australia, Canberra, Retrieved 15/06/09 from http://www.artpages.com.au/johnmac/Age_learn_report.pdf

McIver, W. J., Jr., & Elmagarmid, A. K. (2002). *Advances in digital government: Technology, human factors, and policy.* Boston, MA: Kluwer Academic Publishers. doi:10.1007/b116295

Melarkode, A., From-Poulson, M., & Warnakulasuriya, S. (2004). Delivering agility through IT. *Business Strategy Review., 15*(3), 45–50. doi:10.1111/j.0955-6419.2004.00327.x

Michael, N., & Margaret, R. (2007, July). Creating Older Adults Technology Training Policies: Lessons from Community Practices. *Australian Journal of Adult Learning, 47*(2), 308–324.

Microsoft Corporation. (2006). *Microsoft Corporation Annual Report 2006.* Retrieved March 1, 2008, from http://www.microsoft.com/MS_2006_AnnualReport.doc

Microsoft Corporation. (2007). *Microsoft Corporation Annual Report 2007.* Retrieved on March 1, 2008, from http://www.microsoft.com/MS_2007_AnnualReport.doc

Miller, M. (2009). *Cloud computing: Web-based applications that change the way you work and collaborate online.* Indianapolis, Indiana: Que Publishing.

Miller, M. J. (2002). Beyond the Box: Driving the Next Billion. *PC Magazine, 21*(15), 7.

Ministry of Finance. (2006). *Belediyeler Seçilmiş Mali Büyüklükler.* [Municipal Fiscal Accounts]. Ankara. Retrieved October 21, 2009, from http://www.muhasebat.gov.tr

Ministry of Finance. (2009). *Kamu Hesapları Bülteni* [Public Accounts Report]. Ankara. Retrieved October 21, 2009, from http://www.muhasebat.gov.tr

Ministry of Information Technology. (2009).Retrieved from: http://www.mit.gov.in/default.aspx?id=832 accessed on 03.03.09.

Mishra, D.C. (2007). Sixty years of Development of E-Governance in India (1947-2007). *Are there Lessons for Developing Countries?,* ICEGOV2007, December 10-13, Macao, ACM978-1-59593-822-0/07/12.

Misra, H. K. (2009), *Managing Rural Citizen Interfaces in E-Governance Systems: A Study in Indian Context, ICEGOV2009,* November 10-13, 2009, Bogota, Colombia, Proceedings of ACM, pp.155-162

Misra, H. K. (2009). *Governance of Rural Information and Communication Technology: Opportunities and Challenges.* New Delhi: Academic Foundation.

Misra, H. K., & Hiremath, B. N. (2006). *Citizen-led Participatory E-Governance Initiatives: An Architectural Perspective*, IIM Lucknow. *Metamorphosis*, *5*(2), 133–148.

Misra, H. K., & Hiremath, B. N. (2009). *Livelihood Perspective of Rural Information Infrastructure and E-Governance Readiness in India: A Case Based Study*, IRMA Working Paper Series 215, IRMA, Anand, India.

Moller, J. E., & Vosegaard, H. (2008). Experiences with electronic health records. *IEEE IT Professional*, *10*(2), 19–23. doi:10.1109/MITP.2008.25

Moore, J. F. (1996). *The Death of Competition: Leadership and Strategy in the Age of Business Ecosystems.* Winchester, UK: J. Wiley & Sons.

Moynihan, D. P. (2008). Combining structural forms in the search for policy tools: Incident command systems in US crisis management. *Governance - an International Journal of Policy and Administration, 21*(2), 205-229.

Murty, S. A. (2005, Spring). The Future of Rural Social Work. *Administration in Social Work*, *6*(1), 132–144.

Musso, J., Weare, C., & Hale, M. (2000). Designing Web Technologies for Local Governance Reform: Good Management or Good Democracy? *Political Communication*, *17*, 1–19. doi:10.1080/105846000198486

Myers, M. (1997). Qualitative research in information systems. *Management Information Systems Quarterly*, *21*(2), 241–242. doi:10.2307/249422

Nairn, M. P. G. (2005). *New Australian Government Chief Information Officer.* Media Release. Senator the Hon Eric Abetz. Special Minister of State. Australia.

Naralan, A. (2008). Belediyelerin Resmi İnternet Sitesi Sahipliği ile Siyasi Partiler ve Nüfus Arasındaki İlişki [Relations among website ownership of municipalities, population and political parties]. *Cumhuriyet Üniversitesi İktisadi ve İdari Bilimler Fakültesi Dergisi*, *9*(2), 63–77.

NASW. (2006a). *National Association of Social Workers Policy Statements. National Association of Social Workers: 2006-2009.* Washington, D.C.: NASW Press.

NASW. (2006b). *Social work speaks. National Association of Social Workers.* Washington, D.C.: NASW Press.

NASW. (2006c). Community Development: The Community Development policy statement. In NASW's Social Work Speaks 2009-2012, Washington, DC: National Association of Social Workers, pp.56-60.

NCA. (2003). *Informatization: White Paper*, National Computerization Agency (NCA), Seoul, Rep. of Korea

Ndubisi, N. D., Jantan, M., & Richerdson, S. (2001). Is the technology acceptance model valid for entrepreneurs? Model testing and examining usage determinants. *Asian Academy of Management Journal*, *6*(2), 31–54.

Nelson, G. B. (2004). *Real Time Decision Support: Creating a Flexible Architecture for Real Time Analytics, SUGI29.* Data Warehousing, Management and Quality. NESSI. (2006). *Strategic Research Agenda* (*Vol. 1*). Framing the Future of the Service.

Network Security Journal. (2007). *Microsoft Opens Its Arms to Open Source*, Retrieved February 16, 2008, from http://www.networksecurityjournal.com/features/microsoft-open-source-lab/.

Newburn, T. (2001). The Commodification of Policing: Security Networks in the late Modern City. *Urban Studies (Edinburgh, Scotland)*, *38*(5/6), 829–848. doi:10.1080/00420980123025

News Report (2007). South Africa Adopts Open Source Software Policy. November 1.

Nonnaly, J. C. (1978). *Psychometric theory.* New York: McGraw Hill.

Normann, R., & Ramirez, R. (1993). From value chain to value constellation: designing interactive strategy. *Harvard Business Review, 71*(4), 65–77. PubMed

Norris, P. (2001). *Digital Divide: Civic Engagement, Information Poverty, and the Internet Wordwide.* Cambridge: Cambridge University Press.

Novell (2007). *Novell 2007 Annual Report.* Retrieved March 1, 2008, from http://www.novell.com/novell_annualreport_2007.pdf

O'Looney, J. A. (2002). *Wiring governments: Challenges and possibilities for public managers.* London: Quorum Books.

OASIS. (2006). *Reference Model for Service Oriented Architecture 1.0.* Retrieved from http://www.oasis-open.org/committees/ tc_home.php?wg_abbrev=soa-rm, August 2006.

OASIS. (2009). Business Process Execution Language v 2.0. Retrieved from http://docs.oasis-open.org/wsbpel/2.0/OS/wsbpel-v2.0-OS.html on 22/10/2009.

OASIS. (2009). Security Assertion Markup Language (SAML). Retrieved from http://www.oasis-open.org/committees/tc_home.php?wg_abbrev=security on 22/10/2009.

OASIS. (2009). Web Services Atomic Transaction (WS-AtomicTransaction). Retrieved from http://docs.oasis-open.org/ws-tx/wsat/2006/06 on 22/10/2009.

OECD (2004). Organisation for Economic Co-operation and Development, *Annual Report*, 2004.

OECD. (2000). *OECD Best Practices for Budget Transparency.* Public Management Service Public Management Committee.

OECD. (2001a). *Cities for Citizens: Improving Metropolitan Governance* (pp. 39–43). Paris: OECD Publications.

OECD. (2001b). *Citizens as Partners: Information, Communication and public Participation in Policy Making* (pp. 20–22). Paris: OECD Publications.

Office of Government Commerce (OGC). (2002). *Policy on the use of Open Source Software.* July 2002, Retrieved September 7, 2009, from http://www.ogc.gov.uk/index.asp?docid=2190#finalreport.

Office of Management and Budget (OMB). (2004) *memorandum M-04-16 "Software Acquisition"* of July 1, 2004 Retrieved September 7, 2009, from http://www.dwheeler.com/oss_fs_why.html.

O'Hear, S. (2006). Web's second phase puts users in control, Tuesday June 20 2006, The Guardian Education. Retrieved from http://education.guardian.co.uk/elearning/story/0,1801086,00.html on 21 November 2008.

Ojamo, M. (2008). *The Finnish register of visual impairment. Annual statistics 2007*: National research and development centre for welfare and health in Finland and the Finnish federation of the visually impaired.

Oliver, E. L., & Sanders, L. (2004). *E-government reconsidered: Renewal of governance for the knowledge age.* Saskatoon, Canada: Saskatchewan Institute of Public Policy.

OMG. (2007). *OMG Unified Modeling Language (OMG UML),* Superstructure, V2.1.2, 585-603. Retrieved April 1. 2008. from http://www.omg.org/docs/formal/07-11-02.pdf

Orlikowski, W. J. (2000). Using Technology and Constituting Structures: A Practice Lens for Studying Technology in Organizations. *Organization Science, 11*(4), 404–428. doi:10.1287/orsc.11.4.404.14600

Osborne, D., & Gaebler, T. (1992). *Reinventing government how the entrepreneurial spirit is transforming the public sector.* London: Addison-Wesley Publishing Co.

Ozaygen, A. L. (2005). *Diffusion of Free/Open Source Software as Innovation: A Case Study of METU,* METU STPS-Working Paper, October 25, 2005.

Paas, L., & Creech, H. (2008). Current Uses and Trends in ICTs supporting Education for Sustainable Development. Winnipeg: IISD http:www.iisd.org

Pacific Council on International Policy. (2002). *Roadmap for E-Government in the Developing World: 10 Questions E-Government Leaders Should Ask Themselves*. CA, USA: Pacific Council on International Policy.

Palvia, S. C. J., & Sharma, S. S. S. (2007). *E-Government and E-Governance: Definitions/Domain Framework and Status around the World*. Paper presented at the Fifth International Conference on E-Governance, Hyderabad, India. Retrieved October 21, 2009, from http://www.iceg.net/2007/books/1/1_369.pdf

Paquet, G. (1999). *Governance through social learning*. Ottawa: University of Ottawa Press.

Paquet, G., & Roy, J. (1998). Governance in Canada: Competition, cooperation in business-government-society relations. *Version VI* (Ottawa: University of Ottawa, Fall): 229-230.

Parasuraman, A. (2000). Technology readiness index (TRI): A multiple-item scale to measure readiness to embrace new technologies. *Journal of Service Research*, *2*(4), 307–320. doi:10.1177/109467050024001

Parasuraman, A., & Colby, C. L. (2001). *Techno-ready marketing: How and why your customers adopt technology*. New York: The Free Press.

Parloff, R. (2004). Redmond's Open Door Policy. *Fortune*, *150*(8), 43–44.

Parry, T. (2007). *The Role of Fiscal Transparency in Sustaining Growth and Stability in Latin America*, Working Paper (Paper No WP/07/220), IMF, Washington D.C.

Pascual, P. J. (2003). *e-Government*, e-ASEAN Task Force, UNDP-APDIP, Malaysia

Pérez, C. C., Bolívar, M. P. R., & Hernández, A. M. L. (2008). e-Government process and incentives for online public financial information. *Online Information Review*, *32*(3), 379–400. doi:10.1108/14684520810889682

Pérez, C. C., Hernández, A. M. L., & Bolívar, M. P. R. (2005). Citizens' Access to on-line governmental financial information: Practices in the European Union countries. *Government Information Quarterly*, *22*, 258–276. doi:10.1016/j.giq.2005.02.002

Perry, J, L Paas, L Pinter, N Sharma, J Belali, M Eugenia-Arreola, E Santer (2009). *Sustaining the IEA capacity building network Draft manuscript prepared for IISD and UNEP Nairobi.*

Perry, R. W. (1995). The structure and function of community emergency operations centres. *Disaster Prevention and Management*, *4*(5), 37–41. doi:10.1108/09653569510100983

Perry, R. W. (2003). Emergency Operations Centres in an Era of Terrorism: Policy and Management Functions. *Journal of Contingencies and Crisis Management*, *11*(4), 151–159. doi:10.1111/j.0966-0879.2003.01104001.x

Perry, R. W. (2004). Disaster Exercise Outcomes for Professional Emergency Personnel and Citizen Volunteers. *Journal of Contingencies and Crisis Management*, *12*(2), 64–75. doi:10.1111/j.0966-0879.2004.00436.x

Pervan, G. (1998). How chief executive officers in large organisations view the management of their information systems. *Journal of Information Technology*, *13*, 95–109. doi:10.1080/026839698344882

Petter, J., Byrnes, P., & Choi, D. (2002). Social Work Speaks: Community Development, *Policy statement approved by the NASW Delegate Assembly,* Washington, DC. *NASW Press*, *2002*, 56–60.

Pfitzmann, A., & Wolf, G. (2000). Properties of protection goals and their integration into a user interface. *International Journal of Computer and Telecommunication*, *32*(6), 669–683.

Pierson, J., & Lievens, B. (2005). Configuring Living Labs for a 'thick' Understanding of Innovation. *Proceedings of EPIC Conference*, 114-127.

Pintér, L., Zahedi, K., & Cressman, D. (2000). *Capacity building for integrated environmental assessment and reporting training manual* Winnipeg: IISD for UNEP http://www.iisd.org/pdf/geo_manual_2.pdf

Pistore, M., Traverso, P., Paolucci, M., & Wagner, M. (2009). From Software Services to a Future Internet of Services. In G. Tselentis, et al. (Eds.), *Towards the Future Internet*. IOS Press.

Planning Commission. (2001). *Government of India, Report of The Working Group on Convergence and E-Governance for Tenth Five Year Plan* (2002-2007), New Delhi, November, p6-25.

Polanksy, M., Inuganti, T., & Wiggins, S. (2004). The 21st Century CIO. *Business Strategy Review.*, *15*(2), 29–33. doi:10.1111/j.0955-6419.2004.00310.x

Porter, M., & Millar, V. (1985). How information gives you competitive advantage. *Harvard Business Review*, *63*(4), 149–174.

Prabhu, C. S. R. (2005). *E-Governance: Concepts and Case Studies*. Delhi: Prentice Hall of India Private Limited.

Prahalad, C. K., & Ramaswamy, V. (2000). Co-opting customer competence. *Harvard Business Review*, *78*(1), 79–87.

Prahalad, C. K., & Ramaswamy, V. (2003). The new frontier of experience innovation. *Sloan Management Review*, *44*(4), 12–18.

Prahalad, C. K., & Ramaswamy, V. (2004). *The Future of Competition: Co-Creating Unique Value with Customers*, New York: Harvard Business School Press, ISBN 978-1578519538.

Premchand, A. (2002). Fiscal Transparency and Accountability: Idea and Reality. In *United Nations. Globalization and new challenges of public finance: Financial management, transparency and accountability*. New York: Department of Economic and Social Affairs.

Public Financial Management and Control Law. *Laws of Turkish Republic*, No 5018 of 2003. Retrieved October 21, 2009, from http://www.tbmm.gov.tr

Rahman, H. (2004). Empowering Marginal Communities with Interactive Education Systems, Commonwealth Open Learning (COL). *3rd Pan-Commonwealth Forum on Open Learning* (PCF3), Dunedin, New Zealand, July 4-8, 2004.

Rahman, H. (2006). Empowerment of Marginal Communities Through Information Driven Learning. In H. Rahman (Ed.), *Empowering Marginal Communities with Information Networking* (pp. 16–42). Hershey, PA: IDEA Group Publishing.

Rahman, H. (2007). Role of ICTs in Socioeconomic Development and Poverty Reduction. In H. Rahman (Ed.), *Information and Communication Technologies for Economic and Regional Developments* (pp. 180–219). Hershey, PA: Idea Group Inc.

Rahman, H. (2008). An Overview on Strategic ICT Implementations Toward Developing Knowledge Societies. In H. Rahman (Ed.), *Developing Successful ICT Strategies: Competitive Advantages in a Global Knowledge-Driven Society* (pp. 1–39). Hershey, PA: Information Science Reference.

Rahman, H. (2009). Local E-Government Management: A Wider Window of E-Governance. In H. Rahman (Ed.), *Handbook of Research on E-Government Readiness for Information and Service Exchange: Utilizing Progressive Information Communication Technologies* (pp. 295–323). Hershey: Information Science Reference.

Rainford, S. (2006). *e-Sri Lanka: An Integrated Approach to e-Government Case Study, Asia Pacific Development Information Programme (APDIP),* Bangkok

Ramayah, T., Ramoo, V., Amlus, I., (2008). Profiling online and manual tax filers: Results from an exploratory study in Penang Malaysia. *Labuan e-Journal of Muamalat and Society*, 2, 1-8.

Rapoza, J. (2007). OLPC Remains Laudable. *eWeek.* 24(35), 64.

Regulation on Activity Reports of Public Administrations. *Regulations of Turkish Republic*, No 26111 of 2006. Retrieved October 21, 2009, from http://www.bumko.gov.tr

Regulation on the Procedures and the Methods Related to Implementation of the Right to Information Law. *Regulations of Turkish Republic*, No 25445 of 2004. Retrieved October 21, 2009, from http://www.mevzuat.gov.tr

Resnikoff, S., Pascolini, D., Etya'ale, D., Kocur, I., Pararajasegaram, R., Pokharel, G. P., et al. (2004). Global data on visual impairment in the year 2002. *Bulletin of the World Health Organization*, *82*, 844–851. PubMed

Retrieved April 17, 2009, from http://www.sikayetim.com/

Retrieved April 21, 2009, from http://www.sikayetiniz.com/

Retrieved April 21, 2009, from http://www.SikayetVar.com/

Retrieved July 20, 2009, from http://www.turkiye.gov.tr

Retrieved July 23, 2009, from http://e-devlet.com

Riga Declaration, (2006). *Internet for all: EU ministers commit to an inclusive and barrier-free information society*, press release of June, IP/06/769.

Right to Information Law. *Laws of Turkish Republic*, No 4982 of 2003. Retrieved October 21, 2009, from http://www.tbmm.gov.tr

Riley, T. B. (2001). Electronic governance: Living and working in the wired world. Commonwealth Centre for Electronic Governance, August. (http://www.electronicgov.net/pubs/research_papers/index.shtml).

Riley, T. B. (2003). E-government vs E-governance: Examining the differences in a changing public sector climate. *International Tracking Survey Report* (No. 4). Commonwealth Centre for Electronic Governance (http://www.electronicgov.net).

Roberts, F. S. (1979). *Measurement Theory with Applications decisionmaking, Utility, and Social Sciences*. Reading, MA: Addison-Wesley Publishing Company.

Robinson, S. (1998). Telecentres in Mexico: The first phase. *Paper presented to the UNRISD Conference.*

Rogers, E. (1995). *Diffusion of Innovations*. New York: The Free Press.

Rosell, S. A. (1999). *Renewing governance: Governing by learning in the information age*. Toronto: Oxford University Press.

Rosenberg, J., & Remy, D. (2004). *Securing Web Services with WS-Security: Demystifying WS-Security*. WS-Policy, SAML, XML Signature, and XML Encryption, Pearson Higher Education.

Rosenfeld, S., Kiss, S., & Siler, S. (2007). *Privacy, security, and the regional health information organization*. California Healthcare Foundation.

Rubaii-Barrett, N., & Wise, L. R. (2008). Disability Access and E-Government: An Empirical Analysis of State Practices. *Journal of Disability Policy Studies, 19*(1), 52–64. doi:10.1177/1044207307311533

Rust, R. T., & Kannan, P. K. (2003). E-Service: A New Paradigm for Business in the Electronic Environment. *Communications of the ACM, 46*(6), 37–42. doi:10.1145/777313.777336

Rust, R. T., & Lemon, K. N. (2001). E-Service and the Consumer. *International Journal of Electronic Commerce, 5*(3), 85–101.

Saelee, K. (2002). *Sustainable use of Biological Resources, Indigenous Peoples' Contributions to COP-8 of the* (pp. 227–243). CBD.

Sawhney, M., & Parikh, D. (2001). Where value lives in a networked world. *Harvard Business Review, 79*(1), 79–90. PubMed

Sawhney, M., Balasubramanian, S., & Krishnan, V. V. (2003). Creating growth with services. *Sloan Management Review, 45*(2), 34–44.

Schick, A. (1999). *A Contemporary Approach to Public Expenditure Management. World Bank Institute: Governance*. Regulation, and Finance Division.

Schneider, D., & Vaught, B. (1993). A comparison of job satisfaction between public and private sector managers. *Public Administration Quarterly., 17*(1), 68–83.

Schweik, C. M., & English, R. C. (2007, November). Brook's Versus Linus' Law: An Empirical Test of Open Source Projects. *Paper presented at the Association for Public Policy Analysis and Management Conference*, Washington D.C.

SDNP. (2001). *Project Implementation Plan: PIP,). Sustainable Development Networking Programme, Bangladesh, Version-D, 2001.* Available at www.sdnbd.org

SDNP. (2003). *Status Report of Sustainable Development Networking Programme (SDNP): Bangladesh Institute of Development Studies*, September 30, 2003. Available at www.sdnbd.org

SDNP. (2004) *Sustainable Development Networking Programme: Final Assessment,* Report of an independent external assessment, February, 2004. Available at www.sdnbd.org

Seely-Brown, J 2002 GROWING UP DIGITAL: How the web changes work, education, and the ways people learn *United States Distance Learning Association USDLA Journal* 16(2): http://www.usdla.org/html/journal/FEB02_Issue/article01.html Accessed 26 May 2009

Segars, A. H., & Grover, V. (1993). Re-examining perceived ease of use and usefulness: A confirmatory factor analysis. *Management Information Systems Quarterly, 17*(1), 517–725. doi:10.2307/249590

Seiferth, C. Justin (2009). *Open Source and These United States.* Retrieved September 7, 2009, from http://skyscraper.fortunecity.com/mondo/841/documents/99-184.html.

Sekaran, U. (2003). *Research methods for business: A skill building approach.* India: John Wiley & Son, Inc.

Seventh Global Forum. (2006). *On Reinventing Government.* Retrieved February 3, 2006, from http://www.7thglobalforum.org

Shaffer, C. R., & Anundsen, K. (1993). *Creating community anywhere.* New York: Tarcher/Perigree.

Shafie, S. (2007). E-government initiatives in Malaysia and the role of the national archives of Malaysia in digital records management, Conference paper on "Development of E-Government and Digital Records Management" at: *The 8th General Conference of* Teo, T.S. H., (2001). Demographic and motivation variable associated with internet usage activities. *Internet Research: Electronic Networking Application and Policy, 1*(2), 125-137

Shiang, J. (2008). *Change and Adaptation of Stakeholder Relationships in e-Governance.* Paper presented at Fourth International Conference on e-Government, Melbourne, Australia. Retrieved October 21, 2009, from http://web.thu.edu.tw/jshiang/www/iceg2008.pdf

Shirky, C. (2003). Social Software: A New Generation of Tools. *Esther Dyson's Monthly Report* (10).

Siemens, G. (2005). Connectivism: A learning theory for the digital age. *International Journal of Instructional Technology & Distance Learning, 2*(1). http://www.itdl.org/Journal/Jan_05/article01.htm and http://www.connectivism.ca/about.html Accessed 26 May 2009.

Silcock, R. (2001). What is e-government. *Parliamentary Affairs, 54,* 88–91. doi:10.1093/pa/54.1.88

Simon, K. D. (2005). The Value of Open Standards and Open-Source Software in Government Environments. *IBM Systems Journal, 44*(2), 227–238. doi:10.1147/sj.442.0227

Siochrú, S. Ó. (2002*). Sustainable Development Networking Programme, Bangladesh: Final Report*, December 2002. Available at www.sdnbd.org

Siochrú, S. Ó., Girard, B., et al. (2002). *Global media governance. A beginner's guide.* Lanham, Rowman & Littlefield Publishers.

Slim, H., & Thompson, P. (1993). *Listening for a Change: Oral History and Development.* London: Panos Publications.

Snellen, I. Th. M. (2000). Territorializing governance and the state: Policy dimensions of Geographic Information Systems. *Information Infrastructure and Policy, 6,* 131–138.

Software Productivity Research – SPR. (2002). *Counting Rules for Function Points and Feature Points,* Retrieved January 3, 2005, from http://www.spr.com

Songan, P., Hamid, K. A., Yeo, A., Gnaniah, J., & Zen, H. (2004). Community Informatics: Challenges in Bridging the Digital Divide. In H.M. Khalid, H.M., M.G. Helander, M.G. & A.W. Yeo, A.W. (Eds.). *Work with Computing Systems 2004*, Kuala Lumpur: Damai Sciences.pp. 267-270

Spergel, I. A. (1987). Community development. In A. Minahan (Ed.-in-Chief), *Encyclopedia of social work* (18th ed., Vol. 1, pp. 299–308). Silver Spring, MD: NASW Press.

Spil, Ton A.M., & Schuring, R.W. (2005). *E-Health systems diffusion and use: The innovation, the user and the USE IT model.* Hershey, PA: Idea Group Publishing.

State Planning Organization. (2003). *e-Transformation Turkey Project Short term Action, Plan: 2003-2004.* Retrieved February 15, 2008, from http://www.bilgitoplumu.gov.tr/eng/docs

State Planning Organization. (2005). *e-Transformation Turkey Project 2005 Action Plan.* Retrieved February 15, 2008, from http://www.bilgitoplumu.gov.tr/eng/docs

State Planning Organization. (2006a). *Bilgi Toplumu Stratejisi (2006-2010)* (Pub. No. 2699). [Information Society Strategy], Ankara.

State Planning Organization. (2006a). *Turkish Information Society Strategy (2006-2010).* Retrieved February 15, 2008, from http://www.bilgitoplumu.gov.tr/eng/docs/Information_Society_Strategy.pdf

State Planning Organization. (2006b). *Turkish Information Society Strategy (2006-2010).* Retrieved Feb. 15, 2008, from http://www.bilgitoplumu.gov.tr/eng/docs/Action_Plan.pdf

State Planning Organization. (2009). *Bilgi Toplumu Stratejisi Eylem Planı (2006-2010) Değerlendirme Raporu 3* [Evaluation Report 3 of the Information Society Strategy Action Plan (2006-2010)], Ankara.

Stauss, B. (2002). The dimensions of complain satisfaction: process and outcome complaint satisfaction versus cold fact and warm act complaint satisfaction. *Managing Service Quality, 12*(3), 173. doi:10.1108/09604520210429240

Stillitoe, P. (1998). The Development of Indigenous Knowledge: A new applied anthropology. In *Current Anthropology,* 49 (2).223-253, April 1998.

Stinchcomb, J. B., & Ordaz, F. (2007). The Integration of Two "Brotherhoods" into One Organizational Culture: A Psycho-social Perspective on Merging Police and Fire Services. *Public Organization Review, 7,* 143–161. doi:10.1007/s11115-006-0026-8

Strategy, L. Lisbon European Council 23 and 24 March 2000 Presidency Conclusions (2000). Retrieved from http://www.europarl.europa.eu/summits/lis1_en.htm

Struska, Z. (2007). *The concept comparison of BORMp method with Use Case Points.* Paper presented at the International Conference on Software Engineering Theory and Practice (SETP-07). Orlando, USAYang, X., Takahashi, D., & Fei, H. (2007). Telemedicine usage and potentials. *Proceedings of Wireless Communications and Networking Conference* (pp. 2736-2740). IEEE Computer Society Press.

Struska, Z., & Pergl, R. (2009). *BORM Points: Introduction and results of practical testing. Enterprise Information Systems.* Proceeding from ICEIS 2009, 590-599. Heidelberg, Germany: Springer Verlag.

Suh, J., & Chen, D. H. C. (2007). (Eds.). *Korea as a knowledge economy: evolutionary process and lessons learned,* The World Bank, Washington DC.

Suomi, R. (2005). Introducing electronic patient records to hospitals: Innovation adoption paths. In A. M. Ton (Ed.), *Spil & Roel W. Schuring, E-Health systems diffusion and use: The innovation, the user and the USE IT model* (pp. 129–146). Hershey, PA: Idea Group Publishing.

Synnott, W., & Gruber, W. (1981). *Information Resource Management: Opportunities and Strategies for the 1980s.* New York: John Wiley & Sons.

Szczepanska, A. M., Bergquist, M., & Ljundberg, J. (2005). High noon at OS corral: Duels and shoot-outs in open source discourse. In J. Feller, et al. (Eds.), *Perspectives on Free and Open Source Software* (pp. 431–446). Cambridge, Mass.: The MIT Press.

Tandon, et. al. (2007). Progress in Community Health Partnerships: Research, Education, and Action, Spring 2007 • vol 1.1, The Johns Hopkins University Press, pp.11-30 (1)

Tapscott, D. (1997). *The digital economy: Promise and peril in the age of networked intelligence.* New York: McGraw Hill.

Taste, W., J. & Wierman, M. J. (2007). Consensus and dissention: A measure of ordinal dispersion. *International Journal of Approximate Reasoning, 45,* 531–545. doi:10.1016/j.ijar.2006.06.024

The Helsinki Manifesto. (2006). http://elivinglab.org/files/Helsinki_Manifesto_201106.pdf

Tiffin, J., & Rajasingham, L. (1995). *Search of the Virtual Class*. London: Routledge. doi:10.4324/9780203291184

Timur, N., & Sariyer, N. (2004). Complaint collecting methods for tools of customer satisfaction – A case of automotive agents in Kayseri. [Abstract]. *Erciyes University Journal of Social Sciences Institute*, *17*(2), 9–32.

tOSSad (2007). *Current Status of FOSS: D18, Version 2.3.* Retrieved February 13, 2008, from http://www.tOSSd.org

Traunmuller, R., & Lenk, K. (1996). *New public management and enabling technologies, advanced IT tools. Edward.* London: Chapman and Hall.

Tripp, S., & Bichelmeyer, B. (1990). Rapid prototyping: An alternative instructional design strategy. *Educational Technology Research and Development*, *38*(1), 31–44. doi:10.1007/BF02298246

Turkish Statistical Institute. (2006, January). 2005 Yılı Belediye Web Hizmetleri Araştırması, [Municipality Web Services Survey 2005], *Haber Bülteni*. Retrieved October 21, 2009, from http://www.tuik.gov.tr

Turkish Statistical Institute. (2007, August). 2007 Yılı Hanehalkı Bilişim Teknolojileri Kullanım Araştırması Revize Sonuçları [Revised Results of the Information and Communication Technology Usage Survey on Households and Individuals 2007]. Retrieved October 22, 2009, from http://www.tuik.gov.tr

Turkish Statistical Institute. (2009, August). 2009 Yılı Hanehalkı Bilişim Teknolojileri Kullanım Araştırması Sonuçları, [The results of 2009 Information and Communication Technology Usage Survey on Households and Individuals], *Haber Bülteni*. Retrieved October 21, 2009, from http://www.tuik.gov.tr

Tyagi, S. (2006). RESTful Web Services. Retrieved from http://java.sun.com/developer/technicalArticles/WebServices/restful/ on 22/10/2009.

UN (2006). E-procurement, a joint publication of Economic and Social Commission for Asia and the Pacific (UNESCAP), Asian Development Bank (ADB) Institute, and Public Procurement Service of the Republic of Korea, United Nations publication

UN. (2008). *UN E-Government Survey*. New York: From E-Government to Connected E-Governance.

UNDP. (1991). *Human Development Report. United nations Development Programme (UNDP).* Oxford University Press.

UNDP. (1998). *Human Development Report*. UNDP, Rosemberg & Seller.

UNDP. (2001). *Human Development Report: Making New Technologies Work for Human Development*. UNDP.

UNDP. (2005). *Promoting ICT for Human Development in Asia: Realizing the Millennium Development Goals, Regional Human Development Report*. Elsevier.

UNDP. (2007). *e-Government Interoperability: Guide, UNDP*, Bangkok

UNEP, (2007a). Environment fund budgets: proposed biennial programme and support budget for 2008 - 2009: Report of the Executive Director (UNEP/GC/24/9)

UNEP, (2007b). Proposed Medium-Term Strategy 2010–2013 (UNEP/GCSS.X/8)

Upbin, B. (2007). The Next Billion. *Forbes*, *180*(10), 48–56.

Vakil, A. C. (1997). Confronting the classification problem:toward a taxonomy of NGOs. *World Development*, *25*, 2057–2070. doi:10.1016/S0305-750X(97)00098-3

Van Lier, A. F. (2009). *Luhmann ontmoet The Matrix. Uitwisselen en delen van informatie in netcentrische omgevingen*. Delft: Eburon Academic Publishers.

Vaus, D. (2006). *Analyzing social science data*. London: Sage Publications, Ltd. eGovernment for Development (eGov4Dev). Success and failure rates of egovernment in developing/transitional Countries: at: http://www.egov4dev.org/success/sfrates.shtml, [accessed on 20 Feb. 2009].

Venkatesh, V., Morris, M. G., Davis, G. B., & Davis, F. D. (2003). User acceptance of information technology: toward a unified view. *Management Information Systems Quarterly*, *27*(3), 425–478.

Von Lubitz, D.K.J.E., Beakley, J.E., & Patricelli, F. (2008). Disaster Management: The Structure, Function, and Significance of Network-Centric Operations, *Journal of Homeland Security and Emergency Management*, *5*(2), article 42,1-24.

W3C (2009). *RDF Annotations (RDFa),* Retrieved from http://www.w3.org/TR/xhtml-rdfa-primer/ on 22/10/2009.

W3C (2009). *RDF Schema (RDFS).* Retrieved from http://www.w3.org/TR/rdf-schema/ on 22/10/2009.

W3C (2009). *Resource Description Framework (RDF*). Retrieved from http://www.w3.org/RDF/ on 22/10/2009.

W3C (2009). *Simple Object Access Protocol (SOAP)* Retrieved from http://www.w3.org/TR/soap/ on 22/10/2009.

Wagenaar, P., Boersma, F. K., Groenewegen, P., & Niemandsverdriet, P. (2009). 'Implementing C2000 in the Dutch police region 'Hollands-Midden', for publication in: Meijer, A., Boersma, F.K., & Wagenaar, P. (eds). *ICTs, Citizens & Governance: After the Hype! Amsterdam: IOS Press series "Innovation and the Public Sector",* 119-134.

Wallauer, J., Macedo, D., Andrade, R., & von Wangenheim, A. (2008). Building a national telemedicine network. *IEEE IT Professional*, *10*(2), 12–17. doi:10.1109/MITP.2008.23

Walter, P. (2003). Surveillance and Security: A Dodgy Relationship. *Journal of Contingencies and Crisis Management*, *11*(1), 19–24. doi:10.1111/1468-5973.1101004

Walters, D., & Lancaster, G. (1999). Value and information: concepts and issues for management. *Management Decision*, *37*(8), 643–656. doi:10.1108/00251749910291613

Weare, C., Musso, J. A., & Hale, M. L. (1999). Electronic Democracy and the Diffusion of Municipal Web Pages in California. *Administration & Society*, *31*(1), 3–27. doi:10.1177/009539999400935475

Wegweiser Gmb, H. Berlin. (2007). *Monitoring eHealth & Gesundheitswirtschaft 2007/2008.*

Weil, M. O., & Gamble, D. N. (1995). Community practice models. In R. L. Edwards (Ed.-in-Chief), *Encyclopedia of social work* (19th ed., Vol. 1, pp. 577–594). Washington, DC: NASW Press.

Wellenius, B. (2003). Sustainable Telecenters, *Private Sector and Infrastructure Network*, World Bank, Note number 251, January 2003.

Wescott, C., Pizarro, M., & Schiavo-Campo, S. (2000). The Role of Information and Communication Technology in Improving Public Administration In S. Schiavo-Campo & P. Sundaram (Eds.), *To Serve And To Preserve: Improving Public Administration In A Competitive World* (pp. 673-701). Retrieved October 21, 2009, from http://www.adb.org/documents/manuals/serve_and_preserve

White, G. (2005). Beyond the horseless carriage: Harnessing the potential of ICT in education and training *Education.au limited* http://www.educationau.edu.au/jahia/webdav/site/myjahiasite/shared/papers/horseless_carriages_GW.pdf Accessed 26 May 2009

White, J. D. (2007). *Managing information in the public sector.* New York: M.E. Sharpe.

Wiig, K. (2004). *People-focused knowledge management: How effective decision making leads to corporate success.* Amsterdam: Elsevier.

Wimmer, M. A. (2003). *Knowledge management in electronic government.* New York: Springer. doi:10.1007/3-540-44836-5

Wood, L. (2006). *Philosophy of Software.* 1-5, Retrieved January 20, 2008, from http://www.q-d.com

World Bank. (2000). *World Development Report 1999/2000.* Washington, DC: World Bank.

World Health Organisation. (2009). *Causes of blindness and visual impairment.* Retrieved 14.4.2009, 2009, from http://www.who.int/blindness/causes/en/

Yajiong, X., & Huigang, L. (2007). Analysis of telemedicine diffusion: The case of China. *IEEE Transactions on Information Technology in Biomedicine*, *11*(2), 231–233. PubMed doi:10.1109/TITB.2006.879599

Yıldız, M. (1999). Yerel Yönetimde Yeni Bir Katılım Kanalı Internet: ABD'de ve Türkiye'de Elektronik Bilgi Ağları [A New Way to Participation in Local Government (Internet): Electronic Information Networks in USA and Turkey]. Çağdaş Yerel Yönetimler, 8(4), 144-156.

Yildiz, M. 2004. *Peeking into the Black Box of E-government Policy-making: The Case of Turkey.* Unpublished doctoral dissertation, Indiana University-Bloomington.

Yurcik, W., Sharma, A., & Doss, D. (2002). False impressions: contrasting perceptions of security as a major impediment to achieving survivable systems. *IEEE/CERT/SEI Fourth Information Survivability Workshop (ISW-2002)*, Canada: IEEE Computer Society Press, Vancouver, BC.

Zambrano, R. (2003). *Mission Report: SDNP Bangladesh.* 22 – 27 February 200. Available at www.sdnbd.org

About the Contributors

Hakikur Rahman, PhD. is Founder-Principal of Institute of Computer Management & Science (ICMS), and President of ICMS Foundation Bangladesh. He is currently serving as a Post-Doctoral researcher at the University of Minho, Portugal. He is an Adjunct Faculty of the Bangabandhu Sheikh Mujibur Rahman Agricultural University (BSMRAU), and a former faculty of the International University of Business Agriculture and Technology (IUBAT), Bangladesh. He served Sustainable Development Networking Foundation (SDNF) as its Executive Director (CEO) from January 2007 to December 2007, the transformed entity of the Sustainable Development Networking Programme (SDNP) in Bangladesh where he was working as the National Project Coordinator since December 1999 (1999-2006). SDNP is a global initiative of UNDP and it completed its activity in Bangladesh on December 31, 2006. Before joining SDNP he worked as the Director, Computer Division, Bangladesh Open University. He also served the South Asia Foundation Bangladesh Chapter as Secretary-Coordinator (2001-2008) and Head Examiner, Computer, Bangladesh Technical Education Board (1996-2008). Graduating from the Bangladesh University of Engineering and Technology (BUET) in 1981, he has done his Master's of Engineering from the American University of Beirut (AUB) in 1986 and completed his PhD in Computer Engineering from the Ansted University, UK in 2001.

* * *

Abdul Raufu Ambali has obtained his PhD from International Islamic University Malaysia, Department of Political Science in year 2005 and joined University Technology MARA (UiTM), Shah Alam, Malaysia. The author is a prolific writer in public policy, public administration, e-government and governance issues. He is a senior lecturer and coordinator of research methodology and data analysis. The author has successfully supervised many under and postgraduate research projects at Faculty of Administrative Science and Policy Studies, UiTM. With his interdisciplinary research background and experience, he has tremendously contributed to many international and local journals, chapters in books as well as conferences within and outside Asia.

Maria Eugenia Arreola is a Programme Officer in the Capacity Development Branch of the UNEP's Division of Early Warning and Assessment (DEWA). She is the team lead for design and implementation of a web-based platform called MENTOR (Marketplace for ENvironmental Training and On-line Resources) which disseminates tools, guidelines, methodologies, e-Learning courses and best practices in support to UNEP's capacity development initiatives. In 2001, Maria Eugenia joined UNEP's Regional

Office for Latin American and the Caribbean where she was responsible for designing and implementing UNEP's Integrated Environmental Assessment Methodology- IEA/GEO on both the city and national level. Prior to joining UNEP, she worked at the Mexico Nature Conservation Fund as Manager of the Capacity Building Programme for environmental NGOs in Mexico. She has presented papers in a special UN session at Online EDUCA 2007; in the 3rd e-Learning Africa Conference 2008; in Online EDUCA Berlin 2009, and in the 4th e-Learning Africa Conference Dakar 2009. Maria Eugenia holds a Bachelor of Arts in International Relations, a Masters in Environmental Management, a post graduate Diploma in Environmental Law and a Certificate as Expert of New Learning Technology from Furtwangen University of Applied Sciences.

Johara Bellali has been involved in the UNEP Integrated Environment Assessment capacity development process since October 2008 when she joined UNEP's Division of Early Warning and Assessments (DEWA). She holds a M.Sc. in Global Development Management and a B.Eng. in Environment Engineering (Land and Water). She worked for the Global Environment Facility at UNDP managing the national portfolio for five environmental conventions in Niger and in particular the Climate Change convention in Vietnam. She managed the Engineering department for the humanitarian NGO Mercy Corps in Meulaboh, Indonesia after the Tsunami and worked with local NGOs in land degradation, water and sanitation and organic farming in Mauritania, Guatemala, Northern India, Vietnam and Kenya. She is a member of the British Institute of Civil Engineers.

Turksel Kaya Bensghir, Assoc. Prof. Dr. of Public Administration Institute for Turkey and the Middle East (PAITME). She is Director of TODAIE eGovernment Center. Kaya Bensghir received her Ph. D. in Business Administration at Gazi University. She is author of Information Technology and Organizational Change (1996), co-author of several books, and has published many articles. She has been teaching and giving seminars on Management Information System, System Analysis and E-Government. Her research interests are information systems and organizational change, e-government, e-signature, ICT outsourcing, Geographic Information System, website management, MIS Discipline, Knowledge Management in Public Organizations, ICT training in management schools and the usage of Open Source Code in public organizations.

Kees Boersma is Associate Professor at the VU University Amsterdam and research manger of the Department of Culture, Organization and Management. His research interest is in 'science and technology studies', 'business history', and in 'organizational culture and power'. He is teacher in the courses Organizational Politics, Organizational and Management Theory, and Technology and Culture.

Tolga Demirbaş is a research assistant at Uludag University, Faculty of Economics and Administrative Sciences in Bursa, Turkey. He received his PhD in public budgeting and fiscal planning from the Institute of Social Sciences, Uludag University in 2006. His research interests concern public budgeting reforms, performance budgeting and auditing, local government finance and fiscal transparency.

Peter Groenewegen is Professor of Organization Science and head of the Department of Organization Science at the VU University. His research interests are in social networks within and between organizations and the role of scientific expertise in policy making.

Adamantios Koumpis heads the Research Programmes Division of ALTEC S.A., which he founded at 1996 (then as independent division of Unisoft S.A.). His previous job position was at the Institute of Computer Science, FORTH, at Heraklio, Crete, where he worked at the Rehabilitation Tele-Informatics and Human-Computer Interaction Group in several EC RTD projects (RACE, ACTS and TAP). He is author of research papers, technical reports and Project deliverables and has successfully lead many industrial and European research projects in the areas of E-Commerce, public sector and business enterprise re-organisation and information logistics, concerning linking of data/information repositories with knowledge management and business engineering models. Adamantios holds a PhD degree from the University of Kingston, UK and a Bachelor degree from the University of Crete,Greece.

Irene Krebs, Graduate engineer (Diploma), specialist translator, Dr.-Ing., Honorary Professor; since 1989 research associate at the Brandenburg University of Technology Cottbus (BTU) at the Chair for Industrial Information Technology; Honorary Professor at the University of Potsdam, Human-scientific Faculty, Institute for Business and Employment Studies; since 1989 research associate at the BTU Cottbus; 1989 – 1994 at the Chair for Automation Technology (fields of activity: teaching: automata theory, mathematical methods of simulation, SPS programming, petri networks, research: modeling and development of information systems in industry); since September 1994 at the Chair for Industrial Information Technology (fields of activity: teaching: information systems in administration, ERP systems, business process modeling, data bases, data base management systems, interfaces, research: modeling and development of information systems for both production and near-production and administrative areas, among others eGovernment, eParticipation); doctoral thesis in 2001 (topic "Production-oriented Information Systems in Administration"); since 2002 lectureship at the University of Potsdam, Institute for Business and Employment Studies/Technology: "eBusiness – Systems and Application"; in 2004 conferment of degree of Honorary Professor at the University of Potsdam; member of Association of Computer Science (GI), technical committee for computer science in administration; member of management of degree course "eBusiness"; coeditor, author and coauthor of approx. 50 publications.

Rachel Lawry is an Honours graduate from Deakin University has presented papers at various conferences and won the University's Vice-Chancellor's Prize for the Best essay, piece of creative writing, work in the visual or performing arts, construction of experimental or field work, or piece of scientific writing in 2006. She is now working as a Human Resource Manager in a major bank in Australia while furthering her postgraduate education.

Harekrishna Misra is a professor in the area of IT & Information Systems Group at the Institute of Rural Management Anand. He is an Electronics and Communication Engineer, has Post-graduate Diploma in Business Management degree in Systems and Operations Management from XIM-Bhubaneswar and has Masters Degree in Software Systems from BITS-Pilani. He also holds a doctorate degree from Utkal University, Bhubaneswar, in the area of Information Systems Management. He has around 28 years of experience in industry and academia in the fields of IT infrastructure management, communication, and networks. His current research interests include software engineering (process modelling), e-governance, information systems management in development organisations, e-Business for rural enterprises and ICT enabled value chain in rural enterprises. His current interests include information systems modelling related to business and development processes with citizen participation. He is a life member of Institution of Engineers (India), member of IEEE, Association of Computing

Machinery (ACM) and Association of Information Systems, USA. He is in the reviewers' panel of the Computing Reviews-ACM. He has widely published in national and international reputed and refereed Journals. He has also participated in technical as well as programme committees and presented papers in national and international refereed academic conferences.

Francesco Molinari holds a MA in Public Management (Siena University, 2005) and a degree in Social and Economic Disciplines (Milan "L. Bocconi" University, 1990). Independent consultant for several public and private organisations, including ALTEC SA, for which account he leaded the TELL-ME consortium. Since 1995 he has been Economic & Financial Manager at a Development Agency with 800+ associated industrial SMEs. Since 2002 a Manager at local Chamber of Commerce and until now member of Massa City Mayor Administrative Staff. Since 2003 a contract Professor at Pisa University, he has been advisor of the Steering Committee of the e-Government module at the Political Science Faculty. ISince 2003 he has been designer of the e-Government module at the Pisa Faculty of Political Science and more recently, the "animator" of Servizi per la Politica (www.serviziperlapolitica.it), a professional virtual community born in the year 2005 to provide services to policy makers.

Vasiliki Moumtzi is a member of the Research Programmes Division of Altec S.A. in Thessaloniki. She is a graduate Informatics and Communication Engineer from the Informatics and Communications department of Technological Educational Institute of Serres, Greece. She also worked as a researcher at the reactor of Institut fór Festkφrperforschung Forschungszentrum Jólich at Germany and at the accelerator of ISIS Rutherford Appleton Laboratory at England for the demand of her diplomacy program AMphOrEAs(Archaeometric multiphase of ornament & element analysis), approved by the European union. Vasiliki is MSc dedicated at the University of Kingston, UK.

Mustafa Kemal Öktem is an associate professor of public administration in the Department of Political Science and Public Administration at Hacettepe University, Faculty of Economics and Administrative Sciences, Ankara/ Turkey where he received his Ph.D. on "Importance of Organizational Culture on Information Technologies-Organizational Structure Interaction". He has published a number of articles on public administration and edited several books. His area of research interests include "public personnel issues", "information society & public administration", "e-governance", and "organization development". His recent publication includes "IT and Public Administration: Are We Going to Finish Turkish E-Governance in the Black?", TODAIE (eGovernment Centre) Proceedings of eGOVSharE2009 Conference.

Leslie Paas holds Eng.D. and Eng.M. degrees (production and systems) from the Universidade Federal de Santa Catarina, Brazil, specializing in distance instructional design and education technologies. Her BA is in communications and Latin American studies from Simon Fraser University in Vancouver, BC Canada. Leslie has worked with IISD a digital editor for IISD's Earth Negotiations Bulletin, as a consultant on several evaluation projects and as a collaborator on the development of online learning programs, contributing her expertise in the use of information technologies and new media in education and knowledge building.

Jim Perry is HT Morse Distinguished University Professor of Water Quality at the University of Minnesota. He holds a Ph.D. in biology from Idaho State University, and has been at the UofMn more than 27 years. He is an elected Fellow of the Institute of Fisheries Research Biologists. He has been awarded the Meritorious Service Award for support of graduate education, was granted the HT Morse Alumni Award for Outstanding Contributions to Undergraduate Education and elected to the Academy of Distinguished Teachers. He has more than 30 years experience in water quality and environmental management. Dr. Perry has authored more than 120 technical and lay publications on water quality, water resources management, aquatic ecology and international development. He has published two textbooks: the first text in his field (1996 Water Quality: Management of a Natural Resource) and the only text advancing ecosystem management in Central and Eastern Europe (2001 Ecosystem Management in Central and Eastern Europe: Decision Taking for the Future). Jim has served as Director of Graduate Studies in Water Resource Science and in Wildlife Conservation. He served 6 years as Head of the Department of Fisheries, Wildlife and Conservation Biology; 3 as Special Assistant to the Dean of the Graduate School; 5 as Deputy Director of the US/AID Environmental Training Project for Central and Eastern Europe and 12 as Director of the University's Center for Natural Resource Policy and Management. He has held appointments as Fulbright Scholar, Brazil; Visiting Scholar, Oxford University; Senior Fellow, National Academy of Sciences, Poland; and Senior Fellow, American Institute of Indian Studies Delhi and Madras.

László Pintér is Director of the Measurement and Assessment Program of the International Institute for Sustainable Development (IISD), headquartered in Winnipeg, Canada (www.iisd.org). His role is to provide strategic leadership and ensure program influence according to IISD's overall vision and mission. His main interest is in addressing today's fundamental challenges to sustainability by changing the ways we measure progress and by crafting and effectively implementing sustainable development strategies. He holds a Ph.D. from the University of Minnesota, a Masters of Natural Resources Management from the University of Manitoba, Canada, and an M.Sc. in Agronomy from St. Stephen University in Hungary.

Nilsun Sariyer is an Assistant Professor at Faculty of Economics and Business Administration in University of Çanakkale Onsekiz Mart in Turkey. She completed PhD at Institute of Social Sciences in Anadolu University. The title of the thesis is Complaint Collecting Methods for Tools of Customer Satisfaction- a Case of Automotive Agents-. Her research is concentrated in three areas: Consumer Behavior, Customer Relationship Marketing and Service Marketing.

Nalini Sharma has been working with the United Nations Environment Programme since 1998. She holds a MSc. in environmental economics from University of York, UK. For the last five years, she has been with UNEP's Division of Early Warning and Assessment (DEWA) mainly working on Environmental Assessments, including the fourth Global Environmental Outlook (GEO-4) and the International Assessment of Agricultural Science and Technology for Development (IAASTD). More recently, she has been involved in capacity development in Integrated Environmental Assessment (IEA), in particular managing the IEA training package which includes the IEA training manual, conduct of training of trainers' events at the global and regional level, the IEA Community of Practice and the IEA e-Learning modules. Other capacity development work that she has undertaken includes managing the GEO fellowship programme. Previously, she was with UNEP's Division of Environmental Conventions (DEC) as Task Manager of a UNEP/GEF project on biosafety and was involved in biodiversity related conventions.

Mohini Singh is Professor of Information Systems at the School of Business Information Technology at RMIT University in Australia. She earned her PhD from Monash University and has published widely in the areas of E-Business and New Technology and Innovation Management. Her publications comprise books, book chapters, journal and conference papers. She serves as a member on the editorial boards of a number of journals and co-chairs tracks on e-government and IT diffusion at a number of international conferences. The focus of her current research is on IT Management, the diffusion of Web 2.0 technologies in business organisations, mobile technologies and e-government.

Reima Suomi is a professor of Information Systems Science at Turku School of Economics and Business Administration, Finland since 1994. He is a docent for the universities of Turku and Oulu, Finland. Years 1992-93 he spent as a "Vollamtlicher Dozent" in the University of St. Gallen, Switzerland, where he led a research project on business process re-engineering. Currently he concentrates on topics around management of telecommunications, including issues such as management of networks, electronic and mobile commerce, virtual organizations, telework and competitive advantage through telecommunication-based information systems. Different governance structures applied to the management of IS and are enabled by IS belong too to his research agenda, as well as application of information systems in health care. Reima Suomi has together over 300 publications, and has published in journals such as Information & Management, Information Services & Use, Technology Analysis & Strategic Management, The Journal of Strategic Information Systems, Behaviour & Information Technology, Journal of Management History and Information Resources Management Journal. For the academic year 2001-2002 he was a senior researcher "varttunut tutkija" for the academy of Finland. With Paul Jackson he has published the book "Virtual Organization and workplace development with Routhledge, London.

Zdeněk Struska, PhD. Born in 1980 in Česke Budějovice, Czech Republic. Educational background: MSc. in Strategy Management, University of West Bohemia, Pilsen. 2004. Ph.D. degree in Information management, Czech University of Life Sciences, Prague, 2008. Present professional position: From 2005: Consultant in the area of Technology Integration in Deloitte Advisory, Czech Republic. From 2007 to 2009: Assistant Professor of Information Management, Department of Information Engineering, Faculty of Economics and Management, Czech University of Life Sciences in Prague, Kamýcká 129, 16521 Prague 6, Czech Republic.

Jiří Vaníček, PhD born in 1937 in Prague, Czech Republic. Present professional position: Professor of Information Management, Department of Information Engineering (Deputy Head), Faculty of Economics and Management, Czech University of Life Sciences in Prague, Kamýcká 129, 16521 Prague 6, Czech Republic – From 1990 President of the Czech National Standardization Committee for Information Technology and the Czech Republic delegate in ISO/IEC JTC1/SC7 Subcommittee 'Information technology – System and software engineering'. Educational background: MSc. and Ph.D. degree in Mathematics (Functional Analysis and Applied Mathematics), Charles University in Prague; Ph.D. degree in Computer Sciences, Czech Technical University in Prague and Czechoslovak Academy of Sciences, Associate Professor of Computer Science, Czech Technical University in Prague; Full professor of Information Management, Czech University of Life Sciences in Prague, 2000.

Kam Hou Vat is currently an invited lecturer in the Department of Computer and Information Science, under the Faculty of Science and Technology, at the University of Macau, Macau SAR, China. His current research interests include learner-centered design with constructivism in Software Engineering education, architected applications developments for Internet software systems, information systems for learning organization, information technology for knowledge synthesis, and collaborative technologies for electronic organizations and virtual communities.

Dianne Waddell is the Associate Dean (Teaching and Learning) with the Faculty of Business and Law at Deakin University, Melbourne, Australia. She is responsible for the development, implementation and evaluation of postgraduate and undergraduate courses and teaches in the areas of Quality Management, Change Management and Strategic Management. Dianne has published and presented many papers on 'resistance to change', 'leadership', 'e-business', 'quality management', 'family business' and 'forecasting for managers'. Her publications include five books and has taught in both public and private education systems as well as presenting specifically designed industry-based courses. She is a Fellow of the Australian Organisation for Quality (AOQ).

Pieter Wagenaar (fp.wagenaar@fsw.vu.nl) is Assistant Professor at VU University Amsterdam in the group of Governance Studies. His research interests are in the informatization of public administration and in administrative history.

Christopher Wills (Dip SS, MA) is Principal Lecturer in the Faculty of Computing, Information Systems and Mathematics at Kingston University, UK and has been the Director of the University's Centre for Applied Research in Information Systems (CARIS) since 2002. He holds an MA from Brunel University and a Post-Graduate Diploma in Social Studies from Ruskin College Oxford. He is Member of the British Computer Society, the Worshipful Company of Information Technologists and is a Freeman of the City of London. He has taught several postgraduate courses including Participative Information Systems Design, Information Management, Strategic Information Systems, Electronic Governance, Project Management; Threat and Risk Assessment and Legal Frameworks - Privacy and Security. Chris has delivered lecture programmes at the University of Oulu Finland, the University of Vienna and the University of the Aegean. His research interests include Participative Information Systems Design Methodologies; Information Economy; Organisational Behaviour; Industrial Sociology and Social Psychology, Safety Critical Software Quality and Reliability Processes and Metrics; Software Procurement. He has worked with organisations as diverse as the Mass Transit Railway Corporation of Hong Kong and the UK's Defence Research Agency where he applied participative design methods to the development of systems requirement specifications for the British Navy.

Mete Yildiz is an associate professor of public administration in the Department of Political Science and Public Administration at Hacettepe University, Turkey. He received his Ph.D. at Indiana University, Bloomington's School of Public and Environmental Affairs in 2004. Among his research topics are government reform, e-government, public policy, comparative public administration and governance issues. His recent publications includes "Digital Divide in Turkey: A General Assessment", in Ferro, Enrico; Dwivedi, Yogesh K.; Garcia, Ramon G. and Michael D. Williams (Eds.), Overcoming Digital Divides: Constructing an Equitable and Competitive Information Society, Hershey, PA.: Idea Group Publishing, pp. 75-89; E-Government Policy Processes from a Grounded Theory Perspective: The Case of Turkey. Köln: Lambert Academic Publishing.

Martin Závodný born in 1982 in Rýmařov, Czech Republic. Educational background: MSc. in Computer Science, University of Economics in Prague, 2007. Present professional position: from 2007: Postgraduate student of Information Management, Department of Information Engineering, Faculty of Economics and Management, Czech University of Life Sciences in Prague, Kamýcká 129, 16521 Prague 6, Czech Republic. From 2007: Business Consultant in Profinit Czech Republic.

Index

D

E

F

G

N

O

P

Q

R

S

T

U

V

W

LaVergne, TN USA
07 October 2010
199852LV00005B/4/P

9 781616 928148